Second Edition

Multicultural Psychology

Pamela Balls Organista

Gerardo Marín

Kevin M. Chun

All at *University of San Francisco*

ROWMAN & LITTLEFIELD

Lanham • Boulder • New York • London

Executive Editor: Nancy Roberts
Associate Editor: Megan Manzano
Senior Marketing Manager: Amy Whitaker

Credits and acknowledgments for material borrowed from other sources, and reproduced with permission, appear on the appropriate page within the text.

Published by Rowman & Littlefield
A wholly owned subsidiary of The Rowman & Littlefield Publishing Group, Inc.
4501 Forbes Boulevard, Suite 200, Lanham, Maryland 20706
www.rowman.com

Unit A, Whitacre Mews, 26-34 Stannary Street, London SE11 4AB, United Kingdom

British Library Cataloguing in Publication Information Available

Library of Congress Cataloging-in-Publication Data

Names: Balls Organista, Pamela, author. | Marín, Gerardo, author. | Chun, Kevin M., author.
Title: Multicultural psychology / Pamela Balls Organista, University of San Francisco, Gerardo Marín, University of San Francisco, Kevin M. Chun, University of San Francisco.
Other titles: Psychology of ethnic groups in the United States
Description: Second Edition. | Lanham: Rowman & Littlefield, [2018] | "First edition 2010 by SAGE Publications"—T.p. verso. | Revision of: Psychology of ethnic groups in the United States. c2010. | Includes bibliographical references and index.
Identifiers: LCCN 2018001631 (print) | LCCN 2017053446 (ebook) | ISBN 9781538101100 (cloth: alk. paper) | ISBN 9781538101117 (paper: alk. paper) | ISBN 9781538101124 (electronic)
Classification: LCC RC451.5.A2 O74 2018 (ebook) | LCC RC451.5.A2 (print) | DDC 616.890089—dc23
LC record available at https://lccn.loc.gov/2018001631

∞™ The paper used in this publication meets the minimum requirements of American National Standard for Information Sciences—Permanence of Paper for Printed Library Materials, ANSI/NISO Z39.48-1992.

Printed in the United States of America

Contents

In Memoriam: Dr. Gerardo Marín (1947–2018) ix

Preface x

Acknowledgments xiv

Introduction 1

1 Psychology in a Multicultural World 3

Learning about Racial and Ethnic Diversity in Psychology 3

What Is Multicultural Psychology? 5

Multicultural Psychology and Multiculturalism 6
Effects of Living in a Multicultural Society 6

The United States as a Racially and Ethnically Diverse Society 7

Within-Group Diversity 9

Ancestry 9

Race and Ethnicity 11
Multiracial or Multiethnic Background 12
Age Differences 12
Language Use and Proficiency 13
Educational Attainment 13
High School Persistence Rates 14
College Enrollment 14
Socioeconomic Status and Poverty 15
Correlates of Poverty 16

Why Study Multicultural Psychology? 17

Improving Psychological Research 17
Advancing Culturally Diverse Societies 18
Improving the Quality of Health and Human Services 19
Promoting Cultural Competencies 19

Multicultural Psychology, Cultural Psychology, and Cross-Cultural Psychology 20

The Growth of Multicultural Psychology 21

2 Key Theoretical Concepts 29

"Mommy, What Color Are You?" 29

Understanding Culture 30

Dimensions of Culture 31
Cultural Influences on Psychological Processes 32

Understanding Ethnicity 33

The Problems of Ethnic Assessment and Labels 34

Understanding Race 35
Whiteness 36

Social Orientations or Ways of Being 37
Views of the Self Across Cultures 37

Social Stratification 39

Minority Status 42

Power and Privilege 43

3 Responsible Research With Racial and Ethnic Communities 47

"That Is Not Me!!" 47

Responsible, Culturally Appropriate Research 49
A Definition of *Responsible, Culturally Appropriate Research* 50

Implementing Responsible, Culturally Appropriate Research 51
An Initial Consideration: Contextualization 51
Culturally Appropriate Methods 52
Choosing a Research Approach 53
Experiments 53
Interviews and Surveys 54
Focus Groups 54
Case Studies 54
Ethnographies 55
Secondary Data Analysis 55
Community-Based Participatory Research (CBPR) 55

Key Issues in Developing Responsible, Culturally Appropriate Research 58
Instrument Characteristics 58
Psychological Tests 59
Translation of Research Instruments 60
The Translation Process 61
Use of Interpreters 63
Properly Identifying and Describing Participants 64
Intragroup Heterogeneity 64
Disaggregating Participants 65
Migration Rationale and History 70
Culturally Appropriate Analysis of Information or Data 71

The Problem of Limited Participation in Research 72

Ethical Considerations 74
Informed Consent 74
Freedom to Discontinue Participation 74
Respect for Privacy and Confidentiality 75
Appropriate Balance Between Risks or Costs and Benefits 76

4 Acculturation 81

"Call Me Jessie, Not Josefina!" 81

Defining Acculturation 83
Early Definitions 84
Contemporary Definitions 85

Understanding Assimilation and Segmented Assimilation 86

Models of Acculturation 88

The Unidirectional Model of Acculturation 88
Berry's Two-Dimensional Model of Acculturation 89
A Social Context Model of Acculturation 91
The Interactive Acculturation Model (IAM) 92
The Relative Acculturation Extended Model (RAEM) 93

Biculturalism 94

Enculturation 95

Generational Differences and Acculturation 97

Acculturational Stress 98

Acculturative Stress and Reasons for Migration 99

Measuring Acculturation 101

Levels of Acculturation 105

5 Intersecting Identities—Part 1: Racial, Ethnic, and Class Dimensions 109

Who Are You? 109

Understanding the Multiple and Intersecting Dimensions of Identity 110

Defining Racial, Ethnic, and Class Identities 111

Racial Identity 111
Ethnic Identity 112
Components of Ethnic Identity 112
Class Identity 114

Models of Racial and Ethnic Identity Development and Formation 114

Racial Identity Development 114
Evaluating Cross's Model of Racial Identity Development 115
Ethnic Identity Development 117
Factors Shaping Ethnic Identity Development 120
Developmental Factors 120
Family Factors 121
Social Factors 121
Acculturation Factors 122
Biracial/Multiracial Identity Development 122
Biracial Identity Resolution Strategies 124
Stage Models of Biracial Identity Development 125
Evaluating Models of Biracial Identity Development 125

Relationship of Racial, Ethnic, and Class Identities to Psychosocial Adjustment 126

Racial Identity and Adjustment 126
Self-Esteem 126
Psychological Adjustment and Mental Health 127
Risk for Drug Use 127
Physical Health 127
Perceptions of Racism 128
Ethnic Identity and Adjustment 128
Self-Esteem 128
Psychological Adjustment and Mental Health 128
Risk for Drug Use 129
Protection Against Discrimination and Racism 129

Biracial/Multiracial Identities and Adjustment 130
Self-Esteem 130
Psychological Adjustment and Mental Health 130
Class Identity and Adjustment 132
Physical and Mental Health 132

6 Intersecting Identities—Part 2: Gender and Sexuality Dimensions 135

"Why Do We Have to Label Everyone?" 135

Defining Gender and Sexual Identities 136
Gender Identity 136
Sexual Identity 136

Models of Gender and Sexual Identity Development and Formation 137
Gender Typing and Gender Identity Formation 137
Asian American Gender Identity 137
African American Gender Identity 138
Latino/Latina Gender Identity 140
Sexual Identity Formation 142
Navigating Intersecting Racial, Sexual, and Gender Stressors 142

Cultural, Family, and Minority Considerations in Coming Out 144
Asian Americans 144
Latinos 145
African Americans 145

Relationship of Gender and Sexual Identities to Psychosocial Adjustment 146
Gender Identity and Adjustment 146
Psychological Functioning and Physical Health 146
Body Image 147
Risk for Drug Use 147
Sexual Identity and Adjustment 148
Psychological Adjustment and Mental Health 148

7 Family Structure, Relations, and Socialization 153

"In My Family, We Never Openly Say 'I Love You'" 153

An Ecological Perspective of Family Functioning 154

Factors Affecting Family Structures and Household Arrangements 156
Migration 156
Socioeconomic Status (SES) 156
Exposure to Stress and Trauma 157
Cultural Values and Beliefs 157

Family Functioning, Socialization, and Adjustment 158
Parenting Styles 158
Ethnic Minority Fathers 161
Disciplinary Practices 162
Asian American Tiger Moms: Fact or Fiction? 162
Parent-Child Relationships 163
Academic Achievement 164
Couple Relationships 166
Family Stress and Coping 169

8 Stereotypes, Prejudice, and Discrimination 173

A True Story by One of the Authors (G. M.) 173

Understanding Stereotypes 174
Stereotype Content 175
Development of Stereotypes 176
Stereotype Characteristics and Effects 179
Stereotype Threat 179
Stereotypes Influenced by Intersectionalities 180
The Effects of Ethnic Labels on Stereotypes 181

Prejudice and Discrimination 181
Measuring Prejudice and Discrimination 183
The Experience of Discrimination 184
Why Do People Discriminate? 185
The Role of Implicit Attitudes 186
The Role of Disparagement Humor 187

Racism 188
Racial Microaggressions 189

Reducing Prejudice, Discrimination, and Racism 190
Intergroup Contact 191
Dialogue Across Difference 192
School Desegregation 193
Other Promising Practices 193

The Benefits of a Multicultural Society 194

9 Physical Health and Well-Being 199

"Son, I've Lost Something" 199

Influential Models of Health 200
Biomedical Model 200
Biopsychosocial Model 201
Ecological Models 202

Culture, Ethnicity, and Health 203

Health Disparities Among Racial and Ethnic Groups 205
Defining Health Disparities 206
Examples of Health Disparities 207
Mortality 207
Coronary Heart Disease 208
Cancer 211
Diabetes 212
HIV and AIDS 213
Disparities in Health Care Access and Quality 215

Factors Associated With Health Disparities 216
Behavioral Lifestyle 216
Tobacco Use 217
Alcohol Consumption 218
Substance Use and Abuse 219

Acculturation 219
Accessible and Affordable Health Care 221
Poverty and Community Characteristics 221
Undocumented Status 222
Discrimination and Racism 223
Environmental Racism 224
Spirituality and Religion 225

Reducing Racial and Ethnic Health Disparities: The Federal Government's Approach 227

Culturally Competent Health Care 227
Barriers to Health Care at the Organizational Level 228
Barriers to Health Care at the Structural Level 229
Clinical Level of Competent Care 229

10 Psychological Adjustment 233

"He's All Right; He's Just Funny That Way" 233

Mental Health and Psychological Distress 234
A Broader Perspective on Adjustment 234

Prevalence and Risk of Major Psychological Disorders 235
General Epidemiological Surveys 235
Surveys Specific to Ethnic Minority Communities 235
Major Disorders in Ethnic Minority Populations 236
Major Depression 236
Anxiety, Obsessive-Compulsive, and Trauma- and Stressor-Related Disorders 237
Substance-Related and Addictive Disorders 239
Dual Diagnosis 240

Cultural Influences on the Explanation and Expression of Psychological Distress 241
Service Utilization 244

Selected Factors Influencing Effective Delivery of Mental Health Services 244
Immigration and Acculturation Factors 244
Limited Economic Resources 246
Clinician Bias and Client Mistrust 246
Language Barriers 247
Cultural Acceptability Barriers 248

Practical and Ethical Guidelines for Culturally Sensitive Practice 249
Preassessment and Pretherapy Intervention 250
Assessment 250
Nontraditional Interventions 252
Humility in Practice 252
Collaborative Care in Treatment 252
Evidence-Based Treatment 253

Glossary 257
References 265
Photo Credits 305
Index 307

In Memoriam

Dr. Gerardo Marín (1947–2018)

A special dedication to our dear friend, colleague, and coauthor, Gerardo Marín, who passed away shortly after the completion of this book, as it was being prepared for publication. This book simply would not have been possible without his leadership, intellectual prowess, dedication, and tremendous heart. He was recognized nationally and internationally for his scholarship on acculturation, smoking cessation among Latinos, culturally appropriate research methods, and many other pioneering contributions to Latino psychology and multicultural psychology. He also was a very generous, kind, and compassionate mentor to untold numbers of ethnic minority students, scholars, and professional psychologists here at the University of San Francisco and around the world. Although he will be dearly missed, this book is part of his deep and long-lasting professional legacy.

Preface

This book is the end product of more than two decades where we, the authors, have been researching, teaching, and writing about multicultural psychology. All along, we have been interested in advancing our understanding of how psychology can help us identify the roles played by culture, race, gender, and ethnicity in shaping human behavior. We feel that current and future generations of psychologists and other social scientists must properly understand how all of human behavior is shaped by who we are, how we identify ourselves, and how other people react to our many social characteristics, including as a minimum our race or ethnicity, our gender identity, socioeconomic status, educational level, and sexuality. Indeed, in the 21st century it is practically impossible not to encounter cultural, racial, and ethnic diversity among one's friends, neighbors, and colleagues, at school and on the street. Interestingly, the same is true of many other regions and nations across the globe, including Africa, Asia, Europe, and the rest of the Americas.

In writing this book we also wanted to acknowledge that the racial, ethnic, and cultural diversity that we encounter in our lives is a central reason for our nation's richness and strength. As you will see in the book, the coming together of diverse individuals produces effective, innovative, and satisfying experiences that promote personal growth and the development of a responsive civil society. These early decades of the 21st century have brought us events and social circumstances that threaten the quality of our future existence if we allow prejudice and discrimination to prevent our working together to change and improve the world we have created. We hope that by reading this book you will become an informed and culturally competent member of our richly diverse community who will contribute to the applications of psychology to creating a peaceful and prosperous world for all.

This book will help you become familiar with some of the most pressing issues that need to be understood when we study the psychology of all the people who reside in the United States regardless of their personal characteristics. For many of the issues and questions addressed in this book, the final answers are not yet available, but the joint efforts of current and future researchers will provide some much-needed new perspectives. Our hope is that this book will help you to be a conscientious and critical consumer of psychological research. We also hope that the book may interest you in contributing to the important work of building a socially engaged multicultural psychology.

Contemporary psychological research in the United States includes de facto the presence of a variety of members of racial and ethnic groups. One reason for this situation is the high proportion of the country's population that belongs to one of the major racial and ethnic minority groups (African Americans, American Indians and Alaska Natives, Asian Americans, Hispanics/Latinos, and Native Hawai'ian or Other Pacific Islanders). But, as we implied above, demographics is just one argument for the need to study a culturally appropriate psychology. More important is the need to obtain an appropriate understanding of what are accurate and valid scientific findings and what information is tainted by nonrepresentative sampling, poor methodologies, or faulty interpretations. Indeed, it is difficult to accept the implicit premise of some social science research that assumes that members of one culture or ethnic group (usually non-Hispanic Whites) are representative of all humanity. This is what happens when researchers fail to include sufficient numbers of members of appropriate racial, ethnic, and cultural groups in their research projects. Just as psychologists have questioned the validity of behavioral rules derived from research with college undergraduates, social and behavioral scientists must question the validity and reliability of findings based on a select and unique group of individuals from predominantly one race.

Our book is not intended to replace basic psychological books and textbooks. Rather, the book provides a survey of essential issues that need to be understood when studying the behavior of all peoples. We invite you to join us in this exploration of the relationship of race, ethnicity, culture, and psychology as you read the pages that follow.

The next section presents an overview of the book including how it is organized and also how to make best use of its various sections. Although most readers tend to overlook the introduction section in textbooks, we urge you to read it carefully because it will help you to understand the book and to better learn the principles and facts we are presenting.

What Is New in This Second Edition?

In preparing the second edition of *Multicultural Psychology*, we reworked the contents of the original book into an updated and more comprehensive new text that highlights recent developments and findings in the field. Moreover, this second edition emphasizes to a much greater extent the intersections of ethnicity, race, and culture with class, gender, sexual, and religious identity dimensions. Also, we added content from allied fields including cross-cultural psychology and cultural psychology to provide students with a historical and theoretical context for the topics being discussed. This second edition continues to organize the chapters by psychological concept (e.g., acculturation, identity, family and socialization, physical health, psychological adjustment, etc.) in order to help the student develop a comprehensive and integrative understanding of the field. The pedagogical features originally designed to enhance active and engaged learning are retained and updated.

This new version differs from the first edition of the book in a number of areas. We have:

- given greater attention to the intersectionality of key social variables in shaping the attitudes, norms, values, and behaviors of ethnic and racial groups
- added an additional 400-odd references
- added section chapters on major areas in the field not previously covered (e.g., health disparities in quality and access, remote acculturation, approaches to reducing racism)
- reorganized chapter order to better reflect a developmental-learning approach
- updated content to include recent research in psychology and related fields (e.g., new acculturation models, an ecological model of health behavior, the implications of coming out, the *DSM-5* cultural-formulation interview, and cultural concepts of distress and syndromes)
- added coverage of multicultural and multiracial individuals as well as of the processes of biculturalism and identity formation
- included more seminal research from cross-cultural psychology, public health, cultural psychology, and other social and behavioral sciences
- expanded coverage of relevance to majority-minority social interactions (e.g., privilege, White identity development, spirituality)
- provided new coverage of ethnic and racial minority group members who also share other minority status (e.g., sexual and gender minorities)
- offered new coverage of additional areas of concern to individuals studying psychology and ethnic minority groups (e.g., undocumented status, violence, refugees, institutional racism)
- increased the number of basic terms and improved their definitions
- streamlined the presentation of data and research results to facilitate comprehension
- revised and reorganized headings and subheadings for greater conceptual clarity
- shortened paragraphs to enhance comprehension and improve ease of reading
- updated list of resources for each chapter
- updated lecture guides, online resources, and test banks available to instructors
- updated online review materials for students (quizzes, suggested readings, flash cards)

From here, we would like to tell you a little about how the book came to be and who we are.

The Road We Have Traveled

This book is the sixth joint publication we have produced over the course of almost 18 years. As early as 1998, we started to search for a textbook that could be used in courses on multicultural psychology or in courses dedicated to studying racial and ethnic minority groups. There were a few books on the market, but they did not quite fit our understanding of multicultural psychology as a field that was continuously evolving yet also mature enough to offer important contributions to the analysis of diverse human behaviors.

Our early disappointment with available texts led us to edit a book of classic and contemporary readings that was published in 1998 by Routledge, titled *Readings in Ethnic Psychology.* That book was one of the first to use the label *ethnic psychology* to talk about the psychology of ethnic and racial minority groups in the United States. A few years later, we realized that acculturation was one of the key principles in multicultural psychology and that it was time to update the early works in the field, to identify theoretical developments as well as new applications of this construct. We held a national conference at the University of San Francisco centered on acculturation, and some of the presentations from that conference were later collected in the book *Acculturation: Advances in Theory, Measurement, and Applied Research*, published in 2002 by the American Psychological Association. Within a few years, we embarked on the wonderful experience of writing a textbook on the psychology of ethnic and racial minority groups, and in 2009 we published *The Psychology of Ethnic Groups in the United States* with Sage. That book served as the first edition of the textbook you now hold in your hands. By early 2015 we recognized that there were important developments in the field that demanded the writing of a new edition of the last book. For more than two years we have worked on writing an edition that is current and addresses the needs and desires of faculty and students. The result is this second edition that not only has a new title but also adds new topics and is completely updated with a large number of new findings and new citations.

Who We Are

We would like to tell you something about ourselves so that you see how our experiences and lives have shaped what you will read in this book. We feel that a book is an intensely personal communication between authors and readers, and for this reason we have always included a picture of the three of us in our books. Below is a short description of our personal and professional trajectories.

Pamela Balls Organista was born in Saint Louis, Missouri. She attended Washington University in St. Louis where she obtained a BA in psychology and Black studies. She then attended Arizona State University for graduate studies in clinical psychology, obtaining her PhD, and then the University of California, San Francisco, where she completed a postdoctorate in clinical psychology with an emphasis in public service and minorities. She has been at the University of San Francisco (USF) since 1992 and currently serves as associate dean for social sciences and professor of psychology. She was the founding director of ethnic studies in the College of Arts and Sciences at USF. Her research interests have centered on health risks and protective factors in primarily underserved populations including poor medical patients, Mexican migrants, and racial and ethnic minority youth.

Gerardo Marín was born in Pereira, Colombia, and raised in Cali, Colombia. His family migrated to the United States when he was 17 years old. He attended Miami Dade Community College (now known as Miami Dade College) for two years and then transferred to Loyola University Chicago, where he obtained a BS in psychology in 1970. He attended graduate school at DePaul University, obtaining an MS in psychology in 1972 and his PhD in 1979. Gerardo was part of the University of San Francisco in a number of capacities between 1982 and 2015 and was professor emeritus at USF. He published more than 130 articles, chapters, and books, mostly on topics such as acculturation, culturally appropriate research methods, AIDS, and tobacco and alcohol use among racial and ethnic minority groups. He was involved in developing two of the most widely used acculturation scales for Latinos and served as scientific editor for the surgeon general's report on tobacco use among ethnic and racial minorities. He was also interested in cross-cultural psychology and in international activities and was an active member of many international psychological associations. He has been honored by various psychological associations and nongovernmental organizations and was awarded the Surgeon General's Medal and a doctorate *honoris causa* by Pázmány Péter Catholic University in Hungary (Pázmány Péter Katolikus Egyetem).

Kevin M. Chun is a fifth generation Chinese American with long-standing family roots in San Francisco. He received a BS in psychology from Santa Clara University in 1990 and a PhD in clinical psychology from the University of California, Los Angeles, in 1995. While at UCLA, he worked with his mentor and adviser, Dr. Stanley Sue, at the National Research Center on Asian American Mental Health. Kevin completed a psychology internship at VA Palo Alto Health Care System and received an Irvine Scholar Dissertation Fellowship (now known as the Gerardo Marín Diversity Scholars Program) at the University of San Francisco in 1995. Soon after, Kevin joined USF as a full-time faculty member and is currently professor of psychology, Asian Pacific American studies, and critical diversity studies. His research focuses on family acculturation processes and health issues for Chinese American immigrants. Kevin and his UCSF colleague, Dr. Catherine Chesla, received two consecutive R01 grants from the National Institutes of Health to investigate cultural issues in diabetes management for Chinese American immigrant families and to develop the first empirically supported diabetes-management intervention for this ethnic group. Kevin has contributed to a number of scholarly works, including *Handbook of Asian American Psychology* (first and second editions), *Acculturation and Parent-Child Relationships: Measurement and Development*, and *Handbook of Mental Health and Acculturation in Asian American Families*. He was a recipient of the Early Career Award for Distinguished Contributions from the Asian American Psychological Association (AAPA) in 2005 and was appointed fellow of AAPA in 2011.

Acknowledgments

The writing of this second edition has been "in process" for approximately two and a half years, at times delayed by other pressing deadlines or by competing demands on our time. Nevertheless, we are proud of the final product and thankful for all the support we received from many individuals. Jointly, we wish to thank a number of former and current colleagues (faculty and administrators) at the University of San Francisco who have created the institutional climate necessary to make this book a reality and who, by their example and encouragement, made it possible for us to work on our four books that were born out of our collegial and scholarly search for what is best for our students (the search for the *magis* that characterizes Jesuit education). Unfortunately, they are too many to single out individually, but they know the very important role they played in our professional and personal lives.

We also wish to express our sincere thanks to Molly White, associate editor at Rowman & Littlefield, who from the beginning showed enthusiastic support for our proposal and who has been a helpful and much appreciated editor for our project. Thanks are also due to the many students at USF who provided us with feedback on the first edition; to colleagues at other institutions who provided suggestions and feedback to our first edition and to our plans for this second edition; and to the editors at two other textbook publishers who supported our project and provided encouragement and good ideas that made the book much better.

Individually, we also wish to express special thanks to a number of people who have supported us while we wrote the book. We hope they feel proud of their contributions and share in our joy to have completed such an important task.

Pamela is eternally grateful to work collaboratively with her esteemed friends and colleagues Gerardo and Kevin. Together they have had the opportunity to work on several projects (articles, presentations, books, and grants) that reflect the mission of the University of San Francisco and their values—namely, to continually create, through their scholarship and service, a more understanding, just, and inclusive world. As a multicultural team, they are able to address issues through a variety of cultural lenses and provide a complex understanding of the psychosocial challenges, promises, and questions that still remain for ethnic minorities living in the United States. Taking on the writing of this manuscript has been a daunting process, and without the passion and support of others its completion would have been dubious. In particular, Pamela is grateful for her close family and friends. They are upbeat, bright, and good people who never cease to amaze her with their work and commitment to others. She wants to express her thanks to her two sisters, Zoneice and Tunderleauh, and nephews, Demerrio and Tory. She gives special thanks to her husband, Kurt Organista, who continually provides a rich source of inspiration, intellectual collaboration, and loving support. Their beautiful and beloved daughters, Zena Laura and Zara Luz, never fail to make her think and care more deeply, laugh/play, and recognize that they hold a special place of importance in one another's lives. Finally, she wants to express her heartfelt gratitude to her parents, Zevonzell and Cynthia Balls, who provided a good upbringing and home and a strong education to sustain her. Throughout her life, they provided love, encouragement, and belief in her abilities. These gifts are meaningful and invaluable. She dedicates this book to her family, especially in loving memory of her mother.

Gerardo wishes to express a special appreciation to Pamela and Kevin, his respected colleagues who have been part of many "crazy" ideas and who have sustained his interest in these issues and taught him much. His daughter, Melisa (married to Kevin Lindamood), and his son, Andrés Daniel (married to Cassie Weiss), have been instrumental in shaping this and other books and in making them a reality. In particular, he wishes to thank Lois Ann Lorentzen for her constant and caring companionship, her love, her emotional support, her example, and her disappointed face when other things stole time away from writing. Gerardo and Lois live in Fairfax, California, and he is enjoying the life of a busy retiree. Since the first edition of this book was published, Gerardo has been blessed by an increase in the number of granddaughters who have brought much happiness to his life: Sienna M. Lindamood, Sasha

G. Lindamood, and Mia I. Marín. The three not only bring him joy and a sense of hope for the future but also exemplify in their backgrounds the realities of a multicultural society. He would like to dedicate this book to them.

Kevin also wishes to thank his dear friends and colleagues Gerardo and Pamela for their continued friendship and support throughout the years. He continues to be inspired by their professional expertise, intellectual curiosity, and abiding commitment to social justice. Kevin is also grateful for the generous and unconditional support of his partner, Anthony Ng; his family, Wilfred Chun, Annett, Shaun, Garrett, and Harrison Wright, Henry Lum, and William and Yvonne Ng; and his amazing friends and extended family members in the San Francisco Bay Area. He dedicates this book to his late mother, Cynthia Chun Lum, a much-beloved, inspiring, and dedicated public school educator who touched the lives of hundreds of students.

Introduction

You are reading this book in exciting and challenging times. The United States and the rest of the world are experiencing large levels of mobility across borders, bringing people from different cultures into contact with each other. Financial developments in the United States dating back to 2008 have brought economic challenges and difficulties not just to our nation but also to many other countries. The U.S. Census Bureau is predicting that within a generation the country will be so ethnically diverse that White Americans will no longer be the majority. In 2009 we welcomed the inauguration of the first African American president in the more than 200 years of history of the country. The results of the 2016 elections are producing profound social changes, policies, and legislation that affect all Americans and particularly ethnic and racial minorities. These and many other significant events underscore the need for all of us to become more informed about our multicultural society. That was the impetus for writing this book.

Before you start reading Chapter 1, there are a few things we would like to point out that will make your reading more productive.

Intended Audience

This is a textbook intended for undergraduate and graduate students interested in multicultural psychology. As such, we envision it will be assigned in classes as diverse as those exploring ethnicity, race, culture, class, gender, sexualities, minority status, ethnic diversity, and multiculturalism. For a more detailed coverage of the various topics, we have recommended a series of handbooks and other books at the end of each chapter. These additional sources of information will help you gain a comprehensive understanding of the field.

Goal

We wrote this book with the aim of offering a comprehensive overview of the best-quality research in psychology and in other social sciences regarding *ethnic and racial minorities in the United States.* This text focuses primarily on five ethnic and racial minority groups: African Americans, American Indians and Alaska Natives, Asian Americans, Hispanics/Latinos, and Native Hawai'ians and Other Pacific Islanders. Our selection of these five ethnic and racial minority groups is not intended to ignore the fact that there are many other ethnic and racial minorities in the country. Instead, because these five minorities have received the most attention in the multicultural-psychology literature, their experiences allow for in-depth analyses of their psychological experiences, much of which is applicable to other racial and ethnic minority groups. Furthermore, while we are focusing our analysis on racial and ethnic minority groups in the United States, we are also adding research conducted in other countries. Indeed, there is important research conducted with ethnic and racial minorities in other countries that is helpful as we try to understand our realities in the United States. For example, research with individuals of Asian backgrounds living in Canada or Australia, Latinos living in Scandinavia, or Northern Africans living in Southern Europe and in Germany have recently contributed to new developments in the field that are mentioned throughout the book.

A Word about Labels

We realize that during the last few decades ethnic and racial labels have evolved to reflect changes in sociopolitical beliefs and attitudes in the United States. In writing this book, we tried not only to use the ethnic and racial labels used by the U.S. government in conducting the decennial census but also to reflect the most commonly used labels in the social sciences literature at the beginning of the 21st century. As such, we frequently use *African American* instead of *Black* to denote individuals who trace their background to Africa or certain areas of the Caribbean. Likewise, we tend to use *Latino* rather than *Hispanic* or the older label *Spanish American* to designate individuals who trace their background to Latin America. We use *Latino* as an English-language label that includes individuals who self-identify as women, men, or other gender rather than as a Spanish-language label that would optimally require at least two different words (*Latino* and *Latina*). Likewise, we are aware of the need to use inclusive nonbinary labels, but recent suggestions such as *Latin@* or *Latinx* are still nascent terms that have yet to be widely referenced. We made this choice for convenience and ease of reading and not as a way of ignoring a very important segment of the Latino population. We use *Asian American* instead of *Asian*, as found in the census reports, to better represent individuals who reside in the United States and trace their background to one or more of the Asian countries. The label *American Indian* is used to denote those who trace their background to the first peoples of the country, and it often replaces *Native American*. Most likely, by the third edition of this book we will change some of these labels as sociopolitical attitudes and beliefs about ethnicity and race continue to evolve. Likewise, you should be aware that the U.S. Census Bureau is studying a somewhat different set of labels to denote the ethnic and racial groups mentioned above. Those new labels will be analyzed by the Office of Management and Budget in time for the 2020 census.

The Book's Organization

We have endeavored to write the book in a way that is inviting and easy to read by including a number of helpful features. Every chapter begins with a vignette, a short story that illustrates practical applications of key topics and issues that are presented in the chapter. Likewise, you will find boxes throughout the chapters that expand coverage of certain topics by providing added examples of relevant research and extended data and commentary. Do not skip these features, because they will help you to contextualize and punctuate key ideas in the main text of the chapter.

At the end of each chapter you will find three sections that will help you study and remember what the chapter has covered. First, a section called *Key Terms* presents a list of the concepts covered in the chapter that deserve special consideration. These terms also are shown in bold type when they are first discussed in the text of the chapter. You will want to make sure that you can define each of these terms and explain why they are important to the chapter's topics.

Also at the end of each chapter you will find a section called *Learning by Doing*, where we suggest exercises or activities that you can carry out to help improve your understanding of the implications of the theoretical concepts that were included in the chapter. These mini-studies will take a little time and effort but will make concrete the abstract ideas you have studied. Finally, each chapter includes a section labeled *Suggested Further Readings*, where we list books that you may want to consult to gain a deeper understanding of the topics presented in the chapter.

We hope that you enjoy reading this book and that you gain more comprehensive and nuanced perspectives on our multicultural society. Furthermore, we hope that you are able to see the relevance and interactions of ethnicity, race, culture, and other important identity dimensions to core psychology principles and theories and learn how to work and live more effectively in a culturally diverse world.

We would enjoy hearing your thoughts and opinions about our book as well as any suggestions for future revisions. Feel free to contact us by e-mail: Pamela Balls Organista (organistap@usfca.edu) and Kevin M. Chun (chunk@usfca.edu).

Psychology in a Multicultural World 1

Learning about Racial and Ethnic Diversity in Psychology

Lee Yee started his undergraduate studies in biology at a private university in Seattle. His parents were born in New York, and his grandparents came from China in the early 20th century. They were all very proud of Lee's academic accomplishments. Lee's acceptance into college validated their years of sacrifice and hard work to provide Lee the best possible education. Moreover, his plan to later pursue a medical degree was a "dream come true" to his mother. Lee studied hard to obtain the best grades in his courses, but college seemed markedly different from his high school years. For one, he was living away from his home. Two, he no longer had his group of friends—most of Asian descent—for hanging out and socializing. Indeed, he felt somewhat different from his peers, since most of the students in his classes were White Americans. Nevertheless, he managed to pass his freshman-year courses and was determined to pull his grades up higher during his second year. He also needed to take other courses to satisfy his core requirements. He decided that introductory psychology was a good choice since it dealt with the study of human behavior—and, as a future doctor, it might have some relevance to his career. Although he aced the course, he was unhappy with the almost total absence of information about Asian Americans—it almost seemed as if he and other students of color were being ignored by psychology (at least the psychology described in the textbook and in lectures). He also thought that some of the psychological principles mentioned in class were not part of his experience as an Asian American—a feeling that was shared by his roommate, Dwayne, an African American computer science major from Saint Louis, Missouri. Looking for an elective to take, Lee chose a relatively new course in the curriculum: Multicultural Psychology in the United States. The title captured his attention because he hoped to hear about his culture and people like himself and like Dwayne. On the first day of class, the instructor, Dr. Gonzalez, introduced the course by saying, "The purpose of this course is to educate and sensitize you to the major psychological issues facing individuals from different ethnic or racial groups with special attention focused on African Americans, Latinos, Asian Americans, and American Indians. We are going to explore what psychology says about this emerging majority in the country and also what psychology has failed to address." As Lee listened, he got more and more excited. He thought, "Finally, a course about me. And Dr. Gonzalez is an Asian American like myself—the first Asian American professor I've seen here."

The United States can easily be described as a rich and complex cultural, racial, and ethnic mosaic that is a work in progress. With each passing decade, residents and immigrants and their children and grandchildren add to its color and energy, sustaining our historical self-portrait as a diverse nation enriched by the contributions of many different peoples and cultures. Yet this vision and its underlying beliefs of unlimited opportunity, equality, and freedom have been challenged by a long and complicated history centered on our difficulties in understanding and accepting people's differences. Ever since the founding of this country—or even before—skin color, gender, race, national origin, ethnicity, income, and cultural differences have been used to restrict the rights and freedoms of certain groups or allowed to shape the nature of our personal interactions.

The United States has a population that is quite diverse in a number of ways beyond race, ethnicity, or culture. For example, we differ in terms of gender, sexuality, age, socioeconomic status, religious beliefs, physical ability (ableness), nationality, ancestry, educational level, employment, place of residence, and so on. All of these areas of diversity are important since they affect the way we think and act, and they interact with each other in shaping people's beliefs, attitudes, values, and behaviors. For example, Mary, who was raised by an African American family on a farm in rural Illinois, may exhibit attitudes or behaviors that are different from those of her Latina cousin Esperanza, who was raised in the heart of Chicago, or another cousin who lives on a farm in rural Northern California. They share family ties and traditions but differ in how they view the world and how they interact with others and among themselves. This portrait repeats itself across the United States, where families enjoy the riches brought about by diverse cultures, experiences, and ways of living.

Psychologists have made important contributions to our understanding of racial, ethnic, and cultural differences, but we are still struggling to find ways to cogently discuss and examine how race, ethnicity, gender, income, and culture interact in influencing people's behavior. This book is an attempt to summarize the most significant knowledge we have about the psychology of racial and ethnic minority groups hoping to contribute to the development of a respectful, informed, and balanced scientific language. Furthermore, the book should help you identify ways in which you can contribute to building a diverse country that respects and values differences and also benefits from what people with various perspectives and experiences contribute.

This book, therefore, explores differences primarily due to people's race, ethnicity, and culture as they interact with such other characteristics as their gender, social class, and sexuality. The analysis of multiple factors interacting with each other (often labeled **intersectionality** or *intersectional inquiry*) provides not only a more complete and nuanced understanding of human behavior but also a better basis for developing personal and societal interventions to produce change (Cohen & Varnum, 2016; Collins & Bilge, 2016). Indeed, many universities recognize this fact by offering not just courses like Psychology of Ethnic Groups or Multicultural Psychology but also courses such as Psychology of Women, Psychology of Men, Poverty and Psychology, Urban Psychology, and so on. We hope that by reading this book you will become familiar with the field of multicultural psychology and will learn concepts and skills that will help you form meaningful relationships with racial and ethnically diverse individuals. As authors, we also hope that the book will motivate you to learn more about the field and to explore how cultures differ and how they influence people's behavior.

What Is Multicultural Psychology?

The study of multicultural psychology is a fairly recent development in the field, reflecting the contributions that psychology can make to an understanding of the behavior of individuals who differ in a number of characteristics (e.g., gender, ethnicity, race, social class, sexuality, etc.) and of their interactions with those who do not share the same characteristics. As is true with most concepts in psychology and the social sciences, there are differences in the way multicultural psychology has been defined (see Box 1.1), and each definition contributes an important perspective. Nevertheless, there are two central aspects that are shared by these definitions. One is the fact that, as part of psychology, multicultural psychology studies and predicts peoples' values, norms, attitudes, and behaviors. The other common thread refers to the fact that these objects of psychological inquiry are influenced by peoples' culture.

While most definitions of multicultural psychology have seen **culture** as including those attitudes, norms, beliefs, values, and behaviors shaped by an individual's ethnicity and race or national origin, here we propose, agreeing with Hall (2014; see Box 1.1), that cultures are also developed and shaped by individuals' gender, physical and mental abilities, sexuality, social class, and other similar characteristics. In this sense, in this book we define *multicultural psychology* as *the study of human behavior (including attitudes, norms, values, and beliefs) as influenced (1) by a person's cultures interacting with variables as diverse as race, ethnicity, gender, social class, and sexuality and (2) by the person's involvement with other individuals who share or differ in terms of their cultures as influenced in turn by such characteristics as race, ethnicity, gender, and social class.*

Box 1.1

Definitions of *Multicultural Psychology*

Multicultural psychology is the study of cultural (e.g., culture of origin, US cultures) and sociocultural influences (e.g., minority status, discrimination) on behavior. (Hall, 2010, p. 8)

The systematic study of behavior, cognition, and affect in settings where people of different backgrounds interact. (Mio, Barker, & Domenech Rodríguez, 2016, p. 3)

Multicultural psychology is the systematic study of how culture influences affect cognition and behavior. In other words, multicultural psychology is about how culture influences the way people feel, think, and act. Multicultural psychology also considers internal (e.g., within the individual) and external (e.g., the impact of relationships, social, institutional, structural, and community) factors when seeking to understand how culture impacts psychological processes, well-being, and mental health. (University of Rhode Island, Department of Psychology, 2015, p. 1)

Multicultural psychology places a clear emphasis, perhaps it even privileges, the role of context and culture. . . . Multicultural psychology isn't only about studying different people but also about the discovery and study of different constructs, including those that might be culturally specific, rather than universal. (Cauce, 2011, p. 228)

Multicultural psychology views human behavior as influenced by an individual's culture and the cultures surrounding and acting on the individual. Cultures can include ethnicity or race, gender, physical and mental abilities, sexual orientation, socioeconomic status, geography, family background, and many others. (Hall, 2014, p. 3)

Multicultural Psychology and Multiculturalism

Multicultural psychology views **multiculturalism** as a sociopolitical characteristic that defines communities as well as nations (Rattansi, 2011) and is more complex and nuanced than concepts such as *diversity* or *pluralism*. Philosophers, political theorists, ethicists, and social scientists have been studying the concept of multiculturalism and its implications for a number of years, and in the process many critical issues and concerns have been identified. Multiculturalism is defined (Berry & Sam, 2014) as including the "presence of cultural diversity, [where] multiculturalism also requires intercultural contact and equitable participation of all cultural elements in the life of the larger society" (p. 97). While some individuals and some countries, such as Canada and Australia, have embraced the ideal of multiculturalism as a positive characteristic, other countries have been concerned about certain perceived negative effects of multiculturalism, such as discrimination, residential segregation, poverty, inequality, and so on. Other terms such as **interculturalism** and *transnationalism* have been offered primarily by scholars outside the United States as alternatives to the sometimes-maligned term *multiculturalism*. Nevertheless, in the United States, multiculturalism seems to be the preferred term.

In this book we argue that multiculturalism requires an abiding and respectful concern and interest in the lived experiences and human conditions of diverse groups of people. It involves "stepping into another person's shoes" to understand how she or he experiences, views, and interacts with the world. This understanding becomes possible when we delve into a group's psychosocial experiences and when we learn to appreciate and respect what makes us different and unique from each other. Multiculturalism also requires a fair and just process of interactions across groups where cultural differences are respected, individuals value the contributions of others, and social justice prevails (these requirements are often ascribed to the definition of interculturalism). Multiculturalism also implies a personal commitment to critically evaluate one's own **privilege** or preferential standing in the world that is not due to effort or performance (this topic is more fully covered in Chapter 2). Finally, multiculturalism rests on a fundamental belief in the common good and a willingness to contribute to it.

A truly multicultural society is not created by the *mere presence* of individuals who look, act, or think differently from each other because of the color of their skin, the shape of their eyes, their national origin, or their fluency in speaking English, among other factors. The simple *counting* of racially, ethnically, or culturally diverse individuals constitutes what can be called **facial diversity**—that is, using variations in people's physical characteristics such as skin color, eye shape, national origin, or hair texture as proof of the existence of multiculturalism. But facial diversity in itself does not define a truly multicultural society. What is needed to develop a functioning multicultural society is the presence of positive and respectful interpersonal relationships among diverse individuals, the sharing of power and resources, and mutual collaboration and dialogue. Nevertheless, the use of facial diversity as evidence of multiculturalism is very common among politicians, business people, and even scientists. Facial diversity, for example, can be seen when politicians claim cultural diversity in a government when a token number of racial or ethnic minorities is appointed to government posts. Facial diversity can also be seen when university officials claim the existence of a multicultural community on their campuses based on the numbers of racially or ethnically diverse individuals but their students from different ethnic and racial groups seldom have meaningful and shared experiences with one another (such as collaborative classroom relationships or shared extracurricular activities).

Effects of Living in a Multicultural Society

Going beyond facial diversity (that just "counts" the presence of diverse individuals) to building a functioning multicultural community allows individuals to benefit from interacting with people of diverse backgrounds and cultures (Phillips, 2014). For example, research on ethnically diverse school settings has shown that classrooms where individuals of different races and ethnicities interact produce not only greater cultural awareness and interest in studying ethnic and racial groups but also higher levels of academic development and satisfaction and improved student retention rates (Gurin, Dey, Hurtado, & Gurin, 2002; Lopez, 2004). Those students (White as well as African American) who experienced racial diversity in classroom settings showed high levels of civic and interpersonal engagement with diverse others. Interestingly, the research shows that these effects continued well after the students graduated from college. The researchers (Gurin et al., 2002) also found improvements in critical thinking, ability to manage complex and conflictual situations, and preparedness for participating in a racially and ethnically diverse democracy by showing respect for differences across groups. These studies are also covered in Chapter 8, where we talk about prejudice and discrimination.

The positive effects of living in a multicultural society are also found in other settings. For example, work groups that are diverse in terms of their race or ethnicity tend to be more effective and to show more creativity and satisfaction (Stahl, Maznevski, Voigt, & Jonsen, 2009; Stahl, Makela, Zander, & Maznevski, 2010; Phillips, 2014). Likewise, Antonio (2004) found that diverse social groups enhance the intellectual self-confidence of their members and increase people's ability to integrate different perspectives. Indeed, Anthony Marsella (1998), a psychologist from Hawai'i, has argued that "ethnocultural diversity is as important for human survival as is biological diversity because it provides social and psychological options and choices in the face of powerful unpredictable environmental demands" (p. 1288).

The United States as a Racially and Ethnically Diverse Society

The United States is a country with a long and complicated history around racial, ethnic, and cultural differences. A short overview of our history shows how European immigrants joined the peoples of the First Nations in sharing a bountiful land full of promise. Later years brought to our shores more Europeans, many of them fleeing poverty or political and religious persecution. Africans were forced to come to our land under inhumane conditions and to sacrifice their lives at the service of those whose families had arrived a few years before them. Other ethnic and cultural groups were brought together under one flag and one nation through land purchases (as in the case of the Cajuns in Louisiana or Alaskan Natives) or through political agreements (as in the case of Mexicans living in what is now the southwestern United States).

In the 19th and 20th centuries, large groups of Italians, Jews, Irish, Chinese, and Mexicans, among others, came to the United States to contribute to the country's economic growth by performing manual and skilled labor jobs that few people wanted. The latter part of the 20th century and the beginnings of the 21st century have witnessed the continued arrival of individuals from all over the world who eagerly wish to contribute to the advancement of the nation and to enjoy its economic and educational opportunities and freedoms. The end result of these migrations over the course of various centuries is a distinctly diverse society that witnesses the presence on its shores of multiple cultural traditions and that pursues the goal of considering all women and men as having been created equal (Waters & Pineau, 2015).

The cultural and ethnic diversity that characterizes the United States can easily be experienced in our cities and in our small towns where people of many cultures interact with each other, even if not with perfect comfort. Our traditions and our foods celebrate that diversity, and our laws endeavor to support the richness it contributes. Many of us live in ethnically diverse settings where we feel comfortable eating foods from diverse cultures, dancing to a variety of rhythms, or playing or watching sports that come from many cultures. Nevertheless, a truly culturally diverse country is defined by national policies that support, and individual behaviors that demonstrate, an understanding, appreciation, protection, and respect of racial, ethnic, and cultural differences. Indeed, our experiences in sharing cultures and traditions have produced a significant number of individuals who have a bicultural or multicultural identity and who feel comfortable in more than one cultural setting (Hong, 2010; Hong, Zhan, Morris, & Benet-Martínez, 2016).

Unfortunately, these experiences in creating a multicultural society also have brought about stress, discomfort, and irrational fears of foreigners (**xenophobia**). Our history as a country has registered a number of instances where intolerance has been demonstrated through segregation, discrimination, hate, prejudice, and even violence. In this book we wish to celebrate the characteristics and contributions of multicultural individuals and also explore what psychology has to offer to our understanding and prevention of the negative manifestations of intolerance.

In this book, and as mentioned before, we pay particular attention to individuals who self-identify as African Americans or Blacks, American Indians or Alaska Natives, Asian Americans, Hispanics or Latinos, and Native Hawai'ians or Other Pacific Islanders (see Box 1.2 for definitions of various ethnic and racial groups as written in 1997 by the OMB—the Office of Management and Budget). This does not mean that other groups (e.g., Irish Americans, Italian Americans, Arab Americans, German Americans, Filipino Americans, Polish Americans) are not important or have not been studied by psychologists. Instead, the emphasis on the five major groups as defined in 1997 by the OMB and used by many federal and state agencies, such as U.S. Census Bureau, is a way of making the discussion manageable and controlling the length of the book. Furthermore, the majority of multicultural research in psychology focuses on these five groups. Many of the concepts mentioned in the book (e.g., acculturation, ethnic identity, family structure) as applied to the five major ethnic and racial minority groups are also relevant to other groups. It is important to note that other multicultural countries use different ways of addressing these groups; Canada, for example, uses the label *visible minority populations* as equivalent to the label *racial and ethnic minorities* that we use in the United States. Also, Canada refers to the various subgroups in a way that is different from the one we use in the United States (see Box 1.2). In considering visible minority populations, Statistics Canada looks separately at various groups that include seven separate national groups, such Asians, Blacks, Latin Americans, and those with multiple minority status, and the definition excludes aboriginal peoples and Caucasians.

As mentioned in the previous paragraph, the groupings shown in Box 1.2 were approved by the OMB in 1997, and since then a number of analyses and research projects have tried to produce better labels. All along, the OMB (2017) recognizes that

> the categories developed represent a socio-political construct designed to be used in the self-reported or observed collection of data on the race and ethnicity of major broad population groups in this country, and are not genetically-, anthropologically-, or scientifically-based. (p. 4)

These labels are therefore labels of convenience adopted by an agency of the federal government of the United States that, as the OMB states, have no basis in genetics or any science, but they help shape the collection and analysis of data. These assumptions are specific to the United States, and

Box 1.2

Definitions of Racial and Ethnic Groups

African American or Black: A person having origins in any of the Black racial groups of Africa

American Indian or Alaska Native: An individual having origins in any of the original peoples of North and South America (including Central America) and who maintains tribal affiliation or community attachment

Asian or Asian American: A person having origins in any of the original peoples of the Far East, Southeast Asia, or the Indian subcontinent, including, for example, Cambodia, China, India, Japan, Korea, Malaysia, Pakistan, the Philippines, Thailand, and Vietnam

Hispanic or Latino: A person of Cuban, Mexican, Puerto Rican, South or Central American, or other Spanish culture or origin, regardless of race

Native Hawai'ian or Other Pacific Islander: A person having origins in any of the original peoples of Hawai'i, Guam, Samoa, or other Pacific Islands

White or at times non-Hispanic White: A person having origins in any of the original peoples of Europe, the Middle East, or North Africa

Source: Office of Management and Budget, 1997.

other countries have chosen different approaches, such as the United Kingdom, which considers two types of Whites (*White British* and *White Other*) and does not talk about a White race but rather a White ethnicity. In 2017 the OMB considered a number of changes to the categories and standard definitions, including separating those with ancestry in the Middle East and North African countries (MENA countries) from White and creating a separate ethnicity or race for them. If approved, these and other changes will be implemented during the 2020 census.

Within-Group Diversity

It is also important to remember that the labels used in the census reports (such as *Hispanic*, *African American*, or *Asian*) as well as in this book and in most research publications are convenient labels that mask or hide important **within-group variability** or **within-group differences**. These differences among the members of a given ethnic or racial group ("within-group") are the product of variations in age, gender, national origin, socioeconomic status or social class, educational level, employment, and many other characteristics that affect people's behavior. For example, Asian Americans show vast differences in ancestry, with some tracing their ancestral heritage to Japan, others to China, and still others to Vietnam, Laos, Cambodia, Philippines, India, or other Asian regions entirely.

Unfortunately, a number of researchers and authors pay little attention to these within-group differences and assign generalized characteristics (e.g., average income, median educational level) to all members of a racial or ethnic group. This problem can easily be seen for Asian Americans who have been historically stereotyped as the **model minority** or a racial group that is uniformly financially and academically successful and well adjusted. This historical stereotype is often fueled by relatively higher-median household incomes and education levels reported for the larger Asian American population. However, income and education levels vary tremendously across different Asian American subgroups and generational cohorts (Chou & Feagin, 2015). For example, the overall percentage of Asian Americans who held at least a bachelor's degree in 2015 was 53.9 percent, a larger percentage than Whites (32.8 percent) or Latinos (15.5 percent) (Ryan & Bauman, 2016). These data could, at first glance, lead us to talk about Asian Americans as, indeed, a "model minority" in terms of educational attainment. Nevertheless, the use of such averages masks the fact that foreign-born Asian Americans have a much lower percentage (28 percent) of individuals who have achieved a bachelor's degree than all Asian Americans (Musu-Gillette et al., 2016). Furthermore, when those data are disaggregated by specific Asian American ethnicities, the differences are even starker and do not support the stereotype that *all* Asian Americans are highly educated "model minorities."

As you read the rest of this book you will see that, unfortunately, many researchers have ignored these within-group differences (sometimes because of convenience and sometimes because of the lack of sufficient numbers of research participants) and assign modal (or average) characteristics to all members of a given ethnic or racial group. In many cases, these problems lead to the development and perpetuation of certain myths about the characteristics of racial and ethnic minorities, as is the case of the model minority stereotype for Asian Americans. We will return to this topic in Chapter 3, when we discuss the methodological problems of much research in multicultural psychology, and also in Chapter 8, where we analyze the negative consequences of these myths and other stereotypes.

The next sections of this chapter describe a number of important social and demographic characteristics that define the various racial and ethnic groups in the United States. When possible, we also have included in our presentation some information on within-group differences.

Ancestry

The U.S. Census Bureau defines ancestry as the "roots," heritage, descent, ethnic origin, or place of birth of individuals or their parents or grandparents (ancestors). Ancestry does not reflect the level of personal attachment to a given ethnic or national (ancestral) group or culture; it only measures individuals' awareness of their heritage or ancestral roots. Ancestry sometimes correlates with a geographical area or political entity (e.g., Germany, Kenya, China, Colombia), but sometimes it refers to cultural heritage (such as Louisiana's Cajun).

In general, reports of data from the U.S. Census Bureau separate ancestry groups (e.g., Irish Americans, Russian Americans, Palestinians) from the major racial and ethnic groups (African Americans, American Indians and Alaska Natives, Asian Americans, Native Hawai'ians and Pacific Islanders, and Latinos or Hispanics). In this chapter and throughout the book we adopt this differentiation in order to facilitate subsequent research that you may wish to pursue.

Data from the U.S. Census Bureau (from 2010 through 2014, pulled from the American Community Survey) show that a large percentage of the total population of the country traced their **ancestry** back to at least one national group regardless of the length of time they and their families or ancestors had resided in the United States (U.S. Census Bureau, 2014). For example, a large percentage of the country's population reports German ancestry (14.9 percent). As shown in Table 1.1, other ancestries claimed by large percentages of the population of the United States included Irish (10.8 percent), English (8.0 percent), Italian (5.5 percent), Polish (3.0 percent), and French (2.7 percent). While the actual numbers and their percentages in the total population will necessarily change with the passing of time, the significance of a person's ancestry and the rank order of the major ancestries will probably not change radically from what is presented in Table 1.1.

Some of you may have had discussions with parents and other relatives about your ancestry ("where we come from") and how it defines certain traditions (holidays, special meals, gift giving), ways of thinking, and behaviors (whom to befriend, whom to marry, whom to trust). Also, very likely, you may have learned from parents and relatives about how your ancestry is primarily of one origin

TABLE 1.1 Largest Ancestries in the United States

Ancestry	Estimated population, 2014
German	46,047,113
Irish	33,147,639
English	24,382,182
Italian	17,220,604
Polish	9,249,392
French	8,153,515
Scottish	5,365,154
Norwegian	4,444,566
Dutch	4,243,067
Swedish	3,887,273
Scottish-Irish	2,978,827
Russian	2,762,830
French Canadian	2,099,430
Arab	1,927,432
Welsh	1,757,657
Czech	1,419,630
Hungarian	1,406,350
Portuguese	1,340,026
British	1,326,960
Greek	1,295,703
Danish	1,275,222
Jamaican	1,087,185

Source: Based on information from U.S. Census Bureau, 2014.

(e.g., Irish) but combined with others (e.g., English, Italian, German, Kenyan). This is a demonstration of the saliency of ancestry in our lives and of how the lived experiences of our families usually reflect the multiculturalism of the nation (as discussed in the previous paragraphs).

Race and Ethnicity

As mentioned before, the U.S. Census Bureau reports data on six major ethnic or racial groups: African American or Black, American Indian or Alaska Native, Asian, Hispanic, Native Hawaiian or Other Pacific Islander, and White (Box 1.2). The literature and popular use have modified some of these labels, and we have chosen to adopt those modifications in order to provide some consistency. For example, we generally will use *Asian American* to refer to those individuals to whom the U.S. Census Bureau refers as *Asian*. Also, we have chosen to use either *Hispanic* or *Latino* interchangeably. As mentioned in Chapter 3, this last ethnic group has been labeled variously in the last few years (e.g., *Spanish*, *Spanish-Speaking*), and *Latino* has been offered as an alternative to the imposed label of *Hispanic*. Nevertheless, *Latino* is also problematic, since it can be perceived to be a male-centered label (in Spanish, the -o ending denotes a masculine noun or adjective), although in Spanish groups composed of women and men are referred to using the masculine term. Alternatives suggested recently include *Latina/o*, *Latin@s*, or *Latinxs*. We also have chosen to change the spelling of *Hawaiian* to *Hawai'ian* to more accurately reflect the enunciation and representation in the Native Hawai'ian language.

The decennial census in 2010, the most recent available at publication time (see Table 1.2), shows that there were 281,421,906 people residing in the United States (Humes, Jones & Ramirez, 2011). Of these, 63.7 percent (196,817,552) considered themselves White alone (not Hispanic and not biracial). Overall, the largest racial or ethnic minority group was comprised of Latinos (16.3 percent), followed by Blacks/African Americans (12.6 percent), Asian Americans (4.8 percent), and Native Hawai'ian and Other Pacific Islanders (0.2 percent). States with the largest racial or ethnic minority populations were California (22.3 million), Texas (13.7 million), New York (8.1 million), Florida (7.9 million), and Illinois (4.7 million), and the populations of these states, together with the District of Columbia, showed that minority populations were the majority in the state.

As shown in Table 1.2, all racial and ethnic groups exhibited increases in their numbers between the last two U.S. censuses (2000 and 2010). Overall, ethnic and racial minority groups showed a 29 percent growth rate between 2000 and 2010, the largest being experienced in the South and West. The largest increases were found among Asian Americans (43.3 percent) and Latinos (43.0 percent). By the year 2050 it is estimated that more than half of the population of the country will be made up of individuals who identify wholly or partially as ethnic or racial minorities (often referred to as a *majority minority*), with the largest group being Latinos or Hispanics (24.4 percent), followed by

TABLE 1.2 Proportional Representation of Racial and Ethnic Groups

	Percent of U.S. population by year		
	2000 census	2010 census	2050, projected
African Americans	12.3	12.6	12.8
American Indians or Alaska Natives	0.9	0.9	1.0
Asian Americans	3.6	4.8	8.4
Hispanics/Latinos	12.5	16.3	24.4
Native Hawai'ians or Pacific Islanders	0.1	0.2	0.2
Whites	69.1	63.7	47.3

Sources: U.S. Census Bureau, Population Division, 2008; U.S. Census Bureau, 2014; Humes, Jones & Ramirez, 2011.

African Americans (12.8 percent) and Asian Americans (8.4 percent) (Passel & Cohn, 2008; U.S. Census Bureau, Population Division, 2008; U.S. Census Bureau, 2014). Other projections indicate that this transition to a majority-minority population for the whole country will take place as early as 2035 or 2040 (Esri, 2012; Reese-Cassal, 2014).

The various ethnic or racial groups differ in terms of the number of individuals who were born outside the United States and migrated within their lifetimes. According to 2013 data (U.S. Census Bureau, 2014), the highest percentage of individuals born outside the United States are Asian Americans (33 percent) and Latinos (65 percent). The large majority of the other ethnic or racial groups residing in the United States were born in the United States, including American Indians/Alaska Natives (99 percent), Whites (96 percent), African Americans (92 percent), and Pacific Islanders (80 percent) (Musu-Gillette et al., 2016). Among Latinos, the largest percentage of U.S.-born can be found (in descending order) among Puerto Ricans, Mexicans, Dominicans, Cubans, and Salvadorans. Similar within-group variability can be seen among Asian Americans, with the largest percentage of U.S.-born individuals found among the Japanese, Filipino, Vietnamese, Chinese, and South Asian Indian populations.

The numbers presented in Table 1.2 imply that living in the United States provides expanding opportunities to interact with ethnically diverse populations. Reese-Cassal (2014) and colleagues have developed the Esri Diversity Index to "[represent] the likelihood that two persons, chosen at random from the same area, belong to different race or ethnic groups" (p. 3). The index goes from 0, which indicates no diversity, to 100, which denotes complete diversity. The researchers estimate that in 2010 the Esri Diversity Index was 60.6, while in 2019 it is projected to be 65 (a probability of 65 percent that two people randomly chosen would belong to different ethnicities or races).

Multiracial or Multiethnic Background

The 2010 U.S. census shows that approximately 9.3 million people (2.9 percent of the total U.S. population) considered themselves to belong to two or more races. The equivalent data for the 2000 census was 6.8 million, or 2.4 percent of the total population (Jones & Smith, 2003), and 5.3 percent of the population is expected to belong to two or more races by the year 2050 (U.S. Census Bureau, 2014). The largest percentage of people reporting multiple races in the 2010 census were found among Native Hawai'ians and Other Pacific Islanders (55.9 percent) and among American Indians and Alaska Natives (43.8 percent) (Humes, Jones, & Ramirez, 2011). A survey by the Pew Research Center (2015) estimates that multiracial individuals accounted for approximately 6.9 percent of the total U.S. population in 2015. That study also shows that a majority of multiracial individuals (80 percent) were biracial (e.g., White and Latino), with a smaller percentage (10 percent) considered belonging to three races.

The rest of this section presents some of the other important social and demographic characteristics that highlight within-group diversity among various ethnic and racial groups and that need to be taken into consideration when reading or doing research about various minority groups.

Age Differences

Overall, ethnic and racial minority groups are young—particularly those who self-identify as Latino and Asian American. The percentage of the U.S. population between five and 17 years of age (often considered to be of "school age") who are from these two groups has shown a major increase. For example, numbers of school-age Latinos increased from 16 percent of the total school-age U.S. population in 2000 to 24 percent in 2013 (Musu-Gillette et al., 2016). At the same time the population of school-age White children decreased from 62 percent in the year 2000 to 53 percent in 2013. Multiracial individuals are also on average much younger (median age of 19 years) than all single-race individuals (median age of 38 years). In fact, 46 percent of the multiracial population were 18 years of age or younger, compared to 23 percent of the total U.S. population (Pew Research Center, 2015). Schools, therefore, are exhibiting the same major demographic shifts occurring nationally and are being entrusted with teaching more ethnically and racially diverse student populations.

Language Use and Proficiency

Language proficiency is another characteristic varying across and within racial and ethnic groups. Census data show that over recent decades, the number of individuals who speak a language other than English at home has progressively increased. The 2000 census shows that approximately 18 percent of people age five years or older spoke a language other than English at home. The corresponding figure for the 1990 census was 14 percent, and it was 11 percent for the 1980 census (Shin & Bruno, 2003). In the year 2010, approximately 37 million people spoke Spanish (approximately a 232 percent increase over the year 1980).

For the country as a whole, frequently spoken languages, other than English and Spanish, are Chinese (2.8 million), French (2.1 million), German (1.0 million), Tagalog (language of Philippines, 1.6 million), Vietnamese (1.4 million), and Korean (1.1 million) (Ryan, 2013; Shin & Bruno, 2003). Speaking a language other than English does not always result in less fluency in English. Data from the American Community Survey for 2011 show that a large number of those who spoke a language other than English at home also spoke English either "very well" (58.2 percent) or "well" (19.4 percent). English proficiency seemed to be correlated with higher levels of education, naturalization, and with income above the poverty level (Ryan, 2013).

National data for 2013 show a fairly large percentage of public school students considered English-Language Learners (ELLs), particularly among Latinos (29 percent), Asian Americans (20 percent), and Pacific Islanders (14 percent) (Musu-Gillette et al., 2016). This is one of many factors possibly related to gaps in primary and secondary school achievement across ethnic and racial groups that in turn affects future performance in college and in employment settings. For example, the White-Black reading achievement gap in 2013 was 30 points (compared to 24 points in 1992). The White-Latino reading achievement gap in 2013 was 22 points and had changed little since 1992. These data are of concern, since they show that reading achievement among ethnic and racial minority students (at least for African Americans and Latinos) has basically not improved over two decades.

A phenomenon of particular importance among recent immigrants, and particularly among Latinos, is the level of maternal- or ancestral-language maintenance occurring across extended periods of time of residence in the United States and even across generations. Research with Latinos has shown that immigrants maintain proficiency in Spanish even after 50 years of residence in the country and after having achieved proficiency in the use of English (Bahrick, Hall, Goggin, Bahrick, & Berger, 1994). An earlier study with Cuban American youths (Garcia & Diaz, 1992) shows that, while Spanish was preferred by children in preschool, a mixture of English and Spanish became the preferred pattern of usage during the last years of high school, although the social setting (e.g., school, home) in the interaction (e.g., among friends, siblings, parents) moderated which language was used.

Educational Attainment

Historically the United States has been improving the level of educational attainment of its population by supporting compulsory education in primary and secondary schooling and by providing financial support for tertiary (college) education. Data from the 2015 Current Population Survey show that, overall, a high percentage (88.4 percent) of U.S. residents age 25 and older had achieved a secondary school education (high school or GED) with almost one in three adults (32.5 percent) having completed at least a bachelor's degree (Ryan & Bauman, 2016). The data also show that there is no difference in high school attainment between women (88.8 percent) and men (88.0 percent) and very little difference between men (32.3 percent) and women (32.7 percent) who have completed a bachelor's degree or higher. Nevertheless, there are important differences in educational attainment across racial and ethnic groups. Among individuals 25 years or older, Asian Americans (when studied as an aggregate) show the highest levels of educational attainment (53.9 percent) in terms of achieving at least a bachelor's degree as well as an advanced degree (21.4 percent). Latinos, by contrast, show the lowest, with 15.5 percent having completed a bachelor's degree or higher (see Table 1.3). However, these figures mask important differences between different subgroups, as noted in our discussion of within-group variability.

TABLE 1.3 Educational Attainment Rates of Adults Age 25 and Older

	Percent of U.S. population age 25 and older			
	High school graduate or more	Some college or more	Bachelor's degree or more	Advanced degree
All	88.4	58.9	32.5	12.0
Female	88.8	60.1	32.7	12.0
Male	88.0	57.6	32.3	12.0
African American	87.0	52.9	22.5	8.2
Asian American	89.1	70.0	53.9	21.4
Latino	66.7	36.8	15.5	4.7
White (non-Hispanic)	93.3	63.8	36.2	13.5

Source: Data by Ryan & Bauman, 2016.

A number of variables have been proposed to explain the differences in educational achievement across ethnic and racial groups (Kurtz-Costes, Swinton, & Skinner, 2014). An important explanation for these differences in outcomes and student success is the low quality of schools located in poor neighborhoods in terms of facilities, underprepared teachers and limited instructional support, and resources, which affects students' academic involvement and learning. Also relevant are low expectations teachers hold for minority students because of the color of their skin, their limited English-language skills, or their personal experiences. Poverty at home, low parental involvement with the school system due to work schedules or family responsibilities, and lack of immigrant families' familiarity with the U.S. educational system also explain differences in academic achievement across ethnic and racial groups. Educational attainment, therefore, is another relevant variable to disaggregate when reading or conducting research among ethnic and racial minority groups.

High School Persistence Rates

Related to these differences in educational attainment is the rate of *persistence* (measuring the number of students who do not drop out before graduating to the next grade level) in secondary school. Data from 2013 (Musu-Gillete et al., 2016) show important group differences in dropout rates among 16- to 24-year-olds, with American Indians and Alaska Natives exhibiting the highest rate (13 percent), followed in descending order by Latinos (12 percent), African Americans (9 percent), and Asian Americans (2 percent). The dropout rate for Whites was 5 percent. Among racial and ethnic groups, the rate of dropouts was generally higher among those born outside the United States (e.g., 22 percent for immigrant Latinos compared to 8 percent for domestic Latinos). As expected, there are important subgroup differences in dropout rates. For example, among Latinos the largest dropout rates for those 16 to 24 years old were for Guatemalans (27 percent), Hondurans (20 percent), and Salvadorans (13 percent). Among Asian Americans the highest numbers of school dropouts were among Bhutanese (37 percent) and Burmese (21 percent), while the largest subgroups in terms of overall size (Chinese, Filipino, Japanese, Korean) had dropout rates of no more than 2 percent.

College Enrollment

Data from the 2013 American Community Survey (Musu-Gillette et al., 2016) show that, among 18- to 24-year-olds, Asian Americans had the highest college-enrollment percentage (62 percent), followed by Whites (42 percent), African Americans (34 percent), Latinos (34 percent), Pacific

TABLE 1.4 Distribution of Fall 2014 Undergraduate Enrollment at Degree-Granting Institutions in the United States, by Selected Race or Ethnicity and Type of Institution

	Percent of fall 2014 undergraduates			
Institution	**Asian American**	**African American**	**Hispanic**	**White**
Public two-year	40	44	56	39
Public four-year	43	29	29	39
Private nonprofit four-year	14	13	8	17
For-profit	3	14	7	5
Total	100	100	100	100

Source: Ma & Baum, 2016.

Islanders (33 percent), and American Indians/Alaska Natives (32 percent). As expected, there are important within-group differences. Among Latinos, the highest college-participation rates were found among Venezuelans, Peruvians, Costa Ricans, Colombians, and Panamanians. Mexican Americans and Central Americans (from Guatemala, Honduras, Nicaragua, and El Salvador) have some of the lowest college-enrollment rates. Among Asian Americans the highest college-enrollment rates for 18- to 24-year-olds are found among the Chinese, Japanese, Pakistani, Korean, Vietnamese, and Asian Indian populations.

There are differences in the number of ethnic and racial minority students who enroll at certain types of higher education institutions (see Table 1.4). Data from the 2014 Integrated Postsecondary Education Data System (IPEDS, a federal government data collection process) show that among Latinos the highest percentage of higher-education attendees (56 percent) are enrolled at public two-year institutions (commonly referred to as community colleges). Substantial numbers of African Americans (44 percent) also are enrolled in community colleges. The largest percentage of Asian Americans in this cohort (43 percent) are enrolled in public four-year institutions (usually state colleges or universities). Among Whites, similar percentages of students (39 percent) are enrolled in community colleges and in four-year public institutions (Ma & Baum, 2016). Moreover, a large percentage of African Americans (14 percent) are enrolled at for-profit institutions, a higher percentage than found among any other racial or ethnic group.

Socioeconomic Status and Poverty

Significant income differences also exist across the various ethnic and racial groups. U.S. census data for 2014 (DeNavas-Walt & Proctor, 2015) show that the real median household income for the whole country was $53,657. Nevertheless, incomes varied markedly across ethnic and racial groups, with Asian Americans reporting the highest median household income ($74,297), followed by Whites ($60,256); below the nation's median were Latinos ($42,491) and African Americans ($35,398). While these composite amounts are informative, keep in mind that, as mentioned previously, the data mask ethnic and racial subgroup differences (e.g., differences in median income between Chinese Americans and Vietnamese Americans). Also, residential area must be considered when evaluating income differences across ethnic groups. Asian Americans and Latinos primarily reside in metropolitan centers (e.g., San Francisco, Los Angeles, New York City) with higher costs of living, and thus their dollars do not stretch as far in covering home mortgages or rentals, food, and other daily living expenses.

Poverty rates in the United States have been declining over the years, with the exception of the period stretching from 2000 to 2010, when the poverty rates remained fairly stable due to the 2008 national recession. In the 2000 census, approximately 34 million people in the United States

(12.4 percent of the total population) reported incomes below the poverty level. Ten years earlier (1990), 13.1 percent of all U.S. residents had been classified as living below the poverty line. Data from the 2014 Current Population Survey show that almost 15 out of 100 U.S. residents—or 46.7 million people—were living in poverty (DeNavas-Walt & Proctor, 2015). In 2014, African Americans (26.2 percent) experienced the highest rate of poverty, followed by Latinos (23.6 percent) and Asian Americans (12 percent). The poverty rate for non-Hispanic Whites was 12.7 percent.

Disaggregated data by ethnic and racial groups are available for the results of the American Community Surveys covering 2007 to 2011 (Macartney, Bishaw, & Fontenot, 2013), and these data show more detailed information on economic hardship across groups. Among Asian Americans, differences across subgroups included Korean Americans' reporting the highest percentage (15.0 percent) living below the poverty line, followed by Vietnamese (14.7 percent), Chinese (13.4 percent), Japanese (8.2 percent), Asian Indians (8.2 percent), and Filipinos (5.8 percent). Among Latinos, Dominican Americans comprised the largest percentage of individuals living under the poverty line (26.3 percent), followed in descending order by Puerto Ricans (25.6 percent), Guatemalans (24.9 percent), Mexican Americans (24.9 percent), Salvadorans (18.9 percent), and Cubans (16.2 percent).

Correlates of Poverty

There are some social variables that differentiate income and poverty rates across individuals and families. One important correlate is place of birth (in or outside the United States) of individuals. Overall, those born in the United States had a 2014 median income of $54,678, compared with $49,592 for those born outside the United States (by way of comparison, the overall median income for the whole country was $53,657) (DeNavas-Walt & Proctor, 2015). The poverty rate of foreign-born individuals is higher (18.5 percent) than that of the native born (14.2 percent).

Also relevant is the role that family composition plays on income. Data from the 2014 Current Population Survey show that single head of household families, especially those headed by women, experienced greater poverty (30.6 percent for female-headed households and 15.7 percent for male-headed households, compared to 6.2 percent for families with two parents). Other factors relevant in analyzing poverty levels of ethnic minorities include the fact that some ethnic groups (e.g., Latinos, African Americans) are relatively young and tend to have lower levels of educational attainment. On average, those under 18 years of age have a higher poverty rate (21.1 percent) than do individuals ages 18 to 64 years old (13.5 percent) (DeNavas-Walt & Proctor, 2015). The 2014 Current Population Survey data show that 10.1 percent of non-Hispanic Whites reported incomes below poverty (as defined by the U.S. Census Bureau). At the same time, 23.6 percent of Latinos reported earnings below poverty level, compared to 26.2 percent of African Americans and 12 percent of Asian Americans (DeNavas-Walt & Proctor, 2015).

Additionally, working men have higher median earnings ($50,383) than working women ($39,621), and those individuals ages 25 to 34 with a college education have a higher median income ($50,000) than those with only a high school education ($30,000) (Musu-Gillette et al., 2016). Not surprisingly, earning data differ across ethnic and racial groups. The 2014 Current Population Survey (Musu-Gillette et al., 2016) shows that, among adults ages 25 to 34 who had a college education (minimum of a bachelor's degree), Asian Americans had the highest median income ($59,900), followed by Whites ($50,000), Latinos ($45,800), and African Americans ($44,600). As expected, those with only a high school education reported a lower median income: $31,700 among Whites, $28,300 among Latinos, $27,900 among Asian Americans, and $25,000 among African Americans (Musu-Guillette et al., 2016).

Unemployment is obviously an important contributor to poverty, and data from the 2013 American Community Survey (Musu-Gillette et al., 2016) show that African Americans have a disproportionally higher rate of unemployment (12 percent) among those 25 to 64 years old compared with the total population (7 percent) and with other ethnic and racial groups—with Latinos at 8 percent, Whites at 6 percent, and Asian Americans at 5 percent.

Also important, particularly in the case of Latinos and Asian Americans, is the fact that large amounts of income are sent as remittances to their countries of origin in order to help house, feed, and educate children, parents, and other relatives or to help with the damage produced by disasters and armed conflicts. It is estimated that, worldwide, $431.6 billion were sent to countries with developing economies (World Bank, 2016). The Pew Research Center (2014) reported that the largest country receiver of remittances was India, followed by Mexico, China, Philippines, Nigeria, Vietnam, South Korea, Guatemala, El Salvador, Dominican Republic, Honduras, and Germany.

The fact that high levels of poverty exist among members of racial and ethnic groups is a troubling finding not only because it implies that there is no disposable income for savings but also, and more important, because it means that there are daily needs that are not being fully met (nutrition, educational opportunities, housing, transportation). Of particular concern is the fact that large numbers of racial and ethnic minority children (under 18 years of age) live in poverty. In 2013 a high percentage (39 percent) of African American children and of Latino children (30 percent) lived in poverty, compared to Asian American (as a whole) and White children (both at 10 percent) (Musu-Gillette et al., 2016). These figures are of concern because experiences of poverty have significant effects on people's health and behavior (APA Task Force on Socioeconomic Status, 2007), and particularly on a child's intellectual and emotional development (Evans, 2004). For example, a large-scale study on the effects of economic deprivation on early childhood development (Duncan, Brooks-Gunn, & Klebanov, 1994) shows that low family income and poverty status correlated with poor levels of children's cognitive development and social maturity. Furthermore, poverty can be related to lower psychological well-being (Saéz-Santiago & Bernal, 2003), higher risk for depression (Downey & Coyne, 1990), and inferior parenting skills (Rainwater, 1970).

Why Study Multicultural Psychology?

This book is part of recent efforts by researchers and practitioners within the field of psychology to struggle to better understand and appreciate racial and ethnic diversity. In writing this book we are trying to answer many of the questions arising for Lee and Dwayne—the two students in the vignette at the beginning of the chapter—regarding what psychology has to say about their experiences and their culture. The information included in this book will also help you, students of all ethnic and racial groups, to learn how psychology has tried to better understand the effects of a person's culture on behavior and on physical and mental health. As such, the book explores how being exposed to or raised in a particular racial, ethnic, or cultural community influences the way individuals think about the world, the value they place on family interactions, and their expectations for personal relationships. The sections in the following pages summarize some additional compelling reasons to study and perhaps consider a professional career in multicultural psychology.

Improving Psychological Research

What is the relevance of our country's ethnic and racial diversity to psychology? Simply put, our knowledge of human behavior only makes sense when properly contextualized in terms of the characteristics of the population. As Trickett (1996) argues, psychological theory, research, and interventions need to be located within the sociocultural context in which individuals and communities reside. As a matter of fact, much research in multicultural psychology and in cross-cultural psychology suggests that what is appropriate or even valued in one culture may be rejected in others (Sternberg, 2004). For example, Okagaki and Sternberg (1993) find that Hispanic parents tended to define intelligence in their school-age children in terms of skills in social competence, while Asian American and White parents tended to emphasize cognitive skills. At the same time, teachers, reflecting the values of White culture, placed emphasis on cognitive skills and rewarded children in terms of their development of those skills rather than in terms of their social competence. Not surprisingly, Latino children were ranked as less intelligent by those teachers whose conceptions of intelligence differed from what Latino parents valued the most. Indeed, many researchers argue that "the conceptualization, assessment, and development of intelligence [or any other psychological construct] cannot be fully or even meaningfully understood outside their cultural context" (Sternberg, 2004, p. 325). The same statement can be made regarding psychological research and theorizing with members of ethnic and racial groups in a multicultural society. Contextualizing behavior in terms of relevant cultures is therefore one important reason for studying multicultural psychology.

One other important reason for studying the psychology of ethnic and racial minority groups is because it contributes validity and usefulness to the field at large by conducting good, quality research. Ignoring cultural values and expectancies as well as using inappropriate methodological approaches to measurement can produce terribly false information and conclusions with limited external validity (Helms, 2006; Sue, 1999).

Psychology has frequently made embarrassingly erroneous statements in the area of intelligence measurement—statements based on improper conceptualization of the constructs, ignorance of group-specific values, or invalid measurements. It is widely known, for example, that during the infancy of intelligence measurement in the early part of the 20th century, intelligence tests were given to recently landed immigrants in the United States as a way of detecting mental and intellectual deficiencies among that group. Some immigrants were excluded from entry to the United States by simple observation on the part of immigration officials or through examinations and tests that suffered from untrained translators or that had been altered by eliminating items from the original version. Likewise, and not surprisingly, data showed that many immigrants with limited English abilities often scored fairly low in intelligence measures. Indeed, early researchers believed that the majority of the Italian, Hungarian, and Russian immigrants they tested should be considered "morons" or "feeble-minded," even though these researchers failed to consider the fact that many of the test subjects did not speak English and had been asked to complete an intelligence test in a language they neither understood nor spoke. Another significant example of egregious oversight in the field is the argument of the heritability of intelligence as an explanation for lower IQ scores among African Americans (Herrnstein & Murray, 1994), where the effects of culture-specific definitions of intelligence and the pervasive influence of socioeconomic status were ignored while measuring instruments were used that were not culturally appropriate, as they had not been normed or standardized for the populations tested. Proper attention to cultural, racial, and ethnic differences, as required by multicultural psychology, would have allowed those psychologists to properly contextualize their findings and to make scientifically valid observations.

Attention to racial and ethnic variations in psychological theory and instrumentation, of course, does not imply an absolute relativism that would reject all that psychology has produced. It is indeed quite possible that some of the theories and behavioral principles that have evolved over the last 100-plus years of scientific psychology are generalizable or applicable to all racial and ethnic populations and across cultures. In that sense we should be able to use certain psychological principles to explain the behavior of people from different cultures, races, and ethnicities. What is important is to question the a priori assumption of generalizability across ethnicities or cultures. That generalizability needs to be demonstrated by conducting culturally appropriate research (see Chapter 3). This goal of demonstrating generalizability becomes the guiding principle of multicultural psychology as presented throughout this book.

Advancing Culturally Diverse Societies

A number of issues are of relevance when we try to understand how culturally diverse societies can function better by supporting the incorporation of individuals of varying cultural, racial, and ethnic backgrounds and by respecting and celebrating those differences. As shown at the beginning of this chapter, a diverse environment helps individuals improve their learning and performance. For psychologists, therefore, a key concern is how our science can best contribute to those goals of understanding cultures and ethnic differences and promoting individual growth in ethnically and culturally diverse environments.

The proper understanding of contemporary racially and ethnically diverse societies requires input from various disciplines to provide a more appropriate and comprehensive picture of a nation. Berry (2003) argues that an understanding of diverse multicultural societies requires at a minimum the interaction of psychology, sociology, anthropology, and political science, which together provide an understanding of three key aspects of a diverse society: (1) its sociocultural factors (e.g., discrimination, prejudice), (2) public policies (e.g., health care policy, social welfare policy), and (3) the behavior of individuals (e.g., psychological adjustment, coping behavior).

While the emphasis in this book is on psychological research, we have added at times findings and theories from sociology and other social sciences in order to provide a more comprehensive perspective. Indeed, a significant amount of research in the social sciences has helped psychologists develop better studies with racial and ethnic minority communities. Anthropologists, for example, have provided a nuanced understanding of culture by researching how primary social units (such as the family) function and how they influence people's values, beliefs, attitudes, and social behaviors. Sociologists have helped psychologists understand the roles played by groups and other social entities in supporting an individual's development of values and norms as well as the roles played by expectations for the way they and others should behave. Other social sciences have contributed to our knowledge of issues as complex as discrimination, judicial bias, underemployment, homelessness, poor-quality social services, and racial profiling. Multicultural psychologists work in tandem with these social scientists to improve the social conditions of ethnic and racial minority individuals and, by doing so, advance multicultural societies.

A key component of advancing the development of multicultural societies is the contribution psychology can make promoting a fair and just society, where differences are valued and respected. Prejudice and fearmongering make it difficult for individuals to trust each other, show respect for their values and traditions, be able to work together, and share in the benefits of living in multicultural settings. Unfortunately, we have recently seen the results of a "banalization of bigotry," as labeled by the United Nations High Commissioner for Human Rights (Cumming-Bruce, 2016). This process involves use of racist language and the thinking and peddling of fear by politicians and citizens alike to defend persecutions and exterminations; limitations on migration; discrimination in job placement, housing, and law enforcement; and many other shameful acts against those who differ because of their faith, nationality, traditions, and traits. As you will see in this book (particularly in Chapter 8), multicultural psychology has much to contribute to eliminating prejudice and discrimination and to promoting trust and social justice among individuals from diverse races and ethnicities.

Improving the Quality of Health and Human Services

Research with racial and ethnic minority communities also helps service providers (such as counselors, teachers, therapists, physicians, and other health care personnel) to properly support and promote the social, personal, and psychological development of members of the various racial and ethnic communities. For example, to be effective, preventive and therapeutic services in psychology as well as in medicine and public health must reflect the needs of those individuals being served rather than the characteristics of the providers (Rossa, Dumka, Gonzales, & Knight, 2002). To be useful to these communities, psychological research—as well as the research of other social and behavioral sciences—must adhere to standards of scientific integrity and validity including external or ecological validity in research studies (see Chapter 3) (Sue & Sue, 2008; Sue, 1999).

Promoting Cultural Competencies

A major objective of multicultural psychology is the development of culturally competent individuals. We define a **culturally competent individual** as someone who understands and appreciates cultural diversity in others; interacts effectively and meaningfully with individuals who differ on culture, race, ethnicity, gender, social class, sexuality, and so on; and advocates for a society that values and is respectful of diversity.

Efforts at developing culturally competent individuals and institutions were central to efforts of the U.S. federal government when developing services for immigrants, refugees, and cultural minorities. As early as 1965 when the Social Security Amendments were promulgated, the U.S. government expected services to be provided in a culturally and linguistically appropriate manner. Since then, psychology and other allied disciplines have researched the characteristics that define a culturally competent individual. Indeed, the importance of cultural competencies has been highlighted in diverse contexts such as schools (Cuyjet, Linder, Howard-Hamilton, & Cooper, 2016), psychological practice (Lowman, 2013), health care (Rassool, 2014), and organizational management (Borrego & Johnson, 2012; Dolan & Kawamura, 2015). Unfortunately, many models of cultural competence emphasize cognitive and behavioral components while ignoring the role of cultural contexts and related social ecology (Suarez-Balcazar, Balcazar, García-Ramirez, & Taylor-Ritzler, 2014). This important outcome of studying multicultural psychology is explored in greater detail in Chapters 9 and 10 when we analyze cultural competence in health care and in psychological treatment.

As you can see, there are many reasons for studying multicultural psychology, and they all can be subsumed under our need to understand and contribute to the advancement of a diverse society such as the United States. By the time you finish reading this book, you will have acquired a comprehensive and nuanced knowledge of issues such as ethnicity, race, minority status, class differences, and cultural values and their effects on people's behavior. This knowledge should help you become an informed student of human behavior and a culturally competent and engaged citizen.

Multicultural Psychology, Cultural Psychology, and Cross-Cultural Psychology

Psychological literature often uses interchangeably terms as diverse as *multicultural psychology*, *cross-cultural psychology*, *ethnic psychology*, and *cultural psychology* to describe the study of cultural influences on psychological phenomena. While all of them are concerned with "culture" and behavior, they differ in important ways. At this point, it is important to differentiate between cross-cultural psychology and multicultural psychology. While both areas study the effects of culture and cultural differences on people's behavior, they differ in terms of their cultural or geographic areas of emphasis. **Cross-cultural psychology** emphasizes differences in cultural influences across nations or regions of the world. **Multicultural psychology**, however, tends to focus on racial, ethnic, and cultural group differences within a single nation or community (Segall, Lonner, & Berry, 1998). As such, cross-cultural psychology focuses, for example, on studying differences and similarities in moral development in children in the United States and in Mexico, while multicultural psychology would concentrate on studying moral development among Mexican Americans. While both areas attend to cultural issues in research methods (see Chapter 3) and sometimes have overlapping areas of scientific interest (e.g., values, intergroup relations, cognition, psychopathology), they differ in their unit of analysis (who is studied) and location of research—within-country or nation for multicultural psychology, and across countries or cultures for cross-cultural psychology.

There are topical areas that overlap in cross-cultural and multicultural psychology, and these similarities in interests actually enrich their development by cross-fertilizing theoretical advances and empirical discoveries. Nevertheless, care should be taken to not make inappropriate generalizations. Indeed, findings from cross-cultural research must be carefully analyzed before being generalized to an ethnic or racial minority population and vice versa. For example, research on the development of a child's value structure among children in Beijing cannot be generalized to Chinese Americans in San Francisco since both groups of children have been exposed to a number of important differences in child-rearing, including schooling (usually public, government subsidized schools in Beijing) and racial and ethnic diversity of the social environment (greater in San Francisco).

Another important difference between cross-cultural psychology and multicultural psychology is the centrality given to the role played by differences in culture learning (usually called *acculturation*) on an individual's beliefs, values, attitudes, and behaviors. Research in multicultural psychology must take into consideration how acculturation affects people's behavior—if not directly, then at least indirectly (see Chapter 4 for a more thorough discussion of acculturation and its effects on psychological and health outcomes).

Also essential to multicultural psychology is the recognition of the significance of certain social conditions that affect the attitudes and behaviors of ethnic groups, such as often being part of statistical minorities and experiencing the results of social and economic stratification. At the same time, both cross-cultural psychology and multicultural psychology share the belief that in order for psychology to be valid and useful, it must consider the mutual influences that exist between a person's culture and behavior (Segall et al., 1998).

As psychology is an evolving field (see the next section of this chapter), different labels have been preferred by some authors over time, and, as such, we find multicultural psychology sometimes referred to as *ethnic psychology* or *ethnic minority psychology*. In this book, we have chosen to talk about *multicultural psychology* since it seems to be the most frequently used term at the time of our writing, although we used the term *ethnic psychology* in the first edition of the book and in other publications. We consider these changes in labels a sign of lively growth of the field, which is captured throughout this book.

The Growth of Multicultural Psychology

The overlap between multicultural psychology and cross-cultural psychology will be seen throughout this book as principles, and even authors and research findings, from cross-cultural psychology are mentioned. Nevertheless, both fields have become better defined, and an examination of cross-cultural-psychology and of multicultural-psychology textbooks or even research articles will easily show the differences in perspective, individuals studied, and theories or hypotheses. Indeed, the last few years have seen a significant growth in multicultural-psychology publications, including the *Handbook of Racial & Ethnic Minority Psychology* (Bernal, Trimble, Burlew, & Leong, 2003), the collection of articles in *Readings in Ethnic Psychology* (Balls Organista, Chun, & Marín, 1998), handbooks or texts directed at practitioners or clinicians such as the *Handbook of Multicultural Counseling* (Ponterotto, Casas, Suzuki, & Alexander, 2001), and the *Encyclopedia of Race, Ethnicity, and Society* (Schaefer, 2008) and the *APA Handbook of Multicultural Psychology* (Leong, Comas-Díaz, Hall, McLoyd, & Trimble, 2014). These publications join a number of textbooks (e.g., Hall, 2018; Mio, Barker, & Domenech Rodríguez, 2016; Organista, 2007; Sue & Sue, 2008) as well as professional books dealing with methodological concerns in social science research with racial and ethnic populations, such as *Research with Hispanic Populations* (Marín & VanOss Marín, 1991), *Race and Ethnicity in Research Methods* (Stanfield & Dennis, 1993), and *Studying Ethnic Minority and Economically Disadvantaged Populations* (Knight, Roosa, & Umaña-Taylor, 2009). Likewise, a number of journals emphasize racial and ethnic psychological research (see Box 1.3). In addition, most scientific journals in the social and behavioral sciences are now publishing an increasing number of articles dealing with multicultural psychology.

Box 1.3

Selection of Journals Publishing Racial and Ethnic Psychology

Asian American Journal of Psychology
Cultural Diversity & Ethnic Minority Psychology
Equity & Excellence in Education
Ethnic and Racial Studies
Ethnicities
Ethnicity & Health
Hispanic Journal of Behavioral Sciences
International Journal of Intercultural Relations
International Migration Review
The Journal of Black Psychology
The Journal of Educational Issues of Language Minority Students
Journal of Ethnic and Migration Studies
Journal of Immigrant and Minority Health
Journal of Latina/o Psychology
Minority Health

One of the reasons the field of multicultural psychology is rapidly growing in significance and scientific importance is the realization that a psychology based on members of one group alone (usually Whites) does not validly represent the variety and richness of human behavior (this is a topic that we cover at greater length in Chapter 3). Indeed, significant advances in multicultural psychology have been made in other diverse societies such as Australia, Canada, Israel, and the Netherlands as well as in francophone countries (France, Belgium), where the field is often called *psychologie interculturelle* (intercultural psychology).

The achievements and developments we currently witness in multicultural psychology are the result of the efforts of a number of individuals who for decades have advocated the development of a psychology that reflects the social and demographic realities of the country. This history of slow but certain achievements has been well documented (e.g., Holliday & Holmes, 2003; Leong & Okazaki, 2009), and Box 1.4 highlights some of those key developments.

Box 1.4

Some Key Moments in the Development of Multicultural Psychology

1885	The first mental hospital for the exclusive treatment of African Americans is opened near Petersburg, Virginia.
1899	Howard University in Washington, DC, offers its first psychology course.
1920	Francis C. Sumner is the first African American awarded a PhD in psychology.
1928	Howard University establishes a department of psychology.
1937	Alberta B. Turner is the first African American woman to receive a PhD in psychology.
1943	Robert Chin is the first Chinese American to receive a PhD in psychology.
1951	Efraín Sánchez Hidalgo is the first Puerto Rican to receive a PhD in psychology.
1962	Martha Bernal is the first Mexican American woman to be awarded a PhD in psychology.
1963	The American Psychological Association establishes the Ad Hoc Committee on Equality of Opportunity in Psychology to analyze problems in training and employment due to race.
1968	The Association of Black Psychologists (ABPsi) is founded.
1970	The Association of Psychologists por la Raza is founded.
1970	Kenneth B. Clark becomes the first person of color and first African American president of the APA.
1971	The National Institute of Mental Health (NIMH) establishes the Center for Minority Group Mental Health Programs.
1972	The Asian American Psychological Association is founded.
1972	The APA founds the Committee on Women in Psychology.
1974	The APA founds the Minority Fellowship Program.
1974	*The Journal of Black Psychology* is founded.
1975	The Society of Indian Psychologists is founded.
1976	*Psychology of Women Quarterly* begins publication.
1977	The *International Journal of Intercultural Relations* begins publication.
1978	The APA establishes the Ad Hoc Committee on Minority Affairs.
1979	The APA founds the Office of Ethnic Minority Affairs with Esteban Olmedo as its first director.
1979	The National Hispanic Psychological Association is founded.
1979	Amado M. Padilla founds the *Hispanic Journal of Behavioral Sciences*.
1979	The first issue of the *Journal of the Asian American Psychological Association* is published.
1980	The APA establishes the Board of Ethnic Minority Affairs.
1985	The Asian American Psychological Association holds its first convention.

1985	The APA creates Division 44—the Society for the Psychological Study of Lesbian and Gay Issues.
1986	The APA establishes Division 45—the Society for the Psychological Study of Ethnic Minority Issues.
1986	Logan Wright is the first American Indian to become president of the APA.
1988	The APA publishes its "Guidelines for Avoiding Sexism in Psychological Research" (today found online at https://www.apa.org/about/policy/avoiding-sexism.pdf).
1999	First issue of the journal *Cultural Diversity & Ethnic Minority Psychology* is published.
1999	The APA passes a resolution supporting affirmative action and equal opportunity.
1999	Richard M. Suinn is the first Asian American to serve as APA president.
2000	The APA develops "Guidelines for Psychotherapy with Lesbian, Gay, and Bisexual Clients" (today found online at https://www.apa.org/practice/guidelines/glbt.pdf).
2002	Norman B. Anderson becomes the first African American to serve as the APA's chief executive officer.
2002	The National Hispanic Psychological Association changes its name to the National Latino/a Psychological Association.
2003	The *Handbook of Racial & Ethnic Minority Psychology* is published.
2010	Melba Vasquez is elected the first Latina president of the APA.
2010	The *Asian American Journal of Psychology* beings publication under the APA.
2013	The *Journal of Latina/o Psychology* begins publication under the APA.
2014	The APA Handbook of Multicultural Psychology is published.
2017	The APA publishes *Multicultural Guidelines: An Ecological Approach to Context, Identity, and Intersectionality, 2017* (www.apa.org/about/policy/multicultural-guidelines.pdf).

Sources: Based on Holliday & Holmes, 2003; Padilla & Olmedo, 2009.

Nevertheless, attention to multicultural psychology in the United States by professional associations is a somewhat recent phenomenon. Only in 2002 did the American Psychological Association (APA) issue a series of guidelines for the training and professional practice of psychologists (Box 1.5), which were revised fifteen years later (American Psychological Association, 2017). These principles respond to the need for psychologists to be knowledgeable of and proficient in understanding members of various ethnic groups and to be culturally competent in their professional practice whether teaching, conducting research, or applying psychological knowledge. The guidelines are fairly broad but are based on the belief that as social beings we all have attitudes and expectancies that can affect how we treat other individuals, particularly those who differ from ourselves. Furthermore, the APA's guidelines support the notion that much psychological research may be limited in its usefulness and appropriateness by monocultural perspectives of researchers and the lack of diversity (ethnic, gender, socioeconomic status, sexual orientation, etc.) in subject pools, research teams, and peer reviewers. Likewise, the guidelines argue for the need to be sensitive to the social ecology of human behavior, incorporating considerations of context, identity, and intersectionality (as reflected in the organization of this book). According to the APA (2017), the guidelines

> are conceptualized from a need to reconsider diversity and multicultural practice within professional psychology at a different period in time, with intersectionality as its primary purview. The 2017 version of the *Multicultural Guidelines* encourages psychologists to consider how knowledge and understanding of identity develops from and is disseminated with professional psychological practice. Endemic to this understanding is an approach that incorporates developmental and contextual antecedents of identity and how they can be acknowledged, addressed, and embraced to engender more effective models of professional engagement. (p. 6)

Box 1.5

A Selection of APA's 2017 Multicultural Guidelines

- Psychologists seek to recognize and understand that identity and self-definition are fluid and complex and that the interaction between the two is dynamic. To this end, psychologists appreciate that intersectionality is shaped by the multiplicity of the individual's social contexts.
- Psychologists aspire to recognize and understand that, as cultural beings, they hold attitudes and beliefs that can influence their perceptions of and interactions with others as well as their clinical and empirical conceptualization. As such, psychologists strive to move beyond conceptualizations rooted in categorical assumptions, biases, and/or formulations based on limited knowledge about individuals and communities.
- Psychologists strive to recognize and understand the role of language and communication through engagement that is sensitive to the lived experience of the individual, couple, family, group, community, and/or organizations with whom they interact. Psychologists also seek to understand how they bring their own language and communication in their interactions. Psychologists endeavor to be aware of the role of the social and physical environment in the lives of clients, students, research participants, and/or consultees.
- Psychologists aspire to recognize and understand historical and contemporary experiences with power, privilege, and oppression. As such, they seek to address institutional barriers and related inequities, disproportionalities, and disparities of law enforcement, administration of criminal justice, educational, mental health, and other systems as they seek to promote justice, human rights, and access to quality and equitable mental and behavioral health services.
- Psychologists seek to promote culturally adaptive interventions and advocacy within and across systems, including prevention, early intervention, and recovery.
- Psychologists endeavor to examine the profession's assumptions and practices within an international context, whether domestically or internationally based, and consider how this globalization has an impact on the psychologist's self-definition, purpose, role, and function.
- Psychologists seek awareness and understanding of how developmental stages and life transitions intersect the larger biosociocultural context, how identity evolves as a function of such intersections, and how these different socialization and maturation experiences influence worldview and identity.
- Psychologists strive to conduct culturally appropriate and informed research, teaching, supervision, consultation, assessment, interpretation, diagnosis, dissemination, and evaluation of efficacy.

Source: American Psychological Association, 2017.

Pickren (2009) describes the results of the development of a multicultural psychology as a psychology that "will enrich theory, methods, and practices beyond what is available in the Eurocentric or America-centric traditions alone" (p. 431). These new developments are what you will find in the rest of the book. But first it is important to review some of the basic concepts central to understanding a multicultural psychology. That is the basis for Chapter 2.

Chapter Summary

This chapter presents an overview of the field of multicultural psychology and its importance in contemporary American society. While there are many other multicultural societies in the world (Canada, Belgium, Australia, Singapore, Israel), the historical, demographic, political, and economic characteristics of the United States require the development of a unique, or at least distinctive, body of knowledge that addresses the conditions of racial and ethnic groups in this country. An important characteristic of multicultural psychology is the attention given to the interactions of culture, race, and ethnicity with a number of social characteristics (e.g., gender, social class, sexuality). As such, multicultural psychology contributes to the development of psychology as a science and as a profession by properly contextualizing theories and findings in terms of culture, race, ethnicity, and other identity dimensions. Furthermore, the work of multicultural psychologists, as reflected in this book, allows all psychologists to understand the limits in the generalizability of our findings and, in doing so, improve the validity of scientific research. While most of the literature reviewed in this book emphasizes some of the major racial or ethnic groups (African Americans, Alaska Natives, American Indians, Asian Americans, Hawai'ian Natives, and Latinos), the overall findings can be applicable to other racial or ethnic groups in the country. In this sense, multicultural psychology supports the development of scientific behavioral knowledge of the diverse society that is the United States. A comprehensive analysis of these ethnic and racial groups requires that attention be given to within-group variability due to migration history, economic status, educational level, and other relevant variables. The study of multicultural psychology not only produces a more valid core of psychological knowledge but also helps in the training and promotion of culturally competent individuals and organizations.

Key Terms

ancestry 10
cross-cultural psychology 20
culturally competent individual 19
culture 5
facial diversity 6
interculturalism 6
intersectionality 4
model minority 9
multiculturalism 6
multicultural psychology 20
privilege 6
within-group differences 9
within-group variability 9
xenophobia 7

Learning by Doing

- Interview, if possible, your parents, guardians, or caregivers and your uncles and aunts and grandparents, asking them to self-identify in terms of their racial or ethnic backgrounds. Then draw a diagram or family tree in which you indicate the relationship (e.g., who is a parent to whom) and the racial or ethnic label they assign themselves (use the U.S. Census Bureau's terms found in Box 1.2 as well as the label actually used by your interviewees). Then analyze how labels for races or ethnicities have changed over time and how some people prefer very specific labels rather than those used by the U.S. Census Bureau (e.g., Thai rather than Asian American), and indicate how you would define yourself.
- Interview your parents' or caregivers' siblings (your aunts and uncles) and your grandparents, and identify their highest academic achievement and that of their children (your parents, grandparents, aunts and uncles, and cousins). Indicate, for example, whether they have graduated from high school or have completed two years of college, a bachelor's degree, a master's degree, or a doctorate. Note how academic achievement may have changed over generations, and identify how many college graduates have children who also have gone to college.
- Talk to various members of your family (e.g., parents, guardians, and/or their siblings), and draw a diagram that traces who migrated to the United States, when, and from where. Use this information to identify how various cultural groups are represented in your family as well as how multiple combinations of ancestry or national origin are created as you move down the diagram (or family tree).
- Compare data from your institution (from its website or its office of institutional research) on the ethnic and racial background of students with the data found in Table 1.4. Make sure to compare

your institution's data with the relevant type of college or university (e.g., community college, public four-year university, etc.). Identify where your institution does better, the same, or worse in enrolling students of the specified ethnic and racial groups. Try to find out from your institution's admissions office what recruitment plans have produced these results and what plans are in place to increase ethnic and racial diversity. Keep in mind that the data on Table 1.4 are for 2014 (the latest available as of the time of writing this book).

Suggested Further Readings

Below is a list of key seminal books on multicultural psychology and comprehensive compilations of review chapters dealing with the various topics of concern to psychologists and students interested in multicultural psychology.

Amer, M. M., & Awad, G. H. (2016). *Handbook of Arab American psychology.* New York: Routledge.

A comprehensive analysis of the psychology of Arab Americans including basic psychological principles, acculturation, services, and considerations when dealing with special populations such as international students and refugees.

Balls Organista, P., Chun, K. M., & Marín, G. (Eds.). (1998). *Readings in ethnic psychology.* New York: Routledge.

A collection of classic and contemporary research reports on multicultural psychology. The book covers methodological areas as well as topics related to applied fields, including risk behaviors, identity, and psychological interventions.

Belgrave, F. Z., & Allison, K. W. (2006). *African American psychology: From Africa to America.* Thousand Oaks, CA: Sage.

An overview of psychological research with African Americans that incorporates the migration experience of early and recent ancestors.

Bernal, G., Trimble, J. E., Burlew, A. K., & Leong, F. T. L. (Eds.). (2003). *Handbook of racial & ethnic minority psychology.* Thousand Oaks, CA: Sage.

A comprehensive book analyzing most areas of research and practice with racial and ethnic minority groups. The authors include many leaders in the field, and the various chapters are excellent overviews of theories and research findings.

Bolaffi, G., Bracalenti, R., Braham, P., & Gindro, S. (2003). *Dictionary of race, ethnicity & culture.* London: Sage.

A very complete dictionary of terms, topics, and issues related to the study of ethnicity and culture. The majority of the writers are European and contribute perspectives often ignored or unknown in the United States.

Fong, T. P., & Shinagawa, L. H. (2000). *Asian Americans: Experiences and perspectives.* Upper Saddle River, NJ: Prentice Hall.

One of the first books to summarize major areas of research with Asian Americans. A very important source of early material on the topic.

Jackson, Y. K. (Ed.). (2006). *Encyclopedia of multicultural psychology.* Thousand Oaks, CA: Sage.

A useful compilation of research in multicultural psychology with emphasis on all ethnic groups and helpful in gaining a perspective on the types of research psychologists have conducted among racial and ethnic groups.

Leong, F. T. L. (Ed.) (2009). Special issue: History of racial and ethnic minority psychology. *Cultural Diversity & Ethnic Minority Psychology, 15*(4).

A comprehensive review of the history of multicultural psychology with separate articles on psychology and each of the major racial and ethnic minority groups as well as on the APA's Division 45 and the Minority Fellowship Program.

Leong, F. T. L., Inman, A., Ebreo, A., Yang, L. H., Kinoshita, L. M., & Fu, M. (Eds.) (2007). *Handbook of Asian American psychology* (2nd ed.). Thousand Oaks, CA: Sage Publications.

A very complete compilation of significant findings about Asian Americans, with contributions by distinguished researchers.

Leong, F. T. L., Comas-Díaz, L., Hall, G. C. N., McLoyd, V. C., & Trimble, J. E. (Eds.). (2014). *APA handbook of multicultural psychology*. Washington, DC: American Psychological Association.

A comprehensive and up-to-date two-volume analysis of the multicultural psychology literature covering basic and applied themes. An essential source of information for those interested in the field.

Miville, M. L., & Ferguson, A. D. (Eds.) (2014). *Handbook of race-ethnicity and gender in psychology*. New York: Springer.

A comprehensive analysis of the intersections of race, ethnicity, and gender in the psychology of family, social groups, organizations, and clinical settings.

Nadal, K. L. (Ed.) (2011). *Filipino American psychology: A handbook of theory, research, and clinical practice*. Hoboken, NJ: Wiley.

A compilation of seminal articles on the psychology and clinical practice with one of the largest Asian American groups in the United States.

Neville, H. A., Tynes, B. M., & Utsey, S. O. (Eds.). (2008). *Handbook of African American psychology* (2nd ed.). Thousand Oaks, CA: Sage.

A very well-researched summary of research among African Americans by some of the best known and most active psychologists in the field. An essential resource for students and professionals.

Padilla, A. M. (Ed.). (1995). *Hispanic psychology: Critical issues in theory and research*. Thousand Oaks, CA: Sage.

A compilation of key articles from the *Hispanic Journal of Behavioral Sciences* by one of the pioneers in the field.

Root, M. P. P. (Ed.). (1996). *The multiracial experience: Racial borders as the new frontier*. Thousand Oaks, CA: Sage.

A summary of basic and applied psychological and sociological research on multiracial individuals. Very useful for understanding early research on the topic.

Schaefer, R. T. (Ed.). (2008). *Encyclopedia of race, ethnicity, and society* (vols. 1–3). Thousand Oaks, CA: Sage.

A comprehensive encyclopedia addressing research with racial and ethnic minority groups from the perspectives of the various social sciences. An excellent resource for students and researchers.

Velasquez, R. J., Arellano, L. M., & McNeill, B. W. (Eds.). (2004). *The handbook of Chicana/o psychology and mental health*. Mahwah, NJ: Lawrence Erlbaum.

A collection of chapters analyzing psychological issues among Mexican Americans and serves as an introduction to the study of all Latinos.

Key Theoretical Concepts 2

"Mommy, What Color Are You?"

At the end of Sheila's workday, she left to pick up her two-year-old daughter, Laura, at her day care center. As Sheila positioned Laura into her car seat, she detected a very inquisitive look on her daughter's face. Once Sheila strapped on her seat belt, she noticed through her rearview mirror that Laura still looked somewhat puzzled. Laura then asked, "Mommy, what color are you?" What a question! *Sheila thought. How could it be that at the mere age of two Laura was even aware of the idea of color in people? Sheila then wondered,* Is this question about my ethnicity or a question about my race? *She started to feel a moment of discomfort as she stalled for the "correct" answer to her daughter's inquiry . . . should she respond that she is Black . . . African American . . . a person of color? Sheila even started to think that perhaps Laura was asking this question because she was confused by her own sense of identity as a multiethnic person, part African American and part Latino (or is it better to say Mexican American . . . Chicana . . . Hispanic?). As Sheila's pause in her response became more pregnant, she suddenly had an insight:* Why sweat it trying to come up with the perfect answer? I am the parent—I should be the one asking the questions. *So Sheila turned to Laura and asked, "Well, what color do you think I am?" Without hesitation, Laura replied, "Mommy, you're beige!" Sheila laughed and looked at herself in the rearview mirror. Sure enough, her daughter possessed a precocious knack for identifying colors. At a very early age, Laura could discern among various shades of blue—aqua versus turquoise versus navy blue. Indeed, Sheila's "color" is beige. Like many African Americans, Sheila's ancestry is diverse and consists of family members of African, American Indian, and European descent. In addition, Laura is at a developmental age where she can start to recognize distinctions in colors. Had Sheila responded that she was "Black," Laura probably would have looked incredulously at her for failing to recognize that her skin was not even close to that color. Laura even held up her stuffed doggie, Gromit, and noted that he too was beige.*

The moment of confusion described in this vignette is not unusual in discussions centered on topics of ethnicity, race, and culture. Yet it is important to gain a basic understanding of concepts that are pertinent to the study of multicultural psychology—and sensitivity toward the complexity involved in defining these concepts. This chapter begins with a discussion centered on culture—its definition, components, and effects on human behavior. Contemporary definitions of culture, ethnicity, and race are presented together with a discussion of the controversies surrounding the use of race as a biological construct, as opposed to a social construct. In addition, we define social orientations (collectivism and individualism) and cultural views of the self (interdependent and independent self-construals) and their effects on major psychological processes that are presented in later chapters. The chapter concludes by identifying and describing important social conditions that affect the behavior of ethnic minority groups in the United States such as processes that underlie social stratification and the intersectionality between socioeconomic class, education, gender, and other dimensions of stratification.

Throughout this book, we would like to provide a basic understanding of certain constructs that are central to the study of ethnic minority populations in the United States. A **construct** is a term that is frequently used in the field of psychology and refers to a concept or idea based on theory and/or empirical observation. For example, *clinical depression*, *attachment*, and *intelligence* are all constructs that have been studied extensively by psychologists, psychiatrists, and other scientists and professionals (e.g., Ainsworth, 1989; Blatt, 2004; Parker, Fletcher, & Hadzi-Pavlovic, 2012; Sternberg, 1985). Although certain constructs are widely discussed for European Americans, they may not be entirely applicable to the psychological experiences of other ethnic groups. In the case of depression, currently we have theories about the causes and manifestations of major depression that have been formulated, assessed, and tested through empirical or scientific observations (Blatt, 2004). Multicultural and cross-cultural studies have found this construct may have very different meanings and manifestations in different cultural groups throughout the world (Kessler, Birnbaum, et al., 2010) and within the United States (e.g., Perkins, 2014), particularly for new Asian American and Latino immigrants (Balls Organista, Organista, & Kurasaki, 2003; Kaltman, Green, Mete, Shara, & Miranda, 2010; S. Sue, Sue, Sue, & Takeuchi, 1998). Many of the constructs in the field of multicultural psychology have spawned wide-ranging debates in terms of their validity. Throughout this book, we try to briefly summarize the most important of these debates and the varying interpretations of various constructs used in multicultural psychology.

Understanding Culture

Although most of us can readily think of what *culture* might entail, the task of developing a definition that clearly distinguishes culture is very difficult. Much of the difficulty in defining culture lies in the fact that it is a **multidimensional construct**, meaning that it consists of many different elements or components. Although there are many different definitions of culture, many psychologists view **culture** as a set of attitudes, values, beliefs, and norms that are shared within a group and transmitted across generations (Matsumoto & Juang, 2017; Triandis, 1994).

As a multidimensional construct, culture has been viewed as consisting of both internal dimensions and external dimensions. Internal dimensions include attitudes, beliefs, and values. For example, culture can be expressed through the belief in the importance of the family above all other social relationships or through the value placed on personal independence or through a person's positive or negative attitudes regarding certain behaviors such as abstinence, celibacy until marriage, or children's obedience to parents. External dimensions of culture include those social structures and institutions in which culture is expressed within societies. For example, culture can be exhibited through formal, organized social structures and social organizations such as government, education, religion, and political and economic systems. Culture can also be displayed through social-relationship patterns or kinship networks. It is also expressed through individuals' ability to satisfy their psychological needs for affiliation, problem solving, stress reduction, and adaptation to their social environment through adherence to **social norms**. Social norms are explicit and implicit rules regarding the formation and engagement of social relationships and behaviors (Comer, 2015; Gavac, Murrar, & Brauer, 2017). For instance, in patriarchal cultures there is an established hierarchy of power that influences how members relate to the male authority figure in the family; in particular, female family members are socialized to defer to the males' authority in decision-making and rules of the family.

Culture is also dynamic because it constantly changes and develops over time. For example, contemporary American culture is quite different from American culture when this nation was founded. Whether it pertains to music, clothing and food preferences, or social and political attitudes, culture is a living entity that is reconstructed and reenacted by different generations across history. Cultural transformations are due to a number of factors, including increasing globalization in trade and commerce, mass media, and transportation that facilitate and expand the exchange of information, materials, and even peoples. As a result, there are many characterizations of culture as a construct. While a complete catalog of definitions is beyond the scope of this chapter, it is instructive to briefly review the various ways in which culture has been defined by social and behavioral scientists.

Dimensions of Culture

According to Bolaffi et al. (2003), culture has always been thought to represent what is learned and taught, with emphasis being placed on what differentiates one group from another and on the fact that culture has an existence predicated by the group's own reality. They further suggest that the construct of culture has often been defined by emphasis of the researchers involved in writing the definition. For example, from a sociological perspective, Lévi-Strauss (1966) defines culture as a normative construct, while psychoanalytic perspectives usually emphasize culture as a more subconscious process that influences dreams (as Freud suggested; see Jones, 1953) or myths and symbols (as proposed by Jung; see Jung, 1967) or language (as mentioned by Lacan; see Dor, 2001).

From a more psychosocial perspective, Triandis (1994) defines culture as

> a set of human-made objective and subjective elements that in the past have increased the probability of survival and resulted in satisfaction for participants in an ecological niche[] and thus became shared among those who could communicate with each other because they had a common language and they lived in the same time and place. (p. 22)

Examples of objective elements of culture include materials that a group may use, such as machinery, foods, shelter, tools, and dress (Triandis, 2002). Subjective elements of culture are the ways in which a group understands and makes sense of its social environment, including ideas about beauty, spirituality, philosophy, values, money management, and child-rearing (Triandis, 2002).

A somewhat different perspective in defining culture is taken by Kim (2001) by arguing that "culture is the collective utilization of natural and human resources to achieve desired outcomes" (p. 58). Thus, culture is viewed as a process that allows a group to effectively share its resources to accomplish goals that reflect the values, beliefs, and/or behaviors of the members.

Jones (2003) proposes a fairly comprehensive definition of culture. He suggests that culture can be said to include a variety of elements categorized as "*psychological* (patterns of thinking, feeling, behaving, and valuing), *symbolic* (representations of meaningful psychological patterns), *historical* (cultural elements selectively derived and transmitted over time), [and] *dynamic* (cultural elements that both shape meaning and are transformed by events and actions)" (p. 223). Regardless of the definition, culture has been considered by many researchers to be an important construct that helps define the characteristics of a human group, including its psychosocial and behavioral norms and expectancies. In this sense, culture is an important construct in ethnic psychology that allows us to better understand what influences people's behaviors and attitudes.

It is important to note that culture differs from **nationality**, which refers to a person's country of birth or place of citizenship, family origin, or background, and from **ancestry**, which is person's origin, heritage, or descent that is associated with birthplace of self or ancestors. We do not automatically assume that a person's birth or citizenship in a particular country will mean that he or she will adopt the country's prominent cultural norms (Matsumoto & Juang, 2017). However, in general there may be a strong relationship between nationality and culture simply through exposure to common behaviors, customs, beliefs, and attitudes.

Culture is often used interchangeably with *ethnicity* (Betancourt & Lopez, 1993); however, culture is a more general construct that influences ethnicity and ethnic identification by shaping our meaning of ideals and values (Rohner, 1984, as cited in Betancourt & Lopez, 1993), as well as views about our self and about others (Markus & Kitayama, 1991) and the behaviors that are associated with those thoughts (Nisbett, Peng, Choi, & Norenzayan, 2001; Peng & Nisbett, 1999).

For a review of this terminology, see Box 2.1.

Cultural Influences on Psychological Processes

As mentioned in Chapter 1, a significant amount of research has been conducted by cross-cultural psychologists trying to identify how culture influences people's behavior and how individuals from various cultures differ from one another. Such studies, for example, have found that cultures tend to differ in the way in which they process cognitive information (Markus & Kitayama, 1991). East Asians, for instance, tend to make judgments of causality by attending to all details, while Westerners tend to concentrate on specific objects and categories (Nisbett et al., 2001). Other studies have suggested that cultures differ in the way the self is understood in relation to others; some cultures generally value mutual support and reliance on the family, while other cultures promote personal independence (Markus & Kitayama, 1991).

In multicultural psychology, cultural differences and preference for certain values tend to be important in predicting physical and psychological health. For example, Maria Cecilia Zea and colleagues (Zea, Quezada, & Belgrave, 1994) suggest that the cultural values of *allocentrism* (an individual's concern for the group to which he or she belongs) and *familialism* (strong devotion to family) play

Box 2.1

Some Basic Terms

Ancestry: A person's origin, heritage, or descent that is associated with birthplace of self or ancestors

Culture: A set of attitudes, values, beliefs, and norms that are shared within a group and transmitted across generations

Ethnicity: A social group's distinct sense of belongingness as a result of common culture and descent

Nationality: A person's country of birth or descent

Race: A socially constructed concept based on prevailing social and political attitudes; often used to express ambiguous distinctions, promote dominance of certain privileged groups, and oppress groups that are deemed inferior important roles in Latino patients' recovery from disabilities in terms of the emotional and social support received. Sociologists Ronald Angel and Marta Tienda (1982) and Elena Bastida (2001) state that extended family households found among some cultures are particularly important in immigrants' early adjustment to a foreign country. Susan Savage and Mary Gauvain (1998) report that responsibilities assigned to children are influenced by culture-specific expectancies of children's ability to plan at certain ages. Finally, other researchers (e.g., Damron-Rodriguez, Wallace, & Kington, 1994; Tseng & Strelzer, 2008) suggest that the quality of medical care received by ethnic minorities is affected, in part, by cultural values. Issues related to the physical and psychological health of ethnic minority groups are further discussed in Chapters 9 and 10.

Understanding Ethnicity

The term *ethnicity* derives from the Greek word *ethnos*, meaning "a people" as well as "a nation or a crowd" (Bhopal, 2003; Bolaffi et al., 2003). **Ethnicity** refers to a social group's distinct sense of belongingness as a result of common culture and descent (Al-Issa, 1997; Jones, 1992). Sociologist Max Weber considered ethnicity derived from the belief in shared origins that members of a group hold without a direct correspondence to a nation or a race and that manifests itself through commonly practiced customs and memories of the group's history (Bolaffi et al., 2003).

Similar to culture, ethnicity can reflect several different dimensions that can be used in defining the construct. For example, some authors see ethnicity as including three components: (1) group membership, either by choice or externally imposed, that allows a differentiation of **in-groups** (i.e., groups that maintain respect, esteem, and loyalty and, consequently, are more desirable) and **out-groups** (i.e., groups that are subjected to disapproval, contempt, and competition and, consequently, are less desirable), (2) emphasis on a common identity, and (3) the assignment of specific beliefs or behaviors (stereotypes) to members of the group by individuals who belong to other ethnic groups (Bolaffi et al., 2003). At the same time, Jean Phinney (1996) suggests that

> there are at least three aspects of ethnicity that may account for its psychological importance. These include (a) the cultural values, attitudes, and behaviors that distinguish ethnic groups, (b) the subjective sense of ethnic group membership (i.e., ethnic identity) that is held by group members, and (c) the experiences associated with minority status, including powerlessness, discrimination, and prejudice. (p. 919)

Ethnic identity is a relatively new construct that grew out of the ethnic-consciousness movements of the early 1970s in reaction to historically oppressive racial typologies. Ethnicity nonetheless is similar to *race* in that both are social constructions.

Marger (2015) states that ethnic groups possess unique cultural traits. Ethnic groups exist within a larger cultural and social system but maintain behavior characteristics that distinguish them from other groups within a given society. For example, the practice of Kwanzaa by some African Americans can differentiate their distinctive African-based values from those reflected in the traditional Christian holiday celebration of Christmas. Common traditions also support a sense of community among members of ethnic groups. There is also a sense of communion primarily derived from a shared ancestry or heritage. Ethnic group membership is acquired at birth by virtue of one's parents and/or the culture in which one is raised. Membership is reinforced by the cultural values, symbols, beliefs, and practices that people are exposed to as they grow up, as well as by the distinctions that members of other ethnic groups make as they ascribe group membership based on commonly held beliefs and attitudes, physical characteristics (phenotype), group-valued practices, and personal identification.

Members of an ethnic group can have the potential to interpret what occurs in their group as being correct and "best" compared to other ethnic groups. They may perceive their customs, traditions, and values as being more universal, and thus they might believe that everyone should embrace them. They may favor those from their own ethnic group and/or feel negative toward others outside their group. All of these descriptions are related to the concept of **ethnocentrism**, the bias of viewing one's own ethnic group as superior to others (Brewer & Campbell, 1976). As discussed more thoroughly in

Chapter 8, this ethnocentrism is closely related to negative stereotyping (prejudice) of members of other ethnic groups and to discriminatory practices against them. Our earlier history as a nation saw the curtailment of basic rights and benefits based on many of those prejudicial attitudes borne out of ethnocentric thinking. As such, during the first years of our nation, voting rights to women and Blacks and to those without land were not granted. Chinese Americans were not allowed to own property or to live in European American neighborhoods in many major cities until the mid-1950s. Blacks brought to the country as enslaved laborers were not even given the care that sometimes was freely accorded to animals. In recent history, Blacks and other ethnic minority groups were not allowed admission to certain institutions of higher learning, and, even when granted, they were excluded from certain social clubs or fraternities or sororities. In addition, Mexican Americans were forbidden to use Spanish in school. All of these inhumanities were institutionalized and supported by ethnocentric beliefs.

The Problems of Ethnic Assessment and Labels

The assessment of ethnicity is often problematic. As reviewed in the next chapter, many people often are dismayed by the limitation of "checking the one box" that best describes their ethnicity. Most measures rely on self-definitions of ethnicity where the person is given the "choice" of which box to check, but this self-assessment ignores the fact that sometimes ethnicity cannot be limited to broad categories such as Asian or Hispanic because the boxes do not reflect the heterogeneity that may exist within any one group, nor will the boxes reflect the multiple ethnicities that may exist within any one individual. The option of marking "Other" in response to these categories is wholly unsatisfying for those who embrace their multiple ethnicities and wish to explicitly identify them when asked.

There can also be uncertainty about the "correct" label when choices are provided. In the vignette that opens this chapter, Sheila wonders which ethnic label—"African American" or "Black"—she should use to appropriately identify her ethnicity to her daughter. The African American label reflects contemporary usage and recognition of her ethnocultural roots rather than skin-color characteristics. However, others with black skin would agree with then–Illinois senator Barack Obama in saying that "some of the patterns of struggle and degradation that Blacks here in the United States experienced aren't that different from the colonial experiences in the Caribbean or the African Continent" (quoted in Swarns, 2004, p. 1). Indeed, a number of African Americans prefer to be called "Black," particularly those who recently migrated (from Africa or the Caribbean) as well as some of their children (Swarns, 2004). Also, some individuals believe that positively affirming one's "Blackness" is a political statement that neutralizes historically negative representations of "dark" racial skin color or phenotype.

As a further example, the use of the labels "Latino" and "Hispanic" interchangeably reflects contemporary usage in the literature. Despite continuing debate and arguments to favor one term over the other (Marín & Marín, 1991; Taylor, Lopez, Martínez, & Velasco, 2012), current usage patterns in psychology do not necessarily show any particular preference. This is consistent with a recent national bilingual survey of 1,220 Hispanic adults conducted by the Pew Research Center (Taylor et al., 2012). More than half of the respondents (54 percent) say they most often identify themselves by their family's country of origin (e.g., "Mexican," "Cuban," or "Dominican"). Only 24 percent say they prefer the terms "Hispanic" or "Latino" to commonly describe their identity. And 21 percent use the term "American" most often. Ethnic identity, the sense of oneself as belonging to a particular ethnic group (or groups), and assessment of ethnicity are addressed in detail in Chapter 5.

Some authors have criticized the use of the construct of ethnicity in social science research because they feel that it represents a "construction of Western colonial culture" (Bolaffi et al., 2003) and that it carries the assumption of culture that is primitive, simplistic, and strikingly unusual. As such, the word *ethnicity* is sometimes used to describe a sort of exoticism often represented in terms such as *ethnic music*, *ethnic art*, or *ethnic food*, which can best be described by emphasizing their place in a group's folklore. Other researchers favor the use of *ethnicity* because it supports the development of a supportive "collective ego" (Comaroff, 1987) for members of groups who share common histories or characteristics. In this book, we use *ethnicity* as a way to identify those groups that share not only a history but also social structures and psychosocial characteristics such as attitudes, beliefs, and values. Ethnicity, as used in this book, does not refer to underdevelopment or exotic groups.

Understanding Race

Ethnicity is often used interchangeably with the term *race*; however, these terms are different. Although all humans belong to one species, Homo sapiens, biologists and anthropologists have attempted to classify and categorize physical and biological traits that may differ among populations. We often observe others and inquire or make assumptions (not necessarily accurate) about their racial background. In our opening vignette, Sheila initially thought that Laura's question—"What color are you?"—was an inquiry about her race.

Historically, studying race based on contrived or visible physical differences between groups of people was particularly popular during the 18th, 19th, and early 20th centuries. The inherent flaws in discerning reliable and valid physical and biological indicators of racial distinctions are illustrated by early research in physical and cultural anthropology (Guthrie, 1998). Researchers used a variety of dubious strategies to classify racial groups, including assessment of cranium or brain size, skeletal structures, and behavioral observation. Robert Guthrie (1998) reviewed the work of several prominent anthropologists who developed race measurement methods—such as Aleš Hrdlička, who described precise instructions for using a spinning color top to measure skin pigment, and Felix von Luschan, who invented a porcelain scale of skin color that required holding up various colored blocks next to the skin until a match was made between the shade and the subject's skin color. Similarly, other scientists developed methods and instruments to measure observable anatomical features (i.e., phenotypes), such as hair texture (to distinguish between "straight," "curly or wavy," "frizzy," or "woolly" forms of hair), hair color (use of a color wheel to distinguish color variations between blond, red, brunette, and black), and differences in thickness of lips, length of head, height of nose, and other body features (Guthrie, 1998). However, there was no consensus about which of these types of characteristics, phenotypes, genotypes (measurements based on genetic traits inherited from one's parents), and/or anatomical traits would be used consistently in defining race.

Many of the earliest racial categories included distinct categories for Caucasoid, Mongoloid, and Negroid people. However, some systems also included separate categories for certain indigenous groups (e.g., aborigines, Bushmen). These systems were based on oversimplified and stereotypical physical markers that exist at least to some degree among groups. However, clearly this classification is imprecise and ignores large segments within populations that do not fit neatly into narrow and fixed categories. For example, where do you place groups that have mixed ancestry, like many from Indonesia or Mestizo (mixture of indigenous tribes and Spanish ancestry) groups from Latin America?

Although scientific studies on racial differences flourished particularly during the 19th century, the classification of race has perhaps spawned the greatest level of controversy and argument among psychologists and those in related disciplines. Racial categories are arbitrary and contingent on the goals and theories of the classifier (Marger, 2015). Generally, most analyses yield the conclusion that it is difficult at best, or nearly impossible, to distinguish clear-cut "pure" races with consistent physical features, genetic markers, and other biological indicators that separate one group from another (Betancourt & Lopez, 1993; Yee, Fairchild, Weizmann, & Wyatt, 1993; Zuckerman, 1998). Some differences between groups aside, the relative proximity and mobility of diverse groups over the past centuries, the high level of mixing (also known as *genetic interchangeability*) of groups, and adaptations to changing environments have all led to more complex phenotypic traits. Indeed, Jackson (1992) concluded that "the zoological definition of race, based on significant genetic differences, cannot be legitimately applied to contemporary humans" (p. 120). Moreover, many agree that a greater level of diversity can be found within any one "racial" group than between various racial groups (Marks, 1995; Okazaki & Sue, 1998; Zuckerman, 1998).

Race is socially constructed based on prevailing social and political attitudes. As a sociopolitical construct, race is used to express ambiguous racial distinctions, promote dominance of certain privileged groups, and oppress groups that are deemed "inferior." History shows us that "race" is often used to promote racism and prejudice. Labeling racial groups can create negative stereotypes and myths about the nature of different groups—hence, the individuality of the person is suppressed, and, consequently, his or her humanity can become less salient.

As noted later on in this text (Chapter 8 and elsewhere), criticism of racial labels does not negate the terrible impact of racism and racial distinctions in the history of the United States and the suffering of many individuals that has resulted because of the color of their skin or of traits perceived to be associated with genetic or biological characteristics. The random and abhorrent killings of American Indians, the perversity of slavery of African Americans, and the unfairness of policies discriminating or segregating access or services to African Americans and Asian Americans are examples of how "racial differences" have been used to partly justify the destruction of the goals of equity and justice enshrined in the U.S. Constitution. The reality of these social and political consequences leads researchers to argue that race and racial identity, specifically, can be important constructs for study when we want to understand the psychological effects of social marginalization, discrimination, and prejudice for certain groups that have been racialized (Helms, 1990).

Whiteness

Research in the social sciences—especially in sociology and critical race studies—and in education has recently given more attention to **Whiteness** and to Whites as a "cultural" group (Twine & Gallagher, 2008). This research recognizes that individuals whose skin color is light ("white") share experiences and attitudes that differentiate them from others whose skin color is darker. Similar to other cultures, these shared experiences go beyond the social and economic privileges that historically have been awarded to lighter-skinned individuals and include the assumption of commonly held or generalized attitudes and values among Whites. Twine and Gallagher (2008) note that since the 1990s the number of scholarly works on the study of Whiteness and White identity has surged, particularly in the United States.

In an overview of the interdisciplinary field of Whiteness studies, an emerging body of research is described that builds upon earlier writings on racial identity development. In these contemporary studies, the formation, destabilization, and maintenance of White identity, culture, and privilege are explored through inventive methodologies—for example, critical analyses of "racial-consciousness biographies" (written accounts of how Whites perceive and negotiate their Whiteness in their everyday private and public lives), Internet sites, newspapers, music, and other popular media (Twine & Gallagher, 2008). Psychological scholarship that includes Whiteness in the study of culture and race allows greater critical analysis of all people and can promote an intersectional approach being applied in terms of the complex influence of factors such as gender, class, disabilities, and sexual orientations given the great diversity among Whites (Dottolo & Kaschak, 2015). Moreover, Whites can be researched and viewed less as the standard or norm in psychology (Morawski, 2004).

The study of Whiteness has not been without its critics, within both academic circles and the popular media. For example, in a *New York Times* article, Talbot (1997) charged that this represents the "academic trend du jour," a trendy exploration of an ill-defined concept that makes racial categories necessary and absolute. In contrast, Twine and Gallagher (2008) note that the steady proliferation of empirical work has produced hundreds of books, qualitative studies, and scholarly articles that challenge our current racial categories and social hierarchies. Similarly, Hattam (2001) states that research on Whiteness has produced some important results that allow for a more complete cultural understanding of the major racial groups "of color" (African Americans, American Indians and Alaska Natives, Asian Americans, and Latinos). In particular, Hattam (2001) argues that research on Whiteness has allowed U.S. social scientists to validate a historical perspective on the construct of "race" as well as emphasize the role of class and social privilege in people's ethnic identification. Helfand and Lippin (2002) further suggest that "Whiteness is an historical, cultural, social, and political category" created in part by the fact that "Whiteness is so often invisible to White people but not invisible to people of color" (p. 12).

Social Orientations or Ways of Being

Hofstede (1980), in his influential book on cultural values, defines **cultural dimensions** as "a broad tendency to prefer certain states of affairs over others" (p. 19). It is in that sense that cultural dimensions are discussed here. They are perceived to be frequently found (modal) preferences for certain behaviors or beliefs or worldviews held by group members, defined by culture, nationality, or ethnicity, that vary in terms of intensity (i.e., personal relevance) and direction (e.g., certain outcomes are positive while others are evaluated as negative) or modality (Hofstede, 1980; Kluckhohn, 1961) and serve to differentiate members of one ethnic or cultural group from those of another. These constructs have received names as varied as *value structures* (Hofstede, 1980), *cultural dimensions* or value orientations (Kluckhohn & Strodtbeck, 1961), and *cultural syndromes* (Triandis, 1994). Researchers working with members of ethnic groups often use these basic cultural dimensions to explain behavioral or cognitive differences across ethnic groups identified in their studies.

Characterizing societies or ethnic groups by using certain general dimensions or cultural dimensions is obviously a process of simplification and of blurring individual differences. Nevertheless, the use of cultural dimensions allows the prediction and explanation of the normative (or modal) behaviors of certain cultural or ethnic groups. While at times these efforts have been fraught with methodological limitations, the overall result has been heuristically and practically important.

Research in psychology and anthropology has produced a large number of social orientations that are perceived as being related to people's preferred orientation or ways of being. Many of these dimensions are perceived to be specific to a given culture while others are more general. For example, Latin Americans and Latinos are described in the literature as valuing positive interpersonal relations, a social script defined as *simpatía* (Triandis, Marín, Lisansky & Betancourt, 1984) that is somewhat related to the Japanese social script of *amae* or the Filipino *delicadeza*. In addition, Asian cultures are often described as placing special value on "face saving," protection of one's integrity within close interpersonal relationships (Zane & Mak, 2003). Researchers also have identified social dimensions that seem to be central to a large number of cultures and ethnic groups. Among these are familialism, allocentrism, and interdependence. We review some of these dimensions below, and others are summarized in later chapters.

Views of the Self Across Cultures

It is proposed that individuals from cultures that emphasize responsibility toward others are more likely to make **interdependent construals of the self** in which they tend to value interpersonal relationships and see others as integral to their self-conceptualization. According to Markus and Kitayama (1991), interdependent persons view their behavior as greatly influenced by the thoughts, actions, and beliefs of others in their community. Interdependent construals are more commonly associated with societies such as those of Africa, Asia, and Latin America (Constantine, Gainor, Ahluwalia, & Berkel, 2003; Markus & Kitayama, 1991). **Independent construals of the self**, in which individuality and one's unique thoughts, emotions, and behaviors are distinguished from those of others, tend to be best exemplified by societies such as the United States, Canada, and Germany (Constantine et al., 2003; Markus & Kitayama, 1991). As expected, data from cross-cultural studies indicate that **collectivistic cultures** (cultures focused on the community as a whole) are more highly correlated with interdependent self-construals, while **individualistic cultures** (cultures focused on individual autonomy) are more associated with independent self-construals (e.g., Chia, Allred, Cheng, & Chuang, 1999; Morling & Fiske, 1999; Singelis, 1994).

However, in other empirical studies and critical analyses, psychologists question the clear dichotomy between interdependent versus independent constructs and collectivistic versus individualistic constructs. Several argue that these constructs should be more accurately conceptualized and measured as complex phenomena that can even coexist within many individuals and social relationships (e.g., Emde & Buchsbaum, 1990; Grotevant, 1998; Guisenger & Blatt, 1994; Neff, 2003; Triandis, 1995; Triandis & Gelfand, 1998). For example, Neff (2003) notes that many of the classic studies that explored infant attachment to caregiver (e.g., Ainsworth, 1967; Bowlby, 1969) suggest that a secure, stable, interdependent relationship between the caregiver and child facilitates the infant's autonomous exploration of the world. Furthermore, research on parenting styles indicates that an authoritative style (i.e., supportive and warm, yet with firm limits and adaptable to the child's needs) actually stimulates greater independence and self-confidence as well as social adaptability and skills in children (e.g., Steinberg, 2001). Neff and her colleagues (Neff & Harter, 2002a, 2002b, 2003), as well as others, propose that a balance between independence and interdependence is needed for positive self-development and harmonious personal relationships. However, while this balance may be desirable in several instances, it is also important to consider that an individual's self-construal or social orientation may be more adaptive in certain cultural contexts but less so in others.

Researchers suggest that closely associated with the social dimension of individualism are personal values such as autonomy, privacy, self-reliance, and competition as well as societal institutions that are person-centered and individually oriented. Collectivism, however, has been associated with such behaviors and attitudes as (1) holding group-centered values where members of a given society or group are concerned about how their actions impact others, (2) greater valuing of the views and needs of the members of the in-group even if it means personal sacrifices, (3) sharing resources without concern for individual utilitarian considerations, (4) holding beliefs that are similar to those of the members of the in-group, (5) accepting the group's norms, and (6) accepting values such as interdependence, cooperation, and sociability (Hui & Triandis, 1986; Triandis, 1990, 1994).

A more recent trend in research is to study how these self-constructs may be composed of differing components or subtypes. Triandis and his associates (Triandis, 1995; Triandis & Gelfand, 1998), for example, describe two types of individualism—**horizontal individualism** and **vertical individualism**. Horizontal individualism refers to cultures that value the individual but not necessarily a societal hierarchical structure. Vertical individualism refers to a cultural orientation that values the individual but also societal competitiveness that leads to upward mobility. According to Triandis and Gelfand (1998), a capitalist society like the United States might best exemplify vertical individualism. Likewise, collectivism can be conceptualized as running along horizontal and vertical axes: **Horizontal collectivism** represents a cultural orientation that favors commonality among individuals and interdependence—but not with the control of authoritarian force. **Vertical collectivism** represents a cultural orientation that also values interdependence and deference to the common needs of the community, but deference or submission to a higher authority is also supported. Although this is an influential multidimensional model, studies designed to demonstrate the applicability of these constructs across a variety of cultures have been limited in number (Gouveia, Clemente, & Espinosa, 2003).

According to other studies, the importance placed on independence or interdependence can vary in hierarchical social structures. For instance, Neff (2001) studied rights and responsibilities within marital relationships among lower-middle-class Hindu Indians. She found that support for characteristics and behaviors consistent with independence was much more emphasized for husbands, while support for interdependence was more emphasized for wives. Interestingly, however, many within the group were critical of this imbalance and restraint placed on women's autonomy.

Future chapters include a more thorough discussion of other social scripts and of the way in which people's behaviors and attitudes are influenced by these social orientations or cultural dimensions. For example, we describe the role of familialism in supporting individuals' actions in Chapter 7 and discuss the relationship of culture-specific patterns to ethnic, racial, and gender identities in Chapters 5 and 6. Nevertheless, it is important to mention here that acculturation (the culture learning process described in Chapter 4) differentially affects these social dimensions. Specific components or aspects of these dimensions that are central to a culture are less affected by the process of acculturation and assimilation than more peripheral aspects.

An important caveat to the literature on social dimensions is the danger of assuming a "damaging-culture" perspective (Buriel, 1984; Ramirez & Castaneda, 1974) or a victim-blaming approach (Ryan, 1972). This perspective would explain problems experienced by members of an ethnic group (e.g., poverty, unemployment, crime) by referencing the group's culture or the relevant cultural syndrome or social script rather than the political, social, and economic conditions that are more directly related to the problems. The cultural dimensions discussed here are of help in describing general cultural patterns, in helping individuals to better comprehend how cultures differ, in developing research protocols and intervention strategies that are culturally appropriate, and in training professionals who will be culturally sensitive and capable (Marín, 1993).

Nevertheless, the social conditions experienced by many members of the major ethnic groups should not be construed to be the direct result of the cultural dimensions described in this book. Such an approach to the social sciences would be not only simplistic but also naive and prejudicial.

Social Stratification

As noted earlier, many "differences" do not fully represent innate or biological distinctions; instead, they more strongly represent social constructions that are formed within a social context. Hence, it is important to look at the way in which societies are designed to empower or disenfranchise individuals or groups. **Social stratification** describes a society's system for distributing resources and rewards among various groups. The question, in any given society, is who receives wealth, power, freedom, and prestige? When a social system is stratified, there is a structured hierarchy in which groups receive differential access to society's rewards. Because this text is focused on culture and ethnicity, it is important to consider how our society determines social stratification based on people's culture and ethnicity, but there are also other dimensions such as age, gender, socioeconomic standing, and sexual orientation that are interrelated and simultaneously impact social systems.

Stratification systems are not unique to the United States or other industrialized countries; they occur in many different countries and can change over time. Social stratification can be illustrated by slave, caste, or class systems (Rothman, 2005). Slave systems consist of those in bondage (slaves) and those who are free (masters or freemen). In the United States, we tend to think of slavery as being a thing of the past, something that ended roughly two centuries ago. Yet modern slavery is very much a part of our world. There are millions of cases of children and adults who are held against their will and must work hard labor in inhumane working conditions to pay their "debt" owed to their masters or who are sold or forced into slavery systems. Slave industry can take the form of forced labor on farms or plantations, in factories, or within the sex-trade industry. This form of stratification is particularly evident in poor, less industrialized countries where women and children and sometimes men are forced to labor long hours in component factories or sewing industries in order to save enough money to pay the owners for their housing and sustenance with little recourse to other sorts of employment. Sex workers in many countries also face similar conditions where prostitution is one of very few options for avoiding extreme poverty and where the proceeds are seldom enough for these individuals to gain independence from their masters. Caste systems are social strata determined by fixed family patterns in which children are born into the caste of their parents. Caste systems have existed for centuries in certain countries, although, currently, in certain areas they have lessened in their rigidity due to the introduction of more democratic ideals, modernization, and exposure to other cultures' alternative religions and media.

Within more industrialized countries like the United States, **class systems** have been the most popular form of social stratification. Class systems are hierarchies based on some key social criterion. One of the best-known models of a class system is the one proposed by Karl Marx. His model emphasizes economics as the basis for stratification. Two groups are distinguished—the ruling class and the working class. This two-tier model states that the "haves" are members of the ruling class that have ownership and authority over production and resources (e.g., commerce, transportation, food production, media). The "have-nots" are members of the working class who can only provide labor in order to obtain any type of resource.

In general, social classes are constituted of individuals who share an equal likelihood of acquiring society's wealth, resources, and rewards. Rothman (2005) describes a contemporary class typology that is based on society's economic system. In this system, many of the difficulties faced by members of society are directly linked to their place in the social class hierarchy. Groups are categorized as "the elite," "the upper middle class," "the lower middle class," "the working class," and "the poor." At the top of the stratification system is the elite class, which exercises a potent level of power over economic, political, and social entities. The elite are made up of some of the wealthiest individuals, who have derived their power from wealth and property. Sometimes this wealth is inherited over generations within families (e.g., the Bush, Getty, Heinz, or Kennedy families). In other cases, the wealth that characterizes the elite is acquired through innovation, investments, or the development of industries (as in the case of the founders of McDonald's, Walmart, or Microsoft). Interestingly, the elite class in the United States constitutes only about 1 percent of the total population, and yet it holds approximately 38 percent of the total national wealth. The top 20 percent of households (those with incomes of $180,000 a year or more) hold more than 80 percent of the nation's wealth (Mantsios, 2004; Mishel, Bernstein, & Boushey, 2003). In contrast, the bottom 60 percent of the American population holds less than 6 percent of the national wealth. The relationship between these classes inevitably leads to conflict and struggle over this inequitable system.

Another classic model is offered by Max Weber (as described in Gerth & Mills, 1946). Similar to Marx and others, Weber acknowledges the significant role of economic factors in establishing a social hierarchy. In addition, Weber notes the role of social classes that express lifestyle-group differences in terms of their ability to acquire material possessions, property, and access to education, among other resources. **Socioeconomic status (SES)** is often highly correlated with social class, because economic status usually relates to social opportunities and lifestyle, at least in the United States. Weber's model also gives attention to political parties that wield authority within the system. Political parties are any groups that assert influence toward community change; contemporary examples would include labor unions, consumer and environmental protection agencies, organizations for professional groups (e.g., psychologists, social workers, teachers), ethnic organizations (e.g., the National Association for the Advancement of Colored People), and formal political parties (e.g., Democrat, Republican, Green). Membership in a powerful party that wields authority can influence one's ability to reap consequent benefits from social and political changes that support an individual. Conversely, members of weak political parties may be unable to move ahead within society due to failure to effectively change the social and political climate or laws that can protect their interests.

An alternative model of social stratification is described by Marger (2015) and adapted from a **distributive system model** developed by Gerhard Lenski (1966). This multidimensional model is based on parallel class systems where each system represents a social dimension such as education, wealth and property acquisition, and occupation (see Figure 2.1). Marger notes that there is remarkable consistency across class systems, especially within a diverse society. As such, individuals in a particular class will exert a similar level of power and benefit from relevant levels of privilege no matter what social dimension is examined. For example, those who are ranked high within the education class system (e.g., those who achieve a graduate school degree) will similarly rank high on the hierarchies of the other class systems—economic wealth, professional occupation, and so on—whereas those who are ranked low within the education class system (e.g., those who achieve only a grade school or high school education) will rank low on other social strata.

There is, however, complexity in any class system distribution. For instance, if we attempted to examine stratification among various ethnic minority groups, an "ethnic class system," there are problems inherent in ranking as though certain ethnic groups are worse off than other groups. For instance, ranking Asian Americans above Hispanic Americans, African Americans, or American Indians in an ethnic class system can inadvertently perpetuate the model minority stereotype—that is, that Asians are the ideal of all ethnic minority groups. Also, such ranking would overlook significant social and economic hardships faced by certain Asian American subgroups (e.g., Southeast Asian refugees) that are hidden or obscured by this broad ethnic category.

It is important to note that many, including Marger (2015), also acknowledge that these patterns are not immune to exceptions. There are, for example, well-educated individuals who do not enjoy authority and rank high across all social dimensions and certain individuals who have relatively limited schooling and are generally ranked lower on the education hierarchy yet who nonetheless succeed in other social dimensions. Marger (2015) notes, however, that such exceptions tend to be infrequent due to institutionalized forms of discrimination that make it difficult for certain groups to gain upward mobility. This is most apparent when considering how many wealthy people obtain entrance at the

The Distributive System

The political class system	The property class system	The occupational class system	The education class system
The elite	The upper class	Capitalists	Highly Educated Graduate/Professional
The bureaucracy Ⓐ	The upper middle class Ⓐ	Professionals, managers, entrepreneurs Ⓐ	College/Technical Ⓐ
The electorate Ⓑ	The middle class Ⓑ	Skilled workers, technicians Ⓑ	Trade School Ⓑ
The apolitical populace Ⓒ	The working class	Unskilled workers Ⓒ	High School Ⓒ
	The poor Ⓒ The underclass	The unemployed	Grade School or Below

Source: Adapted from Marger (2015), also adapted from Lenski (1966).

FIG. 2.1 The Distributive System of American Society (A, B, and C represent three individuals).

most elite academic academies. Is this simply a matter of character or intelligence or real differences in access and power that make upward mobility possible?

Missing from the model in Figure 2.1 is the inclusion of gender as another social dimension that intersects the class systems that shape our society. **Gender** refers to the socially and psychologically defined and acquired characteristics that distinguish being male from being female, whereas sex describes the biological and physiological characteristics of men and women (Santrock, 2005). Although this may sound like a straightforward distinction, some social scientists argue that, in order to understand gender in our society, one must look at the complex interaction of biological, psychosocial, and cognitive influences on gender (Deaux, 1999; Santrock, 2005). Moreover, gender definitions and expectations can change within any historical point in time; thus, gender has evolved over the course of civilizations and across cultures.

Within a stratified system, we can see that there are differences between the ranking of men and women within particular class systems. Perhaps an area where this is most salient is in the occupational class system. The disparity between payment for the work of women and men has been well documented (Rothman, 2005). Despite working more hours than men and doing more than their fair share of work worldwide, only roughly one-third of women receive payment for labor compared to three -fourths of men (Rothman, 2005). Even now in contemporary U.S. society, women (no matter what their overall class status, including racial or ethnic class) perform more unpaid work (e.g., housework, childcare, eldercare) than men (Rothman, 2005). Power or wealth can help reduce these unpaid hours, however, because the affluent can afford to hire others to do domestic chores and dependent-care services. Clearly, unpaid work is essential to the survival of families and homes, but the fact that much of the work is unpaid testifies to the inequity of value and reward that are placed on "real work" (i.e., paid labor) versus "responsibilities" (i.e., work that supports the house and dependents) that may be restricted based on gender roles.

Likewise, sexual orientation is another form of social stratification. This is perhaps most poignantly illustrated by continuing discrimination and hate crimes that are directed toward gays and lesbians. Also, homophobic political rhetoric in the ongoing debate on same-sex marriage echoes discriminatory attitudes that fueled the antimiscegenation laws that made interracial marriage a crime. Such instances of discrimination and hate are often pronounced for gays and lesbians of color because they can be considered minorities within a minority community. Indeed, the terms *double jeopardy*, *triple jeopardy*, and even *multiple jeopardy* are used to refer to multiple minority statuses that may characterize an individual (Lindsay, 1979). For example, a woman who is an ethnic minority and lesbian may be considered at increased risk for stress related to experiences as a member of all three groups (Bowleg, Huang, Brooks, Black, & Burkholder, 2003). These and other related issues pertaining to experiences of ethnic minority gays and lesbians are discussed in detail in Chapter 6.

No matter what theoretical model of stratification is examined, it is clear that social class status can have a powerful influence on individuals' and families' access to resources that benefit adjustment, such as those related to health, education, and living in a safe environment. As such, any stratification system will ultimately impact the psychological and physical well-being of its members. As reported in Chapter 1, members of ethnic minority groups show a disproportionately high level of poverty relative to Whites. This is especially true for American Indians and Alaska Natives, African Americans, Latinos, and Southeast Asian refugee groups. Of additional concern is the toll of poverty on children and their development that is associated with limits in the level and type of social and cultural stimulation and the quality and quantity of nutritional intake (Allen, 1970).

Low SES children are more likely to be exposed to violence, environmental toxins, poor quality of food, and improper housing or homelessness than are higher-level SES children (Santrock, 2004). When poverty becomes long-term, these dangerous conditions predictably lead to a host of negative outcomes for children into middle adulthood, including lower functioning in terms of behavioral, psychological, and medical problems (Schoon et al., 2002). (See Chapters 9 and 10 for more information on the physical and psychosocial adjustment of ethnic groups.)

Many stratification systems exist for many years and even centuries in certain societies. Sustaining a system of inequality is contingent upon having an *ideology* or set of beliefs that supports and justifies the imbalance. Social scientists point to many ideologies that may support our U.S. stratified structure. The most popular include racism, sexism, and **meritocracy**—the perception that those who receive the rewards (e.g., the upper class) have done so based solely on the strength of their own efforts. If you work hard enough, you can make it in our society. Implicit (and often explicit) in this rationale is that those who have not made it (e.g., the lower class or the underclass) failed because of a lack of ability or character.

Minority Status

Minority status can be defined in a number of ways. On a broad social level, the term **minority** has been used to refer to groups that have limited power and access to society's wealth and resources, resulting from discrimination and subjugation by the dominant society (Alvidrez, Azocar, & Miranda, 1996). Hence, being deemed an ethnic person is not necessarily interchangeable with being deemed a minority person. For instance, there are currently people in the United States—like Italian Americans or Irish Americans—who are members of ethnic groups but, due to assimilation processes, are not typically considered minorities. Berry (1998) notes that minorities' disempowerment and discrimination are often determined by the characteristics of the dominant groups, such as their openness to share privilege and status, the nature of relationships between groups (e.g., positive or tension-filled), and levels of tolerance or embracement of difference or diversity. Other important features of minority status include the following:

- *Minority status is unrelated to population size.* Minority groups can represent a significant percentage of an entire population, but their access to society's wealth and resources can still be limited.
- *Individual characteristics are overlooked.* If you belong to a minority group, your individual attributes, including your individual talents and achievements, do not protect you against discrimination and prejudice. You will still be viewed through the lens of negative stereotypes attached to

your group; thus, upward socioeconomic mobility and social prestige are not guaranteed, despite your individual efforts.

- *Minority status is socially defined.* The dominant group has the power to determine which social markers or criteria define minority group status (e.g., gender, race, ethnicity, sexual orientation, religious identity) and how to differentially allocate society's wealth and resources accordingly.
- *Minority groups are not necessarily "powerless."* Minority groups may be lacking in financial and material resources and representation in institutional positions of power, but they can still possess social capital or important social networks and relations that help promote self-empowerment, civic engagement, and group well-being.

Regardless of the rationale for the label of *minority*—ethnicity, sexuality, religious beliefs, or cultural traditions—continued discrimination in the United States not only is countercultural but also cannot be part of a truly diverse society. The minority label has received its share of criticism as the result of its implication of subordination to a dominant group rather than emphasizing the unique characteristics of a group that make it distinct and vibrant. Members of the **dominant group** are advantaged socially, politically, and economically within society. Because of these advantages, the cultural norms and values of the dominant group become the standard. Also, the dominant group has the power to determine the flow and composition of immigrants to their nation. Historically, groups that have similar racial, cultural, and religious identities to the dominant group are given preferential consideration in becoming full citizens. In this context, some believe that minority groups become defined in terms of their deficits in relation to dominant groups, blurring their strengths in the process (Berry, 1998). Obviously, many authors who use the word *minorities* to refer to African Americans or Asian Americans or other ethnic groups are using the term as a shorthand descriptor devoid (at least partly) of negative connotations.

Power and Privilege

Some researchers have begun addressing the conditions under which privilege ensues. *Privilege* is usually defined as the unfair advantages and benefits afforded people who hold a dominant position within a social-stratification system. While equity in access and opportunities are valued goals of our society as we strive to follow Martin Luther King Jr.'s dictum that people should "not be judged by the color of their skin but by the content of their character" (National Archive, n.d.), equality of opportunities and the elimination of prejudice still have yet to be achieved (Crosby, Iyer, Clayton, & Downing, 2003; Sue, 2003). Some individuals are assigned privileges and benefits or entitlements as a by-product of their skin color.

Peggy McIntosh (2004) popularized the concept of *White privilege* in her often-cited work based on her experiences teaching women's studies courses. She noted that while several men were willing to acknowledge that women were disadvantaged in many situations (e.g., job upward mobility), they had difficulty admitting that they themselves were privileged in many situations as a consequence of sexism. In a sense, we are taught that it is important to recognize the painful consequences of bigotry; yet we are not taught to look at ourselves as possible beneficiaries of someone's oppression.

McIntosh (2004) applied this analysis to a self-examination on race and found that she, too, as a White woman living in the United States, was privileged by the simple fact of living in a society where racism and ethnic and racial discrimination exist. She cited several examples of the ways that her privilege can be experienced on a daily basis, such as noting, "I can go shopping alone most of the time fairly well assured that I will not be followed or harassed by store detectives," "I can swear, or dress in secondhand clothes, or not answer letters, without having people attribute these choices to the bad morals, the poverty, or the illiteracy of my race," and "If a traffic cop pulls me over or if the IRS audits my tax return, I can be sure I haven't been singled out because of my race" (McIntosh 2004).

Asian American psychologist Derald Wing Sue (2004) further acknowledges that not only is there disproportioned access to society's rewards, but these advantages are also unearned and accrued to "White people by virtue of a system normed on the experiences, values, and perceptions of their group" (p. 764). In addition, White privilege can influence and limit racial interactions (Lucal, 1996), since individuals may choose not to interact with others perceived as less worthy or less accomplished due to lacking some of the benefits that the privileged have received.

Privilege is not only exhibited in race and gender matters; there are other privilege statuses, including heterosexual privilege, middle- and upper-class privilege, physically and mentally abled privilege, and so on (McIntosh, 2004; Rosenblum & Travis, 2015). While the idea of privilege can be seemingly simple and straightforward, the reactions of those that are "privileged" can be complex. Consistent with McIntosh's male colleagues' reaction, a limited number of studies conducted typically with students such as counselor trainees or undergraduates support that there is resistance to acknowledging privileged status (Hays & Chang, 2003). Often there is difficulty in recognizing gains that are received on the backs of others who are less privileged. One hardly wants to adopt the title of "oppressor," and there is the associated guilt that may accompany any acknowledgment of unfair advantage over others. Moreover, one of the basic ways that privilege statuses are maintained is by ideologies—many of which are similar to those that support social stratification. If we believe that life is fair and that we live in an unbiased society that truly rewards the best and brightest, these ideals will alleviate our discomfort over inequality. Similarly, the **just world hypothesis** states that our thoughts about experiences are influenced by our need to believe that the world is a just place in which good people are rewarded for their positive deeds and bad people are punished for their wicked ways (Lerner, 1980). Adhering to this sort of viewpoint can provide at least an illusion of safety (if one has a positive sense of self) and an explanation for meaningless tragedies. Yet the risk of a just world view is that it can lead to a *blaming the victim* mentality in which one reasons that, if bad things happen to a person, then the person must have done something wrong to trigger this outcome, and, hence, they got what they deserved.

One final matter on privilege is that as a social construct it is possible that individuals can simultaneously be members of groups that are oppressed *and* oppressive in their power. For example, a middle-class, heterosexual, Alaska Native woman may be privileged in terms of her class and sexual orientation but subjugated due to her ethnicity and gender status. Because the acceptance or recognition of the existence of privilege is likely to be suppressed, she will be more likely to be aware of the ways in which being Alaska Native and a woman are likely to hamper her chances of equality in society. Yet she will have to deal with the privileges and challenges experienced within the context of her self and social environment. Rosenblum and Travis (2015) argue that, despite the coexistence of both privilege and oppression within any one person, stigma is so pervasive and strong in our society that oppression can often trump privileges that one's other statuses might offer. They point to health, housing, economic, hiring, and promotion disparities as evidence that inequality is a strong and persistent force that must be continually addressed. Consequently, we need to take an intersectional approach to look at ethnicity, class, gender, and other dimensions that may converge to place particular groups at high risk for disempowerment and disadvantage.

Chapter Summary

This chapter reviews a number of constructs that are important in the field of multicultural psychology and related fields of study. Many of the constructs such as race, ethnicity, and culture share similar challenges: They have multiple dimensions that define them, and these multiple meanings can often prove to be controversial and lead to misunderstandings and poor science. Nevertheless, at their best, they provide fruitful insights into the nature of human beings—those aspects that serve to join us together as a human race and those that distinguish our unique behaviors, thoughts, values, and histories that enrich our diversity. These are some of the basic constructs that will be revisited throughout the text. In addition, other constructs such as acculturation and intersectional identities of race, ethnicity, class, gender, and sexuality will be examined in depth in later chapters of this book. We have also sought to provide a social context for the study of ethnic groups in the United States by discussing societal stratification and the nature of privilege that impact the quality of life of multicultural groups.

Key Terms

ancestry 32
class system 39
collectivistic culture 37
construct 30
cultural dimensions 37
culture 30
distributive system model 40
dominant group 43
ethnicity 33
ethnocentrism 33
gender 41
horizontal collectivism 38
horizontal individualism 38
independent construal of the self 37
individualistic culture 37
in-group 33
interdependent construal of the self 37
just world hypothesis 44
meritocracy 42
minority 42
multidimensional construct 30
nationality 32
out-group 33
race 32
social norms 31
social stratification 39
socioeconomic status (SES) 40
vertical collectivism 38
vertical individualism 38
Whiteness 36

Learning by Doing

- Respond to the following three questions:
  1. What is your ethnicity?
  2. What is your culture?
  3. What is your race?

  Was there any overlap in your answers? How were you able to distinguish among ethnicity versus culture versus race?
- Think of the various ways in which you are "privileged." Generate a list of at least 10 activities or behaviors that you can engage in without question because of who you are as a person with certain statuses (e.g., status afforded your gender, ethnicity, SES, age, sexuality). Now imagine that one of your statuses changed: for example, you and your parents (or significant other) lose all financial resources and housing due to a natural disaster and a crash in the stock market. How would the list of privileges change now that you are at a lower level of economic stability? Would some of the privileges disappear? Would new privileges appear? Alter the list accordingly.

Suggested Further Readings

Guthrie, R. V. (1998). *Even the rat was white: A historical view of psychology* (2nd ed.). Needham Heights, MA: Allyn & Bacon.

Classic historical overview and critique of the measurement of race and racial differences. It also provides an account of the early contributions of African Americans to the field of psychology.

Jacobson, M. F. (1998). *Whiteness of a different color: European immigrants and the alchemy of race.* Cambridge, MA: Harvard University Press.

A historical analysis of "Whiteness" as a racial identity that has undergone various conceptualizations over time.

Marger, M. N. (Ed.) (2015). *Race and ethnic relations: American and global perspectives* (10th ed.). Stamford, CT: Wadsworth/Cengage Learning.

An exploration of social-stratification patterns of race and ethnic relations in the United States and abroad (e.g., South Africa, Brazil, Canada, Northern Ireland).

Montagu, A. (1974). *Man's most dangerous myth: The fallacy of race* (5th ed.). New York: Oxford University Press.
Classic analysis of the "myth" of race. Provides evidence that many alleged racial differences are illusory or insignificant.

Omi, M., & Winant, H. (2013). *Racial formation in the United States* (3rd ed.). New York: Routledge.
A scholarly contribution to the argument that race is more accurately defined as a social construct as opposed to a biological construct. Documents the changing conceptualizations of race in the United States and the influence of political factors on our views of race.

Rosenblum, K. E., & Travis, T.-M. C. (2015). *The meaning of difference: American constructions of race and ethnicity, sex and gender, social class, sexuality, and disability* (7th ed.). New York: McGraw-Hill.
Textbook reader of the construction, experience, and sociological meaning of difference across the dimensions of race, ethnicity, sex, gender, social class, sexuality, and disability. Writings include works by noted scholars, journalists, artists, and activists.

Rothman, R. A. (2005). *Inequality and stratification: Race, class, and gender* (5th ed.). New York: Routledge.
A straightforward analysis of how the intersection of race, ethnicity, class, and gender relates to social, political, and economic inequality.

Tatum, B. D. (2003). *"Why are all the Black kids sitting together in the cafeteria?" and other conversations about race.* New York: Basic Books.
A psychologist's examination of the development of racial identity in Blacks and how to address issues of racism within a multicultural context. The text manages to be both analytical and readable through the use of personal anecdotes and reflections, thus making it a good choice for a wide audience—from high school youths to scholars—interested in these topics.

3 Responsible Research With Racial and Ethnic Communities

"That Is Not Me!!"

While reading a psychology textbook, Angelina, a Filipino American nursing student, was surprised to read that the authors talked about Asian Americans as a single group and made generalizations that did not reflect her family or herself. The authors talked about how Asian Americans were a "model minority" that had achieved great academic and economic success in the country. The authors suggested that this level of success was due to their long history of living in the United States and to their proficiency in speaking English. They concluded that, due to these circumstances, traditional cultural values such as the significance of the family in decision-making had become less relevant. Angelina was confused by those statements. She was an immigrant to the United States, and so were all of her close relatives. Having arrived in the United States six years earlier, she was still trying to master English since the family primarily spoke Tagalog in the Philippines as well as after their arrival in this country. Working overtime, and at times two jobs, her parents had been able to help her pay for the portion of college tuition not covered by scholarships, loans, and federal and state aid. She felt that she didn't fit the description in the textbook, and none of her Filipino American high school friends were that different from herself. In class the next day, she asked two Asian American friends how accurate they thought the textbook description was. Sophia, a Vietnamese American born in the United States, said that her parents were still working two shifts and that she was the only sibling in her family who was attending college. Ronald, a Chinese American also born in the United States, reported that his father had gone to college while his mother worked at the shop set up by his grandfather and preferred to speak Cantonese as opposed to English. After a long discussion at the campus juice bar, the three concluded that the authors of the textbook had failed to realize that there were many differences among Asian Americans based not just on their ancestral countries but also on how long they had lived in the United States, the opportunities they had had for employment and education, the level and types of prejudice they had experienced, and many other variables. While Angelina, Sophia, and Ronald shared some cultural values that made them comfortable interacting with each other, they also agreed that their lives and experiences were so different that, at times, the label "Asian American" was of little value.

Psychology, like any other science, must rely on research to properly develop and test theories and hypotheses about human behavior. In this chapter you will read about some important issues to consider when reading or carrying out psychological research with racial and ethnic minority groups. We are not trying to make a researcher out of you but, rather, a good consumer of science who is aware of the complexities and limitations of conducting psychological research in multicultural settings. We hope to provide you with the perspectives and tools to be able to question the validity of statements you may find in the press about ethnic and racial minority groups and even to question some of the content in your psychology textbooks. We hope when you read statements such as those Angelina read about Filipino American families (in the introductory vignette) that you will be able to question the cultural appropriateness of the research often cited in support of those statements.

Unfortunately, much of the early (and some contemporary) findings in multicultural psychology have been the result of projects carried out by psychologists and other social scientists who either were unaware of or ignored the special requirements involved in conducting responsible, culturally appropriate research with multicultural populations. The list of potential pitfalls is long as you will see in this chapter and includes issues as diverse as the false assumption that all members of a group are alike, the use of poorly developed measurement instruments, inadequate translation and adaptation procedures, the lack of cultural awareness on the part of the researchers, failure to consult with the community being studied, biased interpretation of results, and many other oversights and poor practices (Burlew, 2003; Okazaki & Sue, 1995). Proper attention to all of these factors is part of developing and using responsible, culturally appropriate methodologies.

The end result of the failure to use culturally appropriate methodologies has been the production of research findings that are of limited validity and minimal practical use. Fortunately, we have made significant strides in improving our research methodologies in the last few decades, and we are now able to rapidly build a better science of multicultural psychology. The methodological issues covered in this chapter will allow you to better analyze what you read in textbooks and scientific journals or even the popular press regarding ethnic and racial minority groups. This chapter does not replace methodological handbooks that explain basic research methodologies and books specifically written to guide researchers working with racial or ethnic populations. Rather, we hope to provide you with an overview of the challenges that researchers face when studying racial and ethnic groups that in turn will guide you in reflecting on the usefulness of research findings.

This chapter begins with a description of what is involved in conducting research that is responsible, sensitive, and responsive to the characteristics of the groups being studied, what we call **responsible, culturally appropriate research**. Subsequent sections summarize some of the most serious methodological problems that researchers need to address when investigating racial or ethnic populations, including threats to the validity of some psychological instruments and the difficulties involved in obtaining an appropriate linguistic version or translation. It should be noted that these issues are relevant to quantitative research as well as to methods that are qualitative in nature. Obviously some problems or concerns, by their nature, are more relevant to methods that rely on the collection of data (quantitative methods) while other problems are more germane to research approaches that rely on qualitative evidence such as verbal or written statements, behavioral observations, documents, and similar strategies.

Many of the issues discussed in this chapter are complex, and at times we assume that you already have some familiarity with research methodology in psychology or in the social sciences. Nevertheless, remember that the goal of this chapter is not to train you in methodology but, rather, to help you become a good consumer of research in multicultural psychology.

Responsible, Culturally Appropriate Research

In general, the goal of researchers working with racial and ethnic populations should be to conduct responsible, culturally appropriate research or what other researchers have called "culturally sensitive research" (Rogler, 1999a). We prefer to use the term *responsible, culturally appropriate research* to indicate that there are specific requirements that should be met in order to have valid and reliable research with racial and ethnic populations (*culturally appropriate research*) that includes being aware and respectful (*responsible*) of cultural, racial, or ethnic characteristics and differences and sensitive to unique ethical concerns.

The concerns for using responsible, culturally appropriate research methodologies are multifold. On the one hand, researchers believe that valid, reliable, and culturally appropriate research is a human right and a basic requirement in the scientific development of multicultural psychology. These beliefs are based on various international declarations and covenants, as well as on statements by professional groups, as shown in Box 3.1. You may also recall that in Chapter 1 (Box 1.5) we quoted the APA's (2017) Multicultural Guidelines, which ask, like the previous version (APA, 2002b), that psychologists use a "cultural lens" during their professional practice as they recognize that their own attitudes and beliefs affect how they think, feel, and act toward individuals who are different from themselves. These interpersonal relationships, as well as the concern for how culture, race, and ethnicity affect human

Box 3.1

Declarations Supporting the Need for Responsible, Culturally Appropriate Research

- [It is a human right] to enjoy the benefits of scientific progress and its applications. (United Nations General Assembly, 1966)
- Challenge some of the historical notions, traditional methods, and theoretical underpinnings upon which Western psychology was initially predicated, but also offer us a unique opportunity to articulate the profound importance of valuing individual and cultural diversity in the research that we conduct. (Council of National Psychological Associations for the Advancement of Ethnic Minority Interests, 2000)
- Culturally sensitive psychological researchers are encouraged to recognize the importance of conducting culture-centered and ethical psychological research among persons from ethnic, linguistic, and racial minority backgrounds. (American Psychological Association, 2002b)
- The cardinal principle of modern research ethics . . . is respect for human dignity. This principle aspires to protect the multiple and interdependent interests of the person—from bodily to psychological to cultural integrity. (Health Canada, 2007)
- Educational researchers . . . are sensitive to cultural, individual, role differences in teaching, studying, and providing services to groups of people with distinctive characteristics. They strive to eliminate bias in their professional activities, and they do not tolerate any forms of discrimination based on race; ethnicity; cultural; national origin; gender; sexual orientation; gender identity; age; religion; language; disability; health conditions; socioeconomic status; or marital, domestic or parental status. (American Educational Research Association, 2011)
- Researchers should take responsibility for the trustworthiness of their research. . . . Researchers should employ appropriate research methods, base conclusions on critical analysis of the evidence, and report findings and interpretations fully and objectively. (*The Singapore statement on research integrity*, 2010)

- Adherence to the concept of moral right is an essential component of respect for the dignity of persons. Rights to privacy, self-determination, personal liberty and natural justice are of particular importance to psychologists, and they have a responsibility to protect and promote these rights in their research activities. As such, psychologists have a responsibility to develop and follow procedures for valid consent, confidentiality, anonymity, fair treatment and due process that are consistent with those rights . . . psychologists respect the knowledge, insight, experience and expertise of participants and potential participants. They respect individual, cultural and role differences, including those involving age, sex, disability, education, ethnicity, gender, language, national origin, religion, sexual orientation, marital or family situation and socio-economic status. (The British Psychological Society, 2010)
- All vulnerable groups and individuals should receive specifically considered protection. Medical research with a vulnerable group is only justified if the research is responsive to the health needs or priorities of this group and the research cannot be carried out in a non-vulnerable group. In addition, this group should stand to benefit from the knowledge, practices or interventions that result from the research. (World Medical Association, 1964/2013)

behavior, are of course central to multicultural psychology. Research must therefore properly reflect these characteristics by using culturally appropriate theories, hypotheses, methods, analytic techniques, and interpretative approaches (Okazaki & Sue, 1995).

A Definition of *Responsible, Culturally Appropriate Research*

Over the past few years, a number of characteristics have been identified to define the essence of conducting responsible, culturally appropriate research. These concerns can also be found in defining the components of culturally appropriate professional practice. These efforts have been present in many countries, and not only in psychology but also in fields as diverse as health promotion, nursing, anthropology, sociology, and communications. As shown in Box 3.2, the term *culturally appropriate* has been defined as having various characteristics depending on the field, but there are some common threads that we will use to define **culturally appropriate research** in psychology.

Box 3.2

Various Perspectives on Cultural Appropriateness

Culturally appropriate communication . . .

[finds] a way to communicate effectively that also respects and accepts cultural differences. (Department of Families, Community Services and Indigenous Affairs, Government of Australia, n.d.)

Culturally appropriate community interventions . . .

[meet] each of the following characteristics: (a) The intervention is based on the cultural values of the group, (b) the strategies that make up the intervention reflect the subjective culture (attitudes, expectancies, norms) of the group, and (c) the components that make up the strategies reflect the behavioral preferences and expectations of the group's members. (Marín, 1993, p. 376)

Culturally appropriate health services . . .

provide effective, equitable, understandable, and respectful quality care and services that are responsive to diverse cultural health beliefs and practices, preferred languages, health literacy and other communication needs. (Office of Minority Health, U.S. Department of Health and Human Services, n.d.)

Cultural competence . . .

requires organizations and their personnel to (1) value diversity, (2) assess themselves, (3) manage the dynamics of difference, (4) acquire and institutionalize cultural knowledge, and (5) adapt to diversity and the cultural contexts of individuals and communities served. (National Center for Cultural Competence, Georgetown University, n.d.)

Box 3.3

Characteristics of Culturally Appropriate Research

Culturally appropriate research . . .

- is based on theories and hypotheses that are sensitive to cultural variations.
- uses methods that are appropriate, familiar, and relevant.
- provides analyses that are contextualized and take into consideration culture and other relevant characteristics of the population (e.g., gender, class, migration status).
- adheres to widely accepted principles for ethical, valid, and reliable research.

In this book, we present culturally appropriate research as involving four basic components (see Box 3.3). First, culturally appropriate research demands the development and testing of theories and hypotheses that are sensitive to and respectful of cultural variations and that appropriately reflect the role of culture, race, and ethnicity in shaping behavior. A second requirement is the use of research methods that are appropriate, familiar, and relevant to the question being researched as well as to the members of the racial or ethnic group being studied. Third, culturally appropriate research implies that the analysis and interpretation of data and other results of a research project must take into consideration not only the culture that characterizes participants but also other relevant variables, such as their gender, socioeconomic conditions, educational level, and migration history. Fourth, culturally appropriate research involves strict adherence to principles of ethical and responsible behavior in all aspects of the research project. Obviously, conducting culturally appropriate research does not mean ignoring the more common requirements for good research, such as being grounded in theory or testing properly derived hypotheses or utilizing methods that produce valid and reliable observations. Rather, the requirements of culturally appropriate research must be added to those of otherwise valid investigations.

Implementing Responsible, Culturally Appropriate Research

From the definition of responsible, culturally appropriate research mentioned above, we can derive at least three major areas that merit particular attention on the part of readers and consumers of psychological research. First is the need to determine whether the researchers used culturally appropriate research methods and instrumentation. A second central concern is determining how well the researchers identified and sampled the participants so that biases and overgeneralizations were controlled or eliminated. Finally, there is a need to establish the validity and cultural appropriateness of the interpretation of the results. These three areas are covered next. A later section of the chapter is dedicated to ethical concerns of particular significance when conducting research in multicultural psychology.

An Initial Consideration: Contextualization

The development of culturally appropriate research is undergirded with the basic commitment to sensitivity to the proper historical and cultural context of the issues to be studied and to the contemporary situational variables (time, politics, social climate) that are relevant. This process of **contextualization** can be defined as the recognition of the role that social and cultural contexts (situations or characteristics) have in shaping human behavior. Researchers and research consumers alike need to be aware of the social context in which a project took place, since its geographical setting, date, cultural mores, and generalized attitudes play an important role in shaping the process, the results, and the analysis of the information collected.

The need to consider the historical and social context in which human artifacts (e.g., books, paintings, scientific theories) were produced has been quite common among scholars in literary criticism and comparative literature but notably absent among social and behavioral scientists. For example, it is not difficult to find the influence of the American South in Mark Twain's writings. The analysis of those influences is part of the work of literary critics and researchers and becomes a central component of their writings. Your literature instructors have probably talked about how books such as *Huckleberry Finn* or *The Kite Runner* or movies such as *Gone With the Wind* or *Star Wars* can best be understood when we consider the history and politics of the times as well as the social and economic conditions of the people who lived during the period when the book was being written or the movie was being produced.

Like poets and novelists, social scientists of necessity reflect the culture to which they belong and the social conditions in which they live. For example, Freud's work was heavily influenced by the prudish Viennese culture into which he was born, and Skinner's understanding of behavior was shaped by the individualistic Anglo-Saxon culture in which he was raised. Their cultural experiences significantly shaped the theories they developed to explain human behavior.

The development of culturally appropriate research procedures requires, therefore, that researchers recognize the role that their culture plays in the development of their view of human behavior and that the theories and methods to be used properly reflect the culture of the group or groups being studied. As Gardiner (2001) suggests, this contextualization implies that "behavior cannot be studied meaningfully or fully understood independent of the context in which it takes place" (p. 102). Indeed, one of the strengths of qualitative research (ethnographies, structured observations, focus groups, interviews of informers, document analysis, etc.) is the emphasis that researchers place on understanding the meaning and nature of people's action by defining the context in which they occur (Chun, Morera, Andal, & Skewes, 2008).

Culturally Appropriate Methods

As mentioned above, one important component of culturally appropriate research is the use of research methods or approaches that are relevant to the racial, ethnic, or cultural group being studied. This implies that all research approaches and instruments must be appropriately relevant to the issue in question, be familiar to the respondents being studied, and include responses or behaviors that the participants can produce. For example, it would be inappropriate to ask blind persons to point at images on a computer as they answer a series of questions being posed to them. Equally inappropriate would be to ask individuals with limited fluency in English to answer survey questions that are in English or to take a psychological test in a language that they do not fully control. Unfortunately, the psychological literature often includes studies where people are asked to perform tasks that are beyond their capacity or experience or to answer tests and surveys in languages they do not fully understand. Indeed, as mentioned in Chapter 1, a number of immigrants coming to the United States through Ellis Island were required to take an intelligence test in English even if they were unable to speak the language. This procedure led to the exclusion from the country of a number of poorly educated or functionally illiterate European immigrants and prospective immigrants who did not speak English.

To better understand the importance of using culturally relevant methods and instruments, assume for a moment that you are not familiar with the rules of soccer. Your mathematics teacher decides to make a quiz fun and uses soccer-related questions to check on your ability to add and subtract. One question asks, *How many players will finish the game against the Panthers if they lose two players during the first half of the game (one expelled and the other relieved for injury) and the team is allowed to replace them with only one player?* If you are not familiar with soccer rules (and don't know how many players are allowed on the field at the start of a game), you most likely will be unable to properly answer the question even though you are quite capable of adding and subtracting. Something similar can happen when culturally inappropriate methods or instruments are used in psychological research. The individuals may very well be able to perform a task or to report an attitude or value, but the approach used to elicit their responses is unknown to them or inappropriate to their culture.

The need for culturally appropriate research procedures can also be seen in a study of family dynamics and decision-making among Puerto Ricans (Rogler, 1999b). In the original plan, the respondents would be asked to identify who in the family decides such significant issues as where to vacation, which school the children should attend, and the type of insurance to purchase. During pretesting, the researchers found that these concerns were irrelevant to poor Puerto Rican families, since they seldom (if ever) had those choices. Family decision-making revolved instead around more basic survival issues and did not resemble the issues facing middle-class families in the United States. As such, in order to be culturally appropriate, the study needed to address decision-making about issues relevant to family survival rather than about such personally irrelevant issues as where to vacation or which type of insurance to buy. As Rogler (1999b) states, "the concept of decision-making presupposed a situation in which families made choices in an open, companionate relationship between spouses. . . . Just as poverty severely constricted choices, it severely constricted decision-making" (p. 430). In this case, the research method was appropriate (an interview), but the initial content was not (the questions about vacations and insurance).

Choosing a Research Approach

As you have read in other textbooks in psychology or in other social sciences, psychologists have used a number of different research approaches (or designs) to study and predict behavior. In this section, we review the most-frequently used methodological approaches to research in order to refresh your mind. Keep in mind that most research designs have limitations when working with multicultural communities and that these problems decrease their usefulness as a research method.

In order to prevent or solve methodological limitations and difficulties when working with ethnic and racial communities, various authors have suggested that researchers should use a multimethod approach where a variety of research methods are used and the results are compared across methods (**triangulation**) in order to obtain a better approximation to the reality being studied. Indeed, Cauce (2011) argues that

> multicultural psychology *is* incompatible with a psychological science that is narrow in its methods and at the extreme end of positivism in its epistemological grounding. There is no question that to better understand, assess, study, and appropriately intervene in our richly varied multicultural world will require us to draw upon a broader and more diverse array of methods. (p. 230)

Experiments Experimentation in psychology has a long history and has been offered as the strongest approach to testing hypotheses. The interest in experimentation in psychology is related to our concern for demonstrating the validity of our science and to our desire to imitate the methods and approaches of the physical and biological sciences. As you recall, in an experiment the researcher manipulates a variable (the *independent variable*) and measures the effects of this manipulation on a second variable (the *dependent variable*). In addition, the researcher controls—as much as possible—other variables and conditions (time, social and environmental characteristics, etc.) and also includes a *control group* that is also observed as the group that experienced the manipulation of the independent variable (*experimental group*) but does not receive the manipulation (or *treatment*). In a true *experiment* the participants (or *subjects*) are randomly assigned to either the experimental group or the control group. When random assignment does not take place or is not possible, then the research design is called a *quasi-experiment*, since control over relevant variables cannot be guaranteed.

You are probably familiar with *laboratory experiments*, those conducted in a controlled and isolated environment such as the psychology department laboratory. In these experiments, the researcher tries to control all relevant variables, but in the process, the *generalizability* or external validity (and applicability) of the experimental situation is diminished. You probably recall how sterile and unique the laboratory cubicles were and how seldom will you ever encounter such settings outside the university. To solve some of these difficulties, researchers have used **field experiments** that resemble the laboratory experiments but take place in real-world settings (e.g., offices, factories, shopping malls, restaurants), and the variables manipulated are not unusual or contrived (e.g., amount of money spent at a shop, quantity of alcoholic beverages consumed, number of objects assembled in an hour).

One of the main weaknesses of experimental research in general and in multicultural psychology in particular is the reduced number of variables studied due to the need to control the effects of one or very few independent variables. By limiting the quantity of variables studied, experimental research ignores the interactions or intersectionality (see Chapter 1) of relevant and important variables or conditions. In real life, as mentioned in previous chapters, many variables interact with each other and affect the behavior of individuals. Another limitation of experiments in multicultural settings, particularly laboratory experiments, is that many are conducted in university settings and usually with college students as participants. This aspect limits how generalizable the results are, since college students account for a small percentage of the country's population and because racial and ethnic populations are typically underrepresented at most colleges.

Interviews and Surveys The use of surveys and interviews is common in some areas of psychology and in other social sciences, as well as in applied fields such as public health, sociology, public opinion, management, and educational research, among other fields. You are probably quite familiar with these research methods, as you use them when you evaluate your professor or when answering surveys about your satisfaction with a given product or service. Both approaches (interviews and surveys) involve developing questions (either open-ended or close-ended) that are given to the respondents or asked by the researchers. Depending on the design of the study, the respondents are chosen randomly or are asked to participate in convenient settings (e.g., classrooms, shopping malls, offices, churches). The questions can be asked in person (verbally or on paper), by telephone, or over the Internet (email, social media, websites, or apps).

A number of difficulties are present in the use of interviews or surveys among racial and ethnic communities. Foremost among these is the need to maintain confidentiality (a topic covered in greater detail later on this chapter). Also often problematic is the proper design and adaptation of the instruments, including the inclusion of respectful approaches to obtaining participation and the appropriate translation of the questions. Also of relevance are the differences among ethnic and racial groups in their willingness to disclose personal or attitudinal information. For example, in a recent study on willingness to share biometric information to employers, researchers found that Latinos and Whites differed in their acquiescence to sharing such information (Carpenter, Maasberg, Hicks, & Chen, 2016). In that study, Latinos felt more vulnerable than Whites when sharing biometric information with their employers, even if the information could be helpful in dealing with crisis and emergency situations. These issues are also covered in greater detail later on in this chapter.

Focus Groups The use of focus groups is an exploratory research approach in which researchers put together a small group of individuals (sometimes randomly chosen or sometimes a convenient sample) and the group is asked to discuss a particular issue or to react to certain stimuli (e.g., a new product, a statement, pictures, packages, advertisements). Depending on their objectives, focus groups can be very useful in providing researchers with a comprehensive perspective on a problem or a topic. As you can tell from the description, focus groups are limited in their generalizability (how representative can a small group of individuals be of a whole community?) and depend very heavily on the expertise of the group leader or facilitator in charge of directing the discussion toward the expected goals. In addition, among ethnic and racial groups, cultural standards for social interactions (e.g., saving face, preference for not disagreeing with others in public) can significantly influence results.

Case Studies In implementing a case study, researchers conduct an in-depth analysis of an individual or a group or institution utilizing a number of research approaches—particularly interviews, surveys, observation, and the analysis of documents and archives. The goal is to identify central characteristics and patterns of individual or group functioning that can be used for developing individual or group strategies for change (as in psychological therapy) or for the change or design of innovative systems approaches (as in developing a more efficient client management system). A key problem with case studies is that their effectiveness depends entirely on the sensitivity and analytic and integrative skills of the researcher. In uses of case studies with racial and ethnic groups, the knowledge and sensitivity of the researcher to the culture of the group being studied becomes essential. This contextualization (as mentioned above) is of foremost importance in order to present a nuanced perspective of the observed individuals or groups.

Ethnographies This is a research approach common in anthropology that is sometimes used by other social sciences, including sociology and multicultural psychology. An ethnography of a group requires that the researcher become immersed in the group and its culture, social institutions, and activities. The researcher observes and takes notes on everyday activities of the group, participates in conversations or activities with the community, and writes down the experiences and, often, reactions to what has been observed. Often recordings (voice and/or video) are also made to exemplify what the researcher observed. Like a case study, this approach provides a holistic perspective on a group or community compiled over a substantial period of time (from months to years). A major difficulty with this approach is the limitation in the validity of the analysis and the interpretation produced by possibly limited knowledge and familiarity with the group's culture. Frequently the ethnographer is an individual from outside the community, an advantage in contributing some objectivity to the observations but a disadvantage in lacking a complete and nuanced understanding of the group's culture, which can lead to improper assumptions or conclusions. As discussed later in the ethics section of this chapter, in the past some ethnographies with racial and ethnic groups used deceitful approaches in order to gain entry into the community or failed to engage community members in the interpretation of the observations. These are particularly problematic limitations of this method.

Secondary Data Analysis Often a researcher wishes to explore a question that requires large numbers of respondents or the reanalysis of data collected for other purposes (e.g., data from the decennial census, information from student transcripts, results of employee evaluations). This approach of analyzing previously collected data is often referred to as *secondary data analysis.* Its advantage resides in the ability of the researcher to explore a question with large numbers of respondents or in settings from which it may be impossible or difficult to collect original data or information (Donnellan & Lucas, 2014). In this case, the researcher uses data files culled from a variety of sources, such as national or international studies of certain phenomena (e.g., school achievement in countries belonging to the OECD—Organisation for Economic Co-operation and Development—national health status surveys) or data already archived in an institution or similar setting (e.g., records of lengths of calls using mobile telephones, immigration records, data on student attendance at basketball games).

An important advantage of secondary data analysis is the relatively easy accessibility to large data or information sets and their possible representativeness. The major limitation of this approach is that often the data are collected for specific purposes (e.g., levels of broadband usage by owners of mobile telephones, amount of money spent by tourists, levels of consumption of alcoholic beverages at resorts) and may not include the variables the researcher needs in order to properly answer a question or test a hypothesis. The use of these archives may be of limited value when studying racial and ethnic groups if proper disaggregation is not possible given the absence of essential indicators like ethnic or racial group identification, social class, educational status, migration history, and so on. Nevertheless, this approach has produced very important results with racial and ethnic communities particularly in a number of fields and particularly in the area of health promotion.

Community-Based Participatory Research (CBPR) **Community-based participatory research**, or CBPR (also known as participatory action research, or PAR), is a recently developed holistic approach to conducting research particularly among ethnic or racial minority groups. In this type of research, scientists work in collaboration with community partners (e.g., community agency staff, residents and leaders, medical or mental health patients, homeless shelter residents—those people affected by the research question and findings) to promote the health and well-being of a community (Israel, Eng, Schultz, & Parker, 2005; McIntyre, 2008). Since you may not have encountered this research approach in your other courses, we describe CBPR in greater detail than we do other research methods that are likely more familiar to you.

One of the hallmarks of CBPR is the collaboration between researchers and community partners throughout all stages of a study—the identification of the study question, formulation of the research design, implementation of methods and data collection, data analysis, and dissemination of findings. Hence, for the researcher, the focus is not on conducting research *on* community members; instead, the focus is on conducting research *with* them (Israel et al., 2005; McIntyre, 2008). As such, the researchers' perspective is changed from working with "research subjects" to "respecting participants" (Bromley, Mikesell, Jones, & Khodyakov, 2015). The importance of this basic CBPR tenet becomes all the more apparent when considering that racial or ethnic minority communities are often wary of researchers, given their historical experiences of discrimination and prejudice in society, past negative experiences with researchers, or unfamiliarity with empirical investigations. Much of their fear and trepidation about research, however, can be allayed by including them as equal partners in a shared CBPR endeavor with the explicit aim of serving their community. Other key principles of CBPR also have special significance for ethnic minority psychology research. According to Israel et al. (2005), a community-based participatory research project has several important facets:

- *CBPR builds on existing community strengths and resources.* A CBPR study can identify and expand cultural support networks and resources to enhance an ethnic or racial minority community's ability to safeguard and promote the health of its members. For instance, CBPR investigators may help different community organizations and agencies (e.g., neighborhood churches and temples, community health clinics, schools, social service agencies) strengthen or expand their collaborative relationships, particularly if they share common goals and overlapping interests in certain community health issues. In addition, this collaboration between researchers and communities allows for the protection of the community and supports the design of ethical procedures (Shore, Ford, Wat, Brayboy, Isaacs, Park, Streinick, & Seifer, 2015).
- *CBPR integrates knowledge and intervention for the mutual benefit of all partners.* CBPR research is not only concerned with making contributions to our general body of knowledge or scholarship but also committed to ensuring that the findings are translated and made meaningful to those in the community for their benefit. CBPR researchers are thus expected to work with all partners to best determine how study findings can inform public policy and culturally appropriate interventions that benefit the community at large. Indeed, in an analysis of 51 CBPR projects dealing with HIV among Canadian indigenous communities, researchers found that involvement of community elders was essential in their service as counselors and promoters of the study and as resources on the community's history, culture, and local context (Flicker et al., 2015).
- *CBPR promotes a cooperative process of mutual learning and empowerment that addresses social inequalities or disparities.* Both researchers and community partners learn from each other and share their knowledge with one another in an egalitarian working relationship. Researchers learn about the cultural beliefs, norms, worldviews, or "local theories" of an ethnic community from their community partners, while community partners learn more about scientific inquiry from researchers. This mutual learning process helps to ground the study methods and findings in the cultural beliefs and life perspectives of an ethnic or racial community, and it allows community members to develop new research skills and knowledge—all of which can help address a community's health and social concerns (Jernigan, Jacob, Tribal Community Research Team, & Styne, 2015).
- *CBPR disseminates findings and knowledge to all partners.* Researchers are expected to discuss the study data with community partners and to solicit their feedback prior to publishing or presenting

study findings. In addition, community partners are duly acknowledged on all study publications and, in some instances, are enlisted as coauthors. The entire CBPR team also makes a concerted effort to publicize their study findings in the ethnic languages and media of the community to ensure that it reaches their target audience. A key idea behind this principle is joint ownership of the study by all research partners.

- *CBPR focuses on long-term commitments and sustainable relationships among partners.* Many CBPR interventions striving to promote health and well-being in a community require sustained and joint efforts over extended periods of time before their benefits or anticipated effects can be fully realized. With this in mind, CBPR is based on the understanding that researchers will not simply leave the community once they have gathered their data but will remain a supportive and committed partner with the community until their mutually established goals are fulfilled. This requires that all partners develop permanent and stable relationships and communication channels for sustained collaboration and support once research funding has ended.

All three of the authors of this textbook have conducted CBPR with ethnic minority communities to develop responsible, culturally appropriate health interventions. For instance, Kevin Chun and Catherine Chesla, his colleague at the University of California, San Francisco, received a four-year CBPR grant from the National Institutes of Health for their Chinese Family Diabetes Project. A major aim of this project was to develop the first empirically supported type 2 diabetes management intervention for Chinese American immigrants. These researchers and their university research staff worked closely with two community partners in San Francisco's Chinatown—Cameron House and Northeast Medical Services—both highly respected in the Chinese American immigrant community, with long-standing records of community service. Together these researchers and community partners strived to integrate local theories or knowledge from Chinese American immigrants in adapting and testing a cognitive behavioral intervention for type 2 diabetes management. Specifically, community agency staff shared their insights and expertise on Chinese cultural norms, beliefs, and values, which informed the content and application of the intervention protocol. In addition, the university researchers helped community agency staff develop new research skills, general diabetes knowledge, and cognitive behavioral intervention techniques that can be used well beyond the duration of the study. To further ensure that the study was grounded in the cultural worldviews and daily lives of Chinese American immigrants, this CBPR study also enlisted local Chinese American community leaders, health professionals, and immigrant community members to serve on a community advisory board, which provided important guidance and feedback on research methods. All partners in this CBPR project jointly developed culturally appropriate strategies to promote the study in the local Chinese American immigrant community and to disseminate the study findings. Strategies for promotion and dissemination included working with local Chinese-language media—specifically, Cantonese and Mandarin television and radio outlets and newspapers that reach a wide audience of monolingual Chinese-language immigrant households. Through this partnership between academia and the community, the CBPR team hoped to strengthen their collaborative relationships and, most important, to improve the health and well-being of this traditionally underserved Asian American population.

CBPR is a promising methodology in multicultural psychology that has been used with a variety of ethnic or racial groups, including African Americans (Corrigan, Kraus, Burks, & Schmidt, 2015), American Indians (Langdon et al., 2016), Arab Americans (Aroian, 2016), Chinese Americans (Chang, Simon, & Dong, 2016), Korean Americans (Rhodes, Song, Nam, Choi, & Choi, 2015), Latinos (Garcia-Huidobro et al., 2016), and Native Hawai'ians (Spencer, 2015). The commitment to engaging the community in the research process as partners rather than just objects of study is not only a central characteristics CBPR's approach but also one of its great advantages. This process guarantees that the project will show respect for the community's culture and that findings will be interpreted accurately, eliminating prejudices and stereotypes. Particularly important is the fact that CBPR has been used in a number of psychological and health promotion efforts (Blumenthal, DiClemente, Braithwaite, & Smith, 2013; Zane, Bernal, & Leong, 2016) where researchers report finding a receptive audience in the community to accept and implement the results of the study and to adopt healthier lifestyles.

Key Issues in Developing Responsible, Culturally Appropriate Research

Certain important components of a research project deserve special attention when studying multicultural communities. As a whole, these considerations define the cultural appropriateness of a research project, and they are applicable to all research methods or approaches. As you will see in the following, there is great complexity involved in designing a good research study with racial and ethnic minority groups (Pernice, 1994), including the selection of measuring instruments, translation or adaptation of procedures and instruments, sampling and identification of participants, and respectful analysis and reporting of the results.

Instrument Characteristics

Determining which psychological instruments to use in research is probably one of the most difficult decisions made by researchers. You have certainly read in other courses in psychology and in the social sciences about the two key issues that characterize a measurement instrument. As a minimum, there is a need to identify instruments or tools that properly and accurately measure the variable or variables being investigated. This is usually referred to as the **validity** of the instrument. In addition, there is a need to make sure that the instrument is consistent, that it will produce the same or extremely similar results every time it is used. This characteristic is called **reliability**. There are various ways in which reliability and validity are measured, and you can consult a research methods book to get a more complete perspective.

Nevertheless, we wish to highlight the importance of a type of validity—**external validity**—that refers to the generalizability of a measure or of certain research findings. Indeed, a central concern of multicultural psychology is making sure that research findings are externally valid and that they are appropriately generalizable across persons, settings, ethnic, and racial groups. Some researchers using qualitative methods (particularly outside the United States) refer to this process of demonstrating the generalizability or external validity of research findings as **transferability**. Of concern, therefore, is the fact that, if we wish to talk about findings being externally valid, we want to make sure that what is found in a laboratory is also found outside its walls.

Likewise, in establishing the external validity of a research project we wish to make sure that the testing environment (e.g., the laboratory, clinic) did not determine or affect the results and that the methods and procedures approximate as much as possible the real world. This type of external validity is often called **ecological validity** and is often assumed to be of particular importance in multicultural research. As consumers (or researchers) of multicultural psychology research, we expect, therefore, that there should be external validity in research findings within racial or ethnic groups irrespective of the various social characteristics that differentiate individuals (e.g., gender, class, education). At a minimum, we expect researchers to show that results are generalizable across a number of settings and variables and, importantly, to individuals who were not part of the study.

Another significant issue when analyzing the cultural appropriateness of measurement tools is the expectation that the instrument (e.g., observation guides, interview questions, tasks to be performed, surveys, tests) must be equivalent across groups (Bravo, 2003; Okazaki & Sue, 1995) and properly reflect the values, characteristics, and experiences of the population in which it is being used. One initial concern, as noted earlier, is the expectation that an instrument be in a language in which the respondent is fluent so that questions are fully understood and answered. The same can be said about the instrument's reading level, which may not be appropriate to the abilities of the intended participants because it is too difficult or too complex or even too simple.

The difficulties with establishing the cultural appropriateness of various psychological tests or other "paper-and-pencil" (written) instruments, such as surveys and other questionnaires, go beyond the language used. How appropriately an instrument reflects a concept as defined within the culture of a group is also relevant here. This type of validity has been called **conceptual equivalence** (Okazaki & Sue, 1995) or **construct validity**. It is important, therefore, to analyze this type of validity whenever a research instrument is used in groups different from those for which it was originally developed. The concern of the researcher must be to use instruments that validly measure a concept ("construct") or behavior in a way that has equivalent meanings across groups and is relevant to the group in which it is being used. For example, research with Latinos has shown that, in many cases, distant relatives (aunts, uncles, second cousins) are considered family members for whom one should feel not only respect but also a sense of responsibility and admiration and whose advice should be sought (Sabogal, Marín, Otero-Sabogal, Marín, & Pérez-Stable, 1987). Interviewers or researchers using questionnaires or tests analyzing the nature of family relations among Latinos should therefore go beyond asking questions about how the respondent interacts with parents and siblings to include other members of the family such as grandparents, uncles, aunts, and second cousins and putative relatives such as godparents and in-laws. In this way, the instrument will have construct validity, since the construct of Latino family relations is accurately and completely measured.

Two additional issues are of importance in the selection of instruments in research with ethnic and racial minority groups. Given their importance, we consider them separately in the following. One of special importance to psychological research—and also sometimes research in public health, nursing, sociology, and related fields—is the potential for difficulty encountered when using psychological tests among ethnic and racial minority populations. The other major issue that you should be aware of as a culturally appropriate consumer of research is the need encountered by various researchers to translate questions, procedures, and other instruments into a language different from the one in which they were originally written.

Psychological Tests The American Psychological Association (Turner, DeMersr, Fox, & Reed, 2001) has stated that consideration of ethnic, racial, and cultural variables is of particular importance in the selection of tests to be used in a research project or during professional practice. The APA further supports the notion that there are a number of issues associated with the use of tests among diverse populations that should be of concern to researchers. These include the need for identifying construct equivalence (or construct validity, as defined above), controlling the possible presence of test bias, and using proper procedures for examining between-group differences. Also relevant is the level of cultural competence of the researcher and of the institution as well as the realization that all human beings exhibit certain levels of cultural biases that color the way in which we perceive reality (Roysircar, 2014). Indeed, Roysircar (2005) argues that "multiculturally competent psychologists know that their worldview is neither universal nor objective, and, therefore, they are always aware of their own cultural assumptions." (p. 20). In 2017, the International Test Commission released guidelines for the translation and adaptation of tests.[1] These guidelines are usually comprehensive in nature and apply to the use of psychological tests among ethnic or racial minorities as well as cross-cultural or cross-national comparisons.

While an analysis of these issues is beyond the scope of this book, students of multicultural psychology should be aware of the fact that psychological tests, even well-known and often-used tests, may produce invalid results when utilized with populations that were not included in the development of the instrument, or when the instrument was not properly adapted and analyzed. Indeed, Padilla (2001) suggests that "the reliability and validity of a test used with individuals of different cultural or linguistic groups who were not included in the standardization group are questionable" (p. 6).

[1] Visit the Internal Test Commission online at https://www.intestcom.org.

Translation of Research Instruments The difficulties encountered by investigators interested in studying individuals who are not fluent speakers of the researchers' language has led to the use of translated research instruments. Nevertheless, as you will see in the following, translation is a complex and difficult process. The decision to choose a language or languages in designing the materials to be presented to participants is a particularly sensitive step in the research process. It is possible that in studying racial or ethnic communities researchers will find individuals unable to participate in English because of limited language skills as well as participants preferring to use a heritage or ancestral language because of comfort or fluency. Limiting participation to only those who are fluent or willing to participate in English will significantly limit the validity of a study and the generalizability (external validity) of its findings (Knight, Roosa, & Umaña-Taylor, 2009).

Another issue to consider is the fact that researchers have learned that among bilinguals certain emotions or attitudes are more prevalent or easier to express when using one language over the other (Costa et al., 2014; Harris, Aycicegi, & Gleason, 2003). These differences will affect the results of studies across ethnic or racial groups and seriously impact recall of events and moral decisions. For example, when making moral judgments, individuals using a second language have been found to make more lenient evaluations of moral transgressions and to consider violations of social norms less harshly (Geipel, Hadjichristidis, & Surian, 2015). Other researchers have found that recall of an event is more accurate when there is concordance or agreement between the language used for encoding (language used when the event took place) and for decoding (language used when recalling the event) (Marian & Neisser, 2000). As such, researchers may find that reports of behaviors or events may differ in accuracy when the individual is asked to recall in a second language (e.g., a questionnaire in English) when the event took place while speaking another language or while being in a different linguistic environment (e.g., socializing with other Arab Americans). As you read research projects with ethnic or racial populations in the United States, you will want to identify how researchers dealt with limited English-language fluency (particularly among certain Asian Americans and Latinos) and how regional variations in vocabulary or grammar were included for use by those racial minority communities that speak English. Also important is to consider whether the issue being studied could be susceptible to the reduced activation of social and moral norms experienced by bilinguals when using a second language.

In an important article Vijver and Hambleton (1996) described three types of bias in cross-cultural research of relevance when considering the translation of instruments: (1) *construct bias*, where the concept or construct being analyzed (e.g., need for achievement, independence, individualism) has different meaning or implications in each culture, (2) *method bias*, or factors associated with the application of the instrument and the type of response individuals provide that influence those responses (e.g., the tendency to agree with the statements being presented by the researcher, what is often called **acquiescent response**), and (3) *item bias*, which refers to aspects of the question or item (e.g., wording, content) that have different meanings or implications across cultures. Obviously, the best way to avoid all of these biases is to have the interview, test, or instrument undergo a more complex process than just translating it from one language to another, so as to make sure that the items are relevant to the culture (avoiding construct bias), are presented in an appropriate fashion (avoiding method bias), and are properly worded (avoiding item bias).

One of the problems related to the translation of instruments that have undergone lengthy psychometric analysis (often referred to as **standardized instruments**) is the possibility of responses being partially influenced by the new wording. For example, a number of studies have looked at a well-known measure of depression (the Center for Epidemiological Studies Depression Scale, or the CES-D) and its translation and adaptation to Spanish. These studies are indicative of the problems associated with using instruments developed for one culture in studying another group even after proper translation procedures have been followed, and these problems pertain not just to tests but also to questions used in interviews or in observational studies. One problem faced by researchers using the CES-D in their investigations was how to properly translate items that use informal or colloquial statements such as "shaking the blues." In many cases, these colloquial statements do not have proper equivalents in other languages and are meaningless if literally translated ("shaking the blues" would become "shaking the blue colors" if literally translated into Spanish).

A second possible problem with the translation of a psychological test is related to the internal structure of the instrument. Although some research (e.g., Roberts, Vernon, & Rhoades, 1989) shows that translation of the CES-D does not affect the statistical characteristics of the test, specifically its dimensionality and reliability, other studies (e.g., Golding & Aneshensel, 1989; Guarnaccia, Angel, & Worobey, 1989; Posner, Stewart, Marín, & Pérez-Stable, 2001) show that the internal dimensionality of the instrument is indeed different in English and in Spanish. These results could mean that, while the wording of the items is similar in both languages, the way the items are being interpreted by respondents in English and in Spanish is so different that they could be answering what in practice amounts to two different tests. Furthermore, responses to at least some items seem to differ based on the birthplace (abroad or in the United States) of the respondents, indicating that acculturation (see Chapter 4) or generational history affects the way they interpret the various questions (Golding, Aneshensel, & Hough, 1991).

Given the above difficulties, some researchers (particularly cross-cultural psychologists) have argued that instead of translating instruments, researchers should develop new instruments (particularly psychological tests) that deal with universal issues or topics (also known as **etic constructs**) while using group-specific descriptions and concepts (indigenous or **emic**). This strategy of using an etic-emic approach to instrument development is often perceived as a better way to develop culturally appropriate instruments for measuring indigenous concepts (Cheung et al., 1996; Cheung, van de Vijver, & Leong, 2011). Indeed, these authors have used this approach for the development of personality measures in China and South Africa with the goal of creating "a richer and more integrated and balanced view of the universal and culture-specific aspects of a target construct or theory than could be obtained by the use of an emic or etic method separately" (Cheung, van de Vijver, & Leong, 2011, p. 597).

The Translation Process As suggested by Sperber, Devellis, and Boehlecke (1994), the goal in translating is "to adapt the instrument in a culturally relevant and comprehensible form while maintaining the meaning of the original items" (p. 502). Suggestions for translating questionnaires, interviews, and other instruments have been made in the research literature for many years, particularly in the works of cross-cultural investigators and multicultural psychologists (e.g., Brislin, 1980; Brislin, Lonner, & Thorndike, 1973; Marín & Marín, 1991). There is much controversy about the goals of translating and best procedures to follow despite the significance of the translation process not only in multicultural psychology research but also in areas as diverse as politics (translations of legal proceedings and meetings), entertainment (movie or show dubbing and subtitling), and literature (books, poems, music). In the last few years, machine-assisted translation (computerized translation procedures) has become more prevalent, its quality indeed improved. Nevertheless, using these computerized translation programs and apps must be done with great care (or best avoided for research purposes). We are all familiar with the nonsense that at times (or often) comes out when we ask our computers to translate an e-mail or a Facebook or WhatsApp message. Currently the use of machine-assisted translation produces not only wrong translations but also significant problems with grammar, sentence structure, and other important characteristics. This means that for the foreseeable future we will need to rely on humans to translate our instruments and other research tools. In the following section we briefly discuss some of the most common approaches to translation these instruments allow, along with this technology's limitations.

The simplest and less valid translation process uses one language as the original or standard while the instrument is translated into the target language by an experienced or volunteer translator. The translator creates a new version of the instrument in the target language, usually adopting a fairly literal, word-for-word approach to translation, and the process ends at that point. This approach is frequently known as *forward translation* or *one-way translation*. A researcher would be using forward translation were she to ask Thuan, her Vietnamese American student, to translate a survey from English into Vietnamese and were she to then take Thuan's new text as the final version of the survey to be used for interviewing other Vietnamese Americans. Sometimes various translators are asked to produce different forward translations in different languages, and the various target language versions are compared (a process often called *reconciliation*) in order to revise and refine each translation before a final version is reached. This forward translation approach is of limited use, since it considers neither any linguistic limitations of the translator nor the variability in culture-specific meanings of words or concepts that may be unfamiliar to the translator. Unfortunately, this translation approach was used in much early research in multicultural psychology.

An alternative translation approach has been called **double translation** (Marín & Marín, 1991) or **back translation** by other authors (e.g., Brislin, 1980). This approach, often considered one of the best procedures currently available for translating instruments, involves the use of at least two bilingual translators and a significant level of consultation within the research team and across translators. This translation procedure has a number of possible variations, but it involves going back and forth across languages, trying to obtain translations that are appropriate to the language and culture of the respondents and that do not differ significantly in meaning from the intended goal of the project. This comparison process of various versions of back translations is called *harmonization*. For example, in a double translation process, one translator (Translator A) takes the original version of the instrument written in the original language (for example, French Version 1) and translates it into the target language (for example, Mandarin), producing Mandarin Version 1. A second translator (Translator B) then takes the first target language version of the instrument (Mandarin Version 1) and translates it into the original language without consulting with Translator A, thus producing French Version 2. Once the two original language versions (French Version 1 and French Version 2) are ready, the researchers compare the instruments in order to identify problems with the translations (odd wording, improper meaning, incomplete sentences, etc.). At this stage, the researchers can engage the translators in discussions as to what was done and how to resolve any discrepancies. A repetition of the process is often recommended (from French Version 2 to Mandarin Version 2 to French Version 3) with the same or different translators. The consultation and modification process continues until researchers and translators are satisfied that the resulting linguistic versions are similar and equally useful in each language. See Box 3.4 for an example of the double translation procedure.

In a complete double translation process, researchers often add a step called *cognitive debriefing*, where the final version of the instrument in the target language is tested in a small group of individuals who resemble the intended respondents, in order to identify alternative words that could be used as well as to check how understandable the translation is and to ascertain the cultural relevance of the new version. Also common to the process is the involvement of native speakers of the target language, proficient in the original language, who are asked to review the instrument and, at times, participate in the cognitive debriefing.

The difficulties inherent in using some of these discussed instrument translation methods (expensive, time consuming, problems with translating between different linguistic families, difficulty identifying capable bilinguals, etc.) have motivated researchers to explore alternative approaches (Cha, Kim,

Box 3.4

Example of the Double Translation Procedure

Original language, version 1 (English)
"I often feel hungry when studying."

Target language, version 1 (Spanish)
"Frecuentemente, siento hambre cuando estudio."

Original language, version 2 (English)
"Frequently, I feel hunger when I study."

Target language, version 2 (Spanish)
"Frecuentemente me siento con hambre cuando estoy estudiando."

Original language version 3 (English)
"Often I feel hungry when studying."

& Erlen, 2007). In general, these new approaches combine aspects of the methods described above with some of the research strategies used in CBPR (see again the section on community-based participatory research). For example, Sumathipala and Murray (2000) report the effectiveness of mixing the use of teams of translators not only to translate the instrument (in this case from English to Sinhala, the language of Sri Lanka) but also to discuss how best to modify the final instrument in order to obtain an appropriate translation. This is a particularly useful approach when translating from English or other languages of the same or a related linguistic family (for example, Spanish, Portuguese, French, Italian) to another linguistic family (for example, translating into Arabic, Russian, Hindi, Hungarian, Chinese, Japanese) where grammar is quite different from that of English. An example of combining translation approaches with CBPR methodologies can be found in a study with Hmong communities in the United States (Baker et al., 2010) that used what the researchers called a *process-based universalistic approach* to translate a survey dealing with immunizations. In that project, members from the community were involved in identifying the best version of the instrument that guaranteed full equivalence (conceptual, semantic, measurement, functional, etc.) across cultures and after implementing modifications of the back translation strategy.

As an alternative to the double translation procedure, Erkut and colleagues (Erkut, Alarcon, Coll, Tropp, & Garcia, 1999) have suggested what they call the **dual focus approach to translation**, which also incorporates steps often used in CBPR studies. In this approach, bilingual and bicultural research teams work together to plan the research project and develop the instruments to be used. During the initial stage, members of the team become familiar with the literature, making sure that the concepts and constructs to be used in the research project are equally valid in all cultures. Then all members of the research team work to guarantee that the words to be used in all language versions are equivalent in their emotional meaning (affect), familiarity, and ease of comprehension (clarity). Focus groups made up of indigenous informants review the instrument and provide feedback as to its linguistic and cultural appropriateness. Psychometric and statistical analyses are then conducted to establish the usefulness and internal consistency of the instruments in the research enterprise.

Use of Interpreters In some situations or research projects, interpreters translate instructions or questions to the respondents as they are being verbalized by the researcher, clinician, nurse, or therapist. This approach, while not ideal, may become necessary for certain qualitative research projects, such as when conducting field studies, ethnographies, interviews, and focus groups or while carrying out initial exploratory visits to communities to be studied. The use of interpreters, however, is fraught with problems. Research on the use of interpreters in medical settings, for example, shows that interpreters usually do not properly transmit information to patients or to health personnel, mostly because they don't understand what is being said, they lack enough cultural and/or personal sensitivity, they fail to understand colloquial expressions or dialects, they fail to pay attention to nonverbal communication, or they inappropriately translate words that have various meanings (Brooks, 1992; Nápoles, Santoyo-Olsson, Karliner, Gregorich, & Pérez-Stable, 2015). The use of interpreters or translators can also create other complications, such as the interpreter responding to or taking issue with the interviewee's responses, the translator inputting her or his own beliefs or perspectives while translating the question or prompt, and the interviewee losing interest in the study as the interpreter takes time to communicate with the researcher.

Despite these limitations, evidence suggests that well-trained interpreters can provide fairly accurate translations. Research in medical settings (Nápoles et al., 2015) shows that, overall, interpreters properly translate 70 percent of statements made and professional translators make fewer mistakes (25 percent) than ad hoc translators (54 percent). Some researchers (Lie, 2006) argue that interpreters should be part of the research team and should be used not just for translating but also to help the researcher obtain a context in which the study is being conducted (in a sense, becoming "key informants"). At the same time, this new role for interpreters presents the danger that they may influence the results in providing specific cues to the participants or explaining the meaning of the questions by going beyond the actual wording of the question or prompt. Other potential difficulties with the use of interpreters as suggested by Lie include differences in social status between interpreter and participant (for example, differing social classes or familial roles when a child translates for parents or other adults), poor interpreter linguistic skills, and difficulties establishing rapport because of either personality or differences in ancestry.

In general, the use of interpreters should be avoided or used sparingly in research. And when reviewing research where interpreters have been used to collect information, be careful to identify situations or topics that may have been subject to misinterpretation or mistranslation, and pay particular attention to how those problems could affect the validity of the information. If translators have been used, ascertain whether they were properly trained and had the experience and background knowledge needed to produce an accurate translation to researchers as well as to research participants.

Properly Identifying and Describing Participants

The proper identification and description of participants in a research project is important in helping students and other researchers understand the implications and generalizability of the results. This concern is of particular importance when conducting research with racial and ethnic groups, since a number of approaches can be taken to describing individuals forming an ethnic or racial group in the United States. For example, basic demographic information provides an understanding of a group's size (usually based on self-identification), along with such socioeconomic characteristics as median age, average income, and mean level of formal education. At the same time, historical information can be used to understand the reasons for the group's presence in the country, their level of involvement with the dominant culture(s), or their current social and political status.

Probably the most important consideration when planning research with ethnic or racial minority groups is the need to consider the heterogeneity present in all ethnic or racial groups. Related to this concern is the need to disaggregate the data by the relevant sociocultural variables—that is, reporting data by smaller groupings than the use of the entire ethnic or racial group. As discussed in Chapter 1, important differences are found within any given ethnic or racial group that are based not only on ancestry (for example, country or culture of origin) but also on sociocultural variables (for example, educational level, social class, generational history). These additional variables defining an ethnic or racial group are described in the following sections of this chapter.

Intragroup Heterogeneity In our opening vignette, Angelina encountered one initial basic problem with most early research among ethnic or racial groups when reading her textbook: The faulty assumption by many researchers that all members of an ethnic or racial group are similar and share a number of characteristics allows researchers to cluster diverse individuals into one single entity. This phenomenon, often called the **assumption of intragroup homogeneity**, pervades much research currently found in the literature. Indeed, in Chapter 1 we see how important within-group differences in the demographic characteristics abound among various racial and ethnic groups. And, as you will see in this chapter, important within-group differences in many sociocultural and psychological variables must be taken into consideration when conducting or reading research in multicultural psychology. Various authors (for example, Bledsoe & Hopson, 2009) suggest that assuming homogeneity across diverse cultural, ethnic, or racial groups is an example of unethical research with underserved populations.

The overriding principle in defining the members of an ethnic group is the belief that what may unite these individuals is a shared culture and traditions that are valued and/or defended and that have survived migrations, the passing of time, and the onslaught of a massive globalizing culture. Many of these defining characteristics are partially subsumed in the ethnic or racial label used to identify members of the group, and those labels can be self-assigned (for example, African American or Latino) or imposed by other groups (for example, Black or Hispanic).

It is indeed common in the United States to use labels based on ancestry, race, or ethnicity—such as Asian American, Hispanic, African American, Latino, American Indian, Mexican American, Vietnamese American, Chinese American, Cuban American, Puerto Rican, Filipino American, or Laotian American. These labels and others, as mentioned in Chapter 1, imply that a number of characteristics define or are shared by individuals comprising these groups and that these characteristics usually go beyond common ancestry or national or cultural origin. Nevertheless, there is a need to understand that these ethnic or racial or cultural labels are **labels of convenience** that allow researchers, politicians, care providers, educators, researchers, and others to identify individuals who share some general characteristics. Those labels neither necessarily reflect intragroup homogeneity or complete similarity nor necessarily imply common psychological characteristics (Okazaki & Sue, 1995; Weiss & Weiss, 2002).

It is important, therefore, to remember great variability exists within the various ethnic and racial groups found in the United States—in terms of migration history, socioeconomic characteristics (educational level, income, average age), and psychological variables. Ethnic labels provide a convenient shorthand for discussion of a group of individuals sharing *some* characteristics. Indeed, research shows that members of a given ethnic or racial group perceive significant heterogeneity within their own group but assume that other ethnic or racial groups experience homogeneity in values, attitudes, and behaviors (Lee & Ottati, 1993).

Racial or ethnic labels nevertheless denote groups that include significant intragroup variability, and these labels are not equivalent to the groupings used in the natural sciences, as when botanists group plants, zoologists group animal families, or biologists categorize blood types. For example, individuals who consider themselves Chinese Americans vary in any number of characteristics, including immigration history. Some came to the United States to work on the construction of the railroads, while others migrated to join those early relatives. Another group of Chinese Americans fled the Communist revolution and the war with Japan, while still others came to the United States when Hong Kong was ceded back to the People's Republic of China. Recently, Chinese from the southern provinces of the People's Republic have been coming to the United States in search of economic advancement. At the same time, there are Chinese Americans who were born in the United States or whose parents, and often grandparents, were also born in the United States.

These differences in immigration histories of various Chinese Americans are also often reflected in the various groups' average educational levels and in their average incomes, and English-language fluency, among other characteristics. While all of these groups can be described as Chinese Americans who share certain cultural values, they also differ in terms of a number of variables. The same variability can be found among other Asian American groups as well as among African Americans, American Indians, Native Hawai'ians, and Latinos. Thus, researchers and consumers of research must pay attention to the variability that exists not only within the larger labels used to identify ethnic or racial groups (see Box 1.2) but also within the more specific labels (for example, Chinese Americans, Filipino Americans, and Vietnamese Americans, all of whom are generally considered Asian Americans). The examination of this intragroup variability is often called **disaggregation** of results.

Disaggregating Participants You may recall how in the vignette at the beginning of this chapter Angelina and her friends were unhappy with what they read in their textbooks because they could not fully identify with the ethnic groups being described. What explains those differences in people's behaviors and attitudes is the variability discussed earlier. It is necessary, therefore, that researchers properly define their respondents or research participants by describing the individual characteristics differentiating members of the group.

Culturally appropriate research demands proper disaggregation or sampling and reporting of relevant characteristics that produce differences within and across ethnic groups. We see in Chapter 1 how important it is to disaggregate members of racial and ethnic groups in terms of key demographic characteristics like gender, national origin or ancestry, social class, and educational level. The process of disaggregation implies that, in addition to including information on typical sociodemographic parameters (gender, generation, education, age), researchers must study participants who are members of ethnic groups in terms of other relevant variables like immigration status, literacy, acculturation level, and language preference and use (Baluja, Park, & Myers, 2003). The description of respondents and analysis of the information or data must address each of these characteristics in order to more properly identify research participants (Okazaki & Sue, 1995) and produce a better, more valid multicultural psychology.

The proper disaggregation of research participants allows students of multicultural psychology to better understand a social phenomenon. A study of the rates of tobacco use (or prevalence) among

Latinos exemplifies the need to properly disaggregate research findings: The study (Marín, Pérez-Stable, & Marín, 1989) showed that acculturation (or rate of learning of a new culture; see Chapter 4) differentially affected the rate at which male and female Latinos smoked cigarettes. Highest rates of cigarette smoking were found among the less acculturated men, while among women the highest rates of cigarette smoking were found among the highly acculturated. Ignoring the need to differentiate respondents by gender and acculturation could have led researchers to propose erroneous conclusions about the rates of cigarette smoking among Latinos. Another study on tobacco use among racial and ethnic minorities (Sakuma et al., 2016) shows not only differences in prevalence (occurrence) of cigarette smoking across racial and ethnic groups but also that residence in California has a marked effect on overall prevalence and intensity of cigarette smoking across groups. The data show that California has a greater percentage of former smokers than other states across all ethnic groups and also a lower number of heavy smokers when controlling for the effects of age, gender, and education. In this study, disaggregating by state of residence was an essential component that allowed a more nuanced perspective on the phenomenon studied.

Unfortunately, at times researchers have not been sensitive to the need to properly identify respondents and appropriately disaggregate information. While by now most researchers are aware of the need to define racial and ethnic groups at least by the major categories (see Box 1.2) used by the U.S. Department of Commerce in the decennial census, we must acknowledge the limits of these overarching labels, keeping in mind that there are more than 300 distinct ethnic or ancestral groups and that approximately 500 American Indian tribes were identified in the 1990 census.

And so we see that it is essential for researchers to differentiate within-group communities so that among Asian Americans, for example, Chinese Americans are differentiated from Laotian or Korean or Vietnamese or Filipino Americans. This within-group variability is also found among Latinos (Mexican Americans differing from Salvadoran or Cuban or Puerto Rican or Colombian Americans), as well as among African Americans (Haitians differing from Jamaicans, Kenyans, or Belizeans). For example, the category "Asian American and Pacific Islander" includes more than 57 national heritages or ancestries as well as people who, as a group, use more than 100 languages. Latinos include individuals who trace their roots to more than 34 different countries, and, while most (but not all) speak Spanish or Portuguese, there are variations in lilt, accent, and voice inflection as well as vocabulary. To better understand this complexity, look at Box 3.5 to see the great intragroup variability in national background or ancestry existing among Asian Americans and Latinos in the United States.

Box 3.5

Examples of Diversity Within Ethnic or Racial Groups

Asian Americans include individuals tracing their ancestry or cultural origin to countries or areas of the world such as:

Bangladesh
Bhutan
Cambodia
China
Hong Kong
India
Indonesia
Japan
Korea
Laos
Malaysia
Myanmar (Burma)
Nepal
Pakistan
Philippines
Singapore
Sri Lanka
Taiwan
Thailand
Vietnam

Latinos/Hispanics include individuals tracing their ancestry to countries such as:

Argentina
Bolivia
Brazil
Dominican Republic
Ecuador
El Salvador
Panama
Paraguay
Peru

Chile	Guatemala	Puerto Rico
Colombia	Honduras	Spain
Costa Rica	Mexico	Uruguay
Cuba	Nicaragua	Venezuela

While the argument can be made that using labels to identify the larger racial and ethnic groups is valid and relevant to some extent (for example, Latinos irrespective of national origin do share some basic common values like familialism or finding emotional and social support among relatives), in many cases the differences within an ethnic group are as large as they are across ethnic groups (for example, dietary habits, academic achievement, school persistence, prevalence of certain diseases). As a matter of fact, members of a given racial or ethnic group often are very sensitive to ways in which the various subgroups differ, and within-group variability may often be invoked by respondents as a way of differentiating themselves from other subgroups (for example, Cuban Americans differing from Puerto Rican or Mexican Americans). Researchers must therefore precisely report how they identified and selected research participants in order to present information that is useful and valid to the student of multicultural psychology.

Parenting by individuals from different ethnic or cultural backgrounds is also generating an interesting and important phenomenon in the United States that has implications for our research and for understanding our contemporary culture. Parenting by individuals of diverse ethnic or racial backgrounds and ethnic intermarriage are producing a noticeable increase in the number of individuals tracing their ethnic background to more than one ethnic or ancestral group (*multiethnic* or *multiracial individuals*). While this is not a new phenomenon, respondents were first able to indicate that they belonged to more than one race in the 2000 U.S. decennial census. Indeed, data from that census show that approximately 2.6 percent of the total U.S. population indicated belonging to two or more races, and 5.4 percent of adults married and living with a spouse indicated having married someone of a different race or ethnicity, compared with 4.5 percent of 1990 U.S. census respondents (Farley, 2002). These figures indicate that the probability of encountering multiethnic respondents is rapidly increasing and that researchers need to be aware of this possibility not just in terms of drafting appropriate identifiers but also in deciding how to properly treat their responses.

Unfortunately, few researchers sample ethnic individuals who represent the diversity present in the various communities, and even fewer report the results of disaggregating or separating for each of the values or dimensions of each variable. As educated consumers of psychological research, multicultural psychology students should keep these variables in mind and investigate how researchers included them or failed to consider these types of within-group variability. Variables where significant within-group variability exists among ethnic communities include the following categories.

- *Gender*: It is now fairly common for researchers in the social and behavioral sciences to always consider gender when selecting a sample and to analyze and interpret the results of the study according to the gender of the participants. Indeed, a large number of publications have supported the need for this approach, and various funding agencies (for example, the U.S. Public Health Service, the Centers for Disease Control and Prevention) have required since 1986 the inclusion of men and women in all studies (except when not possible, such as in the case of studies of cervical or prostate cancer). The inclusion of men and women in any sample is of obvious importance, since their development and social experiences vary, resulting in a diversity of behaviors, attitudes, and values. For example, researchers polling peoples' opinions about welfare reform would want to analyze differences in opinions among men and women, among adults of childbearing age, and among older individuals. Failure to include those gender- and age-specific groups could provide biased perspectives on the issues under study.

  Also relevant is consideration of any role played by gender typing, gender stereotyping, and gender-based prejudice and discrimination. It is a well-established fact that women and men differ in the ways they are treated by others in terms of variables as diverse as pay levels, expected behaviors (for example, cooking, driving, making decisions), and perceptions. The type of situation presented to respondents in a study as well as the topic of a study may contaminate the data, and researchers need to be aware of this confounding factor.

- *Rural/urban residence*: Much research tends to ignore differences that may exist between those raised or who reside in small towns and rural communities and those from large metropolitan areas. Nevertheless, research is available that shows important differences between residents of rural and urban areas, including their mental health (Marsella, 1998), levels of resiliency or psychological strength, and risk levels. A study with indigenous people in Chiapas, Mexico, for example, showed that rural participants showed different self-concepts (giving more value to social referents) than did urban respondents (who gave greater value to individualized or personal referents) despite the fact that all participants shared the same culture (Esteban-Guitart, Perera, Monreal-Bosch, & Bastiani, 2016). These rural/urban differences are of particular significance when studying ethnic or racial groups where large numbers of the participants were raised or currently reside in small towns. Indeed, this pattern holds true for African Americans and other U.S.-born ethnic or racial minorities who have worked in agriculture, as well as for individuals who have recently migrated from rural Asia or Latin America. Growing up in small rural areas can influence people's vision of the world, making it different from the worldviews of individuals raised in large metropolitan areas like New York, Miami, Chicago, or Los Angeles.
- *Social class*: It is not uncommon for social and behavioral researchers to consider social class variables as important modifiers of a person's attitudes, norms, values, and behaviors. Whether measured by complex indices or by indicators (for example, educational level, employment category, family income), social class or socioeconomic status can be a powerful modifier of a person's worldview and behavior (APA Task Force on Socioeconomic Status, 2007; Evans, 2004). For members of ethnic or racial groups, the experiences of belonging to a given ethnic or cultural group interact with their social class so that the latter may in some cases powerfully override certain racial- or ethnic-specific characteristics. As such, Korean Americans living in poverty may experience specific attitudes and behaviors that are more closely related to their social class (and therefore found among Whites or African Americans of the same social class status) than to the fact that they are Korean Americans. Researchers must therefore be careful to differentiate as much as possible the effects of social class and socioeconomic conditions from those of ethnic or racial group membership.

  Poverty has indeed been shown to have an effect on people's lives, development, and attitudes that goes beyond simple lifestyle deprivations. For example, research has shown that poverty status affects not only children's development (Duncan, Brooks-Gunn, & Klebanov, 1994) but also their psychosocial adjustment (Westermeyer, Callies, & Neider, 1990), as well as their overall health status (Stein, Nyamathi, & Kington, 1997). In these and other studies, experiencing poverty has been found to produce long-term effects on people's health and psychological well-being (APA Task Force on Socioeconomic Status, 2007). It is therefore of particular importance that researchers consider the possible modifying effects of social class or poverty in the responses and behaviors of the individuals being studied.
- *Generational status*: There is a substantial body of research suggesting that the generational status of individuals produces important behavioral and attitudinal differences across groups. As could be expected, the experiences of immigrants are rather different from those of their children and grandchildren who were born in the United States. Language use and proficiency, for example, can be expected to vary across generations, as can levels of familiarity with cultural products (meals, music, literature, holidays), expectations, and other relevant concepts and experiences.

  While the generational level of ethnic participants may not have been as important for those groups that came to the United States at the end of the 19th century and beginning of the 20th century (where assimilationist perspectives were strong and fairly well accepted by immigrants), the same is not true for the cultural and ancestral groups that have recently arrived in the country. Many of these latter immigrants try to maintain language proficiency and cultural traditions as a way of defining their self-concept and personal identity as well as that of their children. Moreover, the "melting pot" phenomenon in immigrant assimilation may have been true for some groups (possibly Italians, Irish, and Jews of the early 20th century) but may be less true for other recent immigrants (Glazer & Moynihan, 1963). As such, it becomes important for researchers and students alike to properly understand the generational history of those individuals being studied.

Indeed, various analyses have shown that considering a respondent's generation provides a better and more complex description of various psychological phenomena than when generational status is ignored. For example, Baluja, Park, and Myers (2003) found that differentiating between first and second generation Asian Americans allowed them to better understand differences in cigarette smoking: First generation Asian Americans showed a lower proportion of individuals who smoked (prevalence) than what was found among second generation Asian Americans. The data from that study also showed that there were differences across countries of origin, supporting the need to disaggregate results by more than one variable.

Box 3.6 describes the most commonly used **generation** labels found in the literature of the social sciences. While these labels and their definitions are useful to better understand the migration history of individuals and their families, they are labels of convenience that may not properly address the characteristics of all members of ethnic groups. Estimates (Perlmann, 2002) drawn from the 2000 decennial census show that third generation individuals (grandchildren of immigrants) are normally born within 40 years of the time of arrival of the immigrants themselves (generally aged around 20 at time of immigration). Fourth generation individuals are usually born around 70 years after the arrival of the immigrants. At the same time, analysis of census information of Italian immigrants shows that third generation Italians tended to *intermarry* (that is, marrying outside their ethnic or ancestral group) in fairly large percentages (62 percent), and the same was true for fourth generation Italian Americans (89 percent). Therefore, our immigration experiences in the 20th and 21st centuries would show that, within a window of less than 70 years, intermarriage (or outmarriage) is highly likely to occur, generating a large number of multiethnic individuals.

Typically, generational levels are defined as being based on place of birth and familial history but not on the age of the respondents. As shown in Box 3.6, first generation members of ethnic or racial groups are considered those who immigrate into a new culture—for example, a Vietnamese refugee who arrived in the United States after the U.S.-Vietnam war or a Russian first coming to the United States after the collapse of the Soviet Union.

Sociologists Alejandro Portes and Rubén Rumbaut (Rumbaut & Portes, 2001; Portes & Rumbaut, 2001, 2014) have frequently advocated for the need to separately analyze individuals from various generations (disaggregating by generation) since the experiences of a first generation individual can differ across a number of situations from those of a second generation person. Indeed, generational differences can be expected in terms of levels of educational achievement, language proficiency, civic

Box 3.6

Definition of Generational Levels

First Generation: Individual has immigrated to the United States and expects to remain in the country permanently or for a very long time

1.5 Generation: Individual migrated to the United States as a preadolescent

Second Generation: Individual is born in the United States of parents who were both first generation

Mixed Second Generation: Individual is born in the United States with one parent being born in the United States and the other being a first generation; also called *2.5 generation*

Third Generation: Individual and parents born in the United States with at least one grandparent being first generation

Fourth Generation: Individual born in the United States with no grandparent being an immigrant

Source: Based on Portes & Rumbaut, 2001.

incorporation, and employment status. All of these variables are relevant in defining socioeconomic status, acculturation, and level of involvement with a majority culture and will probably impact the characteristics of the participants in a study.

The importance of considering the generational history of ethnic or racial minority groups can be seen in a longitudinal study of children of immigrants (either 1.5 generation or second generation) conducted by Portes and Rumbaut (2014). These children of immigrants were found to perform

> better academically than their native-parentage peers, graduating from high school and going on to college, working hard at their first jobs, and taking the first steps toward independent entrepreneurship. Even children of families with no money and little or no human capital can move forward, riding on their own determination and strategic supports from their families and significant others. (p. 303)

The researchers also find that as generational levels increased, acculturation to the majority culture (see Chapter 4) also increased and the respondents exhibited a decrease or "dampening" in what they called the "immigrant drive" to succeed. This decrease in the immigrant drive was manifested in lower school commitment and lower academic achievement among some third and fourth generation individuals.

Research has likewise shown that generational history interacts with other variables (for example, social class, preferred language) to differentially affect people's behavior even in somewhat unexpected areas such as health status. In a large-scale analysis of data from more than 3,000 Mexican American elderly (Afable-Munsuz, Gregorich, Markides, & Pérez-Stable, 2013), researchers find that the presence of diabetes among the respondents was dependent on their generational history and language preference interacting with social class. In that study, participants from lower social classes who preferred to speak in Spanish (a proxy measure for low acculturation; see Chapter 4) showed an increased risk of experiencing diabetes from the first to the third generations. At the same time, English-speaking, higher social class respondents showed lower risk for diabetes among second and third generation respondents.

As could be expected, generational levels have been found to influence many other variables as diverse as English-language proficiency (Sodowsky, Lai, & Plake, 1991), mental health status (Vega, Gil, & Kolody, 2002), alcohol drinking patterns (Golding, Burnam, Benjamin, & Wells, 1992), and cigarette smoking (Markides, Coreil, & Ray, 1987). It is therefore imperative that studies with ethnic or racial minority populations disaggregate the results by the generational level of the respondents. Unfortunately, this has seldom been done in much of multicultural psychology research.

Migration Rationale and History Some researchers (for example, Ogbu, 1978) argue that people's behaviors in a new environment or culture can be significantly influenced by the reason for their migration experience. Ogbu suggests that the voluntary or involuntary nature of the migration experience can affect people's education and overall socioeconomic success in the new country. **Voluntary immigrants** for Ogbu are those who choose to migrate searching for economic and educational improvements. **Involuntary immigrants**, by contrast, are those individuals who have been enslaved or colonized and may have experienced difficulties assimilating (for example, American Indians, African Americans, Native Hawai'ians) or those who were forced to leave their country of origin because of political conditions (for example, refugees and asylum seekers). While the data supporting these assumptions are not very conclusive, involuntary immigrants are usually characterized as faring poorly in academic settings, having school adjustment difficulties, and experiencing scholarly failure. Ogbu further argues that in part this is due to their refusal to accept the values of the "host" culture, which in turn can be expected to lead to failure in academic pursuits and poorer future employment opportunities.

Ogbu's hypothesis is of interest in that it provides insights into certain attitudinal conflicts experienced by various ethnic or racial groups that may in turn affect their performance and generalized willingness to adapt to or learn the new culture. Of particular importance is the distinction that can be drawn from Ogbu's (1978) typology when applied to individuals from various generations who are members of the same family unit. For example, immigrant parents who choose to migrate in search of economic advancement can be considered voluntary immigrants. At the same time, their small children who are forced to relocate because of their parents' decision can be considered involuntary immigrants. Differences in attitudes and in the ease of acculturation (see Chapter 4) can be expected in these two groups of individuals.

Portes and Rumbaut (2014) also present a typology of immigrants, this time based on the legal process they followed to migrate. At one end of the continuum are **unauthorized migrants** (also known as **undocumented migrants** or pejoratively as "illegal immigrants"). These are individuals who have entered or remained in the country without proper documentation (such as a visa) or have overstayed a time-limited permit (for example, an expired tourist visa). A second category are those who enter the country as legal, **temporary migrants**, individuals who receive a permit to live and work in the United States for limited periods of time, such as au pairs or farm laborers with H-2 visas, or skilled workers, such as software engineers who receive H-1B visas. This second category also includes **sojourners**, those individuals temporarily in the country as tourists or foreign students. A third category of immigrants includes those individuals who can be considered legal, **permanent migrants**, who entered the country with an immigrant visa (or "green card") that allows them to live and work permanently in the United States and eventually to become citizens. A fourth category of immigrants are **refugees** or **asylees**, who receive temporary, long-term permission to live and work in the United States (and sometimes permission to apply for permanent residency and eventual citizenship) due to political or human rights abuses in their country of origin (for example, Vietnamese after the Vietnam War, Cubans after the Cuban revolution, Russians and Ukrainians after the 1990 political changes, Syrians in 2016, or some Central Americans who received temporary protected status (TPS) in the 1990s and 2000s). As is true for Ogbu's categories, these typologies are important to consider when studying the social, political, and attitudinal characteristics of ethnic or racial minority groups, since they can affect an individual's values, behavior, and motivation to be part of the new culture.

This section of the chapter emphasizes the need for researchers to properly define the characteristics of their respondents by going beyond large and usually uninformative labels such as "Asian Americans" or "Latinos." As a student of multicultural psychology, you should be aware of the differences that exist within each ethnic group in terms of generation or factors such as gender, age, economic and educational status, acculturation (see Chapter 4), and experiences of prejudice and discrimination (see Chapter 8). This section of the chapter complements the information presented in Chapter 1 on how ethnic or racial groups differ not just across groups but also within. As mentioned in the vignette that introduced this chapter, Angelina could not recognize herself as an Asian American when reading her textbooks since the authors had failed to indicate the differences that exist within and across various Asian American groups. One key lesson from this chapter is that it is difficult to properly understand ethnic or racial groups unless the data and information are properly disaggregated by other relevant variables such as gender, generational history, migration motivation, and educational status. These variables or personal characteristics have been found to produce differences in attitudes, behaviors, and perceptions and also to interact with each other (Bleidorn et al., 2016).

Culturally Appropriate Analysis of Information or Data

In carrying out culturally appropriate research, there is a need for researchers to be aware of their own cultural background and social status and the effects those variables can have on their interpretation of the results of a study. Often we tend to misinterpret behaviors that are different from those that are familiar or frequent among our friends and relatives. Indeed, in his famous book *Even the Rat Was White* African American psychologist Robert Guthrie (1998, 2004) properly pointed out how much of psychological research had ignored the nuances and variability produced by differences in ethnicity, race, and other variables. This one-sided perspective of human behavior (when in extreme cases researchers, subjects, and even laboratory rats were white) challenges the generalizability of our findings. One extreme manifestation, as noted by Padilla (2001), is the fact that any deviation from White middle-class norms is often interpreted as a deficit or a problem that requires alleviation or intervention. Also relevant is the faulty explanation of differences found among racial and ethnic groups as manifestations of culture-specific behavior (Okazaki & Sue, 1995) by underestimating possible pathology by attributing findings to cultural norms. As such, there is need, as Okazaki and Sue suggested, to avoid "possible cultural bias, either in overpathologizing or underpathologizing ethnic minorities when interpreting ethnic or racial differences on [psychological] assessment measures" (p. 373).

A related problem is the assumption that research in multicultural psychology must include a comparison of the ethnic or racial group with a "control" or "comparison" group of White participants. These comparisons often have an implied gradation of goodness or appropriateness where the group-specific characteristics of a dominant group are set as the standard (the "gold standard") that other groups must meet and against which deficits are identified. This approach has two limitations. First, it fails to acknowledge not only cultural variations but also the important effects of such social conditions as discrimination, poverty, unemployment, and malnutrition on people's lives. Second, setting one group as a "control" group ignores the fact that the comparison of one group against another is not necessarily more informative than research that explores an issue or tests a hypothesis within members of one ethnic group alone.

The expectation of Whites serving as the "control" or "comparison" group is an example of biases inherent in the research process that promotes the assumption of a deficit model to describe the behavior of ethnic or racial groups (Bernal & Scharrón–del Río, 2001). Generally, **deficit models** assume that any behavior that is different from what is found among Whites can be explained by invoking social, cultural, intellectual, or psychological limitations ("deficits") on the part of the members of the ethnic group. An equally absurd approach would be to set the behavior of residents of the United States as the standard against which the behavior of people from other countries should be compared. For example, the developmental study of friendship patterns among African American children is as valuable as the same analysis conducted among Asian Americans or Whites. Likewise, the comparison across groups of those findings is valuable, but the standard against which the findings are compared should not be the African American pattern of development or that of the White children. Using one pattern as the gold standard against which the others are compared in effect introduces biases in the interpretation of the results: the belief in the supremacy of one culture over another.

The Problem of Limited Participation in Research

One of the serious issues limiting the usefulness and generalizability of much multicultural psychology research is the fact that in a number of cases, participation by ethnic or racial community members is not as large (representative) or as continuous (in terms of length of participation) as could be expected. These limitations in the size or representativeness of the samples used in research restrict the potential usefulness of the results for advancing theory or psychological applications.

In general, there are a number of variables that produce concerns or outright refusals to participate in research by ethnic or racial minority individuals. These problems are structural, cultural, and linguistic and are often associated with the topic being researched, the community being studied, or the procedures being implemented. Box 3.7 summarizes some of the most frequent problems researchers encounter in obtaining participation in a research project.

The problems listed in Box 3.7 have been found not only by researchers working with multicultural communities within the context of psychological research but also by those conducting studies in public health, anthropology, medicine, and a number of other fields (e.g., Brown, Fouad, Basen-Engquist, & Tortolero-Luna, 2000). Not surprisingly, researchers studying some sensitive topics (drug use, HIV/AIDS, religiosity, sexual behavior) have additional difficulties in obtaining participation. For example, involvement in HIV/AIDS research by ethnic or racial groups can be affected by cultural, normative, and political attitudes held by members of specific groups. Researchers have argued, for example, that some African Americans refuse to participate in HIV/AIDS research and interventions due to variables such as negative attitudes toward homosexuality, the perception by some that AIDS is racial genocide, a distrust of medical research (Shavers-Hornaday, Lynch, Burmeister, & Torner, 1997), and viewing illness as a punishment for sins (Icard, Zamora-Hernandez, Spencer, & Catalano, 1996).

It is not uncommon in ethnic or racial minority communities to question the actual benefit to the participants or to the community that can be derived from the research procedure. Some Native

American communities have developed their own review process whereby researchers are expected to properly and completely explain the purpose of the study and to give back to the community by, at a minimum, providing progress reports, reports on the study's results, and data files. While the formal procedures in other ethnic communities may not necessarily match the organizational structure of Native American tribes and nations, they may informally exist through the roles played by ministers and priests, local government officials (ward chairs, council members, mayors), and community organizers. In the end, full participation benefits the community (Trimble, Scharrón–del Río, & Casillas, 2014), but, unfortunately, a number of researchers have treated ethnic minority communities without respect for their autonomy and personal integrity and more like laboratory rats than human beings. Exploitative situations view participants as research subjects to be observed and measured as objects rather than as individuals (Chaudhary, 2004).

As you can see from the list of problems in Box 3.7, the key principle in obtaining collaboration from research participants is establishing a trusting relationship (Hosokawa, 2010). A participant or respondent who does not trust the researcher or the research project will tend to be less open and forthcoming, less participative, and will probably be more likely to provide incomplete or invalid responses and drop out of the study. This process of earning trust is even more important in research with racial and ethnic minorities in general, and particularly when the researcher is not a member of the same race or ethnicity as the participants.

As you read reports on research studies conducted with ethnic or racial groups, you may want to ascertain how trust was established and how much attention was paid by the researcher in establishing a connection and gaining trust from the respondents (Hosokawa, 2010). You can use the contents of Box 3.7 to establish how much attention researchers have paid to trust building in conducting a study

Box 3.7

Problems Often Associated With Decreased Participation in Multicultural Psychology Research

1. **History of negative interactions with community.** Previous researchers have evidenced carelessness or lack of respect or have committed outright abuse of community members.
2. **Lack of information on the study's purpose.** Researchers provide insufficient information on the rationale for the study and fail to combat fears that the information is being collected for nefarious commercial purposes (for sales, fraud, identity theft) or for government agencies (the IRS, immigration offices).
3. **Logistical issues.** Difficulties in reaching research sites (hospitals, universities, clinics) because of cost or distance, the lack of substitute care for children or adults who depend on the research participant for their care, the interference and time conflicts with job schedules or housework, and the level of English language proficiency required may prevent participation.
4. **Questions about the usefulness of the study.** A lack of understanding or complete information about the study's potential benefits to the individual, the community, or society may limit participation. Also relevant here is the absence of procedures for the researchers to "give back" to the participants and their community (copies of results, presentations, etc.).
5. **Structural issues.** The length of the procedures and of the study, sponsorship, the number of follow-ups, the possible side effects, the cost, and confidentiality procedures may all contribute to suppressing participation.
6. **Cultural variables.** Beliefs and attitudes toward medical care or psychological interventions, beliefs about the origin and treatment of certain illnesses and conditions, beliefs about modesty or privacy, community- or culturally based beliefs about disclosure of sensitive information or discussion of sensitive topics.

you are reading or studying. The validity of results where no effort was made to establishing trust should be considered with concern.

Ethical Considerations

Research with ethnic or racial minority communities must be conducted within the constraints of ethical procedures for research with human populations. These, of course, include informed consent, freedom to discontinue participation, respect for an individual's privacy and confidentiality, and appropriate balance between risk and benefit. Nevertheless, research with racial or ethnic minority populations also requires that the researcher consider special circumstances associated with projects involving communities that generally have limited social, economic, or political power. Some of these specific concerns have already been addressed in the previous pages of this chapter and include the often-limited level of community member involvement in the planning and implementation of a research project and the potential for bias and ethnocentric interpretation of results. Additional aspects of the traditional ethical concerns in conducting research with ethnic or racial minority communities are addressed briefly in the paragraphs that follow. Studying these concerns will sensitize you as future researchers or consumers of psychological research to the complexities involved in multicultural psychology research.

Informed Consent

Basic to research with human participants is the need to obtain **informed consent** for participation. The concept of informed consent implies that the participants are properly informed as to the purpose of the study, its procedures, its potential benefits, and its risks; the voluntary nature of their participation; and their ability to ask questions of the researchers. Often, participants are asked to sign a form that indicates that they understand the procedures, its risks, and its potential benefits and that they acknowledge their ability to discontinue participation.

Unfortunately, many informed consent forms are drafted in legalistic wording that is difficult to understand by the majority of the people—and certainly by individuals with limited linguistic fluency or educational achievement. As a general principle, informed consent procedures should be designed in a way that is respectful and consistent with the group's culture and its related values, attitudes, and beliefs (Bernal, Cumba-Avilés, & Rodriguez-Quintana, 2014). Having consent forms available in the respondents' preferred language (a requirement with most human-subject protection boards or institutional review boards, or IRBs) is often not enough to guarantee comprehension and appropriateness of the forms or the procedures. The need for full disclosure in informed consent has been supported (see Box 3.1) by national and international codes of behavior, including the Helsinki agreements on participation of human subjects in biomedical research (Macklin, 2000). There are, of course, some situations in which informed consent is difficult to obtain (for example, when conducting large-scale observational studies, such as the behavior of sports fans in a stadium), and researchers are required to ensure that individual and personal information is protected.

Freedom to Discontinue Participation

Research conducted with human beings must guarantee participants the *freedom to discontinue participation* in the research project whenever they wish. This assurance allows individuals to stop participation in a study when they feel uncomfortable or feel that the project does not meet their expectations. A problem, of course, arises when participants feel they cannot or should not discontinue participation or when they are not aware of being part of a research project. This ethical difficulty often arises when there are social or cultural pressures that make it difficult for individuals to stop participation. For example, members of ethnic or racial minority communities may feel that they "should" or "must" continue participation in a research project for reasons as varied as the fear of damaging the relationship between researcher and participant, fear of retribution or concerns about insulting the researcher or the institution sponsoring the study, or fear of losing financial, health, psychological, or educational benefits that the study was providing. Also relevant here is the situation where research participants are provided a stipend to cover transportation costs or the time spent in the study and may feel that a contractual relationship has been established that does not "really" allow them to stop participation.

While the situations mentioned above are not necessarily unique to ethnic or racial minority participants in research projects, cultural expectancies and social conditions (such as poverty or welfare needs) may make it more difficult for ethnic or racial minority research participants to stop their involvement with the project. It is quite possible, for example, that participants with limited financial resources may feel that they cannot afford to lose the promised stipend even when it is handed to the participants ahead of their participation in the project. Likewise, a mother may feel that she or her children can be "blacklisted" for medical care or educational programs at school if she or someone in her family refuses to participate in a research project. Refusal to become involved in a study can also be a reality in cultures where authority figures such as teachers, lawyers, physicians, or religious or community leaders are given special status and where community members are expected to comply with their wishes or ideas.

Respect for Privacy and Confidentiality

Most researchers—particularly those conducting qualitative research, such as ethnographies and community interviews—spend a considerable amount of time and effort preserving the confidentiality of the research communities and participants by deleting identifying information from research protocols, assigning pseudonyms to participants, and using invented names for communities. Nevertheless, sometimes efforts at maintaining confidentiality are not sufficient to reduce discomfort among research participants. Allen (1997), for example, describes the reaction of shock and unhappiness when members of a small community in the Chesapeake Bay found out that the sociologist who had visited them and whom they had welcomed into their own homes was "using" them for her research. While the name of the community was disguised in the report of the study, it was not difficult for its members to find out that they were the community involved in the study, which included descriptions of some of its members in less than positive ways.

There are, of course, other situations that can potentially complicate the need to protect privacy. Large-scale studies that identify communities or members of ethnic groups as having certain characteristics run the risk of failing to protect required confidentiality of the findings. In these cases, specific communities can be improperly identified in research reports or press releases as "violent," or "drug-ridden," "involving unwed mothers," or "including abusive husbands." These large-scale characterizations perpetuate myths and improperly characterize communities and their members.

Another challenge to protecting privacy emerges when vulnerable respondents are asked to provide information that they do not have and cannot provide or where disclosure of certain facts can bring embarrassment and distress to the respondents. A good example of this situation is when children at school are asked to provide information about their parents and grandparents without attention being given to the fact that, in many cases, they may not have the information being asked for or that this type of disclosure may bring embarrassment to the children. Such is the case when adopted or foster children are asked to report the culture or background of their unknown parents and grandparents. A similar situation occurs with children in single-parent or same-gender households when asked about behaviors by a particular member of what some consider a "typical" household composed of a married heterosexual couple who have children of their own. Having to report that there is no "dad" at home or that the male head-of-household is an adoptive father or stepfather or that there are two dads or two moms can bring about embarrassment and distress. Likewise, children and adults may find it difficult and embarrassing to report personal information such as parental use of tobacco or alcoholic beverages, food preferences, time spent away from home, or even levels of use of television or the Internet.

The issue here, of course, is that researchers should never assume that certain behaviors that are normative in their own culture are also normative in another group—a central principle of culturally appropriate research. Knowledge of the culture and the involvement of community researchers is key to avoiding embarrassing questions based on religious, cultural, or traditional differences. A seemingly innocent question (for example, "What did Santa bring you?" or "How often do you go to church?") can produce emotional discomfort to the participants when those beliefs or behaviors are not normative in their own culture or family.

Appropriate Balance Between Risks or Costs and Benefits

Ethical research procedures require that a proper balance be reached in terms of the costs incurred by the participants and the risks associated with participation in comparison to the benefits that they or the community will receive. Costs to the individual may include time spent in participating, lost wages, physical or psychological effort, embarrassment suffered when disclosing attitudes or behaviors, and threats to health or well-being implied in the research procedures.

The argument has been made that the **cost/benefit** or **risk/benefit balance** has not been present in numerous research projects with ethnic or racial minority populations. For example, some ethnic community members perceive social science research as a form of exploitation in which individuals from the dominant culture reap the benefits of the data collection effort through publications, presentations, grants, and awards (Blauner & Wellman, 1973; Hirsch, 1973). These gains are often obtained at the expense (time, effort, stigmatization, significant disclosure demands) of members of ethnic or racial communities who are improperly rewarded or who feel obligated to participate by high-pressure recruitment techniques including large payments or stipends offered as compensation for their participation.

Furthermore, in many cases, members of ethnic or racial communities do not see the results of the study, since reports are usually not presented to the community or since benefits in improved health or education are seldom or never made available to the community studied. This situation has led some individuals to advocate that only minority scientists should have access to minority communities (Baca Zinn, 1979; Moore, 1973; Wilson, 1974) so that at least one or a few members of the group reap some benefits from the research process.

Particularly problematic are situations where the cost/benefit ratio involves significant levels of deception of the participants or when the study involves the use of placebos or the withholding of educational or employment services or medical treatment. Wheeler (1997), for example, reports on 15 studies of HIV-infected women in Africa, Thailand, and the Dominican Republic who were provided placebos instead of appropriate medication. Obviously, this type of research presents serious ethical concerns when individuals are being prevented from receiving life-saving treatment in order to have a "better" or more controlled research project that includes the use of placebos or control conditions that require withholding of treatment.

A notorious example of improper risk/benefit balance is the study of the progression of syphilis conducted among African American men in Tuskegee, Alabama (Gray, 1998). In that research project (see Box 3.8), African American patients were purposely not given the proper treatment to alleviate syphilis so that researchers could study the natural progression of the illness. Although an effective treatment for syphilis was available at the time, this group of men was deprived of the treatment by officials from the U.S. Public Health Service. In a book describing the project, Fred Gray (1998) summarizes the study:

> The government used 623 men as human guinea pigs in a misguided 40-year medical experiment. That in itself would have been bad enough. The moral and ethical injury was compounded by the fact that all of these men were African American, predominantly poor and uneducated, and were deliberately kept in the dark about what was happening to them. (p. 14)

That lack of sensitivity and respect for these individuals still affects the credibility of biobehavioral and medical research among certain ethnic or racial groups and other underserved communities such as the deaf and the poor (McKee, Schlehofer, & Thew, 2013; Pacheco et al., 2013; Rencher & Wolf, 2013; Shavers-Hornaday et al., 1997).

Box 3.8

The Tuskegee Syphilis Study

In 1932, officials from the U.S. Public Health Service designed a study to analyze the effects of untreated syphilis, a sexually transmitted disease that can ultimately cause death. A total of 623 African American men from Macon County, Alabama, were involved in what became known as the Tuskegee Syphilis Study. Approximately half of the men who participated in the study had been diagnosed as having untreated syphilis, and the other half served as a control group. During the study, the men were given physical exams, vitamins, and some free meals. Some syphilitics were told (without explanation) that they had "bad blood," while others were told nothing. The men were not told that they were part of a study, and these men never gave consent to participate in a research project. Researchers followed the men through free physical exams and autopsies on those who had died in order to measure the progression of the illness. While penicillin was available during the period of the study, none of the men with syphilis was offered or given that life-saving treatment.

In 1972 (40 years after the beginning of the study), the media disclosed the existence of the research project, and the men who were still alive learned, many for the first time, of what had happened to them. In 1973 a lawsuit was filed on behalf of the Tuskegee men for violations of the U.S. and Alabama constitutions, civil rights law, and the federal common law. The study was officially terminated by the Centers for Disease Control in 1972. It was not until 1997, however, that President Clinton addressed survivors and relatives of the study, saying, "The United States government did something that was wrong—deeply, profoundly, morally wrong. It was an outrage to our commitment to integrity and equality for all our citizens. . . . The American people are sorry—for the loss, for the years of hurt" (Gray, 1998, p. 13).

The conditions under which this study was conducted showed complete disregard for the human rights of the research participants. Not surprisingly, this study, as well as others conducted with minority populations or prisoners or individuals in developing countries, led many racial and ethnic minority communities to distrust much biomedical research.

Unfortunately, Tuskegee has not been an isolated case of abuse of research participants in large-scale projects. About 15 years after the beginning of the Tuskegee study, more than 5,000 Guatemalans were intentionally infected with bacteria that causes sexually transmitted diseases (STDs). The men and women infected were never told about what was being done and were never asked for their consent. Many of those individuals were left untreated, and those who survived are currently living with the effects of STDs (Rodriguez & Garcia, 2013). In 2010, President Barack Obama apologized to the victims, but there has been little done to alleviate or compensate them or their families. More recently (1989), a study among the Havasupai in Arizona misused blood samples collected to study type 2 diabetes to study schizophrenia, inbreeding, and other topics, all of this without the consent of the participants or of the tribe. A lawsuit by the tribe was filed for lack of informed consent, violation of civil rights given the misuse of blood samples, failure to receive approval for the use of the data previously collected, and violations of confidentiality. The suit was settled out of court and involved compensation to participants, return of DNA samples, and funds for a clinic and a school (Pacheco et al., 2013).

In any study with ethnic or racial minority communities, efforts must be made to properly balance the ratio of cost and benefit to the members of the community as compared to those of the researchers and of the scientific community in general. Part of analyzing that cost/benefit ratio requires understanding the level of stigmatization participation in a study may bring to the respondents (for example, for visiting a mobile health unit or clinic parked in their neighborhood, being identified as an individual with a psychological or addictive problem, being removed from a classroom for "special" activities, or receiving visits at home from people from the local university). Also relevant is the personal and psychological cost incurred by members of ethnic or racial minority communities where displacement to a research site may involve more costs than the transport fare and may include changes in work schedule and difficulties with childcare or the care of ailing adults.

This chapter reviews some of the key concerns about the design, implementation, and analysis of research with multicultural populations. The key principle involved is recognizing that the unique characteristics of ethnic or racial minority populations demand special attention be given to developing respectful, responsible, and culturally appropriate research. This concern does not imply that basic principles of valid research need be abandoned, but rather that additional special attention should be given to certain group-specific characteristics of the population studied. This culturally appropriate approach forces researchers to "decolonize" their methodology, where a **colonizing perspective** assumes that culture is irrelevant and that the majority culture is the baseline against which other cultures are compared. This point is made by Bernal et al. (2014) when they argue that

> to decolonize research methods, all aspects of the research process should be taken into account, including the social, economic, and political context in which the research is conducted. . . . Questioning the ecological validity of the research at each step of the research process is essential. (p. 119)

Simonds and Christopher (2013) also suggest that decolonizing research involves incorporating indigenous methodologies that go beyond deductive reasoning and involves frequent reflection on the research process.

Chapter Summary

This chapter addresses a number of concerns related to conducting research with ethnic populations in order to produce valid and reliable findings while guaranteeing and respecting the personal and emotional integrity of the participants. We argue for the need to develop responsible, culturally appropriate research that respects the culture of the research participants and that includes methods and analyses sensitive to a culture's characteristics. Developing culturally appropriate research is a complex and time-consuming activity. It goes beyond the proper translation and adaptation of questions, tests, and questionnaires. Culturally appropriate methodologies include such additional steps as using culturally relevant theories, developing and testing culturally appropriate hypotheses, using appropriate methodologies, properly disaggregating participants, and implementing appropriate interpretation of results. In analyzing research findings, it becomes essential to consider a number of contextual variables that may moderate the significance and direction of the results. Researchers and analysts must be willing to explore alternative explanations to their findings that go beyond simply assigning causality to racial or ethnic group membership. The possible influence of factors such as poverty, discrimination, segregation, limited academic preparation, and migration history must be considered relevant to the phenomenon being studied before concluding the factors to be due to cultural, racial, or ethnic differences.

Key Terms

1.5 generation 69
acquiescent response 60
assumption of intragroup homogeneity 64
asylee 71
back translation 62
colonizing perspective 78
community-based participatory research (CBPR) 55
conceptual equivalence 58
construct validity 58
contextualization 51
cost/benefit balance 76
culturally appropriate research 50
deficit model 72
disaggregation 65
double translation 62
dual focus translation 63
ecological validity 58
emic construct 61
etic construct 61
external validity 58
field experiment 53
first generation 69
fourth generation 69
generation 69
informed consent 74

involuntary immigrant 70
label of convenience 64
mixed second generation 69
permanent migrant 71
refugee 71
reliability 58
responsible, culturally appropriate research 48
risk/benefit balance 76
second generation 69
sojourner 71
standardized instrument 60
temporary migrant 71
third generation 69
transferability 58
triangulation 53
unauthorized migrant 71
undocumented migrant 71
validity 58
voluntary immigrant 70

Learning by Doing

- Review a recent research article in a psychology journal that includes members of at least one ethnic or racial group. Summarize how well the researchers identified the participants (for example, ethnic or racial group and subgroup membership, gender, educational level, socioeconomic status, generational history, acculturation level). For each of the variables that the researchers failed to use in disaggregating the participants, indicate how the results or the findings may have been different.
- Interview members of your family or a friend's family, and build a generational history tree where you place the respondent at the bottom of the generational tree, and then identify the "tree branches" based on the national or ancestral origin of each individual. In this sense, identify where the respondent's parents or guardians, grandparents, and great-grandparents were born. Then indicate the generation of each level of the tree (for example, first generation, second generation) and the ethnic or racial labels used by each generation.

Suggested Further Readings

Amer, M. M., & Awad, G. H. (2016). *Handbook of Arab American Psychology*. New York: Routledge.
A comprehensive handbook on psychological research and practice among Arab Americans, with particular attention being given to cultural competence and cultural appropriateness.

Dunbar, G. (2005). *Evaluating research methods in psychology: A case study approach*. New York: Wiley-Blackwell.
An overview of classic and contemporary research in psychology from different fields and varying theoretical perspectives. The book encourages readers to question the choices made by researchers and to analyze the appropriateness of the methodological components of studies as well as the interpretation of results.

Hargittai, E. (Ed.) (2009). *Research confidential: Solutions to problems most social scientists pretend they never had*. Ann Arbor: University of Michigan Press.
A behind-the-scenes analysis of the various practical and ethical problems researchers often encounter when conducting social science research. A comprehensive perspective on the complexities involved in conducting research with human participants.

Hosokawa, F. (2010). *Building trust: Doing research to understand ethnic communities*. Lanham, MD: Lexington Books.
A readable and very helpful compendium of practices necessary to building trust between researchers and participants or communities, this book includes a variety of examples and disaggregates recommendations according to specific ethnic or racial communities.

Jason, L. A., Keys, C. B., Suarez-Balcazar, Y., Taylor, R. R., & Davis, M. I. (2003). *Participatory community research: Theories and methods in action*. Washington, DC: American Psychological Association.
A comprehensive analysis of participatory community research by some of the pioneers in the field. Their experience conducting this type of research permeates the book's content and serves as a guide to those interested in not only reading but also conducting participatory community research.

Leong, F. T. L., Comas-Díaz, L., Hall, G. C. N., McLoyd, V. C., & Trimble, J. E. (Eds.) (2014). *APA Handbook of multicultural psychology*. Washington, DC: American Psychological Association.

A two-volume compendium of reviews of the literature on multicultural psychology written by well-known and experienced researchers and practitioners. A required resource in the field of multicultural psychology.

Marín, G., & Marín, B.V. (1991). *Research with Hispanic populations: Vol. 23, Applied social research methods series.* Newbury Park, CA: Sage.

A practical and easy-to-read book looking at the difficulties of conducting culturally appropriate research with Latinos. The contents of the book are also relevant to research with other ethnic minority groups. The book serves as important background for those researching racial or ethnic minority groups, as well as for those reading research reports.

Mertens, D. M., & Ginsberg, P. E. (Eds.) (2009). *The handbook of social research ethics.* Los Angeles: Sage.

A comprehensive resource on ethical issues faced by researchers when conducting social research among various communities and using different research approaches. The book presents a very complete analysis of ethical considerations that must be part of any social research project.

Ratner, C. (1997). *Cultural psychology and qualitative methodology.* New York: Plenum.

A classic book exploring the intersection of culture and research within the perspectives of qualitative methodologies. The book explores culture from different perspectives and using different theoretical backgrounds.

Smith, J. A. (2008). *Qualitative psychology: A practical guide*. Thousand Oaks, CA: Sage.

An excellent source of practical information for students and researchers interested in understanding or conducting qualitative research.

Stanfield, J. H., II, & Dennis, R. M. (Eds.). (1993). *Race and ethnicity in research methods.* Newbury Park, CA: Sage.

A classic book introducing the concerns social science researchers (primarily sociologists and anthropologists) need to address when studying ethnic or racial minority individuals. The authors' recommendations continue to be useful despite the passing of time since the book's first publication.

Suzuki, L. A., & Ponterotto, J. G. (Eds.). (2008). *Handbook of multicultural assessment.* San Francisco: Jossey-Bass.

An all-inclusive overview of issues related to the psychological assessment of ethnic or racial minority individuals and communities. Of particular importance in understanding issues related to measures of basic psychological processes as well as abnormal behavior.

Acculturation 4

"Call Me Jessie, Not Josefina!"

Josefina was born in Chicago's heavily Latino Pilsen neighborhood. Carlos and Maria, her parents, left Puerto Rico in their early 20s and met in Chicago while working at a factory. Carlos and Maria miss the island and their relatives and Puerto Rican food and culture. Fortunately, Pilsen has a good number of markets that sell all the food staples that Carlos and Maria miss, including plantains and gandules. *Carlos often expresses concern for how his kids are not as respectful and courteous as he had been as a teen and blames the American culture for having spoiled his children. He always speaks in Spanish to them, and he is often accused by his children of being old-fashioned. Maria speaks English more fluently than her husband and feels perfectly comfortable among her White friends as well as among her Latino neighbors. Josefina is fully bilingual, having learned Spanish at home and English while attending school. She is as comfortable eating rice with* gandules *as she is eating a hamburger at the fast-food outlet. She loves rock and rap music and is quite at ease dancing salsa. Among her best friends in high school were a non-Latino White boy (to whom she was "Jessie") and two Latinas (one from Puerto Rico, and the other a Mexican American). As a junior in high school, Josefina met Robert, a White teen who shared many of Josefina's interests in the arts and in music. Robert often walked Josefina home from school, and at times they would listen to music in the living room within view of the kitchen where Maria prepared the evening meal. In April,*

Robert asked Josefina to the junior prom. She ran home and yelled at the door, "Mami, guess what? Robert asked me to the prom." From the back of the apartment, Carlos shouted back, "Tienes que llevar un chaperón [You have to bring a chaperone]." Josefina retorted, "I'll die if you force me to do that. Nobody brings chaperones; this is the United States. Papi, olvídate de Puerto Rico [Dad, forget Puerto Rico]." The discussions lasted many days, and in the end Josefina did not go to the junior prom because her father never gave up on the idea of a chaperone. Josefina's senior year in high school was a stressful one for the Martinez family. Josefina was intent on getting good grades and a good ACT score that would allow her to get a scholarship to one of the private Catholic universities on the North Shore of Chicago—close enough to the family home, yet far enough away to justify staying in the residence halls. She insisted on being addressed as Jessie rather than Josefina and would only speak English at home. She often spent long hours on the phone speaking in English to all her friends. When the time came for the senior prom, Carlos again insisted that a chaperone was required but relented after talking with his neighbors, who assured him that in the United States it was appropriate for a girl to go to a dance without a chaperone.

Acculturation is, arguably, one of the most frequently mentioned constructs or concepts in multicultural psychology. Indeed, researchers often include some measure of acculturation in their studies in order to analyze differences within racial or ethnic groups and to understand the relationship of acculturation to psychosocial behavior, adjustment, and health. It is not unusual, therefore, to read in the psychological literature how acculturation is related to a person's level of adaptability to new social situations or to job satisfaction, depression, cigarette smoking, or alcohol use. Likewise, acculturation has been associated with phenomena as varied as intergenerational family conflict, academic performance, and utilization of mental health services. This chapter examines acculturation and the related constructs of assimilation, enculturation, and biculturalism, their definitions, and issues related to their measurement and their effects on people's lives.

Despite the growing attention given to acculturation in the psychological literature, this construct or concept has a history of relative benign neglect. Since the beginnings of the 20th century, a select group of social scientists, primarily anthropologists and sociologists, has been advocating for more studies of acculturation, a request that has intensified over the recent past years (e.g., Brown & Zagefka, 2011; Sam & Berry, 2016). Early social scientists defined acculturation as a process of change that occurs when individuals from different cultures interact and share a common geographical space following migration, political conquest, or forced relocation. As you will see later on in this chapter, the definition of acculturation has been further refined to consider not only the various conditions under which it occurs but also its diverse correlates and effects.

It should be noted that acculturation is not a phenomenon unique to the United States or to countries that have experienced significant migratory waves. Many nations around the world include a variety of ethnic or cultural groups within their boundaries that have shared a given geographical space for centuries, as in the case of Spain, where Basques, Catalans, Galicians, and other cultural groups have shared parts of the Iberian Peninsula. The current phenomenon of **globalization** also can be seen as promoting some type of acculturation around the world by facilitating personal mobility across borders and the sharing of cultures and values through music, electronic and print media, and education. For example, the values reflected in songs by American rappers, Icelandic singer Bjork, or the Irish group U2 are heard throughout the world in the same way that the British magazine *The Economist* or the U.S.-produced magazine *Newsweek* or the *International New York Times* can be found in magazine kiosks almost everywhere around the world. This "cultural globalization" also affects people's beliefs, values, and behaviors to such an extent that we can argue, together with various authors (for example, Ozer, 2013; van Oudenhoven & Ward, 2013), that there are very few "monocultural" or "majority" societies that have not been affected by the cultures of other countries due to people mobility, technological advances, economic globalization, and the international sharing of cultural products.

Acculturation has such theoretical and practical significance in multicultural psychology that much of the rest of this book will refer to its influence in the same fashion as culture, race, and ethnicity.

Indeed, much of the behavior of Carlos, Maria, and Josefina as described in the vignette that begins this chapter reflects their cultural heritage as well as differences in their levels of acculturation. As is often found among first generation individuals who show low levels of acculturation, Carlos struggles to maintain not only the language of his country of origin but also its cultural practices and values. Maria, also a first generation individual but more acculturated than Carlos, has learned English, has a number of friends who are not Latinos, and feels comfortable interacting with people of diverse ethnic backgrounds. Josefina, as a more acculturated, second generation Latina, often finds herself in conflict with the traditional practices of her parents' country of origin. While bilingual, she prefers to speak in English; she changes her name to "Jessie" and considers some practices that were normative in Puerto Rico to be old-fashioned, although she enjoys its food, music, and other cultural expressions.

Defining Acculturation

In the simplest terms, acculturation can be defined as a culture learning process experienced by individuals or groups that are exposed to a new culture. While this process can occur among tourists and individuals who travel briefly abroad or outside their culture, such as international students or overseas employees (also called *sojourners*; see Chapter 3), in this chapter we are concerned primarily with acculturation as experienced by individuals who are exposed to and learn a new culture over lengthier periods of time. As such, we are interested in studying individuals who experience a new culture due to permanent or long-term resettlement and relocation. This long-term exposure to a new culture can occur among a variety of individuals, such as those who willingly migrate to a new culture or nation, those born to immigrant parents or grandparents, and those who seek refuge and protection in a new country or who are forced to reside in a new nation due to political decisions that redraw national borders. For example, when a large part of the southwestern United States was ceded by Mexico after the U.S.-Mexican war in the 1840s, the Mexicans who resided in what is now Texas, Arizona, New Mexico, Nevada, Utah, and California were exposed to the European American culture of the eastern United States. Consequently, the Mexicans had to undergo an imposed process of culture learning. The European American newcomers also had to undergo a process of acculturation to the Mexican and Spanish culture of the residents in the area. At a fairly superficial level, we could argue that this process of culture learning forced the original residents (the Mexicans) to learn to speak English and eat hot dogs while the newly arrived (eastern U.S. citizens) learned some Spanish and began to appreciate tacos and tortillas. As psychologists, we are interested in understanding the extent of these changes in behavior as well as in trying to determine how exposure to one culture affects the values, attitudes, and psychological well-being of both the recently arrived and long-term residents of a given area.

As mentioned previously, the process of acculturation is not limited to individuals who are forced to change their nationality because of political events, such as the ones described above or those experienced recently in Southern and Central Europe (for example, during the break of the former Yugoslavia or Czechoslovakia, or the refugee crisis of Syrians and Afghanis fleeing their countries), parts of Africa (for example, when Sudan was broken into two nations), and Asia (when Hong Kong and Macau were ceded to the People's Republic of China). Immigrants and short-term "foreign workers" or "guest workers" also experience acculturation processes as they change their residence and are exposed to a new culture. Forced relocation and enslavement, as happened with Africans to the United States and to other countries in the Americas, also produced the process of culture learning that we call acculturation. Also important to remember is the fact that the receiving or "host" ethnic or cultural group undergoes the process of acculturation as its members are exposed to new ways of thinking and acting. In that fashion, we can talk about acculturation promoting the development of bicultural individuals in nations or cultures where two or more cultures come in contact with each other and where their residents learn the attitudes, values, behavior, and other cultural aspects of the racial or ethnic groups with whom they interact. Multicultural societies like the United States that have been created by the contributions of immigrants from many places are enriched by the presence of multiple cultures where diverse groups share their beliefs, values, attitudes, and ways of behaving.

Also important is the fact that the process of acculturation can be a long-term phenomenon affecting various generations of individuals. Indeed, acculturation is not limited to immigrants but also takes place among their children and grandchildren. In fact, individuals are changing and learning new values, attitudes, and behaviors whenever two or more cultures come in contact with one another. Acculturation is therefore a fluid process and is not time constrained and, as seen later on in this chapter, can take many forms and produce various changes even within a given family (as seen in the vignette at the beginning of this chapter).

Before delving more deeply into the meaning of acculturation and its implications on psychological research, it is important to mention that other social scientists often use different or related terms to refer to what we here call acculturation. It is not uncommon, for example, to read sociological and anthropological literature that uses terms such as **incorporation** or **assimilation** to refer to concepts fairly similar to what psychologists term *acculturation*. Indeed, much contemporary research in sociology and anthropology uses words such as **cultural assimilation** and **cultural integration** to define the acculturation process of individuals and groups. This variability in terminology lends itself to confusion not only based on the possible differing meanings but also because there is a difference in emphasis. By using terms such as *incorporation* and *assimilation*, sociologists and anthropologists tend to emphasize the characteristics of the larger groups, such as when studies address the characteristics of an ethnic or racial group that facilitate or promote its "civic incorporation" by becoming citizens, voting, participating in town hall meetings, and so on. Psychologists, however, tend to emphasize the more personal characteristics of the process demonstrated through changes in personal values or beliefs or behavior generally analyzed from a more individualized perspective.

Unfortunately, these variations in terminology and emphasis have undermined the advancement of the field and of our understanding of the acculturation process when there is little cross-fertilization between fields. While most of the literature cited in this chapter comes from psychologists, we have endeavored to include relevant works by sociologists, anthropologists, and other social scientists, since their perspectives enrich our understanding of what is a very complex human activity.

Early Definitions

The term *acculturation* has been used in social science literature since the end of the 19th century (Berry & Sam, 2016a). The definition of the term has changed with the passing of time and has evolved from an emphasis on unidirectional cultural imitation of one culture by an immigrant to attention being given to mutual changes brought about by continuity of contact across diverse cultural groups. One of the earliest and most useful definitions of acculturation emphasized direct contact across ethnic or racial groups and the fact that both groups would undergo changes: "Acculturation comprehends those phenomena which result when groups of individuals having different cultures come into continuous first-hand contact, with subsequent changes in the original culture patterns of either or both groups" (Redfield, Linton, & Herskovits, 1936, p. 149).

A subsequent definition proposed the idea that there could be multiple causes for acculturation and that its effects could be not only varied but also observed and measured over varying amounts of time. Acculturation is

> culture change that is initiated by the conjunction of two or more autonomous cultural systems. Acculturative change may be the consequence of direct cultural transmission; it may be derived from non-cultural causes, such as ecological or demographic modification induced by an impinging culture; it may be delayed, as with internal adjustments following upon the acceptance of alien traits or patterns; or it may be a reactive adaptation of transitional modes of life. (Social Science Research Council, 1954, p. 974)

In his influential analysis of assimilation in the United States, sociologist Milton Gordon (1964) suggests that acculturation must be differentiated from **structural assimilation**, whereby the latter is defined as the incorporation of members of ethnic or racial groups into primary relationships with individuals from the dominant or majority group in contexts as varied as social clubs and marriage.

At the same time, Gordon defines acculturation as the adoption of the cultural norms and behavioral patterns of the dominant group (often called the *core culture*), a process he considered as an essential component of the experiences of members of minority ethnic or racial groups. Gordon's definition of acculturation influenced social science literature for many decades and determined our understanding of acculturation as those changes occurring in the new (often, immigrant) group as it tries to emulate or imitate the dominant or majority group. Gordon also suggests that the changes implied in the acculturation process were more rapid among external traits (such as clothing, language, outward expression of emotions), while the more intrinsic personal characteristics (such as values, norms, or religious beliefs) would take longer to change, if they changed at all.

More recently, sociologist Herbert Gans (1999) has defined acculturation as "the newcomers' adoption of the culture—that is, the behavior patterns or practices, values, rules, symbols, and so forth, of the host society (or rather an overly homogenized and reified conception of it)" (p. 162). This definition is significant because it moves closer to a psychosocial understanding of the concept and it acknowledges that a group's culture is an abstraction that is considered as something concrete (what he calls a "reified conception"). At the same time, Gans defines assimilation as an interactive process (that may not require changes in the person's values or beliefs as acculturation does) and that can best be characterized by behaviors where "the newcomers move out of formal and informal ethnic associations and other social institutions and into the host society's non-ethnic ones" (p. 162). Gans suggests that this distinction allows for the assimilation and acculturation processes to proceed at different speeds. This perspective is particularly important because it reflects the realities of assimilation being driven externally by social stratification or socioeconomic class as well as by prejudice and discrimination that may speed or slow down the ethnic group's assimilation (or incorporation, as some other researchers would call it) into the social and civic fabric of the dominant group or of the receiving host country or culture. It is important to remember that these processes are not unique to immigrants but that their children and grandchildren may also experience them.

Contemporary Definitions

Dissatisfaction with some of the limitations inherent in the older definitions of acculturation has led some psychologists and other researchers to propose more comprehensive definitions that take into consideration the fact that acculturation is a process that affects the diverse psychosocial characteristics and behaviors of individuals and groups and that these changes take place at different rates. These newer conceptualizations of acculturation do not negate the changing processes of cultures experienced by groups that come in contact with each other (an interest of sociologists and anthropologists) but highlight the emphasis of psychology on individual characteristics (Berry & Sam, 2016b).

In 2004, the IOM (International Organization for Migration of the United Nations) defined acculturation as "the progressive adoption of elements of a foreign culture (ideas, words, values, norms, behavior and institutions) by persons, groups or classes of a given culture." Unfortunately, this recent definition is limited by its overemphasis on the adoption of a culture's characteristics, while selective adoption or even rejection are also potential results in situations of group contact (Berry & Sam, 2016b).

In this book, we define **acculturation** as follows:

> A dynamic and multidimensional process of change or adaptation that occurs when distinct cultures come into sustained contact. It involves different degrees and instances of culture learning (change) as well as maintenance that are contingent upon individual, group, and environmental factors. Acculturation is dynamic because it is a continuous and fluctuating process, and it is multidimensional because it involves numerous aspects of psychosocial functioning and can result in multiple adaptation outcomes. Furthermore, acculturation can involve the contact of various cultures at the same time and as such is not limited to the interactions of two cultures or racial or ethnic groups.

In general, researchers have emphasized the acculturational experiences of individuals who migrate or whose families migrated in the recent past. These studies have analyzed how individuals learn a new culture and its related attitudes, values, norms, and behaviors. Unfortunately, little attention has been given to the changes that these groups produce in the "host" or receiving society. Evident in most of the definitions of acculturation reviewed above is the assumption that immigrants and their descendants learn about the new culture, but little is said about the fact that the host or receiving culture is in turn modified by their presence. Our definition of acculturation addresses this limitation of previous definitions. Likewise, relatively little attention has been given to the acculturation process of the children and grandchildren of immigrants who also are exposed to this multidimensional process of personal development. Also absent from much research on acculturation, whether in the United States or in other nations, is the fact that contemporary events (wars, international agreements, persecutions, economic crises, natural disasters, human right abuses, etc.) are producing significant movements of individuals who are helping to shape many nations as multicultural countries where individuals from many cultures and nationalities are sharing a specific locale. These human movements (some large, as the migration of Central Americans to the United States or of Middle Easterners to Europe; some smaller, as the movement of northern South Americans to the southern nations of Argentina and Chile) are producing multicultural settings where individuals are exposed to a variety of cultures in the same place. For example, Los Angeles is home to large numbers of first and second generation Latinos (Mexican, Salvadorans), Asians (Chinese, Koreans, Vietnamese), and African Americans who interact with Whites and with each other. As such, it is difficult to speak only of newly arrived Latinos from Central America acculturating to the White Anglo-Saxon culture when they are interacting with Latinos from other cultures and ethnicities, Asians from a number of cultures, and African Americans. The end result is therefore a multifactorial acculturation process that is creating a unique multicultural society.

This multicultural process is an important aspect of the acculturation process as currently experienced by residents of large cities in the United States (for example, Los Angeles, San Francisco, Chicago, New York, Miami, Orlando) and around the world (London, Paris, Hong Kong, Singapore, Cape Town, Madrid, Amsterdam). As a matter of convenience, much contemporary psychological research on acculturation addresses the relationships between two cultures or ethnic/racial groups (for example, Asian Americans and Whites in the United States), but the reality is that more than two cultures are usually impacting individuals. This "convenient" bicultural approach to acculturation is a serious limitation of much currently available psychological research.

Understanding Assimilation and Segmented Assimilation

Countries such as the United States that saw significant migratory waves during the 19th and early 20th centuries experienced calls from politicians and social scientists to try to create a common culture made up of many—a concept enshrined in its national ethos as *E pluribus unum* (Out of many, one). This push toward assimilation generally implied that immigrants would need to subdue or reject those values, attitudes, and behaviors that had characterized their cultures of origin as they learned and internalized the cultural characteristics perceived to define White, Anglo-Saxon Protestants. At the same time that a variety of social forces and institutions (e.g., schools, churches) were pushing for cultural and behavioral assimilation, various early migrant groups established strong communities (e.g., Little Italy, Chinatown, Irish and Polish neighborhoods) that reinforced their ties to the culture of origin while supporting a process of biculturalism that would allow them to work effectively in both cultural communities.

In many cases, assimilation in the early 19th and 20th centuries was also promoted through indirect methods, such as what the sociologist Alejandro Portes (1999) calls "symbolic violence," which is exemplified by immigrants disembarking at Ellis Island (New York) and at Angel Island (California) being forced to assume anglicized names whenever immigration officers did not know how or care to properly spell the names of members of immigrant groups. For example, Portes reports a German Jew who, when stressed upon being questioned by immigration officers, said, "Schoyn vergessen" (Yiddish for "I forget"), and was thereafter known as "Sean Ferguson."

The contributions of multicultural psychology researchers have produced an evaluation of the usefulness of the construct of assimilation. Indeed, Alba and Nee (1999) noted that "assimilation has come to be viewed by social scientists as a worn-out theory that imposes ethnocentric and patronizing demands on minority peoples struggling to retain their cultural and ethnic integrity" (p. 137). While Alba and Nee argue that assimilation as a construct in the social sciences is still useful, the term has been misused to imply the assumed inevitable outcome of absorption of minorities into an theoretically more homogeneous or common culture. In this sense, assimilation is a problematic term.

As a matter of fact, anthropologist Nancy Foner (1999) argues that the traditional concept of assimilation is an inaccurate description of the lives of immigrants and of those undergoing processes of culture learning. Foner proposes that assimilation is too simplistic a concept to analyze people's lives in this country since there is "no undifferentiated, monolithic 'American' culture" (p. 260). This criticism of traditional assimilationist thinking in the social sciences has given birth to the new construct of "segmented assimilation," which more appropriately defines the changes in social behavior that take place as people acculturate (Portes, 1999).

Segmented assimilation is defined by Foner (1999) as a process of assimilation into a particular social segment ranging from the middle to the lower classes. Indeed, sociologists (Rumbaut & Portes, 2001; Zhou, 1999) argue that the path taken in segmented assimilation depends on factors such as varying economic opportunity and other structural constraints, the pervasiveness of racial and ethnic discrimination, and the segment of American society to which the immigrants are exposed more frequently. In that sense, Rumbaut and Portes suggest that

> one path may follow the so-called straight line theory . . . of assimilation into the middle-class dominant; an opposite type of adaptation may lead to downward mobility and assimilation into the inner-city underclass; yet another may combine upward mobility and heightened ethnic awareness within solidaristic immigrant enclaves. (p. 188)

Foner (1999) further argues that the process of segmented assimilation does not necessarily imply the complete internalization of the new values and behaviors. In this sense, we could expect behavioral changes that reflect or resemble those of members of the dominant or majority group (segmented assimilation) although the individual may not have completely internalized their values or attitudes (acculturation). This is indeed an important differentiation in terms and in processes that helps us to better understand the changes that immigrants and those of later generations undergo as they learn new cultures. The end result of these two processes is that the cultures of immigrant minority ethnic groups can very well differ from those of the dominant or majority culture as well as from the culture of origin and in different areas of a person's life. We could then witness a process of the creation of what practically could be considered a new ethnicity (a hyphenated ethnicity such as "Filipino-Americans" or "Mexican-Americans") that benefits from multiple perspectives and cultures. Foner quotes the groundbreaking works of William Thomas and Florian Znaniecki (1918) on Polish Americans at the beginning of the 20th century when they concluded that there had been the

> creation of a society in which structure and prevalent attitudes is neither Polish nor American but constitutes a specific new product whose raw materials have been partly drawn from Polish traditions, partly from the new conditions in which the immigrants live, and partly from American social values as the immigrant sees and interprets them. (Foner, 1999, p. 108)

This process of segmented assimilation is also called **ethnogenesis** by some researchers (Foner, 1999) where culture contact can be expected to produce a mixed set of values and behaviors that characterize the specific ethnic or racial group and that are somewhat different from those of the original or ancestral culture or of those of the dominant group. Ethnogenesis defines the process that produces changes in certain values and attitudes and their related behaviors that affect not only clothing styles, musical preferences, or speech patterns but also religious beliefs and basic cultural values. For example, Foner (1999) describes how Jamaican immigrants to the United States change their gender-role expectations for men by making them more responsible for home duties without giving up the perception of the home as the woman's domain. Other studies have shown changes among Vietnamese Americans in the definition of kinship (i.e., who is considered a relative) and the perception of who belongs to the extended family (Kibria, 1993) or differentiations in the meaning of basic cultural values such as familialism among Latinos (Sabogal et al., 1987).

Returning to our opening vignette, we could very well expect that in Chicago's neighborhood of Pilsen frequent interactions between Puerto Rican, Mexican, Central American, and South American immigrants and African Americans create mixed cultures for each of these groups. We could hypothesize that the Puerto Rican American "culture" in which Josefina was raised was a combination of traditional Puerto Rican attitudes and values (such as the need for chaperones) together with the cultural characteristics of the groups that shared the neighborhood or the larger Chicago metropolitan area (which may not adhere to the importance of chaperones), as well as a Puerto Rican American component that may have evolved over the years as more second and third generation individuals inhabit the area. Examples of popular-culture manifestations of this ethnogenesis can be seen in bilingual songs (like the 2017 hit "Despacito"), urban and rap music, or the recent emergence of music mixing reggae and rap rhythms and sung in mixtures of English and Spanish—such as can be found in the music of hip-hop group Orishas, which mixes Cuban and Caribbean rhythms with rap, or in the music of other popular contemporary artists like Gwen Stefani.

Models of Acculturation

The fact that acculturation has been of interest to a variety of social scientists including anthropologists, sociologists, and psychologists is reflected in the different definitions of the term as seen previously as well as in the type of acculturation effects that are studied, as you will read in this section of the chapter. As could be expected, a concept of such importance as acculturation has been studied from a variety of perspectives and using different theoretical models. In this chapter you will read about the most recent models of acculturation that better reflect the contemporary definitions of acculturation.

The Unidirectional Model of Acculturation

As mentioned above, much of the early research on acculturation suffered severe conceptual limitations, including a simplistic assumption that acculturation inevitably leads to a weakening of one's original cultural identity and practices. This assumption reflects a **unidirectional model of acculturation**, in which culture change is thought to occur in one direction—people *move away* from their culture of origin and *toward* the dominant group during resettlement in a new country and/or upon exposure to a new culture. This unidirectional, bipolar model of acculturation was predominant in the United States at the beginning of the 20th century and reflected the "melting pot" paradigm, wherein newcomers were expected to mimic as much as possible the members of the "host" or dominant group. In short, acculturation was perceived as assimilation to the dominant or host culture (Ozer, 2013).

Figure 4.1 shows a hypothetical unidirectional model of acculturation in which individuals who share a Chinese ancestral or heritage culture are assumed to "move" toward a U.S. White culture by learning the values, norms, and attitudes of the latter and giving up their heritage cultural components. This assumption about the unidirectionality of the acculturation process (inherent in Gordon's definition of acculturation, mentioned previously) has been criticized by a number of researchers (see Chun, Balls Organista, & Marín, 2003) who prefer to think of acculturation as a more complex phenomenon that considers at least two cultural dimensions where, like Josefina, an individual may retain some aspects of the culture of origin and also learn and favor aspects of the new culture. This more complex

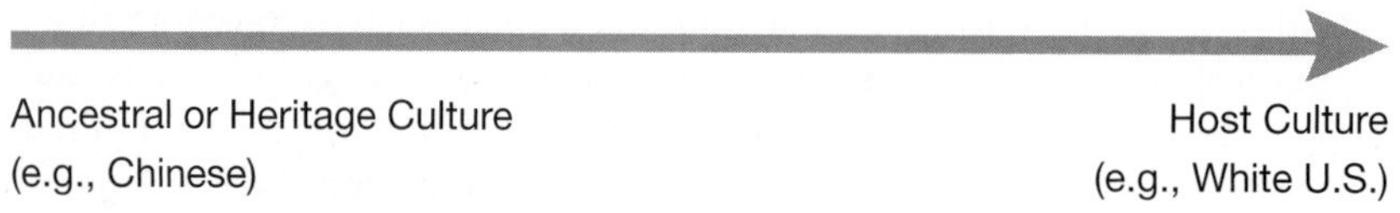

Ancestral or Heritage Culture (e.g., Chinese) → Host Culture (e.g., White U.S.)

FIG. 4.1 The Unidirectional Model of Acculturation.

understanding of acculturation is often perceived as promoting a society characterized by individuals who are comfortable in various cultural settings, producing what is often termed a "cultural mosaic" rather than a melting pot.

Berry's Two-Dimensional Model of Acculturation

For more than three decades, Canadian psychologist John Berry (2003) has advocated a comprehensive framework for understanding the progression and changes implied in the acculturation process as they affect the individual and social groups. Berry's model has been used in a large number of studies and has served as the basis for refinements in our understanding of acculturation, as you will see in the subsequent models discussed in this section of the chapter.

Berry (2003) suggests that, as a result of exposure to one or more new cultures, an individual experiences at least three types of changes or reactions. At one level is the process of deciding how much of the ancestral or heritage identity they wish to retain and acquire from the new host culture(s). A second component of the model concerns the behavioral shifts that affect the way the individual acts in areas as diverse as speech patterns, eating habits, clothing styles, or even self-identity. A third component covers acculturative stress, which includes emotional reactions on the part of the individual to the exposure to other culture(s) and can include anxiety and depression (Berry, 1980; Sam & Berry, 2006, 2016). At the social group level, acculturation impacts groups in terms of a variety of areas, including their structure, economic resources, and political impact. Much research addressing Berry's model has emphasized the individual aspects of the model rather than the societal implications, probably because of the attention the model has received among psychologists. Another important contribution of Berry's model has been its emphasis on the relationship between acculturation and stress among individuals. A later section in this chapter explores acculturative stress in greater detail, but at this point it is important to consider that acculturative stress is related to factors as varied as the need to learn new behaviors, beliefs, and attitudes and the realization of how different or even incompatible two cultures can be. For example, an immigrant from India may, after residing for a while in the United States, start wearing saris less frequently and self-identify as an "Asian American" rather than "Indian." At the same time, these acculturative experiences may produce personal and interpersonal conflicts regarding deeply ingrained cultural practices or values (e.g., arranged marriages or vegetarian diets) that may in turn promote feelings of anxiety or even psychological depression.

One of Berry's most important contributions to the study of acculturation has been his insistence on the need to consider the multiple types of attitudinal responses that an individual can have to acculturation. While initially Berry (1980) talked about "varieties of acculturation," the term he currently prefers is "acculturation strategies" or "acculturation modes" (Berry, 2003). An individual's choice of a strategy depends on such previous circumstances as the person's level of involvement with each culture as well as specific attitudinal and behavioral preferences and characteristics. The choice of a particular **acculturative strategy** would reflect the attitudes or orientation that an individual assumes toward the culture of origin (or "heritage culture") and toward the other group or groups. This model therefore requires considering two dimensions. One reflects the individual's positive or negative attitude toward maintenance of the heritage culture and identity. The second dimension (also from a negative to positive continuum) classifies the individual in terms of the preferred level and type of interaction with another group or groups.

For Berry (2003), an individual's acculturation can therefore be described as approaching one of four different strategies (see Figure 4.2) that are the product of the interaction of the dimensions mentioned previously:

1. *Assimilation*: The individual wishes to diminish or decrease the significance of the culture of origin (represented in Figure 4.2 as a "negative" attitude toward keeping the heritage culture) and desires to identify and interact primarily with the other culture, typically with the dominant

		Attitude Toward Keeping Heritage Culture and Identity	
		Positive	**Negative**
Attitude Toward Learning and Interacting With New Culture	**Positive**	Integration	Assimilation
	Negative	Separation	Marginalization

Source: Based on Berry (2003)

FIG. 4.2 Acculturation Strategies in Berry's Model.

culture if one comes from an ethnic minority group (represented in Figure 4.2 as a "positive" attitude toward learning the new culture).

2. *Separation*: The individual wishes to hold on to the original culture and avoids interacting or learning about the other culture(s).
3. *Marginalization*: The individual shows little involvement in maintaining the culture of origin or in learning about the other culture(s).
4. *Integration*: The individual shows an interest in maintaining the original culture and in learning and participating in the other culture(s).

In general, the fewest behavioral and attitudinal changes on the part of the individual can be found among those who have chosen the *separation* strategy and the largest number among those using the *assimilation* strategy (Berry, 2003). *Integration*, and to some extent *marginalization*, implies a selective process of maintenance and rejection that involves a moderate level of behavioral changes. Research tends to show that integration is probably the most frequently chosen acculturative strategy and that marginalization is the least often chosen alternative (Navas et al., 2005).

In terms of acculturative stress, Berry (2003) suggests that integration implies the lowest levels of stress while marginalization would be associated with the highest levels of stress. By choosing an integration strategy, acculturating individuals can be expected to experience lower levels of personal stress since they are able to acquire the cultural characteristics of the new culture (as expected by members of the new culture or group) while continuing to value the culture of heritage (as possibly expected by parents, siblings, and friends). At the same time, assimilation and separation strategies would be associated with moderate levels of stress since they imply a selection process that may not be supported or appreciated by the individual's relatives or friends.

As can be expected from the above description of Berry's (2003) strategies for acculturation, marginalization can result in serious psychological problems for individuals resorting to or being forced to assume such a strategy. As a matter of fact, Berry suggests that marginalization is likely to be the result of failed attempts at assimilation combined with experiences of discrimination. Furthermore, Berry argues that individuals can choose integration as an acculturation strategy primarily in societies that have open and inclusive orientations toward ethnic and cultural diversity indicated by the value placed on multiculturalism, relatively low levels of ethnic prejudice and discrimination, an absence of intergroup hatred, and a generalized sense of identification with the culture of the larger society. Whether an acculturation strategy is imposed or freely chosen also affects acculturation stress levels. For example, separation as a strategy can be less stressful if it is chosen rather than forced on individuals, as could be the case in examples of group segregation.

The members of the Martinez family as described at the beginning of the chapter can be considered to exhibit at least three of Berry's acculturation strategies. Carlos, through his emphasis on maintaining the Puerto Rican culture in his life and in his family, could be viewed as having primarily adopted a separation strategy. His wife's behavior could be an example of an integration strategy, given her bilingual skills and bicultural friendships. Their daughter Jessie could be considered an example of an assimilation strategy, particularly during her senior year, when she chose to separate herself as much as possible from the Puerto Rican heritage of her family.

In general, Berry's model of acculturation has been found useful in a variety of settings (see, for example, Sam & Berry, 2006, 2016). While measuring the four strategies is at times difficult, the Bidimensional Acculturation Scale for Hispanics, or BAS (Marín & Gamba, 1996), produces scores that can be easily related to Berry's four acculturational strategies. Studies with Korean Americans (Lee, Sobal, & Frongillo, 2003) and with Vietnamese Americans (Pham & Harris, 2001) have also found that the model was applicable to describing the acculturational experiences of the groups being studied.

Nevertheless, some authors (Del Pilar & Udasco, 2004) have questioned the practical possibility of marginalization where individuals show little interest in maintaining the culture of origin or learning a new culture. These authors argue that, even in cases of colonization and discrimination, individuals reframe or reformulate their culture of origin rather than losing the culture and being left "cultureless." Another possible limitation to Berry's model is its applicability to individuals who belong to more than two ethnicities or cultures. While the model does not intrinsically ignore persons who have more than two ethnic or racial heritages, it is much more difficult to apply in those conditions. For example, a child born of Chinese and Latino parents can choose an integration strategy into the dominant White culture while maintaining the Chinese and Latino heritage learned from the parents. The difficulties for the model's usefulness arise when the hypothetical individual wishes to diminish the significance of one of the cultures of origin while maintaining the other (for example, maintaining the Chinese heritage while decreasing the significance of the Latino heritage). In these types of cases, the model is more difficult to use since it does not provide a predictable outcome.

A Social Context Model of Acculturation

A different model of the acculturation process has been suggested by Rumbaut and Portes (2001). Reflecting its sociological roots, the model emphasizes the social context in which acculturation takes place rather than individual processes that are the basis of psychological models of acculturation. Rumbaut and Portes suggest that the results of the acculturation process, particularly for second generation individuals, are dependent on background factors of the immigrant parents such as their personal characteristics (or "human capital"), the structure of the family, parental levels of civic incorporation, experiences with discrimination, and the presence of ethnic subcultures in which the second generation individuals are raised.

This model of acculturation (Rumbaut & Portes, 2001; Ferguson & Birman, 2016) emphasizing the social context in acculturation suggests two possible extreme outcomes. At one end is a process of ***downward assimilation*** that is the result of divergent levels of acculturation between parents and children (see the following section on generational differences in acculturation) as well as the experiences of racial and ethnic discrimination and negative experiences in the labor market and residential environments. At the other end of the continuum is a process of engagement with and acceptance of two cultures or biculturalism (as discussed in greater detail in the following section) that is produced by the selective acculturation of the parents, the presence of supportive ethnic networks, and the presence of community resources and strong familial and community networks. This process of selective acculturation characterized by biculturalism is said to lead to "better psychosocial and achievement outcomes because it preserves bonds across immigrant generations and gives children a clear reference point to guide their future lives" (Rumbaut & Portes, 2001, p. 309).

A study with Soviet Jewish refugees in the United States (Birman & Trickett, 2001) showed that there were indeed generational differences in civic incorporation and acculturation with the older first generation refugees maintaining Russian-language proficiency to a greater extent than their children regardless of their length of residence in the United States. The children, probably due to the support system they encountered, exhibited a greater sense of Russian identity than the parents, although behaviorally they showed the greatest level of acculturation, probably exhibiting the biculturalism proposed by Rumbaut and Portes's model and reinforcing the importance of the social context in promoting acculturation and adaptation to a new culture (Birman, Trickett, & Buchanan, 2005).

The Interactive Acculturation Model (IAM)

Work by a group of Canadian psychologists led by Richard Bourhis (Bourhis, Moise, Perreault, & Senécal, 1997) has extended Berry's model of acculturation, paying particular attention to the perspectives and attitudes of the acculturating group as well as to those of the host cultural group. The Interactive Acculturation Model (IAM) emphasizes the relationship between acculturation and intergroup relations as well as language-based identity. The IAM recognizes that the acculturating group as well as the host cultural group will have attitudes toward each other based on the origin of the immigrant group as well as on its political, demographic, and socioeconomic characteristics (gender, age, class). As a fluid model of acculturation, the IAM also recognizes that the acculturating strategies and attitudes of the nondominant group will vary across generations and the level of social mobility achieved in the host country.

Bourhis and colleagues (1997) developed the IAM in order to "present a nondeterministic, more dynamic account of immigrant and host community acculturation in multicultural settings" (p. 379). As mentioned previously, the IAM considers the interaction of the acculturational attitudes and strategies of immigrants and of host communities. In terms of the ethnic or racial minority community, the IAM (see the first row of Figure 4.3) uses Berry's strategies, except that the marginalization strategy is divided into two: individualism and anomie following research reported earlier by Berry (1980). Individuals experiencing cultural alienation or anomie are considered those who reject identification with the heritage group as well as with the host group. At the same time, some acculturating individuals who also reject identifying with heritage and host cultures may assume an "individualist" acculturation strategy wherein they prefer to identify as individuals rather than as members of either the heritage or the host group. The second component of the IAM is made up of five possible attitudes the host community assumes toward the acculturation of immigrants or minority ethnic/racial individuals (see the first column of Figure 4.3). Bourhis and colleagues suggest the following possibilities:

1. *Integration*: The host community accepts and values the maintenance of the heritage culture and welcomes the adoption of components of the host culture on the part of the minority cultural group.
2. *Assimilation*: The host community expects minority members to relinquish their heritage culture in order to join the dominant or majority culture.
3. *Segregation*: The host community distances themselves from the newcomers, expecting them to not adopt the dominant culture, and, as the label implies, preferring minimal interactions and separate communities.
4. *Exclusion*: The host community feels newcomers or minority groups should not retain their heritage culture and should not be culturally or socially incorporated into the dominant culture.
5. *Individualism*: The host community considers themselves and immigrants as individuals, and group categories are considered inappropriate and cultural maintenance or adoption an irrelevant concept.

The two perspectives and five strategies of each perspective can be combined in a five-by-five cross-table to identify the nature (problematic, consensus, conflict) of the interactions between acculturating individuals and the host culture and to identify the acculturational pressures and stress experienced by both communities (thereby being designated an "interactive" model). Figure 4.3 presents the possible cross-table and the related relational outcomes. As shown in Figure 4.3, when both the host dominant members and the immigrant group favor an integrationist strategy to acculturation, there is consensus across both groups and positive relationships can be expected. Nevertheless, if the host society prefers an integrationist strategy while the minority community (or individual) favors a separationist strategy (third box from left on top of table), the relationship between both groups (or between host group and individual) will be conflictual.

Acculturation Orientations For Immigrants

Acculturation Orientations For Dominant Community	Integration	Assimilation	Separation	Anomie	Individualism
Integration	consensus	problematic	conflict	problematic	problematic
Assimilation	problematic	consensus	conflict	problematic	problematic
Segregation	conflict	conflict	conflict	conflict	conflict
Exclusion	conflict	conflict	conflict	conflict	conflict
Individualism	problematic	problematic	problematic	problematic	consensus

Source: Based on Bourhis et al., 1997

FIG. 4.3 Interactional Outcomes According to the IAM.

Bourhis and colleagues (1997) argue that this type of analysis of the *relational outcomes* of acculturation strategies is important in predicting "patterns of intercultural communications between immigrants and host community members, interethnic attitudes and stereotypes, acculturative stress, and discrimination between immigrant and host majority members in domains such as housing, employment, schooling, the police, and the judiciary" (p. 383). The IAM makes an important contribution to the study of acculturation by signaling that acculturating individuals not only have different strategies to pursue but also need to deal with varying acculturational attitudes and expectations on the part of the host community (Ngo, 2008). Furthermore, the IAM allows for an analysis of the multiple acculturational strategies required of racial or ethnic minority individuals as they interact with diverse multicultural host communities. Indeed, a study by Bourhis and his colleagues (Bourhis, Montaruli, El-Geledi, Harvey, & Barrette, 2010) showed the usefulness of the IAM in understanding the acculturational experiences of ethnic or racial minorities in two multicultural cities (Montreal and Los Angeles). Nevertheless, some authors (Ngo, 2008) have argued that, while the IAM is an improvement over traditional models of acculturation, it still fails to properly account for the changes that take place among host communities and seems to imply that change is only expected on the part of the ethnic or racial group members. As such, Ngo argues that the IAM "remains focused on the failure of immigrants to successfully acculturate into the dominant culture" and therefore fails to properly account for what some European researchers have identified as the necessary **mutuality in acculturation** in plural societies (Horenczyk, Jasinskaja-Lahti, Sam, & Vedder, 2013) where host and immigrant groups change as a reciprocal function of their interactions and exposure to their cultures.

The IAM is a promising model that deserves further testing and refinement. Unfortunately, the authors have not defined yet the meaning and implications of the various possible outcomes of the interactions between both communities (Figure 4.3), a factor of importance in order to use the model as a predictive tool. The conceptual complexity implied in 25 different outcomes also makes it difficult to develop appropriate and manageable measuring instruments. Nevertheless, the IAM is an important step in moving the field toward realizing that acculturation is a very complex phenomenon that cannot be properly understood by using simple, unidirectional models. Further support for the complexity of studying acculturation can be found in the next model.

The Relative Acculturation Extended Model (RAEM)

Another acculturation model somewhat related to the IAM and to Berry's model is the Relative Acculturation Extended Model, or RAEM, developed by a team of psychologists in Spain (Navas et al., 2005). This model has been used to study the acculturational experiences of a number of individuals in Europe and in other countries, including the experiences of Northern Africans, Sub-Saharan Africans,

Romanians, New Zealanders, Turks, and Spaniards. The RAEM differs from the previous two models in emphasizing the fact that all cultural groups (host as well as immigrant) undergo a process of acculturation and make specific choices of acculturational attitudes and strategies ("real" choices) while aware of a variety of possible choices ("ideal") that are sometimes presented as optimal outcomes of the acculturation process. The "real" choices are those strategies that the immigrants and the host culture members report having adopted, while the "ideal" are those strategies that the immigrants would like to adopt and those that the host community would like to see in the acculturating individuals. The differences between real and ideal choices (or "planes," according to the authors) are relevant to better understanding variables such as acceptance, social integration, civic involvement, sense of belonging, and discrimination.

Another contribution made by the RAEM model is the suggestion that these acculturative choices (or strategies as described in Barry's model) can vary across different spheres or domains of activity (for example, political, employment, economic, social, familial, religious). As such, it would be possible to find an individual who adopts "a 'separation' strategy with regard to choosing a spouse, 'assimilation' in dress codes and 'integration' with regard to food or to celebrating holidays" (Navas et al., 2005, p. 29). In summary, the RAEM argues that acculturation is a complex process that occurs at multiple levels and is experienced by the host culture and the members of immigrant groups. Various strategies can therefore be adopted depending on the domain of activity being considered, whether familial, religious, or any other sphere of activity.

While the RAEM is relatively new, various studies (for example, Rojas, Navas, Sayans-Jimenez, & Cuadrado, 2014; Ward & Kus, 2012) have shown its effectiveness in portraying the complexity of the acculturation process in terms of individuals who experience the changes implied in acculturation, the multiple areas that are affected (attitudes and behaviors as a minimum), and the variability in acculturational strategies that are chosen by the acculturating individuals. A very rich model, the RAEM forces us to move beyond a naive approach to acculturation as a simplistic phenomenon that affects primarily a newcomer group and that assumes a generalized strategy being adopted in all areas of human behavior and interaction.

Biculturalism

Biculturalism is one of the outcomes of the acculturation process that is mentioned in most acculturative models. For example, individuals choosing the integration strategy in Berry's acculturation model can be considered bicultural. Indeed, various researchers (e.g., Buriel & Saenz, 1980; LaFromboise, Coleman, & Gerton, 1993; Nguyen & Benet-Martínez, 2007; Szapocznik & Kurtines, 1980; Tadmor & Tetlock, 2006) suggest that special attention should be given to understanding those individuals who are knowledgeable about two cultures and who feel perfectly comfortable interacting in either culture group. For example, an immigrant from Vietnam to the United States can become a bicultural Vietnamese American after not just learning English but also incorporating values and behaviors that define the "mainstream" U.S. culture while maintaining a significant proportion of the values and behaviors that characterize Vietnam.

Biculturalism is present not just among immigrants or members of a majority or dominant culture but also among the children of ethnically mixed households or families. Households where one parent is a member of one ethnic or cultural group (for example, White non-Hispanic) and the other parent belongs to a different ethnic group (for example, African American) are likely to raise children who exhibit the characteristics of biculturalism by engagement with both cultures. Parents can choose to foster a home environment that allows their children to learn both cultures and to feel comfortable in either one. The multicultural nature of the population of the United States, where people of various races and ethnicities live and work in close proximity, can be expected to generate biracial or bicultural families. For example, the 2010 U.S. census showed that 9 million people (or 2.9 percent of the total population) saw themselves as belonging to more than one race (Jones & Bullock, 2012). The largest proportion involved combinations of White and Black (20 percent) and White and Asian (18 percent), followed by White and American Indian and Alaska Native (16 percent). As suggested by the various acculturation models, the external conditions of exposure to more than one culture (whether in society or in the family) alone do not necessarily produce truly bicultural individuals. There is a need for the presence of family and social conditions that reinforce bicultural identity and behavior and for the individual's active acceptance of the cultures (Root, 2003).

Although psychological research on the adaptiveness of bicultural individuals is limited (Rudmin, 2003), the literature shows that biculturals have some special characteristics that distinguish them from others (LaFromboise et al., 1993). Generally, bicultural individuals are proficient not just at using the language of both cultural groups (if they differ) but also, and more important, in understanding the values of both groups and the associated behavioral expectancies. Bicultural individuals have been shown to have significant integrative cognitive flexibility by easily switching from one cultural framework to the other when exposed to culture-specific symbols or to cultural stimuli that are present in the social environment (Hong, Morris, Chiu, & Benet-Martínez, 2000; Tadmor & Tetlock, 2006). Other studies (Miranda & Umhoefer, 1998) have found that, when compared to monoculturals, bicultural individuals tend to show psychological well-being that includes lower levels of depression and greater sense of self-worth (Birman, 1998), higher self-esteem, generalized optimism, and positive family relations (Schwartz, Unger, et al., 2015). LaFromboise et al. (1993) suggest that, among bicultural individuals,

> in addition to having a strong and stable sense of personal identity, another affective element of bicultural competence is the ability to develop and maintain positive attitudes toward one's culture of origin and the second culture in which he or she is attempting to acquire competence. (p. 408)

In addition, LaFromboise and colleagues argue that people who develop bicultural competencies exhibit better physical and mental health and "outperform their monoculturally competent peers in vocational and academic endeavors" (p. 409). Nevertheless, much of this research measures associations among variables since it is correlational in nature and causality or the direction of the biculturalism/well-being relationship remains a matter of conjecture.

As mentioned previously, biculturalism usually involves **bilingualism**—or the learning of at least two languages with varying levels of proficiency. Research is quite conclusive about the benefits of bilingualism among children and adults. For example, infants raised in bilingual environments exhibit heightened cognitive abilities when compared to those raised in monolingual environments even before they learn to speak (Kovács & Mehler, 2009). In general, bilinguals exhibit greater creativity (Adesope, Lavin, Thompson, & Ungerleider, 2010) and flexibility in cognition as well as in visual perception when trying to identify objects or processing an idea (Chabal & Marian, 2015). Bilingualism also has been associated with greater tolerance of ambiguity and increased acceptance of cultural differences as well as with optimism, innovative thinking, and risk-taking (Dewaele & Wei, 2013; Nguyen & Kellogg, 2010). Research with older adults has shown that bilingualism protects against cognitive decline including the onset of dementia and other symptoms of Alzheimer's disease (Bialystok, Craik, & Luk, 2012). While the study of bilingualism is not part of this book, you may want to keep in mind these findings about its correlates as you analyze the cognitive and behavioral characteristics of members of racial or ethnic minority groups.

Enculturation

Enculturation is a concept used by social scientists to mean various aspects of the process of culture learning. Initially, anthropologists and sociologists used the term to define the process by which children learn the culture of the family in which they have been born. Recently, this process has been labeled *socialization* by psychologists and other behavioral scientists. Others have used the term *enculturation* to define the process of culture learning of the host or dominant culture that is now better understood as acculturation. At the same time, the term *enculturation* has been used to define ancestral culture learning on the part of acculturating individuals. As such, individuals who endeavor to learn or affirm their culture of origin are often described as undergoing a process of **enculturation** (Soldier, 1985). This phenomenon is often found among individuals who are two or more generations removed from the direct experience of a particular ancestry or culture and who wish now to rediscover those cultural and ethnic roots that shape part of their attitudinal and behavioral repertoire (Hansen, 1952). For example, Goering (1971) found that ethnicity and the sense of belonging to an ethnic group was of greater importance to third generation Irish Americans and Italian Americans than to first generation immigrants.

In this sense, enculturation can be perceived to be an active reclaiming of an individual's heritage that may have been lost or diminished during the process of acculturation. As suggested by various acculturation models, certain behaviors or attitudes and even values tend to become less salient or less personally important from one generation to the next (Rumbaut & Portes, 2001). Even by the second generation (that is, individuals who were born in the United States to immigrants), some behaviors and some cultural characteristics start to disappear. These changes usually occur at what Marín (1992) calls the superficial and intermediate levels of cultural change that often involve changes in eating habits, variations in preference for ethnic or heritage media, and less frequent use of ethnic social scripts (a culture's mores or preferred behavioral patterns). By contrast, individuals who wish to enculturate would try to recover those practices and beliefs that were lost or had become less salient in previous generations and make them more central to their own (Soldier, 1985; Wilbert, 1976).

Research with Native Americans (Zimmerman, Ramirez-Valles, Washienko, Walter, & Dyer, 1996) has shown that enculturation can be measured by evaluating individuals' sense of pride and interest in their culture including the importance assigned to maintaining Native American practices and values, the level of knowledge of traditional culture that they are able to report, and their overall sense of pride in being Native American. Also relevant in this enculturation process was the level of involvement in ethnic activities such as sweat lodges, powwows, learning lodges, and fasting. A study with Louisiana Cajuns (Henry & Bankston, 1999) finds that, while significant acculturation had taken place across generations, a recent resurgence in enculturation focused on their Cajun identity and Acadian heritage, including such behaviors as learning French (even if they seldom used it) and fostering a sense of ethnic pride that went beyond their social status.

Unfortunately, enculturation has received little attention from researchers. Nevertheless, there is evidence of renewed interest in "one's own roots" on the part of individuals who are second, third, or higher generation or who had stopped considering themselves a "hyphenated American" (as in "Italian-American" or "Irish-American"). This concern is being shown in terms of increased interest in genealogies, visiting ancestral homes, consuming heritage media, and learning the language and culture of those relatives who first migrated to the United States. This last phenomenon is called **remote enculturation** and refers to the learning of one's heritage from a remote location (the host community) or through short-term exposure (for example, visits, vacations) and not by direct, long-term personal exposure to the heritage community, its culture, and its manifestations (Ferguson, Costigan, Clarke, & Ge, 2016). The process of remote enculturation has been shown to correlate with overall well-being in terms of positive psychological, academic, and health outcomes (Rivas-Drake et al., 2014). Remote enculturation is facilitated by the availability of heritage media (radio and television programs such as those available on cable TV, ethnic soaps, world music), ease of communicating via the Internet (SMS, e-mail, Twitter, various apps, or even voice through services such as Skype and WhatsApp). Likewise, remote enculturation is supported by a number of activities, like visits to ancestral homes during holidays and to international sports events such as the World Cup and the Olympics, where individuals can interact with relatives, friends, or even new acquaintances from the heritage culture.

A related topic to remote enculturation is **remote acculturation**, which refers to an individual's acculturating to a remote culture to which they have not been directly exposed and/or is not their ancestral culture (Adams & Abubakar, 2016). This process has been primarily studied among non-Western contexts, such as in South Africa and Jamaica, where individuals have become familiar (acculturated) to Western (primarily U.S.) cultural manifestations and characteristics through the pop and urban culture of the last few decades (Ferguson & Birman, 2016). Global mass media and global marketing of consumer goods have promoted contact with values, beliefs, and behaviors that resemble those of the United States and other Western societies. The study of remote enculturation and acculturation is of particular importance because it helps us better understand how acculturation can differ among migrants (given that some may have already undergone some level of remote acculturation). The processes that define remote acculturation and remote enculturation can then be compared with acculturation in order to identify critical patterns in culture learning and in the adoption of new cultural traditions and behaviors.

Generational Differences and Acculturation

Much research on acculturation has emphasized the fact that across generations members of ethnic groups differ in their levels and speeds of acculturation. In general, second and third generation individuals tend to exhibit greater levels of acculturation to the host culture than do first generation members of an ethnic group (Perez & Padilla, 2000). These variations in complexity, level, and speed of acculturation are not surprising, since they tend to be related to length of residence in the host country as well as to the greater exposure to acculturating institutions (schools, churches, social groups) often experienced by second and higher generation members (van Oudenhoven, Stuart, & Tip, 2016). Indeed, researchers argue that young individuals facing acculturative pressures must balance by negotiating and consolidating the values and behaviors of their ancestral culture with those of the host society. The search for balance in the acculturation process has been found to characterize the acculturation choices made by adolescents as in the case of Muslim adolescents in New Zealand (Stuart & Ward, 2011). The concept of balance was defined by the authors as "the dynamic process through which one could minimize the risks of negotiating their multiple social worlds and meet the variety of expectations that were placed upon them" (p. 263).

The phenomenon of generational differences in acculturation is best exemplified when the first generation adults have migrated as adults and either have brought young children along or had children after arriving in the United States. In some cases, the first generation adult immigrants experience difficulties in becoming proficient in the language or in understanding the requirements of civil society for full incorporation (e.g., passing driving tests, becoming naturalized citizens), while their children because of their upbringing in schools are more proficient in English and are better able, in some cases, to navigate the requirements of a bureaucracy. Some researchers have indeed noted how the children of immigrants (even when first generation themselves) become their "parents' parents" by being translators and information brokers in the family. These differential patterns of acculturation, labeled **dissonant acculturation** by Portes (1999) or **acculturation mismatch/gap** by others (Lui, 2015; Telzer, 2010), often produce intergenerational conflicts in the family and in some cases have been associated with behavioral problems in second generation children, including abuse of drugs, truancy, and disciplinary problems (Szapocznik & Kurtines, 1980), as well as with poor educational outcomes by the children (Lui, 2015).

The role reversals (as when children take on responsibilities usually assigned to parents in the family) are often perceived as undercutting parental authority and limiting the role of parents in controlling adolescents. The acculturation process and a renewed sense of independence probably also contribute to these difficulties in the behavior of second generation adolescents. Nevertheless, we should keep in mind that intergenerational conflict is not an exclusive phenomenon among immigrants (Berrol, 1995) but something that seems to be central to the value American society places on independence. A study by Carola Suárez-Orozco and Marcelo Suárez-Orozco (1995) shows that, while intergenerational conflict was present among Latinos and Whites, it was more common and more extended among Whites. At the same time, Zhou (1999) suggests that immigrant children who live in inner cities and who rebel against parental values and their mobility expectations are likely to experience downward mobility and to develop an adversarial outlook as a response to the discrimination they experience and the limited opportunities to move upwardly in social class. A recent study in Germany found that a significant proportion of intergenerational conflict among immigrants occurs when parents and children disagree on the level and quality of the interaction of the immigrant child with peers from the host society (Titzmann & Sonnenberg, 2016).

Acculturational Stress

The challenges and difficulties experienced by acculturating individuals have been labeled by many authors as **acculturational stress** (or **acculturative stress**). The constellation of pressures to change and the presence of unfamiliar external social and physical environmental conditions are hypothesized to produce stressful conditions on acculturating individuals. Indeed, much psychological literature proposes that acculturative stresses (and the ability to cope with stress) are "inherent and inevitable aspects of acculturating experiences and processes" (Kuo, 2014). Successfully coping with those stressful conditions is related to an overall sense of well-being and to physical and mental health correlates. Acculturational stresses can involve situations encountered prior to the migration experience (often associated with the need to migrate) and with postmigration (changes in social status, relocation, prejudice and discrimination, logistics associated with living in a new environment). For example, an immigrant arriving in the United States will need in many cases to learn a new language, master new social conventions related to group and interpersonal behavior (when to shake hands, how to address superiors, how much interpersonal distance to keep), gain skills at dealing with government bureaucracies and civic entities (how to get a Social Security card, how to obtain a driver's license, how to enroll children in school), learn to perform job skills that may be very different from those used in the past (how to use an English-language keyboard, how to use a machine at work), learn daily logistics (how to use public transportation, where to get stamps, how to get a mobile telephone), and learn and respect new cultural values (individualism, competition, trust in civic institutions). In many cases, these situations must be handled with little previous preparation and over a short period of time. While all geographic dislocation is difficult (even when a New Yorker moves to Los Angeles), crossing cultures can be even more complex given the variety and intricacy of changes that are implied in such a move. Furthermore, the conditions that are related to acculturative stress do not disappear after a few months but may be present over a period of many years. As you can probably attest, acculturational stress is not limited to immigrants and refugees but is also experienced by short-term mobility across cultures, as happens with sojourners (Safdar & Berno, 2016; Ward & Mak, 2016) such as international tourists, students, diplomats, and corporate employees temporarily relocating to another country.

Acculturative stress can also occur at a family level where varying levels of acculturation of the parents are compared to their children's, a situation that increases the likelihood for parent-child conflict and marital discord. Nevertheless, certain personal traits (being a younger versus an older adult), abilities and skills (being bicultural, having a high level of formal education), acculturation strategies chosen (integration versus marginalization), and goals and motives (feeling "pulled" toward a host country by greater economic and educational opportunities versus being "pushed" out of one's country of origin due to war, poverty, unemployment) may serve as protective or causal factors for acculturative stress.

Indeed, the level of acculturative stress experienced is related to a number of variables. For example, research with Latino adults (Miranda & Matheny, 2000) shows that acculturative stress is related to low levels of cohesion in the family, poor English-language ability, and the length of residence in the United States. Subsequent research (Rodriguez, Myers, Mira, Flores, & Garcia-Hernandez, 2002) shows that acculturative stress is related to linguistic competence (perceived pressures to learn a language, speaking with an accent), pressures to assimilate, and pressures against acculturation (people's rejection of the individual espousing dominant cultural values). This last study finds that the language competency variables seem to be the most important sources of acculturative stress. Not surprisingly, the significance of language competency in promoting acculturative stress is more marked among recent immigrants (Gil & Vega, 1996) and is often produced by the presence of members of the same ethnic group who are already proficient in the majority language (Holleran, 2003).

A study with Cambodian and Vietnamese refugees (Nwadiora & McAdoo, 1996) also shows the significant impact of English-language deficiencies in producing acculturative stress together with unemployment and limited levels of formal education. Negative reactions from members of the dominant group may also elevate an individual's acculturative stress. Studies with Latinos (Sanchez & Fernandez, 1993) and with Arab Americans (Faragallah, Schumm, & Webb, 1997) show that experiences of discrimination or social rejection are related to acculturative stress. Furthermore, a study with Latinos shows that acculturative stress (manifested as generalized anxiety disorders) is highly correlated with fear of deportation (Salas-Wright, Robles, Vaughn, Cordova, & Perez-Figueroa (2015).

Both women and men seem to experience fairly similar levels of acculturative stress, at least among refugees (Nwadiora & McAdoo, 1996), and it seems to be more likely among those who migrate after 12 years of age (Mena, Padilla, & Maldonado, 1987). Also, Padilla and Perez (2003) have argued that acculturation is most difficult for individuals who are visibly different from the dominant group in terms of skin color and language spoken. Among immigrants, the realization that relatives and friends left behind are no longer a source of emotional, personal, and financial support can also produce acculturative stress. Likewise, the acculturation process may create a type of "survivor's guilt," where stress is felt by acculturating individuals who realize that their friends and relatives back home will not have the same experiences and opportunities that they are able to enjoy in the new country.

It should be noted that the acculturation process is not necessarily always stressful. As Rogler, Cortes, and Malgady (1991) note, acculturating individuals also have positive experiences, including feeling safer and better off than those in their country of origin. In addition, immigrants often experience positive incidents in their new culture with new friends and coworkers and may enjoy newly discovered foods, entertainment, sights, and conveniences that balance to some extent the impact of the acculturative stressors. Nevertheless, the positive effects of these new experiences may decrease after the novelty wears off, and acculturating individuals often need to cope with experiences of prejudice and discrimination and the realization that, in many cases, their socioeconomic status is not rapidly improving, that only a few drive fancy cars, or that not everybody in the country lives in the homes portrayed in Hollywood movies. Indeed, the shattering of numerous myths about the United States—the ability to improve one's life if only you work hard enough or the more improbable images of "streets paved with gold" or "dollars hanging from trees"—can be particularly stressful for immigrants as they acculturate. Likewise, acculturative stress is generated as individuals must cope with the stratification processes of society in the United States, where, in many cases, the color of their skin or the culture of origin or the use of accented speech determines the type of societal rewards and opportunities a person is able to receive. The poor quality of schools in many ethnic neighborhoods, for example, limits the potential for social advancement of many first and second generation individuals, circumscribing the kinds of employment they can obtain or the possibility of attending college.

The literature on acculturative stress, as is true in the stress literature in general, emphasizes the important role coping strategies play in facilitating adaptation and well-being (van der Zee, Benet-Martínez, & van Oudenhoven, 2016). In a review of the literature on acculturative stress, Kuo (2014) suggests that active and problem-focused coping strategies support not only personal adaptation but also generalized emotional well-being. At the same time, Kuo suggests that there is strong evidence to show that "avoidance coping strategies" create difficulties in adjustment and personal well-being. Kuo's review further shows that the cognitive appraisal of the stressful situation together with the coping mechanisms chosen can jointly lead to either adaptive or detrimental outcomes. Another recent analysis of the literature on acculturational stress (van der Zee et al., 2016) shows that active coping strategies (for example, seeking a job, making friends, learning the new language) protect individuals from stress and are associated with lower levels of depression and anxiety (Burrow-Sanchez, Ortiz-Jensen, Corrales, & Meyers, 2015).

Acculturative Stress and Reasons for Migration

An important consideration when analyzing acculturative stress is the reason or the causes for migration. The nature of the migration experience (for example, whether it was voluntary or forced) can be expected to affect the disposition of the immigrant toward the new culture and its people. Ogbu (1978) argues that voluntary migrants—that is, those who choose to migrate for employment or for educational or economic improvement—will react differently to the new experiences than will those who have been enslaved, colonized, or forced to migrate or relocate for political reasons, such as American Indians, African Americans, Puerto Ricans, or some Asian Americans. For Ogbu, involuntary migrants (and by extension their children and grandchildren) have greater difficulty accepting the values of the mainstream or "host" culture, which in turn leads to failure in academic activities and to low-status employment.

Some authors (e.g., Burnam, Hough, Karno, Escobar, & Telles, 1987) suggest that in a process of selective migration among voluntary immigrants, the strongest ("migration of the fittest") or the most creative and healthiest or the risk-takers or the youngest tend to choose to migrate. This is known as the **selective migration hypothesis**. This hypothesis, if true, would argue that members of a first generation cohort would be less likely to exhibit adjustment and health problems than those belonging to a second or higher generation. Mental health research (Vega, Warheit, Buhl-Autg, & Meinhardt, 1984) indeed shows that the mental health status of Mexican American immigrants is similar to Mexicans (in Mexico), while U.S.-born Mexican Americans (second generation) exhibit poorer mental health conditions. A related **social stress hypothesis** suggests that the members of second and higher generation groups exhibit poorer mental and physical health not because they are less strong or less able to withstand acculturative stress but rather because they bear the brunt of discrimination and prejudice in our society. In addition, the social stress hypothesis endorses the assumption that immigrants are better able to maintain and use the protective cultural traditions of origin that in turn support better physical health and stronger mental health (Escobar, 1998).

Research on physical health (Nguyen, 2006; Sam, 2006; Sam, Jasinskaja-Lahti, Ryder, & Hassan, 2016) seems to shed some light on the complexity of this phenomenon. Early research (Kleinman, Fingerhut, & Prager, 1991) find that immigrant Mexican American women had rates of children with low and very low birth weight comparable to those found among White women. Furthermore, Guendelman and colleagues (Guendelman, Gould, Hudes, & Eskenazi, 1990) find that second generation Mexican American women were more likely to have low birth weight babies than were first generation mothers. These results (sometimes referred to as the Hispanic paradox or the **immigrant health paradox**) seemed contradictory since immigrant mothers tended to be less educated and poorer and to have less access to medical care. Nevertheless, subsequent research finds that the improved health status does not necessarily remain consistent over time (Guendelman & English, 1995). Furthermore, more sensitive analysis of the data show that the low birth weight phenomenon was related to a complex interaction of predictor variables such as the language ability of the mothers, their socioeconomic conditions, and their reason for migration. We could assume therefore that the explanation is more complex than first suggested by the selective migration hypothesis or the social stress hypothesis and that the results of the acculturation process can best be explained as an interaction of multiple variables including at a minimum the preexisting conditions (physical as well as mental status) of the immigrants, their reasons for migrating, their ability to cope with acculturative stresses, access and patterns of use of health care and support systems, experiences of prejudice and discrimination, and social and environmental characteristics of their living environment. A recent comprehensive analysis of the *immigrant paradox* (Garcia Coll & Marks, 2012) shows the protective role of biculturalism and bilingualism among second and third generation immigrants. Furthermore, as argued by Nguyen (2006), most studies have failed to properly measure the role of acculturation in explaining these findings and instead have used indicators or correlates of acculturation that may have different effects on people's behavior.

Another related effect of the process of acculturation is the role that ethnic enclaves have on people's health and welfare. One positive element of residing in ethnic enclaves (for example, Chinatowns, Little Saigons, barrios) is the support that they provide in culture and language maintenance. Residence in an ethnic enclave allows first and even second generation individuals to maintain the ancestral language, form friendships with people who share the same culture and values, and prevent some of the stresses associated with living in a truly foreign environment. Nevertheless, some authors also propose that residence in ethnic enclaves (or the "ethnic inner city") can have negative consequences. Zhou (1999) suggests that, indeed, immigrants who reside in an ethnic inner-city enclave tend to have children who face an adversarial outlook within the community, and this situation can lead first and second generation children to perform less well in school (so as to not be labeled "Whites" or "turncoats") and to avoid stigmatization of being considered foreigners in their own world. These children not only reject "nerdy" and "uncool" attitudes toward school (Gibson, 1989) but also adopt linguistic patterns and behaviors of the inner city. In addition, hostile and unwelcoming environments may lead observers (teachers, community leaders, other adults) to assume that these children will "naturally" fail and in this fashion to support a self-fulfilling prophesy wherein these students receive less constructive feedback and less attention from the teachers.

Measuring Acculturation

This section of the chapter presents a summary of the approaches used to measure the acculturation process. An understanding of the methods used to measure acculturation is important because, in some instances, theoretical or methodological characteristics of the various measures become confounding factors when trying to analyze the findings of studies exploring the relevance of acculturation. Indeed, some of the discrepancies across studies that are found in the literature can often be explained by the limited validity in the way acculturation was defined or conceptualized by the researchers or to such methodological limitations as poorly constructed instrumentation or incomplete measures.

Acculturation has been measured using a variety of social science methods, including case studies, observations, interviews, and surveys. Nevertheless, the majority of procedures developed for measuring acculturation have relied on self-report paper-and-pencil instruments, where individuals are asked to indicate their attitudes, norms, or values or to report on the frequency or presence of certain behaviors. For example, a large number of acculturation scales ask respondents to report how well they speak, write, or understand English and/or the language of origin. A Korean American, for example, would be asked to indicate how well she speaks Korean, usually on a Likert-type scale, where responses can range from "very well" to "very poorly" or "not at all." Another item or question could ask respondents to report on their proficiency in English. Other acculturation scales use a single item to determine the person's proficiency in English and in Korean, going from one extreme to another, with such optional responses as "speak only Korean at home" to "speak only English at home."

Most acculturation scales include a wide range of behaviors and attitudes or values and frequently are designed for one major ethnic group (for example, Asian Americans) or for a subgroup (for example, Vietnamese Americans or Chinese Americans). Among the behaviors often included in acculturation scales are language use, preference, and fluidity; media usage patterns; ethnic friendship preferences; food consumption patterns; knowledge of cultural traditions and values; ethnic self-identification; perceived prejudice and discrimination; and cultural values or scripts, such as familialism (family orientation and devotion) or time orientation (personal significance of time and timeliness), or group-specific cultural scripts, such as *simpatía* (value placed on positive social relations).

As suggested by Zane and Mak (2003) and others (for example, Celenk & van de Vijver, 2014; Marín & Gamba, 1996), the measurement of acculturation in psychological research has varied in terms of conceptual approaches, domains measured, psychometric characteristics of the acculturation construct, and populations sampled. While some scales consider acculturation as a unidirectional process with possible responses going in one direction from the culture of origin to the new culture, others consider the process as bidirectional, taking place in two different fields (one related to the culture of origin and another to the new culture). An acculturation scale for Chinese Americans based on a unidirectional conceptualization of acculturation, for example, would ask respondents to indicate the ethnicity of close friends in a Likert-type scale that goes from "only White Americans" to "only Chinese," including a midpoint of "half White Americans and half Chinese."

The unidirectional approach to the measurement of acculturation has fallen into disfavor because it implies a zero-sum approach to culture learning (Rogler et al., 1991), wherein gains in one culture imply losses in the other culture. For example, gains in English proficiency would imply losses in proficiency in the language of origin, or, in the above example, increases in friends who are White would imply decreases in the number of Chinese friends.

Most recent research favors a multidirectional conceptualization of acculturation, where the acculturating individual is free to move from one end to the other of each culture or "cultural field." The most significant contribution of this bidirectional or multidirectional conceptualization is its recognition that individuals can learn a new culture's behaviors or values without having to give up aspects of the culture of origin. For example, a Japanese American can self-report proficiency in English that can vary from "not at all" at one extreme to "excellent" at the other. This rating is independent of the respondent's self-reported knowledge of Japanese, which can also vary from "not at all" to "excellent." In a five-point Likert-type scale, the Japanese American could mark a five ("excellent") for knowledge of Japanese and a three ("average") for knowledge of English. In a few months, the same individual could indicate a four ("good") for knowledge of English without necessarily having to indicate a lowering of his knowledge of Japanese.

As mentioned previously, acculturation scales also vary in terms of the behavioral areas or domains that they measure. Probably the most frequently used domain is related to language proficiency, preference, and use and sometimes specifying the social context in which the language is used (Kang, 2006; Zane & Mak, 2003). Often respondents are asked to report on linguistic preferences and proficiency in selected situations and for English as well as for the ancestral language of origin. For example, the Bidimensional Acculturation Scale for Hispanics (Marín & Gamba, 1996) asks respondents to report proficiency in English and in Spanish separately while speaking, reading, writing, listening to the radio, listening to music, and watching television (see Box 4.1).

Another frequently used behavioral domain involves preferences for the ethnicity of the individuals with whom one socializes. For example, the original African American Acculturation Scale (Landrine & Klonoff, 1996) includes items measuring the ethnicity of friends, of people one feels comfortable

Box 4.1

Examples of Acculturation Scale Items

Language Use Subscale

1. How often do you speak English?
2. How often do you speak in English with your friends?
3. How often do you think in English?
4. How often do you speak Spanish?
5. How often do you speak in Spanish with your friends?
6. How often do you think in Spanish?

Linguistic Proficiency Subscale

7. How well do you speak English?
8. How well do you read in English?
9. How well do you understand television programs in English?
10. How well do you understand radio programs in English?
11. How well do you write in English?
12. How well do you understand music in English?
13. How well do you speak Spanish?
14. How well do you read in Spanish?
15. How well do you understand television programs in Spanish?
16. How well do you understand radio programs in Spanish?
17. How well do you write in Spanish?
18. How well do you understand music in Spanish?

Electronic Media Subscale

19. How often do you watch television programs in English?
20. How often do you listen to radio programs in English?
21. How often do you listen to music in English?
22. How often do you watch television programs in Spanish?
23. How often do you listen to radio programs in Spanish?
24. How often do you listen to music in Spanish?

The response categories for items 1 through 6, and items 19 through 24 are *almost always* (scored as 4), *often* (scored as 3), *sometimes* (scored as 2), and *almost never* (scored as 1).

The response categories for items 7 through 18 are *very well* (scored as 4), *well* (scored as 3), *poorly* (scored as 2), and *very poorly* (scored as 1).

Source: Bidimensional Acculturation Scale for Hispanics (Marín & Gamba, 1996).

having around them, of the person they admire the most, of the people they trust, of the members of their church, and of the neighborhood in which they grew up. One other type of question frequently used in acculturation scales is related to the preference individuals report for media use, including printed media such as newspapers or magazines, television programming, radio stations, and social media (English-language or mainstream outlets or ethnic-specific). Other types of questions often used to measure acculturation are knowledge of culture-specific symbols or events (such as the meaning of the Fourth of July holiday or the colors of a flag) or familiarity with religious or patriotic figures (for example, "Who was Gandhi?" "Who was Bolívar?").

The reliance on language-use and -proficiency items in most acculturation scales has been criticized for a number of reasons. First is the concern that linguistic abilities or preferences are just a small, if not insignificant, aspect of a person's life and that changes may reflect the effects of various circumstances that may or may not properly measure psychological acculturation (Chiriboga, 2004). For example, schooling and job requirements may externally modify linguistic practices of immigrants and second generation individuals without necessarily reflecting internal or more personal acculturation changes. At the same time, the ethnic composition of certain neighborhoods in large urban environments (Miami, New York, Chicago, Los Angeles, San Francisco) may make it possible for older individuals to function in their language of origin without having to learn much English. Likewise, prohibitions against the use of languages other than English, as existed in the past (and currently exist in some places of employment), may also spuriously contribute to acculturation scores that do not reflect psychological acculturation.

Furthermore, generational differences in language use have been well documented, which could reflect behavioral preferences that are not related to acculturational changes at the more basic level of values and attitudes. For example, Fishman (1965/2000) suggests that adult immigrants continue to use the mother tongue in the majority of settings while second generation individuals tend to use it only at home with parents and other relatives who may continue to use the mother tongue. The majority of third generation individuals generally exhibit little proficiency in the heritage tongue, using the dominant language for most interactions. These patterns can therefore produce spurious correlations in acculturation scales that rely on language proficiency or preference items to measure such a fairly complex construct since there are external factors that may moderate the choice of language used (Kang, 2006). An additional limitation of most acculturation scales is their failure to ascertain or measure if the behavioral or attitudinal choices have been freely made by the individual or if they have been imposed by environmental conditions or pressures from others. For example, the choice of English-language television may be the result of an individual's personal choice or the result of pressures from parents to avoid television in other languages or due to the fact that there are no ethnic stations available in the place of residence. Each of these situations could have varying implications for the measurement of the individual's acculturation level.

These differences in domains, theoretical conceptualizations, and directionality contribute to the difficulties in understanding inconsistencies in psychological research dealing with acculturation among ethnic groups in the United States. Cabassa (2003) suggests that measures of acculturation need to become more complex by increasing the number of areas that are measured so that the whole range of experiences lived by an acculturating individual can be evaluated (at home, school, work, while shopping, when accompanied by friends, or alone). This is indeed a very important issue that has plagued researchers as they try to balance the need for comprehensiveness in the measure and the need for controlling the length of the instrument for practical reasons (Serrano & Anderson, 2003; Wallen, Feldman, & Anliker, 2002). Nguyen (2006) also criticizes much of the current research on acculturation in the United States because of its lack of strong theoretical conceptual frameworks and its frequent lack of attention to social and structural contexts. The more recent models of acculturation—such as the RAEM and IAM (reviewed in the previous)—have tried to solve these limitations in the literature. Further criticisms of current measuring approaches of acculturation include the reliance on paper-and-pencil instruments at the expense of other methodological approaches, including qualitative methods and mixed-method approaches, as well as the need to analyze such a complex phenomenon from a longitudinal perspective rather than in a cross-sectional (one-time) approach (Ozer, 2013; Stuart & Ward, 2011).

Despite the theoretical and methodological advantages of some approaches or of some scales over others, we can expect that the problem of limited comparability across measures will continue. Indeed, the last decades have seen the creation of a substantial number of acculturation scales as well as the revision of scales that had been in existence for a few years. There are acculturation scales for the major ethnic groups, including African Americans, Asian Americans, and Latinos, as well as for specific subgroups, like Arab Americans (Wrobel, 2016), Japanese Americans (Meredith, Wenger, Liu, Harada, & Kahn, 2000), Puerto Ricans (Tropp, Erkut, Coll, Alarcón, & Garcia, 1999), Khmer (Lim, Heiby, Brislin, & Griffin, 2002), Vietnamese (Nguyen & von Eye, 2002), East Asians (Barry, 2001), Southeast Asians (Anderson et al., 1993), Chinese Americans (Gupta & Yick, 2001), and Greek Americans (Harris & Verven, 1996, 1998), as well as acculturation among deaf people (Maxwell-McCaw & Zea, 2011) and among American Indians (Winterowd, Montgomery, Stumblingbear, Harless, & Hicks, 2008).

Also, some scales have tried to measure acculturation within multicultural groups by using items that do not explicitly address a given language (e.g., Vietnamese, Spanish) or the values and attitudes related to a particular culture. These scales are meant to be used in situations where it is difficult to develop group-specific acculturation scales or where the group being studied includes individuals from multiple ethnicities. Examples of these multicultural acculturation scales include the Stephenson Multigroup Acculturation Scale (Stephenson, 2000), one developed specifically for adolescents (Unger et al., 2002), and one more recently developed in Australia to measure acculturation and resilience (Khawaja, Moisuc, & Ramirez, 2014). As a matter of fact, Celenk and van de Vijver (2014) have compiled a list of measures that are available in the public domain and compared them across a number of variables including their conceptual background, psychometric characteristics, validity, and reliability. Some of the most frequently used scales are listed in Box 4.2.

Box 4.2

Frequently Used Acculturation Scales by Ethnic or Racial Minority Group

African Americans

African American Acculturation Scale (AAAS)

(Landrine & Klonoff, 1994, 1995, 1996)

Measures eight dimensions with 74 items: family structures and practices (e.g., child taking, extended family, informal adoption), socialization practices, preference for things African American (e.g., music, magazines), consumption of traditional foods (e.g., collard greens, ham hocks), health beliefs, religious beliefs and practices, belief in superstitions, and attitudes of cultural mistrust.

African American Acculturation Scale

(Snowden & Hines, 1999)

Includes 10 items related to media preferences, ethnic/racial characteristics of friends, church congregation, neighborhood, attitudes toward interracial marriage and familial dependence, and comfort interacting with Whites.

Measurement of Acculturation Strategies for People of African Descent

(Obasi & Leong, 2010)

Uses 45 items to measure various acculturational strategies such as pride, child-rearing practices, friendship patterns, religiosity, celebration preferences, and so on.

Asian Americans

Suinn-Lew Asian Self-Identity Acculturation Scale

(Suinn, Rickard-Figueroa, Lew, & Vigil, 1987)

A unidimensional 21-item scale measuring language use, friendship patterns, and ethnic identity.

Asian American Values Scale—Multidimensional

(Kim, Li, & Ng, 2005)

An instrument of 36 items that measures various Asian values (e.g., collectivism, humility, emotional self-control, filial piety).

Asian American Multidimensional Acculturation Scale

(Chung, Kim, & Abreu, 2004)
A multidimensional scale with 45 items measuring cultural behavior, identity, and knowledge.

Latinos/Hispanics

Acculturation Rating Scale for Mexican Americans–Revised (ARSMA–R)

(Cuellar, Arnold, & Gonzalez, 1995)
A bidimensional scale that measures language proficiency, linguistic preference, and ethnic identification and allows researchers to classify respondents in terms of Berry's four acculturative strategies.

Short Acculturation Scale for Hispanics (SASH)

(Marín, Sabogal, Marín, Otero-Sabogal, & Pérez-Stable, 1987)
A 12-item unidimensional scale that asks respondents to identify their level of involvement with Latino and White cultures. A language use/preference factor allows researchers to quickly classify individuals as Latino oriented or White oriented.

Bidimensional Acculturation Scale for Hispanics (BAS)

(Marín & Gamba, 1996)
Includes 12 items for each cultural domain—Hispanic versus non-Hispanic White—that measure three acculturative areas: language use, linguistic proficiency, and patterns of use of electronic media.

Native Americans

Native American Acculturation Scale

(Garrett & Pichette, 2000)
Includes 20 multiple-choice items addressing identity, language use, ethnicity of friends, attitudes, and behaviors.

Levels of Acculturation

Various authors have expressed concerns regarding the fact that the literature on acculturation tends to confuse central or core aspects of acculturation from those that are less important or even peripheral to the process (Chiriboga, 2004; Marín, 1992; Zane & Mak, 2003). Indeed, changes in behavior and attitudes produced by exposure to a new culture can be observed at three different levels (Marín, 1992) depending on the length of exposure and the personal significance of the behaviors or values. Probably the most superficial level, and therefore most easily changed, involves learning and/or forgetting facts and behaviors that are characteristic of an ethnic group or culture but have generally lower personal significance (e.g., meanings of holidays, ancestral food likings, and media preferences). A second, more intermediate level involves changes in frequently performed behaviors that are of relative or moderate personal value or significance (e.g., language preference, ethnicity of friends). Finally, the third and most basic level involves modifications in an individual's core values (beliefs in justice, the value of the family). Most research on acculturation has been concentrated on the first two levels, probably because of the difficulty in identifying operational definitions and developing culturally appropriate measures for basic cultural values. Indeed, the analysis by Zane and Mak (2003) of 22 frequently used acculturation scales found that only five included the measurement of cultural values.

For example, among Latinos, length of residence in the United States is related to changes at the superficial level, such as patterns of media use. As such, Latinos who have lived in the United States the longest period of time show an increased preference for mass media in English rather than in Spanish (Alcalay et al., 1987–1988). Other studies have shown that, as acculturation proceeds in terms of increased length of residence and personal involvement with a new culture, changes in areas such as linguistic proficiency and ethnic preferences for friends also occur (Cuellar et al., 1995; Cuellar, Harris, & Jasso, 1980; Marín et al., 1987). Finally, research has shown that, while changes at the more basic level of cultural and personal values occur as a result of acculturation among Latinos, they tend to be less frequent and to take more time (Cuellar et al., 1995; Sabogal et al., 1987).

It is important to note that, in this age of globalization and internationalized mass media, changes related to the most superficial levels of acculturation can be the product of circumstances that have little to do with psychological acculturation. As many international travelers note, the influence of Hollywood films and of international mass media such as the BBC, the *International New York Times*, or CNN can be seen everywhere, including in the most remote of places. This internationalization of electronic and print mass media makes it possible for some aspects of the culture of the United States to be transmitted via movies, radio, and television programs. As such, recent immigrants to the United States can easily report familiarity with our cultural icons and events (Coca-Cola, McDonald's, KFC, Pepsi, rap music, movie actors, the Fourth of July, the Super Bowl, or NBA teams) immediately upon arriving and before being exposed to the acculturational process of living in a new culture. This familiarity with certain cultural products may potentially modify or buffer acculturative stress among those individuals who may find a supportive image in the product or idea that is not totally unfamiliar to them.

Chapter Summary

This chapter has presented an overview of acculturation as one of the most significant concepts in multicultural psychology. Acculturation has received a considerable amount of attention on the part of many researchers and is a concept or construct often mentioned when trying to predict or explain the behavior of individuals who are exposed to a new culture. Despite acculturation's relatively short history, important changes have occurred in the ways in which it is defined, how it is measured, and how its effects and correlates are studied. Individuals vary in the acculturation strategies they choose, and these can in turn be related to acculturative stress. The role of acculturation in shaping behaviors and attitudes is so strong that fairly clear patterns can be identified despite the variety of ethnic groups studied and the methodological limitations of some studies in terms of the measurements used or the limited samples studied.

Despite the large number of studies on the psychology of acculturation, the field still needs better-defined multidimensional models of acculturation, improved measuring methodologies that include the triangulation of various research methods, and the benefits of testing hypotheses across cultures. At the same time, it is important to keep in mind the admonition proposed by some authors (e.g., Hunt, Schneider, & Comer, 2004) that, at times, acculturation effects on health may be better explained by socioeconomic status or discrimination rather than by vague cultural differences.

Research has shown that individuals exposed to a new culture undergo a process of change in their worldviews, their attitudes, their values, and their behaviors and that these changes show varying patterns across individuals as a function of their migration and generational history. As Berry (2003) notes, it is important to remember that many people have undergone and continue to experience the effects of acculturation and that most have survived and have been able to function in a productive way. Acculturation therefore does not imply either social or psychological pathology, despite the significant emphasis that researchers, primarily psychologists, have placed on the negative aspects of acculturation. Except for some significant work on biculturalism (Chun, Kwan, Strycker, & Chesla, 2016), a substantial number of studies have primarily searched for the negative consequences of the acculturation process (Chun et al., 2003). One other important consideration is the fact that acculturation takes place within a socioecological context where the family, school, work, and society in general affect the nature of the process and promote acculturative change and, possibly, acculturative stress (Ward & Geeraert, 2016).

Key Terms

acculturation 85
acculturational/acculturative stress 98
acculturation mismatch/gap 97
acculturative strategy 89
assimilation 84
biculturalism 94
bilingualism 95
cultural assimilation 84
cultural integration 84
dissonant acculturation 97
enculturation 96
ethnogenesis 87
globalization 82
immigrant health paradox 100

incorporation 84
mutuality in acculturation 93
remote acculturation 96
remote enculturation 96
segmented assimilation 87
selective migration hypothesis 100
social stress hypothesis 100
structural assimilation 84
unidirectional model of acculturation 88

Learning by Doing

- Answer the items of the Bidimensional Acculturation Scale found in Box 4.1, and score your responses by computing an average of your responses to items dealing with English and another average for the items dealing with Spanish. Analyze the differences in both averages based on your background and exposure to Latino culture. You can compute the average for your English-related questions by adding your responses to questions 1–3, 7–12, and 19–21 and then dividing by 12. Your average (or mean) for the Spanish-related questions can be computed by adding your responses to the other items and dividing by 12. The range of each mean score should be between 1 and 4.
- Interview five people of varying ethnic backgrounds, and ask them to indicate what practices, attitudes, and beliefs characterize their ethnic group. You can ask, for example, about dating practices, who makes financial decisions at home, attitudes about women working outside the house, religious practices, the role of adults toward their aging parents, how involved men are in child-rearing, and whether men cook the family's meals. Find out whether grandparents and parents held or hold the same beliefs and carried or carry out the same practices.
- Interview first and second generation immigrants, and have them report on preferred language use in various settings and explore the role of external factors in shaping those preferences or practices. For example, ask which language they prefer at home, with their parents, with their children, at religious services, and when watching television or movies.
- Imagine that you are about to move permanently to a new city where you do not speak the language. Make a list of the things you would need to do within the first five days in order to have a life that resembles your current conditions. Rate how stressful (on a scale of 1–10, with 10 being the highest level of stress) achieving each of those outcomes would be to you. Consider, for example, renting an apartment, getting a telephone landline installed, registering children for school, managing the public transportation system, buying groceries when you cannot read the labels, opening a bank account, buying stamps, getting a driver's license, getting a government-issued identification card, and learning what is appropriate to wear when going to school, looking for a job, or going to a party.

Suggested Further Readings

Berry, J. W. (2003). Conceptual approaches to acculturation. In K. M. Chun, P. Balls Organista, & G. Marín (Eds.), *Acculturation: Advances in theory, measurement, and applied research* (pp. 17–37). Washington, DC: American Psychological Association.

A comprehensive and updated overview of Berry's acculturation model and his perspectives on the model's implications.

Chun, K. M., Balls Organista, P., & Marín, G. (Eds.). (2003). *Acculturation: Advances in theory, measurement, and applied research.* Washington, DC: American Psychological Association.

A presentation of comprehensive summaries and analyses of current perspectives on acculturation theories and their applications. The book includes contributions by some of the key contributors to our understanding of this complex process among ethnic minority groups in the United States.

Jacoby, T. (Ed.). (2004). *Reinventing the melting pot: The new immigrants and what it means to be American.* New York: Basic Books.

An excellent analysis of the processes and difficulties facing recent immigrants to the United States. The book analyzes various models of acculturation and social integration within the older perspectives of assimilation.

LaFromboise, T., Coleman, H. L. K., & Gerton, J. (1993). Psychological impact of biculturalism: Evidence and theory. *Psychological Bulletin, 114*, 395–412.
A classic article on the effects of biculturalism that shows the positive results of learning more than one culture.

Padilla, A. M. (Ed.). (1980). *Acculturation: Theory, models, and some new findings.* Boulder, CO: Westview.
A presentation of a number of acculturation models and their implications for Latino families. A classic in the field.

Root, M. P. P. (1996). *The multiracial experience: Racial borders as the new frontier*. Thousand Oaks, CA: Sage.
An advocacy for the need for social scientists to focus on the social and psychological characteristics of individuals of multiple ethnic backgrounds. This book updates previous work by the same author and identifies important areas of research as the nation becomes more multiracial and multiethnic.

Rumbaut, R. G., & Portes, A. (Eds.). (2001). *Ethnicities: Children of immigrants in America*. Berkeley: University of California Press.
An important analysis of the experiences and characteristics of second generation individuals (the children of immigrants) primarily from sociological and anthropological perspectives. The book is based on the researcher's comprehensive studies of immigrants to the United States.

Sam, D. L., & Berry, J. W. (Eds.). (2016). *The Cambridge handbook of acculturation psychology* (2nd ed.). Cambridge: Cambridge University Press.
An international collection of chapters analyzing research and theoretical perspectives on acculturation. The book benefits from the authors' experiences around the world and among individuals who differ in their migration patterns and acculturational perspectives.

Intersecting Identities—Part 1 5
Racial, Ethnic, and Class Dimensions

Who Are You?

On the first day of classes, Thalia and her classmates were asked by their personality psychology professor to write their response to the question, "Who am I?" Thalia's first impulse was to write down "A woman," while Ibrahim, her friend sitting next to her, wrote, "A Muslim." After a few seconds, Thalia decided to add more descriptions to her answer and wrote, "A feminist, granddaughter of Salvadoran refugees, working-class." She then turned to Mohamed and asked him to show her what he'd written. He showed her his first answer; then he said, "You, know, I'm more than that. I'm a man, an American whose grandparents came from Lebanon, a White guy." Thalia and Ibrahim looked curiously at each other, and Thalia said to Ibrahim, "I wonder what Esperanza wrote." Both turned their heads to where Esperanza was sitting and asked about her responses. Esperanza had written "Mexican American, Catholic, middle-class." Thalia then asked Esperanza, "What about being a woman, a feminist activist?" Esperanza answered, "Yes, but that's not as important to me as being an American with Mexican grandparents and being a practicing Catholic." Ibrahim then said, "Yes! To me, being an American Muslim is more important than being a man or anything else." After class, Thalia, Ibrahim, and Esperanza continued their discussion about why some characteristics are more important than others and how together they helped define who they are—not just men or women, not just Catholics or Muslims, but the three of them sharing a common thread of being Americans. Thalia then mentioned that this activity had shown how a number of characteristics define who they are but that, in some cases, one or two seem more important than others.

Understanding the Multiple and Intersecting Dimensions of Identity

How do you define your personal identity? Is it even possible to categorize yourself in one particular way? Are certain facets of your identity, like your ethnicity, race, and gender, more important to you than your social class, religious background, or other identity dimensions? Does it depend on the social context, including whom you are with, what you are doing, and where you are at any given moment?

Imagine how Mohamed, the man described in the vignette, might respond when asked, "Who are you?" At first glance, this may seem like a simple question, but Mohamed doesn't solely define himself as a Muslim man. Many identity dimensions matter to him and influence his everyday life in complex ways. His experiences show that *multiple and intersecting* dimensions can inform a person's overall sense of identity. The term **intersecting identities** refers to multiple and closely linked identities that interact in meaningful ways, contributing to unique life experiences. Many of them are very salient, like ethnicity and gender were for the students in the vignette. Others may not be as salient (social class, sexuality, migration history, etc.). You might experience significant psychological distress if your self-identity includes multiple, intersecting dimensions of minority status (Nadal et al., 2015) or "intersecting oppressions" (Parent, DeBlaere, & Moradi, 2013).

Because people define themselves in numerous ways, tremendous "heterogeneity and hybridity" or *diversity* is seen within and across different identity groupings. Diverse identities in turn lead to varied physical and psychological outcomes captured by statistical "interaction effects" between identity dimensions. For instance, race- and gender-interaction effects on health have been well documented. In one study of White, African, Mexican, Puerto Rican, and Cuban Americans (Read & Gorman, 2006), women in general had poorer functional health than men. However, when race and gender were both examined, African American women had lower scores on all health measures (self-rated health, daily physical functioning, and being diagnosed with a life-threatening medical condition like heart disease, diabetes, or cancer) than did White and African American men, even after controlling for socioeconomic status. Race and gender interactions likewise influence mental health. In a study of African American adolescent males (Rogers, Scott, & Way, 2015), racial identity alone was not related to depression, but having both positive racial *and* gender identities did significantly reduce depression risk, highlighting the intersectional nature of these identity dimensions.

Finally, gender attitudes are affected by race and gender interactions. African Americans in general show more critical understanding of the origins and extent of gender inequality than do Whites. However, when gender is also considered, African American women show greater recognition and critical understanding of gender inequality, while White men are the least likely to perceive and understand it (Kane, 2000). African American women's distinct perspectives and life experiences, shaped by the intersection of gender, race, and class, produced the "womanist" movement. Ethnic minority women and their allies initiated this movement as an alternative framework to feminism, which had failed to recognize racism, ethnocentrism, and poverty as equivalent concerns to sexism (Lyons, Carlson, Thurm, Grant, & Gipson, 2006).

By fully attending to such diverse psychological experiences within and across identity groupings, we can develop a more accurate and rich understanding of psychological phenomena in a multicultural context. Because racial, ethnic, class, gender, and sexual identities have received wide attention in multicultural psychology research, we explore these identity dimensions in this and the following chapter. In both chapters we discuss how these identities are conceptualized and defined, how they develop and form across the life span, and how they affect psychological functioning.

Multicultural psychologists view racial, ethnic, class, and gender identities as **social constructions**, meaning that their definitions and categorizations are based on prevailing sociopolitical attitudes and historical forces in society rather than biological or genetic factors. Sexual identity, however, is believed to represent a nature and nurture interaction (Rosario & Schrimshaw, 2014), although more research is needed to more fully understand its basis or etiology.

Defining Racial, Ethnic, and Class Identities

Racial Identity

Racial identity refers to identification with a socially defined racial category or phenotype that is influenced by racial stratification and historical oppression of racial minorities (Gillem, Cohn, & Throne, 2001; Helms & Cook, 1999). Thus, racial identity reflects an individual's awareness of and psychological responses to racial oppression formed through **racial socialization**—the process of learning about and ascribing meaning and value to socially constructed racial hierarchies and categories.

Multicultural psychologists have debated whether racial and ethnic identity should be conceptualized and studied as distinct or equivalent constructs. Much of the confusion in distinguishing racial from ethnic identity stems from continued uncertainty about the actual meanings of *culture*, *ethnicity*, and *race* (Trimble, 2007). Furthermore, racial and ethnic identities share a few general characteristics that make it difficult to tell them apart. Both racial and ethnic identity (1) involve a sense of belonging to a group, (2) arise from a process of learning about one's group, (3) vary in importance and salience across time and context, (4) are associated with specific cultural behaviors and values, attitudes toward one's own group, and responses to discrimination (Phinney & Ong, 2007), and (5) are social constructions.

Some researchers investigating children and youths propose using the term *ethnic-racial identity*, because both identities share similar components and developmental patterns, are measured in overlapping ways, and are experienced similarly in childhood through young adulthood (Umaña-Taylor et al., 2014). Still, other researchers believe that racial identity and ethnic identity are distinct but overlapping constructs that can be studied separately in meaningful ways (Lee & Ahn, 2013). Researching racial identity, for instance, can provide insights to individual and group experiences of racism and racial stratification, Black racial awareness and consciousness (Neville & Cross, 2017), and racial minority status and its effects on racial identity formation (Cokley, 2007).

Another example of this diversity in thinking about race and ethnicity is the use of labels to identify individuals from specific ancestry, heritage, ethnicity, or race. As mentioned in Chapter 1, we have made some specific choices about which labels to use to denote ethnicities or races, but as labels of convenience they are not necessarily the most precise ones, and some researchers or individuals may actually object to our using them. One case in point is the use of a "racial" label, White, to denote individuals who share a particular phenotype (lighter skin color) and whose ancestry can be traced to Europe, West Asia (also known as the Middle East), and Northern Africa (also known together as the MENA countries). To somehow differentiate these constructs of race and ethnicity, we usually use the label "White" to denote a particular phenotype or race and "European American" to denote the ethnicity or ancestry often associated with such phenotype. Since sometimes it is difficult to discern if researchers were studying Whites or European Americans, and because of common usage, you will see how we use *White* more frequently than *European American*. Hopefully this will not prove confusing.

Regardless of whether ethnicity and race are conceptualized as similar or distinct constructs, racial labels or categories should never be used to explain behavior or psychological functioning, because they lack conceptual meaning and often reflect researchers' racial beliefs and biases rather than study participants' actual behaviors and characteristics (Helms, Jernigan, & Mascher, 2005). In this case, racial group differences on any dependent variable (for example, psychological distress, educational achievement) should not simply be explained as "racial differences," because this doesn't really tell us anything. Are these racial differences due to economic disparity, parenting practices, racial socialization, school environments, acculturation, or other factors? Instead, researchers should focus their attention on identifying and studying *latent constructs*—underlying reasons for racial group differences—rather than basing conclusions on unspecified, or assumed, racial attributes of psychological functioning, which perpetuates racial stereotypes (Helms et al., 2005).

Ethnic Identity

Ethnic identity refers to an individual's subjective sense of membership and belonging to an ethnic group, which includes their attitudes, beliefs, knowledge, feelings, and behaviors associated with that particular ethnic group (Cokley, 2007; Ponterotto, Gretchen, Utsey, Stracuzzi, & Saya, 2003; Rotheram & Phinney, 1987). Ethnic identity is formed through **cultural socialization**, or the process of learning about and ascribing meaning and value to the cultural heritage and practices of socially constructed ethnic groupings or categories (Cokley, 2007; Helms, 2007).

Jean Phinney, leading investigator of ethnic identity, believes that ethnic identity is an aspect of social identity as studied in social psychology. Ethnic identity is thus part of your self-concept, which is based on your understanding of your membership in a particular social group (or groups) and the value and emotional significance attached to that membership (Phinney, 1990).

Components of Ethnic Identity Phinney and Ong (2007) have expanded their original conceptualization of ethnic identity by outlining the many different components of this construct, which we describe below (for a summary, see Box 5.1).

1. *Self-categorization and labeling* refers to the types of labels and categories that people use to describe their membership in an ethnic group. Although this is the most basic component of ethnic identification, it can be difficult to measure using traditional paper-and-pencil measures, because people describe or label their ethnic heritage or ancestry in multiple ways, depending on their personal beliefs, acculturation levels, and social context. For instance, a person of Chinese descent might self-identify as Chinese, Asian, Chinese American, Asian American, or Asian Pacific Islander depending on whom they are with and how others view them.
2. *Commitment and attachment* are defined as an individual's sense of belonging and emotional ties to their ethnic group. This is another important component to consider, because people might use a particular ethnic label to describe themselves, yet feel distant or detached from their ethnic

Box 5.1

Components of Ethnic Identity

Self-Categorization and Labeling: Ethnic labels and categories used to describe oneself
Commitment and Attachment: A sense of belonging and emotional ties to one's ethnic group
Exploration: Seeking information and experiences related to one's ethnic heritage by participating in cultural activities
Ethnic Behaviors: Behaviors and practices associated with one's ethnic group
Evaluation and In-Group Attitudes: Positive or negative attitudes about one's ethnic group, or level of comfort with one's ethnic group membership
Values and Beliefs: Endorsement and promotion of one's ethnic group's belief system and values
Importance and Salience: The extent to which ethnicity is an important part of one's life
Ethnic Identity and National Identity: The relationship between one's identification with a particular ethnic group and with a particular nation or country

Source: Phinney & Ong, 2007.

group. If you feel a strong attachment or an emotional bond to your ethnic group and are personally invested in your ethnic group membership, then you show a *commitment* to an ethnic identity. However, commitment to an ethnic identity does not necessarily mean that you have a stable and secure ethnic identity; commitment can be based on how your parents or role models identify themselves without understanding what your own ethnic identity actually means. Commitment to an ethnic identity without exploring or understanding its meaning is called *foreclosure*.

3. *Exploration* involves seeking information and experiences about your ethnic heritage through a wide range of activities that can include participating in cultural events and holidays, reading, and talking to family and ethnic community members to learn about your ethnic heritage or ancestry, practices, and traditions. Exploring your ethnic heritage, which can be a lifetime pursuit, is essential to forming a secure and positive ethnic identity, particularly during your adolescence, when identity formation is an important developmental task.
4. *Ethnic behaviors* include any behaviors and practices associated with your ethnic group, including eating your ethnic group's foods, speaking your ethnic group's language, practicing your group's religious rituals and traditions, and socializing with fellow ethnic group members.
5. *Evaluation and in-group attitudes* encompass positive or negative attitudes about your ethnic group—or how comfortable you feel about your ethnic group membership. This component can operate independently from the others. For example, ethnic minorities who participate in their ethnic traditions and self-identify with their ethnic group can still have negative attitudes about their group and favor the dominant group, particularly if they have experienced racial discrimination and have internalized negative stereotypes about their ethnicity.
6. *Values and beliefs* associated with your ethnic group are another important component of your ethnic identity. The extent to which you endorse and promote your ethnic group's beliefs and values can reflect your closeness to your group. Measuring and analyzing this component poses some challenges, because ethnic group members might not agree about the specific values and beliefs of their group, and measures of a particular group's values and beliefs may not be relevant to other groups, making comparative analyses impossible.
7. *Importance and salience* refer to the extent to which your ethnicity is an important part of your life. The importance and salience of ethnic identity varies across different individuals and across time; ethnic identity is more important and salient for ethnic minorities compared to dominant group members, due to experiences of racial stratification and discrimination. Also, individuals with strong ethnic identities tend to report greater ethnic identity salience on a daily basis than do those who have a weaker or low ethnic identity.
8. *Ethnic identity and national (or American) identity* are addressed by Phinney and Ong (2007), who believe that ethnic identity is more fully understood when it is examined vis-à-vis national identity, because both represent prominent, albeit independent, group identities in many people's lives. In the United States, for instance, being an American and being a member of one's ethnic group are equally important and meaningful to many ethnic minorities. The relationship between ethnic and national identity varies across individuals, showing either positive or negative correlations or no correlation at all. Contrary to popular stereotypes, having pride in one's ethnic group membership and maintaining a strong ethnic identity do not weaken or compromise one's national identity or sense of being an American.

When considering all of these ethnic identity components, it's clear that no single component fully captures your ethnic identity. Experiences and expressions of ethnic identity are wide ranging, especially when considering people's different experiences for each component. People who use the same ethnic label to describe themselves might have altogether different attitudes, views, and feelings about their ethnic group, leading to diverse experiences and psychosocial issues around their ethnicity. In short, evaluating ethnic identity solely on the basis of someone's ethnic label is akin to judging a book solely on the basis of its cover. To really understand the meaning and significance of ethnic identity, all of its cognitive, emotional, and behavioral components must be explored.

Class Identity

Class or socioeconomic status (SES) refers to one's financial and social standing. As noted in Chapter 2, different socioeconomic groups or classes have different access to society's wealth and resources, which produces distinct life experiences and even different attitudes, values, and behaviors unique to their class groupings. Compared to racial and ethnic identities, class identity is relatively more "invisible," because it's not always easily detected or noticed; yet it also influences psychological functioning in important ways (Thomas & Azmitia, 2014).

Socioeconomic status (SES) can be examined on multiple levels, including neighborhood SES (e.g., educational levels and median household incomes of neighborhood residents), family SES (e.g., family income and family assets and savings), and individual SES (individual education levels, occupations, and incomes) (Chen & Paterson, 2006). It is important to consider these different levels of SES because each may have its own relationship to psychological adjustment and distinct implications for interventions. For instance, if neighborhood rather than individual SES is a stronger predictor of health and well-being, then community-level interventions targeting neighborhood SES disparities might be more effective than individual-level interventions.

Researchers have also found that subjective self-perceptions of economic status is an equally or even more powerful predictor of health and adjustment because it involves self-perceived ability to meet daily needs and consequent stress from economic pressures. One study (Barrera, Caples, & Tein, 2001) identified a cross-culturally valid construct of subjective sense of economic hardship for African American, Mexican American (both English- and Spanish-speaking), and European American urban parents. The study assessed (1) the inability to afford specific necessities for living, (2) a general sense that financial obligations outstrip the family's ability to meet them, (3) behavioral attempts to reduce expenses or generate more income to meet obligations, and (4) hopelessness that the future will bring a brighter financial outlook. These findings show the great variability of areas that shape a person's subjective sense of economic status. Subjective impressions of socioeconomic standing can vary by race. For instance, African Americans are less likely to self-identify as middle or upper class compared to Whites with similar wealth, education, income, and occupations (Speer, 2016).

In summary, by considering both objective and subjective definitions of class identity, multicultural psychologists can more clearly understand how SES affects health and psychosocial functioning for diverse groups.

Models of Racial and Ethnic Identity Development and Formation

Racial Identity Development

Racial identity development models are informed by a social constructionist perspective of race, such that racial identity is viewed as a response to racial hierarchies and racial oppression in society (Helms, 1995). Research on racial identity development has mostly focused on the formation of Black racial identity, an area of scholarship that was sparked by the critical examination of race and race relations between African Americans and Whites during the U.S. civil rights movement.

One of the first and most widely referenced models of Black racial identity development was established by a pioneering researcher in this area of study, William E. Cross Jr., who bases his model of racial identity development on his "theory of nigresence" (1971, 1995). *Nigresence* is a French term for "turning Black." Cross uses this term to describe the process of accepting and affirming a Black identity in the context of American race relations (Vandiver, 2001). Cross's original model (1971) proposes that Black Americans progress through a series of five racial identity stages reflecting different attitudes, feelings, and responses toward racism in their lives. He labels these five sequential stages as preencounter, encounter, immersion-emersion, internalization, and internalization-commitment (see Box 5.2).

In the *preencounter* stage of Cross's model, individuals adopt a pro-White identity by favoring dominant group attitudes and behaviors while denigrating and deemphasizing their Black identity,

Box 5.2

Cross's Stages of Racial Identity Formation

1. **Preencounter:** Pro-White racial identity and devaluation of own Black racial identity
2. **Encounter:** Initial recognition of the importance of race and questioning of previously held racial beliefs
3. **Immersion-emersion:** Full immersion into Black culture; development of a pro-Black identity, which can lead to anger and hatred toward Whites; emergence from these negative emotions to a point of greater understanding and rational evaluation of race
4. **Internalization:** Acceptance of Black racial identity on an emotional and intellectual level; race and racial identity are no longer central concerns in daily life
5. **Internalization-commitment:** Fully internalized positive Black racial identity and commitment to promoting racial equality, including supporting civil rights of other disenfranchised racial groups

Sources: Cross 1971, 1995.

resulting in low self-esteem and internalized racism. Individuals in this first stage might say things like "I hate being Black" or "I can't stand my Black facial features." In the *encounter* stage, individuals begin to recognize the importance of race and racial issues in American society, begin to question previously held beliefs and attitudes about race, and reevaluate their racial identity following a personal event (e.g., witnessing or experiencing racism for the first time, meeting a racial peer who exhibits racial pride and defies negative racial stereotypes). The next stage, *immersion-emersion*, occurs when individuals fully *immerse* themselves in Black culture (e.g., adopting an African name, favoring clothing and music associated with Black culture, exclusively socializing with other Blacks, increasing involvement in Black organizations and activities) and develop a strong pro-Black identity that idealizes or romanticizes Black culture. Strong anti-White racial attitudes also arise during this third stage, which can generate feelings of anger or hatred toward the White dominant group and racial oppression. *Emersion* occurs when individuals gradually emerge from and relinquish their anti-White stance, achieve greater calm, and take a more rational approach to reevaluating the meaning of race and racial identity in their lives. This eventually leads to *internalization*, when individuals accept their Black identity on an emotional and intellectual level. In this stage, a stable Black identity is established, but race and racial identity are no longer central concerns in one's daily life. Instead, racial identity recedes to the background of one's daily activities and is viewed in the same light as other aspects of the self. Finally, in *internalization-commitment*, individuals fully internalize a positive and secure Black identity and commit themselves to promoting racial equality and civil rights through social activism.

Evaluating Cross's Model of Racial Identity Development Since Cross initially presented his Model of Racial Identity Development, he and other researchers have recommended a number of revisions and updates to this original model of nigresence. Namely, there is growing recognition that Cross's proposed stages are too rigid in how they portray racial identity development. Although people's responses to racism can change and grow, racial identity development may not necessarily occur in such a fixed and linear fashion; people of varied ages can show many different features of racial identity development simultaneously and might even regress to earlier stages depending on social and life circumstances (Parham, White, & Ajamu, 2000). For instance, a person might move away from an anti-White stance as seen during emersion but then revert back to this stance and reenter immersion when experiencing racism. Thus, the notion of a developmental hierarchy of racial attitudes, beliefs, and behaviors in Cross's model is problematic and not fully supported by current research (Chavez-Korell & Vandiver, 2012; Quintana, 2007).

Additionally, the proposed stages in Cross's original model are more complex and layered than originally assumed. Cross and his colleagues have acknowledged this point and in subsequent studies have identified additional racial identity dimensions or experiences in the preencounter, immersion-emersion, and internalization stages (Vandiver, 2001; Vandiver, Fhagen-Smith, Cokley, Cross, & Worrell, 2001). For instance, an expanded model of Cross's nigresence proposes three different preencounter identities, two separate immersion identities, and two internalization identities, underscoring that multiple attitudes, feelings, and responses to racism can occur in a single stage (Vandiver et al., 2001). Cross (1995) later found few differences between the internalization and internalization-commitment stages, and thus combined both of them under internalization.

Despite some of the conceptual limitations to Cross's model and the need for more comprehensive validation studies, research shows that personal events (for example, experiencing racism, new educational experiences, increased politically activism) can indeed spark racial identity exploration, heighten sensitivity to racial discrimination, and lead to more positive racial attitudes (Neville & Cross, 2017). Additionally, Cross's model has sparked much scholarship and debate on the nature of racial identity and how it unfolds in racially oppressive societies.

Cross's racial identity model also has influenced models of minority, ethnic, feminist, womanist, lesbian, and gay identity development and has led to the creation of widely used racial identity measures like the Cross Racial Identity Scale (CRIS), a measure of nigresence (Sussman, Beaujean, Worrell, & Watson, 2012; Worrell, Mendoza-Denton, Telesford, Simmons, & Martin, 2011), and the People of Color Racial Identity Attitudes Scale (PRIAS), which has been successfully used with Asian Americans and other racial minorities (Miller, Alvarez, Li, Chen, & Iwamoto, 2016). Cross and his colleagues fully acknowledge that identifying the many possible ideologies and responses to race is an ongoing journey, often leading to more, unexpected findings that require further investigation (Vandiver, 2001). This research has also motivated investigators to explore White racial identity (see Box 5.3 for a discussion on this issue).

Multicultural psychologists believe that studying all forms of racial identity, including White racial identity, is important for a number of reasons. First, by including Whites in studies of race, we fundamentally dismantle the dynamics of racial privilege. By acknowledging that racial identity is relevant to all groups, we create new and expanded opportunities to engage and involve all racial groups in questioning racial stratification. Second, including Whites is essential to understanding the full range

Box 5.3

Should White Racial Identity Be Studied?

Do White people have a racial identity, and, if so, what are the potential benefits of studying it? Compared to the vast body of research on racial minority identity, fewer studies examine White racial identity. This research disparity in many ways reflects the shortage of meaningful and in-depth racial analyses and dialogue in U.S. society. As noted in Chapters 1 and 2, people often find it difficult to engage one another on racial topics out of fear or concern that it will quickly become personalized, emotional, and confusing. Lack of attention to White racial identity, both in U.S. society and in psychological research, also is related to racial stratification and privilege, which frame racial issues as relevant only to minority persons or people of color. If you are a member of any dominant group, you really don't have to think about the identity dimension defining your dominant group status, whether it's your race, gender, class, sexual orientation, or any other dimension. That's the nature of privilege that comes with dominant group membership. For racial minorities, however, their racial features are socially constructed markers, imposed by the dominant group, that define their experiences of prejudice and discrimination. Matters of race are therefore front and center in many racial minorities' daily lives, even when they don't want them to be, which can lead to greater exploration, discussion, and awareness of their racial minority identities.

of racial identity experiences across diverse groups, thereby improving our scientific knowledge of this construct. In sum, studying White racial identity is simply good science with promising social benefits.

The nascent body of White racial identity research has revealed a number of interesting findings. Studies show that Whites' responses to race, racial attitudes, and identity formations are broad in scope and can be quite distinct from those of racial minorities. In a qualitative study of White middle-aged U.S. Midwesterners (Dottolo & Stewart, 2013), participants expressed confusion, responded negatively to, or failed to understand the relevance of questions about their White racial identity. When asked about White privilege, their responses included ambivalence, confusion, anxiety, and denial. For those acknowledging White privilege, they could not fully articulate or understand its meaning, instead simply describing it as freedom from having to know about racial oppression or contrasting it with minority disadvantage (e.g., not having to face racial prejudice), which in turn made their lives easier. Reports of White racial identity, however, can differ across various segments of the White population. In another qualitative study, White persons engaged in antiracist activism (Malott, Paone, Schaefle, Cates, & Haizlip, 2015) more clearly articulated the nature of White privilege and felt that their racial privilege made it difficult, if not impossible, to develop a positive White racial identity that was completely free from historically oppressive racial hierarchies. To resolve this dilemma, these participants believed it was more realistic to seek out living and work spaces that were less racially oppressive and to continue their work against White privilege.

Similar to research findings for racial minorities, White racial identity status and development affects a number of psychological outcomes. For instance, White racial identity characterized by positive and nonracist understandings of Whiteness and comfort and ease with interracial contact is associated with lower fear responses when thinking about challenging racial encounters (Siegel & Carter, 2014). Likewise, among White college students, "openness to diversity," or appreciation of cultural differences, strengthens White empathy toward racial minorities' experiences of racism in ways that extend beyond having pluralistic and egalitarian racial attitudes (Chao, Wei, Spanierman, Longo, & Northart, 2015). And among White psychology counselors, advanced White racial identity development, which includes improved racial understandings and awareness, confers greater multicultural counseling knowledge, skills, and abilities (Johnson & Jackson Williams, 2015).

Ethnic Identity Development

Ethnic identity development models propose that a stable and secure identity can be achieved through exploration, reflection, and experience. However, ethnic identity models primarily focus on individuals' ethnic group ties and membership rather than responses to racism and racial oppression. Also, ethnic-identity research mostly involves Latino and Asian Americans, while racial identity research mostly studies African Americans. Such differences may reflect researchers' biases about life experiences and conditions of different minority groups (Phinney & Ong, 2007) and the historical racialization of African Americans in research, which emphasizes their race over their ethnicity or culture (Landrine & Klonoff, 1996). Nonetheless, racial and ethnic identity development are relevant to all minority groups because of shared experiences of racial oppression, and both constructs can affect their psychosocial adjustment in important ways.

Jean Phinney (1992) first developed a stage model of ethnic identity formation based on ego identity development theory, key ideas from Cross's racial identity development model, and her own research with adolescents. In Phinney's model, ethnic identity formation begins with an initial stage of indifference, confusion, or minimal awareness around ethnicity, followed by later stages involving more complex thinking about ethnic group membership and greater appreciation for multiculturalism. Some studies support this developmental progression and report that it can coincide with age and maturation (e.g., Ponterotto & Park-Taylor, 2007; Quintana, 2007). However, other studies show that ethnic identity development does not follow fixed stages, instead fluctuating, sometimes on a daily basis, depending on changing situational contexts and individual factors. In a study of Chinese American adolescents, the extent to which they reported feeling "Chinese"—an experience called *ethnic salience*—changed depending on what they were doing, whom they were with, and what types

Box 5.4

Self-Report Items Assessing Exploration and Commitment on the Multigroup Ethnic Identity Measure–Revised (MEIM–R)

Exploration

- I have spent time trying to find out more about my ethnic group, such as its history, traditions, and customs.
- I have often done things that will help me understand my ethnic background better.
- I have often talked to other people in order to learn more about my ethnic group.

Commitment

- I have a strong sense of belonging to my own ethnic group.
- I understand pretty well what my ethnic group membership means to me.
- I feel a strong attachment toward my own ethnic group.

Source: Phinney & Ong, 2007.

of situations they encountered. As might be expected, they were more likely to feel Chinese when they were participating in ethnic behaviors (e.g., speaking Chinese, eating Chinese food) and were in the presence of other Chinese people, including their family members (Yip & Fuligni, 2002).

Ethnic identity development can also vary by gender. African American girls, for instance, show faster ethnic identity formation than African American boys, possibly because they participate in cultural and ethnic customs more than boys and act as key carriers of African American cultural values and traditions (Phinney & Rosenthal, 1992).

In light of the stage model's limitations, Phinney and Ong (2007) offered a revised *process* model that emphasizes the two previously described ethnic identity components of exploration and commitment, which they believe lies at the core of ethnic identity development. Empirical evidence suggests that these two processes are highly related to each other, supporting the theory that exploration is unlikely without a certain degree of commitment and that stronger commitment results from heightened exploration (Phinney & Ong, 2007). The Multigroup Ethnic Identity Measure–Revised (MEIM–R; Phinney & Ong, 2007) can be used to evaluate both processes (see Box 5.4 for examples of items used in the scale) and identify four different ethnic identity statuses (see Table 5.1).

TABLE 5.1 Four Possible Ethnic Identity Statuses Based on Ethnic Identity Exploration and Commitment

		Exploration of ethnic identity	
		Yes	**No**
Commitment to an ethnic identity	**Yes**	Achieved ethnic identity	Identity foreclosure
	No	Moratorium	Identity diffusion

As shown in Table 5.1, Phinney and Ong (2007) identify four possible ethnic identity statuses based on an individual's exploration of ethnic identity and commitment to an ethnic identity. Each of these four statuses is explained in greater detail in the following:

- **Identity diffusion** is characterized by the absence of ethnic identity exploration and commitment. Individuals show little (if any) interest in ethnic and racial issues, have no commitment to any particular ethnic group, and have not explored the meaning of their ethnicity; in short, ethnicity is simply a nonissue with this identity status. For instance, in a study of adolescents (Phinney, 1989, 1992), an African American female exhibiting identity diffusion asked, "Why do I need to learn about who was the first Black woman to do this or that? I'm just not too interested." In the same study, a Mexican American adolescent male likewise stated, "My parents tell me . . . about where they lived, but what do I care? I've never lived there." Individuals who experience identity diffusion may not have faced or been exposed to ethnic issues in their life (e.g., discrimination and prejudice based on ethnic group membership) and thus have few or no opinions or thoughts on this subject. In such cases, there is minimal acknowledgment and awareness of ethnic group differences and little understanding and knowledge of one's own ethnicity and of other ethnic groups. If asked about their ethnicity, people in diffusion might confound nationality with ethnicity by self-identifying as "American" without much thought or consideration about what this actually means. For instance, European Americans who grew up in predominantly European American neighborhoods and schools, may have never faced ethnic discrimination or considered the meaning of their ethnicity, and thus pay little attention to racial issues, may indeed experience diffusion.
- **Identity foreclosure** involves commitment to an ethnic identity without exploration. Unlike diffusion, individuals who exhibit foreclosure claim an ethnic identity, usually based on their parents' and family's ethnic identification, without exploring its meaning. This was expressed by a Mexican American adolescent male who said, "I don't go looking for my culture. I just go by what my parents say and do, and what they tell me to do, the way they are" (Phinney, 1992). In this case, the ethnic label, cultural values, and attitudes of the parents and family are adopted without independently forming an ethnic identity through questioning and exploration. This might include readily accepting both positive and negative views of one's ethnic group without question. Ethnic minorities might even show a preference to belonging to the dominant group. An Asian American adolescent male exhibiting foreclosure explained, "If I could have chosen, I would choose to be American White, because it's America and I would then be in my country" (Phinney, 1992). In some cases, ethnic minorities showing foreclosure also prefer dominant group physical characteristics and traits and may alter their physical appearance accordingly. For instance, some Asian Americans opt for cosmetic surgery to modify the epicanthal fold or crease on their eyelids in an attempt to look White. Also, in the African American community, individuals might artificially lighten their skin tone. Some ethnic minorities also might internalize negative attitudes and stereotypes about their own ethnic group. This can be seen in ethnic minorities who criticize or put down their own ethnic group or only date European Americans believing that ethnic minorities are less attractive.
- **Moratorium** involves ethnic identity exploration without commitment. Individuals begin showing an interest in their ethnic background by asking questions and learning about their ethnic practices and traditions. Also, individuals may begin to read about their ethnic group, participate in their group's cultural activities or organizations, and gain a heightened political consciousness. A Mexican American female teen discussed this process by saying, "I want to know what to do and how our culture is different from others. Going to festivals and cultural events helps me to learn more about my own culture and about myself" (Phinney, 1992). Active exploration of one's ethnic identity can be sparked by a shocking personal or social event that challenges previously held racial beliefs and attitudes. For ethnic minorities, this might entail experiencing racism for the first time, which challenges their indifferent racial attitudes and beliefs. Likewise, ethnic minorities who might have once preferred dominant group membership will begin to realize that

they will never be fully accepted or treated equally by dominant group members. They may thus gain a greater awareness of the negative effects of racism on their personal lives and realize that dominant group cultural values and beliefs may not be beneficial or relevant to them. Ethnic minorities also might acquire new information that forces them to reevaluate their previously held negative views and stereotypes about their own ethnic group. For instance, Asian Americans who initially believe that Asians are nonassertive might encounter a civic leader in their ethnic community who shatters this stereotype. Likewise, a Latino who feels ashamed of his cultural upbringing may meet another Latino who is proud of his cultural heritage. These types of new information or shocking experiences can raise the fundamental question about the meaning of one's ethnicity for the first time, leading to a crisis of identity, as noted by one Japanese American male adolescent: "There are a lot of non-Japanese people around me, and it gets pretty confusing to try and decide who I am" (Phinney, 1992). An identity crisis in moratorium sparks a personal search for an ethnic identity that incorporates a new and growing appreciation of one's ethnic group and allows for unique self-expression of one's ethnic group membership.

- **Achieved ethnic identity** is found when both ethnic identity exploration and commitment occur. Individuals finally develop an inner sense of security with their ethnic identity and can appreciate the unique features of their own culture and of other cultures. Ethnic diversity and multiculturalism are valued. Identity conflicts and problems are resolved, and negative images and stereotypes of their ethnic group are replaced with feelings of positive self-worth and self-acceptance. There is a greater sense of control and flexibility in defining oneself; rigid and narrow ethnic categorizations are eschewed in favor of an ethnic identity that is congruent with their self-concept and allows them to feel comfortable in their own skin. A Mexican American female teen explained, "People put me down because I'm a Mexican, but I don't care anymore. I can accept myself more." An African American girl expressed similar sentiments:

> I used to want to be White, because I wanted long, flowing hair. And I wanted to be real light. I used to think being light was prettier, but now I think there are pretty dark-skinned girls and pretty light-skinned girls. I don't want to be White now. I'm happy being Black. (Phinney, 1992)

In support of this process model, various studies have confirmed these four different ethnic identity statuses for diverse adolescent groups (Yip, 2014) and have shown that greater exploration and understanding of ethnic group membership can follow personal experiences of prejudice (Syed & Azmitia, 2010). Ethnic identity formation, however, may not always develop in predictable and orderly ways (e.g., with exploration preceding commitment) but may instead show tremendous variation (Huang & Stormshak, 2011; Meeus, 2011) that is more easily detected when examining individuals rather than groups (Kiang, Witkow, Baldelomar, & Fuligni, 2010).

Factors Shaping Ethnic Identity Development A burgeoning body of research shows that ethnic identity development is shaped by a dynamic interplay of individual, social, and environmental factors. In particular, studies have highlighted developmental, family, social, and acculturation factors that potentially elicit different experiences, expressions, and views of one's ethnicity. In the following pages, we explain the role played by each of these factors.

Developmental Factors. Studies have shown that developmental stage, abilities, and tasks affect ethnic and racial identity development (Umaña-Taylor et al., 2014). According to Eriksonian theory, the primary developmental task during adolescence is to form a secure and stable identity through exploration and questioning of one's group affiliations and personal beliefs, values, and goals (Erikson, 1950). Research shows that ethnic and racial identity formation can follow this developmental trajectory with heightened exploration and questioning of ethnicity and ethnic group membership occurring in adolescence. During this developmental stage, adolescents begin to develop an ethnic group consciousness (Quintana, 1998) and begin to think about their group identity in more abstract ways (e.g., ethnic heritage, birthplace, ethnic beliefs, and values) that are perceived as stable across different contexts and part of a unified sense of self (e.g., a bicultural Mexican American identity) (Phinney, 1993). This normative process of actively searching for an ethnic or racial identity during adolescence does not necessarily elicit an identity crisis involving heightened levels of stress and conflict as once assumed. Instead, exploration and questioning of one's ethnicity and race may be much more subtle and gradual, beginning in early adolescence and lasting until late adolescence and possibly early adulthood (Phinney, 1992; Quintana, 2007).

Family Factors. In many respects, the family is where an individual's ethnic identity development first begins. Parents teach their children about the cultural beliefs, values, traditions, and expectations of their ethnic group and in that process convey what it means to be a member of the ethnic group. Parents can also impart positive or negative views and attitudes about their own ethnic group and about others, which can further influence their offspring's ethnic self-identification. Research shows that Mexican-origin mothers who endorse traditional *familismo* values and have actively explored their own ethnic identity are especially likely to be invested in teaching their children about their ethnic group (Derlan, Umaña-Taylor, Updegraff, & Jahromi, 2016). Also, studies have shown that children are more likely to develop strong ethnic identities if their parents possess strong ethnic identities themselves (Farver, Narang, & Bhadha, 2002) and if they come from families that are highly invested in positive ethnic and cultural socialization (Douglass & Umaña-Taylor, 2015; Gonzales-Backen & Umaña-Taylor, 2011), including imparting strong cultural knowledge and pride (Gartner, Kiang, & Supple, 2014).

Social Factors. Minority status and community characteristics are key social factors that influence ethnic identity development. For minority youths, ethnicity is often the most important part of their identity due to the presence of racial stratification (Phinney, 1993). Minority status can thus heighten "ethnic self-awareness," or the degree to which individuals are consciously aware of their ethnicity. Asian American college students in Boston, for instance, showed greater ethnic self-awareness than did their European American counterparts when they were perceived to be the ethnic minority in a social situation (Kim-Ju & Liem, 2003). Interestingly, the Asian American students in this study also showed heightened ethnic self-awareness when they were the ethnic majority in a social situation, largely because they were unaccustomed to this type of social setting. Heightened ethnic self-awareness can enhance ethnic identity development even when it's induced by stereotyping and discrimination. For example, Asian American adolescents exposed to the model minority stereotype exhibit positive ethnic identity development over time (Thompson, Kiang, & Witkow, 2016), and ethnic-racial microaggressions are positively correlated with Native American young adults' ethnic identification (Jones & Galliher, 2015). These findings support the idea that key personal events, including experiences of discrimination, prejudice, and stereotyping, can trigger ethnic exploration, increase ethnic awareness, and potentially strengthen ethnic identification as proposed in Phinney and Ong's (2007) process model. Still, there is an important caveat: minority status can also contribute to internalized racism, which can undermine a secure and stable ethnic identity (Hipolito-Delgado, 2016).

Community characteristics also play an important role in ethnic identity development. Ethnic density of one's neighborhood, ethnic composition of family and social networks, and daily settings (e.g., schools and neighborhoods) potentially have more effects on ethnic identity formation and psychological adaptation than national immigration and cultural diversity policies (Phinney, Horenczyk, Liebkind, & Vedder, 2001). African American adolescents, for example, report more positive feelings and sense of belonging to their ethnic group when they have a greater percentage of African American friends (Derlan & Umaña-Taylor, 2015). Also, Asian U.S. high school students with strong ethnic identification feel more positively about their ethnicity if they are surrounded by other Asians in White-majority schools or schools with no clear ethnic majority (Yip, Douglass, & Shelton, 2013).

Acculturation Factors. Acculturation effects on ethnic identity development have been reported for Asian American and Latino groups. Among Asian American and Latino college students, those who are recent immigrants from limited-English-proficient families and ethnically similar immigrant neighborhoods show the strongest ethnic identities throughout college compared to their more acculturated peers (Sears, Fu, Henry, & Bui, 2003). Studies also report an overall weakening of ethnic identity with acculturation, although this seems to be an oversimplification; different ethnic identity components may be stable and resilient to cultural shifts while others are more susceptible to change. For instance, cultural values, positive attitudes and feelings about one's ethnic group, and ethnic loyalty are more resilient to acculturation than knowledge and awareness of one's cultural heritage (Phinney & Rosenthal, 1992; Sabogal et al., 1987). Also, studies have found that ethnic identity loss during acculturation can be prevented with enculturation interventions that promote active learning and retention of cultural practices and rituals (Schweigman, Soto, Wright, & Unger, 2011).

Different acculturation modes also have variable effects on ethnic identity development. In one study, South Asian Indian adolescents exhibiting integration reported stronger ethnic identities, greater ethnic identity exploration and understanding, and more appreciation of other ethnic groups compared to those exhibiting marginalization or separation (Farver et al., 2002). Likewise, biculturalism and integration are linked to significant ethnic identity exploration for Mexican and Mexican American adolescents (Matsunaga, Hecht, Elek, & Ndiaye, 2010).

Biracial/Multiracial Identity Development

> I have been queried about my racial identity (or, erroneously, my "nationality"). People, mostly White, have wondered why I do not choose to "pass" as White. Other people, mostly Black, have demanded to know why I say I am biracial instead of "just admitting" I am Black. I have been scrutinized and found to be "not Black enough" by some, whereas others have deemed me "too into racial issues." People have given me advice on how I should talk, think, act, and feel about myself racially. Repeatedly, people have tried to define my existence for me. . . . What this has done is forced me to examine myself. (Williams, 1999, p. 34)

This passage illustrates the distinct ethnic identity issues and challenges often faced by multiracial persons in their daily lives. These types of negative racial experiences contribute to an **otherness status**, which is a form of social marginalization and social isolation on the basis of race, including societal pressures to "fit" into specific racial categorizations (Root, 1990). Otherness status is literally seen on demographic forms and questionnaires that require multiracial people to check the "other" box if they do not fit into specified racial categories. The meaning of this term, *other*, not only is vague and confusing but also overlooks the fact that multiracial individuals may identify themselves in multiple ways.

In a comprehensive review of multiracial identity research, Shih and Sanchez (2005) summarized key psychosocial issues complicating multiracial identity development as follows:

- *Conflict between private and public definitions*: Multiracial individuals often feel conflicted when their private definitions of their selves do not match how the public or society defines them. In these situations, feelings of frustration and marginalization arise from social pressures to meet public expectations and views of their racial heritage.
- *Justifying identity choices*: Multiracial persons typically have to justify how they define themselves, particularly when faced with ongoing questions about and challenges to their membership in different ethnic groups. This can lead to self-doubt and constant introspection and questioning about their identity selection.
- *Forced-choice dilemmas*: Multiracial individuals face social pressures to define themselves in one particular way, whether it's a single racial category, a mixed-race identity, or some other identity that does not allow for more fluid and integrated experiences of one's multiracial self. Feelings of

distress, guilt, and fragmentation can occur in these situations when multiracial individuals feel like they have to reject or deny a part of their racial heritage to fit into these limiting categories.

- *Lack of role models*: Multiracial individuals face the added challenge of finding positive multiracial role models in the community who can either help steward them through their identity search or show them possible ways to lead healthy and racially integrated lives. Multiracial public figures who might serve as role models are often rendered invisible in the media when they are cast as monoracial. For example, Tiger Woods, one of the most highly regarded golfers of his time, is often exclusively portrayed as an African American athlete even though his mother is Asian American.
- *Conflicting messages*: Multiracial youths are often exposed to conflicting racial messages from their families and communities. In their interracial families, parents might directly or indirectly communicate to their multiracial children that race is not necessarily an issue and that different racial groups live in peaceful coexistence. Parents might also communicate that people unconditionally accept their multiracial heritage. However, when multiracial children enter the community they are confronted with racial discrimination, prejudice, and interracial conflict, leaving them feeling confused, distressed, and unable to integrate their multiple racial identities.
- *Double rejection*: Multiracial persons often face rejection by the dominant group and other ethnic minority groups, particularly if people do not associate their physical features with a particular racial group. This experience of double rejection results in isolation, psychological stress, and the lack of a stable and supportive reference group for their identity search.

Some researchers believe that these psychosocial issues associated with multiracial identity require a new and more complex understanding of identity development than what is proposed in monoracial or monoethnic identity models (Gaither, 2015; Marks, Patton, & Coll, 2011). One study of African and White biracial teens, for instance, showed that their search for an identity is much more layered and complex than those of monoracial teens (Gillem et al., 2001). These biracial African and White teens faced challenges in integrating multiple racial identities, negotiating conflicted dominant group and ethnic minority group relations, and gaining both groups' acceptance. Although this proved stressful, some of these biracial teens developed a more sensitive and balanced understanding of dominant and minority groups, particularly if they had positive and loving relationships with both monoracial parents. Other studies have likewise shown that biracial adolescents experience their ethnicity and race in distinct ways. In a study of ethnically diverse high school students from the Southwestern United States (self-identified Black, White, Asian, Latino, Asian/White, Black/White, Latino/White, Asian/Black, Asian/Latino, and Black/Latino students), biracial adolescents reported stronger ethnic identities than their monoracial White peers but weaker ethnic identities than their monoracial minority peers (Bracey, Bamaca, & Umaña-Taylor, 2004). These findings suggest that biracial teens are more likely than monoracial White teens to explore their ethnic identities because they must cope with more complicated and pressing racial identity issues. However, these issues can lead to confusion and weaker ethnic identity commitment.

Finally, research shows that biracial identity choice is influenced by parental ethnic identification and socioeconomic class. In this case, part-White biracial persons' ethnic identities are closely aligned with their parents', particularly if the children feel close to them (Stepney, Sanchez, & Handy, 2015), and middle-class biracials are more likely than working-class biracials to claim a biracial identity, possibly due to a class-related desire to emphasize their individuality and uniqueness (Townsend, Fryberg, Wilkins, & Markus, 2012).

Current monoracial identity development models do not fully capture these unique multiracial experiences. Poston (1990) summarized the specific shortcomings of monoracial identity models:

1. *Monoracial identity models do not allow for the integration of more than one group identity.* The process of integrating and negotiating different, and at times conflicting, group identities, as in the case of negotiating minority and dominant group identities, is often entirely overlooked by monoracial identity models.

2. *Monoracial identity models imply that multiracial individuals must reject one or more of their ethnic affiliations.* Cross's model, for instance, proposes that Blacks who enter the immersion stage may develop anti-White and pro-Black attitudes. This poses problems for biracial Black and White persons, however, because they cannot necessarily reject a part of themselves, particularly if they have positive relationships with a dominant group parent or family member.
3. *Monoracial identity models assume acceptance from the minority group of origin.* In Cross's immersion-emersion and internalization stages, acceptance by the Black community is assumed and in many respects required for the formation of a stable and secure Black racial identity. However, biracial Black and White individuals may face discrimination and rejection in the Black community, especially if they have physical features perceived to be more similar to Whites'.

Biracial identity development models have been developed to address these limitations to monoracial identity frameworks. Most of these models propose that healthy identity development involves first moving from a diffuse or unspecified racial identity to a monoracial identity imposed by society, typically eliciting feelings of ambivalence and struggle, until a distinct biracial identity is individually defined and established (Gillem et al., 2001).

Biracial Identity Resolution Strategies One of the first models of biracial identity development was proposed by Maria Root, a pioneering researcher of biracial and multiracial identity experiences. Based on her clinical work with biracial adolescents, Root (1990) believed that biracial identity conflicts and issues, particularly pressures to compartmentalize different parts of one's racial heritage, are typically resolved in one of four different ways:

1. *Acceptance of the identity society assigns.* This resolution typically occurs in racially oppressive societies where biracial individuals do not have the freedom to choose their racial identity. In these societies, an ethnic minority group identity is typically imposed on a biracial individual if he or she has physical features that are associated with the minority group. This can be a positive resolution if the biracial individual feels a sense of belonging to the racial group to which he or she is assigned. For instance, a biracial Black and White individual who is assigned a Black identity by society may feel supported and fully accepted by his or her African American extended family, which can then become a stable and secure reference group.
2. *Identification with both racial groups.* Individuals who follow this resolution are likely to self-identify in a biracial manner by describing their racial background as "part African American, part White" or "mixed," for example. This can be a positive resolution strategy if their personality remains consistent across groups and they are fully accepted by both groups. Biracial individuals who exhibit this resolution tend to view their mixed race heritage as a positive marker of their uniqueness and individuality. Root believed that this may be the most idealistic identity resolution and may only occur in those regions of the country where there is greater tolerance and high numbers of mixed marriages and biracial children.
3. *Identification with a single racial group.* Although this resolution looks like the first resolution, individuals who exhibit this resolution actively select their racial identity even if it is different from the identity that family members and society assign or possibly conflicts with their physical features. This resolution can be a positive experience if biracial individuals are not marginalized by their selected groups and they do not suppress their other race. Difficulties arise when their chosen group membership is contested or questioned by their reference group, requiring them to develop coping strategies to deal with this situation.
4. *Identification as a new racial group.* Feeling kinship with other biracial individuals more than with any other racial group is a main feature of this resolution strategy. Shared social-marginalization experiences may encourage biracial individuals to bond with one another and form a new racial group. Root (1990) believes that this resolution strategy is seen in the hapa haole community (half White, half Asian) in Hawai'i. Biracial individuals in this community often move fluidly between different racial groups without feeling constrained to any particular racial label. They

view themselves as being apart from specific racial groups yet do not feel marginalized, because they have a new and stable biracial reference group.

Stage Models of Biracial Identity Development More recent stage models of biracial identity development have expanded on some of Maria Root's key ideas. For example, Collins (2000) believes that biracial identity development occurs along a progressive, stage-like sequence as depicted in monoethnic and monoracial identity development stage models. Like others studying the biracial experience, however, Collins emphasizes that biracial persons face different identity questions and issues. Based on interviews with biracial individuals of Japanese and European American descent, he outlines four different phases of development, which he labels phase I, questioning and confusion; phase II, refusal and suppression; phase III, infusion and exploration; and phase IV, resolution and acceptance. These phases are described in greater detailed in the following.

- *Phase I, questioning and confusion*: This phase is characterized by constant feelings of differentness, confusion, and discomfort as one struggles to formulate a racial identity without a clear reference group. Ongoing questions by others about one's racial background (e.g., constantly facing the question "What are you?") coupled with persistent discrimination and stigmatization contribute to feelings of alienation and isolation during this phase.
- *Phase II, refusal and suppression*: After facing constant questions and challenges around their racial background, individuals attempt to define themselves in this phase. This is a crucial phase of development because individuals strive to identify with a clear reference group or search for multiple reference groups. Individuals may choose one group over the other during this time and deny or suppress the identity that they have rejected. A positive identity can begin to develop if biracial individuals have the opportunity to socialize and interact with people from culturally diverse backgrounds, other biracial people, and role models in the community who affirm individual difference. Biracial individuals thus begin to formulate an identity based on their social interactions outside of the family during this stage.
- *Phase III, infusion and exploration*: This stage is marked by confusion and guilt due to choosing one identity over the other, leading the biracial individual to ask, "What about my other half?" They may feel uncomfortable with their selected identity and may attempt to integrate their other identity. During this time, overidentification with their rejected identity can occur. For instance, biracial Japanese and White individuals who have identified solely as a European American while rejecting or suppressing their Japanese heritage in phase II may feel guilty about this and self-identify exclusively as a Japanese American in this phase.
- *Phase IV, resolution and acceptance*: Biracial individuals enter this phase when they fully accept their biracial identity, marked by such statements as "I am who I am." An integrated sense of self is established by treating both of their racial heritages as equally important aspects of the self. This experience of recognizing and valuing each side of their identity is akin to blending individual colors from a color palette—when two distinct racial identities are fused together, forming an altogether new biracial identity that is appreciated and affirmed for its uniqueness.

Evaluating Models of Biracial Identity Development The identity development models offered by Root and Collins highlight a number of important distinctions between biracial and monoracial identity development. In sum, biracial individuals face added questions and challenges to their identity early in their lives that can generate internal conflict, confusion, and even guilt over their racial group membership. A stable and secure biracial identity can be achieved, however, if they can successfully navigate social and family pressures to define themselves in certain ways and learn to develop a positive identity that matches how they feel and experience their mixed race heritage. Supportive family environments, multicultural communities, and biracial or multiracial social networks that affirm and value multiracial identity can facilitate this process and help diffuse otherness status.

As with monoracial and monoethnic identity development models, more research is needed to support the basic principles and features of biracial identity models. The notion that identity development follows distinct sequential stages or phases, as proposed in Collins's model, requires added investigation or new models altogether. In this latter regard, researchers have proposed an alternative *ecological model* to better understand the dynamic and multifaceted nature of biracial and multiracial identity development. According to this model, mixed race persons' identity choices and experiences can fluctuate and vary widely depending on their daily living environments or ecologies (Gonzales-Backen, 2013). Ethnic composition, cultural-socialization experiences, and racial messages can vary across their immediate family, school, and peer settings, leading to multiple identity formations and adjustment patterns. In support of this ecological model, a study of Asian-White biracial adults showed that different cultural-socialization experiences generate different identity profiles (Chong & Kuo, 2015). Study participants who identified equally as Asian-White reported more Asian cultural-socialization experiences than those favoring one identity. Also, mainly Asian-identified participants reported less White cultural socialization than those who were mostly White or Asian-White identified.

More research also is needed to understand identity development for people with three or more ethnicities or races. People with more than two racial backgrounds (e.g., a person with African American, Asian American, and Latino heritages) may have qualitatively different identity experiences than biracial and monoracial people. The fundamental questions faced by biracial individuals—"Who am I?" "Which racial groups do I belong to?" "How do I integrate my different races?"—can assume added complexity when negotiating more racial reference groups and race relations.

Addressing these and other biracial and multiracial research issues comes with a number of investigative challenges (Root, 1998). Finding and recruiting a diverse pool of biracial and multiracial study participants is particularly challenging. Typically, researchers look for specific racial or ethnic groups based on a person's last name, but this method is unfeasible or nearly impossible to follow, because mixed race heritage cannot be detected in this way. Using convenience samples (e.g., targeting biracial student organizations on college campuses or biracial social organizations for study recruitment) may bias or skew research results. Although these research issues are difficult to address, they warrant special consideration because biracial and multiracial persons are the fastest-growing racial population in the United States, as discussed in Chapter 1.

Relationship of Racial, Ethnic, and Class Identities to Psychosocial Adjustment

Different dimensions of the self affect psychological functioning and overall mental health in variable and important ways. This section highlights key research findings on the relationship of ethnic, racial, biracial and multiracial, and class identities to multiple health and psychological outcomes.

Racial Identity and Adjustment

Not surprisingly, an individual's racial identity affects their psychological adjustment at different levels and in a number of possible ways. In the following, we summarize some of the important research findings in this area.

Self-Esteem African Americans with strong racial group identification and positive racial group evaluations report higher self-esteem and greater mastery or sense of control over their life than do those with weaker and negative ethnic identification (Hughes, Kiecolt, Keith, & Demo, 2015). Racial identity is linked with self-esteem through racial identity schemas. **Racial identity schemas** are a set of race-related beliefs and emotional responses that individuals are socialized into during their development, influencing how race-related information is interpreted and internalized as part of an overall individual identity (Alvarez & Helms, 2001). Different racial identity schemas are tied to different stages of racial identity development and self-esteem levels. For example, among Asian Americans, more sophisticated racial identity schemas (i.e., immersion-emersion and integrative awareness) were positively related to collective self-esteem (the quality of a person's evaluation of himself or herself as a member of a racial group), while less sophisticated schemas (i.e., conformity) were negatively associated with collective self-esteem. Some studies suggest that minority status and racial stigmatization may not uniformly lead to poor self-esteem, but this might be due to other factors (for example, individualism, willingness to talk about oneself) affecting responses to self-esteem questionnaires (Quintana, 2007).

Psychological Adjustment and Mental Health Advanced racial identity status also provides mental health benefits (Forsyth & Carter, 2012). Asian Pacific Islander American college students who have positive feelings about their racial group, otherwise known as **high private regard**, report less anxiety than do those with low private regard (French, Tran, & Chávez, 2013). For African American adults, depression, anger, confusion, and psychological tension are positively correlated with preencounter racial attitudes (for example, devaluing one's Blackness) and are negatively related to internalization-commitment attitudes (for example, a positive commitment to other Blacks) (Carter & Reynolds, 2011).

Neighborhood characteristics appear to moderate the effects of racial identity status on depression. In a study of African American emerging adults, high private regard was associated with less depressive symptoms, especially if they lived in neighborhoods with few African Americans, which potentially increased positive racial identity awareness (Hurd, Sellers, Cogburn, Butler-Barnes, & Zimmerman, 2013). Also, African American children are at lower risk for depression and are protected against the negative effects of criminal victimization when they live in neighborhoods characterized by strong racial identification and racial pride (Simons et al., 2002). The cultural values and traditions in these neighborhoods can foster meaning, belonging, and optimism among African American youths in the face of stressful and violent living conditions.

Risk for Drug Use Risk for drug use can be exacerbated by actual or imagined instances of racial discrimination. For example, African American young adults who report low racial identification and socialize mostly with White peers are especially likely to use alcohol (Stock et al., 2013). Furthermore, in a longitudinal study of African American adolescents (Fuller-Rowell et al., 2012), reports of discrimination were related to higher substance use throughout their high school attendance. Interestingly, such discrimination effects on substance use were less likely if these adolescents believed that others perceived their racial group negatively (known as *low public regard*), suggesting that realistic racial perceptions guard against negative effects from discrimination. In another study of African American young adults, imagining personal experience of racial discrimination increased willingness to use drugs, but only if the young adults reported low racial identification (Stock, Gibbons, Walsh, & Gerrard, 2011).

Physical Health Socially constructed racial categories and identities are intimately tied to health outcomes. For example, one study found that African Americans and Latinos were less likely than Whites to receive smoking cessation advice from their health care providers (Houston, Scarinci, Person, & Greene, 2005). Reasons for these racial differences were not explored, but they might stem from racial discrimination and racial stereotyping in the health care system and, for Latinos, language barriers. In that study, racial identity also interacted with other identity dimensions in affecting health care advice. For example, smoking counseling differences found between African Americans and Whites were greater among lower income persons without health insurance.

Racial discrimination can adversely affect other physical health outcomes, but racial identity and related racial attitudes mediate and moderate this relationship. African American youths who face significant racial discrimination have higher cytokine levels and correspondingly low-grade bodily inflammation, increasing their risk at a later age for chronic diseases often associated with aging, such as cardiovascular heart disease (Brody, Yu, Miller, & Chen, 2015). However, a positive racial identity mitigates these negative health effects from discrimination. Similarly, racial discrimination is negatively related to diastolic blood pressure for African Americans who accurately detect low public regard of their racial group and view the African American experience as being unique (Neblett & Carter, 2012). Finally, African American men who internalize negative racial group attitudes and underreport or deny racial discrimination are particularly at risk for poor cardiovascular-health outcomes (Chae, Lincoln, Adler, & Syme, 2010).

Perceptions of Racism Stages of racial identity development affect perceptions of racism. Asian Americans who showed features of immersion (idealizing their own racial group and devaluing Whites) were more likely to report racism and race-related stress, most likely due to their increased sensitivity to and awareness of racial issues (Concepcion, Kohatsu, & Yeh, 2013). Among a national sample of African Americans, those least likely to report experiencing or witnessing racism against their family tended to exhibit Cross's preencounter stage of racial identity development. Again, this stage is characterized by weak Black racial identification, preference for dominant group culture and assimilation, and denial of prejudice against Blacks (Hyers, 2001). Although those exhibiting preencounter features reported high life satisfaction, they possessed low self-esteem, possibly because they attributed their experiences of racism to their own actions rather than to racial stratification.

Ethnic Identity and Adjustment

As detailed in the following, ethnic identity has been found to affect various areas of an individual's psychological adjustment, often in manners similar to the effects of racial identity.

Self-Esteem Phinney (1992) finds that a strong ethnic identity (self-identifying with one's ethnic group, participating in one's ethnic group traditions and cultural practices, feeling a sense of belonging and membership to one's ethnic group, and having a secure sense of one's ethnicity) was positively related to self-esteem for American high schoolers of Asian, African, Hispanic, European Americans, and multiethnic descent. By college age, however, this relationship only held true for ethnic minorities indicating that ethnicity was more likely to remain an important part of their lives compared to their White peers (Phinney, 1992).

Studies also show that ethnic identity effects on self-esteem vary across ethnic minority groups due to differences in developmental abilities and racial stratification experiences (Negy, Shreve, Jensen, & Uddin, 2003), ethnic affirmation levels (Romero, Edwards, Fryberg, & Orduña, 2014), the ethnic identity component being examined (Gonzales-Backen, Bámaca-Colbert, & Allen, 2016), the importance of ethnicity in a person's life (Phinney, 1990), levels of parental support (Chang, Han, Lee, & Qin, 2015), and how individuals respond to and deal with their ethnicity in their daily lives (Phinney, Lochner, & Murphy, 1990). Ethnic composition of one's residence is another important factor that moderates the relationship between ethnic identification and self-esteem. One study found that ethnic identity was related to self-esteem for Latinos only if they resided in areas where their specific Latino group was the largest Latino population (Umaña-Taylor, Diversi, & Fine, 2002).

Psychological Adjustment and Mental Health With the substantial growth in ethnic identity research, researchers can now better examine ethnic identity effects on mental health using meta-analytic techniques that pool together numerous research findings. A meta-analysis of 46 studies of ethnic minority youths shows that positive feelings about their ethnic group have small to medium effects in increasing positive social functioning, self-esteem, well-being, and academic achievement and in reducing depression, risky health behaviors, and internalizing and externalizing problems (Rivas-Drake, Syed, et al., 2014). In another meta-analysis of 45 studies of minority students, ethnic identity had small but significantly positive effects on academic achievement (Miller-Cotto & Byrnes, 2016), while a meta-analysis of 184 studies of ethnic minorities found an overall modest relationship between ethnic identity and personal well-being that was stronger for adolescents and young adults than for those over 40 years of age (Smith & Silva, 2011).

Positive effects of ethnic identification on psychological adjustment may be related to variable effects of ethnic identity components on coping skills and abilities. For instance, one study found that high affirmation and belonging, ethnic identity achievement, and high involvement in ethnic behaviors were significantly related to coping strategies. For African American students, these three indicators of a strong ethnic identity are related to desirable coping behaviors (for example, cognitive restructuring) and, for European American students, to infrequent use of negative coping strategies (such as self-criticism and blaming others) (Zaff, Blount, Phillips, & Cohen, 2002).

A study of urban African American adolescents from low-SES families similarly found that a strong and positive ethnic identity is associated with more active coping (active exploration and evaluation of a problem, developing effective problem-solving strategies), less acceptance of aggression, and fewer aggressive behaviors (McMahon & Watts, 2002). This finding still held true even when self-worth and self-esteem were controlled, suggesting that a strong ethnic identity had its own independent effects on psychological well-being. Thus, having a strong and positive ethnic identity was independently related to positive coping and less aggression for this sample of adolescents. Other studies have likewise shown that a strong ethnic identity is related to positive coping skills, a sense of mastery in meeting life's challenges, and optimism (Phinney & Rosenthal, 1992) and generally results in less loneliness and depression for African American, Mexican American, and White middle school students (Roberts et al., 1999).

Still, the relationship between ethnic identity and psychological and mental health can vary according to the saliency or centrality of ethnicity in daily life. Chinese American adolescents with strong ethnic identification reported less anxiety and depression and more positive well-being when their ethnicity was salient or central to their daily activities and social settings (Yip & Fuligni, 2002). Research also shows that the effects of ethnic identity on psychological outcomes can vary by ethnic group (Rivas-Drake, Seaton, et al., 2014), ethnic identity component examined (Serrano-Villar & Calzada, 2016), levels of religious commitment (Ajibade, Hook, Utsey, Davis, & Van Tongeren, 2016), and self-esteem and optimism (Smokowski, Evans, Cotter, & Webber, 2014).

Risk for Drug Use Positive ethnic identification involving strong affirmation, sense of belonging and commitment (Skewes & Blume, 2015), and strong cultural participation and socialization (Brown, Dickerson, & D'Amico, 2016) have been found to reduce substance abuse risk. Similarly, among ethnically diverse seventh graders, strong ethnic affiliation, attachment, and pride were linked to stronger personal antidrug beliefs and greater concern over friends' reactions to drug use (Marsiglia, Kulis, Hecht, & Sills, 2004). Interestingly, this finding was particularly true for European American students and less so for American Indians and Mexican Americans, possibly due to differences in salience or importance of their ethnicity in their daily lives. The European American students in this study were a numerical minority in their schools and neighborhoods; thus, their ethnic identity was perhaps more salient and closely attached to their daily functioning than was true for their ethnic minority peers.

Protection Against Discrimination and Racism Among Filipino Americans, ethnic pride and cultural involvement and commitment buffers stress from perceived discrimination and reduces depression risk (Mossakowski, 2003). Also, Latino adolescents with secure and positive ethnic identities are more resistant to negative ethnic group information (Phinney, Chavira, & Tate, 1993) and negative discrimination effects on their educational beliefs and aspirations (Mroczkowski & Sánchez, 2015). For African American adolescents, a positive ethnic identity buffers against negative effects of discrimination on academic performance and classroom behavior (Wong, Eccles, & Sameroff, 2003) and against online discrimination effects on anxiety levels (Tynes, Umaña-Taylor, Rose, Lin, & Anderson, 2012). However, ethnic identity does not always protect against negative discrimination effects for Asian American college students because it does not necessarily impart specific coping skills in dealing with discrimination (Lee, 2003).

Understanding how ethnic identity buffers against discrimination is complicated and requires careful attention to research design (e.g., participants' developmental abilities, sources and types of discrimination examined) for accurate results (Umaña-Taylor, 2016). For example, protective effects from ethnic identity may be a complex interaction between discrimination levels in one's environment and strength of ethnic identification. When faced with frequent discrimination, Latino, Asian, and African American youths with weak ethnic identification have higher self-esteem than those youths with strong ethnic identification. However, those who have strong ethnic identification tend to have higher self-esteem in environments with low discrimination (Quintana, 2007).

Biracial/Multiracial Identities and Adjustment

Research with biracial or multiracial individuals has also shown important relationships between their identity and adjustment in areas similar to those mentioned previously for ethnic and racial identities.

Self-Esteem In a study of biracial and monoracial adolescents, strong ethnic identification was positively related to higher self-esteem (Bracey et al., 2004). This finding suggests that ethnic identification serves as a protective factor against discrimination and racial stereotypes by offering adolescents expanded support from multiple racial groups during identity formation.

Psychological Adjustment and Mental Health Early theories of multiracial psychological adjustment suggested uniform and consistent patterns of identity conflicts, psychological distress, and poor psychological outcomes (Root, 1992). However, more recent research shows mixed or positive adjustment patterns. For instance, although studies report higher depression for multiracial high schoolers than for their monoracial peers (Fisher, Reynolds, Hsu, Barnes, & Tyler, 2014), other studies report less depression and greater self-acceptance and self-esteem for multiracial university students who experience ethnic identity resolution and affirmation (Brittian, Umaña-Taylor, & Derlan, 2013). Also, Asian-White biracials with integrated biracial identities are less psychologically distressed than those who are mostly White-identified, possibly due to greater sociocultural support and sense of belonging to multiple ethnic groups (Chong & Kuo, 2015). Multiracial identity may also encourage more flexible and effective cognitive coping strategies to navigate diverse identities and sociocultural environments (Gaither, 2015).

Shih and Sanchez (2005) arrive at the following conclusions in their review of the literature on multiracial individuals and their psychological adjustment:

1. *There is evidence for both positive and negative psychological adjustment among multiracial individuals.* This contradicts traditional theories proposing uniform patterns of identity conflict and maladjustment. Thus, it appears that multiracial identity can provide important resources, like expanded support from multiple ethnic communities, contributing to personal resilience rather than to stress.
2. *The direction of study findings is influenced by research strategies and methods.* In this case, findings vary by:
    a. *The types of populations that were studied.* Studies reporting negative psychological adjustment (e.g., higher levels of depression, problem behaviors, poor school performance, and low self-esteem) typically focused on clinical samples, while those reporting positive adjustment (e.g., happiness, high self-esteem) examined nonclinical samples.
    b. *The historical period when the study was conducted.* More negative outcomes (e.g., social rejection and isolation) were reported in studies that were conducted before the 1990s, while more positive outcomes (e.g., social acceptance and improved peer relationships) are reported in more recent studies. This trend suggests that social attitudes toward interracial marriages and the multiracial community may be improving. Conversely, this trend may also reflect improvements in study methods and sample selection.

c. *The psychological outcome under examination and the monoracial ethnicity of the comparison group.* When compared with monoracial Whites, multiracial individuals appeared to have more negative outcomes (e.g., depression and behavioral problems). However, when multiracial individuals were compared with monoracial minorities, their psychological adjustment patterns varied according to the outcome studied (for example, multiracials tend to show stronger academic performance but less racial pride than monoracial ethnic minorities).

In sum, the relationship between multiracial identity and psychological adjustment is much more complex than originally proposed in earlier psychological theories. These earlier theories characterized the multiracial experience as being fraught with chronic identity conflicts, high levels of psychological distress, and poor psychological outcomes. However, researchers now acknowledge more variable adjustment patterns, as proposed by the risk and resilience theory (Yoo, Jackson, Guevarra, Miller, & Harrington, 2016). According to this theory, multiracial adjustment is affected by a constellation of risk factors (e.g., discrimination) and resiliency factors (e.g., engagement with multicultural community), none of which consistently generate positive or negative outcomes. Instead, the psychological effects of both factors depend on multiracial persons' daily living environments or ecologies and on individual, social, and community factors.

Box 5.5 reproduces a case study of a recent research project that shows the various factors affecting the relationship between race and ethnic identity and a person's adjustment.

Box 5.5

How Does Family Environment Affect Multiracial Identity Development?

A study found that multiracial college students were more conflicted about their ethnic identity around their peers and reported more adjustment difficulties at college if they came from families that did not support their mixed race heritage (Jourdan, 2006). Thus, a family environment that promotes positive exploration and discussion of mixed-race identity can reduce risk for identity conflicts and psychosocial problems. The importance of family environment on multiracial identity development was highlighted by the experiences of Kevin, a mixed-race college student in this study:

> Kevin's mother is Chinese, and his father is African American and Caucasian. He explained that his ethnic identity was a source of contention in his family. Throughout his life, Kevin received mixed messages from his family regarding his ethnic identity. . . . Kevin did not have a home environment that allowed him to share his thoughts and feelings regarding his ethnic identity; thus, he was unable to develop a secure ethnic identity, making him feel unconnected to all ethnic groups. . . . He asserted that his maternal grandmother did not accept his father because his father is African American and Caucasian. Kevin stated that this family experience led him to conclude that all Chinese people were racist. Furthermore, he explained that his father told him that all Chinese people were evil and that he should identify as African American. . . . He has heard negative and confusing information about all facets of his ethnic background from different members of his family; thus, he does not feel connected to a particular ethnic group. He stated, "I decided my ethnicity is Kevin. I don't really think I have an ethnicity anyway. I feel very alienated from all groups—Blacks, Chinese, Whites, everyone. I find the most amount of exclusion from Chinese." . . . He then described a feeling of being different every time he walked into a college classroom; he also reported that he wanted to escape whenever he was in a room of people who were White. In an attempt to form a connection with people in college, Kevin became involved with an African American group and a Chinese American group on campus. However, he did not feel connected to either of these groups. He explained, "I guess when I went to meet with the Chinese people, they didn't know what the hell I was. So how the hell could they feel like any bond with me? I would just meet with the Chinese people and they didn't even know what to make of me, you know, let alone feel any sense of camaraderie, you know, like they were all

under the yoke of a common oppressor. And the same thing with Black people, they don't know what the f@*! I am, how the hell can they ever, you know, feel that way." Kevin went on to explain that people always viewed him as being different, thus creating a barrier in his interactions with others. As a result, he said that he constantly felt insecure and rejected. . . . He stated that he had never formed a close connection with a particular ethnic group and instead felt rejected by all ethnic groups. (Jourdan, 2006, pp. 332–338)

As you read this case, you may want to consider the following questions: What are the key psychosocial difficulties that Kevin is facing? How are these issues tied to his family's responses to race? Do Kevin's identity experiences reflect any features of Root's or Collins's models of biracial identity development? If so, which ones?

Class Identity and Adjustment

As mentioned at the beginning of this chapter and in other chapters of this book, socioeconomic status (SES) is an important indicator of class identity that is often intertwined with racial identity. Much research in psychology and other social sciences has analyzed these relationships, and we include some of those findings in other chapters. Here we wish to concentrate in the relationship between class identity and health.

Physical and Mental Health Health research continues to reveal significant health disparities between racial minorities and Whites, caused by the combined effects of economic hardship and racial stratification. SES, race, and health are linked together in a number of ways that we summarize below (see Chapters 9 and 10 for a more thorough discussion).

Specifically, social class and health have been found to show that:

1. Racism and institutionalized discrimination prevent racial and ethnic minorities from gaining upward social mobility that can improve health outcomes.
2. Disproportionately more racial and ethnic minorities conduct their daily lives in impoverished and stressful living and work environments that contribute to chronic and disabling physical health conditions.
3. Low-SES ethnic and racial minorities face cumulative stressors and disadvantages throughout the course of their life, leading to a "weathering" of their health as they age and a shortened life span.
4. Ethnic and racial minorities may somatize their stress from racial discrimination and poverty, which can negatively affect their perceptions of their overall health and well-being (Sudano & Baker, 2006).

Still, the ways in which SES affects health are not always clear; thus, researchers are beginning to examine the different facets or dimensions of SES to determine whether they have independent and complex pathways to health. For instance, a community study of low-SES Mexican Americans found that **objective social status** (individual income, educational level, and occupation), rather than **subjective social status** (self-perceived social position in society), was more strongly related to health outcomes (Franzini & Fernandez-Esquer, 2006). Likewise, objective reports of economic hassles or stressors are robustly related to depression for Mexican American youths living in an ethnic enclave (García, Manongdo, & Ozechowski, 2014). However, other studies show that subjective SES is a better health predictor. For low-SES, Spanish-speaking Mexican American mothers, their subjective economic stress predicts higher cortisol (a stress hormone) levels, but only if they had low family support (Jewell, Luecken, Gress-Smith, Crnic, & Gonzales, 2015). Subjective rather than objective socioeconomic indicators also show a stronger relationship to multiple health and psychological outcomes for Asian Americans (Gong, Xu, & Takeuchi, 2012).

Studies have also found that "neighborhood SES" and "family SES" have independent relationships to health. In a study (Chen & Paterson, 2006) of White and African American adolescent health, neighborhood SES was a composite of neighborhood educational levels, family employment status, median family income, and median value of owner-occupied homes, while family SES was based on household income and a family's liquid assets or savings. Findings showed that low neighborhood SES was positively related to adolescent obesity and exposure to discrimination. Thus, people living in low-SES neighborhoods may experience greater stress from discrimination and consequent health problems. Low-SES neighborhoods also tend to lack safe and clean civic spaces (e.g., public parks, hiking and walking paths) and healthy food options, preventing adolescents from engaging in outdoor physical activities and maintaining a healthy diet. This study found that family SES was also negatively related to adolescent obesity, suggesting that poor families may not be able to afford healthy food options, organized physical activities for their children, and preventative health care (Chen & Paterson, 2006). A study of African American, Latino, and White youths likewise found that social disadvantages experienced on individual and neighborhood levels increased risk for developing unhealthy behaviors that contribute to cardiovascular disease, such as poor dietary habits, low physical activity, and cigarette smoking (Lee & Cubbin, 2002).

Low SES and race have also been associated with health disparities in HIV treatment and survival rates. One study reported that HIV-infected ethnic minority adults with low-SES backgrounds receive fewer health care services, including effective and expensive antiretroviral treatment (Cunningham et al., 2005). This same study also found that HIV-infected impoverished individuals of all ethnicities had an 89 percent greater risk of death than did wealthier individuals, and those with less than a high school education had a 53 percent greater risk of death than did those with more formal education.

Chapter Summary

In this chapter, we examine the interrelationship between different facets of individual and group identities. All of these facets—racial, ethnic, class identities—are complex in their development, interaction with one another, and expression in our daily lives. The preponderance of identity research is based on African American, Asian American, and Hispanic/Latino study samples with relatively less attention afforded to American Indians. As such, much more research on these underrepresented topics and populations is needed to better understand the broad range of human experience associated with multiple intersecting identities. The next chapter summarizes research on two other importance aspects of a person's identity: gender and sexuality.

Key Terms

achieved ethnic identity 120
cultural socialization 112
ethnic identity 112
high private regard 127
identity diffusion 119
identity foreclosure 119
intersecting identities 110
moratorium 119
objective social status 132
otherness status 122
racial identity 111
racial identity schemas 126
racial socialization 111
social constructions 111
subjective social status 132

Learning by Doing

- Trace your ethnic identity development by thinking about how you have experienced your race or ethnicity throughout the course of your life. Below are some questions you may ask yourself:

1. What components of ethnic or racial identity are most salient to your daily life?
2. Has the way in which you identify yourself and how you feel about your ethnic or racial group membership changed or remained the same? What do you think are some factors that have contributed to this?
3. Consider Phinney's early model of ethnic identity development.
4. What stage of ethnic identity development would you place yourself in? Why?
5. If you are biracial or multiracial, what identity resolution strategy in Root's model captures your identity experiences?
6. What contextual factors have influenced your ethnic or racial identity development?
7. Do you feel that these models of ethnic, racial, and biracial identity development capture your personal search for an ethnic identity? What do you think are the strengths and limitations of these models?
8. How do other facets of your identity intersect with your ethnicity or race to shape who you are today?

Suggested Further Readings

Benet-Martínez, V., & Hong, Y.-Y. (2014). *The Oxford handbook of multicultural identity.* New York: Oxford University Press.

In-depth review of theory and scholarly research on the psychological underpinnings of multiculturalism and multicultural identities.

Lott, B. (2010). *Multiculturalism and diversity: A social psychological perspective.* West Sussex, UK: Wiley-Blackwell.

A brief analysis of the various aspects of the experience of modern individuals as their behavior is affected by the intersectionality of culture, ethnicity, gender, social class, and sexual identity.

Philip, C. (2007). *Asian American identities: Racial and ethnic identity issues in the twenty-first century.* Amherst, NY: Cambria Press.

A comprehensive overview of the historical, psychological, and social issues surrounding the development of Asian American identity.

Santos, C. E., & Umaña-Taylor, A. J. (2015). *Studying ethnic identity: Methodological and conceptual approaches across disciplines.* Washington, DC: American Psychological Association.

Interdisciplinary review of ethnic identity theory, measurement, and innovative research methods by leading scholars in the field.

Singley, B. (Ed.). (2002). *When race becomes real: Black and White writers confront their personal histories.* Chicago: Lawrence Hill.

Compilation of essays from a talented group of writers who expose the long and challenging legacy of race in the United States and the meanings of racial identity in their personal lives.

Intersecting Identities—Part 2 6
Gender and Sexuality Dimensions

"Why Do We Have to Label Everyone?"

"Growing up in Odessa, Texas, in the early 1970s was an experience," remarked Damon, a 35-year-old African American male. As a child, he never really questioned why a railroad track divided the African American and European American neighborhoods. However, he remembered his mother's warnings that White people couldn't really be trusted and to be wary of them. Damon didn't fully understand her; he never really spent a lot of time with European Americans, and he rarely thought about race. This changed, however, when he attended a rural Northeastern college and noticed very few African Americans there and even fewer in the local community. When he went to local stores, employees would single him out and follow him, thinking that he would shoplift, while White customers were left alone. In a stressful turn of events, Damon's two European American male roommates began taunting him with racial slurs and even threatened his life, although Damon hadn't done anything to provoke them. Damon began to wonder why people reacted so violently to his skin color. He was confronted with added questions about his identity as he slowly came out and self-identified as a gay man. Upon moving to San Francisco after finishing college, he found many new friends, but the predominantly gay European American community was not entirely inviting or friendly. At gay social venues and events, he seemed mostly invisible to the European American clientele and sometimes overheard racist remarks about African Americans and other racial minority groups.

Looking for other African American gay men for support, he discovered that some preferred to exclusively date and socialize with White men because they didn't find racial minority men attractive. And in the heterosexual African American community, Damon found that some were homophobic and avoided discussing gay issues. Damon commented to a good friend, "In the gay community, I'm not totally accepted because I'm Black, and in the Black community I'm not fully accepted because I'm gay. And growing up in Texas, people were also obsessed with racial categories. Why do we have to label everyone?"

Defining Gender and Sexual Identities

In Chapter 5 we discussed the interactions that ethnicity, race, and class have in shaping an individual's identity and human behavior in general. In this chapter, we concentrate on two other important human conditions that moderate and influence a person's identity: gender and sexual identity. As shown in the vignette at the beginning of this chapter, dimensions such as race, gender, and sexuality frequently interact with each other in shaping how we relate with others and, in many cases, how we develop attitudes and beliefs.

Gender Identity

There are two important concepts to consider when analyzing the intersection of gender with other social conditions in shaping a person's identity. One is **gender typing**—that is, the process by which you learn the behaviors, interests, and abilities that are associated with being masculine or feminine in a given culture. The other is **gender identity**—your fundamental sense of being male or female, shaped by gender typing, yet sometimes independent of social and cultural norms and rules for gender (Wade & Tavris, 2017). Overall, culture plays an integral role in shaping societal assumptions and expectations about male and female **gender roles**—or the expected responsibilities and abilities of men and women. For instance, in Chinese culture, Confucian philosophy outlines hierarchical family roles based on gender and age, generally requiring wives to assume a more nurturing family role and husbands to assume more family leadership roles.

Such gender roles and expectations are not based on actual biological sex differences or abilities but are instead established by cultural beliefs and values and by cultural and social structures and institutions (Pyke & Johnson, 2003). This is evidenced by variable definitions of gender identity and gender roles across cultural and ethnic groups, historical periods, and acculturation experiences (Chun & Akutsu, 2003). Another example is the cultural notion of "two-spirited" or cross-gender individuals among American Indians and Alaska Natives, which speaks to gender diversity across different cultural traditions. **Two-spirited individuals** are considered blessed with both male and female spirits, and many fulfilled spiritual, sacred, and ceremonial tribal roles (Balsam, Huang, Fieland, Simoni, & Walters, 2004; Garnets, 2002). Thus, two-spirited persons are historically valued members in their tribes who are viewed as having special spiritual gifts and powers. Their very presence challenges dominant Western understandings of gender identity, which favor dichotomous gender categories and treat gender nonconformity as abnormal psychological functioning.

Sexual Identity

Sexual identity or sexual orientation encompasses the broad range of sexual, emotional, and erotic attractions that exist among individuals (Wade & Tavris, 2017). Advances in sexual identity research (for example, Garnets, 2002; Rosario & Schrimshaw, 2014) highlight the following key features of sexual identity:

- Sexual identities are considered complex, multidimensional, and fluid, reflecting the fact that people of the same gender can be sexually, emotionally, and erotically attracted to one another in many different ways. This counters older, more simplistic views of sexual identity that were typically restricted to "heterosexual" and "homosexual" categorizations and overlooked the broad continuum of sexuality within and between these categorizations.

- Sexual identity is experienced and expressed in many different ways; it encompasses erotic-emotional behaviors and fantasies, emotional attachments, self-identification, and current relationship status *in addition to* sexual behavior. In the past, sexual behavior was thought to be the defining feature of sexual identity; however, sexual behaviors and sexual fantasies can be independent from sexual identity.
- Sexual identity or sexual orientation can change across a person's lifetime and across different social and cultural contexts, whereas in the past it was thought to be fixed and unchanging. Changes are most likely to be seen in sexual activity and identification during adolescence and emerging adulthood but can also occur later in life.

Sexual identity formation and experiences among ethnic and racial minorities can differ from those of European Americans. As seen in Damon's experiences in the vignette opening the chapter, forming an integrated sense of self and developing social bonds with different ethnic and sexual communities are complicated by multiple minority identities. For lesbian and bisexual women of color, sexism can be an additional stressor that challenges their identity formation.

Models of Gender and Sexual Identity Development and Formation

Gender Typing and Gender Identity Formation

A relatively new body of multicultural psychology research has begun to examine how cultural beliefs and values influence gender typing and gender identity development. Ethnic minorities may engage in gender typing by early socialization of their members around culturally acceptable gender behaviors and beliefs about manhood and womanhood. However, the gender identity of individual members may not necessarily conform to their group's cultural beliefs about gender. Gender can therefore be represented and expressed in multiple ways within any ethnic group. Research with Asian Americans, African Americans, and Latinos/Latinas indicates that a broad array of cultural, social, and political factors shape how gender is represented and expressed in each of these ethnic communities. We describe these in the following paragraphs.

Asian American Gender Identity Asian American gender identity research shows links between Confucian principles and family and social roles for men and women. This philosophical tradition, with roots in sixth-century China (Solomon & Higgins, 1997), promotes as mentioned previously, patriarchal family and social structures giving men greater family and social authority and privileges than women (Lee, 1997). Men are expected to be heads of their households and primary family providers, while women are expected to fulfill more nurturing and supportive family roles, including caring for children and attending to daily household chores. These gender role expectations are associated with specific gender typing experiences: Men are taught to sustain their family's public status and reputation and to meet their parents' wishes and familial obligations as standard-bearers of their family name (Liu, 2002). These gender role expectations and gender typing experiences are particularly salient for the oldest sons, who are typically given the most family and social privileges and, upon reaching adulthood, are expected to assume a family leadership role. Asian American women who live in these patriarchal environments have altogether different gender typing experiences; Confucian principles instruct them to assume a secondary role to their husbands and to subsume their individual needs and wishes to those of their husband, in-laws, and children. Such gender typing experiences in patriarchal societies—which generally afford greater status and privilege to men—can heighten risk for domestic violence by condoning male power assertion and domination over women (Kim, Lau, & Chang, 2007).

Still, some researchers believe that these Asian American gender representations are limiting, historically imposed by the dominant group, and based on negative stereotypes that overlook diverse Asian American gender identities. For instance, studies have found that Asian American men may not necessarily follow "traditional" Confucian family roles but may instead share in domestic tasks and household responsibilities with their wives (Chua & Fujino, 1999). Additionally, Asian American women in patriarchal environments may appear to be secondary to their husbands, but this might only be true in public; behind closed doors wives can influence family decision-making by practicing their authority discreetly so that their husbands do not lose face (Lee, 1997). Finally, newer waves of Asian immigrant women are rapidly breaking away from traditional gender role expectations by joining the workforce in greater numbers and achieving greater earning power and financial independence (Kawahara & Fu, 2007). Thus, Asian American men and women construct their gender identities in multiple ways that defy one-dimensional and rigid gender stereotypes. If this is the case, then why do we see highly stereotyped gender images of Asian Americans in the media?

Television shows, movies, and the Internet abound with images of the passive and emasculated Asian American male, the emotionally detached and unaffectionate Asian American father and husband, the hypersexual or subservient Asian American female "geisha," and the hyperfeminine and fragile Asian female "lotus blossom." Researchers believe that racial stratification and racial oppression lie at the heart of this matter (Espiritu, 1997).

In a study of U.S.- and foreign-born Korean and Vietnamese women (Pyke & Johnson, 2003), the nature and effects of "controlling images" on Asian American gender identities were explored. **Controlling images** are stereotyped and negative racial and gender images intended to subordinate minority groups and justify and affirm dominant group power and norms. For the Korean and Vietnamese women in this study, controlling images negatively affected how they constructed and enacted gender in their daily lives in several ways. First, the controlling image of Asian American men as domineering and patriarchal led these women to believe that individual freedom and egalitarian relationships could only be achieved with White men, which discouraged some from having relationships with Asian American men. Second, the controlling image of Asian American women as subservient, passive, and quiet caused some women to believe that losing or rejecting their Asian heritage was necessary to be independent and assertive. Likewise, these women reported that White men sometimes believed that Asian women would be more subservient in relationships. Finally, controlling images of both genders obscured or dismissed variations in their gender behaviors, including reversals in their expected gender roles or hierarchies.

In short, controlling racial and gender images produce tension and conflict in Asian American relationships, and they often discourage Asian American women from seeking relationships with Asian American men. Also, controlling images glorify the White dominant world as a place of absolute gender equity, causing Asian American men and women to believe that their ethnic and gender identities are incompatible or at odds. They might therefore believe that a positive, egalitarian, or flexible gender identity is only possible by renouncing their ethnic heritage and assimilating into White culture.

Asian American masculinities are challenged and complicated by gender-related stress from racist images or acts that are perceived as threats to Asian American manhood. Because Asian American men face emasculating racial-gender stereotypes, they feel pressured to follow White masculine norms, feel socially alienated and disempowered, and encounter restricted opportunities and resources to fulfill masculine gender expectations, such as being the family provider (Liu & Wong, 2016). These experiences of gender-related stress thus undermine Asian American men's sense of masculinity, self-efficacy in fulfilling their social gender roles, and overall well-being.

African American Gender Identity African American gender identities have also been distorted and stereotyped by controlling images. Historically, African American men have often been wrongly stereotyped as being deviant, irresponsible, and neglectful in their family and social roles. Popular media images of the angry and hypersexual Black man, the chronic substance abuser, and the absent African American father have sustained these negative stereotypes. As with other ethnic minority groups, these controlling images ignore diverse and positive gender constructions, and they dehumanize African American men and restrict their social mobility.

One qualitative study (Hammond & Mattis, 2005) attempted to uncover the broadest possible range of African American male gender constructions by asking African American men one open-ended question: "What does manhood mean to you?" Fifteen different dimensions of African American manhood emerged in response to this question; the most frequently occurring dimension—"responsibility-accountability"—was mentioned by almost half of all respondents. This dimension emphasized taking responsibility for the welfare of family and others, and being accountable for personal actions, thoughts, and behaviors, which directly contradicted negative stereotypes and controlling images of African American men. Additional analyses highlighted four larger, interrelated categories of African American manhood. First, manhood was described in the context of relationships including being connected to God, themselves, family, community, and others. Second, manhood was portrayed as a fluid and adaptive process in which positive male traits developed with time and life experience. Third, manhood was seen as a redemptive process; by becoming an active family and community member, past mistakes and behaviors could be corrected or rectified and one's humanity regained. Fourth, being proactive was considered a requirement of manhood, including being a smart and independent thinker, anticipating threats or barriers to healthy identity development, and initiating positive behaviors that nurtured male identity.

All of these findings point to multilayered African American masculinities that defy one-dimensional gender and racial stereotypes. Moreover, respondents' frequent mentioning of responsibility-accountability, and the shared view that manhood involves social and spiritual interconnectedness, life experience, redemption, and proactive behaviors, reflects their desire to dismantle negative stereotypes and frame their manhood in more humane terms.

Another qualitative study of African American men (Rogers, Sperry, & Levant, 2015) found both similar and different gender identity constructions than the study above. When asked a general question about their masculinity—"What does it mean to be a man?"—respondents also offered a wide range of responses but emphasized more traditional Western male roles and traits (e.g., being a family provider and protector, leadership, strength, toughness, withholding emotions, heterosexuality). Responses to a second question on intersecting racial-gender identities—"What does it mean to be an African American man?"—elicited responses of "racist gender role strain" or experiences of interpersonal and institutional racism that threaten African American masculinity and gender roles. Respondents used positive coping strategies to deal with this strain (for example, caring for family and community, learning about their cultural history, and being mentally tough, physically strong, and spiritually grounded), which ultimately led them to form a culturally unique African American male identity and set of behaviors.

African American women also exhibit diverse gender identity traits and characteristics that defy stereotyped, negative controlling images. For instance, African American girls are socialized at an early age to develop flexible gender roles to cope with the realities of discrimination and economic marginalization of African American men. In a study of African American youths, girls endorsed both traditional masculine traits (e.g., independence and bravery) and feminine traits (e.g., kindness and sensitivity) needed to form and sustain a positive identity and counter negative gender and racial images and attitudes in society (Skinner & McHale, 2017). African American women's gender role beliefs likewise embody *agency* (belief or confidence in one's ability to meet life's challenges) and *caretaking* (belief in taking care of and providing for the well-being of others), both of which signal strength and resilience in the face of adversity (Belgrave, Abrams, Hood, Moore, & Nguyen, 2016).

Last, African American girls and young women experience **gendered racial socialization**—a socialization process in which their families teach them about what it means to be African American and female in a society that devalues both social identities. This socialization process includes imparting positive messages, beliefs, and skills to cope with this "double jeopardy" status. In a study of African American girls and young women, gendered racial socialization included a broad set of messages emphasizing gendered racial pride and empowerment (having positive internal self-worth and positive views of physical features), family expectations and responsibilities (fulfilling gender role duties in the family), and sisterhood (drawing from the strength and resiliency of African American women and mothers) (Brown, Blackmon, Rosnick, Griffin-Fennell, & White-Johnson, 2017).

Researchers have explored whether African and European American women understand femininity differently. One study found both distinct and common constructions of femininity for African and European American women (Cole & Zucker, 2007). In regard to commonalties, both African and European American women believed that femininity includes three primary components: (1) a *feminine appearance*, or wearing feminine clothes, grooming, and the presentation of one's home; (2) *feminine traits or demeanor*, encompassing socially desirable traits for women; and (3) *traditional gender role ideology*, or a fundamental belief that women and men are best suited to fulfill different roles and duties, with women being the best candidates for domestic roles and men being highly suited for work and leadership roles. Still, this shared view of femininity did not mean that both ethnic groups experienced its components similarly. African American women were more interested than European American women in maintaining a feminine appearance but more likely to describe themselves as feminists. Furthermore, European American women who self-identified as feminists predictably rejected traditional gender role ideology, but this was not true for self-identified African American feminists. African American women thus appeared to have culturally distinct notions of feminism that contradicted European American feminist beliefs. Although Cole and Zucker (2007) acknowledge that these differences might reflect a lack of specificity in how feminism was defined and measured (participants were simply asked to rate their agreement with the statement "I am a feminist"), they noted that other studies have likewise found different interpretations and experiences of feminism for African American women. For instance, they note that African American women who work outside of the home still believe that their husbands should be traditional family providers because it was essential for their husbands' self-esteem and masculinity.

Latino/Latina Gender Identity Much of the scholarship on Latino and Latina gender identities has focused on the constructs of "machismo" and "marianismo," respectively. Traditionally, **machismo** refers to a broad set of stereotyped hypermasculine Latino traits that include male dominance, aggression, fearlessness, bravery, authoritarianism, promiscuous behavior, virility, excessive alcohol use, stoicism, reserved or restricted emotions and aloofness, sexism, oppressive and controlling behaviors toward women and children, autonomy, strength, bravado, responsibility, honor, respect, and being a good provider and protector of women, children, and less fortunate members of society (Torres, Solberg, & Carlstrom, 2002). These stereotyped traits have contributed to narrow and rigid representations of Latino gender identity seen in a number of controlling images, including the overly possessive and emotionally volatile Latino husband, the emotionally distant and authoritarian Latino father, and the promiscuous Latin lover. Again, these types of controlling images discount or dismiss alternative manifestations of Latino masculinities and are often used by the dominant group to justify and sustain racial stratification.

The counterpart to machismo is **marianismo** (or the cult of Maria, the Virgin Mary, or the Madonna), which refers to a broad set of stereotyped feminine traits that idealize the moral virtues and personal character of Latinas. Marianismo is often used to elevate Latinas' gender identity by casting them as being morally and spiritually superior to Latino men, possessing an innate ability to endure hardship and suffering, and being self-sacrificing, humble, modest, reserved, giving, and generous. Some researchers believe that, although these virtuous qualities are based on narrow gender stereotypes, they are not entirely detrimental because they offer positive Latina gender representations that express loyalty, compassion, and generosity.

There continues to be much debate over the meaning and significance of both machismo and marianismo to Latino/Latina gender identity and typing and to overall psychosocial functioning. This debate has included new critical interpretations of these gender constructs that call attention to their overlooked multidimensional and complex characteristics. For instance, one study (Torres et al., 2002) found that traditional definitions of machismo (e.g., authoritarian, emotionally restrictive, controlling) were endorsed by only a minority of their diverse sample of Mexican American, Puerto Rican, Cuban, Central and South American, and multiracial Latino men. Instead, Latino participants defined and expressed machismo in more complicated ways, revealing five distinct dimensions to this construct:

- *Contemporary masculinity*: Flexible gender roles characterized by a preference for cooperation and harmony, less demand for family respect and obedience, and less traditional views of male and female gender roles. They also reported less conflict over their life roles.
- *Machismo*: Respect for family remains an important concern, but it is expressed within a caring and emotionally expressive context without demands for control and dominance.
- *Traditional machismo*: Dominant and rigid male gender behaviors characterized by demands for family respect and obedience, holding traditional views of male and female gender roles, being highly conflicted with balancing life roles, emotionally reserved, and more controlling. Latinos who fell into this category seemed to embody many of the negative hypermasculine stereotypes of machismo.
- *Conflicted/compassionate machismo*: Emphasizes maintaining tradition and defining masculinity through success and achievement. At the same time, there are attempts at being emotionally expressive and empathic in relationships. Men in this category struggle to balance various roles and relationships and may experience gender identity conflicts when attempting to meet different, and at times conflicting, cultural, relational, and societal gender expectations.
- *Contemporary machismo*: Values harmonious family relationships and attempts to achieve them by being aware of emotions and expressing them effectively. Although achievement and success is tied to masculinity, balance between work, family, and leisure is valued. Men in this category thus show a strong connection to their families and an "emerging machismo" that successfully integrates cultural tradition, relationships, and societal demands into a masculine identity.

Researchers have proposed an additional Latino masculine identity construct—*caballerismo*—that embodies many of the positive Latino masculine traits noted above and can be understood as a counterpart to traditional definitions of machismo. **Caballerismo** is defined as a positive set of Latino masculine attitudes, beliefs, and traits that emphasize being the primary family provider and protector and valuing honor, dignity, respect for others, emotional responsiveness, collaboration, and flexible masculine role behaviors (Liang, Salcedo, & Miller, 2011). Caballerismo is related to an important social script (or value) of Latino culture that is usually labeled *simpatía* (Triandis et al., 1984).

A more complex understanding of marianismo is also beginning to emerge in multicultural research. A study of Mexican American adolescents (Piña-Watson, Castillo, Jung, Ojeda, & Castillo-Reyes, 2014) demonstrated that marianismo also is a multidimensional construct that is part of gender typing for both boys and girls, although each gender emphasizes different dimensions. Five different beliefs or dimensions of marianismo were confirmed in this study:

- *Family pillar*: Latinas should maintain family harmony and child-rearing; this belief is influenced by the cultural values of *familismo* and *simpatía*.
- *Virtuous and chaste*: Latinas are expected to be abstinent until marriage, respect their bodies, and be modest in sexual matters; this belief is influenced by *respeto*.
- *Subordinate to others*: Latinas should show obedience and respect for Latino family hierarchies; this too is influenced by *respeto*.
- *Self-silencing to maintain harmony*: Latinas should minimize interpersonal confrontation and conflict; this also is influenced by *simpatía*.
- *Spiritual pillar*: Latinas should be spiritual leaders in their families.

Compared to the Latina girls in that study, Latino boys more strongly endorsed "self-silencing to maintain harmony" and "subordinate to others" as important dimensions of marianismo, a concerning finding given its negative implications for Latino girls' mental health and academic outcomes. Latina girls, however, more strongly endorsed the "family pillar" and "spiritual pillar" dimensions, which they may have viewed as conferring more power over men in their families and communities.

These multidimensional features of machismo and marianismo underscore the need to move away from one-dimensional gender-racial stereotypes to more accurately understand Latinos' and

Latinas' diverse gender understandings and experiences. Moving away from these stereotypes involves refuting the idea that Latino masculinity solely embodies traditional machismo and that Latinas define and value marianismo in uniform ways. Arguing against Latino male stereotypes, one study (Abreu, Goodyear, Campos, & Newcomb, 2000) found that Latino adolescent boys with strong ethnic identification did not endorse traditional male gender roles. Instead, European American adolescents in that study were more likely to endorse traditional male gender roles, which again argues against the notion that traditional machismo is part and parcel of being a Latino man.

In summary, the cultural histories and traditions, social conditions, and minority status of ethnic minority groups intimately shape their gender typing practices and gender identity development. Historically controlling gender and racial images have been imposed on ethnic minorities in the popular media, ultimately limiting our understanding of their diverse gender identities and behaviors. New research on ethnic minority gender identity, however, is beginning to reveal a clearer picture of the complex ways in which persons of color construct and experience gender in their daily lives.

Sexual Identity Formation

Understanding how ethnic and racial minorities construct their sexual identities still requires much exploration because research mostly focuses on the experiences of gay European American men. A few studies indicate that ethnic minorities' coming-out process can be qualitatively different than those of European Americans or Whites due to their minority status and to cultural factors. In regard to minority factors, LGBTQ persons of color experience **double minority status** because they face homophobia in their ethnic communities and in larger society and face racial discrimination in the predominantly White LGBTQ community. For ethnic minority lesbians, sexism presents added challenges to their sexual identity formation. In terms of cultural factors, cultural beliefs and values regarding marriage and relationships, traditional gender roles, family role expectations, and cultural norms around discussing sex complicate LGBTQ identity exploration and formation.

Also, ethnic minorities who view the LGBTQ community as being exclusively White might feel as if they have to reject their ethnic heritage to self-identify as LGBTQ. Consequently, ethnic minority LGBTQ persons potentially face isolation, discrimination, and marginalization in the dominant society and in their own families and ethnic communities. Such experiences require LGBTQ ethnic minorities to negotiate multiple, often competing, cultural and social demands, which can undermine an integrated sexual identity (Sarno, Mohr, Jackson, & Fassinger, 2015). The following outlines the different types of intersecting stressors that LGBTQ ethnic minorities face and their effects on identity formation and integration. We will then take a closer look at specific cultural and family issues in sexual identity disclosure, or coming out, for different ethnic minority groups.

Navigating Intersecting Racial, Sexual, and Gender Stressors LGBTQ ethnic minorities encounter different types of intersecting stressors or oppressions, including racial, sexual, and gender-related microaggressions. In a study of LGBTQ ethnic minorities (Balsam, Molina, Beadnell, Simoni, & Walters, 2011), three classes of intersecting microaggressions were reported: racism in LGBT communities, heterosexism in racial/ethnic minority communities, and racism in dating and close relationships. In this study, participants' income and education were unrelated to microaggressions, indicating that all LGBTQ persons of color encountered them regardless of their social position. Still, these microaggressions were more likely to be reported by men versus women, by lesbians and gay men versus bisexual women and men, and by Asian Americans versus African Americans and Latinos. This latter finding supports past findings that dominant group and ethnic minority gay men perceive Asian American gay men as less sexually desirable due to negative controlling images, as previously discussed. Heterosexism in racial/ethnic minority communities proved to be particularly damaging to all LGBTQ ethnic minorities' mental health because of potential loss of valued cultural support networks to deal with racism.

Sexual identity among ethnic minority lesbians is complicated by experiences of sexism in addition to heterosexism and racism in dominant culture and in their own ethnic minority communities (Greene, 1997). One qualitative study found that African American lesbians employed a "Don't ask, don't tell" coping strategy to navigate their sexual identity development in their families and communities (Miller, 2011). This strategy involved hiding their lesbian identity in their families and communities to maintain valued support, especially for dealing with racism and sexism in their daily lives. Although this strategy created space to develop their lesbian identity (e.g., bringing a partner as a "friend" to family functions) and allowed for tacit or unspoken family acceptance of their sexual identity, respondents felt the need to seek their own community of African American lesbians and other strong African American women to fully integrate their racial, gender, and sexual minority identities.

Intersecting stressors have also been reported for Asian American lesbian and bisexual women (AA LBW). One study (Sung, Szymanski, & Henrichs-Beck, 2015) found that invisibility and lack of representation of AA LBW in the LGBTQ community and in larger society, and sexual objectification and exoticization by White men and women, were especially distressing for their AA LBW participants. To deal with these stressors, AA LBW participants used passive coping strategies (e.g., staying silent about their sexual identity) and active empowerment strategies (e.g., engaging in social activism) that directly challenged intersecting racial, gender, and sexual oppressions. Despite facing intersecting minority stressors, participants said that being AA LBW had its benefits as well, such as being free from oppressive gender roles or expressions of sexuality and being more empathic toward others, which is similarly reported by White LGBs in other studies. However, AA LBW participants also noted culturally distinct benefits of their AA LGB identity, such as possessing a unique intersectional perspective on the world and being able to draw on their Asian culture as a source of strength and resilience.

Not surprisingly, intersectional oppressions or stressors may inhibit or delay LGBTQ people of color's sexual explorations and expressions, and integration of their salient self-identities. A study of African American and Latina lesbians showed that their sexual identity development was more similar to each other than that of European American lesbians (Parks, Hughes, & Matthews, 2004). In general, women of color in this study were younger when they began to question their sexual orientation and spent more time deciding whether they were lesbian compared to European Americans. Additionally, lesbians of color reported significantly less disclosure to persons outside of their families than White lesbians. When age was considered, older women of color were somewhat more likely than their younger counterparts to have disclosed their sexual identity to family members, whereas older White women were far less likely than younger White women to have done so.

In a study of African American, Latino, and European American youths who self-identified as gay, lesbian, or bisexual, ethnic differences were found for sexual identity integration but not for identity formation (Rosario, Schrimshaw, & Hunter, 2004). **Identity formation** in this study was defined as a part of the coming-out process involving becoming aware of one's sexual preferences and initial exploration of lesbian, gay, or bisexual identities, whereas **identity integration** comes later and involves accepting one's sexual identities, overcoming internalized homophobia by adopting positive attitudes about one's sexuality, experiencing greater comfort in disclosing one's sexual identity to others, and engaging more with LBG communities.

All of the youth participants in the study by Rosario, Scrimshaw, and Hunter (2004) progressed similarly in their identity formation by experiencing its developmental milestones at the same point in their lives regardless of their ethnicity. However, when it came to identity integration, African American youths were less engaged with the gay, lesbian, and bisexual community, felt less comfortable with others knowing about their sexual identities, and had disclosed their sexual identities to fewer people compared to European Americans. Interestingly, this changed with time; these same African American youths formed a stronger integrated sexual identity than did European American youths over one year, suggesting that they became even more committed to their sexual identities once they overcame cultural pressures against self-identifying as gay, lesbian, or bisexual. For Latino youths, sexual identity formation and integration were sometimes similar to both African and European American youths. Specifically, Latino youths were similar to European American youths in their comfort level with others knowing about their sexuality; yet they were similar to African American youths in disclosing it to fewer people. These somewhat contradictory findings reflect Latino cultural values of *familismo*, which promotes family support and cohesion, and *respeto*, or respect for family elders and authority figures. Latino gay, lesbian, and bisexual youths may feel comfortable about their sexuality knowing that their families will always support and accept them, yet feel reluctant to disclose it to their families and potentially upset older family members.

The importance of family relationships to LGBTQ racial ethnic minorities' identity formation and integration cannot be understated. In fact, research findings suggest that minority families' full acceptance and support of their children's sexual orientation is not just helpful but also essential to their children's identity integration (Kennedy & Dalla, 2014). However, LGBTQ people of color often find it difficult or impossible to gain unconditional family acceptance due to homonegative cultural beliefs or values tied to traditional gender role expectations. For instance, one study found that Black and Latino parents possessed significant **homonegativity**, or negative attitudes and beliefs about homosexuality, which led them to reject their children's sexual minority identities (Richter, Lindahl, & Malik, 2017).

Multicultural psychology researchers have begun to more closely examine the many different family, cultural, and minority factors affecting racial and ethnic minorities' coming-out processes. This includes gaining a better understanding of how specific cultural values, beliefs, norms, and family relationships influence this process across different ethnic groups as outlined in the following sections.

Cultural, Family, and Minority Considerations in Coming Out

Asian Americans

Coming out for Asian American LGBTQ persons often requires navigating multiple cultural family and gender role expectations, cultural communication norms, a collectivistic social orientation, interdependent views of the self, racial stereotypes (e.g., the model minority stereotype, perpetual foreigner stereotype), and, for those recently arrived to the United States, anti-immigrant sentiments. The extent to which these cultural, family, and minority issues influence the coming-out process depend on AA LGBTQs' acculturation levels, family dynamics, and residential demographics. An exhaustive review of AA LGBTQ research revealed that AA LGBTQ persons encounter more racial and sexual minority stressors than any other sexual minority ethnic group and are at risk for being pathologized by health care professionals who are unfamiliar with the many cultural and family issues that must be navigated (Choi & Israel, 2016).

Chan (1995) outlines the following cultural factors that can complicate the coming-out process for Asian American LGBTQ persons:

- *Distinct cultural conceptualizations of sexuality*: Asian Americans and other ethnic minority groups may not necessarily identify with fixed and rigid sexual categories like "homosexual" or "bisexual" as defined by the dominant group. Instead, they may experience and view their sexuality along a more fluid and broader continuum.
- *Lack of identification with the gay and bisexual community*: Asian Americans, like other ethnic and racial minorities, may be reluctant to identify with the gay, lesbian, and bisexual communities, which are mostly European American. Furthermore, if Asian Americans experience or witness racial discrimination by European American gays, lesbians, and bisexuals, they may find it especially difficult to integrate their ethnic and sexual identities.
- *Concerns that one's ethnic identity will be negated or overlooked by others*: Asian Americans may be hesitant to self-identify as gay or lesbian because others might then solely focus on their sexual orientation and completely disregard or ignore the significance of their ethnicity to the overall sense of self.
- *Distinctions between private and public selves*: For traditionally identified Asian Americans, sexuality and sexual behaviors are considered private rather than public matters (Chan, 1995). Thus, sexual identity is considered part of the private self that is left to one's own discretion. The public self, however, conforms to behaviors that bring honor to one's family. Because coming out is a

very public statement, it violates cultural norms for keeping sexual matters private, particularly when it is potentially stigmatizing or shameful to one's family. Keeping sexual matters private is even enforced for heterosexual Asian Americans. Asian American kids from traditionally identified families often report rarely seeing their parents kiss, hug, or hold hands with each other in public. Imagine, then, the conflict that many gay and lesbian Asian Americans experience as they come to terms with expressing their own sexuality that might be considered a cultural taboo. As such, Asian American gays and lesbians may be more likely to come out to people from other ethnic groups rather than to their own families or ethnic communities (Hom, 1996).

- *Familial obligation*: Similar to other collectivistic cultures, Asian Americans may hide their gay and lesbian sexual identities due to family expectations and obligations. The expression of sexuality among traditionally identified Asian Americans is mainly reserved for procreation and the continuation of the family name. This is especially the case for sons, who are expected to produce heirs who will carry on the family name and family traditions.

Asian American sexual minorities with solid social and economic support and resources, bicultural skills, strong ethnic identities, and greater acculturation are more likely to successfully navigate these cultural challenges, cope with intersecting stressors, and form a positive Asian American sexual minority identity (Vu, Choi, & Do, 2011). Also, having a supportive sibling who can serve as a bridge to traditionally oriented Asian American parents facilitates coming out, which in turn can enhance siblings' own personal growth, understanding of intersectional oppressions, and commitment to social justice (Huang, Chen, & Ponterotto, 2016). In contrast, endorsing traditional Asian values emphasizing heterosexuality increases internalized homonegativity or homophobia and inhibits Asian American LGBTQ persons' willingness to come out to family and others (Szymanski & Sung, 2013).

Latinos

Many of the aforementioned cultural, familial, and minority stressors for Asian American LGBTQ persons are also relevant to Latino coming-out experiences. However, cultural norms and beliefs around traditional machismo and marianismo exert culturally distinct pressures on Latino sexual minorities to fulfill certain gender roles, resulting in gender role strain and psychological distress. In a study of Latino college men (Eaton & Rios, 2017), the majority of participants reported negative social and family reactions to their sexual identity disclosure. Negative reactions included loss of valued social and family relationships, threats of physical harm or being kicked out of their family homes, being pathologized as sinners or sexual deviants, and dealing with significant others who only focused on how they were personally affected by the coming-out process (for example, parents who were mainly concerned about how they would be viewed in public). To cope with these negative reactions, most Latino participants reinterpreted or cognitively reframed them, which involved denying (e.g., "It never really happened to me") or minimizing their occurrence (e.g., the negative reaction was motivated by the individual's personality traits, not by discrimination), blaming themselves (e.g., feeling that they could control or were responsible for the negative reactions), or mentally distancing themselves from the LGBTQ community. Finally, Latino participants highlighted collectivistic concerns over preserving group and family harmony and highlighted maintaining cultural values of *respeto* and *familismo* as reasons for struggling over whether to come out to their family and friends.

African Americans

A qualitative study of African American gay men and their parents (LaSala & Frierson, 2012) revealed both similar and different coming-out experiences compared to European American gay men and their parents. Ethnic similarities included gay men distancing themselves from their parents when becoming aware of their sexual orientation, but before coming out, for self-protection and to avoid family conflict. African and European American parents were alike in their shared experience of guilt when they first learned about their son's gay identity and in their eventual acceptance of their son's sexual orientation with time and support from trusted others. Unlike European Americans, however, gay

African American men and their parents worried about cultural pressures to meet rigid hypermasculine gender role expectations in their families and ethnic community. Racial stratification compels African American men to exhibit public and family displays of strength, toughness, stoicism, and authority; to mask vulnerability; and, in some instances, to embody hyperheterosexuality that can manifest as homophobia. Thus, many African American gay men and their parents in this study felt that coming out required careful negotiation of cultural, racial, gender, and sexual identities. Although the African American parents in this study initially responded negatively to their sons' coming out, none rejected their sons, and they eventually fully accepted their sons' gay identity by keeping an open mind and processing their feelings and concerns with confidants.

The concept of homonegativity, or the intellectual disapproval of homosexuality, as different from homophobia (negative emotions and feelings toward homosexuality and homosexuals), has received significant levels of attention among African American men. Internalized homonegativity has been closely studied because of its potential for inhibiting African American sexual identity formation, disclosure, and willingness to seek same-sex sexual health services and resources. A large, U.S. multisite study examined correlates of internalized homonegativity for African American men who have sex with men (MSM) (Quinn et al., 2015). Study findings revealed that higher religiosity or church involvement, higher levels of masculinity, and being an MSM who self-identifies as bisexual or heterosexual predicted high internalized homonegativity. Religiosity placed African American MSMs in a particular bind because African American churches offered important support and protection against racism and strengthened racial pride and identity but in some instances conveyed anti-gay messages. Still, study findings revealed that active participation and involvement in a gay-identified community and resilience or a strong belief in one's own personal competence, coupled with self-acceptance, were important protective factors that guarded against internalized homonegativity for that African American MSM sample.

In sum, sexual identity development is a complex balancing act for many ethnic minorities, in which competing concerns and demands associated with their sexual orientation, ethnicity, race, culture, and gender must be negotiated and reconciled. Forming an integrated sense of self is complicated by socially stratified environments where being anything other than heterosexual is considered deviant and cause for social marginalization or even violence. Variations in ethnic minorities' sexual identities are innumerable because sexuality represents a broad continuum of experiences and expressions that transcends fixed, binary categorizations. No single factor can reliably predict one's sexual orientation, whether it is heterosexual, homosexual, bisexual, or otherwise (Rosario & Schrimshaw, 2014). Likewise, there is no single pattern for sexual identity development. Researchers are beginning to acknowledge these facts by moving away from older, fixed, and static notions of sexual identity development and by more fully attending to the effects of intersecting identity stressors. Sexual identity formation is in many ways an individual journey, and "sexual identity" is more accurately framed as "sexual identities" to reflect the tremendous diversity and heterogeneity witnessed in all ethnic and racial communities.

Relationship of Gender and Sexual Identities to Psychosocial Adjustment

Different dimensions of the self affect psychological functioning and overall mental health in variable and important ways. The following section highlights key research findings on the relationship of gender and sexual identities to multiple indices of individual health and well-being.

Gender Identity and Adjustment

Psychological Functioning and Physical Health A comprehensive research review on masculinity and its mental and physical health effects for U.S. men of color pointed to mixed and complex findings (Griffith, Gunter, & Watkins, 2012). Although findings across studies varied by definitions of masculinity and gender roles and health outcomes examined, they generally trended in expected ways: Nontraditional masculinity is associated with personal wellness, masculinity is positively correlated with steroid use, alcohol and substance use, and sexual risk-taking, and gender role conflict is positively associated with depression and restrictive emotionality.

In a rare study of transgender youths of color with diverse sexual identities (Singh, 2013), multiple examples of resiliency in coping with transprejudice and racism and safeguarding psychological well-being were identified. In that study, transgender youths of color relied on relational resilience strategies, such as finding their space in the larger LGBTQ youth community, using social media to connect with other transgender youths of color and adults to affirm their identity, and practicing self-advocacy in their educational and community settings.

Researchers have also examined gender effects on psychological functioning and health for specific ethnic groups.

- For Asian American men, gender role conflicts over expectations to succeed and compete, inhibiting emotions and affectionate behavior toward other men, and balancing work and family demands are associated with negative self-esteem (Shek & McEwen, 2012). Also, subjective masculinity stress or perceived stress related to being a man is positively related to psychological distress for Asian male international college students in the United States, especially if they view their masculinity as a prominent feature of their self-concept (Wong, Tsai, Liu, Zhu, & Wei, 2014).
- For African American men, gender role conflict and strain, or the inability to fulfill traditional African American male gender roles due to racism and discrimination, is associated with psychological distress (Wade & Rochlen, 2013). Among African American adolescent girls, androgyny or equal endorsement of masculine and feminine behaviors and traits is associated with less anxiety. Nevertheless, findings also showed that greater masculine role orientation intensified negative effects of daily hassles on psychological functioning, possibly due to related expectations for emotional restraint or stoicism when coping with stress (Cooper, Guthrie, Brown, & Metzger, 2011).
- A study of Latino adults (Central American, Cuban, Dominican, Mexican, Puerto Rican, South American, and other Latino backgrounds) showed that certain aspects of traditional machismo (hypermasculinity, dominance, sexism, emotional restrictiveness) and marianismo (being a source of strength and spiritual leader for the family) are associated with more negative cognitions (cynicism and hostility) and emotions (depression, anxiety, and anger) regardless of Latino background and acculturation levels (Nuñez et al., 2016). Still, an in-depth research review of Latino gender role effects on psychological outcomes concluded that Latino gender roles and attitudes affect psychological functioning in ways that are not always consistent or predictable (Miville, Mendez, & Louie, 2016).

Body Image In a predominantly African American sample of urban elementary school children, higher feminine identification was unrelated to body image contrary to expectations (Lyons et al., 2006). This finding suggests that African American girls may have a broader notion of femininity as a result of racial socialization—which emphasizes women's competence, resourcefulness, and versatility—and resisting narrow gender role definitions imposed by the dominant group. In this same study, a masculine gender role was positively associated with body image, suggesting that certain traditional masculine traits (e.g., instrumental behaviors or assertiveness) foster a positive self-concept, including positive thoughts about one's body and physical skills. For the boys in this sample, their interest and participation in sports may be an important moderator in this relationship, influencing their perceived competencies in physical activities and ultimately their body image. Finally, in a separate study of adolescent Latinas, stronger traditional gender role views were related to more physical appearance concerns and disordered eating, while the opposite was true for adolescent Latinos (Lopez, Corona, & Halfond, 2013).

Risk for Drug Use In a study of predominantly Mexican American eighth-grade students, gender identity proved to be a much more powerful predictor of drug use than did a person's gender label (Kulis, Marsiglia, & Hurdle, 2003). Specifically, four different gender identity dimensions had differential relationships with drug use behaviors and attitudes. These four different gender dimensions included *aggressive masculinity* (dominance and control over others), *assertive masculinity* (confidence and assertiveness), *affective femininity* (nurturing and expressive aspects of femininity), and *submissive femininity* (dependence and inadequacy). In general, aggressive masculinity was consistently associated with undesirable outcomes, while the other three gender identity dimensions were associated with more positive outcomes. Specifically, aggressive masculinity was tied to more drug use (alcohol, cigarettes, and marijuana), earlier drug initiation, and weaker antidrug attitudes. In contrast, assertive masculinity, affective femininity, and submissive femininity had selected protective effects: Assertive masculinity was associated with less lifetime alcohol and cigarette use and stronger antidrug attitudes, affective femininity was associated with lower lifetime use for all three drugs and with stronger antidrug attitudes, and submissive femininity was associated with lower alcohol and marijuana use.

Kulis and colleagues (2003) assert that these positive outcomes from these latter three identity dimensions may mirror positive and adaptive qualities of machismo and marianismo. Still, the relationship between these gender identity dimensions and drug outcomes often involved complex interactions with other personal characteristics. For example, the impact of gender identity dimensions on drug outcome was strongly mediated by acculturation. Submissive femininity was only a significant protector against marijuana use for more acculturated Mexican Americans, while aggressive masculinity was related to greater use of all three drugs for more acculturated Mexican Americans and to more marijuana use for less acculturated Mexican Americans.

Sexual Identity and Adjustment

Psychological Adjustment and Mental Health A study of Latino gay men showed that they experienced a unique set of stressors and resultant psychological stress linked to their intersecting sexual, ethnic, and class identities (Diaz, Ayala, & Bein, 2004). The Latino gay men in this study reported multiple instances of verbal and physical abuse, rude mistreatment, and discrimination based on their sexual orientation and their ethnicity. Moreover, many reported feeling uncomfortable in gay venues because of racism and racially based sexual objectification in the gay community, mostly consisting of White middle-class men. Latino gay men reported, for instance, that White men often approached and viewed them as exotic sex objects because of their race. In addition to these racial and sexual identity stressors, these Latino men also reported financial stressors, including inability to pay for basic food and shelter. High psychological distress was associated with exposure to these racial, sexual, and financial stressors, contributing to risky sex practices (engaging in sex while under the influence of drugs or alcohol, being with sex partners who resisted condom use) in an attempt to alleviate their stress and anxiety. These findings thus illustrated that psychological distress from racism, financial hardship, and homophobia elevates Latino gay men's risk for HIV infection.

Other studies of ethnic and racial minority LGBT (lesbian, gay, bisexual, and transgender) individuals likewise report high levels of psychological distress. In a study of American Indian "two-spirited" individuals who self-identify as lesbian, gay, bisexual, or unsure and who embody both feminine and masculine spirits, high rates of alcohol use were reported as a means to increase their sociability, decrease feelings of inferiority, manage their mood, and relieve tension (Balsam et al., 2004).

Still, other studies indicate that not all ethnic minority LGBTs are at increased risk for psychological difficulties. In one study of same-sex-attracted middle and high school students, African Americans and Whites reported more suicidal thoughts than did other-sex-attracted youths, but this was not the case for Latino or Asian/Pacific Islander same-sex-attracted youths (Consolacion, Russell, & Sue, 2004). Study results also showed higher levels of depression for Latino, African American, and White same-sex-attracted youths compared to other-sex-attracted youths, but this was not true for same-sex-attracted Asian/Pacific Islanders. Finally, only African American and White same-sex-attracted youths reported lower self-esteem than did other-sex-attracted youths. The authors of this study note that these findings indicate that ethnic minority same-sex-attracted youths exhibit variable risk for psychological difficulties. They clearly state, however, that the nonsignificant findings for some of the ethnic minority participants—namely, for Asian/Pacific Islanders—do not necessarily mean that they do not face multiple minority stressors. Rather, some ethnic minority LGBTs might effectively adapt to discrimination by "readjusting" their identity and focusing on the least-disparaged or -oppressed identity in a given social situation.

Researchers continue to test the **minority stress theory**, which proposes that intersecting stressors from multiple minority social positions increase the risk for psychological and health problems. As shown in the following, empirical support for this theory is quite extensive:

- South Asian American LGBQ adults experience significant racist incidents, heterosexist discrimination, and internalized heterosexism that compound their psychological distress (Sandil, Robinson, Brewster, Wong, & Geiger, 2015).
- Asian American LGBTQs experience heightened psychological distress from heterosexism in communities of color, race-related dating and relationship problems in the LGBTQ community, internalized heterosexism, and the condition of being out (Szymanski & Sung, 2010).
- African American LGB adolescents report significant antigay and racist discrimination, both of which independently contribute to depression and suicidal ideation (Thoma & Huebner, 2013).
- African American lesbian and bisexual women are at greater risk for diabetes and hypertension than are White lesbian and bisexual women (Molina, Lehavot, Beadnell, & Simoni, 2014).
- Black and Latina sexual minority women suffer from substance abuse problems at rates that are four times higher than ethnically similar heterosexual women and two times higher than for White lesbian women (Mereish & Bradford, 2014).
- Young Black gay men show higher levels of cortisol (a stress hormone tied to diabetes and heart disease) than do young White gay men (Cook, Juster, Calebs, Heinze, & Miller, 2017).
- Low SES racial minority transgender persons (with diverse sexual orientations) report more anxiety than do high SES White transgender persons (with diverse sexual orientations) (Budge, Thai, Tebbe, & Howard, 2016).

Researchers caution, however, that, although intersectional minority identities increase LGBTQ ethnic-racial minorities' risk for psychological and health problems, their effects vary across health outcomes and are not always additive in nature, instead representing complex interactions (Hsieh & Ruther, 2016). Also, each minority identity can affect psychological functioning and health in different and independent ways. For example, in a study of Asian American gay men, sexual minority stress predicted psychological distress, but racial minority stress did not. This finding was related to the fact that antigay discrimination, unlike racism, predicted lower self-esteem, which in turn predicted greater distress (Chen & Tryon, 2012).

Distinct psychological effects across minority identity dimensions are also witnessed for Black gay and bisexual emerging adult men. One study showed that racial identity, but not sexual identity, predicted risky sex behaviors for this group of men (Walker, Longmire-Avital, & Golub, 2015). Specifically, study participants whose Black identities were central to their self-concept and who perceived that society had positive views of Blacks were less likely to engage in risky sex. The researchers explained Black GB participants may have established their racial identities earlier in their lives, which may account for this stronger relationship with racial identity.

Finally, a large-scale study of African American, Asian and Pacific Islander American (APIA), and Latino men who have sex with men (MSM) found a positive relationship between reports of discrimination and psychological distress. However, different types of discrimination varied across groups and had, in some instances, group-specific psychological effects. For instance, African American and Latinos MSMs were more likely to report racism in the general community than were APIA MSMs, but APIA MSMs reported more racism in the mainstream gay community. Also, mainstream gay community racism was associated with anxiety only for APIA MSMs, which again indicates their relatively lower social position in racial hierarchies of perceived sexual attractiveness and desirability (Choi, Paul, Ayala, Boylan, & Gregorich, 2013).

Multicultural psychologists have also tried to determine whether coming out has mental health benefits for LGBTQ persons of color. One study found that Latina lesbians who come out to nonfamily members are less likely to be depressed (Aranda et al., 2015). This finding is significant because, unlike the African and European American lesbians in that study, Latina lesbians reported more depression than both groups and were the least likely to come out to their families. Thus, receiving emotional support from friends and coworkers while striving to maintain family relations may be important to Latina lesbians during their coming-out process.

Data from the National Latino and Asian American Study, however, revealed that coming out may not necessarily benefit mental health. Results showed that Asian Americans and Latinos who came out as lesbian, gay, or bisexual experienced more daily discrimination and higher psychological distress than did their ethnic peers who had same-gender sex but had not come out as LGB (Chae & Ayala, 2010).

Although LGBTQ persons of color must contend with multiple minority stressors, research suggests that resilience, or strength amid adversity, is not an exceptional or rare trait for this population. A qualitative study found that resilience was widely seen among their young Black gay and bisexual male (YBGBM) respondents who expressed it in many different ways in their daily lives (Wilson et al., 2016). Moreover, study findings indicate that, for LGBTQ persons of color, strong self-efficacy, mastery, and control beliefs promote positive psychological health in ways that extend beyond the psychological benefits of social support.

Chapter Summary

In this chapter, we discuss how gender and sexual identities are complex in their development, interaction with one another, and expression in our daily lives. Although multicultural psychology research focuses on racial, ethnic, gender, and class identity dimensions, studies on sexual identities among people of color are currently garnering greater attention in the field. With greater attention focused on how all of these identity dimensions intersect and affect psychological and physical health, more innovative, complex, and effective health interventions can be developed for diverse segments within ethnic and racial minority populations.

Key Terms

caballerismo 141
controlling images 138
double minority status 142
gendered racial socialization 139
gender identity 136
gender roles 136
gender typing 136
homonegativity 144
machismo 140
marianismo 140
minority stress theory 149
sexual identity 136
sexual identity formation 143
sexual identity integration 143
two-spirited individual 136

Learning by Doing

- Thinking about your experiences growing up, try to answer the following questions:
  1. What are the masculine and feminine ideologies or beliefs that are taught in your cultural groups and families?
  2. How might they shape your daily life, including your comfort level in asking questions and participating in classroom discussion, your social interactions with your friends and coworkers, and your perceived family duties and responsibilities?
  3. In what ways do your cultural gender roles affect how you act, feel, and think?

Suggested Further Readings

Greene, B. (Ed.). (1997). *Ethnic and cultural diversity among lesbians and gay men: Vol. 3, Psychological perspectives on lesbian and gay issues series.* Thousand Oaks, CA: Sage.

A pioneering overview of psychological issues for lesbian and gay people of color, covering key empirical, theoretical, and clinical topics.

Landrine, H., & Russo, N. F. (2010). *Handbook of diversity in feminist psychology.* New York: Springer Publishing Co.

A handbook presenting a multicultural approach to diversity in feminist psychology. It comprehensively discusses the cutting edge of feminist discourse, covering major topics such as multicultural feminist theory, gender discrimination, aging, health and therapy, violence and harassment, politics and policy, and much more. Special emphasis is given to the intersectionality of minority identities such as race, ethnicity, social class, sexual preference, and other socially constructed status differences among women.

Nadal, K. L. (2013). *That's so gay! Microaggressions and the lesbian, gay, bisexual, and transgender community.* Washington, DC: American Psychological Association.

A thought-provoking review of the literature on discrimination and microaggressions toward LGBT people. The book includes a generous use of case examples that will help in discussion groups and will support students and professionals who want to adopt LGBT–accepting worldviews and practices.

Suggested Further Readings

7 Family Structure, Relations, and Socialization

"In My Family, We Never Openly Say 'I Love You'"

Jon is a 39-year-old, first generation Chinese American and the oldest son in his family. When he was a teenager, his parents moved the family from Hong Kong to the United States in search of greater educational opportunities for their children. Although Jon describes his parents as caring and kind, he often wishes that they were more verbally expressive and open with him. Whenever Jon visits his parents for dinner, he notices that they "never really talk about anything." To Jon's dismay, his parents rarely ask him about his life and almost never inquire about his thoughts and feelings about personal matters. Instead, his parents typically ask seemingly superficial questions—"Why do you look so thin? Have you been eating?" "Have you spoken to your sister or grandmother lately?" After Jon answers these questions, he notices that they often just sit in silence for the rest of the meal. Jon never thought twice about his interactions with his parents until he spent time with his friends' families. On one occasion, he had dinner with his fourth generation Chinese American friend, Chris, and Chris's family. Jon was surprised to see that Chris and his family freely talked about how they were feeling and how they were doing in their lives. Jon was especially taken aback when Chris's mother hugged her son and told him that she loved him. Afterward, Jon told Chris, "In my family, we never say, 'I love you.'" Jon is becoming frustrated because he wants to share his feelings with his parents, particularly his concerns over his family responsibilities. As the oldest son in his family, Jon's parents expect him to support and house them when they retire. Jon is conflicted about this idea; he doesn't want to be a "bad son," but he also wants to "do his own thing" and be completely independent at times. He feels guilty about this because his parents' sacrifices allowed him to graduate from a prestigious college and become financially successful. Also, Jon appreciates his parents' weekly delivery of home-cooked Chinese meals, which he views as cultural expressions of their love. Consequently, Jon is reluctant to discuss his concerns with his parents because he doesn't want to appear disrespectful and insensitive. What should Jon do?

How would you describe your relationship with your family? Does your culture have specific rules and expectations about how you should behave with certain family members? For instance, are you expected to act differently with older members than with those who are younger or of similar age to you? When you were growing up, did your parents encourage you to freely express your feelings and thoughts to them, or did they simply expect you to obey them and follow their wishes? Your family relationships, family communication styles, and parenting can be understood from different cultural perspectives. Your culture essentially provides you with a set of rules and expectations about how families should ideally function in the world. Jon's experiences highlight family communication styles and family role expectations seen in many first generation Asian American immigrant households. He struggles to negotiate his family's collectivistic norms, which compel him to consider the needs and concerns of his parents over his own. Additionally, certain teachings from Confucian philosophy—namely, showing respect toward elders and fulfilling family obligations as the oldest son—influence his interactions with his parents. As Jon spends time with more acculturated Asian American families like Chris's, or with families who have different cultural traditions, he feels more at odds with his parents' cultural family role and relationship expectations. This chapter explores these and other ethnic minority family issues by highlighting how cultural norms, values, and beliefs influence family life from an ecological perspective of family functioning.

An Ecological Perspective of Family Functioning

According to an **ecological perspective** of family functioning, family well-being and development are shaped by different **ecologies**, or social contexts and relationships, that are part of each family member's life (Bronfenbrenner, 1986; Bronfenbrenner & Morris, 1998) (see Figure 7.1). The immediate home environment might be the first thing that comes to mind when thinking of the effects of social context on family functioning. For instance, ethnic minority homes that are bicultural, collectivistic, and multigenerational are more likely to have positive child-rearing goals that in turn contribute to healthy child development (Harrison, Wilson, Pine, Chan, & Buriel, 1990). Family ecologies also include a wide range of social settings and relationships outside of the home. Children spend a large part of their day at school, in their peer groups, and in recreational organizations. Parents' daily lives also unfold in different settings, like their workplaces and adult social circles. All of these different social settings and relationships influence how family members grow, develop, and relate to one another. In the vignette opening this chapter, Jon's social interactions with Chris's family shifted his own cultural attitudes on family communication, which in turn affected his relationship with his parents. Jon's peer circle thus significantly influenced his behavior and family interactions at home as proposed by the ecological perspective of family functioning.

An ecological perspective also recognizes that ethnic minority families face distinct environmental challenges or stressors that can disrupt their overall functioning and well-being. In particular, two specific ecological challenges—*minority status* and *acculturation*—have been highlighted in the multicultural psychology literature (McLoyd, Cauce, Takeuchi, & Wilson, 2000; Yee, Huang, & Lew, 1998). As outlined in Chapter 2, minority status results from social stratification and having restricted access to society's wealth and resources. Ethnic minority families face historical barriers to quality education, affordable health care, high-income jobs, safe neighborhoods, and even healthy living environments. In this chapter we discuss how these barriers contribute to family stress and psychosocial problems.

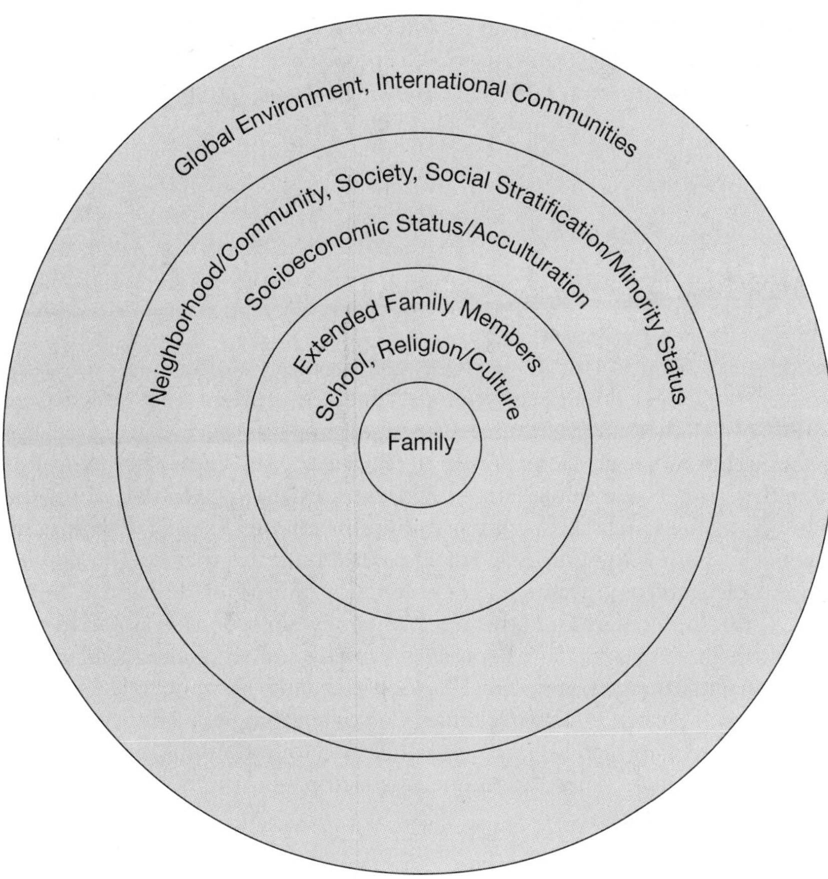

Source: Bronfenbrenner (1986); Bronfenbrenner & Morris (1998).
FIG. 7.1 Ethnic Minority Family Ecologies.

Immigrant and refugee families face the added ecological challenge of acculturation. As mentioned in Chapter 4, acculturation can be a stressful experience when individuals are unable to meet the demands of new cultural environments, including demands to learn a new language and cultural norms and values. As seen in this chapter, such instances of acculturative stress can strain family relationships when parents and their children adjust to a new culture at different rates.

Although an ecological perspective highlights environmental and social factors that impact family functioning, families are far from being passive entities. **Family agency**, or a family's capacity to actively promote and safeguard its own welfare and development, illustrates this point. Family agency is seen in many different ways, including when families transform or shape their social environments and social institutions with which they come into contact. For instance, research shows that many immigrant Latino and Asian American families actively participate in civic life through their churches or religious organizations (Lorentzen, Chun, Gonzalez, & Do, 2009). Religious activities—whether centered on political advocacy for immigrant rights or gang prevention activities for youths—can help immigrant families build certain strengths and skills that promote their growth and development. Family agency is also exercised when families effectively respond to the demands of daily living (e.g., securing food and shelter, locating public transportation, enrolling children in school), fulfill normative developmental tasks (e.g., adjusting to the birth of a new infant, altering family roles and responsibilities), and cope with unexpected crises (e.g., responding to medical emergencies, enduring forced relocation to another country).

In sum, the many different environments and social relationships in family members' daily lives shape family functioning. Families can likewise change or alter their environments to enhance their development and adaptation to new cultural settings. The added stressors of discrimination and prejudice complicate families' abilities to meet their daily needs and negotiate normative life transitions. Therefore, the diverse life experiences of ethnic minority families can only be fully appreciated by exploring the cultural, socioeconomic, and historical contexts in which they occur.

Factors Affecting Family Structures and Household Arrangements

How do you define a family? This appears to be a simple question until you consider all of the different family arrangements that are seen in American society today. The *nuclear family*—a family consisting of a father, mother, and their children—was once considered the standard unit of American family life in social science research. However, shifting sociopolitical attitudes toward gender roles and marriage, and fluctuating divorce rates in the United States, have pushed for broader definitions of the family. Historical assumptions about nuclear family functioning have also been questioned. Research with families across the world indicates that nuclear families do not necessarily function in isolation from extended kin and are not universally individualistic as once proposed (Georgas et al., 2001). Furthermore, the nuclear family unit overlooks variations in how ethnic minority families organize and sustain themselves. In addition to nuclear family households, ethnic minority families maintain multigenerational households, single-parent households, and households headed by grandparents or other family relatives. In some ethnic minority communities, these types of households are more "normative" than the nuclear family household and form the foundation for healthy family functioning. There are numerous factors contributing to diverse family structures across ethnic minority groups.

Migration

Multigenerational or extended family households are formed when new immigrants to the United States join family members or relatives who have gained legal citizenship and can sponsor their immigration. The Asian American and Latino communities have the highest proportion of new immigrants to the United States and are more likely to live in multigenerational homes than are European Americans (Vespa, Lewis, & Kerider, 2013). Often, such extended households offer essential support to new immigrants who face acculturation stressors like learning the English language, adjusting to American cultural norms, and maintaining their cultural identity and traditions in the United States.

Socioeconomic Status (SES)

Family income and economic resources also influence ethnic minority family structures. As noted in Chapter 1, a significant proportion of ethnic minority families fall below the federal poverty line, which is an approximately $25,000 annual income for a family of four (U.S. Department of Health and Human Services, 2017). Poor ethnic minority families must often pool their limited resources together in extended- or multiple-family households to meet their basic living needs. Multiple-family households are those where families share a roof even though they are biologically unrelated. In addition to consolidating capital, extended- or multiple-family households provide instrumental family support to its members in the form of shared childcare and assistance with daily chores and household duties. The influence of SES on family household composition can also be seen for more affluent ethnic minority families. High-SES ethnic minority families sometimes maintain dual or multiple residences in different countries. For example, some Asian nationals might have a primary residence in Asia while maintaining a secondary U.S. residence. This dual or transnational family residence is often established so children can receive an American education. Youths in these secondary homes are called *parachute kids* because they land temporarily in the United States, where they live alone or with siblings until they finish their schooling. This living arrangement can be stressful for immigrant youths because they are isolated from their families while facing academic demands and acculturation stressors.

Exposure to Stress and Trauma

Disrupted family systems can result from war and civil strife, natural disasters, and stress from racial and social stratification. In regard to war and civil strife, Southeast Asian refugee families endured tremendous loss of life and property, separation from family members, and treacherous migration and refugee camp experiences that threatened their survival and in many cases permanently altered their family composition (Abueg & Chun, 1996). In one of the first large-scale mental health needs assessment studies of Southeast Asian refugees, 55 percent of the entire sample reported separations from or deaths of family members, with 30 percent experiencing multiple separations or losses from the Vietnam War and related civil strife in their home countries (Gong-Guy, 1987). For the Cambodian women in this study, more than one in five experienced the death of their husbands. Upon their arrival to the United States, many Southeast Asian refugees encountered acculturation stressors, which exacerbated their stress and increased their risk for family dysfunction. Complicating matters was the possibility of persecution and death if these families ever returned to their home countries to search for family members who had been left behind.

African Americans and American Indians have also experienced high levels of stress from the historical legacy of racial and social stratification in the United States. During the time of slavery, slave masters forcibly separated African family members from one another in an attempt to weaken or destroy their family bonds and ties to their homelands (Schaefer, 1996). For American Indians, removal from tribal homelands and forced youth enrollment in American boarding schools, where they were isolated from their families and tribes and prohibited from practicing their culture, represented significant family stressors (Sue & Sue, 1999).

Institutionalized oppression and social marginalization continue to impact African American and American Indian family structures. Impoverished and dangerous living conditions, chronic exposure to racism and discrimination, and limited opportunities for educational and economic advancement increase family stress, which in turn heightens risk for marital divorce or separation or loss of family members from stress-related illnesses. This can partly explain the high rate of single-parent households in African American and American Indian communities. Approximately 30 percent of African American and 20 percent of American Indian family households are headed by single women, compared to 8 percent for European American households (Vespa et al., 2013). Children from disrupted family systems may be placed in family members' and relatives' homes. These family arrangements are often stereotyped as being pathological or dysfunctional because they do not conform to the nuclear family structure. However, it is wrong to equate family structure with family functioning (Hill, 1998). Furthermore, diverse ethnic minority family structures can actually reflect family resilience and family agency or adaptation to chronically stressful life conditions. Finally, extended or single-parent households, contrary to negative stereotypes, can be nurturing family environments. It is not uncommon for African American children to be raised in large extended families consisting of "blood" and "nonblood" relatives who act as important role models and share in child-rearing or parenting (Franklin, Boyd-Franklin, & Draper, 2002). Also, one-parent African American families can exhibit flexible family roles and strong kinship bonds that foster more family cohesiveness than do many two-parent families (Hill, 1998).

Cultural Values and Beliefs

A family's cultural beliefs, attitudes, and values related to family life also shape their organization and structure. Generally speaking, Asian Americans, African Americans, Latinos, and American Indians historically share a collectivistic social orientation that promotes strong kinship ties, close family living arrangements, extended family households, and family obligation or duty to the family. For Latinos, this is witnessed in **familism** or **familismo**, which is defined as being strongly grounded in one's family, valuing family closeness and cohesion, emphasizing family responsibilities over individual needs or goals (Parke, Coltrane, Borthwick-Duffy, Powers, & Adams, 2004), preferring to live near family, and relying on them for emotional and instrumental support (Gil, Wagner, & Vega, 2000). Findings on the nature and effects of familism and family obligation on ethnic minority family life tend to be mixed. Studies with Latinos show that familism strengthens family cooperation, family contact, and extended family support (Parke et al., 2004) and improves Latino youths' psychological functioning, especially during adolescence (Stein et al., 2014). Studies of other minority groups, however, show that the weight of family obligation causes distress and family conflict. Korean and Korean American caregivers, for instance, feel burdened and distressed by family expectations to care for elderly members with dementia (Youn, Knight, Jeong, & Benton, 1999).

The influence of cultural values on family structures is also seen in Asian American families who follow Confucian principles on family relations, roles, and duties. Confucian teachings support a **patrilineal** family structure that gives greater authority, privileges, and status to older males in the family (Ching, McDermott, Fukunaga, & Yanagida, 1995; Park & Cho, 1995). This type of family structure is thus hierarchical in nature: The father is the figurative family head, responsible for providing for the family and making family decisions. Also, children are expected to show **filial piety**, or respect for the needs and concerns of the family over their own, especially when elderly family members are concerned. When the oldest son comes of age, he is expected to assume the mantle of family leadership by caring for his elderly parents and providing instrumental support to other family members.

Two-way communication or negotiation between parents and children is prohibited in patrilineal families. Family conflict can arise when children become socialized to American culture and desire more open communication with their parents (as was the case for Jon in the vignette at the beginning of the chapter). Still, these Confucian family teachings, as with familism, should not be overgeneralized. Asian American families may follow only some Confucian teachings or none at all depending on their acculturation levels. Also, patrilineal Asian American families are not necessarily experts in Confucian philosophy but may simply follow it without much thought as part of their family traditions. In short, ethnic minority families understand and follow cultural practices in diverse ways depending on their cultural knowledge, socialization, and acculturation strategies.

Family Functioning, Socialization, and Adjustment

Do ethnic minority family members relate to each other in culturally unique ways? How do ethnic minority parents teach their children essential life skills and lessons? Does acculturation affect married couples' gender roles and attitudes? What are the distinct challenges that ethnic minority families face, and how do they cope with them? These questions are related to ethnic minority family functioning, socialization, and adjustment. Much of the research focuses on parenting and parent-child relationships, academic achievement, couple relationships, and family stress and coping. The following sections highlight major research findings in these areas.

Parenting Styles

Developmental psychologists have extensively studied how parents socialize, nurture, and discipline their children and how parenting affects children's overall adjustment and development. One widely referenced parenting model specifies three primary parenting methods or styles based on observations and interviews of mostly European American, middle-class parents with preschool-age children (Baumrind, 1971, 1980): **Authoritarian parenting** is characterized by highly controlling, demanding, and overly strict parenting. Parents falling under this category emphasize obedience and respect for authority and place high standards on their children. Children are not allowed to negotiate

TABLE 7.1 Parenting Styles: Baumrind's Classification

Parenting style	Examples
Authoritarian parenting	
• controlling	"Do as I say. I'm the parent!"
• demanding	
• overly strict	
• no negotiation	
• demanding obedience	
• maintaining high standards	
Authoritative parenting	
• placing limits while encouraging independence	"It isn't like you to behave this way. Let's talk about what's going on."
• fostering parent-child communication	
• maintaining high standards	
Permissive parenting	
• exhibiting little control and involvement	"Whatever you want to do is fine with me."
• allowing child do whatever they wish	

Sources: Baumrind, 1971, 1980.

or openly disagree with their parents, and if parents perceive any transgressions, they use punitive disciplinary measures. **Authoritative parenting** reflects more of a democratic or reciprocal parent-child relationship; parents set high standards and place demands on their children, but they allow their children to share their opinions and concerns without unduly imposing their parental authority or will. In regard to discipline, parents favor reasoning and explanation for their rules or decisions over physical punishment. Also, parents encourage their children to be independent and to reflect on their actions and behaviors. Parents who exhibit **permissive parenting** do not place high standards on their children, exercise little parental control, and can be neglectful of their parental responsibilities. These parents tend to believe that children should be allowed to follow their own impulses and desires without parental monitoring or interference. Permissive parents are thus less concerned with child discipline than are authoritarian and authoritative parents, and may consult with their children on family policies or decisions (see Table 7.1).

Past research with White children indicates that authoritative parenting is the most effective parenting style and produces better childhood outcomes than do authoritarian or permissive parenting. Specifically, children who have authoritative parents tend to be more intellectually curious, self-controlled, self-reliant, and content compared to children from authoritarian or permissive households (Berns, 2004). Some multicultural psychology researchers have questioned the generalizability of these findings, however, given the ethnic homogeneity of the study samples. Furthermore, widely reported effects of authoritarian, authoritative, and permissive parenting styles on childhood adjustment are not always seen in ethnic minority families due to their different cultural views on parenting. African Americans who are asked to evaluate videos of African American mother-daughter interactions tend to see less parental restriction and less conflict compared to non–African Americans watching the same videos (McLoyd et al., 2000). Also, American Indian parents have culture-specific beliefs about the causes of parent-child conflict and what constitutes effective parenting (Ayers, Kulis, & Tsethlikai, 2017).

Mandara and Murray (2002) have developed three new categories of parenting styles that overlap with the authoritarian, authoritative, and permissive categories but also incorporate distinct cultural features of African American parenting (see Table 7.2).

TABLE 7.2 African American Parenting Styles

Parenting style	Outcomes
Conflict-authoritarian	
• demonstrating little concern or warmth • overly strict • maintaining high standards, but controlling	• high familial conflict • distress • moderate racial socialization
Cohesive-authoritative	
• concerned and warm • engaged • structured and supportive • encouraging independence • maintaining high standards without being controlling	• high self-esteem in children • high proactive racial socialization • low defensive racial socialization • high emotional stability in children
Defensive-neglectful	
• neglectful • exhibiting little concern or emotional affection • placing little importance on child's growth and achievement • highly critical • maintaining rigid family hierarchies • punitive	• high family conflict • chaotic family relationships • high defensive racial socialization • low empowering racial socialization

Source: Mandara & Murray, 2002.

- **Conflict-authoritarian:** Similar to an authoritarian parenting style, parents exhibiting a conflict-authoritarian parenting style show little concern and warmth toward their children, are overly strict and controlling toward their children, and disallow their children from expressing their feelings or questioning family rules. Although parents in this category also emphasize achievement like parents who are cohesive-authoritative, their drive for achievement is not necessarily focused on intellectual activities. Also, children may feel conflicted about meeting parental demands because their family environments and activities tend to be unstructured and their parents can be neglectful. Other features of this category include high levels of family conflict, distressed family relationships, and moderate levels of racial socialization. The demographic characteristics of the African American families categorized as conflict-authoritarian in this study (Mandara & Murray, 2002) were the following: (1) 63 percent were headed by married couples, (2) parents had moderate levels of formal education, (3) the average number of children in the household (2.7) was greater than in cohesive-authoritative families but fewer than in defensive-neglectful families, (4) their average annual income was lower than that of cohesive-authoritative households but higher than that of defensive-neglectful families, and (5) they attended church often and held religion in high regard.
- **Cohesive-authoritative:** Parents using the cohesive-authoritative parenting style express concern and warmth toward their children, engage them in intellectual activities, and provide a structured and supportive family environment. Similar to the authoritative parenting style, cohesive-authoritative parents emphasize the personal growth and independence of their children, encourage their children to express themselves openly, value achievement and high standards without being overly rigid or controlling, and tend to avoid punitive disciplinary measures. Some distinct cultural features of this parenting category include high *proactive racial socialization*—meaning parents emphasize positive racial identity and pride in their racial group—and low defensive racial socialization—meaning parents neither teach their children to dislike other racial

groups nor teach them to imitate White behaviors. In this study sample (Mandara & Murray, 2002), African American families who were cohesive-authoritative possessed the following characteristics: (1) 58 percent were headed by married couples, (2) parents had completed more formal education and had higher annual incomes (approximately $32,000) than parents in the other two categories, (3) parents had an average of two children, (4) they attended church on a regular basis, and (5) they exhibited high overall family functioning.

- **Defensive-neglectful:** Proportionally fewer families in this study (Mandara & Murray, 2002) fell into the defensive-neglectful category. However, the relatively few who were classified as defensive-neglectful showed the greatest risk for poor family functioning, reflected by high family conflict and chaotic family relationships. Parents also exhibit neglectful parenting, show little concern and emotional affection toward their children, and place little importance on their child's personal growth and academic achievement. Similar to conflict-authoritarian parents, defensive-neglectful parents could be highly critical of their children and used punitive discipline methods and had rigid and hierarchical family structures. Other features of defensive-neglectful parenting included high levels of defensive racial socialization—where parents taught their children to dislike other racial groups while failing to promote racial pride—and low levels of empowering racial socialization—a form of proactive racial socialization that promotes positive racial identification and a belief in overcoming life obstacles despite racial barriers. The demographic background of defensive-neglectful families in this study included the following: (1) parents had significantly lower educational levels and average annual incomes than did parents in the other two categories, (2) they had an average of three children, and (3) they attended church less frequently than did families from the other two categories.

Finally, Mandara and Murray (2002) found that these three family types were related to African American adolescent self-esteem, ethnic identity, and adjustment. Adolescents who had cohesive-authoritative parents had the highest self-esteem, were more likely to participate in cultural activities and traditions, and valued African American culture more than did their peers from conflict-authoritarian and defensive-neglectful families. Finally, adolescents from cohesive-authoritative families were more emotionally stable than their counterparts in the other two categories. These findings indicate that aspects of authoritative parenting are tied to positive family functioning and childhood adjustment for both African American and White families.

Other studies similarly found important links between features of authoritative parenting and ethnic minority child and family functioning. Authoritative parenting reduces Latino youths' alcohol use and binge drinking (Merianos, King, Vidourek, & Nabors, 2015), and parental warmth and responsive parenting improves African American children's attachment to their parents (Dexter, Wong, Stacks, Beeghly, & Barnett, 2013). Also, parental warmth and monitoring improves African American and Latino youths' academic outcomes (Lowe & Dotterer, 2013).

Ethnic Minority Fathers A growing body of research on fathers is also improving our understanding of ethnic minority parenting. Studies show that young African American men who are emotionally close to their fathers are more likely to experience positive emotional relationships in general, which in turn makes them more involved with their own children, especially with their young daughters (Brown, Kogan, & Kim, 2017). Interestingly, neighborhood characteristics and developmental stage can influence which fathering style benefits youth the most. In a study of Mexican-origin fathers and their children (White, Liu, Gonzales, Knight, & Tein, 2016), authoritative fathering guarded against internalizing symptoms (i.e., generalized anxiety, depression, and social phobia) during early adolescence, but only for those living in economically depressed neighborhoods. Also, under the same adverse neighborhood conditions, a culturally unique form of "no-nonsense" fathering (harsh and demanding yet accepting) improved Mexican-origin youths' mental health over time as they moved from early to middle adolescence. No-nonsense fathering is considered culturally adaptive because it helps prepare Mexican-origin children to deal with stressful neighborhood environments. African American fathers may likewise show culturally adaptive parenting styles. One qualitative study (Doyle et al., 2015) found that African American fathers emphasized close monitoring, discipline, encouragement (rather than open expressions of love and nurturance), and managing or restricting emotions when parenting their preadolescent sons. Close monitoring was an adaptive response to perceived neighborhood risk for gang activity and crime, while managing emotions and encouragement reflected African American fathers' masculine ideologies or gender attitudes.

Disciplinary Practices Studies also show that ethnic groups might view parenting and child discipline methods in culturally distinct ways. One study (Whaley, 2000) shows that White parents viewed spanking as a "parent-oriented" form of physical discipline that promotes obedience to parents. However, African American parents viewed spanking as both a parent-oriented and a "child-oriented" form of physical discipline. In this latter case, African American parents also believed that spanking helped their children become self-respecting and responsible adults. A study of Chinese American parents showed that cultural values influence parents' use of physical discipline in multifaceted ways (Lau, 2010). In this study, belief in firm parental control was associated with using physical discipline only for highly acculturated Chinese American parents. Also, physical discipline was less likely to be used if Chinese American parents valued emotional self-restraint.

Although cultural views of spanking may vary, research suggests that it should be used sparingly, if at all, because of its potentially negative effects on child and youth development. Among African American and Hispanic mothers, endorsement of spanking predicted short-term reductions in their children's internalizing problems during early childhood but was related to increased internalizing and externalizing problems over time (Coley, Kull, & Carrano, 2014). Thus, physical discipline and power-assertive parenting may have short-term benefits but also model aggressive behaviors, inhibit positive interpersonal skills development, and weaken parent-child emotional bonds. Potentially harmful effects of physical discipline may be even more pronounced for ethnic minority youths who are genetically more emotionally sensitive and reactive to harsh parenting (Brody et al., 2014).

Asian American Tiger Moms: Fact or Fiction? Asian American mothers and their children also possess culturally distinct views of parenting and child discipline that can be misinterpreted. In this case, Asian American mothers are frequently stereotyped as ruthless "Tiger Moms" in the popular media and even in psychological research (Lau & Fung, 2013). This includes characterizing Chinese American mothers as authoritarian, restrictive, and controlling. However, this rigid portrayal of Chinese mothers overlooks certain Chinese parenting beliefs and attitudes. In one study (Chao, 1994), Chinese American mothers of preschool-age children scored higher than did their White counterparts on standard measures of authoritarian parenting and parental control. However, these same Chinese mothers, unlike the White mothers, were also more likely to endorse Chinese child-rearing practices related to child "training" even after controlling for mothers' scores on authoritarian and parental control measures. Although the Chinese concept of training overlaps with authoritarian features of parental authority, parental control, and high parental standards, it is a culturally distinct parenting concept because it also involves highly supportive and caring parenting. Furthermore, this Chinese notion of training involves different motives than those underlying authoritarian parenting; it aims to teach children culturally appropriate behaviors and skills to help them achieve academic success and meet societal and family expectations.

These cultural differences might partially explain why high parental control or parental monitoring does not consistently predict poor Asian American youth adjustment and Asian American family functioning. In a study of Chinese American adolescents, those who reported close parental monitoring (e.g., parents' desire to know their whereabouts, who they were with, and whether they complied with a set bedtime) were at lower risk for depression than were their peers who reported less parental monitoring (Kim & Ge, 2000). This unexpected finding is similar to other findings showing that Korean adolescents may associate parental control with parental warmth and attentiveness (Rohner & Pettengill, 1985) and that immigrant Chinese parents are more likely to report positive relationships with their children if they view themselves as competent parents and in control of their children (Ying, 1999).

More recent research continues to debunk the Asian tiger mom stereotype. A study of Chinese American parents showed that although "tiger parenting" does exist as a unique parenting style involving both negative (e.g., hostility) and positive (warmth) dimensions, it was not the most typical Chinese American parenting style, nor did it produce the best academic and youth mental health outcomes (Kim, Wang, Orozco-Lapray, Shen, & Murtuza, 2013). Another study found that first generation Chinese American immigrant mothers favored a bicultural parenting style that included both U.S. and Chinese cultural parenting practices (Cheah, Leung, & Zhou, 2013). This involved supporting their child's autonomy and individuality while maintaining their sense of interpersonal relatedness and family centeredness, all of which were considered essential for their children to thrive in bicultural environments. Lastly, a study of Chinese mothers in Nanjing, China (Way et al., 2013), revealed that "Chinese" tiger mothering might not even exist in modern-day China! Although the Chinese mothers in this study wanted their children to succeed academically, they were mostly concerned with raising socially and emotionally well-adjusted children who could take care of themselves and secure employment as adults. Thus, rather than being obsessed with their children's school grades, they wanted their children to simply be happy by developing their interpersonal skills and exercising their personal freedom to meet the new cultural, social, and economic realities of a rapidly modernizing China.

Parent-Child Relationships

Research on ethnic minority parent-child relationships has examined the quality and tone of parent-child interaction, the types of issues that tend to elicit conflict, possible reasons for such conflict, and the psychological consequences of parent-child discord. Most of the research on parent-child conflict actually focuses on parents and their adolescent offspring due to a number of developmental changes during adolescence. The adolescent years are marked by a restructuring of family and social relationships during which teens can become more argumentative and rebellious and experience greater mood fluctuations (Cole, Cole, & Lightfoot, 2005). Multicultural psychology researchers are interested in understanding cultural issues in parent-child conflict, including whether it's related to specific cultural practices and beliefs and parent-child acculturation differences.

Research on conflict issues indicates that ethnic minority parents and their adolescent offspring tend to argue about mundane, daily activities of family life such as chores, homework, academic achievement, and choice of activities. However, parent-adolescent disagreements can vary by generational status, age, ethnicity, gender, and family income. For instance, African American parents and their offspring report fewer disagreements about chores over time, possibly due to a cultural emphasis on responsibility and collectivism (Smetana & Gaines, 1999).

Conflict issues can also involve disagreement about specific cultural values. For Asian American parents and their adolescents, this includes conflicts over autonomy, familial obligation or family responsibilities, respecting elders, traditional gender role expectations, cultural expressions of affection, academic achievement, career choice, and dating (Chun & Akutsu, 2003). Disagreements over cultural values can also vary by gender and with acculturation. In a study of immigrant Vietnamese adolescents (Rosenthal, Ranieri, & Klimidis, 1996), endorsement of traditional family values (e.g., support of traditional gender roles, filial obligation, respect for elders, dating and marriage, and expression of feelings) decreased with acculturation, while endorsement of autonomy and independence increased for all adolescents. However, this pattern was stronger for girls than boys. The girls valued traditional values less and were more likely than boys to report more conflict with their parents if they perceived a discrepancy in values between themselves and their parents. These findings suggest that Vietnamese immigrant girls experience more acculturation difficulties and potentially more conflict with their parents because of strict gender role expectations and perceived double standards in their families. The potential for parent-child conflict resulting from an *acculturation gap*, or different parent-child acculturation levels, has been well-documented in multicultural psychology research. In meta-analyses of 68 studies of Asian American and Latino families (Lui, 2015), acculturation gap or mismatch between parents and their children was significantly related to intergenerational conflict, which in turn predicted more mental health problems for children.

Some researchers believe that these instances of parent-adolescent conflict are not entirely related to acculturation or to specific features of a culture. Phinney and her colleagues (Phinney, Ong, & Madden, 2000) finds that parents tend to endorse family obligation more so than do their adolescent offspring regardless of their ethnic backgrounds. This finding suggests that parents are generally inclined to maintain existing norms and expectations while adolescents generally tend to question them regardless of their immigrant or nonimmigrant background. The effects of parent-adolescent disagreements over values on youth functioning might also be similar across ethnic groups. One study finds that parent-adolescent disagreement on family obligation is associated with less life satisfaction for both Vietnamese and European American adolescents (Phinney & Ong, 2002).

Parent-adolescent conflict can become even more complicated when there are language differences. Children who are more proficient in English than their immigrant parents may be placed in the role of "language brokers" for their families (Chao, 2006). This can be a stressful experience for youths who are expected to assume adult roles and responsibilities such as paying household bills, assisting siblings in the educational system, and serving as interpreters for their parents during medical exams. At the same time, these youths may be required to shift back into their role as a child in home settings. Past research shows that these role shifts and language brokering duties in immigrant households can lead to youth depression and anxiety (Chun, 2006).

With the onset of adolescence, youths often desire greater **individuation** or separation from their parents and increased contacts outside of the home, which can weaken parent-adolescent closeness. These developmental changes can be even more pronounced for Asian American and Latino adolescents who prefer to speak another language than their immigrant parents. Adolescents who speak with their parents in different languages (e.g., mother speaks in Spanish, and her adolescent offspring replies in English) reported fewer conversations with them and more emotional distance compared to adolescents who speak the same language (Tseng & Fuligni, 2000). Such instances of "nonreciprocal language use" may result in miscommunication or misunderstandings, especially when it comes to expressing emotions or difficult concerns (Tseng & Fuligni, 2000).

Acculturation also seems to influence reported communication difficulties. Chinese immigrant mothers who perceive a significant acculturation gap between themselves and their children are more likely to report communication problems with them (Buki, Ma, Strom, & Strom, 2003). In those ethnic minority families that have open and effective parent-adolescent communication, adolescent offspring tend to show better psychosocial adjustment. For African American and Latino families, open and receptive communication between mothers and adolescents about sex decreases the likelihood that adolescents will participate in sexual risk-taking behaviors (Kotchick, Dorsey, Miller, & Forehand, 1999).

Academic Achievement

Do you feel that the color of your skin affects how your teachers and fellow students interact with you in the classroom? Did anyone in your family ever attend college, and did this influence your selection of a university and major, your preparation for the ACT or the SAT, and your current study habits? When you study long hours in the library, do you see it as a means of getting ahead in life and possibly as a means of helping your entire family move ahead too, or do you experience your studies simply as an intellectual exercise or perhaps sheer drudgery? These types of questions revolve around the key issues of race and immigrant effects on ethnic minority academic achievement.

In regard to racial effects, racial group membership often determines the challenges that families face in securing a quality education for their children and accessing educational resources. This is most apparent when considering the characteristics and resources of public schools in racially stratified neighborhoods and cities. Public schools in predominantly ethnic minority districts are typically located in unhealthy and stressful environments (near freeways or busy intersections, high-density and high-crime areas), have physical facilities that are in disrepair, lack up-to-date instructional materials and equipment (textbooks, computer labs, and Internet access), have little or no honors or advanced-placement courses (which are needed for admission to prestigious colleges), and lack essential support staff (e.g., college guidance counselors, health staff, academic tutors). Contrast this situation with the environments and resources of public schools in predominantly upper- to middle-class neighborhoods where mostly dominant group members reside. Often, it resembles a tale of two cities on all of these dimensions of school environment and instructional resources. Thus, the race toward educational success does not always begin on a level playing field for ethnic minority students, especially if their family members have little or no formal education, as seen in many immigrant households.

Complicating matters is the issue of **racial tracking** in the educational system. Ethnic minority youths are more likely to be overlooked for placement in honors or advanced academic courses beginning in elementary school regardless of their academic abilities and potential. Unfortunately, talented ethnic minority students are "tracked" into remedial or regular courses that do not match their academic skills and intellect, preventing them from becoming competitive candidates for college admission. For example, African Americans are overplaced in special educational services (Losen & Orfield, 2002) and are less likely to be identified for gifted and talented programs (D. Y. Ford, Harris, Tyson, & Frazier Trotman, 2002). In a longitudinal study following more than 2,000 students from 9th to 12th grade, African American students were less likely than White non-Hispanic students to be moved into honors or advanced math courses (Hallinan, 1996).

Racial tracking is tied to teachers' and educational administrators' racial stereotypes of ethnic-minority students. African American students are rated more negatively (less cognitive ability, less motivated, less verbal) than Asian or White students. Teachers' low expectations and negative racial views negatively affect African American youths' self-concepts, motivation, academic achievement, and future ambitions and can thus become self-fulfilling prophecies (Franklin et al., 2002). Ethnic minority parents can prevent negative racial views from affecting their children's academic progress by strengthening their ethnic and racial identities and becoming involved with their children's academics (McGill, Hughes, Alicea, & Way, 2012). Also, ethnic minority students' own intrinsic motivation to succeed and their families' support for education can help them overcome negative racial stereotypes. Studies find that poor African American and Latino families with elementary school children are enthusiastic about education, strive to provide supportive environments for academic achievement, and hold high expectations for academic success (Stevenson, Chen, & Uttal, 1990). Furthermore, Mexican American teens with formally educated, supportive, and involved parents possess high educational aspirations (Plunkett & Bamaca-Gomez, 2003).

Research on immigrant effects has examined whether immigrant youths' family environments, cultural beliefs, and individual attributes affect their academic performance. Much of this research attempts to explain why certain immigrant groups like Chinese, Japanese, and Korean Americans show high academic achievement despite facing economic hardship and insufficient educational resources. Studies typically compare GPAs, achievement test scores, and college performance between foreign- and U.S.-born student populations. Additionally, family characteristics, including cultural beliefs about education, are compared for immigrant and nonimmigrant groups. Generally speaking, immigrant students perform as well as American-born students; however, differences in academic achievement arise when demographic factors are closely examined. In a study of 12th graders enrolled in public education (Fuligni & Witkow, 2004), both immigrant and American-born students basically showed the same academic progress into college even though the immigrant students had added responsibilities for making financial contributions to their households. Differences in academic achievement were revealed when students' ethnicity and family SES and the educational backgrounds of their parents were analyzed. Latino and Filipino American students from low-SES families, and those who had parents with little formal education, showed low achievement in some areas in college. However, high aspirations for educational achievement and familial obligation or a sense of duty to one's family promoted academic success. Another study similarly found that low-income Latino adolescents who valued "respeto" were motivated to "give back" to and honor their immigrant parents' struggles by succeeding in school (Ceballo, Maurizi, Suarez, & Aretakis, 2014).

These findings suggest that family background, resources, and cultural values play an important role in ethnic minority students' educational success. Societal and historical conditions and perceived opportunities for upward mobility in a racially stratified society also shape academic achievement. Sue and Okazaki (1990) hypothesize that Asian Americans' educational success can be explained by **relative functionalism**. According to this hypothesis, Asian Americans tend to view education as a means for upward mobility. Sue and Okazaki explain that certain occupations and career paths that do not require a formal education (e.g., those in the entertainment and sports industries and in organized labor) have been historically closed to Asian Americans due to institutional racism and discrimination. Evidence for this lies in the conspicuous absence of highly visible Asian Americans in film, television, and sports. However, careers requiring a formal education (e.g., engineering, medicine, and law) have been less restrictive to Asian Americans and are viewed as viable means for getting ahead. Consequently, Asian American students who equate studying with social and economic upward mobility are more likely to focus on their studies and academic achievement. In support of this hypothesis, past studies show that Asian American students are more likely to view and experience their studies as an effective and positive means to becoming successful in life (Alva, 1993; Asakawa & Csikszentmihalyi, 1998).

An alternative theory (Zhou & Lee, 2017) proposes that Asian American educational success can be attributed to (1) hyperselectivity of talented Asian immigrants to the United States due to U.S. immigration policies favoring the highly skilled and educated, (2) a "success frame," or belief that education is essential for success, and (3) access to ethnic educational resources and support. According to this theory, hyperselected Asian immigrant groups pursue their educational and career goals from more socially advantageous starting points and are socialized by their families to concentrate their efforts on academic success for upward socioeconomic mobility. Access to specialized academic tutoring, studying, exam preparation, and enrichment programs in their ethnic communities further their academic pursuits and chances for educational success. However, Asian American students must also contend with the model minority stereotype, which portrays all Asian American students as high-achieving academic whiz kids. Although Asian Americans' academic performance may get an initial boost from this stereotype from educators, it later creates a "bamboo ceiling," or barrier to leadership positions in the workplace, by creating much higher standards for success. Evidence for this can be seen in the noticeable absence of Asian American corporate executive officers, even in the technology industry where they are overrepresented.

Much has been written on the negative effects of the model minority stereotype on Asian American youths' school adjustment and overall well-being (e.g., Leong et al., 2007). This stereotype is particularly burdensome for certain Asian American subgroups like Southeast Asian refugees and other marginalized Asian American youths who experience academic difficulties, elevated school-dropout rates, and elevated risk for delinquency. Moreover, this stereotype is especially problematic because it has been historically used to reinforce stratification by pitting ethnic minority groups against one another and obscuring the real effects of racial and social stratification on educational performance.

Couple Relationships

Gender roles and attitudes, predictors of marital conflict and divorce, and cultural issues and risk factors for domestic violence are main topics of ethnic minority couple research. In regard to gender roles, investigators have examined how certain cultural beliefs or value systems inform responsibilities and duties, communication patterns and styles, and interactions between men and women. Often, families socialize their children around cultural gender role expectations early in their development. In a study of Chinese American teens (Fuligni, Yip, & Tseng, 2002), girls showed more family involvement and family obligations than did boys, such as sharing a family meal, helping with house cleaning, running errands, caring for siblings, or cooking meals. These same girls were also more likely than boys to experience daily conflicts with their parents over negotiating these family obligations with time spent with friends and studying. These findings indicate that Chinese American girls are more likely than boys to struggle with gender role expectations to fulfill daily family and household duties.

Similar gender role expectations have been reported for Latino couples. Researchers have commented that Latino men are socialized to assume a dominant position in couple relationships and to provide for and protect their wives and families (Grebler, Moore, & Guzman, 1973). Women in return are expected to follow their husbands, maintain the household, and perform daily child-rearing duties. These types of Latino/Latina gender role prescriptions—often characterized as machismo and marianismo for men and women, respectively—are defined and discussed at length in Chapter 6. Suffice it to say, the cultural meaning and subtle nuances of Latino and Latina gender roles are often overlooked in research, which unfortunately perpetuates one-dimensional racial stereotypes (Torres et al., 2002). As explained in Chapter 6, Latino/Latina gender behaviors and attitudes vary according to individual backgrounds and life experiences. For instance, studies indicate that Latinos/Latinas with more formal education and longer U.S. residency are less likely to endorse traditional gender roles than are newer Latino/Latina immigrants with less education (Chun & Akutsu, 2003).

African American men and women may exhibit more egalitarian gender roles partly due to historical job discrimination, which prevented African American men from becoming sole family breadwinners or providers (S. A. Hill, 2001). African American women thus continue to make important economic contributions to their families by seeking gainful employment and sharing household duties with their husbands.

Research on marital conflict shows that ethnicity is not a reliable predictor of how frequently marital conflict occurs. This refutes racial stereotypes of African Americans as high-conflict couples, which stem from older studies that failed to control for socioeconomic status, educational levels, family structure, and racial discrimination, all of which affect couples' stress levels (McLoyd, Harper, & Copeland, 2001). The negative effects of economic hardship on couples are seen for African American and Latino newlyweds who cite financial difficulties as one of the most pressing stressors in their marriage (Jackson et al., 2016). In a longitudinal study of African American newlywed couples, financial strain during the early years of marriage heightened both husbands' and wives' concerns about marital instability and reduced perceived spousal warmth over time, especially among wives (Barton & Bryant, 2016). Mexican American immigrant couples are likewise adversely affected by financial strain in addition to acculturation stress. For Mexican immigrant couples, economic and acculturation stressors are tied to depressive symptoms, which in turn lead to negative marital interactions and, for the wives, lower marital satisfaction (Helms et al., 2014). Still, other findings suggest that first generation Mexican American couples experience less conflict if they maintain strong family and religious values and beliefs (Orengo-Aguayo, 2015).

Marital conflict can lead to intimate partner violence (IPV), which is considered a serious family, mental, and public health issue in multicultural psychology. Despite the pressing need to address IPV, underreporting and reluctance to seek help, especially among marginalized ethnic minority women, make it difficult to study this issue. A national survey on violence against women showed that minority women were proportionally less likely than European American women to seek professional mental health services for IPV (Cheng & Lo, 2015). Large-scale psychiatric epidemiological survey data indicate that Asian American women may be particularly reluctant to seek help. Compared to Latinos, African Americans, and European Americans, Asian women are less likely to utilize mental health services for IPV after controlling for education, socioeconomic status, type of IPV, and self-perceived mental health status (Cho & Kim, 2012). Underutilization of professional services may reflect cultural preferences for support and assistance from family and friends in addition to other interrelated factors. This is especially seen for new immigrant women who must contend with interrelated cultural, gender, and socioeconomic issues that make it dangerous and potentially life-threatening to report IPV. Asian American immigrant women who experience physical violence might be reluctant to seek help because of loss of face issues and traditional gender role attitudes. **Loss of face** is defined as a person's social integrity, which is tied to one's ability to meet the role responsibilities and expectations of a valued social group like one's family (Zane & Mak, 2003). Asian American women who are battered may be hesitant to report their husbands' violence because they fear it will bring loss of face not only to themselves but also to their entire families. This concern is reinforced by patriarchal family structures that pressure women to assume a passive and obedient role to their husbands (Tang, Cheung, Chen, & Sun, 2002).

Certain cultural values like filial obligation and filial piety, which compel family members to subsume individual desires and needs to the interests and well-being of the entire family, further discourage Asian American women from leaving their abusive husbands (Bhandari Preisser, 1999; Tran & Des Jardins, 2000). In Japanese culture, the concept of **gaman** is a valued cultural trait, ascribing character and strength to those who endure and withstand hardship without complaint (Ho, 1990). Japanese women who endorse this concept might feel that their individual character depends on their ability to endure and remain in an abusive relationship in order to keep the family intact (Ho, 1990). Finally, immigrant women in general are often reluctant to seek help and relocate with their children due to English-language difficulties, economic hardship, and fear of deportation, all of which contribute to feelings of isolation and despair.

The causes of IPV against ethnic minority women involve an interaction between class, culture, gender, and immigration status (Bui & Morash, 1999). This means that a couple's risk for IPV varies depending on each partner's socioeconomic status, cultural beliefs and norms, gender attitudes and beliefs, and acculturation experiences. From a feminist perspective, IPV is not simply an issue of violence but one of control and the familial, social, and historical forces that promote male dominance and control. In a study of South Asian Indian women (Mehrotra, 1999), reported abuse included mental, verbal, emotional, and economic abuse in addition to physical abuse. Economic abuse entailed not being allowed to control economic resources and household finances. One South Asian Indian woman who had a high-paying job reported that her paychecks were directly deposited into her husband's bank account and that she was restricted to a weekly allowance he controlled. The women in this study also reported that their husbands asserted their dominance and control by isolating them from family and friends. The relationship between violence against women and male dominance was found for Korean Americans as well. In one study, severe violence against Korean American wives was four times higher in male-dominant couples in which men held decision-making power compared to that of egalitarian couples with joint family decision-making (Kim & Sung, 2000).

Domestic violence in male-dominant households can also stem from **status inconsistency**, which is a loss of socioeconomic status and occupational prestige following immigration to another country. Immigrant men who held high-paying and prestigious positions in their country of origin are often unable to gain equivalent positions in a new country due to language barriers, lack of similar occupations, difficulties transferring professional degrees and training, and discrimination. Status inconsistency arises when these immigrant men are relegated to lower-paying or low-status jobs or become unemployed, which can damage their self-esteem and lead to frustration, anger, and depression. In one case study (Chun, Akutsu, & Abueg, 1994), a Vietnamese refugee who fled to the United States following the Vietnam War was forced to leave his position as a high-ranking South Vietnamese general and assume a new role as a social worker. For this individual, status inconsistency contributed to depressive symptoms, loss of face, and a feeling of shame. Immigrant men who experience status inconsistency, possess low self-esteem, and cannot effectively manage their anger and frustration are at risk for becoming perpetrators of IPV.

Some immigrant men might also become abusive when feeling threatened by shifting gender roles. Immigrant women who once assumed a secondary role to their husbands may be required to seek gainful employment and help support their family households in the United States. Men with rigid gender role attitudes may react violently to this shift in responsibilities, especially if their wives become the primary or sole household provider and become more independent. In one study (Kim & Zane, 2004), Korean American male batterers showed greater anger and less anger control than White male batterers due to higher occupational and economic stress and possibly due to traditional gender role attitudes. Still, the link between traditional gender role attitudes and IPV may vary depending on a person's educational level, age, and socioeconomic status. In a sample of highly educated, older, upper-middle-class Chinese Americans, there was no relationship between gender role attitudes and domestic violence (Yick, 2000).

Family Stress and Coping

Economic hardship and poverty continue to stress ethnic minority family functioning and relations. The negative impact of poverty on family life is most pronounced for households headed by single women. Poverty rates of children in these households are almost five times that of children in married-couple households (Lugaila & Overturf, 2004). Racial minority children are especially at risk for poverty. The percentage of children under 18 years old who live in poverty is 34 percent for African Americans, 34 percent for American Indians, 28 percent for Latinos, 12 percent for Asian Americans, and 12 percent for Whites (Ryan & Bauman, 2016). As noted in Chapter 1, such aggregate figures for Asian Americans should be interpreted cautiously, because disaggregated analyses of certain subgroups (e.g., Cambodians, Vietnamese, Laotians, and certain first generation immigrant groups) show high variability in socioeconomic status.

There is a growing body of research that examines the effects of economic hardship on ethnic minority youths' well-being. Much of this research points to a **family stress model**, which posits that family environment mediates or is related to the relationship between economic disadvantage and youth adjustment (Hammack, LaVome Robinson, Crawford, & Li, 2004; McLoyd, 1990, 1998; Barajas-Gonzalez & Brooks-Gunn, 2014). One study (White, Liu, Nair, & Tein, 2015) found that Mexican American mothers' financial strain was associated with harsher parenting, which increased adolescent externalizing symptoms (defiance disorder, conduct disorder, and attention deficit hyperactivity disorder symptoms) over time. However, financial strain was less likely to affect adolescents' behaviors if their mothers had strong familism values, which acted as a protective mental health buffer. Likewise, African American mothers faced with economic hardship and community violence are at risk for depressive, anxiety, and hostile symptoms, which can gradually undermine their parenting over time (Borre & Kliewer, 2014).

Family dysfunction in poor ethnic minority families is often misattributed to a *culture of poverty*, characterized by inherently deviant cultural norms and values, particularly among the urban poor. However, this racial stereotype overlooks the fact that structural inequalities and concentrated poverty socially isolate ethnic minority families, which ultimately compromises their overall functioning. In impoverished neighborhoods, important institutions like businesses, schools, social clubs, and community and voluntary organizations decline and often disappear, leaving families without important resources to sustain their development (Rankin & Quane, 2000). Research clearly shows that greater access to capital and financial resources can improve ethnic minority family functioning. For example, when financial resources are perceived as adequate, African American mothers are more likely to perceive themselves as being effective parents. Furthermore, African American mothers who view themselves as effective parents are more likely to create a structured and organized family life for their children (Seaton & Taylor, 2003) and, while raising their children, are more likely to emphasize educational goals, respect for others in the community, and concern for others (Brody, Flor, & Morgan Gibson, 1999).

Some researchers have noted that, although poor ethnic minority families may lack financial capital, they may still have an abundance of **social capital**, which is defined as social support and resources that come from one's social relationships and connections within one's family and community (Fuligni & Yoshikawa, 2003). Social capital can include cultural resources or family traditions that promote mutual support and interdependence. For instance, extended kin support from grandparents is a form of social capital for many ethnic minority families. From a family resource management perspective, grandparents provide valuable human resources in terms of time, human energy, and skills that can help families meet life demands and accomplish their goals (Tam & Detzner, 1998). Grandparents or other relatives can also provide skilled child-rearing and play a key role in the cultural socialization and ethnic identity development of children.

Social capital is also derived from social networks in one's ethnic community, such as those found in religious organizations and churches. Social capital from religious organizations can partly offset the stress of poverty by providing essential cultural, instrumental, and emotional support. A large-scale study of Asian American, Central American, and Mexican American immigrant communities in the San Francisco Bay Area found that religious organizations helped low-income immigrant families develop and thrive by (1) helping them maintain important cultural traditions and transnational family and ethnic community support networks, (2) offsetting status inconsistency by providing leadership roles and opportunities, (3) helping family members cope with acculturation stressors and racial discrimination, and (4) providing culturally appropriate means to address existential and spiritual questions about life changes and hardships (Lorentzen et al., 2009).

Racism and discrimination represent additional stressors for ethnic minority families. One study found that African American children who reside in a highly discriminatory community are at greater risk for depression (Simons et al., 2002). Moreover, this finding was not restricted to those children who were targets of discrimination; simply witnessing incidents of discrimination against members in their ethnic or racial group also increased children's risk for depression. However, living in a neighborhood that displayed ethnic identification and pride lowered risk for childhood depression. Researchers report that chronic racial discrimination exacerbates the negative effects of ongoing life stressors in African American families. For African American mothers, racial discrimination exacerbated their cumulative life stressors, psychological distress, and the negative effects of their psychological distress on their parent-child and couple relationships (Murry, Brown, Brody, Cutrona, & Simons, 2001).

Again, social capital from religious organizations can buffer the harmful effects of racism and discrimination on ethnic minority family functioning. For African Americans, religious organizations offer an environment for positive self-evaluation through prayer along with instrumental and emotional support from fellow church members (Harrison-Hale, McLoyd, & Smedley, 2004). African American churches often serve as an extended family to their members and a community agency by providing homeless shelters, food programs, nursing home programs, counseling, GED preparation programs, and even physical fitness centers (Sanders, 2002).

The benefits of church attendance and church affiliation on African American family functioning are gradually being documented in multicultural psychology research. In African American two-parent families from the rural South, high parental religiosity (measured by church attendance and perceived importance of church) was associated with more cohesive family relationships, less marital conflict, and fewer behavioral and emotional problems in adolescents (Brody, Stoneman, & Flor, 1996). For African American families in the Midwest, regular church attendance by parents was related to fewer parental reports of oppositional behavior, peer conflict, depression, and immaturity in their children (Christian & Barbarin, 2001). African American youths who attended church or religious services on a regular basis were also less likely to engage in premarital intercourse and less likely to use alcohol, cigarettes, and marijuana (Steinman & Zimmerman, 2004).

Chapter Summary

In this chapter, we examine ethnic minority family functioning from an ecological perspective to illustrate how different social relationships, environments, and social institutions shape and are themselves shaped by the collective lives of family members. Diverse patterns of family functioning emerge across ethnic minority families based on their distinct structures and relationships and the varied life demands, stressors, and resources in their respective ecologies. For families of color, the ecological challenges of acculturation and minority status can heighten their family stress and restrict their access to important coping resources, complicating their ability to navigate normative developmental changes and life transitions. Still, ethnic minority families should not be narrowly viewed from a deficit model of family functioning, because doing so completely overlooks their many strengths and family agency. To this end, more multicultural psychologists are focusing their attention on ethnic minority families' resiliency, positive characteristics, and cultural resources that promote and safeguard their development and well-being.

Key Terms

authoritarian parenting 158
authoritative parenting 159
cohesive-authoritative parenting 160
conflict-authoritarian parenting 160
defensive-neglectful parenting 161
ecological perspective 154
ecologies 154
familism/*familismo* 158
family agency 155
family stress model 169
filial piety 158
gaman 168
individuation 164
loss of face 167
patrilineal 158
permissive parenting 159
racial tracking 165
relative functionalism 166
social capital 169
status inconsistency 168

Learning by Doing

- As noted at the beginning of this chapter, the many ways in which family members relate to one another, organize or structure their family roles, and fulfill their daily tasks are influenced by the diverse ecologies that each family member inhabits. Think of your own family for a moment. What is the ecological context of your family life?
- What are the different types of family ecologies that you and your family members inhabit in your daily lives?
- How do these family ecologies shape how your family functions? For example, how do your family members relate to one another, how are duties and tasks assigned to family members, and how does your family meet its daily needs as well as new life challenges?
- If you belong to an ethnic minority family, how have the ecological challenges of minority status and acculturation affected your family life? Have these ecological challenges brought your family members closer together or pulled them apart?
- Can you think of instances in which your family showed "family agency" during difficult or challenging times? How have these instances shaped how you view your family, including what you believe to be your family's strengths and limitations? Do these instances of family agency serve as a source of inspiration and guidance in your daily life? If so, how?

Suggested Further Readings

Bornstein, M. H., & Cote, L. R. (Eds.). (2006). *Acculturation and parent-child relationships: Measurement and development.* Mahwah, NJ: Lawrence Erlbaum.

A seminal book in the field that presents pioneering research on the conceptualization and measurement of acculturation and on acculturation influences on family development and parent-child relations.

Falicov, C. J. (2014). *Latino families in therapy* (2nd ed.). New York: Guilford Press.

A book in which practitioners and students gain an understanding of the family dynamics, migration experiences, ecological stressors, and cultural resources that are frequently shared by Latino families, as well as variations among them.

Juang, L. P., & Umaña-Taylor, A. J. (2012). *Family conflict among Chinese- and Mexican-origin adolescents and their parents in the U.S.* (vol. 2012). San Francisco: Jossey-Bass.

A more nuanced understanding of parent-adolescent conflict in Chinese- and Mexican-origin families in the United States. In their chapters, authors explore key issues related to family conflict, such as acculturation gaps, parent and adolescent internal conflicts, conflict resolution, and seeking out confidants for help in coping with conflict.

McLoyd, V. C., Hill, N. E., & Dodge, K. A. (Eds.). (2005). *African American family life: Ecological and cultural diversity*. New York: Guilford.

An illustration of the diversity of African American family lives, presenting recent research findings on African American family ecologies and family development.

Roosa, M. W., Gonzales, N. A., Knight, G. P., & Vargas, D. A. (2014). Children and families. In F. T. L. Leong, L. Comas-Díaz, G. C. N. Hall, V. C. McLoyd, & J. E. Trimble (Eds.). *APA handbook of multicultural psychology* (vol. 1, pp. 411–427). Washington, DC: American Psychological Association.

A chapter discussing challenges to improving our understanding of U.S. ethnic minority families and children. It also offers cultural perspectives on ethnic minority family and youth research and interventions and makes recommendations to improve future research with these populations.

Sutton, C. E. T., & Broken Nose, M. A. (2005). American Indian families: An overview. In M. McGoldrick, J. Giordano, & N. Garcia-Preto (Eds.), *Ethnicity and family therapy* (3rd ed., pp. 43–54). New York: Guilford.

An invaluable resource for clinicians that covers key cultural, social, and historical factors shaping American Indian family relations and functioning.

Yee, B. W. K., DeBaryshe, B. D., Yuen, S., Kim, S. Y., & McCubbin, H. I. (2007). Asian American and Pacific Islander families: Resiliency and life-span socialization in a cultural context. In F. T. L. Leong, A. G. Inman, A. Ebreo, L. H. Yang, L. Kinoshita, & M. Fu (Eds.), *Handbook of Asian American psychology* (2nd ed., pp. 69–86). Thousand Oaks, CA: Sage.

A presentation of key conceptual frameworks to understanding Asian American family functioning, along with a comprehensive review of Asian American family research topics and findings.

Stereotypes, Prejudice, and Discrimination 8

A True Story by One of the Authors (G. M.)

Having graduated from a Jesuit high school where students were challenged academically and shown respect and personal attention, I was looking forward to starting college but was unprepared for the prejudice I was about to face. Having only just migrated to the United States, I was unaware of options available to college students and so followed the suggestions of our neighbors, enrolling at a large community college. This was in the early 1970s in a Southern state with a large Latino population. One of my freshman courses was an introduction to my major. The course was required and a prerequisite for most other courses in the program. The first day of classes, approximately 50 students filed into the classroom, looking forward to starting a new year. Soon the professor—let's call him Dr. Jones—walked into the classroom, went through the class list, distributed the syllabus, and started to describe what the course was about. As Dr. Jones began describing the tests and projects expected of all students, he raised his voice for all of us to hear and clearly announced, "A word of caution to all of you: I don't like cheaters and people who plagiarize or copy homework assignments from other students." He then looked around and pointed directly at the 10 or so of us who had a Spanish surname and said, "All of you Hispanics, pay attention. I know you all cheat, so the best grade you can get in this class is a C, because I never know if the work is yours or if you just copied it from a friend." Some of us stayed enrolled in the course and indeed got no higher than a C as the final grade. We were too afraid to appeal to staff and faculty about the unfairness of the situation or even to talk about it with others. I then transferred to a Jesuit university in the Midwest, and the rest is history. I often wondered whatever happened to Dr. Jones. In a sense, he is responsible for motivating me to change majors and become a social psychologist and try to understand why people feel and act that way toward those individuals who happen to be different from them.

The purpose of this chapter is to briefly review the psychological literature that deals with some of the attitudinal effects of living in a diverse, multiethnic community. Obviously the sheer magnitude of the topic makes it necessary to limit coverage to certain attitudinal and behavioral effects of being exposed to members of a racially or ethnically diverse social environment. We start this chapter by talking about stereotypes as reactions to encountering diverse individuals and as basic components of the processes of prejudice and discrimination. Stereotypes, prejudice, and discrimination are of particular importance when we study the social and psychological effects of living in a multicultural society. You may have already covered some aspects of these concepts in your foundational courses in psychology, sociology, or ethnic studies classes, and therefore we will only briefly describe them here. We then review ways in which stereotypes, prejudice, discrimination, and racism can be changed or prevented. Finally, we review the benefits that are part of living in a racial and ethnically diverse society—benefits that affect Whites as well as all other members of our multicultural society.

Understanding Stereotypes

Many studies have been carried out by researchers to better understand stereotypes, what they are, how they are formed, and how can they be changed (Hilton & von Hippel, 1996). Here we first analyze how stereotypes have been defined in the literature, since they occupy a particularly important place in our understanding of concepts such as prejudice and discrimination (discussed later on in this chapter).

There have been a large number of definitions of stereotypes, and they tend to consider stereotypes as mental images or generalizations that include personal, social, or ethical characteristics we tend to assign to individuals belonging to members of specific human groups (see Box 8.1). We can, therefore, talk about **ethnic** or **racial stereotypes** as the characteristics ("beliefs" in the APA definition in Box 8.1) that are perceived as common among members of specific ethnic or racial groups (that is, generalized to all members of a group). There are, of course, stereotypes that can be identified for social groups other than racial or ethnic groups, such as those usually assigned to men or women or to nationalities or to specific professions. In this chapter we primarily review ethnic or racial stereotypes and how these stereotypes are usually formed and shaped by experiences with others, by the media, and even by conversations with friends or relatives.

The definitions found in Box 8.1 emphasize the cognitive nature of stereotypes (as generalized *beliefs* about people) that are associated with evaluative or affective reactions. As generalizations, stereotypes can be explained as aiding peoples' process of perception (by simplifying the complexity involved in concentrating on particulars rather than adopting universal ways of thinking). Other than simplifying life, stereotypes can also be seen as the product of social situations (roles, conflict), and at times they can also be used to justify social inequality and in such a fashion support the status quo. As Hilton and von Hippel (1996) suggest, stereotypes have a context-dependent functionality: They emerge when needed in certain contexts. As such, we can use positive stereotypes (for example, trustworthy, dedicated, hardworking) or negative (lazy, unreliable, devious) to define certain groups of individuals who differ from us in terms of their gender, race, or ethnicity (e.g., African American, Asian American, Latino), religion (e.g., Catholic, Muslim, Evangelical), nationality (e.g., German, Italian, Chinese), and sexuality (e.g., straight, lesbian, gay) and even profession (e.g., physician, sales staff, teacher, politician), body type (e.g., skinny, obese), and musical preferences (e.g., classical, country, D&B, salsa, rap).

Researchers studying stereotypes have tried to identify the characteristics most frequently associated with members of specific groups (*stereotype content*) as well as to determine how stable or

Box 8.1

Basic Definitions

Stereotypes

- Beliefs and opinions about the characteristics, attributes, and behaviors of members of various groups (Whitley & Kite, 2006, p. 6)
- Generalized beliefs about groups and their members (American Psychological Association, 2007, p. 475)
- Stereotypes are beliefs about the characteristics, attributes, and behaviors of members of certain groups (Hilton & von Hippel, 1996, p. 240)

Prejudice

- An antipathy based on a faulty and inflexible generalization (Allport, 1954, p. 9)
- An attitudinal dimension that consists of negative or stigmatizing beliefs about a particular group (Dovidio, Brigham, Johnson, & Gaertner, 1996)
- Unfavorable affective reactions to or evaluation of groups and their members (American Psychological Association, 2007, p. 475)

Racism

- The beliefs, attitudes, institutional arrangements, and acts that tend to denigrate individuals or groups because of phenotypic characteristics or ethnic group affiliation (Clark, Anderson, Clark, & Williams, 1999, p. 805)

Discrimination

- Treating people differently from others based primarily on membership in a social group (Whitley & Kite, 2006, p. 8)
- Interpersonal discrimination is differential treatment by individuals toward some groups and their members relative to other groups and their members, and institutional discrimination involves policies and contexts that create, enact, reify, and maintain inequality (American Psychological Association, 2007, p. 475)
- Unfair treatment received because of one's ethnicity (Contrada et al., 2001)

consistent those stereotypes are over time. Other researchers have been concerned about how those stereotypes are formed or changed. This section of the chapter summarizes some important findings in these areas. Unfortunately, much stereotype research has been conducted among college students, limiting the generalizability of the results to the entire population. Indeed, not only do college students represent a small percentage of the population of the country, but they are also unique in their level of education and, in many cases, in the types and intensity of experiences with diverse individuals. Nevertheless, there are some studies that have used national samples of respondents and that allow us to understand the content of stereotypes held by other women and men in the country.

Stereotype Content

The identification of the specific stereotypes assigned to a given group is usually described as the study of **stereotype content**. Surveys with large national samples have shown important differences in the ways racial or ethnic minority groups are perceived in the United States. For example, an analysis of the 1990 General Social Survey, a large-scale survey with a representative sample of the nation's population, shows that Hispanic Americans in general were considered in less positive terms than Whites and than most other racial or ethnic groups (Jews, Blacks, Asians, Southern Whites) included in the survey (Smith, 1990). For example, Hispanics were considered poorer, less intelligent, and less patriotic than all other groups, as well as lazier, more likely to be prone to violence, and more likely to be living off welfare than all other ethnic groups, except for African Americans. A later study also using the General Social Survey (Weaver, 2007) shows interesting differences between Latinos and Whites in the stereotypes they held of each other. White respondents held generally negative stereotypes of Latinos in terms of their wealth, work ethic, intelligence, and violent behavior. Furthermore, they perceived themselves in a more positive fashion than Latinos in each of those four areas. Latinos, by contrast, had favorable images of Whites, and in each of the four characteristics measured in the survey they perceived Whites more positively than they perceived Latinos in general.

Religion is also an important determinant of stereotypes among adults in the United States. A 2017 survey by the Pew Research Center showed that, overall, a national sample of Americans tended to have neutral or positive attitudes toward various religious groups (for example, Evangelicals, Catholics, Jews, Buddhists) except for Muslims. These results were fairly consistent across gender, race, age, ethnicity, and educational level. Nevertheless, there were two interesting exceptions: African Americans did not share in the general negative attitude toward Muslims, and Republicans held much more negative attitudes toward Muslims than Democrats did. Consistent with much research on stereotypes, these respondents elicited those attitudes even though large percentages indicated not knowing anybody who belonged to that particular religious group.

Interestingly, specific personality-based stereotypes are often assigned based on seemingly inconsequential behaviors. A study of stereotypes held of music fans showed that personality traits were assigned by college students to various categories of music enthusiasts: Classical and jazz music admirers were perceived to be agreeable and emotionally stable; rock and electronic music fans were often categorized as being extroverted and open while low on emotional stability (Rentfrow, McDonald, & Oldmeadow, 2009).

While most studies on stereotype content have measured personal attributes, traits, or characteristics of the groups studied, there is also evidence that stereotypes are often assigned to groups in terms of behaviors. For example, Asian Americans are often perceived as being successful and good at mathematics and computer science, stereotypes usually related to the model minority concept we have discussed previously. Other studies (for example, Wong, Owen, Tran, Collins, & Higgins, 2012) have found constellations of positive as well as negative behavioral characteristics assigned to Asian Americans, such as being boring, intelligent, hardworking, bad at interpersonal relations, and unathletic. And members of racial minority groups stereotyped the behavior of White males as competent but cold (Conley, Rabinowitz, & Rabow, 2010). The media often promote these behavioral stereotypes through advertising, movies, and television shows so that certain stereotypical beliefs become urban myths (for example, "White men can't jump," "African Americans are good at basketball," "Asians know kung fu," "Hispanics are all illegal aliens"). In the rest of this chapter we pay little attention to the actual content of stereotypes and rather emphasize how they are shaped and how they influence people's lives and behaviors.

Development of Stereotypes

As mentioned previously, stereotypes are generalized perceptions or beliefs we hold of people who belong to specific groups. In reality, they are overgeneralizations that lead us to ignore the individuality that is part of our humanity. As overgeneralizations, stereotypes can be formed by experiences we have with one or few individuals who are easily identifiable as members of a racial or ethnic group that, in turn, lead us to believe all members share those characteristics. This overgeneralization of beliefs about people is often called the **out-group homogeneity effect**. At school you may have had the experience of meeting an international student from a country whose nationals you had never met (e.g., Kazakhstan). You enjoyed meeting the student—felt she was friendly, smart, intelligent, and open. Next time you talk about people from Kazakhstan, you may very well assign them the same characteristics that you found in this student. Those characteristics have become initial stereotypes that you hold of people from that country. Underlying these beliefs is the out-group homogeneity effect, where unknown groups of individuals (*out-groups*) are perceived to be homogeneous in their beliefs, attitudes, and behaviors.

Devos (2014) suggests that in reviewing the literature in the field there are some motivational dynamics that can be identified as helping explain the development of stereotypes. One of these motivational dynamics is the need or motivation to understand the social environment where the necessity for closure in social perception leads to quick assumptions about people often based on little information, such as first impressions or very limited contact. These easy-to-make assumptions allow the perceiver to think or feel that they understand the situation or the observed behaviors. Another possible motivational dynamic is the need to exert control over our lives, particularly during interpersonal interactions. The acceptance of stereotypes allows individuals to believe not only that they understand the other individual(s) but also that they also accurately comprehend the power structure of the relations. In this case, negative stereotypes can support the belief that the perceiver is superior (more intelligent, more creative, better looking) than the other individual, who is perceived to be less socially powerful. A third possible dynamic is the need to belong, where the perceivers assigns certain traits (usually positive) to those who are like them and a different set of traits to those who are different and "do not belong" to the perceivers' group in terms of gender, phenotype, culture, traditions, or religion. A fourth dynamic is the need for self-enhancement, where the perceiver forms stereotypes that build up their own self-concept (usually positively) and assign or project negative traits to others. As you can see from the descriptions of these motivational dynamics, there are various possible reasons for forming stereotypes (with some overlapping), but they all serve a psychological function to the perceiver. As seen in the next paragraphs, there are other, more external reasons for explaining how stereotypes are formed.

Other than direct interactions with members of a given group (as in the case described above of the student from Kazakhstan), statements by others, particularly people personally important to us, can also be a source of stereotypes. As we grow up, we are often exposed to statements by relatives, friends, teachers, or coaches that help shape the stereotypes we hold of people who belong to certain groups. We may have heard, for example, our parents or teachers say that people from a certain group are intelligent and do well in school or from coaches that members of a racial group are great soccer players. Those statements can be the root for the stereotypes we hold, particularly when they become "confirmed" by personal experiences, such as when you meet a member of the group who exhibits the characteristics you heard about from your parents, teachers, or coaches.

Historical and political events also can influence the formation of stereotypes. Wars, for example, have fostered the development of certain perceptions about the enemy that easily become part of a generalized stereotype of members of that group. We have seen that phenomenon in our country—as when the stereotypes about Germans and Japanese became fairly negative during World War II or as in the case of the Vietnamese during the United States–Vietnam War of the 1960s and 1970s or, more recently, in the case of Muslims after the September 11 tragedy. Likewise, some stereotypes are formed by biased perceptions of national origin or loyalty based on skin color or national heritage. Indeed, research has shown that the definition of *American* is heavily related to Whiteness among Caucasians and even among some ethnic or racial groups (Devos & Banaji, 2005) and that feelings of economic and social inclusion are partly related to skin color.

But personal experiences and historical and political events are not the only ways in which stereotypes are formed. Mass media—electronic or printed—can also contribute to the formation of stereotypes and related misperceptions (Mastro & Tukachinsky, 2012; Peterson, Wingood, DiClemente, Harrington, & Davies, 2007) by, if nothing else, the frequency or absence with which members of an ethnic group are portrayed. For example, an analysis of television commercials broadcast in 1984 during prime time shows that Latinos appeared in approximately 5 percent of commercials, compared with African Americans, who appeared 17 percent of the time; males from either ethnic group appeared at least 2.5 times more frequently than females (Wilkes & Valencia, 1989). These figures, of course, do not appropriately represent the actual number of African Americans and Latinos in the country at that time and further support a notion of an "invisible minority." The passing of time and the increase in the number of Latinos residing in the United States have not produced changes in these indicators, with Latino actors and models being basically absent from the media, including movies and television shows. When portrayed in movies or television programming, Latino males are often represented as violent individuals involved in criminal activities or as service personnel (maids, gardeners, kitchen staff) rather than as managers, teachers, politicians, or doctors (Nicolini, 1987). Other studies have shown how television programming reinforces the stereotypes commonly assigned to ethnic or racial minority group members. For example, a study of recent television programs shows that Asian Americans are infrequently included in the cast of major television shows and, when they do appear, they are often portrayed as "nerdy" and socially outcast (Zhang, 2010). These findings are relevant to the formation and reinforcement of stereotypes because research has found that individuals who watch significant amounts of television programming have strong stereotypes about racial and ethnic minorities (Lee, Bichard, Irey, Walt, & Carlson, 2009).

Another source of ethnic or racial minority stereotyping is advertising and mass marketing. Researchers and community leaders have often decried the negative images of African Americans, Asian Americans, and Latinos promoted by some national advertising campaigns. A classic example is the case of the Frito Bandito animated character used to promote the sale of Fritos corn chips in the late 1960s. The Frito Bandito was portrayed as a mustachioed, sombrero-wearing, heavily accented, pistol-toting Mexican thief who managed to cunningly trick people out of their Fritos. Frito-Lay, distributor of Fritos, finally retired the Bandito in 1971 after mounting pressure from the National Mexican-American Anti-Defamation Committee and other groups (Don Markstein's Toonopedia, 2008).

While the use of negative images related to ethnic and racial minority groups in advertising seems to have decreased significantly in the last decades, the potential for stereotype formation is still there. For instance, in 2002 clothier Abercrombie & Fitch created controversy with its sale of T-shirts featuring caricature faces wearing rice-paddy hats (reminiscent of early 1900s pop culture depictions of Chinese men), printed with slogans such as "Wong Brothers Laundry Service—Two Wongs Can Make It White," "Wok-N-Bowl—Let the Good Times Roll—Chinese Food & Bowling," and "Abercrombie and Fitch Buddha Bash—Get Your Buddha on the Floor" (Strasburg, 2002). There was an immediate outcry from many Asian Americans, especially in the San Francisco Bay Area, who viewed these images as demeaning and disrespectful. Representatives from Abercrombie & Fitch insisted that they were surprised by the negative reaction and had not intended to offend anyone, having developed the product to add "humor" and "levity" to its clothing line (Glionna & Goldman, 2002). Hampton Carney, the company's public relations representative, stated that Abercrombie & Fitch had anticipated that "young Asian shoppers" as well as others would think the images were funny and would recognize this as just another product from a company known for its edginess and for "making fun" of a broad range of subjects from "women to flight attendants to baggage handlers to football coaches to Irish Americans to snow skiers" (Strasburg, 2002). However, within a couple of weeks of the statement, Abercrombie & Fitch pulled the line of T-shirts from its stores nationwide. Unfortunately, these types of ads have not disappeared from television: Consider a recent ad for computer chips showing a White manager surrounded by Black men bowing or a detergent advertisement that turns an African American man into an Asian American to meet the desires of a woman at a laundromat.

Also relevant is the use of images that portray ethnic minority groups in negative ways, such as the mascots of sports teams or product logos that use American Indian or African American symbols or members of certain tribes or nations. For example, it is common for sports teams to be called "Braves," "Indians," or "Patriots" or for products to depict members of ethnic minority groups on their labels (for example, Aunt Jemima, Juan Valdez Coffee). A few years ago, the American Psychological Association (2005) issued a resolution calling for the termination of the use of all Indian mascots, symbols, images, and personalities in schools and university athletic programs. The APA's position rested on growing research indicating that using these images produce negative effects not only on American Indians but also on all students by (1) conveying that it is acceptable to denigrate a culture through inaccurate presentations of American Indian culture, (2) establishing an unfriendly or even hostile learning environment for American Indian students by adopting representations that support negative stereotypes that are prevalent in the mainstream culture, (3) making it difficult for American Indian nations to maintain a level of understanding and respect regarding their culture, spirituality, and traditions, and (4) engaging in a form of discrimination against American Indian nations that can lead to negative interactions between groups and negative mental health consequences for American Indian and Alaska Native people. Indeed, research (for example, Angle, Dagogo-Jack, Forehand, & Perkins, 2017) found that the use of American Indian logos in sports teams (for example, Cleveland Indians, Atlanta Braves) reinforced stereotypes, such as Native Americans' aggressiveness, held by college students who were research participants in the study—particularly among those who were considered liberals.

Stereotype Characteristics and Effects

In general, one key characteristic of stereotypes is the fact that they seem to be rather rigid and difficult to change. Nevertheless, some studies have shown slow but identifiable changes in the content and intensity of stereotypes (Thorndike, 1977). For example, analyzing data from the large, nationwide General Social Survey conducted in 1990, and again in 2000, Weaver (2005) found that the stereotypes Whites held of Latinos' industriousness, wealth, and intelligence had improved over the 10 years that had passed between the surveys. At the same time, the perception African Americans held of Latinos' work ethic had changed little in the same period.

Stereotype Threat Another central characteristic of stereotypes is that they influence people's behavior not just in terms of supporting prejudice and discrimination (as discussed later in this chapter) but also in terms of how people act after internalizing the stereotypes that others have of them. Social psychologist Claude Steele (1997) identified what he terms **stereotype threat**, where negative stereotypes are made apparent, even subtly, leading to a diminished performance among members of minority groups consistent with the stereotype itself. In addition, the threat of fulfilling the negative stereotype occurs in situations that are meaningful to the person's identity (for example, being academically oriented among African Americans or Latinos or being math oriented among women). In one study (Steele & Aronson, 1995), the researchers gave both African American and White college students an academic performance test. In the control condition, respondents were asked to complete a questionnaire that asked general questions about the student's background (age, gender, academic major) prior to the test. In the second condition, participants completed a similar questionnaire that included a question asking about their race (the "race prime condition"). As expected in terms of the concept of stereotype threat, African American students in the race prime condition showed lower performance than African American students in the control condition and than White students in either experimental condition.

Over the past two decades, evidence has been found that is consistent with the construct of stereotype threat with different groups, including women, racial or ethnic minorities, and the elderly; indeed, any group may potentially be vulnerable to stereotype threat in situations that matter to their personal identity (Steele, 1997). Shih, Pittinsky, and Trahan (2006), for example, show that Asian American women performed better on a task involving verbal activities after researchers had made them aware of their gender compared to a situation when their ethnicity or race had been made salient to them before performing the task. In another study, Asian American women performed better on a test of mathematics when their race was highlighted when compared to an experimental condition where they were made particularly aware of their gender (Ambady, Shih, Kim, & Pittinsky, 2001). In these experiments, the research participants were acting according to the stereotype that women generally performing better in verbal rather than quantitative tasks and that Asian Americans usually performing well in quantitative assignments. A study with law school students (Birdsall, Gershenson, & Zuñiga, 2016) also found evidence of the effects of stereotype threat on students' performance and furthermore discovered that student performance was related to the presence of faculty of the same gender or the same race or ethnicity. The gender and ethnicity or race of the faculty in this study were used to decrease perceived validity of a stereotype and correlated with better grades among the students.

According to Steele (1997), stereotype threat is not necessarily about internalizing the stereotype (truly believing, for example, that you are superior intellectually because you are an Asian American person); it is more about identifying with a particular situation (e.g., doing well in an academically challenging situation) and being stereotyped in it (e.g., believing that others will view your performance as evidence that Asian Americans perform better than other racial or ethnic groups in an academically challenging situation). It is encouraging that, if these results are truly situational, the threat could be reduced through interventions—at both individual and institutional levels—geared toward promoting "identity safety" and through other efforts aimed at establishing the value-added benefit of diverse social identities to environments. For instance, school-based interventions might teach students about the expandability of intelligence—that intellectual achievement can continue to grow

(Aronson, Fried, & Good, 2002) and that institutional practices can ensure an increase in fair and valid testing (e.g., Good, Aronson, & Harder, 2008).

Stereotypes Influenced by Intersectionalities Other recent studies show that the nature and content of stereotypes is a complex phenomenon influenced by the intersectionality of a number of variables. One important study analyzed variations in stereotyping when groups were defined by crossing gender and race or ethnicity (Ghavami & Peplau, 2012); researchers discovered that the content of gender-by-ethnicity stereotypes included unique elements that were not the result of just adding gender stereotypes to racial stereotypes. The whole was greater than the sum of its parts: In other words, the stereotypes framing African American women were more complex than the stereotypes framing either African Americans generally or women generally. The study showed that stereotypes reported for African American women, for example, were qualitatively different from those reported for African American men, and the same held true for the other intersectionalities analyzed. As the authors conclude that "ethnic and gender stereotypes are complex and that the intersections of these social categories produce meaningful differences in the way groups are perceived" (p. 113). Unfortunately, much previous research has ignored the possible effect of the intersectionalities of social characteristics and, in doing so, may have overlooked the complexity inherent in the phenomenon being studied (Settles & Buchanan, 2014).

Another line of research on the intersectionalities of stereotyping examines how accented English—spoken by either men or women—affects assumptions of competence of the speaker (Nelson, Signorella, & Botti, 2016). Research tends to show that in most countries (the United States included) indigenous language skills (speaking the language of the host country) plays a significant role in considering a person as a member of the in-group or national group and that this variable is even more important than birthplace (Pew Research Center, 2016). The ability to speak without a noticeable accent was found to be key: Individuals speaking with a nonindigenous accented speech often experience prejudice and suffer discrimination. For example, in one study, job applicants speaking Spanish-accented English were perceived less favorably (Purkiss, Perrewé, Gillespie, Mayes, & Ferris, 2006). Another study looking at the intersection of gender and ethnicity showed that Spanish-accented individuals were more likely to be perceived negatively and that these effects were more pronounced if the speaker was a woman (Nelson et al., 2016). These negative perceptions or stereotypes toward individuals who do not speak with an indigenous accent tend to produce negative self-perceptions or feelings of social isolation. Indeed, studies with individuals who do not speak English with a U.S.-centric accent show that they tend to feel that they do not belong in the country (Gluszek & Dovidio, 2010).

Researchers have also recently examined the intersection of gender with race and ethnicity in terms of the prejudices developed and the discriminations enacted (Miville & Ferguson, 2014). As mentioned at the beginning of the book, intersectionality is an approach to social science research that acknowledges the meaning and consequences to individuals who belong to various social categories (Cole, 2009). As such, researchers have argued for the need to consider the experiences of women of color as different from those of men of color. This concern has motivated some authors (for example, Essed, 1990) to name **gendered racism** when "describ[ing] the multiplicative impact that racism and sexism can have on the lives of men and women of color" (Milville & Ferguson, 2014, p. 10). Examples of gendered racism are seen when media and popular culture magnify or overgeneralize characteristics of men or women from ethnic and racial groups, including playing on stereotypes about physical prowess, sexuality, subservient behavior, or even traits considered positive, such as being conscientious and hardworking. The assumption that African American men are gifted athletes, that Latino men are hypermasculine, or that Asian American women are passive and docile are all examples of gendered racism. These stereotypes can be particularly damaging to the recipient by pressuring them to internalize the content of the gendered racism and think, feel, and act as dictated by the stereotypes. Some argue (e.g., Milville & Ferguson, 2014) that internalized gendered racism manifests itself when certain standards of beauty are maintained (straightening hair, whitening skin) and when certain modes of behavior are pursued (aggressiveness, physical prowess).

Internalizing gendered racism is an emergent area of research that certainly deserves attention and that again emphasizes the need to consider the multiple interacting sources that help shape stereotypes, prejudice, and discrimination.

The Effects of Ethnic Labels on Stereotypes The label used to identify or talk about an ethnic or racial group can be an important determinant of the stereotype used to frame members of that group. Obviously, when individuals use negative or pejorative labels to talk about an ethnic or racial group, we can expect that they also hold negative stereotypes about the group's members. Unfortunately, our history is full of negative labels used to refer to African Americans, Chinese Americans, Japanese Americans, Latinos, and many other groups. And often those labels have been associated with prejudicial attitudes about them as well as discriminatory behaviors.

Interestingly, researchers have also shown that stereotypes vary when groups are identified with labels that are not necessarily negative. In a study with undergraduate college students in Los Angeles (Fairchild & Cozens, 1981), a large proportion of the respondents considered Hispanics and Mexican Americans more positively than they considered individuals identified as "Chicanos." For example, Hispanics were considered talkative and tradition loving by large percentages of the respondents, while Mexican Americans were perceived as tradition loving and ignorant, and Chicanos were seen as ignorant and cruel. When White students from the same university were asked to come up with traits to assign to different Hispanic groups, differential stereotypes were also obtained (Marín, 1984). For example, Hispanics were most frequently considered aggressive (19 percent), poor (16 percent), friendly (16 percent), and family oriented (13 percent), while Mexican Americans were most frequently considered poor (38 percent), aggressive (26 percent), lazy (19 percent), hardworking (16 percent), and family oriented (16 percent). As expected, Chicanos were considered differently from Mexican Americans: aggressive (64 percent), family oriented (12 percent), hardworking (12 percent), and lazy (12 percent). This same study asked respondents to rate each ethnic group and subgroup. The results showed that, in general, Mexican Americans were more positively evaluated than Chicanos, even though both labels indicate the very same national heritage or ancestry.

Prejudice and Discrimination

Box 8.1 (shown previously) shows some representative definitions of prejudice and discrimination. In general, we consider **prejudice** a negative attitude toward members of a particular group based on the stereotypes held by the perceiver. As Allport's definition specifies (see Box 8.1), prejudice is often based on faulty and inflexible generalizations—in other words, well-established unconfirmed beliefs about members of a group. **Discrimination**, however, refers to the actions (behaviors) carried out or planned that negatively affect members of the group that is the object of prejudice. As you are probably aware from reading newspapers and magazines and from a variety of Internet sources, discrimination can take many forms, including interpersonal interactions (for example, not hiring or promoting members of certain groups or refusing to sell them a product) and institutional approaches (such as preventing immigration from certain nations, internment in controlled environments or camps, segregation, and apartheid).

In the vignette at the beginning of this chapter, Dr. Jones exemplified how stereotyping, holding prejudice, and discriminating can reside in one individual and affected the way they act. The professor held the *stereotype* that Latinos were untrustworthy because, according to him, they "all" cheated and plagiarized in their schoolwork. His negative feelings toward actions that compromise academic honesty had been generalized to all Latinos, and he erroneously held on to those *prejudicial attitudes* as characteristics of all Latinos. Furthermore, he felt justified in *discriminating* against all Latinos by only awarding a grade no higher than a C, even to those who excelled in their class performance. So even though he had never met the new Latino students in his class or had any reason to believe that they would cheat on exams and papers, he overgeneralized his stereotypes and prejudices and declared them cheaters, dishonest, and unreliable students.

Box 8.2

Various Forms of Prejudice and Discrimination

Ableism: The marginalization of differently abled individuals with physical or mental limitations or "disabilities"; assumes that the norm is able-bodiedness

Classism: Attitudes, beliefs, behaviors, and institutional practices that justify power differences based on social class with preference being assigned to the upper and middle classes

Heterosexism: Beliefs that promote the idea that heterosexuality is the norm in gender identity and sexual attraction

Ambivalent Sexism: Simultaneous hostility toward nontraditional women and benevolence toward women in traditional subordinate roles

Hostile Sexism: Rejection of women in agentic roles

Benevolent Sexism: Support for women in traditional roles and rejection of women in nontraditional sex roles

Aversive Racism: Egalitarian attitudes and behaviors toward racial differences, but person is influenced by unconscious negative attitudes and beliefs

Symbolic Racism: Negative perceptions of certain groups that are perceived as having violated central values of a society

Source: Adapted from American Psychological Association, Presidential Task Force on Preventing Discrimination and Promoting Diversity, 2012.

As could be expected, there is a significant amount of research on prejudice toward and discrimination against people who differ in terms of gender (e.g., research on sexism), race, sexuality (including homophobic attitudes and behaviors), religious beliefs or practices (such as research on attitudes and behaviors toward Catholics, fundamentalists, Mormons, Muslims), political ideologies, physical characteristics and ability (e.g., discrimination toward persons with physical disabilities, obesity, learning disabilities), and other aspects that define human diversity. These types of prejudice and discrimination are manifested in a variety of ways including jokes (e.g., "How many [insert group name] does it take to change a light bulb?"), statements (e.g., "I don't trust those people; they're always trying to get something for nothing"), attitudes (e.g., "I don't like nurses who are [insert group name]"), and, of course, actions (e.g., not serving people from a certain group at a restaurant or shop). Various types of prejudice and discrimination are defined in Box 8.2. As mentioned previously, discrimination can at times be institutionalized, as it was in the United States when African Americans were not allowed to go to the same schools as Whites, marry Whites, or even drink from the same water fountains as Whites. Other examples of institutionalized discrimination include apartheid in South Africa or in countries where the foreign-born are not allowed to become citizens.

Nevertheless, it is ethnicity, and particularly race, that has received the largest amount of attention in the psychological literature on prejudice and discrimination. A recent study (Lu & Nicholson-Crotty, 2010), for example, finds that attitudes toward Latino immigration were related to the stereotypes that Whites had of Latinos so that those White individuals who had prejudicial attitudes toward Latinos were likely to have negative attitudes toward Latino immigration to the United States. At the same time, Awad and Amayreh (2016) argue that negative stereotypes toward Arabs and Muslims are pervasive and transmitted by various media with a consistent message that supports the othering of Muslims where they are rarely seen as similar to the average American. Indeed, the presence of negative stereotypes toward Muslims has been found to be related to lack of empathy and discriminatory behaviors, including discrimination in employment and housing (Awad & Amayreh, 2016).

A few years ago, the American Psychological Association (2007) issued a resolution condemning discrimination of all types, urging psychologists to study ways to decrease the effects of discrimination. The APA resolution affirmed that not only is discrimination an abridgement or limitation of human rights but, together with stereotypes and prejudice, it also has a number of negative consequences for the individuals who are their target, including distress, anxiety, lower self-esteem, and psychosomatic

Box 8.3

Some Possible Effects of Prejudice and Discrimination

- Negative cognitive, affective, motivational, and behavioral effects among members of stigmatized groups
  - anger and anxiety
  - depression
  - lowered aspirations
- Internalization of stereotypical characteristics
  - self-blame
  - believing negative stereotypes
  - poorer psychological well-being, including lower self-esteem
- Negative intergroup relations including distrust
- Hostile environments
  - feelings of rejection
  - lack of self-confidence
  - fright
- Violence, conflict, and genocide
- Unequal access to education, economic advancement, housing, security, health status, and services
- Damaging effects on perpetrators, including their physical and mental health

Source: American Psychological Association, 2007.

disorders. Indeed, the Latino students in the vignette at the beginning of the chapter who bore the negative effects of Dr. Jones's biases felt intimidated and powerless to change their situation. In addition, stereotypes, prejudice, and discrimination can create negative social environments, including rejection of certain individuals, social disparities (in education, housing, income, health status) and intergroup hostility, conflict, crime, and even genocide. Box 8.3 lists some of the key results of prejudice and discrimination according to the American Psychological Association.

Measuring Prejudice and Discrimination

Prejudice and interpersonal discrimination have been measured using a number of techniques that are common in the social sciences, including surveys and polls as well as measuring reactions to vignettes and having individuals identify their reactions (real or potential) to various situations. The measures of discrimination of particular interest to psychologists deal primarily with interpersonal situations rather than discrimination at the macrosocial level where societal traditions, laws, and practices support discriminatory actions. At the interpersonal level, we study how prejudicial attitudes impact our interactions with others and how those prejudices also impact the recipient of the prejudice. This section of the chapter presents examples of some of the results obtained with the various methods.

Not surprisingly, surveys and polls are frequently used to measure prejudice toward ethnic and racial groups as well as toward other groups. Important nationwide surveys are frequently conducted by research institutions such as the Pew Research Center and the Anti-Defamation League, as well as by pollsters such as Zogby International.

Some surveys and polls, for example, have asked respondents to report their behavior or emotional reactions toward racial and ethnic groups. These studies have shown that just living in an ethnically diverse society does not necessarily promote interactions among multicultural groups, nor does it eliminate prejudice. For example, Weaver's (2007) analysis of a national survey of adults found that Latinos report interacting with Whites in higher proportions than the other way around. While 91 percent of Latinos reported personally knowing a White person, only 75 percent of Whites reported such contact with Latinos. Significantly, approximately 70 percent of Latinos reported feeling close to a White person, but only 48 percent of Whites reported such feelings regarding Latinos. Another study (Alba, Rumbaut, & Marotz, 2005) found that misperceptions about the ethnic composition of the country were related to negative attitudes toward immigration as well as to prejudicial attitudes toward ethnic and racial minority groups. Individuals who erroneously felt that Whites made up half or less of the population of the country were likely to express negative attitudes toward immigrants and toward members of ethnic and racial minority groups. At the beginning of this chapter we also summarize studies on stereotypes toward ethnic, racial, and religious groups where the results showed the important role that pssolitical affiliation and contact have on shaping stereotypes and prejudicial attitudes.

Prejudice and discrimination can also be measured by asking individuals to indicate the type of interpersonal contact or social interaction they feel comfortable engaging in across racial or ethnic groups. This type of measure is usually called **social distance**, which was defined by the sociologist Bogardus (1959) as the level of social comfort and understanding that exists between individuals or groups. Typically, individuals are asked to indicate how likely they are to engage in a variety of activities (for example, having as neighbors, coworkers, in-laws) with individuals or members of specific racial, ethnic, or social groups.

Social distance has been used to measure prejudice across ethnic groups in the United States. In an important study using a national sample of respondents, Weaver (2008) analyzed social distance in 1990 and 2000 toward various racial and ethnic minority groups among African Americans, Asian Americans, Latinos, Jews, and Whites. Weaver measured social distance in two situations: (1) living in a neighborhood where half of the neighbors belonged to each of the five specific ethnic and racial groups, and (2) having a close relative marry an individual from each of the same five groups. The study showed that, in general, there was a tendency toward lower prejudice as measured by social distance between 1990 and 2000. The data from 2000 show a tendency for respondents to be less accepting of ethnic and racial minority group members marrying a close relative than having them as neighbors. Nevertheless, in general, all ethnic and racial groups showed a preference for their own group and had little difficulty expressing preferences for specific ethnic or racial minority groups. Another study (Krysan, Couper, Farley, & Forman, 2009) shows that, among residents of Chicago and Detroit who completed a computer-assisted survey, Whites indicated a preference for all-white neighborhoods, while African Americans reported a preference for racially mixed neighborhoods. Further analyses shows that the stated preferences for a given neighborhood expressed by White respondents were heavily influenced by their stereotypes of African Americans so that when the stereotypes were negative the respondents indicated that they preferred not to live in areas of the city that were heavily populated by African Americans.

Other researchers have used psychological tests and paper-and-pencil instruments to analyze exposure and reactions to racial or ethnic discrimination (Awad & Jackson, 2016; Kwok et al., 2011). One such instrument receiving significant levels of attention is the Perceived Ethnic Discrimination Questionnaire (PEDQ), which has been studied among multicultural groups of college students as well as among Asian Americans (Contrada et al., 2001; Kwok et al., 2011). The PEDQ measures an individual's level of perceived discrimination in areas such as social exclusion, stigmatization, discrimination at work/school, and threat/aggression. Research with Asian Americans who took the PEDQ shows that high levels of perceived discrimination correlated with depression and anxiety (Kwok et al., 2011), indicating discrimination's deleterious effects on its recipient.

The Experience of Discrimination

Whether racism and discrimination are treated as human processes or products of historical conditions (Gaines & Reed, 1995; Pike, 1992; Schuman, Steeh, & Bobo, 1985; Takaki, 1979), their effects have significant implications for the type of society in which we live. Legally, discrimination is forbidden in our country. Nevertheless, there is ample evidence that members of racial and ethnic minority groups continue to experience behaviors that are discriminatory in nature. For example, approximately 21 percent of Chinese Americans have reported being treated unfairly at the beginning of the 21st century because of their race (Goto, Gee, & Takeuchi, 2002), and 98 percent of African Americans reported experiencing discrimination during the 1990s and even more recently (Landrine & Klonoff, 1996; Pew Research Center, 2016). Among Latinos, one study (Pérez, Fortuna, & Alegría, 2008) finds that approximately 30 percent of respondents reported having experienced discrimination and unfair treatment because of their ethnicity. Finally, Filipino Americans also report having experienced discrimination at least one time within the year previous to the study (Alvarez & Juang, 2010). There is evidence, therefore, that members of racial and ethnic minority groups continue to experience discriminatory behaviors even today.

A number of studies show how discrimination specifically continues to shape the life experiences of people in the United States. For example, an analysis (Pattnayak & Leonard, 1991) of positions usually assigned to African American and Hispanic baseball players finds that, while White players tended to play central positions such as pitcher and catcher, African Americans tended to be assigned the outfield and Latino ball players tended to play the infield (primarily shortstop and second base). The authors perceive these frequent assignments as limiting African American and Latino players' opportunities to move into leadership positions once they've stopped playing baseball. Further analyses of the types and frequency of discrimination suffered by racial and ethnic minority individuals show that, among other inequitable treatment, they often receive lower salaries than Whites (Torres, 1992), have a lower number of housing possibilities (Yinger, 1988), and are less likely to be called for a job interview than Whites with identical education, training, and work experiences (Kang, DeCelles, Tilcsik, & Jun, 2016).

The frequency and nature of discriminatory experiences reported by members of various racial and ethnic groups differ in terms of a number of characteristics, including the discriminated's national origin, gender, educational level, and social class. For example, African Americans who trace their origin to the British Caribbean islands tend to report lower levels of discrimination than do African Americans whose ancestry is traced to Africa (Hunter, 2008). Cuban Americans and Latinos with high ethnic identity (placing great importance on their ethnicity) were less likely to report experiences with discrimination than were other Latino groups or individuals who had lower ethnic identity (Pérez et al., 2008). At the same time, darker-skinned Latinos report greater levels of discrimination than do light-skinned Latinos (Araujo-Dawson, 2015). Furthermore, ethnic or racial minority women tend to experience double discrimination based on their gender and on their race or ethnicity, and the discrimination occurs even in early childhood and among school-age children (Chavous, Rivas-Drake, Smalls, Griffin, & Cogburn, 2008).

While some studies on prejudice and discrimination had shown slight decreases in prejudice and discrimination toward racial and ethnic minority groups as well as toward certain religious groups, crimes and prejudicial and abusive verbal attacks have recently increased. For example, a large-scale study of public school students shows that Latino children tended to receive disproportionate amounts of punishment and physical abuse at school and that these experiences were related to Latino students dropping out of high school (Peguero, Bondy, & Shekarkhar, 2017). The country has indeed seen recent increases in verbal attacks on racial and ethnic minorities, including Muslims and Jews. This recent racism has manifested in bomb threats called in to Jewish community centers, desecration of Jewish cemeteries, and calls for limiting migration or tourist visits to citizens of certain countries.

Unfortunately, prejudice and discrimination are not phenomena exclusive to the United States. Human history is full of examples of groups that are often statistical minorities becoming the object of negative stereotypes and discrimination. Whether because of their religion, their history, or their skin color, large segments of humanity have suffered curtailment of services (Ortiz, Baeza-Rivera, Salinas-Oñate, Flynn, & Betancourt, 2016), lack of access to education and jobs, segregation, or even death. The Nazi persecution of Jews in Europe, apartheid in South Africa, and the near extermination of indigenous Indian communities in Latin America are just a few examples of the shameful effects of negative stereotypes based on unjustified reactions to some human characteristics. The importance of the topics covered in this chapter, therefore, go well beyond our national borders.

Why Do People Discriminate?

Previous sections of this chapter present hypotheses for the formation of stereotypes and of prejudicial attitudes. In discussing the rationale for discrimination, many of those ideas are equally appropriate. Nevertheless, as this section of the chapter demonstrates, other important explanations can help us understand why people discriminate.

For example, the Institute of Medicine (2002), in reviewing the literature on health care disparities between Whites and racial and ethnic minority populations, concludes that "indirect evidence indicates that bias, stereotyping, prejudice and clinical uncertainty on the part of health care providers may be contributory factors to racial and ethnic disparities in health care" (p. 140). Many of these effects can be attributed to lack of knowledge and information about members of ethnic minority groups on the part of health care providers who are primarily White and usually uninformed about the cultures and traditions of the patients they treat (see Chapter 10 on physical health and well-being). Indeed, social psychologists (e.g., Fiske, 1998; Pettigrew, 1998) have long argued that lack of contact and poor information often produce stereotyping and assumptions of significant dissimilarity. Nevertheless, contact by itself does not necessarily produce liking, and in some cases it may create or reinforce stereotypes and prejudices and produce stress and frustration.

Misunderstandings and actual ignorance about cultural practices play important roles in the development of prejudicial attitudes and discrimination. Traits valued in one culture (e.g., the personal significance of family members or the desire to allow individuals to save face) can be misinterpreted as a manifestation of exclusionary attitudes or negative personality traits. Indeed, lack of information or uncertainty about people's characteristics has been associated with a number of discriminatory behaviors and with differences in access to services (Balsa & McGuire, 2003; Khan, 2014).

Additional psychological research (Mendes, 2007) has shown the role that uncertainty and unfamiliarity can have in producing certain prejudicial attitudes or behaviors. A study of people's reactions to working with an "unexpected other" (an Asian American speaking with a U.S. Southern accent or lilt) showed that college students performed more poorly in an intellectual task when the partner did not conform to expectations in terms of physical appearance and speech patterns. When faced with the "surprising or unexpected other," individuals showed physical reactions related to stress and were less likely to smile. The researchers argued that those reactions may be related to the fact that uncertainty produces stress on the individual and lowers performance. Avoidance of persons perceived to be different can, therefore, make individuals feel less stress and lead to discriminatory behavior that decreases the likelihood of exposure to the different other.

Other researchers argue that immigrant groups are feared because of the change they may bring about in the community (even though relatives or members of the receiving community may have been immigrants in the past) and that this fear of change may also support the development of prejudicial attitudes and discriminatory behavior (Alba et al., 2005). Also relevant is the fact that, often, racial and ethnic minority groups exhibit demographic characteristics like poverty and lower levels of educational achievement that support the development of prejudice on the part of members of other groups (APA Task Force on Socioeconomic Status, 2007). Interestingly, the experiences of discrimination experienced by many immigrants and the poor in general deprive them of educational and employment opportunities that would help them improve their socioeconomic status. In this vicious cycle, discriminatory experiences perpetuate prejudicial attitudes, which makes it difficult for the victims of discrimination and prejudice to change and improve their socioeconomic conditions, which perpetuates their inadequate education, poverty, and disadvantage in other areas. Indeed, a recent study with a large sample of participants (Hazzouri et al., 2016) shows that cumulative exposure to low income for more than two decades is strongly associated with poor cognitive functioning among young adults. These cognitive deficits are found in verbal memory, processing speed, and executive functions, among other important skills.

The Role of Implicit Attitudes A significant amount of research has recently been produced analyzing the role of explicit and implicit attitudes on prejudice and discrimination (Perugini, 2005). **Implicit attitudes** are usually perceived as affective reactions and associations held by individuals toward other people or toward behaviors that are subtle and not easily verbalized and therefore difficult to measure by surveys or attitude scales. These researchers argue that implicit attitudes are correlated with behaviors even if the individual is not completely conscious of the existence of the attitudes (Nosek, Greenwald, & Banaji, 2005; Shelton, Richeson, Salvatore, & Trawalter, 2005; Ziegert & Hanges, 2005). One approach to measuring implicit associations or attitudes is the Implicit Association Test, or IAT, in which individuals are presented with visual stimuli, like two words or concepts (e.g., *Jewish* and *Good*), and the researchers measure response latency, or the amount of time it takes the individuals to perform a task, such as pushing a button when they feel the words or concepts are related or associated. Other researchers have used level of activity of facial muscles—facial electromyography or EMG—to measure prejudicial attitudes toward people or toward some other stimuli (Vanman, Saltz, Nathan, & Warren, 2004).

While the details of the research methods are beyond this chapter, a recent study finds that, indeed, people have different response time when they hold negative attitudes toward certain groups. For example, Christian students took longer to make associations of Muslim names with positive traits than to associate Christian names with positive characteristics, showing certain levels of implicit prejudice against Muslims (Rowatt, Franklin, & Cotton, 2005). That study also found that anti-Arab racism, authoritarianism, and religious fundamentalism were associated with negative attitudes toward Muslims. As predicted by social identity theory (Tajfel, 1981), the evaluations of Christians toward their own group were more positive and favorable than toward the rejected group or out-group (Muslims), and this was true through self-report measures as well as through procedures designed to measure implicit, less external attitudes.

Prejudice and discrimination, of course, can manifest themselves in actions that at first may seem innocuous. For example, what would you do if you received an e-mail message intended for another student? Do you reply, indicating the mistake, or simply hit the delete button? What if the message says that the student has received a highly competitive scholarship and must reply within 48 hours or lose the money? Finally, what do you think other students would do if the e-mail message were addressed to Hameed? An interesting study (Bushman & Bonacci, 2004) analyzes the reactions of college students to receiving that e-mail message. The participating students had previously filled out an attitude scale measuring their prejudice toward Arab Americans. The authors of the study found that highly prejudiced students were less likely to return the message than were those students with lower prejudice toward Arabs. In other conditions of the experiment, the e-mail was addressed to Brice (no difference in return rates by prejudiced and less prejudiced students) or the content was changed to indicate that the student had not received the scholarship. In this latter condition, the prejudiced students were more likely to return the message than were the less prejudiced. The study showed, therefore, that prejudice can also affect behavior, even when individuals cannot be identified and can act surreptitiously to hurt those that they dislike, as did the prejudiced students, who failed to return the e-mail message.

The Role of Disparagement Humor One fruitful area of recent research on the factors that promote discrimination has been the study of the effects of racial disparagement humor on promoting prejudicial attitudes and discrimination. We have all participated in verbalizing or laughing at disparagement humor that presents two conflicting messages: one that is hostile and disparages the target person and another that implicitly argues that the humorous statement is not really negative since "It's only a joke." In a study analyzing the differential vulnerability of various social groups (Ford, Woodzicka, Triplett, Kochersberger & Holden, 2014), the authors found that disparagement humor promoted discriminatory actions against groups toward which society in general has ambivalent attitudes (such as Muslims). Research participants high in anti-Muslim prejudice were more willing to accept discriminatory activities against Muslims after reading an anti-Muslim joke than they were after reading anti-Muslim texts or other types of jokes. Findings were similar when the research participants were highly prejudiced toward gays and read antigay jokes. Disparagement humor was also found in other studies to serve as a trivializing prompt that in turn served to promote intolerance and as justification for discrimination, particularly among highly prejudiced individuals (Woodzicka & Ford, 2010).

Disparagement humor has been described as influencing discrimination by creating a normative climate of tolerance toward discrimination that decreases the need for self-regulation among highly prejudiced individuals (Ford & Ferguson, 2004). A practical application of these studies on disparagement humor is the fact that a joke is never "just a joke"—not only because it hurts the feelings of the objects of the derision but also because the simple act of telling or hearing the joke can promote or justify discriminatory actions. Importantly, this phenomenon of increased discrimination as associated to disparagement humor has been found not just when analyzing humor toward ethnic, racial, and religious groups (Ford et al., 2014) but also toward LGBTQ individuals and toward women (Ford, Boxer, Armstrong, & Edel, 2008).

Racism

Prejudicial attitudes and discriminatory actions based on a person's or group's racial physical characteristics (often called *phenotype*) are central components of what is often labeled *racism*. While racism is not totally different from discrimination based on race or ethnicity, much research has used the word *racism* to describe prejudice and discrimination toward racial minority groups, particularly those minority groups or individuals that share a number of distinct body characteristics differing from those of most Whites—like darker skin color, almond-shaped eyes, curlier hair, larger or broader nose, and fuller lips.

As is true for many psychosocial phenomena, there are many definitions available in the literature to characterize racism. In an analysis of the psychosocial effects of racism, Clark and colleagues (Clark et al., 1999) define **racism** as "beliefs, attitudes, institutional arrangements, and acts that tend to denigrate individuals or groups because of phenotypic characteristics or ethnic group affiliation" (p. 805). An important aspect of the definition of racism proposed by Clark and his colleagues is that racism can occur across ethnic or racial groups (**intergroup racism**) or within a given group (**intragroup racism**).

Disparities among racial groups in education, health, wealth, poverty, and access to and interactions with legal or judicial services are good examples of the effects of racism in the United States (Neville, Gallardo, & Sue, 2016). Indeed, differences in income (where large percentages of racial and ethnic minorities are poor, underemployed, or unemployed) is just one of many indicators of how race continues to affect the lives of ethnic or racial minorities in the United States. At the same time, a number of events in the recent past (such as the election of President Barack Obama) have led some to argue that the United States is now postracial and that race plays a limited role in people's lives, and events ought to be defined not as "racist" but as isolated events (Bonilla-Silva, 2016). Arguing that race and racism are no longer as important as they have been in the past has led some to argue for a Color-Blind Racial Ideology, or CBRI (Neville et al., 2016). Nevertheless, the argument is often made that what has changed is not the eradication of racism itself but the nature of the phenomenon, where racism has become more subtle and institutionalized (Bonilla-Silva & Dietrich, 2011).

Recently Gullet and West (2016) have identified the differences between a color-blind approach to race (as proposed by the CBRI) and multiculturalism. Both perspectives share the goal of easing interpersonal relations—CBRI by suggesting that all interactions (and their analyses) be blind to racial and ethnic differences, and multiculturalism as a process that acknowledges and in a sense empowers and celebrates all races and ethnicities. The authors further argue that

> in direct contrast to the color-blind perspective of ignoring race, multiculturalism seeks to celebrate the importance and harness the power of the perspectives and experiences that come with each individual's unique background. In the context of interpersonal interactions, the multicultural approach can help people accurately gauge the individual motivations and perspectives of one's cross-race interaction partners. (p. 71)

Substantial evidence shows that individuals targeted by racism, as with discrimination, suffer negative consequences (Clark et al., 1999; King, 2005; Mossakowski, 2003)—such negative consequences include not only loss of access to services and benefits (e.g., to education, jobs, housing, social advancement) but also limits to personal and psychological growth. As a stressor, racism can be expected to produce psychological reactions in the targeted individual, including anger, anxiety, depression, fear, aggression, and poor job satisfaction, as well as a number of physiological reactions, such as hypertension and damage to the immune system (Cokley, McClain, Enciso, & Martinez, 2013). Research indeed has shown that racism produces these effects among Latinos (e.g., Finch, Kolody, & Vega, 2000), African Americans (e.g., Landrine & Klonoff, 1996), and Asian Americans (DeCastro, Gee, & Takeuchi, 2008; Mossakowski, 2003).

Results of a large-scale longitudinal study of people's health (Borrell, Kiefe, Williams, Diez-Roux, & Gordon-Larsen, 2006) show that African Americans who reported experiencing high levels of racism (at school, while getting a job, at work, in public settings) also showed poorer self-reported physical and psychological health, including depression and overall poorer sense of physical well-being. These findings were independent of the respondents' skin tone. A study with college students (King, 2005) also finds that experiences of discrimination are stressful when they are perceived to be central to an individual's self-esteem or self-definition. Furthermore, a large-scale study of Asian Americans (DeCastro et al., 2008; Gee, Ro, Gavin, & Takeuchi, 2008; Gee, Spencer, Chen, & Takeuchi, 2007) shows not only poorer health as a result of discrimination and racism but also engagement in risk behaviors like cigarette smoking.

Studies exploring racism—some of which we have discussed previously—have abounded for a number of years, and, indeed, studies such as those of Clark and Clark (1939) on children's racial preferences have been used in the landmark decision of the United States Supreme Court that made racial discrimination illegal. The Clarks' early study showed that African American children, when given a choice, preferred a White doll to a doll whose skin color was closer to their own. The researchers suggested that the children had internalized a dislike for darker skin on individuals, preferring to play and to hold dolls that differed significantly from themselves in skin color. The findings of those early studies have been replicated with similar results even as late as the 1980s (Powell-Hopson & Hopson, 1988). Nevertheless, a later study by Burnett and Sisson (1995) showed that a large percentage of African American children (46 percent) showed no specific preference for the White or African American doll, with the next-larger group showing a preference for the doll that resembled African Americans (37 percent). The authors argued that as children became older (after preschool years) they tended to prefer Black dolls more than younger children, who often chose White dolls. Overall, these studies suggest that societal racism affects children to the point that they show a rejection of self or at least of others who look like them.

As members of a society that has lived painful examples of racism, we are likely to have learned the racial biases of our parents and grandparents and of society in general. Those perceptions affect our ability to work and study and live in an ethnically and racially diverse environment, and the prejudicial attitudes we have learned can become deterrents in acquiring the appropriate levels of cultural competence to function effectively in a multiculturally diverse world (Sue et al., 2007).

Racial Microaggressions

In a very important article, Asian American psychologist Derald Sue and colleagues (2007) propose that there are a number of relatively small and common behaviors that they term *racial microaggressions* that are racist in nature and that can have an impact in a variety of interpersonal relationships, including therapy and instruction. They define **racial microaggressions** as "brief and commonplace daily verbal, behavioral and environmental indignities, whether intentional or unintentional, that communicate hostile, derogatory, or negative racial slights and insults to the target person or group" (p. 273). Expanding on the definition proposed by Sue and colleagues, we identify microaggressions as those brief, subtle expressions or exchanges (verbal, nonverbal, or physical) that carry a negative connotation and are directed toward people who differ from the originating individual in terms of such characteristics as gender, ethnicity, sexuality, religious beliefs, socioeconomic status, educational level, physical ability, nationality, and accent. Examples of microaggressions include avoiding someone's look, not shaking hands when meeting someone, moving to a different cashier line, and ignoring someone's question or comment.

Sue and colleagues (2007) break microaggressions into three categories: (1) microassaults, (2) microinsults, and (3) microinvalidations. *Microassaults* are explicit statements that constitute a verbal or nonverbal attack on an individual. Examples include name-calling, using racial or ethnic epithets, or using or displaying insulting symbols or behaviors (e.g., referring to someone as "Oriental" or "Spick," displaying a picture of a burning cross or a "sleepy Mexican," or performing certain obscene or insulting hand gestures). *Microinsults* are verbal or nonverbal communications that at minimum are rude but often represent a derogatory reaction to a person's ethnicity, race, or personal characteristics. Examples include questioning the role played by ability or skills in hiring or when a decision is made (for example, when analyzing the student diversity of a classroom, asking, "Did we get the best-qualified students regardless of race?") or ignoring someone's presence or contributions because of their race or ethnicity (such as when a supervisor ignores a question asked by a person of color or a salesperson ignores an ethnic or racial minority individual waiting to be helped at a store). *Microinvalidations* are defined by Sue and colleagues as "communications that exclude, negate, or nullify the psychological thoughts, feelings and experiential reality of a person of color" (p. 274). A poignant example mentioned by Sue and colleagues is when Asian Americans born in the United States are told how well they speak English. Additional examples of microinvalidations are when an ethnic or racial minority individual is told, "We don't do that here," or asked, "Why do you people do that?" when dealing with certain cultural traditions and practices.

Recent work in the field has shown an increase in people's interest in understanding microaggresions as subtle forms of prejudice and discrimination and on training individuals in how to prevent microaggressions (Nadal, 2011). Various authors have produced lists of examples of microaggressions toward racial and ethnic groups as well as toward women and toward those who are differently abled or "disabled." Recently, closer scrutiny has been trained on identifying microaggressions, partly due to the seeming overease with which too many statements and behaviors have been labeled microaggressions and blamed for limiting the quality and length of interpersonal interactions (Lilienfeld, 2017). Further analyses of how these actions are perceived and their effect on people who experience them are considered important steps in advancing the field.

Box 8.4 presents some examples of racial microaggressions identified by Sue and colleagues (2007)—including perceiving individuals as foreigners in their own country, assuming criminality, believing in meritocracy, assuming pathology, and ascribing second-class status. Each type of microaggression is clarified, with examples provided of microaggressive comments that could be made, as well as examples of the messages implied in the microaggression. An examination of this material helps us become aware of how, at times unwittingly, we are able to offend individuals who differ from ourselves. Indeed, awareness of these microaggressions and ways to prevent them can be an important first step toward acquiring the level of cultural competence (or openness to the other) that is a central component of a multicultural individual (Fowers & Davidov, 2006).

Reducing Prejudice, Discrimination, and Racism

A key concern of researchers and policymakers is finding ways to reduce the prejudice, discrimination, and racism learned from early interactions at home, school, and playgrounds and later on while at work and in society in general (Oskamp, 2000; Sampson, 1999). Groups affected by prejudice, discrimination, and racism include racial and ethnic groups demographically in the majority as well as members of groups that are a statistical minority because of their ethnicity, race, body characteristics, religion, gender, and real or perceived power in society, among other defining characteristics.

A number of approaches and strategies have been designed not only to expose individuals to diverse others but also to challenge and change prejudicial attitudes and expectations (Oskamp, 2000)—strategies including desegregating elementary and secondary schools, diversifying children's television programming, offering classes and training workshops on diversity, involving individuals in personal sharing within a diverse context, diversifying universities and their curricula, and developing special advertising campaigns (Adams, Biernat, Branscombe, Crandall, & Wrightsman, 2008; American Psychological Association, Presidential Task Force on Preventing Discrimination and Promoting Diversity, 2012; Dovidio, Glick, & Rudman, 2005; Oskamp, 2000).

While a number of theories and approaches have been proposed to understand the process of prejudice reduction (Oskamp, 2000), intergroup contact is probably one of the most frequently analyzed

Box 8.4

Types and Examples of Microaggressions

- Perceiving an individual as a foreigner in their own country
  - "Where were you born?"
  - "Your English is really good."
- Judging of a person's intelligence based on ethnicity
  - "You are a credit to your people."
  - "You are so smart and well-spoken."
- Being uncomfortable or unwilling to emphasize ethnicity
  - "When I look at you, I don't see your race or skin color."
- Assuming criminality based on race or ethnicity
  - Holding tightly to a bag or a purse when in the presence of a person of color
  - Crossing the street when encountering a person of color
  - Following a person of color around a store to ensure they don't shoplift
- Denying racism
  - "I am not a racist; I have a lot of Spanish friends."
  - "Some of my best friends are Jews."
- Maintaining the myth of meritocracy
  - "Only the best person should be hired."
  - "If you work hard, you can get ahead."
- Pathologizing values or behaviors
  - "Why do you people talk so loud?"
  - "Don't be so quiet."
- Assuming second-class status
  - Person of color being mistaken for service personnel
  - Taxi driver who chooses to not stop for a person of color

Source: Based on Sue et al., 2007.

(Dixon, Durrheim, & Tredoux, 2005). Indeed, many theoretical approaches explain components of the intergroup contact process or are derivations of its propositions. This theoretical approach is considered the basis for building a diverse or multicultural society and was originally proposed by Gordon Allport (1954).

The **contact hypothesis** maintains that prejudicial attitudes and emotions can be changed by bringing together diverse peoples into a specific setting. Indeed, major policy decisions such as the school desegregation ruling of the U.S. Supreme Court in 1954 (*Brown v. Board of Education*) as well as special techniques such as collaborative learning are based on significant psychological research (Clark, Chein, & Cook, 2004) and on the principles proposed by the intergroup contact hypothesis (Adams et al., 2008).

Intergroup Contact

Obviously, putting diverse people together in a group is not enough to change their prejudicial attitudes or discriminatory behavior. As a matter of fact, Allport (1954) initially argued that in order to be effective, **intergroup contact** needed to have four main characteristics: (1) group members needed to be perceived as having equal status at least within the group's activities, (2) the interaction would have institutional support and approval by statements from people in authority or as supported by laws or customs, (3) cooperation across groups would be expected to produce a common goal, and (4) the interaction would allow individuals to get to know each other (often called *acquaintance potential*).

More recently, Pettigrew (1998) suggested the importance of an additional characteristic: the possibility of becoming friends. These five conditions or characteristics of intergroup contact can exist in a variety of settings, including universities and schools, the armed forces, voluntary associations, and work settings. For example, equal employment opportunities and affirmative action policies have made it possible for racial and ethnic minority individuals to join workplaces where they can perform their duties alongside White colleagues on group projects. These settings will necessarily help reduce prejudicial attitudes held by all individuals involved as they share frustrations and successes and together move toward a common goal. The armed forces—which were desegregated by law before civil society was—offer a particularly propitious environment for the five conditions of effective intergroup contact.

A large number of studies have analyzed the effectiveness of contact in bringing about a decrease of prejudice and discrimination (e.g., Chin, 2004; Dovidio et al., 2005; Weaver, 2007). A study with college students (Aberson, Shoemaker, & Tomolillo, 2004) shows that White students who had close friendships with African American or Latino students exhibited lower prejudicial attitudes toward either group than those who did not report such close friendships. Results from numerous additional studies tend to confirm results similar to these and support the effectiveness of the contact hypothesis.

Contact across racial and ethnic groups under the conditions proposed by Allport (1954) and Pettigrew (1998) also produces important personal changes that go beyond eliminating prejudice and discrimination. A recent study with students at two California universities (Santos, Ortiz, Morales, & Rosales, 2007) investigates the effects of campus ethnic diversity on students' personal identity. Overall, a sense of inclusion, belonging, and acceptance was the most frequently mentioned result of being in an ethnically and racially diverse campus environment, although this result was more frequent among ethnic and racial minority students than among Whites. A second result was related to how an ethnically and racially diverse campus helped students develop multicultural competence, and the data show that this effect was equally important for White students as for racial and ethnic minority individuals. Among the negative effects identified, White students frequently mentioned a sense of discomfort with their own racial identity, a response that was less frequent among ethnic or racial minority students. However, as the authors conclude, "for many students, experiencing an ethnically diverse campus community engendered a sense of belonging and inclusion within the institution, which was associated with a more positive and enriched sense of ethnic identity and adjustment to college" (p. 112).

Dialogue Across Difference

An approach to ending discrimination and racism has recently been proposed (Gurin, Nagda & Zúñiga, 2013) that expands the contact hypothesis and concentrates on promoting structured dialogue between diverse individuals. Authors of the book *Dialogue Across Difference* present the results of a large number of studies showing the effectiveness of structured and goal-directed dialogue to moderate or change negative stereotypes and prejudicial attitudes. The research was conducted with college students who agreed to participate in group-based activities within a racially and gender diverse group. Participants carried out a series of tasks and then spent a significant amount of time dialoguing about what had happened in the interaction and reflecting (individually and in group) about the experience, including the observed interactions. The semester-long project had as a goal learning about social justice—"learning that involves understanding social identities and group-based inequalities, encourages building of cross-group relationships, and cultivates social responsibility" (p. 3). The results show that the students increased their intergroup understanding and developed and increased positive intergroup relationships and activities. Interestingly, the results show that the changes in the participants were still present a year after the experience. This promising approach is being replicated in a number of institutions and can become a model for other successful interventions.

School Desegregation

In 1954 the U.S. Supreme Court ruled in *Brown v. Board of Education* that segregated education in schools violated the rights of racial and ethnic minority children and ordered that schools should be desegregated. This landmark decision promulgated the need for all children to receive education of equal quality. In addition, various researchers suggested in a brief filed with the Court that desegregation would have significant positive effects not just on children's learning but also on their social and psychological well-being (Adams et al., 2008; Clark et al., 2004). Over the long term, desegregation has helped temper prejudice, discrimination, and racism among children of the last two or three generations and has allowed children of different races and ethnicities to grow and learn together.

Many studies have been conducted to analyze the positive effects of school desegregation where quality education has been made available to larger numbers of racial and ethnic minority children (e.g., Pettigrew, 2004; Schofield & Hausmann, 2004). At the same time, other researchers argue that, while schools may not be formally segregated, they do not provide equal access to the poor and to many racial and ethnic minorities and, as a consequence, produce significant performance gaps in children's learning across ethnic and racial groups (e.g., Weinstein, Gregory, & Strambler, 2004). Although children of all ethnic and racial backgrounds are no longer limited to segregated schools, school district regulations in many cases produce schools that are fairly homogeneous in the race and ethnicity of their students due to controls on school district borders and areas to be served by specific schools.

As a matter of fact, a study with elementary school children (McGlothlin & Killen, 2006) shows that attending ethnically and racially homogeneous school environments can be related to the development of prejudicial attitudes in children. The study finds that, when asked to interpret an ambiguous social situation, children in primarily White schools were more likely to attribute negative traits to African Americans than to Whites.

Without a doubt, the Supreme Court ruling to desegregate schools in *Brown v. Board of Education* did much to begin to move the treatment of all of our nation's children toward equity, and certainly a huge part of the reason for the shift is because of the nation's developing understanding of matters of race, prejudice, and discrimination—a process in which psychology has played an important role. Nevertheless, much remains to be accomplished before we can consider the treatment of all children to be meaningfully equal (Adams et al., 2008). Fine (2004) calls the Supreme Court's decision "a bold move that harnessed social science to interrupt injustice. The *Brown* decision recast the normative as oppressive; the tolerated as intolerable. . . . But . . . the work of justice theorists and activists is two-fold: to interrupt oppression and then to sustain justice" (p. 509)

Other Promising Practices

In 1997 President Bill Clinton established a project to identify ways in which prejudice could be eliminated in the United States. Members of the President's Initiative on Race, also called the One America Program, held a number of events across the country and produced reports and scientific analyses trying to better understand racism and prejudice while hoping to promote understanding across ethnic and racial groups. As part of this process, social science researchers identified a number of strategies that have been used in order to promote dialogue, support intercultural education and understanding, build community, and solve race-related problems (Oskamp & Jones, 2000). This analysis of 59 high-profile programs dedicated to reducing prejudice and discrimination shows that the largest percentage of programs used primarily educational activities (47 percent) and interethnic dialogue (47 percent), followed by training of community leaders (41 percent), production of educational materials (39 percent), and public events like conferences, lectures, and exhibitions (34 percent). Interestingly, only 29 percent of these programs were dedicated to promoting intergroup contact, despite this strategy's proven effectiveness, as demonstrated in psychological research.

Box 8.5

Strategies to Becoming a Change Agent to Prevent Discrimination

1. **Be a self-explorer.** Constantly analyze your own reactions to social situations, and understand that you are a gendered and cultural (racial or ethnic) human being.
2. **Be a student.** Be a life-long learner in order to educate yourself about your biases (racism, sexism, ableism, heterosexism) and ways to eliminate them.
3. **Be a role model.** Be a vocal advocate for equality, and oppose discrimination in front of others, particularly among children. Model positive interactions with those who are different from yourself.
4. **Be an antiracist, antisexist, anticlassist, and antiheterosexist parent.** Teach your children about prejudice and the various types of discrimination. Encourage your children to experience multicultural environments at home, at school, and at play and in other entertainment contexts.
5. **Be a teacher.** Teach your children and relatives how to value diversity and a multicultural country.
6. **Be an activist.** Speak out when you see injustices. Challenge those who discriminate or express prejudicial and stereotypical attitudes even if the attitudes are presented as jokes.
7. **Be proactive.** Promote the analysis and processing of prejudicial attitudes and situations, particularly with young children and those who look up to you.
8. **Be multicultural.** Create an environment that celebrates diversity—in your private spaces (at home and in your room) and public spaces (at school, work, and elsewhere). Participate in culturally diverse activities and celebrations, and expose yourself to multicultural books and media.

Source: Adapted from American Psychological Association Presidential Task Force on Preventing Discrimination and Promoting Diversity, 2012.

Psychologists have been involved in developing, testing, and promoting many activities as well as testing and promoting more recently developed strategies. These new methods vary in approach, theoretical foundation, and, of course, effectiveness. While some psychologists emphasize the need to train counselors and therapists in prejudice reduction (Pedersen, 2003), others suggest the need to train the general public through educational activities, workshops, and training sessions (Neville et al., 2016). Overall, the various strategies are based on a process of personal change that can be taught or modeled. The American Psychological Association Presidential Task Force on Preventing Discrimination and Promoting Diversity (2012), created by former APA president Melba J. T. Vasquez, suggests a number of strategies that adults—including college students like you—can utilize to promote societal change and model proper behaviors for children and promote social justice in the United States (Box 8.5).

The Benefits of a Multicultural Society

It is important to recognize that our experiences living in an ethnically and racially diverse society like the United States imply being exposed to diverse individuals who differ because of who they are, what they believe, or how they act. Negative by-products we discussed previously include stereotyping, prejudice, and discrimination. At the same time, a diverse environment can also foment important and positive sociopsychological changes in individuals.

As mentioned in Chapter 4, one of the advantages to people living in an ethnically and racially diverse country is their developed ability to work within multicultural settings and to learn the values, norms, and expectancies of cultures other than their own. Research shows that working and studying in ethnically and racially diverse groups has a number of advantages, including developing the ability to identify novel and creative solutions to problems and promoting greater intellectual complexity in discussions (Antonio, Chang, Hakuta, Kenny, Levin, & Milem, 2004).

Furthermore, being exposed to multicultural settings allows individuals to learn about one or more cultures and to become conversant in diverse values, beliefs, norms, and attitudes. This process of biculturation—or of becoming bicultural or multicultural—has a number of advantages, like learning how to function appropriately and with ease in ethnically and racially diverse environments and learning to think creatively, process multiple perspectives, and approach problems from multiple angles. As you may recall from the research mentioned in Chapter 4, bicultural individuals show significant cognitive flexibility by easily switching from one cultural framework to the other when exposed to culture-specific symbols or to cultural stimuli that are present in the social environment (Hong et al., 2000). Furthermore, bicultural individuals tend to show a strong sense of personal identity and positive attitudes toward diverse others (LaFromboise et al., 1993). These positive effects can only be achieved within multicultural settings such as the United States.

Chapter Summary

This chapter examines the consequences of living in a multicultural, diverse society such as the United States. Our contact with individuals who differ in terms of their ethnicity or race produces positive and negative results as we learn how people differ from us in terms of their values, norms, beliefs, opinions, and behaviors. Frequently, we form rigid images or beliefs of the members of an ethnic or racial group, assigning all members of the group a select number of traits or characteristics (stereotypes). Sometimes those characteristics are positive, and often they are negative. Those stereotypes are the basis on which prejudices are created, targeting members of the group. The behavioral correlates of those prejudices often become discriminatory as we behave differentially toward various groups, favoring some and rejecting others. Often in the United States, these discriminatory actions have been based on people's skin color, and the resulting racism has created great pain. But living in an ethnically and racially diverse country need not be a negative experience. Indeed, exposure to people who differ from who we are can offer us important gains in cognitive flexibility, problem-solving skills, and personal growth.

Key Terms

ableism 182
ambivalent sexism 182
aversive racism 182
benevolent sexism 182
classism 182
contact hypothesis 191
discrimination 181
ethnic stereotypes 174
gendered racism 180
heterosexism 182
hostile sexism 182
implicit attitudes 186
intergroup contact 191
intergroup racism 188
intragroup racism 188
out-group homogeneity effect 176
prejudice 181
racial microaggressions 189
racial stereotypes 174
racism 188
social distance 184
stereotype content 175
stereotype threat 179
symbolic racism 182

Learning by Doing

- Analyze how multiculturalism has been incorporated into the curriculum of your university (most data should be available via your school's website) by listing characteristics such as (1) the percentage of majors and minors your school offers that are related to diverse populations in terms of gender, ethnicity, race, nationality, and religious faith, (2) the number of courses offered in your core curriculum or general education requirements that address all types of diversity (gender, race or ethnicity, socioeconomic status, sexualities, physical abilities, national origin, etc.), and (3) cocurricular offerings and research centers that support diversity and multiculturalism. Then analyze the website of another university that is similar to yours in terms of funding (public or private), size (number of students), and geographical location (urban or rural and area of the country), and use the same points of analysis.

- Watch five prime-time television shows and two or three soap operas that attempt to show contemporary life in the United States, and count how many non-White characters are part of the show. Do not analyze programs on ethnic networks such as BET, Telemundo, or Univision. Then analyze the positions or roles of the ethnic or racial minority characters, and compare them to those of the White characters (e.g., how many are portrayed as rich or poor or occupying positions of power, such as doctors or judges, or working in low-paying service occupations, such as maids, nannies, or gardeners). Do the shows include people of color in percentages that reflect the population of the country? What do the differences in power or role significance say to you?
- Review 10 issues of mainstream lifestyle magazines (for example, *People*, *Us Weekly*) and 10 issues of sports magazines (for example, *Sports Illustrated*) and analyze (1) the percentage of individuals of each of the five major ethnic and racial groups that are included in the various issues (African Americans, American Indians, Asian Americans, Latinos, Whites) and (2) the activities in which they are portrayed (for example, playing sports, managing a sports team, caring for children, dancing). How representative are those pictures of the ethnic and racial composition of the country? How do the pictures contribute to the development or support of ethnic and racial stereotypes? Repeat this analysis by using ethnic or racial magazines such as *Ebony*, *Latina*, *¡Hola!*, *People en Español*, and *ALIST*.

Suggested Further Readings

Adams, G., Biernat, M., Branscombe, N. R., Crandall, C. S., & Wrightsman, L. S. (Eds.). (2008). *Commemorating "Brown": The social psychology of racism and discrimination*. Washington, DC: American Psychological Association.

A collection of essays reviewing the implications of the *Brown* decision by the Supreme Court from the perspective of social-psychological theories and research.

American Psychological Association Presidential Task Force on Preventing Discrimination and Promoting Diversity. (2012). *Dual pathways to a better America: Preventing discrimination and promoting diversity*. Washington, DC: American Psychological Association.

A review of the literature on discrimination and ethnic and racial diversity conducted by a panel of distinguished psychologists. The report includes important highlights in the field and makes a number of recommendations for future researchers, policy makers, and educators, as well as for professional associations like the American Psychological Association.

Blaine, B. E. (2007). *Understanding the psychology of diversity*. Thousand Oaks, CA: Sage.

A book including an analysis of such psychological phenomena as categorization and stereotyping and their relationships to attitudes (prejudice) and behavior (discrimination). The book combines research addressing ethnic differences as well as other types of diversity (e.g., social class, sexuality).

Chin, J. L. (Ed.). (2004). *The psychology of prejudice and discrimination: Vol. 2, Ethnicity and multiracial identity series*. Westport, CT: Praeger.

A book including a series of comprehensive reviews of research on various topics related to prejudice and discrimination. An excellent resource for researchers and students interested in gaining a more complete understanding of these complex social issues.

Dovidio, J. F., Glick, P., & Rudman, L. A. (2005). *On the nature of prejudice: Fifty years after Allport*. Malden, MA: Blackwell.

A comprehensive resource that analyzes how our knowledge and understanding of prejudice has changed since the publication of Gordon Allport's important book on the topic. *On the nature of prejudice* is an excellent resource for students wishing to gain a deeper understanding of this complex and important phenomenon and chronicles how far the field has developed.

National Academies of Sciences, Engineering, and Medicine. (2016). *The economic and fiscal consequences of immigration.* Washington DC: The National Academies Press.
A comprehensive analysis of the economic and fiscal consequences of migration, including a historical perspective on migratory trends and the socioeconomic results of migration at the state and national level. An important contribution to a better understanding of some of the common stereotypes regarding the effects of migration.

Neville, H. A., Gallardo, M. E., & Sue, D. W. (Eds.) (2016). *The myth of racial color blindness: Manifestations, dynamics, and impact.* Washington, DC: American Psychological Association.
A well-researched edited collection analyzing the consequences of color-blind perspectives on research and services, compared to a multicultural perspective celebrating racial and ethnic differences. The book includes contributions by various social scientists and delves into the deleterious effect of believing in the myth of color-blindness in settings as diverse as schools, health care services, business organizations, and psychotherapy.

Oskamp, S. (Ed.). (2000). *Reducing prejudice and discrimination.* Mahwah, NJ: Lawrence Erlbaum.
A collection of essays on the theory and practice of reducing prejudice and discrimination by some of the best-known researchers in the field. The book includes comprehensive analyses of the research literature and of its practical implications. Although somewhat old, the book includes seminal analyses of interest to individuals invested in the field.

Sue, D. W. (2003). *Overcoming our racism: The journey to liberation.* San Francisco: Jossey-Bass.
An excellent and practical book explicating approaches individuals, and particularly psychologists, can take to become not only more sensitive to cultural differences but also more respectful of racial and ethnic diversity.

Web Resources

- Reducing Stereotype Threat
  https://teachingcenter.wustl.edu/resources/inclusive-teaching-learning/reducing-stereotype-threat/
  An excellent online resource for overviews of published research on stereotype threat and suggestions on how to prevent stereotype threat
- Understanding Prejudice
  http://www.understandingprejudice.org
  A website offering a large number of resources and activities that promote an understanding of all types of prejudice

A Sample of Organizations Providing Resources on Prejudice and Discrimination

Many of the following organizations specify on their websites notable occasions of discrimination and offer important resources such as data on public opinion and research findings. Our list is not exhaustive but provides a number of important resources to begin learning more about the topics discussed in this chapter.

American Civil Liberties Union (ACLU), https://www.aclu.org
Anti-Defamation League (ADL), https://www.adl.org
Asian American Legal Defense and Education Fund (AALDEF), aaldef.org
Council on American-Islamic Relations (CAIR), https://www.cair.com
Japanese American Citizens League (JACL), https://jacl.org
League of United Latin American Citizens (LULAC), lulac.org
Mexican American Legal Defense and Educational Fund (MALDEF), www.maldef.org
National Urban League, nul.iamempowered.com
National Association for the Advancement of Colored People (NAACP), www.naacp.org
National Council of Negro Women (NCNW), www.ncnw.org
National Congress of American Indians (NCAI), www.ncai.org
Asian Pacific American Advocates (OCA), https://www.ocanational.org
Southern Christian Leadership Conference (SCLC), nationalsclc.org
Southern Poverty Law Center (SPLC), https://www.splcenter.org
UnidosUS (formerly National Council of La Raza, NCLR), https://www.unidosus.org

Physical Health and Well-Being 9

"Son, I've Lost Something"

Carmen is a 42-year-old woman of Mexican and Pima Indian ancestry. She is divorced with three children, who range in age from 13 to 20 years old. Carmen grew up near Tucson, Arizona, and is one of five living children (her oldest brother, Joaquin, died two years ago from a massive heart attack). Her mother, Lucy, died just last year at the age of 63 from a severe stroke due to diabetes complications. Carmen was devastated by the loss of her mother, who had raised her and her siblings almost single-handedly (Carmen's father died from complications related to cirrhosis of the liver at the age of 35, when Carmen was still a small girl).

Carmen vowed that she would not suffer the same fate as her mother and Joaquin. At five feet, two inches, and 170 pounds, Carmen is obese, and she is starting to breathe more heavily and experience joint pain in her ankles, knees, and back. With the support of her sons, she decided to visit her community health center. The news the physician relayed to her, following a physical and laboratory work, was disappointing. Like her mother and brother before her, Carmen's blood pressure is high—160/110. Moreover, the doctor warned her that she appears to be "prediabetic," with blood sugar levels elevated enough to warrant a significant change in diet and an exercise program to reduce her weight.

Carmen met with a dietician, who prescribed a daily meal plan that greatly differed from Carmen's usual food preferences. "Remember, keep it low and small . . . Low salt, low fat, low sugar, and small portions," the dietician advised. "You have trained your body to crave poor foods that will slowly but surely lead to your premature death. But the good news is that you can recondition your body to enjoy these 'healthy' foods."

"Am I killing myself? If this is true, I will stop this right now. But I don't know if I can eat the types of food listed on this plan," Carmen thought. "Lots of fresh vegetables, fresh fruit, 'organic recommended'—this stuff is expensive, and they don't sell this highfalutin food at my little grocery store. And only a little oil: 'Avoid animal fats—for example, lard.' What, no manteca for my fried bread? No pork belly to season my stews?"

No sooner had Carmen made it home than she desperately wanted a good "healthy" meal that would stick to her ribs—meat, potatoes, bread, and, of course, just a little something sweet to top it off. As she bent over to pull out the frying pan and the oil to heat, she felt a sharp pain in her back and soreness in her knees. She stopped herself. "Ay, this is a reminder. I'm too young to have the body of a vieja. I've got to stop the madness! Okay, let's see. I have some carrots in the refrigerator and maybe a little rice; I'll get some of that brown rice later. I'll add in a little piece of chicken—boiled chicken for low fat." As she prepared the meal, she placed the saltshaker out of reach to avoid temptation.

Her youngest son came home after school and asked what Carmen was making. "My new 'healthy' food," she replied. Carmen then took a bite and exclaimed, "Dios mio! Son, I've lost something." "What did you lose, Mom?" "El sabor; this tastes like nothing," she moaned.

The woman in our vignette, Carmen, desperately wants a healthy life. She knows that life can be short, having lost close family members to illness far too soon. Yet her struggles to adopt the changes that her doctor has recommended illustrate some of the many challenges to achieving good health—differences in how we define "healthy" foods, economic barriers to healthy choices, clashes between the cultural meanings of certain foods with medically recommended diets, and lack of or inappropriate communication between health care providers and their patients.

This chapter describes the apparent and persistent health disparities that exist among ethnic or racial minority groups relative to Whites in the United States. Factors that may play a protective or negative role in producing these differences are reviewed, including demographic variables (e.g., gender, income, education), physiological and biological strengths and vulnerabilities, inaccessible and unaffordable health care, racism (social and environmental), and psychological characteristics (e.g., acculturation, stress, lifestyle behaviors). We conclude by examining characteristics of health interventions that demonstrate sensitivity to this large number of important biological, psychological, sociopolitical, and cultural variables.

Influential Models of Health

Biomedical Model

Some of our oldest views of health define it as an absence of disease or illness. Indeed, the popular **biomedical model** maintains that all illnesses can be explained on the basis of unusual physical processes, such as biochemical imbalances or structural abnormalities (Taylor, 2015). Attention is focused on a microlevel of analysis, where organisms (e.g., bacteria, viruses) or physical abnormalities lead to short-term or long-term illness. Hence, prominence is given to the disease process rather than to potentially interrelated psychological or social variables. As such, prevention and treatment are designed to deal with this microlevel of analysis (e.g., using medications, surgery) in hopes of producing a fairly immediate improvement in health.

It is not difficult to recognize why the biomedical perspective has been so dominant in the field of medicine. Its roots are firmly embedded in Descartes' philosophy of **mind-body dualism**, the insistence that the mind is a distinct entity from the physical world, including the body (Deary, 2005). This focused ideology lends itself to research that identifies a single factor (biological malfunctioning) as responsible for the development of an illness. Furthermore, this model clearly emphasizes the need to detect the causes of physical pathology so that prevention methods or a cure might be found (Brannon, Updegraff, & Feist, 2017). Many devastating illnesses like polio and diphtheria are no longer of national concern because of the creation of effective vaccines that can prevent their development. Short-term yet deadly infectious **acute diseases**—ailments that come on rapidly and endure a short period of time (e.g., tuberculosis, pneumonia)—that attacked generations prior to the 21st century are not considered major threats to our longevity, at least in industrialized countries like the United States. Indeed, **chronic diseases** (e.g., cardiovascular or heart disease, cancer, diabetes) are currently the top killers in the United States (National Center for Health Statistics [NCHS], 2006; 2016). *Chronic* refers to the fact that generally these diseases persist for a longer period of time than acute diseases. In addition, while a number of factors may increase risks for the development of chronic diseases, typically significant determinants include people's lifestyles—behaviors highly related to illnesses, like smoking, overeating, and little or no exercise.

Biopsychosocial Model

Over the past few decades, many researchers have argued that a focus on physical and biological problems that lead to illness is shortsighted. Both health and illness are caused by more than the single factor of biological malfunctioning. Psychological and social factors can also determine whether an individual is healthy or sick. The model that best describes this view is the **biopsychosocial model** (Suls & Rothman, 2004). This model maintains that health and illness are caused by multiple factors that can potentially produce multiple effects related to health and disease (see Figure 9.1). According

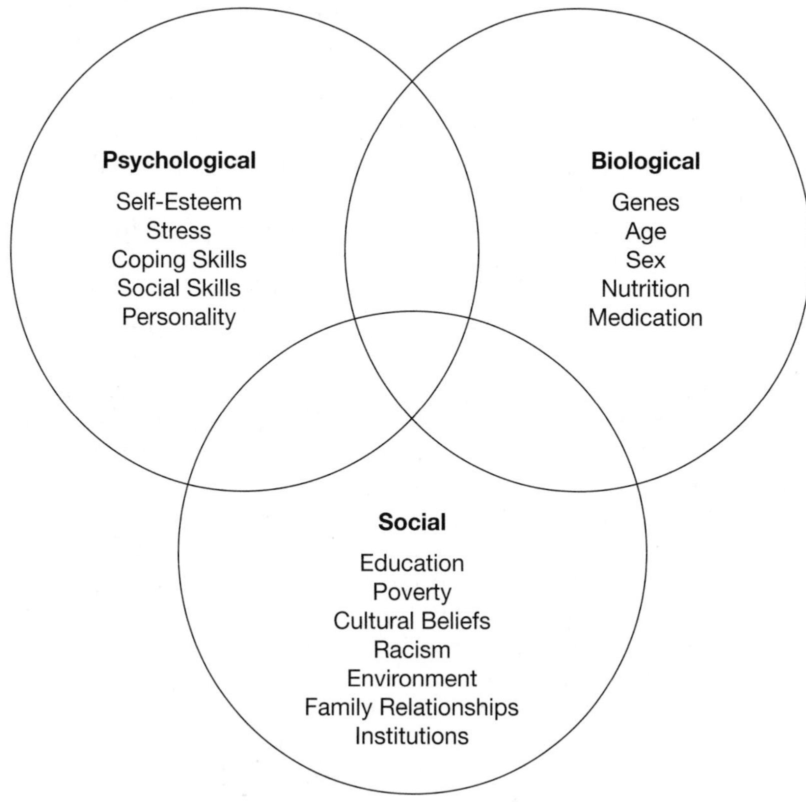

Source: Suls & Rothman, 2004

FIG. 9.1 Biopsychosocial Model: Examples of Biological, Psychological, and Social Factors That May Interact to Increase the Likelihood of Health or Illness

to this model, whether a particular treatment will cure a disease is dependent on psychological and social factors and cannot be explained by biological factors alone. For example, even with some knowledge of the pitfalls of eating certain foods, it is difficult for many to deny themselves the enjoyment of foods that they have eaten since childhood. Carmen's case illustrates that, while certain traditional foods of one's culture may not be necessarily healthy for the body, we need to consider the cultural and personal meanings of food. While food serves nutritional needs, it also serves a person's inner being or soul. To simply prescribe discontinuing certain foods without suggesting alternative foods or healthier recipes that may still nourish the person's soul will leave the individual feeling deprived and craving the forbidden foods more than ever.

An additional distinction of this model is the significance placed on the promotion of health. From this model's perspective, health becomes something one achieves and manages by addressing biological, psychological, and sociological needs rather than something taken for granted or that is simply the by-product of the absence of illness (Taylor, 2015; World Health Organization, 1948). Indeed, a recent study of men's health status (Brown, Hargrove, & Griffith, 2015) with more than 3,000 respondents (African Americans, Latinos, and Whites) shows that socioeconomic status, discrimination, stress, and neighborhood conditions affect health status. These effects were particularly important among African Americans and Latinos. Another study with African Americans (Barber et al., 2016) shows that worsening neighborhood economic and social conditions (including violence) increased the risk of cardiovascular disease among women but not among men. Although no causal relationships can be deduced from the study, the relationship between social conditions and poor health (in this case, cardiovascular disease) confirms the findings from other studies that show that poor social conditions and segregation have serious deleterious effects on people's health, including psychological well-being (Osibogun & Pankey, 2017).

Ecological Models

Recent work in the social sciences and in public health suggests that there is a need for a more comprehensive model of behavior that reflects the interactions or transactions between individuals and the physical and sociocultural environments (Stokols, 1992). This perspective has deep roots in psychological theories where behavioral models of health (such as those proposed by attitude-behavior change) are considered together with "proximal social influences" (friends, family, role models) and with the role played by policies and community characteristics (Sallis & Owen, 2015). A distinct advantage of **ecological models**, according to Sallis and Owen, is the fact that they allow for the integration of multiple theories and models (biomedical models, individual behavior theories) and can serve as a comprehensive approach that incorporates policy issues (such as compulsory vaccinations, limitations in access to tobacco and alcohol by minors, universal health insurance) as well as environmental conditions (for example, pollution, water contamination). Ecological models have been used in a large number of studies designed to analyze and improve the health of many communities, including ethnic or racial communities. These models have also served to shape the U.S. Department of Health and Human Services's (2010) *Healthy People 2020* plan to advance the health status of people in the United States and to eliminate health disparities—a document discussed in the next section.

Sallis and Owen (2015) propose that there are five basic principles that define ecological models. The first, and probably the most basic, is that "ecological models specify that factors at multiple levels, often including intrapersonal, interpersonal, organizational, community, and public policy levels, can influence health behaviors, although the relative influence may vary by target behavior and context" (p. 48). The second principle underscores that a proper understanding of health behavior must include an analysis of social and physical environmental variables—that is, the social and physical situations in which behavior occurs. A third principle emphasizes the fact that all variables interact and that the resulting behavior is the result of these interactions and not of one single variable. As seen in the following section, a number of variables like gender, ethnicity, acculturation, cost of cigarettes, and stress are helpful in understanding, preventing, and treating cigarette smoking. The fourth principle requires that any model be specific to a behavior rather than global in nature (a useful consideration derived from psychological research). As such, an intervention designed to help stop cigarette smoking among Latinos will consider all of the variables mentioned for the third principle, but that intervention will not necessarily be effective in controlling alcohol consumption, although some theoretical principles can be generalizable from one behavior to the next. The final principle suggested by Sallis and Owen, the fifth, is the fact that multilevel interventions are the most effective in producing behavioral changes. As such, a cigarette smoking cessation program would be most effective if it involves culturally appropriate materials on how to quit and the materials are distributed in a community where motivational messages are provided by posters, public service announcements, and sermons at church, together with increases in the cost of cigarettes, limitations in places where cigarettes are sold, and policies that limit the type of places where smoking is allowed.

Despite the fact that ecological models are promising and have been shown to be effective in a large number of cases (Glanz, Rimer, & Viswanath, 2015), they are not as frequent as they should be, probably due to their necessary complexity, the need for interdisciplinary work, and the cost of designing and implementing them. Nevertheless, they can be expected to play a significant role in health promotion in the 21st century.

Culture, Ethnicity, and Health

The roles of culture, race, and ethnicity in determining health and illness are receiving increased attention from psychologists and other social scientists, as well as from many health practitioners. Indeed, in a review of cultural and ethnic factors in health, Berry and Sam (2007) note that our understanding of how these factors relate to health is heightened by the work conducted within a number of varied disciplines, including medical anthropology, transcultural psychiatry, and cross-cultural health psychology. Research findings indicate that differences in health exist on both the individual/psychological and the community/cultural levels in terms of cognitive conceptualizations, attitudes and normative values, behavioral responses to the body, and medical institutions and relationships (Berry & Sam, 2007). For example, knowledge about high blood pressure can be shaped by a community's norms about foods and behaviors that may impact hypertension, but these beliefs can vary from person to person via individual differences (e.g., demographics, comprehension), family practices, and social relationships within a cultural group (Berry & Sam, 2007).

Subgroup differences within racial or ethnic minority populations can bear importance in anticipating health behavior. This is illustrated in a study by Shive and colleagues (2007) in which they examined a nationally representative sample of Asian American subgroups (e.g., Chinese, Vietnamese, Koreans, Japanese, Filipinos, Indians, Laotians) ($N = 6{,}722$). They assessed a number of differences in health behavior, including sources of health information, ethnic/racial preference for physicians, and cancer screening among these groups. Several subgroup differences were noted. For instance, Asian Indians were more likely to use the Internet than Chinese, Koreans, and Filipinos. Koreans were significantly less likely to use printed materials than Filipinos and Japanese. Koreans were the most likely to prefer a physician similar to their own ethnicity, and Indians indicated the least preference. Screening differences were also noted with Vietnamese, the least likely to have a complete physical exam, and Filipinos, the most likely. The percentage of women in the subgroups who did not get a Pap smear for cervical cancer ranged from 15.1 percent for Filipinos to 50 percent for Koreans. Given the variety of differences, Shive et al. (2007) noted the importance of considering the preferences and behaviors of specific groups when planning prevention or health care delivery; this has been one of the central beliefs in developing the culturally appropriate health-related interventions we discuss throughout this chapter.

Carmen's story in our opening vignette highlights the need to consider culture from its most basic components, discussed in Chapter 2: that is, attitudes, values, beliefs, and behavioral norms that are shared within her cultural group and across generations. Carmen is used to the foods of her culture. Exploring how she might define "healthy" foods would likely lead to a response that illustrates that healthy food is food that is familiar in taste and satisfying. Ignoring this value could lead to poor compliance on Carmen's part when changes in diet are required. Instead, some "foodies," nutritionists, and chefs argue that traditional cultural foods can still be enjoyed and, with some adjustments, can be lower in calories, fat, and sodium than the original recipes of our elders (see Box 9.1). Moreover,

Box 9.1

A New Taste of Soul Food

Lindsey Williams was overweight as a child. An admitted "food addict," Lindsey compulsively consumed calorie-, fat-, sugar-, and salt-laden foods. He was also a compulsive dieter—always hungry and starving in order to lose some pounds but consistently rebounding with more weight. Moreover, he is the grandson of one of the most renowned soul food chefs: Sylvia Woods, the "Queen of Soul Food." Her famous restaurant, Sylvia's, is located in the New York neighbourhood of Harlem.

Sylvia's food is enjoyed by locals, tourists, celebrities of film and the music scene, elite athletes, politicians, and other dignitaries. Cooking food is infused in the fiber of Lindsey Williams's family. While working in the music industry as an upper-level promoter and manager, Lindsey felt the toll the increased demands and stress took, and he became morbidly obese. Finally, at the depth of his misery—after losing his job, marriage, house, and cars—he sought out help by joining a support group for food addicts. Building upon insights and social support gained through the group, Lindsey started a physical exercise regime to begin his journey toward recovery and fitness. He also started a new career in catering. Although he'd had an educational upbringing in the family food business, he decided to put a new twist on traditional soul food. He was determined to change the concept of soul food from down-home comfort food that is flavorsome but quite fattening into more sophisticated food that is still big on flavor and familiar in name but made with more wholesome ingredients and designed with more flair. For example, collard greens can be sautéed in olive oil instead of cooked in pork fat; fresh vegetables can be lightly cooked with seasonings rather than using canned vegetables that contain a high level of sodium. Even staples of soul food, such as fried chicken, can be redesigned to be less caloric but still good eating.

Standing at five feet, five inches, Lindsey eventually reduced his weight from 400 pounds to 160 pounds. His catering business became highly successful, and he now oversees Neo Soul Events and Catering. Soul food does not need to be equated with "bad" food. As Sylvia Woods states, "Soul food is just food cooked with a lot of love, and everyone should be able to eat it." Perhaps with continued creativity and lots of love healthier soul food will increasingly become the new traditional food.

Some examples of redesigned traditional meals can be found in numerous cookbooks, such as the following titles:

Beatriz, M. D. (2009). *Latina lite cooking: 200 delicious lowfat recipes from all over the Americas*. New York: Hachette.

Betancourt, M. (2009). *The new Native American Cuisine: Five-star recipes from the chefs of Arizona's Kai Restaurant*. Guilford, CN: Three Forks.

Ferrara, C. (2017). *The healthy wok Chinese cookbook: Simple recipes for cooking healthy versions of your favourite Chinese dishes at home*. Berkeley: Rockridge Press.

Hair, J. (2013). *Steamy Kitchen's healthy Asian favorites: 100 recipes that are fast, fresh, and simple enough for tonight's dinner*. New York: Ten Speed Press.

Kirchner, B. (1994). *The healthy cuisine of India: Recipes from the Bengal region*. Los Angeles: Lowell House.

Martinez, A., & Sosa, A. (2015). *Healthy Latin cooking: Our favorite family recipes remixed*. Lanham, MD: Kyle Books.

Perera, S. (2015). *Best of Sri Lankan food recipes: Healthy Cooking with Coconut and Spices*. N.p.: Xlibris Corp.

Salaman, R. (1996). *Healthy Mediterranean cooking*. London: Francies Lincoln.

Williams, L. (2006). *Neo Soul: Taking Soul Food to a Whole 'Nutha Level*. New York: Avery.

In addition, the USDA has a website dedicated to offering recipes and cooking suggestions for the preparation of healthy ethnic foods, found at https://www.nutrition.gov/subject/shopping-cooking-meal-planning/ethnic-cooking.

you do not have to sacrifice the *sabor* for the health value of foods that are customarily preferred within cultures. This approach has given rise to a number of restaurants and cookbooks that modify traditional and ancestral recipes to improve their nutritional value and eliminate some unhealthy components.

Given that the management and treatment of health problems may vary across cultures and even within subgroups of a particular culture, the need exists to develop more comprehensive and integrative models of human health. Perhaps the ecological model described previously would best highlight the contributions of four major factors—biological, psychological, societal, and cultural—that are intricately interwoven in affecting people's health on both individual and group levels. Theorists, clinicians, and policymakers are compelled to examine these areas in order to offer the most comprehensive conceptualizations of health, illness, and intervention. Hence, multidimensional approaches offer the best promise of achieving parity in good health among various ethnic groups.

Health Disparities Among Racial and Ethnic Groups

A large number of health surveys indicate that ethnic or racial minorities are at higher risk for a number of illnesses relative to non-Hispanic Whites. Many of these findings have been produced by epidemiologists. **Epidemiology** is a special branch of biomedical research devoted to the study of the occurrence of disorders in populations or in special groups and the risk factors associated with these disorders (Tucker, Phillips, Murphy, & Raczynski, 2004). A subspecialty within epidemiology, **psychiatric epidemiology**, focuses on the study of the occurrence of psychiatric disorders and their associated risk factors in populations and in special groups (see Chapter 10 for a discussion of these disorders).

Of particular importance in epidemiology is the provision of information regarding the **prevalence** and the **incidence** of disorders. Prevalence is the *total number of cases* of a problem or disorder occurring in a population of a group at a given time (Tucker et al., 2004). Incidence is the *number of new cases* of a problem or disorder occurring over a specific time period (Tucker et al., 2004). It is useful to compare the incidence and prevalence rates of disorders because these numbers can alert health authorities to the possibility of epidemics. For example, imagine that you have determined that the current prevalence of a disorder in a population is 10,000 cases. Then you determine that the incidence of that same disorder over the past 2 years is 5,000 cases. You now have reason to be alarmed, as you recognize that roughly 50 percent of the cases have been diagnosed in the past two years; the numbers have risen tremendously in a relatively short period of time. As an epidemiologist, you will want to identify factors that may account for these increasing numbers, including the characteristics or behaviors that appear in those who have the disorder (cases) compared to those who are not diagnosed with the disorder (controls). These characteristics or behaviors are what we call **risk factors** (Levy & Brink, 2005).

In identifying prevalence and incidence of diseases, we also can determine the **morbidity**, the proportion of illness or specific disease in a population (Taylor, 2015). The morbidity of a population signals the general health of a group of people. We can also consider the rate of **mortality**, the frequency of death or death rate in a population (Taylor, 2015).

Multicultural psychology and other social and behavioral sciences have much to contribute to the study and elimination of health disparities. The value of social, behavioral, and economic sciences to national priorities has recently been recognized in a report to the National Science Foundation, which uses examples to illustrate how the social and behavioral sciences can contribute to a number of national priorities, including the promotion of health (National Academies of Sciences, Engineering, and Medicine, 2017). This argument has also been proposed by the director of the National Institute on Minority Health and Health Disparities.[1] In that article, Aklin and Pérez-Stable (2017) argue that the social sciences have made a major contribution to the elimination of health disparities by providing the "frameworks necessary for understanding the complexity of health disparities." In support of this claim, Aklin and Pérez-Stable cite the social sciences' clarification of the importance of patient adherence to treatment, the gender and ethnic matching between patient and clinician, the effects of stress on health, and the identification of the role played by the social determinants of health (SDOH), along with the importance of where one works, lives, and plays, all as contributors to health outcomes.

Defining Health Disparities

In the year 2000, a legal definition for *health disparities* was provided through United States Public Law 106–525, also known as the Minority Health and Health Disparities Research and Education Act: "A population is a health disparity population if there is a significant disparity in the overall rate of disease incidence, prevalence, morbidity, mortality or survival rates in the population as compared to the health status of the general population."

These population groups may be characterized by gender, age, ethnicity, ancestry, education, income, social class, disability, geographic location, or sexuality. Hence, in order to demonstrate a disparity, it is necessary to make comparisons of prevalence rates of disorders among ethnic groups, including European Americans or among various groups of interest. Within this text we note the limitations of using a particular group (e.g., White European Americans) as the standard of comparison, but in the case of documenting characteristics that may place certain groups at high risk, large-scale epidemiological studies offer our best glimpse into general trends in the larger population.

The U.S. Department of Health and Human Services periodically publishes *Healthy People*, a report analyzing the health status of residents of the United States and setting goals for improving overall health. Since 2000, the report has emphasized the problem of health disparities, and in *Healthy People 2000* it proposed the goal of reducing health disparities. That goal was modified in 2010 to focus on eliminating health disparities (*Healthy People 2010*), while in the latest version (*Healthy People 2020*) the overall goal was considered achieving health equity, eliminating disparities, and improving the health of all groups. Two important concepts, health equity and health disparities, are guiding current efforts on the part of federal government and state governments in terms of the promotion of health. In *Healthy People 2020*, **health equity** is defined as "attainment of the highest level of health for all people. Achieving health equity requires valuing everyone equally with focused and ongoing societal efforts to address avoidable inequalities, historical and contemporary injustices, and the elimination of health care disparities" (U.S. Department of Health and Human Services, 2010). At the same time, **health disparity** is defined as

> a particular type of health difference that is closely linked with social, economic, and/or environmental disadvantage. Health disparities adversely affect groups of people who have systematically experienced greater obstacles to health based on their racial or ethnic group; religion; socioeconomic status; gender; age; mental health; cognitive, sensory or physical disability; sexual orientation or gender identity; geographic location; or other characteristics historically linked to discrimination or exclusion. (U.S. Department of Health and Human Services, 2010)

This most recent definition of health disparities is a comprehensive acknowledgment of the complexity of the phenomenon as well as a statement of the importance of sociocultural phenomena in determining health status. The definition also implicitly recognizes the role that the social and behavioral sciences play in studying health status and in developing the promotion of health and the prevention of illness.

Although it is useful to make comparisons across groups in order to detect disparity, data are often not available for specific ethnic or ancestral groups. For example, we can list the incidence and prevalence rates of cardiovascular disease in Latinos, but we do not consistently have information on the different subgroups that constitute this large category (Mexican Americans, Puerto Ricans, Cubans, etc.). The same is true for Asian Americans, where we seldom have information for specific ancestries (Chinese Americans, Japanese Americans, Filipino Americans, etc.), and for American Indians (e.g., Hopi, Sioux, Black Foot, and hundreds of other tribes or nations). This situation occurs because epidemiological researchers often group together (aggregate) individuals who share some cultural traits. For example, a recent large-scale study including more than 32,000 respondents (Cheng et al., 2017) combined *all* racial and ethnic minority communities into one group when their use of smokeless tobacco was compared with that of Whites. While the data were useful in identifying likelihood of consumption of smokeless tobacco primarily among younger adults, men, Whites, and nonurban residents, little could be said about ethnic and racial minority groups, given the aggregation of their responses into one group.

Aggregation of data usually takes place because there are very few people in a given subgroup and grouping them within a larger ethnic group may provide certain statistical power that is not available when the subgroups are considered individually. The problems inherent in aggregating data include the possibility that health difficulties may be masked by looking at the overall status of certain ethnic groups. For instance, Chinese Americans and Japanese Americans tend to generally exhibit healthier status than smaller Southeast Asian refugee groups like the Hmong and the Mien, and if all these groups are combined, one could easily conclude that most Asian Americans are fairly healthy (Zane, Takeuchi, & Young, 1994).

Statistics can also be reported in such a way as to diminish the severity of apparent differences in health problems in our country. We could attempt to concentrate on the "good news" (e.g., overall, Americans are living longer now than ever) and not address the persistent and worsening problems at hand. Acknowledging health disparities requires that we consider the possible causes that produced differences in health conditions across groups as well as our responsibility at all levels (e.g., individual, community, national, and political) to take action to diminish and eliminate these inequities.

Examples of Health Disparities

Epidemiological research among ethnic or racial groups shows important differences across and within ethnic groups. For some illnesses (e.g., cancer, heart disease, Alzheimer's disease), racial and ethnic minority groups show morbidity rates that are very different from those of Whites or even some other ethnic groups. For example, in a large-scale study of older adults (the 2006 findings from the National Institute on Aging's longitudinal Health and Retirement Study), the prevalence of Alzheimer's disease varied dramatically when comparing African Americans (325 persons out of 1,000) and Latinos (237 persons out of 1,000) with Whites (98 persons out of 1,000) among adults 75–84 years of age (Lines, Sherif, & Wiener, 2014). Indeed, the literature shows adverse disparities between African Americans and Latinos when compared with Whites in many aspects of Alzheimer's disease, including prevalence, incidence, mortality, participation in clinical trials, use of long-term services, and quality of care (Lines et al., 2014).

Not surprisingly, there has been a marked interest over the last few years in conducting research into why these disparities occur. As detailed later in this chapter, there are multiple possible reasons for these differences in morbidity and mortality, although the research is at times not conclusive. One fairly consistent finding in longitudinal studies (e.g., Link et al., 2017) is that race-based disparities in self-rated health status are consistent across the life span (at least for women) and even transmitted from one generation to the next. In their study, Link and colleagues (2017) analyzed a large number of women across their lives and also included their children who reported disparities in self-rated health that were similar to those of their mothers, particularly after they reached the age of 50. Before addressing the reasons for health disparities, we describe some of the most significant differences in health status across ethnic or racial groups.

Mortality While at times it is difficult to compare information from various studies because of methodological differences, it is possible to identify important disparities in mortality rates. According to a report from the NCHS (the National Center for Health Statistics), within the CDC (the Centers for Disease Control and Prevention), the 2015 estimate for life expectancy in the United States is 78.8 years, and this rate has remained stable since 2012 (Kochanek, Murphy, Xu, & Tejada-Vera, 2016; Xu, Murphy, Kochanek, & Arias, 2016). To see if there are disparities, we can look at whether this average holds up across different groups, including women and men. We find that the current data indicate all-time-high life expectancies for males and females. The 2015 average life expectancy for women is 81.2 years; the average life expectancy for men is 76.3 years (Kochanek et al., 2016; Xu et al., 2016).

Differences in life expectancy across ethnic and racial groups and in comparison with the life expectancy for Whites is one illustration of health disparities in the country. Life expectancy in 2014 and in 2015 for African Americans was 75.5, compared to 78.8 for the whole population of the country and 79.0 for the White population (Kochanek et al, 2016). For Latinos, the 2015 life expectancy was 82 years—higher than that of the country as a whole. These differences have been attributed to a number of possible reasons (Abraído-Lanza, Dohrenwend, Ng-Mak, & Turner, 1999; Kochanek et al., 2016; Palloni & Arias, 2004). One is the *healthy migrant hypothesis*, wherein Latino immigrants would self-select for their good health and robustness. Another explanation has been labeled the *salmon bias effect*, whereby Latinos would return to their country of origin to die or when ill, affecting the mortality rates registered in the United States. A third explanation is the *cultural effects hypothesis*, where Latino cultural characteristics (family support, lifestyles, and social networks) serve as a protective factor to the effects of poverty, discrimination, and minority status. Unfortunately, there is no strong evidence to support any of these hypotheses.

A comparison of death rates is another way to look at disparities across ethnic or racial groups. The 2015 *Health, United States* report issued by the National Center for Health Statistics of the Centers for Disease Control (National Center for Health Statistics, 2016) reports age-adjusted death rates separately for the major ethnic or racial groups. Overall, the death rate for the country between 2013 and 2015 was 729.9 deaths per 100,000 residents. Data (based on death certificates) from the CDC also show that African Americans have the highest death rate (853.9) for the period of 2013 to 2015, followed by non-Hispanic Whites (747.7), American Indians or Alaska Natives (594.1), Latinos (527.8), and Asian Americans or Pacific Islanders (395.9). These data are therefore rather clear that there are notable differences in death rates across ethnic or racial groups. Some of the possible risk factors for these health disparities are discussed later on in this chapter.

Another aspect of mortality, infant mortality, is a particularly good index for detecting group differences, because it is commonly used as a standard indicator of national and worldwide health status. Epidemiologic data reveal that infant mortality rates vary widely across racial or ethnic groups. For example, African Americans (11.1) and American Indians and Alaska Natives (7.9) show infant death rates above the national mean of 5.9 deaths per 1,000 live births (between 2012 and 2014), whereas Whites (5.0), Latinos (5.0), and Asian or Pacific Islanders (4.0) average slightly below the mean (National Center for Health Statistics, 2016). In particular, African Americans show the greatest disparity, with an infant mortality rate of roughly two times the national average (11.1 deaths per 1,000 live births).

Examination of some of the leading causes of death in the United States also illustrates significant differences between groups (see Box 9.2). As an example, heart disease and cancer are the leading causes of death for African Americans, Latinos, Asian Americans, American Indians, and non-Hispanic Whites (see Box 9.2; note that for Asian Americans and Latinos, cancer is the number one cause of death, followed by heart disease). However, after these first two diseases, you will note that differences appear across the groups. For example, unintentional injuries (accidents) have become the third leading cause of death for Latinos and American Indians, whereas stroke (cerebrovascular diseases) is the third leading cause for African Americans and Asian Americans. Chronic liver disease and cirrhosis rank as the fifth and seventh leading cause of death for American Indians and Latinos, respectively, but do not appear in the top 10 for other groups. In addition, African Americans are more likely to die from homicide than are other groups. Similarities and differences across groups lead to questions about whether there are specific vulnerabilities (physiological as well as behavioral) of certain ethnic or racial groups to physical disorders and—equally as important—whether there are protective factors that serve to lower a group's susceptibility to certain diseases.

Coronary Heart Disease In the recent past, coronary heart disease (CHD) deaths have decreased in the United States. From 1950 to 2015, the mortality rate from CHD declined by 29 percent (National Center for Health Statistics, 2017). Despite this pattern, heart disease continues to be the

Box 9.2

The Ten Leading Causes of Death in the United States (2014) Among the Total Population and Across Ethnic Groups: African Americans, Hispanics, Asian Americans, American Indians, and Whites (Non-Hispanics)

Total Population (both sexes, all ages)

1. diseases of the heart
2. malignant neoplasms (cancer)
3. chronic lower respiratory diseases
4. unintentional injuries (accidents)
5. cerebrovascular diseases (e.g., stroke)
6. Alzheimer's disease
7. diabetes mellitus (diabetes)
8. influenza and pneumonia
9. nephritis, nephrotic syndrome, and nephrosis (kidney disease)
10. suicide

African Americans (both sexes, all ages)

1. diseases of the heart
2. malignant neoplasms (cancer)
3. cerebrovascular diseases (e.g., stroke)
4. unintentional injuries (accidents)
5. diabetes mellitus (diabetes)
6. chronic lower respiratory diseases
7. nephritis, nephrotic syndrome, and nephrosis (kidney disease)
8. homicide
9. Alzheimer's disease
10. septicemia (blood poisoning)

Latinos (both sexes, all ages)

1. malignant neoplasms (cancer)
2. diseases of the heart
3. unintentional injuries (accidents)
4. cerebrovascular diseases (e.g., stroke)
5. diabetes mellitus (diabetes)
6. chronic liver disease and cirrhosis
7. Alzheimer's disease
8. chronic lower respiratory diseases
9. influenza and pneumonia
10. nephritis, nephrotic syndrome, and nephrosis (kidney disease)

Asians or Pacific Islanders (both sexes, all ages)

1. malignant neoplasms (cancer)
2. diseases of the heart
3. cerebrovascular diseases (e.g., stroke)
4. unintentional injuries (accidents)
5. diabetes mellitus (diabetes)
6. influenza and pneumonia
7. chronic lower respiratory disease
8. Alzheimer's disease
9. nephritis, nephrotic syndrome, and nephrosis (kidney disease)
10. suicide

American Indians or Alaska Natives (both sexes, all ages)

1. diseases of the heart
2. malignant neoplasms (cancer)
3. unintentional injuries (accidents)
4. chronic liver disease and cirrhosis
5. diabetes mellitus (diabetes)
6. chronic lower respiratory diseases
7. cerebrovascular diseases (e.g., stroke)
8. suicide
9. influenza and pneumonia
10. nephritis, nephrotic syndrome, and nephrosis (liver disease)

Whites (Non-Hispanics, both sexes, all ages)

1. diseases of the heart
2. malignant neoplasms (cancer)
3. chronic lower respiratory diseases
4. unintentional injuries (accidents)
5. cerebrovascular diseases (e.g., stroke)
6. Alzheimer's disease
7. diabetes mellitus (diabetes)
8. influenza and pneumonia
9. suicide
10. nephritis, nephrotic syndrome, and nephrosis (kidney disease)

Source: Heron, 2016.

number one killer in the United States. Although CHD is the top cause of death for all racial and ethnic groups, the prevalence rates for CHD (which includes the diseases of arteriosclerosis—also known as hardening of the arteries—and atherosclerosis—the buildup of atheromas or plaques in the walls of the arteries), stroke, and hypertension (high blood pressure) vary considerably across groups (Myers & Rodriguez, 2003). For instance, in 2015 CHD death rates per 100,000 people were 258.6 for African American males and 211.2 for White males, compared to 165.7 for African American females and 132.4 for White females (National Center for Health Statistics, 2017).

Disparities also exist in the prevalence of risk factors associated with cardiovascular disease. Racial and ethnic minorities have higher rates of hypertension, tend to develop hypertension at an earlier age, and are less likely to undergo treatment to control their high blood pressure than are White non-Hispanics. For example, from 1999 to 2002 the prevalence of hypertension in a sample of 7,000 U.S. adults was 40.5 percent among non-Hispanic Blacks, 27.4 percent among non-Hispanic Whites, and 25.1 percent among Mexican Americans over the age of 20 years (Centers for Disease Control and Prevention, 2005b). Among those adults tested as having hypertension (defined as having an average systolic blood pressure equal to or greater than 140 mm Hg and diastolic blood pressure equal to or greater than 90 mm Hg or taking blood pressure medication), the proportion who were aware of having high blood pressure was 70.3 percent among African Americans, 62 percent among Whites, but only 49.8 percent among Mexican Americans (Centers for Disease Control and Prevention, 2005b). From 1991 to 1999, almost 95 percent of U.S. adults had received a blood pressure screening within the previous two years; however, Hispanics had lower levels of blood pressure screenings than had non-Hispanic Whites or non-Hispanic Blacks (Centers for Disease Control and Prevention, 2002), probably due to the fact that Latinos have the lowest rate of visits to medical providers (O'Hara & Caswell, 2013).

More recent data on the prevalence of hypertension (National Center for Health Statistics, 2016) are reported in the CDC report *Health, United States, 2015.* Among adults aged 20 and over (data for 2011 to 2014), a large percentage of African American men (42.4 percent) and women (44.0 percent) showed hypertension. These figures are notably higher than those found among all other ethnic and racial groups and highlight a troubling aspect of health disparities in the country. As an example, White men and women showed much lower percentages with hypertension (30.2 percent and 28.0 percent, respectively), and the same is true for Latinos (27.7 percent for men and 28.6 percent for women) and Asian Americans (28.0 percent for men and 25.0 percent for women). As could be expected from these data, African Americans report having had a stroke in larger percentages than any other ethnic or racial group (National Center for Health Statistics, 2017).

A longitudinal study of Latinos aged over 50 shows that there were differences in stroke onset based on migration history. Foreign-born Latinos showed a significantly lower stroke risk than did U.S.-born Latinos and even than did Whites (Moon et al., 2012). These findings show a different picture of health disparities than what is true in all cases where a subgroup of Latinos present better health status than other Latinos as well as Whites. The study's authors argue that foreign-born Latinos have a risk factor profile that is different from that of U.S.-born Latinos and even Whites. Unfortunately, the study was not designed to identify those protective variables. It should be noted that these results held even when socioeconomic factors were controlled.

Being overweight and obese are important risks factors for heart disease where we can find disparities across groups.[2] In the United States, being an overweight adult is becoming more and more commonplace. According to a recent survey (National Center for Health Statistics, 2002), in 1999 and 2000, 64 percent of adults were overweight. This figure represents an increase when compared to the rate of 56 percent found among adults surveyed between 1988 and 1994. Similarly, 30 percent reported being obese in 1999 and 2000, whereas 23 percent reported this in the earlier survey. The risk of obesity is particularly significant for women who are African American or Latino (Mexican American) or who belong to certain American Indian or Alaska Native groups, as well as for Pacific Islander women (e.g., Native Hawai'ians and Samoans). As a matter of fact, findings from the National Health and Nutrition Examination Survey (NHANES) indicate that the age-adjusted prevalence rates for obesity are higher for African American women (51 percent are obese and 78 percent overweight) and for Mexican American women (40 percent are obese and 72 percent overweight) than for non-Hispanic White women (31 percent obese and 58 percent overweight) (National Center for Health Statistics, 2002). Likewise, obesity is a problem with children or ethnic or racial minority groups. For example, a recent analysis of the data from the Indian Health Service showed that American Indian or Alaska Native children had a higher prevalence of obesity than all U.S. children (Bullock, Sheff, Moore, & Manson, 2017). In 2015, for example, 18.5 percent of American Indian children aged two were found to be obese, a figure that increased significantly so that 29.7 percent of 19-year-olds were considered obese.

Preventive actions such as regular cholesterol checkups also show disparities for certain racial and ethnic minorities. For instance, an analysis conducted by the NHANES indicated that between 1999 and 2002 the proportion of African Americans and Mexican Americans screened for high blood cholesterol (defined as a total cholesterol level greater than 240 milligrams per deciliter, or a participant reported taking cholesterol-lowering medication) during the preceding five years was lower than the proportion for Whites (Centers for Disease Control and Prevention, 2005b). Interestingly, there are small differences across ethnic or racial groups in adults (20 years or older) reporting high cholesterol (hypercholesterolemia): data for the years 2011–2014 show that 28.7 percent of Whites report high cholesterol, compared to 26.3 percent of Latinos, 26.0 percent of Asians, and 25.2 percent of African Americans (National Center for Health Statistics, 2017). In addition, research has shown that fewer African Americans and Mexican Americans with high blood cholesterol were told by a medical health professional of their diagnosed condition than Whites, with only 42 percent of Mexican Americans aware of their condition (Centers for Disease Control and Prevention, 2005b).

Cancer Cancer represents more than 100 diseases that all result from some malfunction in the cellular programming of our bodies (Kiberstis & Marx, 2002; Taylor, 2015). Although cancer is the second leading cause of death in the United States, recent data indicate that incidence and death rates from all cancers combined decreased since 1975 in men and women overall and in most racial and ethnic populations, with the exception of pancreatic, breast, and uterine cancers and non-Hodgkin lymphoma (Jemal et al., 2008, 2017; National Center for Health Statistics, 2017). Nevertheless, the available epidemiological data indicate that ethnic minority groups (particularly African Americans) suffer disproportionately from cancer. These populations are generally more likely to be diagnosed and die from preventable cancers than the overall U.S. population. They are also likely to be identified much later in the stage of the disease progression than through early screening. Consequently, some may receive little or no treatment, or even treatment that is not at the currently accepted standard of care, and this can lead to greater suffering and pain from terminal cancer. Unfortunately, much research on cancer incidence and prevalence has failed to properly disaggregate by ethnic or racial group or subgroup (Islam, Khan, Kwon, Jang, Ro, & Trinh-Shevrin, 2010; Nguyen, Chawla, Noone, & Srinivasan, 2014). Nevertheless, a significant level of attention has been given to cancer among African Americans and Latinos.

Health disparities among ethnic groups are clearly illustrated by the higher overall cancer incidence and mortality rates of African Americans when compared to other groups. According to the National Cancer Institute (Jemal et al., 2017; National Cancer Institute, 2005), for men and women combined, African Americans have a cancer death rate higher than that of Whites (248.1 versus 195.3 per 100,000). The death rate from cancer for African American men is notably higher than it is for White men (339.4 versus 242.5 per 100,000). Death rates for specific types of cancers further illustrate this disparity. The death rate for lung and bronchus cancer is higher for African American men than for White men (101.3 versus 75.2 per 100,000). The prostate cancer mortality rate for African American men is roughly two and a half times that of White men (68.1 versus 27.7 per 100,000) (National Cancer Institute, 2005).

Paralleling the death rate, certain racial or ethnic groups experience higher rates of specific cancers than do other groups. With the exception of Asian American women, ethnic and racial minority women continue to have the highest incidence rates for cervical cancer (National Center for Health Statistics, 2017), but African American women have the highest death rate for cervical cancer, and Hispanic women have the second highest death rate (National Cancer Institute, 2005). African American men have more cancers of the lung, prostate, colon, and rectum than do non-Hispanic White men (American Cancer Society, 2005; National Cancer Institute, 2005; National Center for Health Statistics, 2017). African American women continue to have the highest rates of mortality from breast cancer (American Cancer Society, 2005; National Cancer Institute, 2005).

While Asians and Pacific Islanders generally experience lower cancer rates overall compared with non-Hispanic Whites and other ethnic or racial minority groups (Jemal et al., 2017; National Center for Health Statistics, 2017), this group and certain subgroups experience higher death and incidence rates for specific cancers. For example, American Indians and Alaska Natives experience one of the highest incidence rates of colon and rectum and stomach cancers (National Center for Health Statistics, 2017).

As you can see from the above data, there are significant disparities in prevalence of and death from various cancers despite the fact that great advances have been made in diagnosis and treatment. Given the significance of social, behavioral, and environmental variables in cancer incidence and prevalence, there is much that multicultural psychologists can contribute to eliminating this type of health disparity as ecological models of health promotion are developed.

Diabetes Diabetes, another comprehensive label including a set of diseases, develops where high blood sugar levels occur as the result of problems in the release or activity of insulin in the body. There are subtypes of diabetes. **Type 1 diabetes**, also referred to as *juvenile-onset diabetes* or *insulin-dependent diabetes mellitus*, is typically associated with biological, genetic, or environmental factors in its development. More common is **type 2 diabetes**, also known as *adult-onset diabetes* or *non-insulin-dependent diabetes mellitus*, which accounts for approximately 90–95 percent of all diagnosed cases of diabetes (National Center for Chronic Disease Prevention and Health Promotion [NCCDPHP], 2002). Older age, obesity, inactive lifestyle, family history of diabetes, and history of gestational (pregnancy-related) diabetes are typical risk factors. Although older age—*adult-onset*—is traditionally associated with increasing risk of type 2 diabetes, many argue that the term *adult onset* is increasingly becoming a misnomer. Over the past 25 years, we have witnessed a larger number of youths diagnosed with this subtype, and the rising prevalence of obesity in youth is commonly associated with this increase (Taylor, 2015).

Although certain types of diabetes are more manageable than others, increasing attention has been placed on positive lifestyle changes that can prevent the serious complications that can result from these diseases, such as blindness, amputation of limbs, cardiovascular disease, and stroke, pain, and premature death. The prevalence and incidence of this disorder have increased sharply over the past 25 years. According to the American Diabetes Association, roughly 30.3 million children and adults (or 9.4 percent of the U.S. population in 2015) had diabetes (American Diabetes Association, 2017).

Ethnic disparities are also found in the case of diabetes. Compared to Whites (9.3 percent), African Americans (17.7 percent), Latinos (16.4 percent), and Asian Americans (16.0 percent) have higher prevalences of diagnosed and undiagnosed diabetes (National Center for Chronic Disease Prevention and Health Promotion, 2017; National Center for Health Statistics, 2017). Although Asian Americans and Pacific Islanders are typically overlooked in diabetes research due to the model minority stereotype and relatively lower obesity rates than found in other ethnic groups (Chesla & Chun, 2005), they likewise suffer from diabetes at almost twice the rate of European Americans (Joslin Diabetes Center, 2018; McNeely & Boyko, 2004). There are important subgroup differences in diagnosed diabetes among adults aged 18 and over. Among Asian Americans, for example, Asian Indians have the highest prevalence (11.2 percent), followed by Filipino Americans (8.9 percent) and Chinese Americans (4.3 percent) (National Center for Chronic Disease Prevention and Health Promotion, 2017). Furthermore, Asian Americans also show significant within-group differences in diabetes screening (Tung, Baig, Huang, Laiteerapong & Chua, 2017). Among Latinos, Mexican Americans (13.8 percent) have the highest prevalence, followed by Puerto Ricans (12.0 percent) and

Cuban Americans (9.0 percent). These subgroup differences in health disparities exemplify the need for proper disaggregation of the data—a message we have offered many times in this book.

Taking a closer look within these ethnic groups, we also see diversity in risk. For example, within Hispanics or Latinos, Puerto Rican men and Mexican American women have some of the highest rates, while Cuban American women have some of the lowest (Myers & Rodriguez, 2003). Pima and Papago Indians have the highest risks of diabetes; it's no wonder that Carmen—a mixture of Mexican and Pima Indian background—has a strong familial and now personal history of this disease (Myers & Rodriguez, 2003; National Center for Chronic Disease Prevention and Health Promotion, 2002).

Complications associated with diabetes are also more prevalent in ethnic minority groups relative to Whites. For example, African Americans and American Indians experience more complications related to diabetes, such as limb amputations and kidney disease, than do Whites (Myers & Rodriguez, 2003). These data point to probably one of the most dramatic health disparities and one area that requires prompt attention since diabetes prevalence has increased in the last three decades (National Center for Health Statistics, 2017). For example, diabetes prevalence among Mexican Americans in the period from 1988 to 1994 was 15.6 percent, while the latest available data (for 2011 to 2014) show a prevalence of 18.0 percent.

HIV and AIDS For people between the ages of 25 and 44 years, HIV infection and AIDS rank as one of the leading causes of death, although the death rates have decreased from 10.2 per 100,000 in 1990 to 1.9 in 2015 (National Center for Health Statistics, 2017). Approximately 40,000 new cases of HIV infection occur each year in the United States, and roughly five million cases occur annually worldwide (National Center for Health Statistics, 2017; National Institute of Allergy and Infectious Diseases, 2004). In recent years, more attention has been given to the disparate number of ethnic or racial minority populations affected by the HIV/AIDS pandemic, especially African Americans. According to reports from the Centers for Disease Control and Prevention, the increased risk among groups is striking: The rates of diagnosis of HIV infection in 2015 (per 100,000 population) were 44.3 for African Americans, 16.4 for Latinos, 14.1 for Native Hawaiians and Other Pacific Islanders, 12.2 for multiracials, 8.8 for American Indians/Alaskan Natives, 5.5 for Asian Americans, and 5.3 for Whites (Centers for Disease Control and Prevention, 2016). More recent analyses (e.g., Mitsch, Hall, & Babu, 2016) find, among those individuals who inject drugs, small decreases in the number of HIV diagnoses among African Americans and Latinos as well as among Whites, but the race-based disparity continues to be of importance, with ethnic and racial minorities faring poorer than Whites. Indeed, nationwide, the number of new cases with HIV diagnosis in 2015 (the latest data available) shows that, out of 39,610 cases, 44.6 percent were among African Americans, 23.5 percent were among Latinos, and 26.5 percent among Whites (National Center for Health Statistics, 2017). Likewise, African Americans show in 2015 a disproportionate burden in terms of AIDS-related death rates (7.9) compared to Whites (1.1) and to the other major ethnic or racial minority groups (National Center for Health Statistics, 2017).

Ethnic minorities also are disproportionately represented in pediatric AIDS cases. For example, although non-Hispanic Blacks are approximately 15 percent of the child population, they represent almost 60 percent of all pediatric AIDS cases (U.S. Department of Health and Human Services, 2006). Moreover, HIV infection is the number one cause of death for African American men ages 35 to 44. HIV/AIDS affects African Americans at a rate that is 10 times greater than that found in the U.S. White population (Karon, Fleming, Steketee, & DeCock, 2001). Since 1996, more AIDS cases have occurred among African Americans than among any other U.S. racial/ethnic population (Centers for Disease Control and Prevention, 2007).

Although intravenous or injection drug users and gay men who engage in unprotected sex maintain the highest risk for HIV infection, alternative routes of transmission exist that increase the vulnerability of minority groups. Approximately 80 percent of HIV-infected women are minorities, and most become infected through heterosexual transmission (Centers for Disease Control and Prevention, 2007). African American women are particularly vulnerable; in 2005 their rate of AIDS diagnosis was

Box 9.3

African Americans at Risk for HIV/AIDS

Disparities in HIV infection and AIDS diagnosis are reported in increasing frequency for African Americans, where African Americans at greatest risk include injection drug users (IDUs). The known risks associated with injection drug use are not new. Even during the earliest years of the HIV epidemic in the 1980s, the possible contamination of blood and associated infections that could occur while engaging in unsterilized needle sharing among drug users was well documented. However, not often discussed were the implications of how this disease could spread among certain groups—especially poor minority groups—at a faster pace because of their heightened risk of needle sharing due to the limited access to clean needles and even to a notion of brotherhood among drug users demonstrated by sharing needles. Exposure through injection drug use is the second leading risk category for HIV/AIDS among African American women (McNair & Prather, 2004).

approximately 4 times the rate for Hispanic women and 23 times the rate for White women (Centers for Disease Control and Prevention, 2005a). More attention is being given to "risky heterosexual sex" that might place women at a heightened vulnerability to contract HIV. (See Box 9.3 for a closer look at African Americans at risk for HIV/AIDS.)

One of the highest risk groups for HIV infection is young African American men who have sex with men (MSM) (Centers for Disease Control and Prevention, 2001). The proportion of African American MSM diagnosed with AIDS increased from 19 percent in 1990 to 34 percent in 1999 (Blair, Fleming, & Karon, 2002). Despite the introduction of highly active antiretroviral therapy in the mid- to late 1990s, African American MSM had a higher number of diseases related to HIV infection and higher mortality rate following the diagnosis of AIDS compared to non-Hispanic Whites and Latino MSM (Blair et al., 2002). In an important study, Hart and Peterson (2004) surveyed a large sample of young African American MSM age 18 to 25 years ($N = 758$) in Atlanta. Respondents were recruited in popular venues (e.g., clubs, organizations, coffeehouses) frequented by African Americans. A significant number, 26.5 percent ($n = 201$), reported engaging in unprotected anal sex. Approximately 16.5 percent engaged in unprotected insertive anal intercourse; a larger number, 18.6 percent, engaged in the even more risky unprotected receptive anal intercourse. The risk of both unprotected receptive and insertive anal intercourse increased among respondents with a main partner as opposed to those who did not have a primary partner. Factors that predicted higher-risk behaviors were unsupportive peer norms regarding the use of condoms and not carrying condoms. Findings suggest that more attention must be given to changing values and beliefs about condoms—in such a way that promotes more positive connotations about having them available and using them.

Men who have sex with men typically have been discussed in the context of gay men's sexuality. Yet many argue that some men are not gay-identified and engage in both unprotected sex with women and secret sex relations with other men. In recent years these men are often referred to as *men on the down-low* or *down-low brothers* (King & Hunter, 2005). Cultural taboos and the stigma of homosexuality, failure of the monogamy ideal, confusion over one's sexual identity, or desire for sexual freedom and exploration are some of the possible reasons for nondisclosure.

An important consideration in the discussion of men on the down-low is the reality that this phenomenon is *not* exclusive to African Americans. Secretly having sex with a person of one's own sex is a behavior that occurs within and across a wide variety of ethnic and racial groups. As Boykin (2005b) argues, "The down-low is just a Black version of 'the closet.' . . . [It] is just a new way of describing a very old thing." Furthermore, people decry the sensationalism of the down-low as a means of further demonizing and pathologizing Black men's sexual behavior—and Black men in general (Boykin, 2005a).

Latinos (up 40.6 percent), American Indians (up 40.3 percent), and Whites (up 23 percent). While the study was not designed to identify reasons for these changes, researchers suggest that society's perception of alcohol consumption had changed in that decade, and stress experienced at work and at home had increased. For ethnic or racial minority groups, discrimination, income disparities, and generalized anxiety may also play an important role. These data are by themselves of concern, but their significance is increased by the role alcohol consumption has in increasing an individual's susceptibility to serious illnesses and its potential role in increasing health disparities.

Substance Use and Abuse Data from the 2014 National Survey on Drug Use and Health (Substance Abuse and Mental Health Services Administration, 2015) show that, among adolescents aged 12 to 17 years, Latinos had the highest rate (10.5 percent) of illicit drug use in the previous month. Next in extent of use were African Americans (9.8 percent), Whites (9.3 percent), and Asian Americans (3.5 percent). Latinos showed a notable increase (from 8.7 percent to 10.5 percent) in use of illicit drugs between 2013 and 2014, while the other racial groups did not show an increase. Overall, poverty was an important variable, with 10.8 percent of adolescents living below the poverty line reporting use of illegal drugs, compared to 9.0 percent to those who were more affluent. For all adolescents, marijuana was the most common substance used (7.4 percent), followed by nonmedical use of psychotherapeutic drugs (2.6 percent). These data point to the need to develop prevention and treatment interventions for Latino adolescents and for those adolescents living below the poverty line.

The above-mentioned 2016 report by the Surgeon General, *Facing Addiction in America*, includes data on use of any illegal substance by individuals 12 years or older. Reported use during the previous 12 months show that the highest percentage (22.9 percent) was reported among American Indians or Alaska Natives. Next were African Americans (20.7 percent), Native Hawai'ians or Other Pacific Islanders (20.5 percent), Whites (17.9 percent), and Latinos (17.2 percent) (U.S. Department of Health and Human Services, 2016a). A noteworthy result was that individuals who considered themselves biracial or multiracial reported illegal drug use in the previous 12 months in the highest percentages (27.1 percent).

The use of prescription opioids has received a significant level of attention, and a presidential committee declared in 2017 that opioid use is a national crisis. This concern is somewhat related to the fact that life expectancy among Whites has shown a decline since 1998 primarily because of drug overdoses (Case & Deaton, 2015). Research suggests that this change in life expectancy is related the U.S. Food and Drug Administration's approval of OxyContin (an addictive pain reliever). Prescriptions of OxyContin showed a rapid uptake in states with large White populations (Van Zee, 2009), with deaths from opioid abuse more than tripling between 2001 and 2014 (National Institute on Drug Abuse, 2015). Given the racialized differences in access to health care and to health insurance, it's striking that the opioid epidemic has become a health problem directly affecting Whites in greater levels than it has affected ethnic or racial minorities (Hansen & Netherland, 2016). Ease of access and a supportive medical and legal environment among White users correlated with increases in use statistics as well as to increases in tragic overdoses. This situation is an example of the way that social and legal conditions affect the members of a specific racial group, in this case Whites.

Acculturation

Different possible health outcomes have been proposed to occur in the process of acculturation. It makes intuitive sense that immigrant groups will experience less stress and health problems with greater acculturation to a new culture. However, a number of findings from epidemiology, sociology, and public health research indicate that foreign-born immigrants fare better than their more acculturated U.S.-born counterparts on psychosocial and health indicators including education, criminal behaviors, and well-being (Nguyen, 2006). This is surprising, given that many immigrants experience a number of barriers that would place them at risk for maladjustment, including low socioeconomic status (SES), poverty, exposure to crime and trauma, minority status, and difficulties accessing health care (Morales, Lara, Kington, Valdez, & Escarce, 2002; Nguyen, 2006). As mentioned before, these findings are termed the **immigrant health paradox** or *epidemiological paradox* because these positive outcomes contradict well-established evidence suggesting that acculturation stress and social and economic factors are important determinants of health and well-being (Morales et al., 2002; Nguyen, 2006). This paradox has been particularly apparent in Latinos, especially Mexican Americans (Morales et al., 2002).

At this time, the reasons for the health paradox are not quite clear. As discussed before in this book, the **selective migration hypothesis** and **social stress hypothesis** describe two different predictions regarding the health outcome of immigrants as they transition and adapt to the United States. Briefly, the selective migration hypothesis or "healthy migrant effect" states that the strongest and healthiest choose to migrate. Thus this select immigrant group would be more robust in terms of health issues than their family members born within the United States. The social stress hypothesis states that generations born in the United States may exhibit poorer health status than do immigrants because of their increased exposure to stressors (e.g., discrimination, racism) and lower presence of protective traditions, behaviors, values, and beliefs that maintained health for earlier generations and that are lost by the latter ones (Escobar, 1998). In addition, some theorists state that the health status of immigrants becomes more similar to the group to which they migrate (Berry, 1998; Lilienfeld, 1972).

Myers and Rodriguez (2003) reviewed a number of studies that investigated the role of acculturation in the co-occurrence of several major medical illnesses. Findings were mixed in terms of the consequences of acculturation on health status. For example, several studies have suggested that overall rates of cancer and diabetes become worse as acculturation level increases, and this risk is related to changes in knowledge, attitudes, and behaviors—especially lifestyle changes such as consuming more processed fatty foods and lack of exercise (e.g., Marks, Garcia, & Solis, 1990; Romero-Gwynn et al., 1993). Myers and Rodriguez (2003) report that some researchers (e.g., Stern et al., 1991) have theorized that as people become more upwardly mobile through the process of acculturation they may become more motivated to live longer, healthier lives and adopt ways of living that avoid negative health behaviors associated with risks for diabetes). Yet other studies have found little or no association between acculturation and certain illnesses, leaving the relationship less clear.

These somewhat contradictory or inconclusive results on the role of acculturation and health have been the object of much research. Recently, Fox, Thayer, and Wadhwa (2017) have suggested that these patterns of results could be the product of methodological and conceptual artifacts on the various studies. They argue that researchers have taken differing approaches in conceptualizing acculturation, with some emphasizing internal attitudes and others considering behavioral (overt) components of acculturation. Fox and colleagues also argue that differences in research on the relationship between acculturation and health could be due to some researchers analyzing acculturation changes at a given point in time while others are looking at lifelong changes. Other problems identified with acculturation and health research are different types of analyses (group-specific or global), lack of attention to biculturalism, and the use of proxy variables such as length of residence in new country or language fluency. As mentioned in the chapter on acculturation, these issues have affected much research on acculturation and its effects on people's behavior and need to be taken into account when analyzing the literature. It is indeed quite possible that discrepancies across studies can be due to some of the methodological artifacts mentioned previously (for example, measuring acculturation using a proxy such as length of residence in new country versus using a multidimensional scale). As the field evolves, we should have a better understanding of the role of acculturation on people's health and therefore be able to design effective interventions. Research with Chinese American immigrants indicates that interventions that strengthen bicultural skills to manage health issues across different cultural settings (e.g., in a Chinese family setting and in a U.S. health care setting) are especially important in mitigating negative acculturation stress effects on immigrants' health (Chun et al., 2016).

Accessible and Affordable Health Care

Clearly one's health status will be influenced by the ability to access and obtain affordable and effective treatment. In many cases ethnic minorities find it difficult, if not impossible, to obtain adequate health insurance coverage because of unemployment or the nature of their employment or having to pay for services out of pocket. An early analysis of the Commonwealth Fund's 2005 Biennial Health Insurance Survey (Doty & Holmgren, 2006) report that insurance coverage was not only inadequate for many ethnic and racial minorities but also, in many cases, nonexistent. This problem was also found in the report on disparities in health care access and quality that was mentioned previously. This situation is particularly problematic for the **working poor**, those who are working at minimum wage or slightly below and whose employer does not provide medical coverage. However, because they are employed, they may not meet the criteria for free or low-cost medical coverage. In the data analyzed by Doty and Holmgren (2006), roughly two-thirds (62 percent) of working-age Latinos and one-third (33 percent) of African Americans were uninsured at one point during the year. This stands in contrast to 20 percent of working-age Whites. In addition, Latinos were *less* likely to have a regular physician, to have been seen by a medical provider in the previous year, or to express confidence in their ability to obtain health care when needed. African Americans were most likely to receive nonurgent treatment through emergency room visits. In addition, low-income African Americans reported the highest number of chronic illnesses and other health problems. Although poverty is tied to one's ability to access and receive adequate medical care (Shi, 2001; see the next section), across all income levels, disparities in access and insurance coverage persisted for ethnic minorities compared to Whites.

Poverty and Community Characteristics

Recently reported data (National Center for Health Statistics, 2016) show that non-Hispanic Whites have a poverty rate of 9.1 percent, whereas the poverty rate for Blacks is 24.1 percent, 21.4 percent for Latinos, and 11.4 percent for Asian Americans. Hence the gap between the rich and the poor across races or ethnic groups is quite wide.

The relationship between poverty (and related characteristics such as unemployment or living within an economically depressed neighborhood) and stress and their consequent negative effects on health status has been examined in a number of studies over the past few decades (e.g., Myers, 2009). Health disparities have been consistently found for individuals that differ in socioeconomic status, with the typical pattern being that those lower in SES are at greater risk for negative health outcomes. The associated health risks of poverty include higher likelihood of low-birth-weight babies, premature death, unintentional injuries, and chronic illness (Aday, 1994; Adler et al., 1994; Williams & Collins, 1995).

In an important longitudinal study on the impact of sustained economic hardship, Lynch, Kaplan, and Shema (1997) examine data from more than 1,000 individuals who were studied since 1965. Results show a significant number of problems associated with people whose income was less than 200 percent of the poverty level. Those who were at this extreme level of poverty were more likely to have problems with managing daily activities (such as cooking, managing income, shopping, walking, eating, using the bathroom, and dressing) and exhibited symptoms of depression. The pattern of results indicated that economic hardship preceded the development of problems in living. Those who were young and healthy when the study began but experienced greater economic hardship over the next 25 years had the worst adjustment.

While it is well known that minority groups are disproportionately represented in low socioeconomic strata in the United States, less recognized is the fact that morbidity and mortality rates continue to be higher for certain ethnic minority groups even when group differences in income and social status are taken into account. For example, Zhou, Dominici, and Louis (2007) studied the relationship between race, SES, and mortality risk in a sample of more than four million Medicare members living in the northeastern United States. Findings show that, overall, there was a statistically higher risk of death for Blacks compared to Whites. Whether risk was examined at an individual level or community level (based on zip code), Blacks fared more poorly in terms of mortality whether SES was or was not adjusted. Even though differences were lower when SES was adjusted at a community level, the fact that differences still existed led to the authors' conclusion that group differences in SES alone do not explain the association between race and mortality—at least for the Medicare population who are 65 years of age or older. It is, however, important to note that reducing SES differences between Blacks and Whites does help to reduce the disparity between their mortality risks.

A related aspect of the relationship between SES and health disparities is the role that health literacy plays in the prevalence and incidence of certain conditions (Schillinger, Barton, Karter, Wang, & Adler, 2006; Berkman, Sheridan, Donahue, Halpern, & Crotty, 2011). **Health literacy** is usually considered the ability that individuals have to obtain, process, and understand information about health and about available services (Baker, 1999). Poor health literacy is usually associated with poverty, low levels of education, and difficulties in speaking or understanding a second language. An analysis of 36 studies on the topic (Mantwill, Monestel-Umaña, & Schultz, 2015) showed that, in general, poor health literacy was a factor in understanding health disparities, although a conclusive statement of the relationship was made difficult by poor methodologies in many of the studies.

Recent work on health disparities has emphasized the important role that the social and economic characteristics of a community have on perpetuating or preventing health disparities. Indeed, poor neighborhoods or communities do not provide the social and physical resources that can affect the health status of their members. Lack of access to community clinics or hospitals, lack of recreational settings such as parks and sports facilities, food stores that do not stock fresh vegetables and fruits, limited medical services, and other common characteristics of poor neighborhoods in the United States are directly associated with poor health promotion and maintenance. Researchers have long argued about the role of these characteristics on people's health (e.g., Wright & Fischer, 2003; Yen & Kaplan, 1999). A recent analysis of these relationships (Bor, Cohen, & Galea, 2017) further argues that other more distal societal characteristics also affect the health status of individuals. Among the factors related to increased inequality (and therefore poorer health) are, Bor and colleagues suggest, the following: unequal access to technological innovations, segregation by income, limited economic mobility, incarceration, and high cost of medical care.

The creation of healthier places is expected to produce better health among its residents, a finding supported by significant numbers of studies and demonstration projects (Dankwa-Mullan & Pérez-Stable, 2016). These **place-based interventions** are defined by Dankwa-Mullan and Pérez-Stable as "approaches for improving health in a geographic location that align[] the community members, businesses, institutions, and other relevant stakeholders in a collaborative and participatory process" (p. 637).

Undocumented Status

Undocumented legal status of immigrants can also affect their health status, given that being undocumented usually prevents access to health insurance, high-quality health care, prescriptions, and certain medical personnel.

One assumption usually found in the literature is that the presence of a large number of undocumented individuals is related to increases in drug problems and in driving under the influence (DUI). These assumptions are often based on the growth rates of undocumented migration from approximately 3.5 million in 1990 to approximately 11 million in 2014 (Warren & Warren, 2013) and increases in fatalities produced by drug overdose and DUI where, for example, fatalities due to drug overdose increased 137 percent from 2000 to 2014 (Rudd, Aleshire, Zibbell, & Gladdden, 2016). Nevertheless, a recent study (Light, Miller, & Kelly, 2017) utilizing large-scale databases, including arrest data from FBI crime reports and the CDC's database on causes of death, shows that increases in undocumented residents in a given area did not produce increases in drug or DUI arrests or in deaths by drug overdose. These results contradict the prejudicial perceptions of the assumed negative role played by undocumented residents and could lend support to the positive healthy behaviors of first generation migrants that we have mentioned throughout this book.

Discrimination and Racism

The lingering aftermath effects of race and ethnicity after socioeconomic status is controlled give us reason to focus on the consequential power of racism. Some have offered explanations for differences in health status that center on the stress produced by long-term exposure to adversity and the oppression of racism (Kawachi, Daniels, & Robinson, 2005; Williams & Collins, 1995). As mentioned above, a report from the Institute of Medicine (Smedley et al., 2003) carefully documents that ethnic or racial minorities receive less intensive and poorer quality of health care than White patients, even when other significant factors (e.g., insurance status, level of income, health symptoms) are equal. Furthermore, recent studies show that racial discrimination plays a significant role in furthering health disparities (Borrell & Dallo, 2008; Borrell & Crawford, 2006). For example, in an analysis of the literature on the health status of White Latinos and of Black Latinos (Cuevas, Dawson, & Williams, 2016), the authors find that the health status (hypertension, depression, overall self-rating of health) of Latinos whose skin color was dark was poorer than that of light-skinned Latinos.

There are daily encounters with discrimination that accompany many of the factors associated with poor health, including impoverished neighborhoods, exposure to violence, poor income, and unemployment (Browning & Cagney, 2003). The regularity of incidents such as being followed by security personnel in a department store for no apparent reason or being overlooked or treated badly by a hostess in a restaurant has been linked to hypertension and coronary heart disease (Lewis et al., 2006). Furthermore, ethnic minorities who perceive and relay incidences of discrimination and racism are more likely to engage in unhealthy behaviors (e.g., smoking) and report more physical and psychological distress than Whites or other ethnic minorities that do not perceive or report similar experiences (Barry & Grilo, 2003; Brondolo, Rieppi, Kelly, & Gerin, 2003; Klonoff & Landrine, 1999; Landrine, Klonoff, Corral, Fernandez, & Roesch, 2006).

A survey conducted by the American Psychological Association in 2015 (American Psychological Association, 2016) found that nearly 70 percent of the population of the United States reported experiencing discriminatory behaviors such as being treated with discourtesy and disrespect or being threatened or harassed. Close to 75 percent of African American adults reported being the target of those behaviors almost on a daily basis. The respondents also reported that those experiences of discrimination or anticipating them were related to high levels of stress, which in turn is associated with poor health.

Smedley (2008), one of the editors of the Institute of Medicine's 2003 report (Smedley et al., 2003), argues that, while it is important to focus on health care and frontline strategies to reduce health disparities, the report stands as a testament to the critical response needed by our sociopolitical and economic systems. Disparities in health primarily mirror the social inequalities and injustices in the United States and are primarily experienced by ethnic minorities and the poor. Inequalities within the broader political, social, and economic policies marginalize and disenfranchise these groups. Hence, Smedley (2008) issues a call to action on government policy reform:

> Eliminating health care inequality requires more than simply expanding insurance coverage among currently un- and underinsured populations. In particular, policymakers must attend to structural and community-level problems, such as the maldistribution of health care resources, the lack of effective mechanisms for underserved communities to participate in health care planning, and the presence of cultural and linguistic barriers in health care settings, to equalize access to high-quality health care. (p. 453)

A broader focus, designed to address the complex interaction of several systems of inequality, would require the identification of multiple targets and levels of intervention. These efforts would include attention to promoting equality on an environmental level (e.g., raising safety standards in the environment—see the following section and Box 9.4), in the educational sphere (e.g., by reducing disparities in school funding), at the employment level (e.g., adequate pay and benefits for work), and with respect to direct service needs—services designed to address cultural needs, values, and behaviors of patients, a topic discussed later in this chapter.

Box 9.4

A Toxic Injustice

Chester, Pennsylvania, houses one of the largest collections of waste facilities in the country. It has the seventh-largest garbage-burning incinerator in the nation. In 1995, adjacent to the incinerator, the nation's largest infectious and chemotherapeutic medical-waste autoclave operated for over a year. Before it was shut down, the plant brought in massive amounts of medical waste (three times more than produced in the state of Pennsylvania). During the plant's operation, it was not unusual to find discarded waste lying in surrounding areas where children played. Several workers at the plant were accidentally stabbed by needles while handling the waste. Some suffered mysterious rashes and other medical problems that were difficult to diagnose. Close to the incinerator and plant is the sewage treatment facility that treats 90 percent of the sewage in Delaware County, as well as sewage from local industries such as ConocoPhillips's oil refinery, Sunoco's oil refinery, Kimberly-Clark's paper mill, and various chemical companies. This toxic sewage sludge is burned in a sludge incinerator, releasing many toxic pollutants into the air, including mercury and arsenic. On average, one new company with toxic potential per year has proposed to build a plant in Chester. In early 2008, a newly formed multiracial, multigenerational, countywide student and community coalition organized and managed to prevent construction of the world's largest tire incinerator.

According to their report, published in 2008, Chester has the highest infant mortality rate and highest percentage of low-weight births in Pennsylvania and a mortality rate and lung cancer rate 60 percent higher than the rest of Delaware County. Sixty percent of children in Chester had significantly high levels of lead in their blood. The rate of poverty is 27 percent, more than twice the national average. More than 80 percent of Chester residents are people of color. Race has been found to be the strongest correlate of exposure to toxic pollution in Delaware County—stronger than income, poverty, childhood poverty, education, job classification, or home ownership (Ewall & ActionPA.org, 2008).

Source: Data from M. Ewall, personal communication, December 29, 2008; Ewall & ActionPA.org, 2008; Energy Justice Network, www.energyjustice.net. For more information on the Chester struggle, see the DelCo Alliance for Environmental Justice website, at www.ejnet.org/chester/.

Environmental Racism

Many researchers argue that residents of ethnic or racial minority communities have been wronged through their disproportionate exposure to environmental health risks. This has been labeled as **environmental racism**, which long-time civil rights activist Reverend Benjamin Chavis Jr. defined as follows:

> Environmental racism is racial discrimination in environmental policymaking. It is racial discrimination in the enforcement of regulations and laws. It is racial discrimination in the deliberate targeting of communities of color for toxic waste disposal and the siting of polluting industries. It is racial discrimination in the official sanctioning of the life-threatening presence of poisons and pollutants in communities of color. And, it is racial discrimination in the history of excluding people of color from the mainstream environmental groups, decision making boards, commissions, and regulatory bodies. (Chavis, 1993, p. 3)

Environmental racism, also sometimes referred to as **environmental injustice**, reflects the historical legacy of exploitation and oppression of various minority groups. Communities with predominantly African American, Hispanic/Latino, American Indian, or Asian American groups (often regardless of class) are more likely to be located near toxic municipal landfills, nuclear waste sites, energy plants, chemical warehouses, garbage incinerators, and other high-risk environmental facilities (Bullard, 1990; Bullard, Mohal, Saha, & Wright, 2007). The costs of such precarious placement are significant, since living close to these types of facilities is linked to higher than normal levels of diseases, including cancer, asthma and other respiratory disorders, skin diseases, low-weight births, blood poisoning, and high mortality rate. Environmental racism is also tied to property devaluation, increases in crime rates, poor quality of surrounding schools, and poor-quality housing. Because risky facilities are located close to neighborhoods, some residents may work at these sites and thus expose themselves to high occupational hazards. See Box 9.4, above, for an example of the situation in Chester, Pennsylvania.

Attempts to rectify these dangers can be addressed through legal and legislative means. In response to public outcry, the Environmental Protection Agency established the Office of Environmental Justice in 1992 (Environmental Protection Agency, 2008). In particular, the Environmental Justice Coordinators' Council consists of frontline staff responsible for ensuring policy input, program development, and implementation of strategies throughout the agency (Environmental Protection Agency, 2018). However, cases of environmental racism can take several years of debate, bureaucracy, and legal maneuvering to clearly establish and receive adequate retribution (if any) for losses incurred. Of the few cases in which damages have been recognized, or plants and other toxic sites shut down, most of the initiative came from grassroots efforts by community residents, advocates, and other concerned citizens. Yet policy must be transformed to realize a diligent commitment to basic human justice.

Also related to environmental justice is the differential availability of basic public services such as potable water, safe gas transportation, appropriate electrical wiring, and lead-free paint. A number of studies have shown how poor neighborhoods and, in many cases, communities primarily housing ethnic or racial minorities suffer from public services of poor quality. These conditions affect important health-promoting behaviors and in some cases (as in the case of lead-based paint) can produce serious illnesses. Consider, for example, the low levels of quality tap water intake found among ethnic and racial minorities that in turn lead to inadequate hydration (Brooks, Gortmaker, Long, Cradock, & Kenney, 2017). Other studies have shown the inadequate safety of tap water in poor neighborhoods and in predominantly African American and Latino communities of (Patel & Schmidt, 2017).

Spirituality and Religion

Dealing with health and other stressful difficulties through the use of spirituality or religion has long been cited as commonplace across many cultural groups. Several reviews have highlighted the link between religiosity (e.g., attending church, adhering to the beliefs and practices of an organized religion) and spirituality (e.g., a search for meaning and values in life; connectedness with others, nature, or higher force) and positive physical and mental health status and longevity (Mueller, Plevak, & Rummans, 2001). Some consider religion and spirituality to be related though different constructs. *Religion* is often associated with one's group participation in an organized formal adherence to doctrine and denominational requirements of a social institution (Hill & Pargament, 2003; Simon, Crowther, & Higgerson, 2007). *Spirituality* is commonly used to refer to the personal, subjective meaning or relationship one has with a higher power that may or may not be related to a religion (Armstrong & Crowther, 2002; Hill & Pargament, 2003). Although these distinctions may assist researchers in discovering the nuanced importance of various aspects of faith, some argue that there are inherent problems with drawing a line between religion and spirituality. Primarily these concerns center on the varied social contexts and personal matters addressed in both religious and spiritual expression. Moreover, many people often experience and view their spiritual expression as one and the same with their religion or general sense of faith (Hill & Pargament, 2003).

Social science research on the relationship between religion and/or spirituality and health for ethnic or racial minority populations has been limited and primarily focused on mainstream denominations of Protestant Christianity; less attention has been given to spirituality and religious issues of newer immigrant populations and ethnic and racial minorities in the United States (Hufford, 2005). Yet there have been some published accounts of cases that emphasize religious considerations in working with diverse cultural groups, and recent publications (e.g., Substance Abuse and Mental Health Services Administration, 2014; Whitley, 2012) highlight the important role played by religion and spirituality in promoting health. As discussed below in Box 9.5, *The Spirit Catches You and You Fall Down: A Hmong Child, Her American Doctors, and the Collision of Two Cultures*, Anne Fadiman's (1997) popular book, focuses on the tragic medical consequences that can occur in the midst of misunderstanding between an immigrant family's Hmong culture and religion and the doctors' biomedical orientation. Further, reviews and ethnographic studies that describe religious healing traditions such as the Afro-Cuban *santería* and Mexican *curanderismo* have heightened awareness of the broad diversity of health beliefs and practices that may be utilized within heterogeneous ethnic communities (e.g., Applewhite, 1995; Holliday, 2008).

The growing research literature on U.S. ethnic and racial minorities suggests a positive relationship between health status and religion and spirituality. For example, religion, prayer, and worship at church are considered dominant features in African American culture (Chatters, Taylor, & Lincoln, 1999). To explore the role of spirituality and religion in assisting a sample of African American women ($N = 18$) to manage breast cancer diagnosis, treatment, and post-treatment, Simon and her colleagues (2007) conducted a series of qualitative interviews. All the women in the study self-identified as

Box 9.5

The Spirit Catches You and You Fall Down

Anne Fadiman's (1997) study of a Hmong family vividly describes the culture clash that exists between Western medicine and the indigenous, spiritual beliefs of an immigrant family from Laos. This is a true story of the Lee family, who immigrate to Merced, California, in 1980.

One year later, their daughter, Lia Lee, is born. Within her first three months of life, Lia suffers her first seizure. Initially, her parents consider treating her with a traditional herbal remedy, but the necessary herbs are not accessible in their new country. They also fear the doctors, due to traumatic experiences related to their time spent in a refugee camp in Thailand. Finally, though, they end up seeking emergency treatment at the Merced Community Medical Center. Lia is diagnosed by her doctors as having epilepsy; however, her parents call it *quag dab peg* [the spirit catches you and you fall down].

Over the next few years, Lia visits the clinic several times. She is treated with a complex combination of drugs to manage the epileptic seizures. Lia's parents have difficulty following the complicated regimen; furthermore, they believe that the medication is making her worse. Consequently, they fail to comply with the doctor's instructions. From the medical point of view, the Lees are seen as negligent and therefore abusive. Eventually, Lia is placed in a foster home to ensure that she is properly treated. Her seizures do not stop. On November 25, 1986, Lia suffers a massive seizure that causes extensive brain damage. She is transported to a pediatric intensive care unit for stabilization. The doctors do not expect Lia to live more than a few days at the most, so they discharge her to her parents. The Lees believe that Lia's soul is lost. Their hope is to help her soul find its way back to her body. They enlist the help of a Hmong shaman to conduct a healing ceremony in their home, a traditional ceremony that involves the sacrifice of a live pig.

The story of Lia transcends a simple language barrier. In this case, the impasse illustrates how culture can shape contrasting worldviews concerning health. The biomedical culture is one that relates the seizure and its effects to the brain's function. Medication that alters physiology through changing brain chemistry will be seen as part of the solution. The Lees' view encompasses their cultural beliefs and spirituality; their understanding of health is tied to their religion that views illness as related to lost souls cured by sacrificial animal shamanism.

In this work, Fadiman makes the case that both the doctors and the parents care about the welfare of Lia but that neither is equipped to handle and understand the contrary nature of the other's culture and manner. Nevertheless, Fadiman acknowledges the importance of medical providers at least exploring the patient's beliefs and seeking cultural interpretation (not just language translation) and guidance about how to best address the clash that will inevitably occur with differences.

Christian, and, interestingly, each respondent mentioned spirituality or religiosity during the interview even before questions on this topic were raised by the researchers. The majority of women indicated that their spirituality and faith were important in supporting them throughout the breast cancer experience in terms of helping them in their reaction to and acceptance of the diagnosis, coping with negative treatment effects, finding meaning in life and desire to live, and finding a reason for their survival. Findings from this and other studies conducted with ethnic minorities suggest that a consideration by health professionals of ways in which they could explore how the patients' commitment toward their spirituality and religion might serve as a means of positive coping in their treatment and recovery from illness could be helpful and empowering to patients. Such an approach exemplifies what is called "culturally competent" health care (see the following section).

Reducing Racial and Ethnic Health Disparities: The Federal Government's Approach

For much of the last few decades, the U.S. Department of Health and Human Services (HHS) and other agencies of the federal government have been concerned with developing plans and funding strategies to reduce or eliminate racial and ethnic health disparities. One approach has been the creation of the Office of Minority Health to oversee and support efforts promoting health among ethnic and racial minorities.[3] OMH, established in 1986 and reauthorized in 2010 by the Patient Protection and Affordable Care Act (also known as Obamacare), has a mission to improve the health of racial and ethnic minority populations and programs by developing health policies and programs that eliminate health disparities. In 2011 HHS and OMH produced a plan to reduce racial and ethnic disparities (U.S. Department of Health and Human Services, 2011) that includes five major goals: (1) to transform health care, (2) strengthen the national health infrastructure and workforce, (3) advance the health, safety, and well-being of the country, (4) advance scientific knowledge and innovation, and (5) increase efficiency, transparency, and accountability. The latest progress report was published in 2015, covering the period of time between 2011 and 2015 (U.S. Department of Health and Human Services, 2015), and it reports on important changes, including the increase in insured individuals brought about by the Patient Protection and Affordable Care Act, the expansion of Medicare services to the indigent and the poor, and the development of a number of innovative strategies to decrease health disparities. One important result of OMH's efforts has been the development of the National Standards for Culturally and Linguistically Appropriate Services (CLAS), which are discussed in the next section of this chapter.

Another important effort on the part of the federal government has been the establishment of the National Institute on Minority Health and Health Disparities (NIMHD)[4] as one of the 27 institutes and centers of the National Institutes of Health (NIH). The current NIMHD was reenvisioned as part of the Patient Protection and Affordable Care Act and traces its roots to a number of offices within the NIH and HHS. The NIMHD has as its goal to raise national awareness about the prevalence and effects of health disparities and promotes the development and implementation of effective interventions at the individual, community, and population levels to reduce and eliminate disparities. The NIMHD funds research projects, supports prevention programs such as Fuel Up to Play 60, which promotes physical activity and nutrition among Latinos, and the Brother, You're on My Mind program, which promotes mental health among African American men.

As you continue to explore issues of health disparities among ethnic and racial minority groups, you may want to periodically consult the websites of the OMH and the NIMHD for updates, current data on disparities and health status, details of interventions, and other useful information.

Culturally Competent Health Care

Given the documented health disparities and multiple factors that can impede or facilitate meeting the health needs of ethnic and racial minorities in the United States, we turn our attention toward **culturally competent health care**. *Cultural competence* in practice is often used interchangeably with related terms such as *cultural sensitivity*, *cultural appropriateness*, *cultural responsiveness*, and *cultural* *awareness*. As mentioned above, provision of culturally competent health services is considered one of the key components in eliminating health disparities and in reaching the goal of health equity as proposed in the *Healthy People 2020* report.

As could be expected, there are a number of definitions as to what constitutes cultural appropriateness in service delivery as well as in terms of the personal characteristics of the service providers. Probably one of the first definitions of cultural competence was proposed by Cross, Bazron, Dennis, & Isaacs (1989), who considered cultural competence to refer to a set of congruent behaviors, attitudes, and policies that are part of a system or are part of professional's repertoire that supports effective interactions with individuals from different cultures. Central to this understanding of cultural competence was the congruence of cognitive and behavioral components that allow institutions and individuals to function effectively in promoting health, personal development, and physical and psychological treatment. In a later definition, Betancourt, Green, Carrillo, and Ananeh-Firempong (2003) defined culturally competent health care as "health care that acknowledges and incorporates—at all levels—the importance of culture, assessment of cross-cultural relations, vigilance toward the dynamics that result from cultural differences, expansion of cultural knowledge, and adaptation of services to meet culturally unique needs" (p. 293). This systematic approach to care recognizes that both social factors (e.g., socioeconomic status, education, risky environments, social stressors) and cultural factors are inextricably intertwined and can contribute to health disparities (Betancourt et al., 2003; Substance Abuse and Mental Health Services Administration, 2014; Smedley, 2008).

As part of their efforts to bridge health disparities, since 2000, and revised in 2010, the Office of Minority Health at the Department of Health and Human Services has been developing and promoting the National Culturally and Linguistically Appropriate Services Standards (CLAS) in Health and Health Care. The standards are designed to promote health equity, improve the quality of services, and contribute to the elimination of health disparities. The current CLAS standards consist of 15 specific requirements divided in three areas: (a) governance, leadership, and workforce, (b) communication and language assistance, and (c) engagement, continuous improvement, and accountability. The standards are based on a principal standard—to "provide effective, equitable, understandable, and respectful quality care and services that are responsive to diverse cultural health beliefs and practices, preferred languages, health literacy, and other communication needs" (U.S. Department of Health and Human Services, n.d.). The standards focus on areas in which many multicultural psychologists have contributed through their theories and their research. The CLAS standards also present specific areas of involvement for future researchers and professionals in terms of delivery services and community interventions in physical and mental health.

The World Health Organization (2012) proposes that many health disparities observed in developed countries such as the United States as well as in evolving economies are due to the nature of the **social determinants of health**, which the WHO defines as those conditions in which individuals are born, grow, live, work, and age. The *Healthy People 2020* report further argues that key social determinants of health in the United States are the socioeconomic status, educational level, and availability of health services, including historical and current discrimination and social injustice[5] (U.S. Department of Health and Human Services, 2010; CMS Office of Minority Health and Rand Corporation, 2017). This perspective that is reflective of an ecological model of health also highlights the significance of the contributions that are expected from the social and behavioral sciences.

In a comprehensive review that examines sociocultural barriers to health care and culturally competent practice, Betancourt and colleagues (2003) identify three levels of health care (organizational, structural, and clinical) at which barriers occur that can lead to health disparities as well as possible targets of intervention.

Barriers to Health Care at the Organizational Level

The first level of barriers to health identified by Betancourt and colleagues (2003) is at the level of the health care organization itself. Availability and acceptability of health care is influenced by whether the administrative leadership and providers reflect the racial and ethnic minorities that they serve. For example, despite the fact that ethnic and racial minorities represent more than 35 percent of the population, they account for less than 2 percent of individuals with senior leadership roles in health care management (Evans, 1999). Whether administrators design programs that are sensitive toward the needs of minority populations will be contingent on awareness gained through experience (e.g., having a shared cultural background and/or exposure to different ethnic groups) and education. However, if administrators lack experience and their education has been limited in terms of not having diversity of curriculum, training, and faculty mentors, there may be a cultural gap between the delivery of health services and the minorities they serve. Interventions designed to promote greater representation of medical professionals and health care managers (e.g., vigorous recruitment and retention of minority medical students, mentoring of minority candidates for upper-level administrative positions) are necessary.

Barriers to Health Care at the Structural Level

This second level of barriers to health proposed by Betancourt and colleagues (2003) refers to those conditions in place that may impede ethnic minority patients from receiving adequate and appropriate health care. Examples of structural barriers include little or no health insurance coverage, lack of prevention and early detection programs, lack of continuity of health care services, long wait times for clinic visits, difficulty in accessing transportation to and from clinics, lack of translated health assessment and educational materials for non-English-speaking or -reading patients, and lack of interpreters to provide assistance in communication between the English-speaking providers and their patients who speak a different language.

Several studies document the importance of ensuring good communication to facilitate accurate understanding, diagnosis, and treatment. Members of diverse cultural groups may conceptualize health, illness, discomfort, and health care practices in different ways. These differences may lead to breakdowns in communication between people from different cultural backgrounds (Angelelli & Geist-Martin, 2005) (see Box 9.5 earlier in this chapter).

Even for patients who have adequate mastery of English, the expression of disease symptoms may differ from majority individuals, which may lead to errors in diagnosis and treatment. Structural interventions are challenging because there are so many possible targets. However, basic to these interventions is a focus on *policy change*. Policy must be influenced on a number of levels—national, state, and local. Electing officials truly committed to culturally competent health care through appropriate assessment, early detection, prevention, and treatment of ethnic or racial minority populations is critical to transforming health care system-wide.

Clinical Level of Competent Care

At its most intimate level, cultural competence begins with the practitioner's ability to relate to the patient in a culturally sensitive manner. Practitioners must be aware of their own attitudes and beliefs (including stereotypes and biases) regarding people of diverse backgrounds. Attitudes and beliefs are shaped by experiences, exposure to other cultures, and the norms of influential individuals and society in general. Culturally competent practitioners are aware that stressful social factors can be possible determinants of health. For example, attempts can be made to understand the patient's experiences dealing with racism and discrimination, poverty, or living in overcrowded or substandard conditions. Learning about patients' stressors as well as strengths and social supports can give a more complete picture of their current health status and potential resources that can assist in patients' recovery.

Additional education may take the form of learning more about culture-specific health interventions. **Complementary health approaches (CHA)** are forms of health interventions that are considered outside the mainstream of conventional Western medicine (see Box 9.6). Previously, these approaches were known as *complementary and alternative medicine*, or CAM, but agencies of HHS proposed that these are health approaches and not "medicine." Although both *complementary*

Box 9.6

Examples of Complementary Health Approaches

Alternative Health Systems

acupuncture
traditional Chinese medicine
healers
Ayurvedic medicine
homeopathic medicine
naturopathic medicine

Mind-Body Therapies

hypnotherapy
patient support groups
meditation
prayer
relaxation techniques
yoga
tai chi

Biologically Based Practices

herbal remedies
dietary supplements
probiotics

Manipulative Practices

chiropractic manipulations
osteopathic manipulations
massage

and *alternative* are used to describe these interventions, the National Center for Complementary and Integrative Health considers the forms of medicine to be different from each other.

Complementary health approaches are used *in combination with* conventional medicine; alternative medicine is used *in place of* conventional medicine. For example, meditation may be used as a complement with cardiovascular drugs to aid a patient's recovery following bypass surgery. A person may elect to use alternative detoxification procedures (to rid the body of toxic elements) to treat cancer instead of conventional surgery, radiation, or chemotherapy. CHA interventions change over time as they demonstrate efficacy and safety and as they are included in conventional treatment or as new developments to health care emerge. Many therapies originally deemed "alternative" have grown in popularity and have demonstrated efficacy especially when combined with other forms of treatment (e.g., meditation, yoga, acupuncture, and some herbal therapies).

CHA use has become increasingly popular among the general population in the United States (Clarke, Black, Stussman, Barnes, & Nahin, 2015; Grzywacz et al., 2005). Recent studies report that nonvitamin, nonmineral dietary supplements were the most commonly used CHA in 2012. Second in popularity were deep breathing exercises, followed by yoga, tai chi, and qigong and by chiropractic and osteopathic manipulation (Clarke et al., 2015). An analysis by race shows that Whites are the most likely to report use of CHA (37.9 percent), followed by Latinos (22.0 percent) and African Americans (19.3 percent). Earlier studies had shown that middle-aged adults (approximately 40 to 60 years of age) are the largest group of consumers (Institute of Medicine, 2005). In a large study using data from the 2002 National Health Survey, Blacks and older adults reported the lowest use of CHA—if prayer is *not* considered; however, when prayer is included as CHA, they have the highest use (Barnes, Powell-Griner, McFann, & Nahin, 2004). In addition, Asian Americans reported a higher use of CHA than did Whites, but use of CHA was lower among Latinos than among Whites (Barnes et al., 2004).

Depending on the culture and environmental context, traditional healers may be herbalists, shamans, *curanderos*, medicine men or women, or other types of religious or spiritual therapists. Some may practice in clinics or offices, but others may practice in homes or religious settings such as churches, temples, or sweat lodges. It is important to inquire and discuss patients' use of other medical interventions, especially if they are taking supplements or engaging in activities that may be contraindicated with conventional medicine. For example, the use of certain popular herbal supplements such as ginkgo biloba, feverfew, and garlic can enhance circulation but should be avoided by people already taking medicines such as blood thinners (anticoagulants) or by people before, during, or after surgery as they can increase bleeding (North American Spine Society, 2006).

As you have seen in this chapter, there are a number of areas that need further research in order to better clarify the relationship between culture and physical health. The health disparities as well as the disparities in health care access and quality are problematic given their impact on a large segment of the population of the country and the problems it brings to many of us. There have been efforts at demanding that research on physical health among ethnic or racial minorities be of excellent quality. Furthermore, government agencies and researchers alike have asked that health promotion interventions be not only culturally sensitive but also properly evaluated as to their effectiveness (Anderson et al., 2003). At the same time, the CDC has established a Community Preventive Services Task Force to, among other things, evaluate the effectiveness of strategies directed at improving health equity (eliminating health disparities) and to identify evidence gaps that can be solved with additional research.[6]

The following chapter analyzes the mental health conditions and treatment possibilities among the racial and ethnic communities in the United States. As is true with physical health, much has been learned and many efforts have been designed to promote the health and well-being of ethnic and racial communities. Unfortunately, much remains to be done.

Chapter Summary

This chapter provides an overview of some of the major health disparities that exist among ethnic and racial minority groups compared to non-Hispanic Whites. We proposed that, rather than focusing solely on biological vulnerabilities or other individual correlates of disease, it is critical to consider multiple determinants of positive or negative health status. Taking a multidimensional approach requires that we prioritize for intervention individual factors—like lifestyle (diet, exercise, smoking, substance use), psychological characteristics (stress, social support), and structural factors (accessible and affordable health care, poverty, social and environmental injustices). There must be a concerted level of commitment among health theorists and providers, policymakers and politicians, as well as concerned individuals and groups to create change in order to achieve equity in health and culturally appropriate services for those in need.

Key Terms

acute diseases 201
biomedical model 200
biopsychosocial model 201
causal factors 216
chronic diseases 201
complementary health approaches (CHA) 229
culturally competent health care 227
ecological models 202
environmental injustice 224
environmental racism 224
epidemiology 205
evidence-based interventions 218
health disparity 206
health equity 206
health literacy 222
immigrant health paradox 220
incidence 205
mind-body dualism 200
morbidity 205
mortality 205
place-based interventions 222
prevalence 205
psychiatric epidemiology 205
risk factors 205
selective migration hypothesis 220
social determinants of health 228
social stress hypothesis 220
type 1 diabetes 212
type 2 diabetes 212
working poor 221

Learning by Doing

- Conduct a taste test with your friends of two types of foods that you like to eat but that can be high in calories, saturated fats, or sodium or treated with hormones, preservatives, or other chemicals. See if you can purchase a "healthy" alternative of the food. You and your friends should taste the foods (regular versus healthy alternatives) side by side. Note your likes and dislikes about each food. Compare your answers. Do the advantages of the healthy alternatives outweigh the disadvantages? How are you and your friends defining a healthy food?

Notes

1 To read this article, visit *Why Social Science?*, blog of the Consortium of Social Science Associations, at http://www.whysocialscience.com/.

2 Overweight and obesity are based on body mass index (BMI is weight in kilograms divided by the square of height in meters). For children and adolescents, overweight is defined as at or above the 95th percentile of the sex-specific BMI for age-growth charts. For adults, obesity is defined as a BMI greater than 30, and extreme obesity is defined as a BMI greater than 40 (Centers for Disease Control and Prevention, 2006).

3 Visit the Office of Minority Health online at https://minorityhealth.hhs.gov.

4 Visit the National Institute on Minority Health and Health Disparities online at https://www.nimhd.nih.gov.

5 Visit the U.S. Department of Health and Human Services' Office of Disease Prevention and Health Promotion online at https://www.healthypeople.gov.

6 The work of the Centers for Disease Control's Community Preventive Services Task Force can be found at https://www.thecommunityguide.org.

Suggested Further Readings

Berry, J. W., & Sam, D. L. (2007). Cultural and ethnic factors in health. In S. Ayers, A. Baum, C. McManus, S. Newman, K. Wallston, J. Weinman, & R. West (Eds.), *Cambridge handbook of psychology, health, and medicine* (2nd ed., pp. 64–70). Cambridge: Cambridge University Press.

An overview of studies from varied disciplines—including cross-cultural health psychology, medical anthropology, and psychiatry—that examines how culture informs our understanding of immigrants' and members of ethnic communities' health status and adjustment.

Kato, P. M., & Mann, T. (Eds.). (1996). *Handbook of diversity issues in health psychology.* New York: Plenum.

An examination of health issues across several groups, including pediatric, adolescent, and elderly populations; men and women; varied sexual orientations; and African Americans, Asian Americans, Latinos, and Native Americans. Attention is also given to the impact of socioeconomic status and the health of ethnic minority populations.

Kazarian, S., & Evans, D. R. (Eds.). (2001). *Handbook of cultural health psychology.* San Diego: Academic Press.

A handbook taking a global perspective on major health issues affecting cultural groups, including cardiovascular/heart disease, cancer, pain, HIV/AIDS, suicide, and health promotion.

LaVeist, T. A. (Ed.). (2002). *Race, ethnicity, and health: A public health reader.* San Francisco: Jossey-Bass.

A reader presenting data on disparities in health outcomes and differential treatment provided in health care settings. Historical and political factors that relate to these differences are addressed.

Marmot, M., & Wilkinson, R. G. (Eds.). (2005). *Social determinants of health* (2nd ed.). New York: Oxford University Press.

An examination of social and economic factors that can lead to various health outcomes. It considers that health is dependent on not just individual behavior but also structural factors (e.g., social, economic, institutional, and policy) and psychosocial environment (e.g., quality of neighborhood, stable workplace).

Substance Abuse and Mental Health Services Administration [SAMHSA]. (2014). *Improving cultural competence.* Treatment Improvement Protocol (TIP) Series No. 59. HHS publication No. (SMA) 14-4849. Rockville, MD: Author. Retrieved from https://store.samhsa.gov/shin/content/SMA14-4849/SMA14-4849.pdf

An excellent compendium of theory and models on what is required to develop cultural competence and culturally appropriate services. A good source of information on key studies, instruments, and resources in the field. A required resource for people interested in health among ethnic or racial minority groups.

Psychological Adjustment 10

"He's All Right; He's Just Funny That Way"

Jerome, a 25-year-old African American man, settles into his chair to watch television. His day at work had not gone well—too many customers demanding his attention. Working at Walmart is not good for the nerves, he concludes. He tries to follow the story line of a television drama but keeps zoning out. At one point, he absentmindedly brushes his fingertips across his face. He is startled to look down at his wet hand. He brings his hand up to his cheek and notices that it is damp with tears. He has been crying, and he can't figure out what is causing this level of distress.

Suddenly, there is an urgent knocking at his front door. Though he does not want company right now, he can hear his mother, Betty, yelling for him to open the door. Jerome pulls himself up from his seat. He feels heavy—his body feels large and out of shape. Further, a weight seems to press down on his shoulders. He steadies himself and breathes a long sigh. "I am carrying the weight of the world," he mutters.

"Where have you been?" his mother exclaims.

"Huh?" Jerome is confused.

"You were supposed to come over for dinner tonight—don't you remember?" Trying as hard as he can to recollect making these plans, Jerome can't. He tells his mother he has no memory of the dinner date, but she is not satisfied. "Something hasn't felt right for the longest time with you. . . . You

keep forgetting things, you don't seem interested in being around your people. . . . You look messed up, too. . . . Actually, you look tired and completely worn out!" Betty barely finishes her sentence when Jerome bursts into tears. He is sobbing uncontrollably. "Son, what's wrong?"

For several minutes, Jerome cannot speak or look at Betty. He struggles to understand the painful thoughts that clutter his mind and never seem to disappear—thoughts like "Why does it seem so hard to get started?" and "Maybe things would be better if I weren't around" and "I feel so blue; life can't get harder than this" and "I can't live like this!"

Finally, Jerome tells his mother, "I'm just so tired, and my head hurts." Betty moves closer to her son and attempts to hug him, but he quickly pulls away. "I don't feel good!"

"Son, you've got to rest and get Jesus back in your life. Call me in the morning."

Jerome mumbles, "Yeah, have a good night." He shuts the door and thinks, "I feel real bad, and my nerves are shot. I need a couple drinks . . . or maybe more."

Outside of Jerome's apartment, Betty looks down and shakes her head. "He's all right . . . he's all right. He's just funny that way."

In this chapter, we discuss psychological distress as well as the variation in psychological adjustment within ethnic groups. Attention is focused on major, highly prevalent disorders like depression, anxiety, and substance use problems and the relationship of cultural, social, and economic risk factors to their development and course. Additional factors that precipitate or guard against psychological distress are examined, like, for example, immigration and acculturation, social class, and availability of social support. We also describe current clinical approaches to understanding the cultural context of mental illness and examine what are termed **cultural idioms of distress** or syndromes—symptom constellations that are considered unique to particular cultural groups. Guidelines and standards from professional psychological organizations support the perspective that culture influences the social behaviors and mental processes of individuals and the provision of mental health services (American Psychological Association, 2017). This chapter concludes with a review of recommendations for those who are committed to improving their awareness of the relationship of ethnic and cultural issues in the provision of professional activities of assessment, intervention, and prevention.

Mental Health and Psychological Distress

A Broader Perspective on Adjustment

Betty tells herself that Jerome is "all right. He's just funny that way." What are the parameters that are used to define psychological distress? How do we distinguish between people who are simply unusual or "funny" and those who are pathologically maladjusted? What needs to be done when people (including family and friends) deny the gravity of symptoms and characteristics that may lead to the conclusion that an individual is mentally ill? The most popular diagnostic system in the United States, the *Diagnostic and Statistical Manual of Mental Disorders: DSM-5* (American Psychiatric Association, 2013), contains criteria for specific disorders. Yet agreement on what constitutes mental distress or illness has been a point of considerable debate, especially when discussed in the context of culture (Comer, 2015; López & Guarnaccia, 2005; Maddux & Winstead, 2005).

Sensitivity to the influence of culture on adjustment would require the integration of multiple disciplines, including anthropology, psychology, and psychiatry, in order to appreciate the limits of traditional diagnosis of disorders like depression, generalized anxiety, and schizophrenia (Kleinman, 1977). In addition, it would be important to recognize how culture can shape one's reaction and possible adaptation to and recovery from mental illness (Kleinman, 1977). As López and Guarnaccia (2000) note, a cultural perspective requires the integration of the "social world" of the individual—an appreciation of social and environmental factors that can influence the adjustment of people on a daily basis. The incidence and prevalence of disorders will tell only part of the story of mental health in ethnic minority populations; we also want to consider variation in the expression of distress, factors that influence the development of illness, and prevention and intervention that facilitate adjustment.

Prevalence and Risk of Major Psychological Disorders

General Epidemiological Surveys

Psychiatric epidemiology is a specialized area within epidemiology (see Chapter 9). While epidemiological research serves to examine the patterns of medical diseases and disease risks among populations, psychiatric epidemiology is designed to examine patterns of mental illness and characteristics that may place particular groups of people at risk. In the past years, that the prevalence of psychiatric disorders in the general U.S. population is high and the age of onset of these disorders tends to be young (e.g., Kessler, Chiu, Demler, & Walters, 2005) has been indicated by a handful of widely cited national epidemiological studies of psychiatric disorders—including the **Epidemiological Catchment Area (ECA) study** (Robins & Regier, 1991), the **National Comorbidity Survey (NCS)** (Kessler et al., 1994), and the **National Comorbidity Survey Replication (NCS-R)** (Kessler et al., 2005; Kessler & Merikangas, 2004). Roughly 30–50 percent of Americans are likely to be diagnosed with a psychological disorder at some point in their life (Kessler et al., 2005). Furthermore, it appears that the first symptoms of these disorders are likely to occur during childhood or adolescence (Kessler et al., 2005).

Although it might seem like a large portion of the U.S. population is at risk, it should be noted that major mental illnesses are particularly pervasive. For example, schizophrenia, bipolar disorder, depression, and panic disorder are found throughout the world among all racial and ethnic groups (U.S. Department of Health and Human Services, 1999). Furthermore, mental illness weighs heavily on the health, well-being, and abilities of peoples from different countries—especially low-income countries—even more so than some of the major acute (e.g., tuberculosis) or chronic (e.g., cardiovascular disease and cancer) diseases (Desjarlais, Eisenberg, Good, & Kleinman, 1996).

As noted in Chapter 9, large-scale population studies tend to compare the prevalence rates of illnesses for ethnic groups to those rates for White European Americans. Despite the critical limitations of such an approach, these gross comparisons consistently yield findings that indicate ethnic minorities are generally overrepresented in the rates of diseases and high mortality. However, the diversity within and across minority groups, as illustrated by differences in educational attainment, income, social mobility, and other indicators of social status, can lead to mixed findings in regard to mental health status. For example, both earlier and more recent epidemiological studies indicate that the prevalence of certain mental disorders for ethnic minorities living in the United States is similar to (or for some mental disorders lower than) that of European Americans (Breslau et al., 2006; Breslau, Kendler, Su, Aguilar-Gaxiola, & Kessler, 2005; U.S. Department of Health and Human Services, 1999; Kessler et al., 1994). However, most of these studies exclusively rely on data gathered from persons living within households; most fail to include those who are homeless or living in treatment centers, shelters, detention centers, jails, or hospitals (U.S. Department of Health and Human Services, 1999). Members of certain ethnic minority groups are more likely to be homeless, be incarcerated, and have children placed in foster care (DHHS, 2001). The vulnerability of these "high-need" groups to psychological disorders is striking. The rate of psychological distress is significantly higher in these groups than in the general population (U.S. Department of Health and Human Services, 1999; Foulks, 2004a).

Hence, the rates of mental health disorders may be suppressed in community surveys that do not include members from these at-risk populations. Finally, studies that report lower than expected lifetime prevalence rates of mental disorders among ethnic minorities have also found that the course of (or persistence of) illnesses may be more severe among minorities than among Whites (e.g., Breslau et al., 2005). For example, compared to Whites, African Americans may have more depressive symptoms that last longer and may be more likely to rate their depression as severe and incapacitating (U.S. Department of Health and Human Services, 2001).

Surveys Specific to Ethnic Minority Communities

Our knowledge regarding mental health among diverse racial and ethnic groups has been heightened by a number of surveys conducted over the past two decades. Nationally representative samples of Latinos (with measures available in Spanish or English, depending on the respondent's preference) and Asian Americans (with measures available in a number of Asian languages—Mandarin,

Cantonese, Tagalog, and Vietnamese—or English, depending on the respondent's preference) were surveyed for the **National Latino and Asian American Study (NLAAS)** (Pennell et al., 2004). The **National Survey of American Life (NSAL)** (Jackson et al., 2004) is a national survey of household residents in the Black population that included 3,570 African Americans and 1,621 Afro-Caribbeans (Blacks of Caribbean descent). The NSAL, the NLAAS, and the NCS-R are known collectively as the **Collaborative Psychiatric Epidemiology Surveys (CPES)** (Neighbors et al., 2007).

American Indians present significant challenges in terms of the traditional national surveys. Given the great cultural and linguistic diversity among the more than 300 federally recognized tribes plus 200 Alaska Native groups, assessing their mental health is difficult. Moreover, American Indians have not been included in sufficient numbers in many national surveys to allow strong estimates of prevalence and incidence of several disorders; yet several smaller-scale studies suggest high rates of disorders, especially those that are alcohol-related and trauma-related (Beals et al., 2005). The **American Indian Services Utilization and Psychiatric Epidemiology Risk and Protective Factors Project (AI-SUPERPFP)** is a rare large-scale survey of 3,084 Southwest and Northern Plains Indians from two tribal groups living near or on home reservations. Tribal members between the ages of 15 and 54 years old were randomly sampled to determine the prevalence of common *DSM-IV* disorders and help-seeking patterns (Beals et al., 2005).

With sizable survey data sets, attention is given to disaggregate groups in terms of ethnicity and culture (e.g., Chinese, Filipino, Vietnamese; Puerto Rican, Mexican, Cuban; Northern Plains Indians and Southwest Indians; or African American and Black Caribbean). Immigration and other cultural variables are included in these studies such as nativity (U.S.-born or foreign-born), years of residence in the United States, language proficiency, age at the time of migration, and generational status. This information is invaluable in gaining insight into multiple variables that may influence the development and prevention of psychological distress and in helping improve the cultural appropriateness of services.

Major Disorders in Ethnic Minority Populations

Although it is beyond the scope of this text to provide a comprehensive examination of the broad array of disorders that may exist within a given population, to get a general picture of psychological distress we can look at a sample of common disorders (e.g., depression, anxiety, and substance use disorders) in terms of their impact on ethnic minorities.

Major Depression Major depression has been examined in a number of epidemiological studies. According to the *DSM-5* (American Psychiatric Association, 2013), the primary symptoms of major depression include depressed mood, an inability for at least the past two weeks to experience pleasure from activities that normally bring enjoyment, plus at least four other psychological symptoms (e.g., feelings of hopelessness, worthlessness, guilt, or suicidal thoughts) and physiological symptoms (e.g., sleep disturbance, appetite changes, attention and concentration difficulties, fatigue). Generally most experts concur that major depression is one of the most common, costly, and disabling of mental disorders on a global level (Compton, Conway, Stinson, & Grant, 2006; Grant et al., 2004). Major depressive disorder held the highest **lifetime prevalence** (i.e., the total number or percentage of individuals in a population who have experienced a particular disorder at some point in their life) of the specific disorders reported in the NCS-R (Kessler et al., 2005). Gender differences are documented for this disorder, with lifetime prevalence of 15 percent for men, compared to 35 percent for women (Kessler et al., 1994). Comparative analyses of data from two large cross-sectional studies indicate that prevalence rates of depression have increased over the past five decades (Compton et al., 2006). This increase was especially significant for Whites, Blacks, and Hispanics. Although a significant increase in prevalence was noted for Hispanics overall, Hispanic men and young Hispanic women (between the ages of 18 and 29) did not demonstrate a significant increase compared to other groups.

In a national sample of approximately 67,500 persons, among adults age 18 or older, the past-year prevalence of major depressive episode was highest among individuals reporting two or more races (10.1 percent), followed by American Indians or Alaska Natives (9.4 percent), Whites (7.6 percent), Hispanics (7.0 percent), and Blacks (6.5 percent) and was lowest for Asian Americans (3.6 percent) (Substance Abuse and Mental Health Services Administration, 2006). These findings support our earlier discussion, in Chapter 5, of the complex relationship between individuals of multiple-race identity and adjustment. Further attention must be focused on multiracial individuals to deepen our understanding of the individual, group, and social factors that may be related to a greater percentage reporting major depression. Looking at the lower level of reported cases, one could initially conclude that the occurrence of major depression in Asian Americans is relatively low. However, in the National Survey on Drug Use and Health (as reported by the Substance Abuse and Mental Health Services Administration, 2006), Asian Americans are not disaggregated into different subgroups (e.g., Vietnamese, Chinese, Japanese Americans); thus, it is difficult to discern how rates of depression might vary between them. For the relatively few studies that actually do examine group-specific rates of depression, the findings can be quite surprising; Southeast Asian refugees, for instance, show rates of depression that are significantly higher than those of the general U.S. population (Abueg & Chun, 1996), underscoring the need for more sophisticated prevalence data on the mental health of Asian Americans.

It is worth more closely examining certain groups' associated risks and protective factors to major depression. In a study on racial and ethnic disparities in depression treatment (Alegría et al., 2008), the authors analyze CPES data from a nationally representative sample of 8,762 persons, finding that significant differences exist in the access to and quality of care for depression in ethnic and racial minority populations. Compared to non-Latino Whites, ethnic minority groups were less likely to receive access to any depression treatment even after controlling for the effects of socioeconomic variables such as poverty, insurance coverage, and education. Specifically, for individuals with depressive disorder, 40.2 percent of non-Latino Whites failed to access any mental health treatment, compared to 63.7 percent of Latinos, 68.7 percent of Asian Americans, and 58.8 percent of African Americans. Alegría and colleagues (2008) propose several factors as possible explanations for these access problems, including the significant underdetection of depression among less acculturated patients and other minority groups (e.g., Rehm et al., 1999), concerns about loss of income that may occur while undergoing treatment, or the stigma that accompanies mental illness (e.g., Schraufnagel, Wagner, Miranda, Peter, & Roy-Byrne, 2006). In addition, Alegría et al. (2008) find that even when treatment was obtained, most people received inadequate care, especially African Americans and Asian Americans in the sample. Overall, Latinos, Asian Americans, and African Americans with depression were 9–23 percentage points less likely to receive care and adequate treatment for their depression compared to non-Latino Whites.

In a recent study, psychosocial predictors for major depressive disorder were examined in a national sample of male Latinos (Ai, Pappas, & Simonsen, 2015). Analyses of NLAAS data indicate that negative interactions within families served as a risk factor for major depression in these men. Family discord was also a strong predictor for suicidal ideation (thoughts about killing oneself). Interestingly, in a parallel study conducted with Latinas, researchers found that negative family interactions predicated generalized anxiety disorder and, to a lesser degree, suicidal ideation rather than major depression (Ai, Weiss, & Ficham, 2014). The researchers suggest gender differences might be due to cultural expectations: Latino men may perceive conflicts and disputes within their families as a personal failure, and this can lead to a great sense of sadness. Latinas, however, may be expected to attend to their family needs more than men may be, which Latinas achieved through positive relationships with children, spouse, and family network in this type of family-centered culture. Hence, family discord may become a stressor for Latinas that leads them to experience more anxiety (Ai et al., 2015).

Anxiety, Obsessive-Compulsive, and Trauma- and Stressor-Related Disorders Several different disorders constitute the class of anxiety disorders in the *DSM-5*, including panic disorder, agoraphobia, social phobia, specific phobia, and generalized anxiety disorder (American Psychiatric

Association, 2013). Obsessive-compulsive disorder and post-traumatic stress disorder (PTSD) had originally been categorized within the major grouping of anxiety disorders in previous diagnostic manuals. This is because, although the disorders have their own distinctive characteristics, most share in common the presence of excessive worrying, nervousness or fear, and persistent uncomfortable psychological and physical symptoms of stress or arousal. Moreover, these symptoms produce significant impairment in the person's life. When classified together, these disorders were the most prevalent of all classes of disorders in their national survey, with lifetime prevalence of 28.8 percent, compared to 20.8 percent for mood disorders and 24.8 percent for substance use disorders (Kessler et al., 2005).

Studies on anxiety and trauma- and stressor-related disorders in Asian American and American Indian populations have been limited compared to those studies that have examined depression (e.g., Gee, 2004; Safren et al., 2000). However, some compelling findings have emerged when specific groups within these minority populations are evaluated. For instance, previous studies on Asian Americans have focused on acculturative stress associated with the experiences of recent immigrants and refugees (Iwamasa, 1997; Lee, Lei, & Sue, 2001). These individuals are particularly susceptible to increased anxiety as they adjust to a new cultural environment in the United States. Southeast Asian refugees are especially at risk for PTSD, in addition to depression, due to their experiences of multiple traumas and stressors spanning four different time periods (Abueg & Chun, 1996).

First, Southeast Asian refugees were exposed to *premigration traumas*, or traumas in their home countries during the Vietnam War era. Such traumas centered on experiences of death and destruction from combat and civil discord, including witnessing the killings of close family members, being separated from their families, losing personal property, and facing political persecution by the government. For instance, former members of the South Vietnamese military were forcibly imprisoned in "reeducation camps," where they faced starvation, hard labor, and torture because of their wartime activities with American troops (Chun et al., 1994). Also, Cambodians faced mass genocide from 1975 to 1979, losing approximately a third of their entire national population under the oppressive rule of Pol Pot and the Khmer Rouge (Kinzie et al., 1990).

Upon fleeing their countries, Southeast Asian refugees then had to cope with *migration traumas*, or traumas incurred during their exodus from their home countries. Such traumas included escaping while being shot at and pursued by the military, fleeing on crowded and unsafe boats, and enduring attacks by pirates who preyed on refugees on the open seas. The large wave of Vietnamese refugees who escaped war-torn Vietnam in the late 1970s and early 1980s, known as the Vietnamese "boat people" in the popular media, suffered greatly from migration-related traumas, with an estimated 200,000 dying at sea (Lee & Lu, 1989).

Next, Southeast Asian refugees endured *encampment traumas and stressors*, or traumas and stressors associated with living in unsafe and unsanitary refugee camps scattered throughout Southeast and East Asia. Refugees applied for entry to countries around the globe while being detained in these camps, often waiting for several months before they knew their fate. Living conditions in the worst camps were highly stressful and dangerous, with refugees being subjected to overcrowding, robbery, rape, and assault (Mollica, 1994).

Finally, Southeast Asian refugees faced *postmigration stressors*, or stressors associated with adjusting to a new cultural environment. As noted throughout this text, these types of stressors are typically classified as *acculturative stressors* and can include pressures to learn a new language and new cultural norms, and any other difficulties in establishing a new life in an unfamiliar country.

As you might expect, the cumulative effects of these four types of traumas and stressors have contributed to some of the highest rates of anxiety disorders and other mental health problems observed for any ethnic minority group. For instance, reported percentages of Southeast Asian psychiatric patients who are diagnosed with PTSD are in excess of 80–90 percent, particularly for the most traumatized refugee groups like the Hmong and Mien (Abueg & Chun, 1996).

Another Asian American group in which problems of anxiety have been noted is college students. Lee and colleagues (2001) highlight a number of studies spanning more than two decades in which findings suggest heightened anxiety symptoms as well as loneliness, isolation, and social interaction difficulties among Asian American students compared to White American students.

In the AI-SUPERPFP (Beals et al., 2005), the most prevalent disorder for American Indian women was post-traumatic stress disorder, while alcohol abuse and dependence were the most common disorders for men. For women in the Southwest tribe, anxiety disorders were more prevalent than either substance use disorders or depressive disorders. However, for Northern Plains women, rates of anxiety and substance use disorders were comparable, and rates of both types of disorders were higher than rates of depressive disorders. The authors note how the historical impact of disease and conflict coupled with the documented high rate of accidents and other frequent traumas within American Indian communities may lead to a greater vulnerability to reexperiencing painful and stressful life events through the expression of PTSD symptoms (Beals et al., 2005).

Attention has also been focused on greater risk of PTSD in Hispanic Americans (Pole, Best, Metzler, & Marmar, 2005). For instance, six months after exposure to Hurricane Andrew, Spanish-speaking Latinos had a significantly higher prevalence rate of PTSD than did African Americans and Whites in a sample of South Florida residents (Perilla, Norris, & Lavizzo, 2002). Similarly, analyses of surveys conducted following the terrorist attacks of September 11, 2001, indicate that 14 percent of Hispanic American residents of New York developed PTSD, compared to 9 percent of African American and 7 percent of White residents (Galea et al., 2002). In addition to heightened risk for PTSD, greater severity of symptoms has been reported among Hispanics diagnosed with PTSD. For example, Hispanic veterans with PTSD reported, on average, more severe symptoms than did veterans of other ethnic groups (Alcántara, Casement, & Lewis-Fernández, 2013), and surveys revealed elevated PTSD symptoms among Hispanic police officers compared to non-Hispanic Whites and African American police officers (Pole et al., 2005).

Explanations for susceptibility to PTSD in Hispanics have included the possible higher presence of dissociative symptoms (i.e., symptoms of an altered state of conscious awareness) as an initial reaction to trauma in Latin American cultures—and dissociation is one of the strongest predictors for later onset of PTSD (Escobar, 1995; Ozer, Best, Lipsey, & Weiss, 2003; Pole et al., 2005). Another explanation offered is that Latinos who maintain a closer adherence to their cultures of origin may tend to view trauma as an inevitable and unchangeable consequence of life (Perilla, Norris, & Levizzo, 2002). Pole and colleagues (2005) suspect that such fatalistic beliefs could potentially impact post-traumatic coping, and this in turn would lead to less effective means of coping among less acculturated Hispanics and heighten the group's sensitivity to PTSD.

As noted earlier, African Americans were found to have generally comparable rates of mental disorders to Whites in the large-scale ECA study when socioeconomic and other demographic factors are controlled (Robins & Regier, 1991). However, among individual anxiety disorders, Zhang and Snowden (1999) find that African Americans were more likely to suffer from phobic disorders than were Whites. Others have reported higher rates of panic disorder (Neal & Turner, 1991) and somatization disorder (multiple physical symptoms with unknown physical causes that are felt to be related to stressors) in African American communities than in other communities (Robins & Regier, 1991; Zhang & Snowden, 1999). Furthermore, findings from descriptive studies have suggested the experience and expression of anxiety symptoms in African Americans are significantly influenced by culture and adaptation in highly stressed environments (Heurtin-Roberts, Snowden, & Miller, 1997).

Substance-Related and Addictive Disorders The term *substance* is used in the *DSM-5* to refer to a variety of drugs that can alter our physical and mental functioning, including prescribed or over-the-counter medications and illegal drugs (American Psychiatric Association, 2013). *Substance use disorder* is considered a maladaptive pattern of behavior in which individuals rely on a drug excessively and persistently to the point that it negatively impacts their personal relationships, occupation, or welfare or the lives of others (American Psychiatric Association, 2013). *Substance-induced disorders* can demonstrate a more advanced pattern that includes the abuse of the drug that leads to intoxication as well as physical changes in the body's response to the drug, such as *tolerance* (where a person needs more and more of the substance to achieve the desired effect) and *withdrawal* (the experience of uncomfortable and even dangerous symptoms when the person tries to either completely discontinue the drug or reduce the amount of drug intake) (American Psychiatric Association, 2013).

In 2005, among individuals 12 years of age and older, the highest rate of substance disorders was among American Indians or Alaska Natives (21.0 percent) (Substance Abuse and Mental Health Services Administration, 2006). The lowest rate of dependence or abuse was among Asians (4.5 percent), whereas comparable rates were reported by Native Hawai'ians or Other Pacific Islanders (11.0 percent), individuals reporting two or more races (10.9 percent), Whites (9.4 percent), Hispanics (9.3 percent), and Blacks (8.5 percent) (Substance Abuse and Mental Health Services Administration, 2006). The elevated rate in American Indians and Alaska Natives relative to other groups is consistent with earlier studies that indicated high rates of substance use problems in American Indian communities—especially alcohol dependence in men (e.g., Kinzie et al., 1992; Kunitz et al., 1999).

Beals and colleagues (2005) examined sex differences in prevalence rates of substance use disorders in American Indians. Although substance use disorders were significantly more prevalent than were either anxiety or depressive disorders in men, as stated previously, anxiety disorders were either more prevalent or comparable to substance use disorders in women.

Dual Diagnosis In our opening vignette, Jerome, in order to deal with his painful feelings of distress, thinks that he needs "a couple drinks . . . or maybe more." If his drinking alcohol to cope with mental anguish becomes routine, excessive, and disruptive, one could question whether Jerome is actually dealing with the problems of abuse and addiction in combination with his poor mood state. When patients are determined to be suffering from more than one disorder, they are said to have **comorbid (co-occurring) disorders**. Comorbidity among psychiatric disorders appears to be high. For example, in the NCS, 56 percent of the respondents with a history of at least one disorder had two or more disorders (Kessler et al., 1994). In the NCS-R, 27.7 percent of respondents had two or more disorders in their lifetime, and 17.3 percent had three or more (Kessler et al., 2005). In the fields of psychiatry and psychology, co-occurring disorder (previously referred to as **dual diagnosis**) is commonly used when describing a person who has a mental disorder and a substance-related disorder (as well as the term **mentally ill and chemical abuser**, or **MICA**). This is because of the well-documented association between mental and substance use disorders. For example, in a national survey of adults, substance use disorders were significantly more common among individuals with mental health problems (e.g., depression, anxiety) than among individuals without these problems: Close to half of the respondents with a substance use disorder had mental health problems, compared with approximately a quarter of all adults (Harris & Edlund, 2005). Moreover, serious mental illness was more than three times higher among adults who had a substance use disorder (Harris & Edlund, 2005).

In the 2014 National Survey on Drug Use and Health (NSDUH) approximately 7.9 million adults 18 years of age and older in the United States had co-occurring disorders (Center for Behavioral Health Statistics and Quality, 2015). The percentage of adults who had a co-occurring substance use disorder was highest among those aged 18–25 (29.3 percent), followed by those aged 26–49 (20.8 percent). These individuals present as some of the most challenging and difficult to manage. In an earlier report, it was noted that, among the estimated cases, less than half (47.0 percent) received treatment for either their mental health disorder or substance use disorder, while far fewer (8.5 percent) received assistance for both mental and substance use disorders. When treatment is provided, it is more than likely for mental health problems rather than substance use problems (Substance Abuse and Mental Health Services Administration, 2006).

Generally, dually diagnosed cases tend to have a poorer prognosis, due to the multiplicative effects of symptoms from more than one disorder, as well as to related psychosocial factors that can impair treatment effectiveness. Many of these factors are present in the high-risk groups discussed earlier in the chapter, such as poverty, homelessness, acting-out behavior, likelihood of criminal history, and problems in social interactions (Bartels et al., 1993).

It is difficult to determine the actual number of ethnic minorities who have co-occurring disorders. It is often challenging to adequately tap into these cases in large-scale surveys. However, findings from the AI-SUPERPFP indicate significant levels of comorbidity among those American Indians with depressive and/or anxiety and substance use disorders (Beals et al., 2005). In clinical settings, it is not unusual for dually diagnosed persons to hide their drug abuse problem or for clinicians to fail to detect the symptoms and as a result underdiagnose this group. Patients may feel compelled to suppress their level of substance abuse due to pragmatic financial reasons in addition to the psychosocial ones. Many treatment agencies receive financial support to treat either mental disorders or substance abuse; only some are equipped and willing to treat both (Sciacca & Thompson, 1996). As such, it is not atypical for the MICA patient to be rejected as inappropriate for treatment in both substance abuse and mental health facilities; these are the people most likely to fall through the cracks, and they deteriorate even further and lose whatever tenuous stability they might have had.

Cultural Influences on the Explanation and Expression of Psychological Distress

Most of the studies reviewed in this chapter have primarily focused on Western expressions of psychological distress and symptoms of major disorders commonly recognized in the United States and in most parts of the world. Although it is necessary to have comparable descriptors of illness across groups in order to compare rates of disorder, there is the concern that we may underestimate rates of mental distress among members of ethnic groups who may express problems in culturally unique ways not commonly seen or not fully understood by many psychologists and other mental health service providers trained in the United States.

The need for increased attention on culture's influence on psychopathology was recognized in the development of the *DSM-IV* and *DSM-5.* López and Guarnaccia (2000) describe the efforts of a National Institute of Mental Health–funded task force charged with developing recommendations for how to incorporate a "cultural perspective" throughout the manual. Three primary contributions were published in the *DSM-IV-TR* (American Psychiatric Association, 2000):

1. the inclusion of how cultural factors can influence the expression, assessment, and prevalence of specific disorders
2. an *outline for cultural formulation* (OCF) of clinical diagnosis to complement the multiaxial assessment
3. a glossary of relevant cultural-bound syndromes (symptom constellations specific to the culture in which they occur) from around the world (López & Guarnaccia, 2000, p. 576)

Although many felt that the *DSM-IV-TR* made some advancement in its recognition of cultural influences on mental health compared to previous editions, some criticism was offered that additional task force recommendations were not addressed and that cultural issues continue to be peripheral in terms of their limited discussion throughout the text and the placement of the relatively brief outline of cultural formation (which lists cultural topics to consider in formulating diagnosis) and a list of culture-bound syndromes in an appendix (López & Guarnaccia, 2000). Still, the inclusion of culture-bound syndromes generated research on these disorders and encouraged clinicians to consider the importance of acculturation and emic cultural expressions of psychological distress (Marín et al., 2003). In addition, over the past two decades, experience and research with the OCF has led to the development of the Cultural Formulation Interview included in the *DSM-5* and described in the following.

The American Psychiatric Association (2013) maintains that even more effort was made to consider cultural issues in the development of the *DSM-5.* Criteria for various disorders were updated to reflect cross-cultural presentations of symptoms and expression of distress. For example, diagnosis should consider the variation in primary somatic and physiological symptoms across cultures in panic attacks (e.g., headaches, uncontrollable crying in one culture versus difficulty breathing in another culture). Further, the *DSM-5* introduced the Cultural Formulation Interview (CFI) to assist the clinician in obtaining further clarity about cultural influences on behavior. Culture-related syndromes as well as cultural idioms of distress, the cultural ways in which distress is communicated or expressed, are presented to facilitate understanding of cultural explanations of symptoms.

The CFI is a 16-question, scripted, semi-structured interview. Informants from the individual's family or extended social network can also provide information on items. Central to the interview is getting a sense of the client's cultural definition of the problem—what they believe may have caused the problem, any support available, cultural issues that may affect the client's ability to cope, and past and present help-seeking, including barriers to obtaining assistance. Twelve supplementary modules can be administered to gather more in-depth information about the items (American Psychiatric Association, 2013; Flett, 2014). Based on their review of research conducted on the OCF, Lewis-Fernandez and colleagues (2014) recommend that standardized training is needed if we are to expect large-scale use of assessment interviews like the CFI. This training can include the development of case stimulations, video vignettes illustrating the CFI in practice, and inclusion of the CFI in psychiatric and applied training curricula. Such systematic instruction will lead to better inquiry into whether direct cultural assessment may lead to more valid diagnosis, effective treatment, and better patient satisfaction and adherence to intervention.

Culture-related syndromes refer to recurrent patterns of unusual behavior and distressing experiences that are typically exhibited in certain areas of the world (American Psychiatric Association, 2013). Although a syndrome may be limited to a certain geographic location or cultural group, it is still considered problematic and may be known by a specific name by those who are likely to suffer from it. What is important to know about these disorders is that many consider their origin, manifestation, and response to social or therapeutic interventions to be heavily influenced by cultural factors within specific, localized societies or cultural groups—hence the term *culture-bound* was used in the previous DSM manual (American Psychiatric Association, 2013). The *DSM-5* includes several examples of cultural syndromes and idioms of distress, but, as noted above, these disorders are described within an appendix when using the manual (see Box 10.1 for examples).

Scientific study on culture-related syndromes has been limited. For many years, social scientists such as Yap (1974) and Guarnaccia and Rogler (1999) have argued that limited research in this area is problematic given the significant number of immigrants who live in the United States. Clinicians are compelled to know what the latest research suggests in order to make accurate and appropriate diagnoses and to develop useful interventions for these disorders. Moreover, the *Diagnostic and Statistical Manual of Mental Disorders* has become increasingly popular internationally. Continuing efforts to increase our understanding of expressions of distress at a cross-cultural level will sustain the utility and significance of the *DSM* within the United States and abroad (Guarnaccia & Rogler, 1999).

It is essential to research that we ask what the relationship of cultural syndromes and idioms of distress is to the *DSM-5* disorders. Our ability to respond to such a query would require a systematic program of research that attempts to address the nature of a syndrome and its relationship to psychiatric disorders (Guarnaccia & Rogler, 1999). The first step would require investigation of the nature of the phenomenon in terms of its distinguishing characteristics. Extensive review of the literature for studies of a particular syndrome is necessary. One should not assume, however, that a disorder's appearance within the literature provides confirmation of its existence. It would be important to also tap into the familiarity and knowledge of a syndrome within a culture—that is, investigate whether members of a particular group recognize (or have experienced) a specific syndrome. This recognition is what is termed *salience of a phenomenon* (Guarnaccia & Rogler, 1999). Investigation through thorough descriptive studies conducted with members of the culture can further document the nature of the characteristics and symptoms or even subtypes that constitute the disorder.

As noted earlier, cultural syndromes are thought to reflect the social and cultural characteristics of the people most likely to be afflicted. As such, research should be designed to illuminate these social and cultural features so that clinicians may know who is at greatest risk (Guarnaccia & Rogler, 1999). The study of these cultural aspects of psychopathology should continue to inspire mental health professionals to go beyond merely describing "rare" and "exotic" cultural syndromes and instead seriously consider culture's profound influence on a broad range of disorders, including those that are well known, so that they can provide culturally competent care (Tseng, 2006).

Box 10.1

Examples of Cultural Concepts of Distress and Cultural Syndromes

***Ataque de nervios* ("attack of nerves")**
This syndrome is primarily reported among individuals of Latino descent. Commonly reported symptoms include uncontrollable screaming or shouting, heightened emotionality and crying spells, attacks of crying, trembling, heat in the chest rising into the head, and verbal or physical aggression. Dissociative experiences (e.g., depersonalization, amnesic episodes), seizure-like or fainting episodes, and suicidal gestures are prominent in some attacks but absent in others. "A general feature of an *ataque de nervios* is a sense of being out of control" (p. 833). Attacks may frequently occur as a direct result of a stressful event. In fewer cases, no particular event may have triggered the attack; instead, the patient's vulnerability to losing control comes from the accumulated experience of suffering.

***Dhat* syndrome**
This term originated in South Asia as a cultural explanation for patients who refer to a broad array of "symptoms such as anxiety, fatigue, weakness, weight loss, impotence, and other multiple somatic complaints, and depressive mood" (p. 833). This is often clinically presented in young male patients who attribute their various symptoms to semen loss. Key features are anxiety and distress about the loss of *dhat* in the absence of any identifiable physiological dysfunction.

***Khyâl cap* ("wind attacks")**
This "syndrome is found among Cambodians in the United States and Cambodia. Common symptoms include those of panic attacks, such as dizziness, heart palpitations, shortness of breath, and cold extremities, as well as other symptoms of anxiety and autonomic arousal" (p. 834). Attacks include stressful thoughts focused on the fear that *khyâl* (a windlike substance) will rise in the body along with blood and produce many of the panic-like symptoms. *Khyâl* attacks may arise without any specific trigger, but many are often precipitated by worrisome thoughts, dizziness upon rising (i.e., orthostasis), offensive odors, and panic feelings associated with being confined in crowds or closed-in spaces (i.e., agoraphobic-like triggers).

***Kufungisisa* ("thinking too much")**
This is a cultural idiom of distress among the Shona of Zimbabwe and cultural explanation for the cause of anxiety, depression, and somatic problems—"e.g., my heart is painful because I think too much" (p. 834). As an idiom of emotional and bodily distress, it is indicative of interpersonal and social difficulties about upsetting thoughts, particularly worries (e.g., marital problems, family problems, economic stressors). As the name implies, rumination, particularly over upsetting thoughts or worries, is one of the central features of *kufungisisa*.

***Maladi moun* ("humanly caused illness" or "sent sickness")**
In Haitian communities *maladi moun* is a cultural explanation for a diversity of medical and psychological disorders caused by interpersonal negative feelings such as envy, jealousy, or hate. These feelings can cause people to harm their adversaries by sending them illnesses such as depression, psychosis, inability to function well on a daily basis, and social and academic failure. The more outwardly successful the person is, the more vulnerable they may be to an illness attack.

***Susto* ("fright")**
Susto comes from the Spanish word for "fright" to describe a sudden intense fear, as of something immediately threatening. It "is a cultural explanation for distress and misfortunate among some Latinos in the United States and among people in Mexico, Central America, and South America" (p. 836). People believe that if a person is suffering from *susto*, their soul is separated from the body, and this leads to sadness, illness, and poor social functioning. Physical symptoms of *susto* can include nervousness, loss of appetite, insomnia, listlessness, muscle tics, cold in the extremities, headache, stomachache, and diarrhea. Emotional and psychosocial symptoms reported include low self-worth or feeling dirty, interpersonal sensitivity, and lack of initiative.

Source: American Psychiatric Association, 2013.

Service Utilization

Underutilization of services is a noted problem in the broad national surveys. Kessler and colleagues (1994), for example, report that less than 40 percent of individuals with a reported disorder during their lifetime had ever received professional treatment and that only 20 percent with a recent disorder had received treatment during the 12 months immediately prior to the research survey. While barriers may exist to some degree for many people living in the United States, there are added obstacles that are specific and more extreme in ethnic minority populations—immigration and acculturation factors, limited economic resources, possible bias and mistrust of mental health professionals, communication barriers, and limited culturally acceptable (or appropriate) treatment interventions.

Selected Factors Influencing Effective Delivery of Mental Health Services

Immigration and Acculturation Factors

A methodological limitation of many of the national epidemiological studies is the reliance on proxy variables (e.g., nativity, increasing years of U.S. residency, language spoken, generation of respondent) to approximate acculturation status. Although not ideal for an in-depth understanding of acculturation as a complex multidimensional process (Marín et al., 2003), these variables do shed light on the importance of cultural and immigration factors in predicting utilization and satisfaction with help received.

Findings regarding utilization are complicated for certain groups. For example, early studies on Asian Americans indicated an underutilization of mental health services (Leong, 1986; Uba, 1994). Yet in a later study Barreto and Segal (2005) concluded that Asian Americans' utilization is much more complex due to significant diversity among the different Asian American subgroups. Based on client and service records in the California Department of Mental Health, East Asians (Chinese, Japanese, and Koreans) used more services than Southeast Asians (Cambodians, Laotians, and Vietnamese), Filipinos, and other Asian groups (Asian Indians, Guamians, Hawai'ian Natives, Samoans, and others) (Barreto & Segal, 2005). In addition, the highest number of patients with a diagnosis of schizophrenia was in the East Asian group, which is consistent with other reports indicating that Asian Americans may eventually use psychiatric services when their symptoms reach a certain point of significant severity (Sue, Sue, Sue, & Takeuchi, 1998). Nevertheless, the finding of greater utilization among East Asians was still significant even when diagnosis was taken into account (Barreto & Segal, 2005). Although Barreto and Segal (2005) did not directly assess the impact of acculturation on utilization, they note that the Asian American subgroups demonstrating the highest level of underutilization are members of populations that are historically more recent in their arrivals to the United States. Furthermore, they speculate that educational achievement is related to service utilization in that the groups with lower levels of attainment (e.g., Southeast Asians) are less likely to use mental health services than those higher in attainment (e.g., East Asians and Filipinos).

A similar pattern of findings is noted in the NLAAS (Abe-Kim et al., 2007), where use of mental health–related services was examined during a 12-month period. In a study of 2,095 Asian American adults (Chinese, Filipino, and Vietnamese participants were targeted, but the sample included individuals of other Asian ancestry), respondents were questioned about their service use and satisfaction with care. They were also assessed for the presence of any psychiatric disorder during the 12-month period according to the *DSM-IV* criteria. Abe-Kim and colleagues (2007) report that Asian Americans appeared to have lower rates of seeking service compared to the general population; 8.6 percent of Asian Americans sought service, while 17.9 percent of the general population sought service according to data from the NCS-R (Wang, Lane, Olfson, Pincus, & Kessler, 2005). Differences in service utilization were noted between U.S.-born Asian Americans and immigrant individuals: Those born in the United States used mental health services at a higher rate than did those who emigrated from abroad (Abe-Kim et al., 2007). Furthermore, generational differences were noted, with third generation respondents being more similar in their service use to the general population, while second generation respondents were more similar to immigrants. Perception of helpfulness of care was also influenced by immigration status: Higher ratings were given by U.S.-born Asian Americans than by immigrants.

Alegría and colleagues (2007) studied the patterns of recent mental health service use among Latinos living in the United States, along with their perceptions of satisfaction with help received. Using data from the NLAAS, four Latino groups—Cuban, Puerto Rican, Mexican, and "other Latino"—were distinguished. Findings indicate overall mental health service use and specialty mental health services (e.g., professional mental health service providers seen in mental health clinics) were significantly higher in Puerto Ricans than in all other Latino groups, with close to one in five Puerto Ricans (19.9 percent) reporting past-year services, compared to one in 10 Mexicans (10.1 percent). Foreign-born Latinos and those who primarily spoke Spanish reported less use of specialty mental health services than did U.S.-born Latinos and those who primarily spoke English, but there were no significant differences in the use of general medical services (e.g., general practitioners, family doctors, or nurses) for mental health problems. In addition, those who had lived in the United States for less than 10 years had significantly lower service use compared to those who had lived in the country for 21 years or more. Mexicans reported lower satisfaction with mental health services than did those in the "other Latino" group. Immigrants who had lived in the United States for five or fewer years reported lower levels of satisfaction with services than did those who had lived in the United States for more than 20 years. Overall, results indicate that cultural factors such as nativity, language, and years of residence in the United States related to mental health service utilization among Latinos. However, another factor—the presence of past-year psychiatric diagnoses—was also important in determining service. These findings only held up when respondents did not meet the criteria for any psychiatric disorders assessed. Puerto Ricans and U.S.-born Latinos still reported higher rates of mental health services than did other Latino subgroups and foreign-born Latinos. Alegría and colleagues (2007) note that cultural and immigration factors are especially important to consider for those Latinos who require preventative or screening services or who are symptomatic but do not yet fulfill criteria to warrant a psychiatric diagnosis.

Chen and Vargas-Busamante (2011) analyzed data from the Medical Expenditure Survey and the National Health Interview Survey from 2002 to 2006. They find that immigrants were significantly less likely to have visited a provider compared to U.S.-born citizens. In addition, analyses suggest that a major deterrent is immigrants' access to care and health care coverage. Improvements in eligibility and accessibility could have significant effects in reducing disparities between U.S.-born citizens and immigrants.

Studies on the role of immigration status or nativity have typically examined Asian or Latino groups. However, as Miranda and colleagues (Miranda, Siddique, Belin, & Kohn-Wood, 2004) note, the Black population of the United States is becoming increasingly diverse. The percentage of foreign-born Blacks in the overall Black population increased from 1.3 to 7.8 percent between 1970 and 2000, with most of the immigrants coming from countries in the Caribbean and Africa (Population Reference Bureau, 2002). Miranda and colleagues (2004) compared the prevalence rates of depression, somatization (physical complaints and ailments), alcohol use, and drug use in a large sample of low-income women who were born in the United States, the Caribbean, or Africa. Results of analyses from data gathered in screening interviews indicate that U.S.-born Black women were 2.94 times more likely to experience depression than were the African-born women and 2.49 times more likely than the Caribbean-born women. Rates of somatization were comparable across all three groups of women. Reported alcohol and drug problems were very low among all groups, with only 1 percent of the women reporting drug or alcohol problems. Similarly, data from the NSAL indicate that increasing years of U.S. residency was associated with increased risk for psychiatric disorders: Black Caribbean immigrants had lower rates of mental disorders than did U.S.-born Black Caribbeans, and Caribbean Black women had lower 12-month and lifetime prevalence rates for anxiety and substance disorders than did African American women (Williams et al., 2007). Even among Caribbean Blacks, first generation Blacks had lower rates of psychiatric disorders compared to U.S.-born Caribbean Blacks. Further, higher generational status was significantly associated with increased risk for disorder. Overall, these results are consistent with studies that compare other U.S.-born ethnic groups (e.g., Mexican Americans, Asian Americans) with their foreign-born counterparts (e.g., Mexican immigrants, Asian immigrants): The longer one lives in the United States may relate to an increased need for mental health services.

Despite this risk, further analyses of NSAL data do not confirm that utilization matches need. Jackson and colleagues (2007) report that African Americans and Caribbean Blacks used formal mental health care services at relatively low rates. In addition, other researchers have noted the tendency of ethnic minorities (e.g., Blacks and Asian Americans) to access mental health services when symptoms become so severe that they warrant urgent or crisis intervention (Sue et al., 1998). Because symptoms of mental illness may occur early in one's life, the ability to access preventative care as well as therapeutic care is critical to long-term prognosis.

Sun and colleagues (Sun, Hoyt, Brockberg, Lam, & Tiwari, 2016) note that the relationship between racial and ethnic minorities' connection with their culture and U.S. culture has generally only a small association with their help-seeking attitudes. However, extensive analyses suggest that this conclusion differs among the various racial and ethnic groups. For instance, culture-based values of self-control and conformity to social norms may be associated with less favorable attitudes toward seeking psychological help among people of Asian descent.

Limited Economic Resources

Financial costs of mental health services can serve as a major deterrent to health care. Similar to physical health access barriers discussed in Chapter 9, ethnic minorities are often plagued by being uninsured—especially the working poor who may not qualify for public assistance but do not earn adequate mental health coverage through benefits. In 2001, the report from the Surgeon General stated that Hispanic Americans are the least likely group to have health insurance (public or private), with a rate of uninsurance at 37 percent, a rate twice that for Whites (U.S. Department of Health and Human Services, 2001).

Lack of adequate health insurance is related to lack of treatment for the major disorders reviewed earlier, including depression (Harman, Edlund, & Fortney, 2004). However, Snowden and Thomas (2000) suggest that the relationship between poverty and mental health treatment, especially in mental health specialty clinics, is not as clear-cut as has been assumed. They note that many poor individuals are able to access care through Medicaid, which provides significant financial support to poor individuals in need of mental health care. In their study, data from a representative sample indicate no significant differences in likelihood of receiving outpatient treatment between African Americans on Medicaid and Whites, but insured African Americans were significantly less likely to receive care (Snowden & Thomas, 2000). This finding suggests that those in the lowest income bracket may be prompted (most likely by serious illnesses) to obtain treatment within public service institutions that must provide treatment to underserved populations (although there is still the question of quality treatment afforded to those who are poor). Yet those who are just outside eligibility for services (e.g., the working poor) may end up with very poor service utilization. Complicating matters, logistical or practical barriers associated with poverty, such as working extended hours and lack of childcare and transportation, further prevent many impoverished ethnic minority families from utilizing essential mental health services (Chun & Akutsu, 1999) and health services in general (Bor et al., 2017).

Clinician Bias and Client Mistrust

Clinician bias plays a significant role in patient diagnosis and treatment. If a person is misdiagnosed, then treatment will likely fail and the patient may be at risk for problems becoming worse as a result of delayed or inappropriate treatment. A number of studies have consistently found evidence that certain groups are less likely to receive appropriate diagnoses. For example, African Americans are more likely to receive diagnoses that are more severe, in terms of level and duration of illness (e.g., schizophrenia), than diagnoses that may be less severe or episodic in nature (e.g., mood disorder)

(López, 1989; Snowden & Cheung, 1990). In one study, African American inpatients were approximately 1.5 times as likely as Whites to be diagnosed with schizophrenia compared to being only 0.60 times as likely to be diagnosed with a mood disorder; for outpatients, the racial discrepancy was less pronounced for patients with mood disorders but was greater for those with schizophrenia (Lawson, Hepler, Holladay, & Cuffel, 1994).

Other studies have found that European Americans and Asians are more likely to receive a mood disorder diagnosis than are African Americans or Hispanics and that Asians and African Americans receive psychotic disorder diagnoses more frequently than European Americans (Foulks, 2004b). In a recent study on diagnosis and race, Schwartz and Feisthamel (2009) reported that counselors were more likely to diagnose schizophrenia and childhood disorders (e.g., attention deficit hyperactivity disorder, conduct disorder) in African Americans than in European Americans.

Whaley (2004) proposes two distinct categories of diagnostic bias: (1) **clinician bias**, defined as the failure to adhere to the diagnostic criteria during psychiatric evaluations, and (2) **cultural bias**, defined as actual ethnic or racial differences in the expression of symptoms being unnoticed or misconstrued by diagnosticians. The achievement of a valid diagnosis requires that both biases be addressed;—that is, adherence to diagnostic criteria is necessary, but attention must also be given to the cultural context in which ethnic minority behavior and emotions are expressed. Cultural bias has been offered, in part, as an explanation of the disproportionate diagnosis of certain disorders in particular ethnic groups (Feisthamel & Schwartz, 2006). Moreover, cultural bias may influence patients' perceptions of the quality of general medical care received and cultural competence of their providers (Johnson, Saha, Arbelaez, Beach, & Cooper, 2004) and raise suspicion and lack of trust toward their clinicians (Whaley, 2004).

Language Barriers

The U.S. Census Bureau recently released data from the American Community Survey indicating that the number of people (five years of age and older) who speak a language other than English at home reached its highest number to date, with an estimated 61.8 million, up 2.2 million from 2010. The largest increases from 2010 to 2013 were for speakers of Spanish, Chinese, and Arabic. Hence, approximately, one in five U.S. residents currently speaks a foreign language at home. Interestingly, of those who speak a foreign language, 25.1 million (41 percent) reported that they speak English less than very well, even though many are not immigrants. Of the approximately 62 million foreign-language speakers, 44 percent (27.2 million) were born in the United States (Camarota & Zeigler, 2014). These findings are consistent with earlier experts' predictions that a growing number of U.S. individuals will be significantly limited in their English proficiency (or will be limited English proficiency [LEP] persons) (Sturgeon, 2005).

The ability of mental health and general health care providers to communicate with and effectively treat these patients is challenging on both legal and professional grounds. In accordance with **Title VI of the 1964 Civil Rights Act**, providers receiving federal financial assistance are required to ensure the availability of appropriate and meaningful access to services even if patients have limited proficiency in English (U.S. Department of Health and Human Services, 2000).

Nonetheless, many LEP or non-English speakers have restricted access to either ethnically or linguistically similar providers (U.S. Department of Health and Human Services, 2001; Snowden, Masland, & Guerrero, 2007). These individuals typically struggle to enter, continue, and demonstrate gains in treatment (Snowden et al., 2007). In addition, they tend to require culturally adapted treatment procedures more than clients who speak English more fluently and are higher in acculturation (Sue, Fujino, Hu, Takeuchi, & Zane, 1991).

Although efforts are made to hire bilingual and bicultural providers, treatment facilities often rely on interpreters to assist in assessment and aspects of intervention. At best, formal interpreters can offer ready and critical assistance to achieve good and sound service to an increasingly diverse patient population. However, there are difficulties inherent in this strategy. Given the diversity of languages and limited number of bilingual staff, some agencies may resort to using informal interpreters (e.g., family members, nonclinical personnel) to provide translation on the spot. Iwamasa and Pai (2003) note how the use of the client's child or grandchild as translator can be in direct opposition to cultural roles assigned to family members and may even violate roles (e.g., a child placed in the position of questioning an elder may be perceived as challenging the elder's ascribed wisdom, respect, and authority). Even using formal interpreters may reduce the exposure and weaken the therapeutic bond between providers and clients, decrease patient confidentiality, lead to misunderstandings due to selective editing of translation, and increase inaccuracy in the *meaning* of what is being said (even if the actual words are accurate) (Sturgeon, 2005). Despite these challenges, research suggests that, in order to provide a minimum level of culturally appropriate intervention, the ability of the therapist or provider to communicate with clients is essential (S. Sue, Zane, Hall, & Berger, 2009).

Cultural Acceptability Barriers

Acceptability barriers focus on cultural ways that individuals and groups cope with various stressors or are encouraged or discouraged from using mental health services. There are several ways in which culture can influence the awareness of mental distress and reactions toward formal mental health care. For example, certain groups such as Asian Americans and Latinos are more likely to express psychiatric distress through somatic or physical symptoms or cultural idioms of distress. For example, for Latino immigrants, *ataque de nervios*, as described earlier in Box 10.1, may reflect cultural patterns that typically characterize maladjustment to stressors (Cortes, 2003). These types of culturally distinct expressions are intimately tied to a culture's views and beliefs about the causes of different psychological disorders. First, Ying (1990) finds that first generation Chinese immigrant women might believe that depression is caused by both somatic and psychological factors, which might explain why some Chinese Americans express their distress through bodily symptoms. It might also explain why some Chinese Americans may be more inclined to initially seek medical assistance from a physician rather than from a mental health professional to resolve their distress. Second, as noted in Chapter 7, problems may be viewed as more appropriately handled within the confines of the family rather than by outsiders. Only when symptoms become severe or acute—or the family is clearly overburdened by the stress and upheaval created by the mental disturbance—will an individual be referred to professional care (Pescosolido, Gardner, & Lubell, 1998). Third, some ethnic minorities may feel less inclined to seek services due to mistrust of health care professionals and lack of confidence that providers will be culturally sensitive to their concerns and experiences (Echeverry, 1997; Sanders Thompson, Bazile, & Akbar, 2004; Whaley, 2001).

Cultural influence is also expressed through attitudes like social stigma toward mental illness that many feel continue to be prominent in the United States. Threats to a person's ability to maintain their job, privacy, and social standing can be heightened when faced with the possibility of being ostracized for mental distress. Research indicates that Asian Americans may be reluctant to pursue mental health services because it can lead to a "loss of face," or feelings of shame and guilt, if they are perceived as being unable to perform important social roles and responsibilities (Zane & Mak, 2003).

There is a tremendous need for more empirical investigation of cultural stigma surrounding mental illness because of its potential effects on acknowledging illness, help seeking, and medication adherence (Corrigan, 2004).

In a study by Anglin, Link, and Phelan (2006), a nationally representative sample of African Americans and Caucasian adults responded to telephone interviews that included vignettes focused on a hypothetical person with a mental illness. Respondents were questioned about their attitudes, beliefs, and opinions about the person. Findings indicated that African Americans were more likely than Caucasians to believe that mentally ill persons were likely to be violent, but African Americans were also more likely to believe that the mentally ill should be given more leniencies in regard to punishment related to violence. We can also consider gender factors that highlight potential ways in which men are socialized to believe that having an illness is akin to being weak, and to idealize being strong. Some researchers suggest for certain groups there is an expectation that life is hard, so feeling blue, hopeless, or anxious at times is natural and inevitable in life (e.g., Sanders Thompson et al., 2004).

Another factor influencing acceptability is whether the person is aware that help is needed or necessary. For instance, Anglin and colleagues (Anglin, Alberti, Link, & Phelan, 2008) examined different reactions to mental health care between a nationally representative sample of White and African American participants. Respondents were given a vignette centered on people living with mental illness. They were then questioned about whether professional mental health providers could provide assistance that would be helpful. They were also asked whether mental health assistance was necessary. Results suggested that, although African Americans were more likely than were Whites to believe that mental health professionals could treat individuals with disorders such as schizophrenia and major depression, African Americans were also more likely to believe that mental health problems could heal on their own. According to these authors, a positive belief in treatment effectiveness may not be sufficient to increase service utilization among groups (e.g., African Americans) who may not believe that treatment is necessary (Anglin et al., 2008).

Breslau and colleagues (2017) examined data sampled from six years of a repeated cross-sectional survey of the U.S. civilian population (N = 232,723). Respondents were identified as perceiving a need for mental health treatment if they had received treatment within the year prior to the study or if they indicated that they had needed but did not receive treatment in that past year. Excluded were respondents who had received treatment but indicated that they had done so because of a legal requirement. Comparisons were made between three non-Hispanic groups (Whites, Blacks, and Asian Americans) and two Hispanic groups (English interviewees and Spanish-speaking interviewees). Controlling for demographic and socioeconomic characteristics and severity of illness, perception of need was less common in all racial and ethnic minority groups compared to Whites. Especially among those with serious mental illness, the largest differences were among Asian Americans and Spanish-speaking Hispanics relative to Whites.

Practical and Ethical Guidelines for Culturally Sensitive Practice

As noted throughout this textbook, when addressing psychological problems (whether they are well-known psychiatric disorders or culture-related syndromes), it will be important to approach culture beyond a simple focus on ethnoracial matters to include intersectional factors such as age, gender, sexual orientation, language, social class, religion, and disability issues. Given the changing demographics of the U.S. population, psychologists and other mental health professionals are increasingly expected to be aware of and relate to inherent cultural differences that may exist among diverse recipients of their services.

Sue and colleagues (2009) state that there are three levels in which cultural competence can be analyzed: (1) the service provider and treatment level, (2) the agency or institutional level (e.g., the planned delivery of services of a clinic, the hiring of diverse personnel, the availability of effective programs for diverse clientele), and (3) the system level (e.g., the broader institutions of care that are available in a community, such as proximate health care clinics and organizations and related community agencies, schools, and churches). Most attention has been given to this first level of analysis, examining the provider or clinician and the appropriateness and effectiveness of the treatment employed.

There are several models and definitions of culturally sensitive practice (Hall, Iwamasa, & Smith, 2003). Many include characteristics of culturally competent practitioners and basic components of effective care that promote cultural awareness. Some of the more recent definitions of culturally competent care describe it as a "system" that values the importance of culture in psychotherapy and includes assessment methods and interventions that are designed to address the unique dynamics that occur in the process of cross-cultural therapy and the needs of diverse clients (Whaley & Davis, 2007).

As presented in Chapter 1, the recently published American Psychological Association's *Multicultural Guidelines: An Ecological Approach to Context, Identity, and Intersectionality* (2017) are updated from the previously released APA guidelines on multicultural education (2003) to reflect the significant development of research and theory concerning various ethnic groups and multicultural contexts. These guidelines serve as an informative call to mental health providers to apply this knowledge and become more culturally competent in their teaching, research, consultation, or practice.

Cultural competence entails a professional approach that considers both developmental and intersectional factors that dynamically influence and shape identities and interactions between people. Hence, according to these guidelines, psychologists must consider the diversity that exists among individuals within a particular group as well as the diversity across distinctive groups. Further, they must consider that they, too, are cultural beings with attitudes, beliefs, and biases that can impact their perceptions and engagement with others as well as their clinical and research conceptualizations. Understanding the influence of historical and current experiences with power, privilege, and oppression is critical in addressing the wider structural contexts that shape adjustment and social justice (American Psychological Association, 2017).

Preassessment and Pretherapy Intervention

Considering the lower rates of therapy and high premature dropout treatment rates for ethnic minorities, some psychologists have recommended instituting orientations for clients unfamiliar with the psychotherapeutic intervention (e.g., Acosta, Yamamoto, & Evans, 1982; Sue, 2006). Orientations need not be long; what is important is that the orientation be intentional in its purpose to demystify therapy and the client's and practitioner's roles in the process of treatment. At the beginning of therapy, clients can be nervous about the nature of therapy and what it means about them that they are obtaining therapy. Therapists can explain what is expected of the client and what the client can expect of the therapist throughout the course of treatment. Encouraging the client to be active and engaged in treatment is important. The first few sessions should help clients prepare for the more active components of therapy. Preparation sessions tend to focus on developing rapport between therapist and client, educating the client about common symptoms of distress, and conducting a thorough assessment of the client's symptoms. Because individuals from culturally different populations may be less familiar with psychological testing than with those from the mainstream, an explanation of assessment procedures may be necessary to reduce clients' discomfort regarding testing.

Assessment

Psychological assessment is conducted in a manner that is sensitive to the client's culture. Sue (2006) notes that cultural competency requiring certain personal characteristics can enhance this process. One of these characteristics is **scientific-mindedness** (the ability to formulate hypotheses rather than hasty conclusions about the nature of the client and their problems). Assessment requires this sort of thoughtfulness, to consider alternative ideas and test assumptions based on sound measures and data in order to reach reliable and valid conclusions. In addition, Sue (2006) notes that culture-specific expertise regarding different ethnic groups (e.g., knowledge regarding their history of oppression, immigration experience, and general belief systems and values) will complement specific strategies and skills.

As highlighted in Box 10.2, assessment is multidimensional in its targets of inquiry through *Awareness* of cultural similarities and differences, *Exploration* of psychosocial stressors, *Information* gathering, *Observation*, and *Utilization* of culturally appropriate measures—AEIOU. A primary aspect of assessment is the awareness of the commonalities and the considerable diversity that exist within ethnic populations. Searching for commonalities and/or generalities can often lead to concerns about potentially stereotyping individuals on the basis of their membership in a certain group. Sue (2006) refers to a characteristic called **dynamic sizing**, in which competent providers have an ability to know when to generalize regarding certain groups and when to individualize their knowledge. Dynamic sizing requires flexibility on the part of the clinician to value the determinants of culture without stereotyping or being overly inclusive of individuals. For example, knowing that Asian Americans may tend to be more collectivistic than individualistic in orientation compared to Whites can be a culturally sound description, or it can run the risk of being an overgeneralization or stereotype. According to Sue (2006), those skilled in dynamic sizing avoid stereotyping individuals while still appreciating the cultural values, beliefs, or practices of a group. The provider needs to consider multiple individual factors (e.g., acculturation, gender, socioeconomic level) that can facilitate general knowledge regarding these groups.

Box 10.2

Assessment From a Cultural Context Perspective—AEIOU

Awareness of within-group differences entails

- consideration of acculturative influences
- consideration of gender issues
- and consideration of SES differences

Exploration of sociocultural stresses considers

- acculturative stress
- and experiences with discrimination or racism (noting the relationship to current psychological distress)

Information gathered includes

- personal and familial immigration and/or migration history
- language ability
- social supports
- community resources
- employment skills and job history
- and cultural identity(ies)

Observation targets

- examination of engagement with the client
- and awareness and interpretation of nonverbal cues

Utilization of culturally sensitive assessment strategies involves

- provision of bilingual services
- use of assessment instruments with demonstrated reliability and validity with specific ethnic populations
- explanation of assessment procedures for individuals less familiar with psychological testing
- and translation of measures, including documents of informed consent

Note: Language should be at a level that is understood by the client.

Assessment also entails the exploration of sociocultural stressors that can lead to poor adjustment in minority populations. In particular, the psychological and physical consequences of acculturative stress have been documented for various groups. For example, Anderson (1991) notes that sources of stress playing a role in the vulnerability of Black Americans are often acculturative in nature. These sources include threats to African-centered or Afrocentric values of present-time orientation, spirituality, group centeredness, and oral expression. These acculturative stressors can require positive adaptation and adequate problem-solving or else produce stressful outcomes in the form of physical disorders and mental distress.

The collection of information in order to understand the client's current circumstances, history, and cultural influences is central to the assessment process. Data gathered can include information regarding the client's personal and familial immigration and/or migration history, language ability, social supports, community resources, employment skills and job history, and cultural identity or identities (American Psychological Association, 2017; Sue, 2006).

A basic aspect of assessment is observation, the first thing that occurs in our face-to-face engagement with each other, and it can be conducted within several different settings. The opportunity to evaluate the client in the home, school, or work setting can be advantageous to capturing a more naturalistic picture of the client's life. As a method of assessment, the provider will be examining the appearance and behavior of the client and the ease or difficulty of establishing rapport. Especially in cross-cultural situations, nonverbal cues require sensitivity and interpretation on the provider's part.

In assessing clinical or research populations, professionals are encouraged to utilize assessment instruments whose validity and reliability have been established for members of the population tested (American Psychological Association, 2017). If validity or reliability has not been established for a particular population, psychologists may use instruments and describe the strengths and limitations of test results, interpretation, and generalizability. In addition, certain established measures may be adapted for use with specific ethnic groups. Strategies utilized in the AI-SUPERPFP show how measures can be modified to provide culturally competent assessment. Because the study was part of a larger collaborative research survey program (CPES), researchers were required to use the NCS's University of Michigan's Composite International Diagnostic Interview (CIDI), but it was tailored for use in American Indian communities (Beals et al., 2002). Focus group interviews were conducted with tribal community members and service providers to help inform the adaptation of the CIDI to the study sample. This led to the elimination of certain items that required more in-depth questioning than a survey interview would permit. For example, concerns were voiced about possible confusion distinguishing between psychotic hallucinations and visions that may be encouraged and sanctioned by certain American Indian cultures, so certain standard questions about psychotic symptoms were dropped. In addition, questions about help-seeking extended beyond mainstream services to include traditional healers that might be utilized by members of the reservation communities such as medicine men and spiritual leaders (Beals et al., 2005).

Nontraditional Interventions

The historical roots of many popular, well-established psychotherapies are embedded in European theories (e.g., psychodynamic) and early to mid-20th-century North American theories (e.g., behavioral and cognitive behavioral) that were not necessarily developed with ethnic minority persons in mind. The possibility of modifying interventions to include more attention to multiculturally sensitive strategies is warranted given this past. Although clinicians may appropriately want to go the route of employing nontraditional interventions, care must be taken to receive appropriate consultation before doing so, because such interventions could possibly lead to negative legal consequences—for example, being accused of facilitating unlicensed practice (California Psychological Association, 2004).

Several modified, culturally adapted interventions have appeared in the research literature over recent decades. Examples include interventions centered on African American girls (Belgrave, 2002) and adults (Longshore & Grills, 2000), American Indians and Alaska Natives (De Coteau, Anderson, & Hope, 2006), Asian American youths and families (Zane, Aoki, Ho, Huang, & Jang, 1998), and Hispanic families (Santisteban, Suarez-Morales, Robbins, & Szapocznik, 2006). Culturally adapted interventions can involve the integration of rituals (e.g., sweat lodges, unity circles), prayer, cultural folklore or sayings, traditional values, and traditional foods (see Sue et al., 2009, for a review of culturally adapted intervention studies).

Humility in Practice

As a learning process, cultural awareness requires not only adherence to sound principles that guide practice but also ongoing education and discoveries of the importance of culture in human behavior across a broad array of groups and individuals. Recognizing the limits of one's competence and obtaining appropriate training, study (e.g., reading of theoretical and applied culture-centered literature), consultation, and supervision are needed to enrich knowledge, skills, and sensitivity to cultural issues. This is often referred to as **cultural humility**. In a concept analysis of 62 recent topical articles, Foronda, Baptiste, Reinholdt, and Ousman (2016) find common attributes used to describe this phenomenon, including openness, self-awareness, lack of ego, supportiveness, self-reflection, and self-critique. Humility was often sparked by diversity and power imbalance. As a result of humility in practice, partnerships based on mutual empowerment, respect, and knowledge were realized. In particular, cultural humility was described as a lifelong process: Learning is ongoing.

Collaborative Care in Treatment

Intervention based on the premise of collaboration between the client and practitioner has been proposed by a number of researchers in the treatment of ethnic minority individuals across different disorders and care settings (Collins, 2012; Davis et al., 2011; Steenbergen-Weijenburg et al., 2010; Woltmann et al., 2012). Central features of this model include educating patients about self-management of symptoms, facilitating ease of clinical information between providers and clients, training providers in preventative and collaborative care resources, providing on-site consultations and community-based resources, and building capacity to provide coordinated care (Collins, 2012; Woltmann et al., 2012). Collaborative care has demonstrated effectiveness in improving access to and quality of mental health care among minorities (Miranda et al., 2003), but further research is needed on the feasibility and effective implementation of this type of care, especially in poor communities challenged by access, affordability, and acceptable care (Collins, 2012).

Evidence-Based Treatment

The need for efficacious treatment leads to another recommendation that has become increasingly popular. This is the idea of **evidence-based treatment**, care that adheres to guidelines that have been tested through rigorous empirical investigation. Indeed, in a supplemental report of the Surgeon General (U.S. Department of Health and Human Services, 2001), providers were strongly encouraged to implement effective treatment based on evidence-based guidelines to improve overall quality of care for minorities. Miranda and colleagues (2005) note that outcome studies of interventions are evaluated in terms of efficacy and effectiveness. Efficacy studies are typically *randomized controlled trials*, designed to determine which particular components of treatment are critical to either predicted positive or negative outcomes. These are rigorous studies that require strict controls over the different treatment groups and conditions so that researchers can be confident in their interpretation of findings. Effectiveness studies may occur in actual community settings (e.g., homes, schools, churches) and may not have the rigor or control of efficacy research studies, but findings can usually be generalized to a broader array of groups or populations (Miranda et al., 2005; Sue et al., 2009). To date, only a few evidence-based treatment studies have been published that have examined the efficacy of treatment for ethnic minority populations despite findings that suggest evidence-based treatments are promising in terms of their effectiveness with ethnic minority children and adults for a wide array of problems, including major mental disorders and family problems (Miranda et al., 2005).

Related to the efficacy and effectiveness of treatment, Santiago and Miranda (2014) examined two recommendations from the Surgeon General's report (1999) that (1) progress be made in increasing the diversity of the mental health workforce to better represent racial and ethnic minority groups in randomized intervention trials and (2) attention be given to including more individuals from racial and ethnic minority groups in clinical trials to better determine whether interventions are equally effective across groups. Data on the workforce were analyzed from research conducted with staff from the American Psychiatric Association, the American Psychological Association, the National Association of Social Workers, and the National Institute of Mental Health and with representatives from professional psychiatric nursing. Ethnic minority representation in studies was examined from data gleaned in clinical trials published between 2001 and 2010. They find that, between 1999 and 2006, the numbers of professionals from racial and ethnic minority groups only slightly increased in psychiatry (17.6–21.4 percent), social work (8.2–12.9 percent), and psychology (6.6–7.8 percent). Progress in diversifying the workforce remains slow, given the continued underrepresentation of minority professionals. There was noted improvement in reporting race and ethnicity in clinical trials from 54 percent in 2001 to 89 percent in 75 studies of similar disorders published by 2010. However, very few analyses specific to race and ethnicity were conducted. This is likely the result of the fact that numbers of diverse participants often remain too low to analyze.

Santiago and Miranda (2014) make the following recommendations for improving ethnic minority representation in the clinical workforce and research in controlled clinical trials: Comprehensive and sustained efforts must be made to significantly eliminate disparities in the number of mental health care providers from racial and ethnic minority groups. The most promising initiatives have started as early as high school to target talented students and sustain intensive support, including research and applied experiences throughout graduate or medical school. And to expand our knowledge of the impact of evidence-based intervention on racial and ethnic minorities, scientists must continue to include members of these groups in their clinical trials and conduct trials that are specifically focused on greatly underrepresented populations in this type of research, such as Asian Americans or Pacific Islanders and American Indians or Alaska Natives. Priority should be given to those studies where there is advanced evidence that a particular invention is promising for diverse groups. Santiago and Miranda (2014) further acknowledged that increasing ethnic minorities' participation in clinical research will also require building community partnerships that will foster a sense of trust given the historical legacy of unethical research conducted by experimenters—for example, the tragic 1932–1972 Tuskegee Syphilis Study. It is hoped that further attention through long-term and sustainable strategies will be given to these important issues to determine the best practices for a diversity of people and issues.

Chapter Summary

This chapter presents a broad overview of psychological distress among the four major ethnic groups. We are only just beginning to get a clearer picture of the prevalence and incidence of mental disorders for groups that have often been underresearched in general population epidemiological studies. These data are invaluable for illuminating the vulnerabilities (risk factors) and strengths (protective factors) of ethnic minority groups and their relation to the development and prevention of mental illness. Further documentation and research of cultural syndromes and idioms of distress will assist in defining and identifying the various expressions of problems and highlight the role of culture in the manifestation of disorders, including the major mental disorders. Finally, with continued attention to empirical outcome studies devoted to the integration of cultural factors and overall culturally competent care, we will begin to guide and shape treatment that is truly effective and worthwhile in producing healthy adjustment in individuals.

Key Terms

American Indian Services Utilization and Psychiatric Epidemiology Risk and Protective Factors Project (AI-SUPERPFP) 236
clinician bias 247
Collaborative Psychiatric Epidemiology Surveys (CPES) 236
comorbid (co-occurring) disorders 240
cultural bias 247
cultural humility 252
cultural idioms of distress 234
culture-related syndromes 242
dual diagnosis 240
dynamic sizing 250
Epidemiological Catchment Area (ECA) study 235
evidence-based treatment 253
lifetime prevalence 236
mentally ill and chemical abuser (MICA) 240
National Comorbidity Survey (NCS) 235
National Comorbidity Survey Replication (NCS-R) 235
National Latino and Asian American Study (NLAAS) 236
National Survey of American Life (NSAL) 236
psychiatric epidemiology 235
scientific-mindedness 250
Title VI of the 1964 Civil Rights Act 247

Learning by Doing

- Generate a list of what you believe are popular, yet distinct, ways for expressing psychological distress within your culture. Ask at least two friends from different cultural backgrounds than your own to also develop lists of the common ways of expressing distress in their respective cultures. Compare the lists. Identify similarities and differences. How does culture shape the expressions of distress that differ among the lists? Does culture still exert an influence on the similar expressions? If yes, what role does it play in these expressions?

Suggested Further Readings

American Psychological Association (2017). *Multicultural guidelines: An ecological approach to context, identity, and intersectionality.* Retrieved from: http://www.apa.org/about/policy/multicultural-guidelines.pdf

Updated guidelines adopted by the American Psychological Association to assist in improving cultural competence in multicultural education, training, research, and clinical and organizational settings of psychologists and related mental health professionals.

Sue, S., & Zane, N. (2006). Ethnic minority populations have been neglected by evidence-based practices. In J. C. Norcross, L. E. Beutler, & R. F. Levant (Eds.), *Evidence-based practices in mental health: Debate and dialogue on the fundamental questions* (pp. 338–345). Washington, DC: American Psychological Association.

Presentation of the challenges in applying evidence-based practices with ethnic minority populations.

Sue, S., Zane, N., Hall, G. C. N., & Berger, L. K. (2009). The case for cultural competence in psychotherapeutic interventions. *Annual Review of Psychology, 60*, 525–548.

A review of different conceptualizations of cultural competency, arguments for and against cultural competency, and examples of cultural competence in practice. Also includes discussion of empirical research that examines the efficacy of cultural competence interventions and newer evidence-based research studies.

Trinh, N. H., Rho, Y., Lu, F., & Sanders, K. M. (Eds.). (2009). *Handbook of mental health and acculturation in Asian American families.* Totowa, NJ: Humana Press.

A look at the acculturation process and the mental health needs of Asian American individuals and their families are examined. Attention is given to the identification of common psychosocial stressors and strengths and resiliency of families. Recommendations for fostering adept clinical insights, assessment strategies, and interventions are provided.

Tseng, W.-S. (2006). From peculiar psychiatric disorders through culture-bound syndromes to culture-related syndromes. *Transcultural Psychiatry, 43*(4), 554–576.

A comprehensive historical overview of the development of concepts about exotic psychiatric disorders to more recent developments in the identification and classification of culture-bound syndromes. Argument is presented for including unique culture-related syndromes in the established psychiatric classification system and promoting the impact of culture on virtually every psychiatric disorder.

Glossary

1.5 generation Individual migrated to the United States as a preadolescent

ableism The marginalization of differently abled individuals with physical or mental limitations or "disabilities"; assumes that the norm is able-bodiedness

acculturation A dynamic and multidimensional process of change or adaptation that occurs when distinct cultures or individuals come into sustained contact. It involves different degrees and instances of culture learning (change) as well as maintenance that are contingent upon individual, group, and environmental factors. Acculturation is dynamic because it is a continuous and fluctuating process, and it is multidimensional because it involves numerous aspects of psychosocial functioning and can result in multiple adaptation outcomes. Furthermore, acculturation can involve the contact of various cultures at the same time and as such is not limited to the interactions of two cultures or racial or ethnic groups; related to *assimilation* and *incorporation*

acculturational/acculturative stress The challenges and difficulties experienced by acculturating individuals; see also *acculturative stress*

acculturation mismatch/gap A differential rate or pattern of acculturation within a family or other group; see also *dissonant acculturation*

acculturative strategy The attitudes or orientation that an individual assumes toward the culture of origin (or "heritage culture") and toward the other group or groups wherein two dimensions are considered—one reflecting the individual's positive or negative attitude toward maintenance of the heritage culture and identity and the second (also from a negative to positive continuum) classifying the individual in terms of the preferred level and type of interaction with another group or groups

achieved ethnic identity An ethnic identity status involving both ethnic identity exploration and commitment

acquiescent response The tendency to agree with the statements being presented by the researcher or another individual

acute disease A short-term ailment

ambivalent sexism Simultaneous hostility toward nontraditional women and benevolence toward women in traditional subordinate roles

American Indian Services Utilization and Psychiatric Epidemiology Risk and Protective Factors Project (AI-SUPERPFP) A rare large-scale survey of 3,084 Southwest and Northern Plains Indians from two tribal groups living near or on home reservations

ancestry A genealogical relationship traced back to at least one national group; a person's origin, heritage, or descent that is associated with birthplace of self or ancestors

assimilation An acculturation strategy experienced by individuals or groups that are exposed to a new culture; involves loss of heritage culture and movement toward new culture; see *acculturation* and *incorporation*

assumption of intragroup homogeneity The faulty assumption by many researchers that all members of an ethnic or racial group are similar and share a number of characteristics

asylee An individual who receives temporary, long-term permission to live and work (and sometimes permission to apply for permanent residency and eventual citizenship) in a country due to political or human rights abuses in their country of origin

authoritarian parenting A parenting style characterized by highly controlling, demanding, and overly strict parenting, where obedience and respect for authority are emphasized and children are held to high standards, are not allowed to negotiate or openly disagree with their parents, and are disciplined punitively if parents perceive any transgressions

authoritative parenting A parenting style reflecting more of a democratic or reciprocal parent-child relationship, in which parents set high standards and place demands on their children; allow their children to share their opinions and concerns without unduly imposing their parental authority or will; in regard to discipline, favor reasoning and explanation for their rules or decisions over physical punishment; and encourage their children to be independent and to reflect on their actions and behaviors

aversive racism Egalitarian attitudes and behaviors toward racial differences, but person is influenced by unconscious negative attitudes and beliefs

back translation The approach for translating instruments that involves the use of at least two bilingual translators, wherein translators go back and forth between the original-language document and the translations, modifying each until wording for each language is found that seems equivalent; see also *double translation*

benevolent sexism Support for women in traditional roles and rejection of women in nontraditional sex roles

biculturalism Knowledge about two cultures, adoption of values and beliefs of both cultures, and feeling perfectly comfortable interacting in either culture group

bilingualism The learning of at least two languages with varying levels of proficiency

biomedical model A framework for understanding health that maintains all illness can be explained on the basis of unusual physical processes, such as biochemical imbalances or structural abnormalities

biopsychosocial model A framework for understanding health that maintains both health and illness are caused by an admixture of biological malfunctioning and psychological and social factors

caballerismo A positive set of Latino masculine attitudes, beliefs, and traits that emphasize being the primary family provider and protector and valuing honor, dignity, respect for others, emotional responsiveness, collaboration, and flexible masculine role behaviors

causal factor A direct cause of the onset of an illness

chronic disease A longer-term ailment

classism Attitudes, beliefs, behaviors, and institutional practices that justify power differences based on social class with preference being assigned to the upper and middle classes

class system A hierarchy based on key social criteria

clinician bias The failure of a clinician to adhere to the diagnostic criteria during psychiatric evaluations

cohesive-authoritative parenting An African American parenting style in which parents express concern and warmth toward their children, engage them in intellectual activities, provide a structured and supportive family environment, emphasize the personal growth and independence of their children, encourage their children to express themselves openly, value achievement and high standards without being overly rigid or controlling, tend to avoid punitive disciplinary measures, and create an environment for proactive racial socialization and low defensive racial socialization

Collaborative Psychiatric Epidemiology Surveys (CPES) A collection of three national epidemiological studies of psychiatric disorders, comprised of the National Comorbidity Survey Replication, the National Latino and Asian American Study, and the National Survey of American Life; see also *National Comorbidity Survey Replication*, *National Latino and Asian American Study*, and *National Survey of American Life*

collectivistic culture A culture focused on the community as a whole

colonizing perspective A worldview assuming that the majority culture is the baseline against which other cultures are compared

community-based participatory research (CBPR) A type of research in which scientists work in collaboration with community partners to promote the health and well-being of a community

comorbid/co-occurring disorders The simultaneous suffering from more than one disorder

complementary health approach (CHA) A form of health interventions considered outside the mainstream of conventional Western medicine

conceptual equivalence How appropriately an instrument reflects a concept as defined within the culture of a group; see also *construct validity*

conflict-authoritarian parenting An African American parenting style in which parents show little concern and warmth toward their children, are overly strict and controlling toward their children, disallow their children from expressing their feelings or questioning family rules, and emphasize achievement not necessarily focused on intellectual activities, resulting in children who may feel conflicted about meeting parental demands (because their family environments and activities tend to be unstructured and their parents can be neglectful), high levels of family conflict, distressed family relationships, and moderate levels of racial socialization

construct A term frequently used in the field of psychology and refers to a concept or idea based on theory and/or empirical observation

construct validity How appropriately an instrument reflects a concept as defined within the culture of a group; see also *conceptual equivalence*

contact hypothesis The suggestion that prejudicial attitudes and emotions can be changed by bringing together diverse peoples into a specific setting

contextualization Understanding how social and cultural contexts shape human behavior

controlling images Stereotyped and negative racial and gender images intended to subordinate minority groups and justify and affirm dominant group power and norms

cost/benefit balance The costs incurred by the participants and the risks associated with participation in a study in comparison to the benefits that they or the community will receive; see also *risk/benefit balance*

cross-cultural psychology The area of psychological study that emphasizes differences in cultural influences across nations or regions of the world

cultural assimilation the acculturation process of individuals and groups; see also *cultural integration*

cultural bias Actual ethnic or racial differences in the expression of symptoms being unnoticed or misconstrued by diagnosticians

cultural dimensions A broad tendency to prefer certain states of affairs over others

cultural humility Recognizing the limits of one's competence and obtaining the appropriate training, study, consultation, and supervision needed to enrich knowledge, skills, and sensitivity to cultural issues

cultural idioms of distress Expressions of distress that reflect a culture's way of experiencing and talking about psychosocial concerns or problems

cultural integration The acculturation process of individuals and groups; see also *cultural assimilation*

culturally appropriate research Research that develops and tests theories and hypotheses that are sensitive to and respectful of cultural variations and that appropriately reflect the role of culture, race, and ethnicity in shaping behavior; that uses research methods that are appropriate, familiar, and relevant to the question being researched as well as to the members of the racial or ethnic group being studied; that implies that the analysis and interpretation of data and other results of a research project must take into consideration not only the culture that characterizes participants but also other relevant variables, such as their gender, socioeconomic conditions, educational level, and migration history; and that involves strict adherence to principles of ethical and responsible behavior in all aspects of the research project

culturally competent health care Health care that acknowledges and incorporates—at all levels—the importance of culture, assessment of cross-cultural relations, vigilance toward the dynamics that result from cultural differences, expansion of cultural knowledge, and adaptation of services to meet culturally unique needs; also known as *culturally sensitive health care*, *culturally appropriate health care*, *culturally responsive health care*, and *culturally aware health care*

culturally competent individual Someone who understands and appreciates cultural diversity in others; interacts effectively and meaningfully with individuals who differ on culture, race, ethnicity, gender, social class, sexuality, and so on; and advocates for a society that values and respects diversity.

cultural socialization The process of learning about one's cultural heritage and practices; underlies ethnic identity formation

culture Those attitudes, norms, beliefs, values, and behaviors shaped by an individual's ethnicity and race or national origin and also developed and shaped by an individual's gender, physical and mental abilities, sexuality, social class, and other similar characteristics

culture-related syndromes Recurrent patterns of unusual behavior or symptoms and distressing experiences typically exhibited in certain areas of the world

defensive-neglectful parenting An African American parenting style showing the greatest risk for poor family functioning, reflected by high family conflict and chaotic family relationships, where parents exhibit neglectful parenting, show little concern and emotional affection toward their children, place little importance on their child's personal growth and academic achievement, can be highly critical of their children, use punitive discipline methods, have rigid and hierarchical family structures, and provide high levels of defensive racial socialization and low levels of empowering racial socialization

deficit model Any psychological model that assumes any behavior differing from what is found among Whites can be explained by invoking social, cultural, intellectual, or psychological limitations on the part of the members of the ethnic or racial group

disaggregation The examination of intragroup variability

discrimination The actions carried out or planned that negatively affect members of a group that is the object of prejudice

dissonant acculturation A differential pattern of acculturation; see also *acculturation mismatch* and *acculturation gap*

distributive system model A multidimensional model based on parallel class systems where each system represents a social dimension such as political force, wealth and property acquisition, and occupation

dominant group Members of society who are advantaged socially, politically, and economically; unrelated to a group's population size

double minority status Belonging to intersecting racial/ethnic and sexual minority groups

double translation See *back translation*

dual diagnosis A commonly used term describing a person who has a mental disorder and a substance-related disorder; see also *mentally ill and chemical abuser (MICA)*

dual focus translation A process of research instrument development in which bilingual and bicultural research teams work together to develop the instruments to be used; the team works to guarantee equivalency in emotional meaning, familiarity, and ease of comprehension of all words in each language version

dynamic sizing A component of competent care in which providers properly discern when to generalize regarding certain groups and when to individualize their knowledge

ecological model A framework for understanding health reflects the interactions or transactions between individuals and their physical and sociocultural environments

ecological perspective The view that a family's well-being and development are shaped by different multiple ecologies

ecological validity The determination that the testing environment did not determine or affect the results and that the methods and procedures approximate as much as possible the real world

ecologies Social contexts and relationships that are part of one's daily life

emic construct A group-specific concept

enculturation The process whereby individuals endeavor to learn or affirm their ancestral culture of origin

environmental injustice Racial discrimination in environmental policymaking; see also *environmental racism*

environmental racism Racial discrimination in environmental policymaking; see also *environmental injustice*

Epidemiological Catchment Area (ECA) study A national epidemiological study of psychiatric disorders

epidemiology A special branch of biomedical research devoted to the study of the occurrence of disorders in populations or in special groups and the risk factors associated with these disorders

ethnic identity An individual's subjective sense of membership and belonging to an ethnic group, which includes their attitudes, beliefs, knowledge, feelings, and behaviors associated with that particular ethnic group

ethnicity A social group's distinct sense of belongingness as a result of common culture and descent

ethnic stereotypes The characteristics that are perceived as common among members of specific ethnic or racial groups; see also *racial stereotypes*

ethnocentrism The bias of viewing one's own ethnic group as superior to others

ethnogenesis A segmented assimilation wherein culture contact can be expected to produce a mixed set of values and behaviors that characterize the specific ethnic or racial group and that are somewhat different from those of the original or ancestral culture or of those of the dominant group

etic construct A universal concept

evidence-based intervention An intervention based on the results of scientific research

evidence-based treatment Care that adheres to guidelines that have been tested through rigorous empirical investigation

external validity The generalizability of a measure or of certain research findings; also known as *generalizability*

facial diversity The simple counting of racially, ethnically, or culturally diverse individuals or, especially, using variations in people's physical characteristics such as skin color, eye shape, national origin, or hair texture as proof of the existence of *multiculturalism*

familism/*familismo* A Latino cultural value; the quality of being strongly grounded in one's family, valuing family closeness and cohesion, emphasizing family responsibilities over individual needs or goals, preferring to live near family, and relying on them for emotional and instrumental support

family agency A family's capacity to actively promote and safeguard its own welfare and development

family stress model The assumption that family environment mediates or is related to the relationship between external stressors and youth adjustment

field experiment An experiment occurring in real-world settings

filial piety An Asian American cultural value; the respect a child has for the needs and concerns of the family over their own

first generation Individual has immigrated to the United States and expects to remain in the country permanently or for a very long time

fourth generation Individual born in the United States with no grandparent being an immigrant

gaman A cultural trait valued in Japanese culture that ascribes character and strength to those who endure and withstand hardship without complaint

gender The socially and psychologically defined and acquired characteristics that distinguish being male from being female

gendered racial socialization A socialization process in which families teach an individual about their race and gender in a society that devalues both social identities

gendered racism The multiplicative impact racism and sexism can have on the lives of men and women of color

gender identity An individual's fundamental sense of being male or female, shaped by gender typing, yet sometimes independent of social and cultural norms and rules for gender

gender roles The expected responsibilities and abilities of men and women

gender typing The process by which an individual learns the behaviors, interests, and abilities associated with being masculine or feminine in a given culture

generation The place of birth and familial history of an individual as they relate to migration

generation 2.5 See *mixed second generation*

globalization A phenomenon promoting some types of acculturation around the world by facilitating personal mobility across borders and the sharing of cultures and values through music, electronic and print media, and education

health disparity The difference in the overall rate of disease incidence, prevalence, morbidity, mortality, or survival rates in the population as compared to the health status of the general population

health equity Attainment of the highest level of health for all people, which requires valuing everyone equally, with focused and ongoing societal efforts to address avoidable inequalities and historical and contemporary injustices, and the elimination of health care disparities

health literacy An individual's ability to obtain, process, and understand information about health and available services

heterosexism Beliefs that promote the idea that heterosexuality is the norm in gender identity and sexual attraction

high private regard Positive feelings about one's racial group

homonegativity Negative attitudes and beliefs about homosexuality

horizontal collectivism A cultural orientation that favors commonality among individuals and interdependence but not with the control of authoritarian force

horizontal individualism A cultural orientation that values the individual but not necessarily a societal hierarchical structure

hostile sexism Rejection of women in agentic roles

identity diffusion The ethnic identity status characterized by the absence of ethnic identity exploration and commitment

identity foreclosure The ethnic identity status involving commitment to an ethnic identity without exploration

immigrant health paradox The finding that recent immigrants tend to show better health status when compared with second generation individuals or even members of the host culture

implicit attitudes Affective reactions and associations held by individuals toward other people or toward behaviors that are subtle and not easily verbalized and therefore difficult to measure by surveys or attitude scales

incidence The number of new cases of a problem or disorder occurring over a specific time period

incorporation A culture learning process experienced by individuals or groups that are exposed to a new culture; see also *acculturation* and *assimilation*

independent construal of the self An understanding of oneself in which individuality and one's unique thoughts, emotions, and behaviors are distinguished from those of others

individualistic culture A culture focused on individual autonomy

individuation Children's separation from their parents and increased contacts outside of the home

informed consent The proper informing of a research participant as to the purpose of the study, its procedures, its potential benefits, and its risks; the voluntary nature of their participation; and their ability to ask questions of the researchers

in-group A group that maintains respect, esteem, and loyalty and, consequently, is perceived as being more desirable

interculturalism A term sometimes offered primarily by non–U.S. scholars to replace the sometimes-maligned term *multiculturalism*; see *multiculturalism* and *transnationalism*

interdependent construal of the self An understanding of oneself in which one tends to value interpersonal relationships and see others as integral to one's self-conceptualization

intergroup contact Putting diverse people together in a group with the aim of breaking down prejudicial attitudes or discriminatory behavior

intergroup racism Racism occurring across ethnic or racial groups

intersecting identities Multiple and closely linked identities that interact in meaningful ways, contributing to unique life experiences

intersectionality The exploration of differences primarily due to people's race, ethnicity, and culture as they interact with such other characteristics as their gender, social class, and sexuality, including the analysis of multiple factors interacting with each other to provide not only a more complete and nuanced understanding of human behavior but also a better basis for developing personal and societal interventions to produce change; also called *intersectional inquiry*

intragroup racism Racism occurring within a given group

involuntary immigrant An individuals who has been enslaved or colonized and may have experienced difficulties assimilating or one who was forced to leave their country of origin because of political conditions

just world hypothesis Our need to believe that the world is a just place in which good people are rewarded for their positive deeds and bad people are punished for their wicked ways

label of convenience A cultural label allowing researchers, politicians, care providers, educators, researchers, and others to identify individuals sharing some general characteristics, where the labels neither necessarily reflect intragroup homogeneity or complete similarity nor necessarily imply common psychological characteristics

lifetime prevalence The total number or percentage of individuals in a population who have experienced a particular disorder at some point in their life

loss of face In Asian American or Asian cultures; perceived threat to a person's social integrity, tied to one's ability to meet the role responsibilities and expectations of a valued social group

machismo A broad set of stereotyped hypermasculine Latino traits that include male dominance, aggression, fearlessness, bravery, authoritarianism, promiscuous behavior, virility, excessive alcohol use, stoicism, reserved or restricted emotions and aloofness, sexism, oppressive and controlling behaviors toward women and children, autonomy, strength, bravado, responsibility, honor, respect, and being a good provider and protector of women, children, and less fortunate members of society

marianismo A broad set of stereotyped feminine traits that idealize the moral virtues and personal character of Latinas, often used to elevate Latinas' gender identity by casting them as being morally and spiritually superior to Latino men, possessing an innate ability to endure hardship and suffering, and being self-sacrificing, humble, modest, reserved, giving, and generous

mentally ill and chemical abuser (MICA) A commonly used term describing a person who has a mental disorder and a substance-related disorder; see also *dual diagnosis*

meritocracy A class structure in which those who receive the rewards have done so based solely on the strength of their own efforts

mind-body dualism The belief that the mind is a distinct entity from the physical world, including the body

minority A member of a group that has limited power and access to society's wealth and resources, resulting from discrimination and subjugation by the dominant society

minority stress theory The theory that intersecting stressors from multiple minority social positions increase the risk for psychological and health problems

mixed second generation An individual born in the United States with one parent being born in the United States and the other being a first generation; also known as generation 2.5 (or 2.5 generation)

model minority A historical stereotype of a particular racial group (e.g., Asian Americans) as being uniformly financially and academically successful and well adjusted

moratorium The ethnic identity status involving ethnic identity exploration without commitment

morbidity The proportion of illness or specific disease in a population

mortality The frequency of death or death rate in a population

multiculturalism A sociopolitical characteristic that defines communities as well as nations and is more complex and nuanced than concepts such as diversity or pluralism

multicultural psychology The study of human behavior as influenced (1) by a person's cultures interacting with variables as diverse as race, ethnicity, gender, social class, and sexuality and (2) by the person's involvement with other individuals who share or differ in terms of their cultures as influenced in turn by such characteristics as race, ethnicity, gender, and social class

multidimensional construct A theoretical entity consisting of many different elements or components

mutuality in acculturation A phenomenon in plural societies where host and immigrant groups change as a reciprocal function of their interactions and exposure to their cultures

National Comorbidity Survey (NCS) A national epidemiological study of psychiatric disorders

National Comorbidity Survey Replication (NCS-R) A national epidemiological study of psychiatric disorders designed to replicate the earlier NCS

nationality A person's country of birth or descent

National Latino and Asian American Study (NLAAS) A survey of mental health among diverse racial and ethnic groups with a nationally representative sample of Latinos and Asian Americans

National Survey of American Life (NSAL) A national survey of household residents in the Black population that includes African Americans and Afro-Caribbeans

objective social status An individual's income, educational level, and occupation

otherness status A form of social marginalization and social isolation experienced by biracial or multiracial persons; includes societal pressures to "fit" into specific racial categorizations

out-group A group that is subjected to disapproval, contempt, and competition and, consequently, is less desirable

out-group homogeneity effect The overgeneralization of beliefs about people

patrilineal Based on Confucian principles; an Asian or Asian American family structure that grants greater authority, privileges, and status to older males in the family

permanent migrant An individual who entered the country with an immigrant visa that allows them to live and work permanently in the United States and eventually become a citizen; sometimes known as *legal immigrant*

permissive parenting A parenting style in which parents do not place high standards on their children, exercise little parental control, can be neglectful of their parental responsibilities, tend to believe that children should be allowed to follow their own impulses and desires without parental monitoring or interference, and, thus, are less concerned with child discipline than are authoritarian and authoritative parents and may consult with their children on family policies or decisions

place-based intervention An approach for improving health in a geographic location that aligns the community members, businesses, institutions, and other relevant stakeholders in a collaborative and participatory process

prevalence The total number of cases of a problem or disorder occurring in a population of a group at a given time

privilege A preferential standing in the world not due to effort or performance

prejudice A negative attitude toward members of a particular group based on the stereotypes held by the perceiver

psychiatric epidemiology A subspecialty within epidemiology focusing on the study of the occurrence of psychiatric disorders and their associated risk factors in populations and in special groups

race A socially constructed concept used to categorize groups or individuals based on prevailing social and political attitudes; often used to express ambiguous physical distinctions, promote dominance of certain privileged groups, and oppress groups that are deemed inferior

racial identity Identification with a socially defined racial category or phenotype that is influenced by racial stratification and historical oppression of racial minorities

racial identity schemas A set of race-related beliefs and emotional responses formed during racial socialization, influencing how race-related information is interpreted and internalized as part of an overall individual identity

racial microaggressions Brief and commonplace daily verbal, behavioral, and environmental indignities, whether intentional or unintentional, that communicate hostile, derogatory, or negative racial slights and insults to the target person or group

racial socialization The process of learning about and ascribing meaning and value to socially constructed racial hierarchies and categories

racial stereotypes The characteristics that are perceived as common among members of specific ethnic or racial groups; see also *ethnic stereotypes*

racial tracking Tendency to place certain ethnic minority students into remedial or regular courses rather than honors or advanced courses regardless of the students' academic abilities and potential

racism Beliefs, attitudes, institutional arrangements, and acts that tend to denigrate individuals or groups because of phenotypic characteristics or ethnic group affiliation

refugee An individual who receives temporary, long-term permission to live and work in the United States (and sometimes permission to apply for permanent residency and eventual citizenship) due to political or human rights abuses in their country of origin; see also *asylee*

relative functionalism A hypothesis for Asian American educational achievement; states that, as Asian Americans have been barred from certain occupations and career paths that do not require a formal education, due to institutional racism and discrimination, Asian American students who equate studying with social and economic upward mobility are more likely to focus on their studies and academic achievement

reliability The quality of producing the same or extremely similar results at every use

remote acculturation Acculturating to a remote culture to which an individual has not been directly exposed and/or that is not their ancestral culture

remote enculturation The learning of one's heritage from a remote location or through short-term exposure and not by direct, long-term personal exposure to the heritage community, its culture, and its manifestations

responsible, culturally appropriate research Research that is responsible, sensitive, and responsive to the characteristics of the groups being studied

risk/benefit balance The costs incurred by the participants and the risks associated with participation in a study in comparison to the benefits that they or the community will receive; see also *cost/benefit balance*

risk factor A characteristic or behavior appearing in individuals who have a disorder

scientific-mindedness A clinician's ability to formulate hypotheses rather than hasty conclusions about the nature of the client and their problems

second generation An individual born in the United States of parents who were both first generation

segmented assimilation A process of assimilation into a particular social segment

selective migration hypothesis The assumption that among voluntary immigrants the strongest, the most creative and healthiest, the risk-takers, or the youngest tend to choose to migrate

sexual identity An individual's identity based on a broad range of sexual, emotional, and erotic attractions

sexual identity formation A part of the coming-out process involving becoming aware of one's sexual preferences and initial exploration of lesbian, gay, or bisexual identities

sexual identity integration Accepting one's sexual identities, overcoming internalized homophobia by adopting positive attitudes about one's sexuality, experiencing greater comfort in disclosing one's sexual identity to others, and engaging more with LBG communities

social capital Social support and resources deriving from one's social relationships and from connections within one's family and community

social construction A construct whose definitions and categorizations are based on prevailing sociopolitical attitudes and historical forces in society rather than biological or genetic factors

social determinants of health Those conditions in which individuals are born, grow, live, work, and age

social distance The type of interpersonal contact or social interaction an individual feels comfortable engaging in across racial or ethnic groups

social norms Explicit and implicit rules regarding the formation and engagement of social relationships and behaviors

social stratification A society's system for distributing resources and rewards among various groups

social stress hypothesis The suggestion that the members of second and higher generation groups exhibit poorer mental and physical health not because they are less strong or less able to withstand acculturative stress but because they bear the brunt of societal discrimination and prejudice

socioeconomic status (SES) The social-economic or class standing of an individual or group often gauged by level of economic, educational, and occupational achievement

sojourner An individual temporarily in the country as tourists or foreign students

standardized instrument A research instrument that has undergone lengthy psychometric analysis

status inconsistency A risk factor for intimate partner violence; loss of socioeconomic status and occupational prestige among immigrant or refugee men following relocation to another country

stereotype content The specific stereotypes assigned to a given group

stereotype threat The diminished performance among members of a given group consistent with negative stereotypes of that group, as a direct result of those stereotypes having been made apparent, even subtly

structural assimilation The incorporation of members of ethnic or racial groups into primary relationships with individuals from the dominant or majority group in contexts as varied as social clubs and marriage

subjective social status An individual's self-perceived social position in society

symbolic racism Negative perceptions of certain groups that are perceived as having violated central values of a society

temporary migrant An individual who receives a permit to live and work in the United States for limited periods of time, such as an au pair or farm laborer with an H-2 visa, or a skilled worker, such as a software engineer who receives an H-1B visa

third generation Individual and parents born in the United States with at least one grandparent being first generation

Title VI of the 1964 Civil Rights Act The U.S. legal provision that service providers receiving federal financial assistance are required to ensure the availability of appropriate and meaningful access to services even if patients have limited proficiency in English

transferability The process of demonstrating the generalizability or external validity of research findings

triangulation Using a multimethod approach where a variety of research methods are used and the results are compared across methods in order to obtain a better approximation to the reality being studied

two-spirited individual A person in American Indian or Native Alaska culture who is considered blessed with both a male and a female spirit

type 1 diabetes A type of diabetes typically associated with biological, genetic, or environmental factors in its development; also referred to as *juvenile-onset diabetes* or *insulin-dependent diabetes mellitus*

type 2 diabetes A type of diabetes typically associated with patients who are of older age, obese, have inactive lifestyles, have family histories of diabetes, or have histories of gestational diabetes; also known as *adult-onset diabetes* or *non-insulin-dependent diabetes mellitus*

unauthorized migrant An individual who has entered or remained in the country without proper documentation or who has overstayed a time-limited permit; sometimes known pejoratively as an *illegal immigrant*; see also *undocumented migrant*

undocumented migrant An individuals who has entered or remained in the country without proper documentation or who has overstayed a time-limited permit; sometimes known pejoratively as an *illegal immigrant*; see also *unauthorized migrants*

unidirectional model of acculturation An understanding of acculturation in which culture change is thought to occur in one direction, wherein people *move away* from their culture of origin and *toward* the dominant group during resettlement in a new country and/or upon exposure to a new culture

validity The quality of properly and accurately measuring the variable or variables being investigated.

vertical collectivism A cultural orientation that values interdependence and deference to the common needs of the community but also supports deference or submission to a higher authority

vertical individualism A cultural orientation that values the individual but also societal competitiveness that leads to upward mobility

voluntary immigrant An individual who chooses to migrate, searching for economic and educational improvements

Whiteness A racial construct that has historically conferred privilege; belonging to a group whose skin color is light, or "white," and sharing experiences and attitudes that differ from others whose skin color is darker

within-group differences The differences among the members of a given ethnic or racial group that are the product of variations in age, gender, national origin, socioeconomic status or social class, educational level, employment, and many other characteristics that affect people's behavior; see also *within-group variability*

within-group variability The differences among the members of a given ethnic or racial group that are the product of variations in age, gender, national origin, socioeconomic status or social class, educational level, employment, and many other characteristics that affect people's behavior; see also *within-group differences*

working poor Those working at minimum wage or slightly below and whose employer does not provide medical coverage

xenophobia An irrational fear of foreigners, resulting in stress and discomfort

References

Abe-Kim, J., Takeuchi, D. T., Hong, S., Zane, N., Sue, S., Spencer, M. S., . . . & Alegría, M. (2007). Use of mental health–related services among immigrant and US-born Asian Americans: Results from the National Latino and Asian American Study. *American Journal of Public Health, 97*, 91–98.

Aberson, C. L., Shoemaker, C., & Tomolillo, C. (2004). Implicit bias and contact: The role of interethnic friendships. *The Journal of Social Psychology, 144*, 335–347.

Abraído-Lanza, A. F., Dohrenwend, B. P., Ng-Mak, D. S., & Turner, J. B. (1999). The Latino mortality paradox: A test of the "salmon bias" and healthy migrant hypotheses. *American Journal of Behavioral Medicine, 89*, 1543–1548.

Abreu, J. M., Goodyear, R. K., Campos, A., & Newcomb, M. D. (2000). Ethnic belonging and traditional masculinity ideology among African Americans, European Americans, and Latinos. *Psychology of Men & Masculinity, 1*, 75–86.

Abueg, F., & Chun, K. M. (1996). Traumatization stress among Asians and Asian Americans. In A. Marsella, M. Friedman, E. Gerrity, & R. Scurfield (Eds.), *Ethnocultural approaches to understanding post-traumatic stress disorder: Issues, research, and clinical applications* (pp. 285–299). Washington, DC: American Psychological Association.

Acosta, F. X., Yamamoto, J., & Evans, L. A. (1982). *Effective psychotherapy for low income and minority patients.* New York: Plenum.

Adams, B. G., & Abubakar, A. (2016). Acculturation in Sub-Saharan Africa. In D. L. Sam & J. W. Berry (Eds.), *The Cambridge handbook of acculturation psychology* (2nd ed., pp. 355–374). Cambridge: Cambridge University Press.

Adams, G., Biernat, M., Branscombe, N. R., Crandall, C. S., & Wrightsman, L. S. (Eds.). (2008). *Commemorating "Brown": The social psychology of racism and discrimination.* Washington, DC: American Psychological Association.

Aday, L. A. (1994). Health status of vulnerable populations. *Annual Review of Public Health, 15*, 487–509.

Adesope, O. O., Lavin, T., Thompson, T., & Ungerleider, C. (2010). A systematic review and meta-analysis of the cognitive correlates of bilingualism. *Review of Educational Research, 80*(2), 207–245.

Adler, N. E., Boyce, T., Chesney, M. A., Cohen, S., Folkman, S., Kahn, R. L., & Syme, S. L. (1994). Socioeconomic status and health: The challenge of the gradient. *American Psychologist, 49*, 15–24.

Afable-Munsuz, A., Gregorich, S. E., Markides, K. S., & Pérez-Stable, E. J. (2013). Diabetes risk in older Mexican Americans: Effects of language acculturation, generation and socioeconomic status. *Journal of Cross Cultural Gerontology, 28*, 359–373.

Agency for Healthcare Research and Quality. (2017). *2016 national healthcare quality and disparities report.* Rockville, MD: Author. Retrieved from https://www.ahrq.gov/research/findings/nhqrdr/nhqdr16/summary.html

Ai, A. L., Pappas, C., & Simonsen, E. (2015). Risk and protective factors for three major mental health problems among Latino American men nationwide. *American Journal of Men's Health, 9*(1), 64–75.

Ai, A. L., Weiss, S. I., & Fincham, F. D. (2014). Family factors contribute to general anxiety disorder and suicidal ideation among Latina Americans. *Women's Health Issues, 24*(3), e345–352.

Ainsworth, M. D. (1967). *Infancy in Uganda: Infant care and the growth of love.* Baltimore: Johns Hopkins University Press.

Ainsworth, M. D. (1989). Attachments beyond infancy. *American Psychologist, 44*, 709–716.

Ajibade, A., Hook, J. N., Utsey, S. O., Davis, D. E., & Van Tongeren, D. R. (2016). Racial/ethnic identity, religious commitment, and well-being in African Americans. *Journal of Black Psychology, 42*, 244–258.

Alba, R., & Nee, V. (1999). Rethinking assimilation theory for a new era of immigration. In C. Hirschman, P. Kasinitz, & J. DeWind (Eds.), *The handbook of international migration: The American experience* (pp. 137–160). New York: Russell Sage Foundation.

Alba, R., Rumbaut, R. G., & Marotz, K. (2005). A distorted nation: Perceptions of racial/ethnic group sizes and attitudes toward immigrants and other minorities. *Social Forces, 84*, 901–919.

Alcalay, R., Sabogal, F., Marín, G., Pérez-Stable, E. J., Marín, B. V., & Otero-Sabogal, R. (1987–1988). Patterns of mass media use among Hispanic smokers: Implications for community interventions. *International Quarterly of Community Health Education, 8*, 341–350.

Alcántara, C., Casement, M. D., & Lewis-Fernández, R. (2013). Conditional risk for PTSD among Latinos: A systematic review of racial/ethnic differences and sociocultural explanations. *Clinical Psychology Review, 33*, 107–119.

Alegría, M., Chatterji, P., Wells, K., Cao, Z., Chen, C., Takeuchi, D., . . . & Meng, X. L. (2008). Disparity in depression treatment among racial and ethnic minority populations in the United States. *Psychiatric Services, 59*, 1264–1272.

Alegría, M., Mulvaney-Day, N., Woo, M., Torres, M., Gao, S., & Oddo, V. (2007). Correlates of past-year mental service use among Latinos: Results from the National Latino and Asian American Study. *American Journal of Public Health, 97*, 76–83.

Al-Issa, I. (1997). Ethnicity, immigration, and psychopathology. In I. Al-Issa & M. Tousignant (Eds.), *Ethnicity, immigration, and psychopathology* (pp. 3–15). New York: Plenum.

Allen, C. (1997). Spies like us: When sociologists deceive their subjects. *Lingua Franca, 7*, 31–39.

Allen, V. L. (Ed.). (1970). *Psychological factors in poverty.* Chicago: Markham Publishing.

Allport, G. W. (1954). *The nature of prejudice.* Cambridge, MA: Addison-Wesley.

Alva, S. A. (1993). Differential patterns of achievement among Asian-American adolescents. *Journal of Youth and Adolescence, 22*, 407–423.

Alvarez, A. N., & Helms, J. E. (2001). Racial identity and reflected appraisals as influences on Asian Americans' racial adjustment. *Cultural Diversity & Ethnic Minority Psychology, 7*, 217–231.

Alvarez, A. N., & Juang, L. (2010). Filipino Americans and racism: A multiple mediation model of coping. *Journal of Counseling Psychology, 57*, 167–178.

Alvidrez, J., Azocar, F., & Miranda, J. (1996). Demystifying the concept of ethnicity for psychotherapy researchers. *Journal of Consulting and Clinical Psychology, 64*, 903–908.

Ambady, N., Shih, M., Kim, A., & Pittinsky, T. L. (2001). Stereotype susceptibility in children: Effects of identity activation on quantitative performance. *Psychological Science, 12*, 385–390.

American Cancer Society. (2005). *Cancer facts & figures 2005.* Retrieved from http://www.cancer.org/docroot/STT/stt_0.asp

American Diabetes Association. (2017). *Statistics About Diabetes.* Retrieved December 31, 2017, from http://www.diabetes.org/diabetes-basics/statistics/

American Educational Research Association. (2011, April 1). AERA Code of ethics: American Educational Research Association approved by the AERA Council, February 2011. *Educational Researcher, 40*(3), 145–156.

American Psychiatric Association. (2000). *Diagnostic and statistical manual of mental disorders: DSM-IV-TR* (4th ed., text rev.). Washington, DC: Author.

American Psychiatric Association. (2013). *Diagnostic and statistical manual of mental disorders: DSM* (5th ed.). Arlington, VA: Author.

American Psychological Association. (2002a). Ethical principles and code of conduct. *American Psychologist, 57*, 1060–1073.

American Psychological Association. (2002b, August). *Guidelines on multicultural education, training, research, practice, and organizational change for psychologists.* Washington, DC: Author.

American Psychological Association. (2003). Guidelines on multicultural education, training, research, practice, and organizational change for psychologists. *American Psychologist, 58*, 377–402.

American Psychological Association. (2005). APA resolution recommending the immediate retirement of American Indian mascots, symbols, images, and personalities by schools, colleges, universities, athletic teams, and organizations. Retrieved from http://www.apa.org/about/policy/mascots.pdf

American Psychological Association. (2007). Resolution on prejudice, stereotypes, and discrimination. *American Psychologist, 62*, 475–481.

American Psychological Association. (2016, March 10). Discrimination linked to increased stress, poorer health, American Psychological Association survey finds. Retrieved from http://www.apa.org/news/press/releases/2016/03/impact-of-discrimination.aspx

American Psychological Association. (2017). *Multicultural guidelines: An ecological approach to context, identity, and intersectionality.* Retrieved from http://www.apa.org/about/policy/multicultural-guidelines.pdf

American Psychological Association Presidential Task Force on Preventing Discrimination and Promoting Diversity. (2012). *Dual pathways to a better America: Preventing discrimination and promoting diversity.* Washington, DC: American Psychological Association.

Anderson, J., Moeschberger, M., Chen, J. M., Kunn, P., Wewers, M., & Guthrie, R. (1993). An acculturation scale for Southeast Asians. *Social Psychiatry and Psychiatric Epidemiology, 28*, 134–141.

Anderson, L. M., Scrimshaw, S. C., Fullilove, M. T., Fielding, J. E., Normand, J., & Task Force on Community Preventive Services (2003). Culturally competent healthcare systems. *American Journal of Preventive Medicine, 24*, 68–79.

Anderson, L. P. (1991). Acculturative stress: A theory of relevance to Black Americans. *Clinical Psychology Review, 11*, 685–702.

Angel, R., & Tienda, M. (1982). Determinants of extended household structure: Cultural pattern or economic need? *American Journal of Sociology, 6*, 1360–1383.

Angelelli, A., & Geist-Martin, P. (2005). Enhancing culturally competent health communication: Constructing understanding between providers and culturally diverse patients. In E. Berlin Ray (Ed.), *Health communication in practice: A case study* (pp. 271–284). Mahwah, NJ: Lawrence Erlbaum.

Angle, J. W., Dagogo-Jack, S., Forehand, M. R., & Perkins, A. (2017). Activating stereotypes with brand imagery: The role of viewer political identity. *Journal of Consumer Psychology, 27*, 84–90.

Anglin, D. M., Alberti, P. M., Link, B. G., & Phelan, J. P. (2008). Racial differences in beliefs about the effectiveness and necessity of mental health treatment. *American Journal of Community Psychology, 42*, 17–24.

Anglin, D. M., Link, B. G., & Phelan, J. C. (2006). Racial differences in stigmatizing attitudes toward people with mental illness. *Psychiatric Services, 57*, 857–862.

Antonio, A. L. (2004). The influence of friendship groups on intellectual self-confidence and educational aspirations in college. *The Journal of Higher Education, 75*, 446–471.

Antonio, A. L., Chang, M. J., Hakuta, K., Kenny, D. A., Levin, S., & Milem, J. F. (2004). Effects of racial diversity on complex thinking in college students. *Psychological Science, 15*, 507–510.

APA Task Force on Socioeconomic Status. (2007). *Report of the APA Task Force on Socioeconomic Status.* Washington, DC: American Psychological Association. Retrieved from https://www.apa.org/pi/ses/resources/publications/task-force-2006.pdf

Applewhite, S. L. (1995). Curanderismo: Demystifying the health beliefs and practices of elderly Mexican Americans. *Health & Social Work, 20*(4), 247–253.

Aranda, F., Matthews, A. K., Hughes, T. L., Muramatsu, N., Wilsnack, S. C., Johnson, T. P., & Riley, B. B. (2015). Coming out in color: Racial/ethnic differences in the relationship between level of sexual identity disclosure and depression among lesbians. *Cultural Diversity and Ethnic Minority Psychology, 21*, 247–257.

Araujo-Dawson, B. (2015). Understanding the complexities of skin color, perceptions of race, and discrimination among Cubans, Dominicans, and Puerto Ricans. *Hispanic Journal of Behavioral Sciences, 37*, 243–256.

Armstrong, T., & Crowther, M. (2002). Spirituality among older African Americans. *Journal of Adult Development, 9*, 3–12.

Aroian, K. J. (2016). Research considerations: Minimizing mistrust and maximizing participation. In M. A. Amer & G. H. Awad (Eds.), *Handbook of Arab American psychology* (pp. 400–413). New York: Routledge.

Aronson, J., Fried, C. B., & Good, C. (2002). Reducing the effects of stereotype threat on African American college students by shaping theories of intelligence. *Journal of Experimental Social Psychology, 38*, 113–125.

Asakawa, K., & Csikszentmihalyi, M. (1998). The quality of experience of Asian American adolescents in academic activities: An exploration of educational achievement. *Journal of Research on Adolescence, 8*, 241–262.

Awad, G., & Jackson, K. M. (2016). The measurement of color-blind racial ideology. In H. A. Neville, M. E. Gallardo, & D. W. Sue. (Eds.), *The myth of color blindness: Manifestations, dynamics, and impact* (pp. 141–156). Washington, DC: American Psychological Association.

Awad, G. H., & Amayreh, W. M. (2016). Discrimination: Heightened prejudice post 9/11 and psychological outcomes. In M. A. Amer & G. H. Awad (Eds.), *Handbook of Arab American psychology* (pp. 63–75). New York: Routledge.

Ayers, S. L., Kulis, S., & Tsethlikai, M. (2017). Assessing parenting and family functioning measures for urban American Indians. *Journal of Community Psychology, 45*(2), 230–249.

Baca Zinn, M. (1979). Field research in minority communities: Ethical, methodological, and political observations by an outsider. *Social Problems, 27*, 209–219.

Bahrick, H. P., Hall, L. K., Goggin, J. P., Bahrick, L. E., & Berger, S. A. (1994). Fifty years of language maintenance and language dominance in bilingual Hispanic immigrants. *Journal of Experimental Psychology: General, 123*(3), 264–283.

Baker, D. L., Meinikow, J., Ly, M. Y., Shoultz, J., Niederhauser, V., & Diaz-Escamilla, R. (2010). Translation of health surveys using mixed methods. *Journal of Nursing Scholarship, 42*, 430–438.

Baker, D. W. (1999). Reading between the lines. *Journal of General and Internal Medicine, 14*, 315–317.

Balls Organista, P., Chun, K. M., & Marín, G. (Eds.). (1998). *Readings in ethnic psychology.* New York: Routledge.

Balls Organista, P., Organista, K. C., & Kurasaki, K. (2003). The relationship between acculturation and ethnic minority mental health. In K. M. Chun, P. Balls Organista, & G. Marín (Eds.), *Acculturation: Advances in theory, measurement, and applied research* (pp. 139–161). Washington, DC: American Psychological Association.

Balsa, A. I., & McGuire, T. G. (2003). Prejudice, clinical uncertainty and stereotyping as sources of health disparities. *Journal of Health Economics, 22*, 89–116.

Balsam, K. F., Huang, B., Fieland, K. C., Simoni, J. M., & Walters, K. L. (2004). Culture, trauma, and wellness: A comparison of heterosexual and lesbian, gay, bisexual, and two-spirit Native Americans. *Cultural Diversity & Ethnic Minority Psychology, 10*, 287–301.

Balsam, K. F., Molina, Y., Beadnell, B., Simoni, J., & Walters, K. (2011). Measuring multiple minority stress: The LGBT People of Color Microaggressions Scale. *Cultural Diversity and Ethnic Minority Psychology, 17*, 163–174.

Baluja, K. F., Park, J., & Myers, D. (2003). Inclusion of immigrant status in smoking prevalence statistics. *American Journal of Public Health, 93*, 642–646.

Barajas-Gonzalez, R. G., & Brooks-Gunn, J. (2014). Income, neighborhood stressors, and harsh parenting: Test of moderation by ethnicity, age, and gender. *Journal of Family Psychology, 28*(6), 855–866.

Barber, S., Hickson, D. A., Wang, X., Sims, M., Nelson, C, & Diez-Roux, A. V. (2016). Neighborhood disadvantage, poor social conditions, and cardiovascular disease incidence among African American adults in the Jackson Heart Study. *American Journal of Public Health, 106*, 2219–2226.

Barnes, A. M., Powell-Griner, E., McFann, K., & Nahin, R. L. (2004). *Complementary and alternative medicine use among adults: United States, 2002. Advance Data from Vital and Health Statistics* (No. 343). Retrieved July 25, 2005, from http://nccam.nih.gov/news/report.pdf

Barrera, M., Jr., Caples, H., & Tein, J.-Y. (2001). The psychological sense of economic hardship: Measurement models, validity, and cross-ethnic equivalence for urban families. *American Journal of Community Psychology, 29*, 493–517.

Barreto, R. M., & Segal, S. P. (2005). Use of mental health services by Asian Americans. *Psychiatric Services, 56*, 746–748.

Barry, D. T. (2001). Assessing culture via the Internet: Methods and techniques for psychological research. *CyberPsychology & Behavior, 4*, 17–21.

Barry, D. T., & Grilo, C. M. (2003). Cultural, self-esteem, and demographic correlates of perception of personal and group discrimination among East Asian immigrants. *American Journal of Orthopsychiatry, 73*, 223–229.

Bartels, S., Teague, G., Drake, R., Clark, R., Bush, P., & Noordsy, D. (1993). Substance abuse in schizophrenia: Service utilization and costs. *The Journal of Nervous and Mental Disease, 181*, 227–232.

Barton, A. W., & Bryant, C. M. (2016). Financial strain, trajectories of marital processes, and African American newlyweds' marital instability. *Journal of Family Psychology, 30*(6), 657–664.

Bastida, E. (2001). Kinship ties of Mexican migrant women on the United States/Mexico border. *Journal of Comparative Family Studies, 32*, 549–572.

Baumrind, D. (1971). Current patterns of parental authority. *Developmental Psychology, 4*(1, part 2), 1–103.

Baumrind, D. (1980). New directions in socialization research. *American Psychologist, 35*, 639–652.

Beals, J., Manson, S. M., Shore, J. H., Friedman, N., Ashcraft, M., Fairbank, J. A., & Schlenger, W. E. (2002). The prevalence of posttraumatic stress disorder among American Indian Vietnam veterans: Disparities and context. *Journal of Traumatic Stress, 15*, 89–97.

Beals, J., Manson, S. M., Whitesell, N. R., Spicer, P., Novins, D. K., & Mitchell, C. M. (2005). Prevalence of *DSM-IV* disorders and attendant help-seeking in 2 American Indian reservation populations. *Archives of General Psychiatry, 62*, 99–108.

Belgrave, F. Z. (2002). Relational theory and cultural enhancement interventions for African American adolescent girls. *Public Health Reports, 117*, 76–81.

Belgrave, F. Z., Abrams, J. A., Hood, K. B., Moore, M. P., & Nguyen, A. B. (2016). Development and validation of a preliminary measure of African American women's gender role beliefs. *Journal of Black Psychology, 42*, 320–342.

Berkman, N. D., Sheridan, S. L., Donahue, K. E., Halpern, D. J., & Crotty, K. (2011). Low health literacy and health outcomes: An updated systematic review. *Annals of Internal Medicine, 155*, 97–107.

Bernal, G., Cumba-Avilés, E., & Rodriguez-Quintana, N. (2014). Methodological challenges in research with ethnic, racial, and ethnocultural groups. In F. T. L. Leong, L. Comas-Díaz, G. C. N. Hall, V. C. McLoyd, & J. E. Trimble (Eds.), *APA handbook of multicultural psychology 1* (vol. 1, pp. 105–123). Washington, DC: American Psychological Association.

Bernal, G., & Scharrón–del Río, M. R. (2001). Are empirically supported treatments valid for ethnic minorities? Toward an alternative approach for treatment research. *Cultural Diversity & Ethnic Minority Psychology, 7*, 328–342.

Bernal, G., Trimble, J. E., Burlew, A. K., & Leong, F. T. L. (Eds.). (2003). *Handbook of racial & ethnic minority psychology.* Thousand Oaks, CA: Sage.

Berns, R. M. (2004). *Child, family, school, community: Socialization and support* (6th ed.). Belmont, CA: Thomson Wadsworth.

Berrol, S. C. (1995). *Growing up American: Immigrant children in America, then and now.* New York: Twayne.

Berry, J. W. (1980). Acculturation as a variety of adaptation. In A. M. Padilla (Ed.), *Acculturation: Theory, models and some new findings* (pp. 9–25). Boulder, CO: Westview.

Berry, J. W. (1998). Acculturative stress. In P. Balls Organista, K. M. Chun, & G. Marín (Eds.), *Readings in ethnic psychology* (pp. 113–117). New York: Routledge.

Berry, J. W. (2003). Conceptual approaches to acculturation. In K. M. Chun, P. Balls Organista, & G. Marín (Eds.), *Acculturation: Advances in theory, measurement, and applied research* (pp. 17–37). Washington, DC: American Psychological Association.

Berry, J. W. (2008). Globalisation and acculturation. *International Journal of Intercultural Relations, 32*(4), 328–336.

Berry, J. W., & Sam, D. L. (2007). Cultural and ethnic factors in health. In S. Ayers, A. Baum, C. McManus, S. Newman, K. Wallston, J. Weinman, & R. West (Eds.), *Cambridge handbook of psychology, health, & medicine* (2nd ed., pp. 64–70). Cambridge: Cambridge University Press.

Berry, J. W., & Sam, D. L. (2014). Multicultural societies. In V. Benet-Martínez & Y.-Y. Hong (Eds.), *The Oxford handbook of multicultural identity* (pp. 97–117). New York: Oxford University Press.

Berry, J. W., & Sam, D. L. (2016a). Introduction. In D. L. Sam & J. W. Berry (Eds.), *The Cambridge handbook of acculturation psychology* (2nd ed., pp. 1–7). Cambridge: Cambridge University Press.

Berry, J. W., & Sam, D. L. (2016b). Theoretical perspectives. In D. L. Sam & J. W. Berry (Eds.), *The Cambridge handbook of acculturation psychology* (2nd ed., pp. 11–29). Cambridge: Cambridge University Press.

Betancourt, H., & López, S. (1993). The study of culture, ethnicity, and race in American psychology. *American Psychologist, 43*, 629–638.

Betancourt, J. R., Green, A. R., Carrillo, J. E., & Ananeh-Firempong, O., II. (2003). Defining cultural competence: A practical framework for addressing racial/ethnic disparities in health and health care. *Public Health Reports, 118*(4), 293–302.

Bhandari Preisser, A. (1999). Domestic violence in South Asian communities in America. *Violence Against Women, 5*, 684–699.

Bhopal, R. (2003). Glossary of terms relating to ethnicity and race: For reflection and debate. *Journal of Epidemiology and Community Health, 58*, 441–445.

Bialystok, E., Craik, F. I. M., & Luk, G. (2012). Bilingualism: Consequences for mind and brain. *American Journal of Human Genetics, 16*, 240–250.

Birdsall, C., Gershenson, S., & Zuñiga, R. (2016, December). *Stereotype threat, role models, and demographic mismatch in an elite professional school setting.* Discussion Paper Series, IZA DP No. 10459. Bonn, Ger.: IZA Institute of Labor Economics. Retrieved from https://www.airweb.org/GrantsAndScholarships/Documents/Grants2016/GershensonScholarlyPaper.pdf

Birman, D. (1998). Biculturalism and perceived competence of Latino immigrant adolescents. *American Journal of Community Psychology, 26*, 335–354.

Birman, D., & Trickett, E. J. (2001). Cultural transitions in first-generation immigrants: Acculturation of Soviet Jewish refugee adolescents and parents. *Journal of Cross-Cultural Psychology, 32*, 456–477.

Birman, D., Trickett, E., & Buchanan, R. M. (2005). A tale of two cities: Replication of a study on the acculturation and adaptation of immigrant adolescents from the former Soviet Union in a different community context. *American Journal of Community Psychology, 35*, 83–101.

Blair, J. M., Fleming, P. L., & Karon, J. M. (2002). Trends in AIDS incidence and survival among racial/ethnic minority men who have sex with men, United States, 1990–1999. *Journal of Acquired Immune Deficiency Syndrome, 31*, 339–347.

Blatt, S. J. (2004). *Experiences of depression: Theoretical, clinical, and research perspectives.* Washington, DC: American Psychological Association.

Blauner, R., & Wellman, D. (1973). Toward the decolonization of social research. In J. A. Ladner (Ed.), *The death of white sociology: Essays on race and culture* (pp. 310–330). New York: Vintage.

Bledsoe, K. L., & Hopson, R. H. (2009). Conducting ethical research in underserved communities. In D. M. Mertens and P. Ginsberg (Eds.), *Handbook of ethics for research in the social sciences.* Thousand Oaks, CA: Sage Publications.

Bleidorn, W., Arslan, R. C., Denissen, J. J. A., Rentfrow, P. J., Gebauer, J. E., Potter, J., & Gosling, S. D. (2016). Age and gender differences in self-esteem: A cross-cultural window. *Journal of Personality and Social Psychology, 111*, 396–410.

Blumenthal, D. S., DiClemente, R. J., Braithwaite, R. L., & Smith, S. A. (Eds.). (2013). *Community-based participatory health research: Issues, methods and translation to practice.* New York: Springer.

Bogardus, E. S. (1959). Race reactions by sexes. *Sociology and Social Research, 43*, 439–441.

Bolaffi, G., Bracalenti, R., Braham, P., & Gindro, S. (Eds.). (2003). *Dictionary of race, ethnicity & culture.* London: Sage.

Bonilla-Silva, E. (2016). Down the rabbit hole: Color-blind racism in Obamerica. In H. A. Neville, M. E. Gallardo, & D. W. Sue. (Eds.), *The myth of color blindness: Manifestations, dynamics, and impact* (pp. 25–38). Washington, DC: American Psychological Association.

Bonilla-Silva, E., & Dietrich, D. (2011). The sweet enchantment of color-blind racism in Obamerica. *Annals of the American Academy of Political and Social Science, 634*, 190–206.

Bor, J., Cohen, G. H., & Galea, S. (2017). Population health in an era of rising income inequalities: USA, 1980–2015. *The Lancet, 389*, 1475–1490.

Borre, A., & Kliewer, W. (2014). Parental strain, mental health problems, and parenting practices: A longitudinal study. *Personality and Individual Differences, 68*, 93–97.

Borrego, E. & Johnson, R. G. (2012). *Cultural competence for public managers: Managing diversity in today's world.* Boca Raton, FL: CRC Press.

Borrell, L. N., & Crawford, N. D. (2006). Race, ethnicity, and self-rated health status in the Behavioral Risk Factor Surveillance System survey. *Hispanic Journal of Behavioral Sciences, 28*, 387–403.

Borrell, L. N., Dallo, F. J. (2008). Self-rated health and race among Hispanic and non-Hispanic adults. *Journal of Immigrant and Minority Health, 10*, 229–238.

Borrell, L. N., Kiefe, C. I., Williams, D. R., Diez-Roux, A. V., & Gordon-Larsen, P. (2006). Self-reported health, perceived racial discrimination, and skin color in African Americans in the CARDIA study. *Social Science & Medicine, 63*, 1415–1427.

Bourhis, R. Y., Moise, L. C., Perreault, S., & Senécal, S. (1997). Towards an interactive acculturation model: A social psychological approach. *International Journal of Psychology, 32*, 369–386.

Bourhis, R. Y., Montaruli, E., El-Geledi, S., Harvey, S.-P., & Barrette, G. (2010). Acculturation in multiple host community settings. *Journal of Social Issues, 66*(4), 780–802.

Bowlby, J. (1969). *Attachment and loss: Vol. 1, Attachment.* New York: Basic Books.

Bowleg, L., Huang, J., Brooks, K., Black, A., & Burkholder, G. (2003). Triple jeopardy and beyond: Multiple minority stress and resilience among Black lesbians. *Journal of Lesbian Studies, 7*(4), 67–108.

Boykin, K. (2005a). *Beyond the down low debate: Sex, lies, and denial in Black America.* New York: Carrol and Graf.

Boykin, K. (2005b, February 3). 10 things you should know about the DL. *Sexuality.* Retrieved from http://www.keithboykin.com/arch/2005/02/03/10_things_you_s, archived at http://archive.li/LrwyR

Bracey, J. R., Bamaca, M. Y., & Umaña-Taylor, A. J. (2004). Examining ethnic identity and self-esteem among biracial and monoracial adolescents. *Journal of Youth and Adolescence, 33*, 123–132.

Brannon, L., Updegraff, J. A., & Feist, J. (2017). *Health psychology: An introduction to behavior and health* (9th ed.). Boston: Cenage Learning.

Bravo, M. (2003). Instrument development: Cultural adaptations for ethnic minority research. In G. Bernal, J. E. Trimble, A. K. Burlew, & F. T. L. Leong (Eds.), *Handbook of racial and ethnic minority psychology* (pp. 220–236). Thousand Oaks, CA: Sage Publications.

Breslau, J., Aguilar-Gaxiola, S., Kendler, K. S., Su, M., Williams, D., & Kessler, R. C. (2006). Specifying race-ethnic differences in risk for psychiatric disorder in the USA national sample. *Psychological Medicine 36*(1), 57–68.

Breslau, J., Cefalu, M., Wong, E. C., Burnam, M. A., Hunter, G. P., Florez, K. R., & Collins, R. L. (2017). Racial/ethnic differences in perception of need for mental health treatment in a US national sample. *Social Psychiatry and Psychiatric Epidemiology, 52*(8), 929–937.

Breslau, J., Kendler, K. S., Su, M., Aguilar-Gaxiola, S., & Kessler, R. C. (2005). Lifetime prevalence and persistence of psychiatric disorders across ethnic groups in the USA. *Psychological Medicine, 35*, 317–327.

Brewer, M. B., & Campbell, D. T. (1976). *Ethnocentrism and intergroup attitudes*. New York: John Wiley.

Brick, L. A., Redding, C. A., Paiva, A. L., & Velicer, W. F. (2017). Intervention effects on stage transitions for adolescent smoking and alcohol use acquisition. *Psychology of Addictive Behaviors, 31*, 614–624.

Brislin, R. W. (1980). Translation and content analysis of oral and written materials. In H. C. Triandis & J. W. Berry (Eds.), *Handbook of cross-cultural psychology* (pp. 389–444). Boston: Allyn & Bacon.

Brislin, R. W., Lonner, W. J., & Thorndike, E. M. (1973). *Cross-cultural research methods*. New York: John Wiley.

The British Psychological Society. (2010). *Code of human research ethics*. Leicester, Eng.: Author. Retrieved from http://www.bps.org.uk/sites/default/files/documents/code_of_human_research_ethics.pdf

Brittian, A. S., Umaña-Taylor, A. J., & Derlan, C. L. (2013). An examination of biracial college youths' family ethnic socialization, ethnic identity, and adjustment: Do self-identification labels and university context matter? *Cultural Diversity and Ethnic Minority Psychology, 19*, 177–189.

Brody, G. H., Flor, D. L., & Morgan Gibson, N. (1999). Linking maternal efficacy beliefs, developmental goals, parenting practices, and child competence in rural single-parent African American families. *Child Development, 70*, 1197–1208.

Brody, G. H., Stoneman, Z., & Flor, D. (1996). Parental religiosity, family processes, and youth competence in rural, two-parent African American families. *Developmental Psychology, 32*, 696–706.

Brody, G. H., Yu, T., Beach, S. R. H., Kogan, S. M., Windle, M., & Philibert, R. A. (2014). Harsh parenting and adolescent health: A longitudinal analysis with genetic moderation. *Health Psychology, 33*(5), 401–409.

Brody, G. H., Yu, T., Miller, G. E., & Chen, E. (2015). Discrimination, racial identity, and cytokine levels among African-American adolescents. *Journal of Adolescent Health, 56*, 496–501.

Bromley, E., Mikesell, L., Jones, F., & Khodyakov, D. (2015). From subject to participant: Ethics and the evolving role of community in health research. *American Journal of Public Health, 105*, 900–908.

Brondolo, E., Rieppi, R., Kelly, K. P., & Gerin, W. (2003). Perceived racism and blood pressure: A review of the literature and conceptual and methodological critique. *Annuals of Behavioral Medicine, 25*, 55–65.

Bronfenbrenner, U. (1986). Ecology of the family as a context for human development: Research perspectives. *Developmental Psychology, 22*, 723–742.

Bronfenbrenner, U., & Morris, P. A. (1998). The ecology of developmental process. In W. Damon (Ed.-in-Chief) & R. M. Lerner (Vol. Ed.), *Handbook of child psychology: Vol. 1, Theoretical models of human development* (5th ed., pp. 993–1028). New York: John Wiley.

Brooks, C. J., Gortmaker, S. L., Long, M. W., Cradock, A. L., & Kenney, E. L. (2017). Racial/ethnic and socioeconomic disparities in hydration status among US adults and the role of tap water and other beverage intake. *American Journal of Public Health, 107*, 1387–1394.

Brooks, T. R. (1992). Pitfalls in communication with Hispanic and African-American patients: Do translators help or harm? *Journal of the National Medical Association, 84*, 941–947.

Brown, D. L., Blackmon, S. K., Rosnick, C. B., Griffin-Fennell, F. D., & White-Johnson, R. L. (2017). Initial development of a gendered-racial socialization scale for african american college women. *Sex Roles, 77*, 178–193.

Brown, D. R., Fouad, M. N., Basen-Engquist, K., & Tortolero-Luna, G. (2000). Recruitment and retention of minority women in cancer screening, prevention, and treatment trials. *Annals of Epidemiology, 10*, S13–S21.

Brown, G. L., Kogan, S. M., & Kim, J. (2017). From fathers to sons: The intergenerational transmission of parenting behavior among African American young men. *Family Process*.

Brown, R., & Zagefka, H. (2011). The dynamics of acculturation: An intergroup perspective. *Advances in Experimental Social Psychology, 44*, 129–183.

Brown, R. A., Dickerson, D. L., & D'Amico, E. J. (2016). Cultural identity among urban american indian/alaska native youth: Implications for alcohol and drug use. *Prevention Science, 17*, 852–861.

Brown, T. H., Hargrove, T. W., & Griffith, D. M. (2015). Racial/ethnic disparities in men's health: Examining psychosocial mechanisms. *Family & Community Health, 38*, 307–318.

Browning, C. R., & Cagney, K. A. (2003). Moving beyond poverty: Neighborhood structure, social processes, and health. *Journal of Health and Social Behavior, 44*, 552–571.

Budge, S. L., Thai, J. L., Tebbe, E. A., & Howard, K. A. S. (2016). The mental health outcomes. *The Counseling Psychologist*, *44*, 1025–1049.

Bui, H., & Morash, M. (1999). Domestic violence in the Vietnamese immigrant community. *Violence Against Women*, *5*, 769–795.

Buki, L. P., Ma, T. C., Strom, R. D., & Strom, S. K. (2003). Chinese immigrant mothers of adolescents: Self-perceptions of acculturation effects on parenting. *Cultural Diversity & Ethnic Minority Psychology*, *9*, 127–140.

Bullard, R. D. (1990). *Dumping in Dixie: Race, class, and environmental quality*. Boulder, CO: Westview.

Bullard, R. D., Mohal, P., Saha, R., & Wright, B. (2007, March). *Toxic wastes and race at twenty*, 1987–2007 (Report prepared for the United Church of Christ Justice and Witness Ministries). Retrieved from http://www.ejrc.cau.edu/TWART-light.pdf

Bullock, A., Sheff, K., Moore, K., & Manson, S. (2017). Obesity and overweight in American Indian and Alaska Native children, 2006–2015. *American Journal of Public Health*, *107*, 1502–1507.

Buriel, R. (1984). Integration with traditional Mexican American culture and sociocultural adjustment. In J. L. Martinez & R. Mendoza (Eds.), *Chicano psychology* (2nd ed., pp. 95–130). New York: Academic Press.

Buriel, R., & Saenz, E. (1980). Psychocultural characteristics of college-bound and noncollege-bound Chicanas. *Journal of Social Psychology*, *110*, 245–251.

Burlew, A. K. (2003). Research with ethnic minorities: Conceptual, methodological, and analytic issues. In G. Bernal, J. E. Trimble, A. K. Burlew, & F. T. L. Leong (Eds.), *Handbook of racial and ethnic minority psychology* (pp. 179–197). Thousand Oaks, CA: Sage Publications.

Burnam, M. A., Hough, R. L., Karno, M., Escobar, J. I., & Telles, C. A. (1987). Acculturation and lifetime prevalence of psychiatric disorders among Mexican Americans in Los Angeles. *Journal of Health and Social Behavior*, *28*, 89–102.

Burnett, M. N., & Sisson, K. (1995). Doll studies revisited: A question of validity. *Journal of Black Psychology*, *21*, 19–29.

Burrow-Sanchez, J. J., Ortiz-Jensen, C., Corrales, C., & Meyers, K. (2015). Acculturation in a pretreatment sample of Latino adolescents: A confirmatory factor analytic study. *Hispanic Journal of Behavioral Sciences*, *37*, 103–117.

Bushman, B. J., & Bonacci, A. M. (2004). You've got mail: Using e-mail to examine the effect of prejudiced attitudes on discrimination against Arabs. *Journal of Experimental Social Psychology*, *40*, 753–759.

Cabassa, L. J. (2003). Measuring acculturation: Where we are and where we need to go. *Hispanic Journal of Behavioral Sciences*, *25*, 127–146.

California Psychological Association. (2004). *Expertise series* (Division I: Clinical and Professional Practice). Retrieved from http://www.cpapsych.org/displaycommon.cfm?an=16

Camarota, S. A., & Zeigler, K. (2014). One in five U.S. residents speaks foreign language at home, record 61.8 million Spanish, Chinese, and Arabic speakers grew most since 2010. *Center for Immigrant Studies*. Retrieved from https://cis.org/sites/cis.org/files/camarota-language.pdf

Carpenter, D., Maasberg, M., Hicks, C., & Chen, X. (2016). A multicultural study of biometric privacy concerns in a fire ground accountability crisis response system. *International Journal of Information Management*, *36*, 735–747.

Carter, R. T., & Reynolds, A. L. (2011). Race-related stress, racial identity status attitudes, and emotional reactions of Black Americans. *Cultural Diversity and Ethnic Minority Psychology*, *17*, 156–162.

Case, A., & Deaton, A. (2015). Rising morbidity and mortality in midlife among White non-Hispanic Americans in the 21st century. *Proceedings of the National cademies of Science USA*, *112*, 15078–15083.

Cauce, A. M. (2011). Is multicultural psychology a-scientific? Diverse methods for diversity research. *Cultural Diversity and Ethnic Minority Psychology*, 17, 228–233.

Ceballo, R., Maurizi, L. K., Suarez, G. A., & Aretakis, M. T. (2014). Gift and sacrifice: Parental involvement in Latino adolescents' education. *Cultural Diversity and Ethnic Minority Psychology*, *20*(1), 116–127.

Celenk, O., & van de Vijver, F. J. R. (2014). Assessment of psychological acculturation and multiculturalism: An overview of measures in the public domain. In V. Benet-Martínez & Y.-Y. Hong (Eds.), *The Oxford handbook of multicultural identity* (pp. 205–226). New York: Oxford University Press.

Center for Behavioral Health Statistics and Quality. (2015). Behavioral health trends in the United States: Results from the 2014 National Survey on Drug Use and Health (HHS Publication No. SMA 15-4927, NSDUH Series H-50). Retrieved from http://www.samhsa.gov/ data/

Centers for Disease Control and Prevention. (2001). HIV incidence among young men who have sex with men—seven U.S. cities, 1994–2000. *Morbidity and Mortality Weekly Report*, *50*(21), 440–444.

Centers for Disease Control and Prevention. (2002). State-specific trends in self-reported blood pressure screening and high blood pressure—United States, 1991–1999. *Morbidity and Mortality Weekly Report*, *51*(21), 456–460.

Centers for Disease Control and Prevention. (2005a). *HIV/AIDS surveillance report* (vol. 17). Atlanta: Author. Retrieved October 21, 2007, from http://www.cdc.gov/hiv/topics/surveillance/resources/reports/

Centers for Disease Control and Prevention. (2005b). Racial/ethnic disparities in prevalence, treatment, and control of hypertension—United States, 1999–2002. *Morbidity and Mortality Weekly Report*, *54*(01), 7–9. Retrieved from https://www.cdc.gov/mmwr/preview/mmwrhtml/mm5401a3.htm

Centers for Disease Control and Prevention. (2006). Deaths: Final data for 2003. *National Vital Statistics*

Reports, 54(13). Retrieved January 15, 2007, from http://www.cdc.gov/nchs/data/nvsr/nvsr54/nvsr54_13.pdf

Centers for Disease Control and Prevention. (2007). *HIV/AIDS surveillance report* (vol. 19). Retrieved from http://www.cdc.gov/hiv/topics/surveillance/resources/reports/

Centers for Disease Control and Prevention. (2016, November). *HIV surveillance report, 2015* (vol. 27). Retreived January 25, 2018, from https://www.cdc.gov/hiv/pdf/library/reports/surveillance/cdc-hiv-surveillance-report-2015-vol-27.pdf

Cha, E.-S., Kim, K. H., & Erlen, J. A. (2007). Translation of scales in cross-cultural research: Issues and techniques. *Journal of Advanced Nursing, 58*, 386–395.

Chabal, S., & Marian, V. (2015). Speakers of different languages process the visual world differently. *Journal of Experimental Psychology: General, 144*, 539–550.

Chae, D. H., & Ayala, G. (2010). Sexual orientation and sexual behavior among Latino and Asian Americans: Implications for unfair treatment and psychological distress. *Journal of Sex Research, 47*, 451–459.

Chae, D. H., Lincoln, K. D., Adler, N. E., & Syme, S. L. (2010). Do experiences of racial discrimination predict cardiovascular disease among African American men? The moderating role of internalized negative racial group attitudes. *Social Science & Medicine, 71*, 1182–1188.

Chan, C. S. (1995). Issues of sexual identity in an ethnic minority: The case of Chinese American lesbians, gay men, and bisexual people. In A. R. D'Augelli & C. J. Patterson (Eds.), *Lesbian, gay, and bisexual identities over the lifespan: Psychological perspectives* (pp. 87–101). New York: Oxford University Press.

Chang, E.-S., Simon, M. A., & Dong, X. Q. (2016). Using community-based participatory research to address Chinese older women's health needs: Toward sustainability. *Journal of Women & Aging, 28*, 276–284.

Chang, T.-F., Han, E.-J., Lee, J.-S., & Qin, D. B. (2015). Korean American adolescent ethnic-identity pride and psychological adjustment: Moderating effects of parental support and school environment. *Asian American Journal of Psychology, 6*, 190–199.

Chao, R. K. (1994). Beyond parental control and authoritarian parenting style: Understanding Chinese parenting through the cultural notion of training. *Child Development, 65*, 1111–1119.

Chao, R. K. (2006). The prevalence and consequences of adolescents' language brokering for their immigrant parents. In M. H. Bornstein & L. R. Cote (Eds.), *Acculturation and parent-child relationships: Measurement and development* (pp. 271–296). Mahwah, NJ: Lawrence Erlbaum.

Chao, R. C.-L., Wei, M., Spanierman, L., Longo, J., & Northart, D. (2015). White racial attitudes and White empathy: The moderation of openness to diversity. *The Counseling Psychologist, 43*, 94–120.

Chatters, L. M., Taylor, R. J., & Lincoln, K. D. (1999). African American religious participation: A multi-sample comparison. *Journal for the Scientific Study of Religion, 38*, 132–145.

Chaudhary, N. (2004). Researching communities: Travails of working in the Indian subcontinent. *Cross-Cultural Psychology Bulletin, 38*(4), 5–13.

Chavez-Korell, S., & Vandiver, B.J. (2012). Are CRIS cluster patterns differentially associated with African American enculturation and social distance? *The Counseling Psychologist, 40*, 755–788.

Chavis, B. (1993). Foreword. In R. D. Bullard (Ed.), *Confronting environmental racism: Voices from the grassroots* (pp. 3–5). Boston: South End Press.

Chavous, T. M., Rivas-Drake, D., Smalls, C., Griffin, T., & Cogburn, C. (2008). Gender matters, too: The influences of school racial discrimination and racial identity on academic engagement outcomes among African American adolescents. *Developmental Psychology, 44*, 637–654.

Cheah, C. S. L., Leung, C. Y. Y., & Zhou, N. (2013). Understanding "tiger parenting" through the perceptions of Chinese immigrant mothers: Can Chinese and U.S. parenting coexist? *Asian American Journal of Psychology, 4*(1), 30–40.

Chen, E., & Paterson, L. Q. (2006). Neighborhood, family, and subjective socioeconomic status: How do they relate to adolescent health? *Health Psychology, 25*, 704–714.

Chen, J., & Vargas-Bustamante, A. (2011). Estimating the effects of immigration status on mental health care utilization in the United States. *Journal of Immigrant Minority Health, 13*, 671–680.

Chen, Y.-C., & Tryon, G. S. (2012). Dual minority stress and Asian American gay men's psychological distress. *Journal of Community Psychology, 40*, 539–554.

Cheng, T. C., & Lo, C. C. (2015). Racial disparities in intimate partner violence and in seeking help with mental health. *Journal of Interpersonal Violence, 30*(18), 3283–3307.

Cheng, Y.-C., Rostron, B. L., Day, H. R., Stanton, C. A., Hull, L. C., Persoskie, A., . . . & Borek, N. (2017). Patterns of use of smokeless tobacco in US adults, 2013–2014. *American Journal of Public Health, 107*(9), 1508–1514.

Chesla, C., & Chun, K. M. (2005). Accommodating type 2 diabetes in the Chinese American family. *Qualitative Health Research, 15*, 240–255.

Chesla, C. A., Chun, K. M., Kwan, C. M., Mullan, J. T., Kwong, Y., Hsu, L., . . . & Waters, C. M. (2013). Testing the efficacy of culturally adapted coping skills for Chinese American immigrants with type 2 diabetes using community-based participatory research. *Research in Nursing and Health, 36*(4), 359–372.

Cheung, F. M., Leung, K., Fan, R. M., Song, W.-Z., Zhang, J.-X., & Zhang, J.-P. (1996). Development of the Chinese Personality Assessment Inventory. *Journal of Cross-Cultural Psychology, 27*, 181–199.

Cheung, F. M., van de Vijver, F. J. R., & Leong, F. T. L. (2011). Toward a new approach to the study of personality in culture. *American Psychologist, 66*, 593–603.

Chia, R. C., Allred, L., Cheng, B., & Chuang, C. J. (1999). "Social" interaction differences between Chinese and Americans. *Psychological Beiträge*, *41*, 84–90.

Chin, J. L. (Ed.). (2004). *The psychology of prejudice and discrimination: Vol. 2, Ethnicity and multiracial identity series.* Westport, CT: Praeger.

Ching, J. W. J., McDermott, J. F., Fukunaga, C., & Yanagida, E. (1995). Perceptions of family values and roles among Japanese Americans: Clinical considerations. *American Journal of Orthopsychiatry*, *65*, 216–224.

Chiriboga, D. A. (2004). Some thoughts on the measurement of acculturation among Mexican American elders. *Hispanic Journal of Behavioral Sciences*, *26*, 274–292.

Cho, H., & Kim, W. J. (2012). Intimate partner violence among Asian Americans and their use of mental health services: Comparisons with White, Black, and Latino victims. *Journal of Immigrant and Minority Health*, *14*(5), 809–815.

Choi, A. Y., & Israel, T. (2016). Centralizing the psychology of sexual minority Asian and Pacific Islander Americans. *Psychology of Sexual Orientation and Gender Diversity*, *3*, 345–356.

Choi, K.-H., Paul, J., Ayala, G., Boylan, R., & Gregorich, S. E. (2013). Experiences of discrimination and their impact on the mental health among African American, Asian and Pacific Islander, and Latino men who have sex with men. *American Journal of Public Health*, *103*, 868–874.

Chong, V., & Kuo, B. C. H. (2015). Racial identity profiles of Asian-White biracial young adults: Testing a theoretical model with cultural and psychological correlates. *Asian American Journal of Psychology*, *6*, 203–212.

Chou, R. S., & Feagin, J. R. (2015). *The myth of the model minority: Asian Americans facing racism.* New York: Taylor & Francis.

Christian, M. D., & Barbarin, O. A. (2001). Cultural resources and psychological adjustment of African American children: Effects of spirituality and racial attribution. *Journal of Black Psychology*, *27*, 43–63.

Chua, P., & Fujino, D. C. (1999). Negotiating new Asian-American masculinities: Attitudes and gender expectations. *The Journal of Men's Studies*, *7*, 391–413.

Chun, K. M. (2006). Conceptual and measurement issues in family acculturation research. In M. H. Bornstein & L. R. Cote (Eds.), *Acculturation and parent-child relationships: Measurement and development* (pp. 63–78). Mahwah, NJ: Lawrence Erlbaum.

Chun, K. M., & Akutsu, P. D. (1999). Utilization of mental health services: Cultural and gender considerations for immigrant and refugee women. In L. Kramer, S. Ivey, & Y. Ying (Eds.), *Immigrant women and the U.S. health care delivery system: From policy to program* (pp. 54–64). San Francisco: Jossey-Bass.

Chun, K. M., & Akutsu, P. D. (2003). Acculturation among ethnic minority families. In K. M. Chun, P. Balls Organista, & G. Marín (Eds.), *Acculturation: Advances in theory, measurement, and applied research* (pp. 95–119). Washington, DC: American Psychological Association.

Chun, K. M., Akutsu, P. D., & Abueg, F. (1994). *A study of Southeast Asian veterans of the Vietnam War.* Paper presented at the 28th annual convention of the Association for Advancement of Behavior Therapy. San Diego, CA.

Chun, K. M., Balls Organista, P., & Marín, G. (Eds.). (2003). *Acculturation: Advances in theory, measurement, and applied research.* Washington, DC: American Psychological Association.

Chun, K. M., & Chesla, C. A. (2004). Cultural issues in disease management for Chinese Americans with type 2 diabetes. *Psychology and Health*, *19*, 767–785.

Chun, K. M., Kwan, C. M. L., Stycker, L. A., & Chesla, C. A. (2016). Acculturation and bicultural efficacy effects on Chinese American immigrants' diabetes and health management. *Journal of Behavioral Medicine*, *39*, 896–907.

Chun, K. M., Morera, O. F., Andal, J. D., & Skewes, M. C. (2008). Conducting research with diverse Asian American groups. In F. T. L. Leong, A. G. Inman, A. Ebreo, L. H. Yang, L. Kinoshita, & M. Fu (Eds.), *Handbook of Asian American psychology* (2nd ed., pp. 47–65). Thousand Oaks, CA: Sage.

Chung, R. H., Kim, B. S., & Abreu, J. M. (2004). Asian American Multidimensional Acculturation Scale: Development, factor, analysis, reliability, and validity. *Cultural Diversity & Ethnic Minority Psychology*, *10*, 66–80.

Clark, K. B., Chein, I., & Cook, S. W. (2004). The effects of segregation and consequences of desegregation. *American Psychologist*, *59*, 495–501.

Clark, K. B., & Clark, M. K. (1939). Segregation as a factor in the racial identification of Negro pre-school children. *Journal of Experimental of Education*, *8*, 161–163.

Clark, R., Anderson, N. B., Clark, V. R., & Williams, D. R. (1999). Racism as a stressor for African Americans: A biopsychosocial model. *American Psychologist*, *54*, 805–816.

Clarke, T. C., Black, L. I., Stussman, B. J. Barnes, P. M., & Nahin, R. L. (2015). Trends in the use of complementary health approaches among adults: United States, 2002–2012. *National Health Statistics Reports*, no. 79. National Center for health Statistics.

CMS Office of Minority Health and Rand Corporation. (2017). *Racial and ethnic disparities by gender in health care in Medicare Advantage.* Baltimore: Author.

Cohen, A. B., & Varnum, M. E. W. (2016). Beyond East vs. West: Social class, region, and religion as forms of culture. *Current Opinion in Psychology*, 8, 5–9.

Cokley, K. (2007). Critical issues in the measurement of ethnic and racial identity: A referendum on the state of the field. *Journal of Counseling Psychology*, *54*, 224–234.

Cokley, K., McClain, S., Enciso, A., & Martinez, M. (2013). An examination of the impact of minority status stress and impostor feelings on the mental health of diverse ethnic minority college students. *Journal of Multicultural Counseling and Development*, *41*, 82–95.

Cole, E. R. (2009). Intersectionality and research in psychology. *American Psychologist*, *64*, 170–180.

Cole, E. R., & Zucker, A. N. (2007). Black and white women's perspectives on femininity. *Cultural Diversity & Ethnic Minority Psychology, 13*, 1–9.

Cole, M., Cole, S. R., & Lightfoot, C. (2005). *The development of children* (5th ed.). New York: Worth Publishers.

Coley, R. L., Kull, M. A., & Carrano, J. (2014). Parental endorsement of spanking and children's internalizing and externalizing problems in African American and Hispanic families. *Journal of Family Psychology, 28*(1), 22–31.

Collins, J. F. (2000). Biracial Japanese American identity: An evolving process. *Cultural Diversity & Ethnic Minority Psychology, 6*, 115–133.

Collins, P. H., & Bilge, S. (2016). *Intersectionality.* Malden, MA: Polity Press.

Collins, P. Y. (2012, September 13). Using collaborative care to reduce racial and ethnic disparities in mental health care. *NAMHC Concept Clearance.* Retrieved from http://www.nimh.nih.gov//about/advisory-boards-and-groups/namhc/index.shtml

Comaroff, J. (1987). Of totemism and ethnicity: Consciousness, practice, and the signs of inequality. *Ethnos, 52*(3–4), 301–323.

Comer, R. J. (2015). *Abnormal psychology* (9th ed.). New York: Worth Publishers.

Compton, W. M., Conway, K. P., Stinson, F. S., & Grant, B. F. (2006). Changes in the prevalence of major depression and comorbid substance use disorders in the United States between 1991–1992 and 2001–2002. *American Journal of Psychiatry, 163*, 2141–2147.

Concepcion, W. R., Kohatsu, E. L., & Yeh, C. J. (2013). Using racial identity and acculturation to analyze experiences of racism among Asian Americans. *Asian American Journal of Psychology, 4*, 136–142.

Conley, T. D., Rabinowitz, J. L., & Rabow, J. (2010). Gordon Gekkos, frat boys and nice guys: The content, dimensions, and structural determinants of multiple ethnic minority groups' stereotypes about White men. *Analyses of Social Issues and Public Policy, 10*, 69–96.

Connolly, C., & Witte, G. (2004, August 27). Poverty rate up 3rd year in a row. *The Washington Post*, p. A01. Retrieved from http://www.washingtonpost.com/wp-dyn/articles/A35175-2004Aug26.html

Consolacion, T. B., Russell, S. T., & Sue, S. (2004). Sex, race/ethnicity, and romantic attractions: Multiple minority status adolescents and mental health. *Cultural Diversity & Ethnic Minority Psychology, 10*, 200–214.

Constantine, M. G., Gainor, K. A., Ahluwalia, M. K., & Berkel, L. A. (2003). Independent and interdependent self-construals, individualism, collectivism, and harmony control in African Americans. *Journal of Black Psychology, 229*, 87–101.

Contrada, R. J., Ashmore, R. D., Gary, M. L., Coups, E., Egeth, J. D., Sewell, A., Ewell, K., Goyal, T. M., & Chasse, V. (2001). Measures of ethnicity-related stress: Psychometric properties, ethnic group differences, and associations with well-being. *Journal of Applied Social Psychology, 31*, 1775–1820.

Cook, S. H., Juster, R.-P., Calebs, B. J., Heinze, J., & Miller, A. L. (2017). Cortisol profiles differ by race/ethnicity among young sexual minority men. *Psychoneuroendocrinology, 75*, 1–4.

Cooper, S. M., Guthrie, B. J., Brown, C., & Metzger, I. (2011). Daily hassles and African American adolescent females' psychological functioning: Direct and interactive associations with gender role orientation. *Sex Roles, 65*, 397–409.

Corrigan, P., Kraus, D., Burks, R., & Schmidt, A. (2015). Community-based participatory research examining the health care needs of African Americans who are homeless with mental illness. *Journal of Health Care for the Poor and Underserved, 26*, 119–133.

Cortes, D. E. (2003). Idioms of distress, acculturation, and depression: The Puerto Rican experience. In K. M. Chun, P. Balls Organista, & G. Marín, *Acculturation: Advances in theory, measurement, and applied research* (pp. 207–222). Washington, DC: American Psychological Association.

Costa, A., Foucart, A., Haykawa, S., Aparici, M., Apesteguia, J., & Keysar, B. (2014). Your morals depend on language. *PLOS One, 9*, e94842.

Council of National Psychological Associations for the Advancement of Ethnic Minority Interests. (2000, January). *Guidelines for research in ethnic minority communities.* Washington, DC: American Psychological Association. Retrieved from https://www.apa.org/pi/oema/resources/cnpaaemi-guidelines.pdf

Crosby, F. J., Iyer, A., Clayton, S., & Downing, R. A. (2003). Affirmative action: Psychological data and the policy debates. *American Psychologist, 58*, 93–115.

Cross, T. L., Bazron, B. J., Dennis, K. W., & Isaacs, M. R. (1989). Towards a culturally competent system of care: A monograph on effective services for minority children who are severely emotionally disturbed. Georgetown University Child Development Center. Washington, DC: CASSP Technical Assistance Center.

Cross, W. E., Jr. (1971). Negro-to-Black conversion experience: Toward a psychology of Black liberation. *Black World, 20*, 13–27.

Cross, W. E., Jr. (1995). The psychology of nigrescence: Revising the cross model. In J. G. Ponterotto, J. M. Casas, L. A. Suzuki, & C. M. Alexander (Eds.), *Handbook of multicultural counseling* (pp. 181–198). Thousand Oaks, CA: Sage.

Cuellar, I., Arnold, B., & Gonzalez, G. (1995). Cognitive referents of acculturation: Assessment of cultural constructs in Mexican Americans. *Journal of Community Psychology, 23*, 339–356.

Cuellar, I., Harris, L. C., & Jasso, R. (1980). An acculturation scale for Mexican American normal and clinical populations. *Hispanic Journal of Behavioral Sciences, 2*, 199–217.

Cuevas, A. G., Dawson, B. A., & Williams, D. R. (2016). Race and skin color in Latino health: An analytic review. *American Journal of Public Health, 106*, 2131–2136.

Cumming-Bruce, N. (2016, September 5). U.N. human rights chief blasts "demagogues" of Western nations. *The New York Times*. Retrieved from https://www.nytimes.com/2016/09/06/world/un-human-rights-chief-blasts-demagogues-of-western-nations.html

Cunningham, W. E., Hays, R. D., Duan, N., Andersen, R., Nakazono, T. T., Bozzette, S. A., & Shapiro, M. F. (2005). The effect of socioeconomic status on the survival of people receiving care for HIV infection in the United States. *Journal of Health Care for the Poor and Underserved, 6*, 655–676.

Cuyjet, M. J., Linder, C., Howard-Hamilton, M. F., & Cooper, D. L. (Eds.) (2016). *Multiculturalism on campus: Theory, models, and practices for understanding diversity and creating inclusion* (2nd ed.). Sterling, VA: Stylus Publishing.

Damron-Rodriguez, J., Wallace, S., & Kington, R. (1994). Service utilization and minority elderly: Appropriateness, accessibility and acceptability. *Gerontology & Geriatrics Education, 15*, 45–63.

Dankwa-Mullan, I., & Pérez-Stable, E. J. (2016). Addressing health disparities is a place-based issue. *American Journal of Public Health, 106*, 637–639.

Davis, T. D., Deen, T., Bryant-Bedell, K., Tate, V., & Fortney, J. (2011). Does minority racial-ethnic status moderate outcomes of collaborative care for depression? *Psychiatric Services, 62*, 1282–1288.

Deary, V. (2005). Explaining the unexplained? Overcoming the distortions of a dualist understanding of medically unexplained illness. *Journal of Mental Health, 14*, 213–221.

Deaux, K. (1999). An overview of research on gender: Four themes from 3 decades. In W. B. Swann Jr., J. H. Langlois, & L. A. Gilbert (Eds.), *Sexism and stereotypes in modern society: The gender science of Janet Taylor Spence* (pp. 11–33). Washington, DC: American Psychological Association.

DeCastro, A. B., Gee, G. C., & Takeuchi, D. T. (2008). Workplace discrimination and health among Filipinos in the United States. *American Journal of Public Health, 98*, 520–526.

De Coteau, T., Anderson, J., & Hope, D. (2006). Adapting manualized treatments: Treating anxiety disorders among Native Americans. *Cognitive and Behavioral Practice, 13*, 304–309.

Del Pilar, J. A., & Udasco, J. O. (2004). Deculturation: Its lack of validity. *Cultural Diversity & Ethnic Minority Psychology, 10*(2), 169–176.

DeNavas-Walt, C., & Proctor, B. D. (2015, September). *Income and poverty in the United States: 2014; Current Population Reports* (P60–252). U.S. Census Bureau. Retrieved from https://www.census.gov/content/dam/Census/library/publications/2015/demo/p60-252.pdf

Department of Families, Community Services and Indigenous Affairs, Government of Australia. (n.d.). *What is "culturally appropriate" communication?* Retrieved January 24, 2018, from http://resources.fahcsia.gov.au/consumertrainingsupportproducts/docs/external/cultural_communication.pdf

Derlan, C. L., & Umaña-Taylor, A. J. (2015). Brief report: Contextual predictors of African American adolescents' ethnic-racial identity affirmation-belonging and resistance to peer pressure. *Journal of Adolescence, 41*, 1–6.

Derlan, C. L., Umaña-Taylor, A. J., Updegraff, K. A., & Jahromi, L. B. (2016). Mothers' characteristics as predictors of adolescents' ethnic-racial identity: An examination of Mexican-origin teen mothers. *Cultural Diversity and Ethnic Minority Psychology, 22*, 453–459.

Desjarlais, R., Eisenberg, L., Good, B., & Kleinman, A. (1996). *World mental health: Problems and priorities in low-income countries*. Oxford: Oxford University Press.

Devos, T. (2014). Stereotypes and intergroup attitudes. . In F. T. L. Leong, L. Comas-Díaz, G. C. N. Hall, V. C. McLoyd, & J. E. Trimble (Eds.), *APA handbook of multicultural psychology* (vol. 1, pp. 341–360). Washington, DC: American Psychological Association.

Devos, T., & Banaji, M. R. (2005). American = White? *Journal of Personality and Social Psychology, 88*, 447–466.

Dewaele, J.-M., & Wei, L. (2013). Is multilingualism linked to a higher tolerance of ambiguity? *Bilingualism: Language and Cognition, 16*(1), 231–240.

Dexter, C. A., Wong, K., Stacks, A. M., Beeghly, M., & Barnett, D. (2013). Parenting and attachment among low-income African American and Caucasian preschoolers. *Journal of Family Psychology, 27*(4), 629–638.

Diaz, R. M., Ayala, G., & Bein, E. (2004). Sexual risk as an outcome of social oppression: Data from a probability sample of Latino gay men in three U.S. cities. *Cultural Diversity & Ethnic Minority Psychology, 10*, 255–267.

Dixon, J., Durrheim, K., & Tredoux, C. (2005). Beyond the optimal contact strategy: A reality check for the contact hypothesis. *American Psychologist, 60*, 697–711.

Dolan, S. L., & Kawamura, K. M. (2015). *Cross cultural competence: A field guide for developing global leaders and managers*. Bingley, UK: Emerald.

Don Markstein's Toonopedia. (2008). *The Frito Bandito*. Retrieved August 8, 2008, from http://www.Toonopedia.com/frito.htm

Donnellan, M. B., & Lucas, R. E. (2014). Secondary analysis of datasets in multicultural settings. . In F. T. L. Leong, L. Comas-Díaz, G. C. N. Hall, V. C. McLoyd, & J. E. Trimble (Eds.), *APA handbook of multicultural psychology* (vol. 1, pp. 161–175). Washington, DC: American Psychological Association.

Dor, J. (2001). *Introduction to the reading of Lacan: The unconscious structured like a language*. New York: Other Press.

Dottolo, A. L., & Kaschak, E. (2015). Whiteness and White privilege. *Women and Therapy, 38*, 179–184.

Dottolo, A. L., & Stewart, A. J. (2013). "I never think about my race": Psychological features of white racial identities. *Qualitative Research in Psychology, 10*, 102–117.

Doty, M. M., & Holmgren, A. L. (2006, August). *Health care disconnect: Gaps in coverage and care for minority adults.* New York: The Commonwealth Fund.

Douglass, S., & Umaña-Taylor, A. J. (2015). Development of ethnic-racial identity among Latino adolescents and the role of family. *Journal of Applied Developmental Psychology, 41*, 90–98.

Dovidio, J. F., Brigham, J. C., Johnson, B. T., & Gaertner, S. L. (1996). Stereotyping, prejudice and discrimination: Another look. In C. N. Macrae, C. Stangor, & M. Hewstone (Eds.), *Stereotypes and stereotyping* (pp. 276–319). New York: Guilford Press.

Dovidio, J. F., Glick, P., & Rudman, L. A. (2005). *On the nature of prejudice: Fifty years after Allport.* Malden, MA: Blackwell.

Downey, G., & Coyne, J. (1990). Children of depressed parents: An integrative review. *Psychological Bulletin, 108*(1), 50–76.

Doyle, O., Clark, T. T., Cryer-Coupet, Q., Nebbitt, V. E., Goldston, D. B., Estroff, S. E., & Magan, I. (2015). Unheard voices: African American fathers speak about their parenting practices. *Psychology of Men & Masculinity, 16*(3), 274–283.

Duncan, G. J., Brooks-Gunn, J., & Klebanov, P. K. (1994). Economic deprivation and early childhood development. *Child Development, 65*(2), 296–318.

Eaton, A. A., & Rios, D. (2017). Social challenges faced by queer Latino college men: Navigating negative responses to coming out in a double minority sample of emerging adults. *Cultural Diversity and Ethnic Minority Psychology, 23.*

Echeverry, J. J. (1997). Treatment barriers: Accessing and accepting professional help. In J. G. Garcia & M. C. Zea (Eds.), *Psychological interventions and research with Latino populations* (pp. 94–107). Boston: Allyn & Bacon.

Emde, R., & Buchsbaum, H. (1990). Didn't you hear my mommy? Autonomy with connectedness in moral self-emergence. In D. Cicchetti & M. Beeghly (Eds.), *The self in transition* (pp. 35–60). Chicago: University of Chicago Press.

Environmental Protection Agency. (2008). *Environmental justice: Basic information, background.* Retrieved November 20, 2008, from http://www.epa.gov/compliance/basics/ejbackground.html

Environmental Protection Agency. (2018). *Frequent questions for specific EPA programs/topics.* Retrieved from https://www.epa.gov/home/frequent-questions-specific-epa-programstopics

Erikson, E. H. (1950). *Childhood and society.* New York: Norton.

Erkut, S., Alarcon, O., Coll, C. G., Tropp, L. R., & Garcia, H. A. (1999). The dual-focus approach to creating bilingual measures. *Journal of Cross-Cultural Psychology, 30*, 206–218.

Escobar, J. I. (1995). Transcultural aspects of dissociative and somatoform disorders. *Psychiatric Clinics of North America, 18*, 555–569.

Escobar, J. I. (1998). Immigration and mental health: Why are immigrants better off? *Archives of General Psychiatry, 55*, 781–782.

Espiritu, Y. L. (1997). *Asian American women and men: Labor, laws, and love.* Thousand Oaks, CA: Sage.

Esri. (2012). *Minority population growth—The new boom: An analysis of America's changing demographics.* Redlands, CA: Author. Retrieved from http://www.esri.com/library/brochures/pdfs/minority-population-growth.pdf2012

Essed, P. (1990). *Everyday racism: Reports from women of two cultures.* Claremont, CA: Hunter House.

Esteban-Guitart, M., Perera, S., Monreal-Bosch, P., & Bastiani, J. (2016). Identity and sociocultural change: Comparing young indigenous people in Chiapas who have different sociodemographic trajectories. *International Journal of Psychology, 53*, 50–68.

Evans, G. W. (2004). The environment of childhood poverty. *American Psychologist, 59*(2), 77–92.

Evans, R. M. (1999). Increasing minority representation in health care management. *Health Forum Journal, 42*, 22.

Ewall, M., & ActionPA.org. (2008, February). Delco Alliance for Environmental Justice. Retrieved from https://www.ejnet.org/chester/delco-ej.pdf

Fadiman, A. (1997). *The spirit catches you and you fall down: A Hmong child, her American doctors, and the collision of two cultures.* New York: Farrar, Straus and Giroux.

Fairchild, H. H., & Cozens, J. A. (1981). Chicano, Hispanic, or Mexican American: What's in a name? *Hispanic Journal of Behavioral Sciences, 3*, 191–198.

Faragallah, M. H., Schumm, W. R., & Webb, F. J. (1997). Acculturation of Arab-American immigrants: An exploratory study. *Journal of Comparative Family Studies, 28*, 182–203.

Farley, R. (2002). Racial identities in 2000: The response to the multiple-race response option. In J. Perlmann & M. C. Waters (Eds.), *The new race question: How the census counts multiracial individuals* (pp. 33–61). New York: Russell Sage Foundation.

Farver, J. A. M., Narang, S. K., & Bhadha, B. R. (2002). East meets West: Ethnic identity, acculturation, and conflict in Asian Indian families. *Journal of Family Psychology, 16*, 338–350.

Feisthamel, K. P., & Schwartz, R. C. (2006). Racial bias in diagnosis: Practical implications for psychotherapists. *Annals of the American Psychotherapy Association, 9*, 10–14.

Ferguson, G. M., & Birman, D. (2016). Acculturation in the United States of America. In D. L. Sam & J. W. Berry (Eds.), *The Cambridge handbook of acculturation psychology* (2nd ed., pp. 396–416). Cambridge: Cambridge University Press.

Ferguson, G. M., Costigan, C. L., Clarke, C. V., & Ge, J. S. (2016). Introducing remote enculturation: Learning your heritage culture from afar. *Child Development Perspectives, 10*, 166–171.

Finch, B. K., Kolody, B., & Vega, W. A. (2000). Perceived discrimination and depression among Mexican-origin adults in California. *Journal of Health and Social Behavior*, *41*, 295–313.

Fine, M. (2004). The power of the *Brown v. Board of Education* decision: Theorizing threats to sustainability. *American Psychologist*, *59*, 502–510.

Fisher, S., Reynolds, J. L., Hsu, W.-W., Barnes, J., & Tyler, K. (2014). Examining multiracial youth in context: Ethnic identity development and mental health outcomes. *Journal of Youth and Adolescence*, *43*, 1688–1699.

Fishman, J. A. (2000). Who speaks what language to whom and when. In W. Li (Ed.), *The bilingualism reader* (pp. 89–106). London: Routledge. (Reprinted from 1965, *La Linguistique*, *2*, 65–88).

Fiske, S. T. (1998). Stereotyping, prejudice, and discrimination. In D. T. Gilbert, S. T. Fiske, & G. Lindzey (Eds.), *The handbook of social psychology* (pp. 357–411). New York: McGraw-Hill.

Flett, M. L. (2014). *Mastering the "DSM- 5": Integrating new and essential measures into your practice*. Eau Claire, WI: PESI Publishing & Media.

Flicker, S., O'Campo, P., Monchalin, R., Thistle, J., Worthington, C., Masching, R., Guta, A., Pooyak, S., Whitebird, W., & Thomas, C. (2015). Research done in "A Good Way": The importance of indigenous elder involvement in HIV community-based research. *American Journal of Public Health*, *105*, 1149–1154.

Foner, N. (1999). The immigrant family: Cultural legacies and cultural changes. In C. Hirschman, P. Kasinitz, & J. DeWind (Eds.), *The handbook of international migration: The American experience* (pp. 257–274). New York: Russell Sage Foundation.

Ford, D. Y., Harris, J. J., III, Tyson, C. A., & Frazier Trotman, M. (2002). Beyond deficit thinking: Providing access for gifted American students. *Roeper Review*, *24*, 52–58.

Ford, T. E., Boxer, C. F., Armstrong, J., & Edel, J. R. More than "just a joke": The prejudice-releasing function of sexist humor. (2008). *Personality and Social Psychology Bulletin*, *34*(2), 159–170.

Ford, T. E., & Ferguson, M. A. (2004). Social consequences of disparagement humor: A prejudiced norm theory. *Personality and Social Psychology Review*, *8*, 79–94.

Ford, T. E., Woodzicka, J. A., Triplett, S. R., Kochersberger, A. O., & Holden, C. J. (2014). Not all groups are equal: Differential vulnerability of social groups to the prejudice-releasing effects of disparagement humor. *Group Processes & Intergroup Relations*, *17*, 178–199.

Foronda, C., Baptiste, D.-L., Reinholdt, M. M., & Ousman, K. (2016). Cultural humility: A concept analysis. *Journal of Transcultural Nursing*, *27*(3), 210–217.

Forsyth, J., & Carter, R. T. (2012). The relationship between racial identity status attitudes, racism-related coping, and mental health among Black Americans. *Cultural Diversity and Ethnic Minority Psychology*, *18*, 128–140.

Foulks, E. F. (2004a). Commentary: Racial bias in diagnosis and medication of mentally ill minorities in prisons and communities. *Journal of the American Academy of Psychiatry and the Law*, *32*, 46.

Foulks, E. F. (2004b). Cultural variables in psychiatry. *Psychiatric Times*, *24*(4), 28–30.

Fowers, B. J., & Davidov, B. J. (2006). The virtue of multiculturalism: Personal transformation, character, and openness to the other. *American Psychologist*, *61*, 581–594.

Fox, M., Thayer, Z., & Wadhwa, P. D. (2017). Assessment of acculturation in minority health research. *Social Science & Medicine*, *176*, 123–132.

Franklin, A. J., Boyd-Franklin, N., & Draper, C. V. (2002). A psychological and educational perspective on Black parenting. In H. P. McAdoo (Ed.), *Black children: Social, educational, and parental environments* (2nd ed., pp. 119–140). Thousand Oaks, CA: Sage.

Franzini, L., & Fernandez-Esquer, M. E. (2006). The association of subjective social status and health in low-income Mexican-origin individuals in Texas. *Social Science & Medicine*, *63*, 788–804.

French, S. E., Tran, N., & Chávez, N. R. (2013). Exploring the effect of in-group and out-group race-related stressors on anxiety among Asian Pacific Islander American students. *Journal of Applied Social Psychology*, *43*(Suppl 2), E339–E350.

Fuligni, A. J., & Witkow, M. (2004). The postsecondary educational progress of youth from immigrant families. *Journal of Research on Adolescence*, *14*, 159–183.

Fuligni, A. J., Yip, T., & Tseng, V. (2002). The impact of family obligation on the daily activities and psychological well-being of Chinese American adolescents. *Child Development*, *73*, 302–314.

Fuligni, A. J., & Yoshikawa, H. (2003). Socioeconomic resources, parenting, and child development among immigrant families. In M. H. Bornstein & R. H. Bradley (Eds.), *Socioeconomic status, parenting, and child development* (pp. 107–124). Mahwah, NJ: Lawrence Erlbaum.

Fuller-Rowell, T. E., Cogburn, C. D., Brodish, A. B., Peck, S. C., Malanchuk, O., & Eccles, J. S. (2012). Racial discrimination and substance use: Longitudinal associations and identity moderators. *Journal of Behavioral Medicine*, *35*, 581–590.

Gaines, S. O., & Reed, E. S. (1995). Prejudice: From Allport to Dubois. *American Psychologist*, *50*, 96–103.

Gaither, S. E. (2015). "Mixed" results: Multiracial research and identity explorations. *Current Directions in Psychological Science*, *24*, 114–119.

Galea, S., Ahern, J., Resnick, H., Kilpatrick, D., Bucuvalas, M., Gold, J., & Vlahov, D. (2002). Psychological sequelae of the September 11 terrorist attacks in New York City. *New England Journal of Medicine*, *346*(13), 982–987.

Gans, H. J. (1999). Toward a reconciliation of "assimilation" and "pluralism": The interplay of acculturation and ethnic retention. In C. Hirschman, P. Kasinitz, & J. DeWind (Eds.), *The handbook of international migration: The American experience* (pp. 161–171). New York: Russell Sage Foundation.

Garcia, R. L., & Diaz, C. F. (1992). The status and use of Spanish and English among Hispanic youth in Dade County (Miami) Florida: A sociolinguistic study, 1989–1991. *Language and Education*, *6*(1), 13–32.

García, J. I. R., Manongdo, J. A., & Ozechowski, T. J. (2014). Depression symptoms among Mexican American youth: Paternal parenting in the context of maternal parenting, economic stress, and youth gender. *Cultural Diversity and Ethnic Minority Psychology, 20*, 27–36.

Garcia Coll, C., & Marks, A. K. (2012). *The immigrant paradox in children and adolescents: Is becoming American a developmental risk?* Washington, DC: American Psychological Association.

Garcia-Huidobro, D., Allen, M., Rosas-Lee, M., Maldonado, F., Gutierrez, L., Svetaz, M. V., & Wieling, E. (2016). Understanding attendance in a community-based parenting intervention for immigrant Latino families. *Health Promotion Practice, 17*, 57–69.

Gardiner, H. W. (2001). Culture, context, and development. In D. Matsumoto (Ed.), *The handbook of culture and psychology* (pp. 101–117). New York: Oxford University Press.

Garnets, L. D. (2002). Sexual orientations in perspective. *Cultural Diversity & Ethnic Minority Psychology, 8*, 115–129.

Garrett, M. T., & Pichette, E. F. (2000). Red as an apple: Native American acculturation and counseling with or without reservation. *Journal of Counseling & Development, 78*, 3–13.

Gartner, M., Kiang, L., & Supple, A. (2014). Prospective links between ethnic socialization, ethnic and American identity, and well-being among Asian-American adolescents. *Journal of Youth and Adolescence, 43*, 1715–1727.

Gavac, S., Murrar, S., & Brauer, M. (2017). Group perception and social norms. In R. Summers (Ed.), *Social psychology: How other people influence our thoughts and actions.* Santa Barbara, CA: ABC-CLIO.

Gee, C. B. (2004). Assessment of anxiety and depression in Asian American youth. *Journal of Clinical Child and Adolescent Psychology, 33*, 269–271.

Gee, G. C., Ro, A., Gavin, A., & Takeuchi, D. T. (2008). Disentangling the effects of racial and weight discrimination on body mass index and obesity among Asian Americans. *American Journal of Public Health, 98*, 493–500.

Gee, G. C., Spencer, M. S., Chen, J., & Takeuchi, D. T. (2007). A nationwide study of discrimination and chronic health conditions among Asian Americans. *American Journal of Public Health, 97*, 1275–1282.

Geipel, J., Hadjichristidis, C., & Surian, L. (2015). How foreign language shapes moral judgment. *Journal of Experimental Social Psychology, 59*, 8–17.

Georgas, J., Mylonas, K., Bafiti, T., Poortinga, Y. H., Christakopoulou, S., Kagitcibasi, C., . . . & Kodiç, Y. (2001). Functional relationships in the nuclear and extended family: A 16-culture study. *International Journal of Psychology, 36*, 289–300.

Gerth, H., & Mills, C. W. (Eds.). (1946). *From Max Weber: Essays in sociology.* New York: Oxford University Press.

Gibson, M. A. (1989). *Accommodation without assimilation: Sikh immigrants in an American high school.* Ithaca, NY: Cornell University Press.

Gil, A. G., & Vega, W. A. (1996). Two different worlds: Acculturation stress and adaptation among Cuban and Nicaraguan families. *Journal of Social and Personal Relationships, 13*, 435–456.

Gil, A. G., Wagner, E. F., & Vega, W. A. (2000). Acculturation, familism, and alcohol use among Latino adolescent males: Longitudinal relations. *Journal of Community Psychology, 28*, 443–458.

Gillem, A. R., Cohn, L. R., & Throne, C. (2001). Black identity in biracial Black/White people: A comparison of Jacqueline who refuses to be exclusively Black and Adolphus who wishes he were. *Cultural Diversity & Ethnic Minority Psychology, 7*, 182–196.

Glanz, K., Rimer, B. H., & Viswanath, K. (Eds.). (2015). *Health behavior: Theory, research, and practice.* San Francisco: Jossey-Bass.

Glazer, N., & Moynihan, D. P. (1963). *Beyond the melting pot.* Cambridge, MA: MIT Press.

Glionna, J. M., & Goldman, A. (2002, April 19). Answering protests, retailer to pull line of T-shirts that mock Asians. *Los Angeles Times*, p. B1.

Gluszek, A. & Dovidio, J. F. (2010). Speaking with a nonnative accent: Perceptions of bias, communication difficulties, and belonging in the United States. *Journal of Language and Social Psychology, 29*, 224–234.

Goering, J. M. (1971). The emergence of ethnic interests: A case of serendipity. *Social Forces, 48*, 379–384.

Golding, J. M., & Aneshensel, C. S. (1989). Factor structure of the Center for Epidemiologic Studies Depression Scale among Mexican Americans and non-Hispanic Whites. *Journal of Consulting and Clinical Psychology, 1*, 163–168.

Golding, J. M., Aneshensel, C. S., & Hough, R. L. (1991). Responses to depression scale items among Mexican-Americans and non-Hispanic Whites. *Journal of Clinical Psychology, 47*, 61–74.

Golding, J. M., Burnam, M. A., Benjamin, B., & Wells, K. B. (1992). Risk factors of secondary depression among Mexican Americans and non-Hispanic Whites. *Journal of Nervous and Mental Disease, 181*, 166–175.

Gong, F., Xu, J., & Takeuchi, D. T. (2012). Beyond conventional socioeconomic status: Examining subjective and objective social status with self-reported health among Asian immigrants. *Journal of Behavioral Medicine, 35*, 407–419.

Gong-Guy, E. (1987). *The California Southeast Asian Mental Health Needs Assessment* (No. 85-76282A-2). Sacramento: California State Department of Mental Health, Asian Community Mental Health Services.

Gonzales-Backen, M. A. (2013). An application of ecological theory to ethnic identity formation among biethnic adolescents. *Family Relations: An Interdisciplinary Journal of Applied Family Studies, 62*, 92–108.

Gonzales-Backen, M. A., Bámaca-Colbert, M. Y., & Allen, K. (2016). Ethnic identity trajectories among Mexican-origin girls during early and middle adolescence: Predicting future psychosocial adjustment. *Developmental Psychology, 52*, 790–797.

Gonzales-Backen, M. A., & Umaña-Taylor, A. J. (2011). Examining the role of physical appearance in Latino adolescents' ethnic identity. *Journal of Adolescence, 34*, 151–162.

Good, C., Aronson, J., & Harder, J. A. (2008). Problems in the pipeline: Stereotype threat and women's achievement in high-level math courses. *Journal of Applied Developmental Psychology, 29*, 17–28.

Gordon, M. (1964). *Assimilation in American life: The role of race, religion, and national origins*. New York: Oxford University Press.

Goto, S. G., Gee, G. C., & Takeuchi, D. T. (2002). Strangers still? The experience of discrimination among Chinese Americans. *Journal of Community Psychology, 30*, 211–224.

Gouveia, V. V., Clemente, M., & Espinosa, B. (2003). The horizontal and vertical attributes of individualism and collectivism in a Spanish population. *The Journal of Social Psychology, 14*, 43–63.

Grant, B. F., Chou, S. P., & Saha, T. D. (2017). Prevalence of 12-month alcohol use, high-risk drinking, and *DSM-IV* alcohol use disorder in the United States, 2001–2002 and 2012–2013. *JAMA Psychiatry, 74*(9), 911–923.

Grant, B. F., Stinson, F. S., Dawson, D. A., Chou, S. P., Dufour, M. C., Compton, W., . . . & Kaplan, K. (2004). Prevalence and co-occurrence of substance use disorders and independent mood and anxiety disorders: Results from the National Epidemiologic Survey on Alcohol and Related Conditions. *Archives of General Psychiatry, 61*, 807–816.

Gray, F. D. (1998). *The Tuskegee syphilis study*. Montgomery, AL: Black Belt Press.

Grebler, L., Moore, J. W., & Guzman, R. C. (1973). The family: Variations in time and space. In L. I. Duran & H. R. Bernard (Eds.), *Introduction to Chicano studies* (pp. 309–331). New York: Macmillan.

Greene, B. (1997). Ethnic minority lesbians and gay men. In B. Greene (Ed.), *Ethnic and cultural diversity among lesbians and gay men* (pp. 216–239). Thousand Oaks, CA: Sage.

Griffith, D. M., Gunter, K., & Watkins, D. C. (2012). Measuring masculinity in research on men of color: Findings and future directions. *American Journal of Public Health, 102*(Suppl 2), S187–S194.

Grotevant, H. (1998). Adolescent development in family contexts. In W. Damon (Ed.-in-Chief) & N. Eisenberg (Vol. Ed.), *Handbook of child psychology: Vol. 3, Social, emotional, and personality development* (5th ed., pp. 1097–1149). New York: John Wiley.

Grzywacz, J. G., Lang, W., Suerken, C., Quandt, S. A., Bell, R. A., & Arcury, T. A. (2005). Age, race, and ethnicity in the use of complementary and alternative medicine for health self-management: Evidence from the 2002 National Health Interview Survey. *Journal of Aging and Health, 17*, 547–572.

Guarnaccia, P. J., Angel, R., & Worobey, J. L. (1989). The factor structure of the CES-D in the Hispanic Health and Nutrition Examination Survey: The influences of ethnicity, gender, and language. *Social Science & Medicine, 29*, 85–94.

Guarnaccia, P. J., & Rogler, L. H. (1999). Research on culture-bound syndromes. *American Journal of Psychiatry, 156*, 13322–13327.

Guendelman, S., & English, P. B. (1995). Effects of United States residence on birth outcomes among Mexican immigrants: An exploratory study. *American Journal of Epidemiology, 142*, S30–S38.

Guendelman, S., Gould, J. B., Hudes, M., & Eskenazi, B. (1990). Generational differences in perinatal health among the Mexican American population: Findings from HHANES 1982–84. *American Journal of Public Health, 80*, S61–S65.

Guisenger, S., & Blatt, S. J. (1994). Individuality and relatedness: Evolution of a fundamental dialectic. *American Psychologist, 49*, 104–111.

Gullett, L., & West, T. V. (2016). Understanding racial color blindness and multiculturalism in interracial relationships: Cognitive and emotional tensions and their implications. In H. A. Neville, M. E. Gallardo, & D. W. Sue (Eds.), *The myth of color blindness: Manifestations, dynamics, and impact* (pp. 69–87). Washington, DC: American Psychological Association.

Gupta, R., & Yick, A. G. (2001). Preliminary validation of the acculturation scale on Chinese Americans. *Journal of Social Work Research & Evaluation, 2*, 43–56.

Gurin, P., Dey, E. L., Hurtado, S., & Gurin, G. (2002). Diversity and higher education: Theory and impact on educational outcomes. *Harvard Educational Review, 72*, 330–366.

Gurin, P., Nagda, B. A., & Zúñiga, X. (2013). *Dialogue across difference*. New York: Russell Sage Foundation.

Guthrie, R. V. (1998). *Even the rat was white: A historical view of psychology*. Boston: Allyn & Bacon.

Guthrie, R. V. (2004). *Even the rat was white: A historical view of psychology* (2nd ed.). Upper Saddle River, NJ: Pearson Education.

Hall, C. C. I. (2014). The evolution of the revolution: The successful establishment of multicultural psychology. In F. T. L. Leong, L. Comas-Díaz, G. C. N. Hall, V. C. McLoyd, & J. E. Trimble (Eds.), *APA handbook of multicultural psychology* (vol. 1, pp. 3–18). Washington, DC: American Psychological Association.

Hall, G. C. N. (2010). *Multicultural psychology*. New York: Routledge.

Hall, G. C. N. (2018). *Multicultural psychology* (3rd ed.). New York: Routledge.

Hall, G. C. N., Iwamasa, G. Y., & Smith, J. N. (2003). Ethical principles of the psychology profession and ethnic minority issues. In W. O'Donohue & K. E. Ferguson (Eds.), *Handbook of professional ethics for psychologists: Issues, questions, and controversies* (pp. 301–318). Thousand Oaks, CA: Sage.

Hallinan, M. T. (1996). Race effects on students' track mobility in high school. *Social Psychology of Education, 1*, 1–24.

Hammack, P. L., LaVome Robinson, W., Crawford, I., & Li, S. T. (2004). Poverty and depressed mood among urban African-American adolescents: A family stress perspective. *Journal of Child and Family Studies, 13*, 309–323.

Hammond, W. P., & Mattis, J. S. (2005). Being a man about it: Manhood meaning among African American men. *Psychology of Men & Masculinity, 6*, 114–126.

Hansen, H., & Netherland, J. (2016). Is the prescription opioid epidemic a White problem? *American Journal of Public Health, 106*, 2127–2128.

Hansen, M. L. (1952). The third generation in America. *Commentary, 14*, 493–500.

Harman, J. S., Edlund, M. J., & Fortney, J. C. (2004). Disparities in the adequacy of depression treatment in the United States. *Psychiatric Services, 55*, 1379–1385.

Harris, A. C., & Verven, R. (1996). The Greek-American acculturation scale: Development and validity. *Psychological Reports, 78*, 599–610.

Harris, A. C., & Verven, R. (1998). Acculturation as a determinant of Greek-American family values. *Psychological Reports, 83*, 1163–1172.

Harris, C., Aycicegi, A., & Gleason, J. B. (2003). Taboo words and reprimands elicit greater autonomic reactivity in a first language than in a second language. *Applied Psycholinguistics, 24*, 561–579.

Harris, K. M., & Edlund, M. J. (2005). Use of mental health care and substance abuse treatment among adults with co-occurring disorders. *Psychiatric Services, 56*, 954–959.

Harrison, A., Wilson, M., Pine, C., Chan, S., & Buriel, R. (1990). Family ecologies of ethnic minority children. *Child Development, 61*, 347–362.

Harrison-Hale, A. O., McLoyd, V. C., & Smedley, B. (2004). Racial and ethnic status: Risk and protective processes among African American families. In K. I. Maton, C. J. Schellenbach, B. J. Leadbeater, & A. L. Solarz (Eds.), *Investing in children, youth, families, and communities* (pp. 269–283). Washington, DC: American Psychological Association.

Hart, T., & Peterson, J. L. (2004). Predictors of risky sexual behavior among young African American men who have sex with men. *American Journal of Public Health, 94*, 1122–1123.

Hattam, V. C. (2001). Whiteness: Theorizing race, eliding ethnicity. *International Labor and Working-Class History, 60*, 61–68.

Hays, D. G., & Chang, C. Y. (2003). White privilege, oppression, and racial identity development: Implications for supervision. *Counselor Education and Supervision, 43*, 134–145.

Hazzouri, A. Z., Elfassy, T., Sidney, S., Jacobs, D., Perez Stable, E. J., & Yaffe, K. (2016). Sustained economic hardship and cognitive function: The coronary artery risk development in young adults study. *American Journal of Preventive Medicine, 52*, 1–9.

Health Canada. (2007, October). *Guiding principles.* Retrieved from https://www.canada.ca/en/health-canada/services/science-research/science-advice-decision-making/research-ethics-board/policy-procedures/guiding-principles.html

Helfand, J., & Lippin, L. (2002). *Understanding Whiteness/unraveling racism: Tools for the journey.* New York: Thomson Learning.

Helms, J. E. (1990). *Black and White racial identity development.* Westport, CT: Greenwood.

Helms, J. E. (1995). An update of Helms' White and people of color racial identity models. In J. G. Ponterotto & J. M. Casas (Eds.), *Handbook of multicultural counseling* (pp. 181–198). Thousand Oaks, CA: Sage.

Helms, J. E. (2006). Fairness is not a validity or cultural bias in racial-group assessment: A quantitative perspective. *American Psychologist, 61*, 845–859.

Helms, J. E., & Cook, D. A. (1999). *Using race and culture in counseling and psychotherapy: Theory and process.* Needham Heights, MA: Allyn & Bacon.

Helms, J. E., Jernigan, M., & Mascher, J. (2005). The meaning of race in psychology and how to change it: A methodological perspective. *American Psychologist, 60*, 27–36.

Helms, H. M., Supple, A. J., Su, J., Rodriguez, Y., Cavanaugh, A. M., & Hengstebeck, N. D. (2014). Economic pressure, cultural adaptation stress, and marital quality among Mexican-origin couples. *Journal of Family Psychology, 28*(1), 77–87.

Henry, J. M., & Bankston, C. L. (1999). Louisiana Cajun ethnicity: Symbolic or structural? *Sociological Spectrum, 19*, 223–248.

Heron, M. (2016). *Leading causes of death for 2014.* National vital statistics reports, vol. 65 no. 5. Hyattsville MD: National Center for Health Statistics.

Herrnstein, R. J., & Murray, C. A. (1994). *The bell curve: Intelligence and class structure in American life.* New York: Free Press.

Heurtin-Roberts, S., Snowden, L. R., & Miller, L. (1997). Expressions of anxiety in African Americans: Ethnography and the ECA studies. *Culture, Medicine, and Psychiatry, 21*, 337–363.

Hill, P. C., & Pargament, K. I. (2003). Advances in the conceptualization and measurement of religion and spirituality: Implications for physical and mental health research. *American Psychologist, 58*, 64–74.

Hill, R. B. (1998). Understanding Black family functioning: A holistic perspective. *Journal of Comparative Family Studies, 29*, 15–25.

Hill, S. A. (2001). Class, race, and gender dimensions of child rearing in African American families. *Journal of Black Studies, 31*, 494–508.

Hilton, J. L., & von Hippel, W. (1996). Stereotypes. *Annual Review of Psychology, 47*, 237–271.

Hipolito-Delgado, C. P. (2016). Internalized racism, perceived racism, and ethnic identity: Exploring their relationship in Latina/o undergraduates. *Journal of College Counseling, 19*, 98–109.

Hirsch, H. (1973). Political scientists and other *camaradas*: Academic myth making and racial stereotypes. In R. O. de la Garza, Z. A. Kruswski, & T. A. Arcinego (Eds.),

Chicanos and Native Americans. Englewood Cliffs, NJ: Prentice Hall.

Ho, C. (1990). An analysis of domestic violence in Asian American communities: A multicultural approach to counseling. *Women and Therapy, 9*, 129–150.

Hofstede, G. (1980). *Culture's consequences: International differences in work-related values.* Newbury Park, CA: Sage.

Holleran, L. K. (2003). Mexican American youth of the Southwest borderlands: Perceptions of ethnicity, acculturation, and race. *Hispanic Journal of Behavioral Sciences, 25*, 352–369.

Holliday, B. G., & Holmes, A. L. (2003). A tale of challenge and change: A history and chronology of ethnic minorities in psychology in the United States. In G. Bernal, J. E. Trimble, A. K. Burlew, & F. T. L. Leong (Eds.), *Handbook of racial & ethnic minority psychology* (pp. 15–64). Thousand Oaks, CA: Sage.

Holliday, K. V. (2008). Religious healing and biomedicine in comparative context. In B. W. McNeill & J. M. Cervantes (Eds.), *Latina/o healing practices: Mestizo and indigenous perspectives* (pp. 249–270). New York: Routledge/Taylor.

Hom, A. Y. (1996). Stories from the homefront: Perspectives of Asian American parents with lesbian daughters and gay sons. In R. Leong (Ed.), *Asian American sexualities: Dimensions of the gay and lesbian experience.* New York: Routledge.

Hong, H.-J. (2010). Bicultural competence and its impact on team effectiveness. *International Journal of Cross-Cultural Management*, 10, 93–120.

Hong, Y.-Y., Morris, M. W., Chiu, C.-y., & Benet-Martínez, V. (2000). Multicultural minds: A dynamic constructivist approach to culture and cognition. *American Psychologist, 55*, 709–720.

Hong, Y.-Y., Zhan, S., Morris, M. W., & Benet-Martínez, V. (2016). Multicultural identity processes. *Current Opinion in Psychology*, 8, 49–53.

Horenczyk, G., Jasinskaja-Lahti, I., Sam, D. L., & Vedder, P. (2013). Mutuality in acculturation: Toward an integration. *Zeitschrift für Psychologie, 221*, 205–213.

Hosokawa, F. (2010). *Building trust: Doing research to understand ethnic communities.* Lanham, MD: Lexington Books.

Houston, T. K., Scarinci, I. C., Person, S. D., & Greene, P. G. (2005). Patient smoking cessation advice by health care providers: The role of ethnicity, socioeconomic status, and health. *American Journal of Public Health, 95*, 1056–1061.

Hsieh, N., & Ruther, M. (2016). Sexual minority health and health risk factors: Intersection effects of gender, race, and sexual identity. *American Journal of Preventive Medicine, 50*, 746–755.

Huang, C. Y., & Stormshak, E. A. (2011). A longitudinal examination of early adolescence ethnic identity trajectories. *Cultural Diversity and Ethnic Minority Psychology, 17*, 261–270.

Huang, J., Chen, E. C., & Ponterotto, J. G. (2016). Heterosexual Chinese Americans' experiences of their lesbian and gay sibling's coming out. *Asian American Journal of Psychology, 7*, 147–158.

Hufford, D. J. (2005). *An analysis of the field of spirituality, religion and health (s/rh).* Retrieved July 5, 2008, from http://www.templetonadvancedresearch program.com/pdf/TARP-Hufford.pdf

Hughes, M., Kiecolt, K. J., Keith, V. M., & Demo, D. H. (2015). Racial identity and well-being among African Americans. *Social Psychology Quarterly, 78*, 25–48.

Hui, C. H., & Triandis, H. C. (1986). Individualism-collectivism: A study of cross- cultural researchers. *Journal of Cross-Cultural Psychology, 17*, 229–244.

Humes, K. R., Jones, N. A., & Ramirez, R. R. (2011, March). *Overview of race and Hispanic origin: 2010; 2010 Census Brief* (C2010BR-02). U.S. Census Bureau Retrieved from https://www.census.gov/prod/cen2010/briefs/c2010br-02.pdf

Hunt, L. M., Schneider, S., & Comer, B. (2004). Should "acculturation" be a variable in health research? A critical review of research on US Hispanics. *Social Science & Medicine, 59*, 973–986.

Hunter, C. D. (2008). Individualistic and collectivistic worldviews: Implications for understanding perceptions of racial discrimination in African Americans and British Caribbean Americans. *Journal of Counseling Psychology, 55*, 321–332.

Hurd, N. M., Sellers, R. M., Cogburn, C. D., Butler-Barnes, S. T., & Zimmerman, M. A. (2013). Racial identity and depressive symptoms among Black emerging adults: The moderating effects of neighborhood racial composition. *Developmental Psychology, 49*, 938–950.

Hurh, W. M., & Kim, K. C. (2010). The "success" image of Asian Americans: Its validity, and its practical and theoretical implications. *Ethnic and Racial Studies, 12*, 512–538.

Hyers, L. L. (2001). African American ethnic identity orientation in two national samples: A secondary survey analysis study. *Journal of Black Psychology, 27*, 139–171.

Icard, L. D., Zamora-Hernandez, C. E., Spencer, M. S., & Catalano, R. (1996). Designing and evaluating strategies to recruit African Americans for AIDS/HIV interventions: Targeting the African-American family. *Ethnicity & Disease, 6*, 301–310.

Institute of Medicine. (2002). *Unequal treatment: Confronting racial and ethnic disparities in health care.* Washington, DC: National Academy of Science.

Institute of Medicine. (2005). *Complementary and alternative medicine in the United States.* Washington, DC: National Academy of Science.

Islam, N. S., Khan, S., Kwon, S., Jang, D., Ro, M., & Trinh-Shevrin, C. (2010). Methodological issues in the collection, analysis, and reporting of granular data in Asian American populations: Historical challenges and potential solutions. *Journal of Health Care for the Poor and Underserved, 21*, 1354–1381.

Israel, B. A., Eng, E., Schultz, A. J., & Parker, E. A. (Eds.). (2005). *Methods in community-based participatory research for health.* San Francisco: Jossey-Bass.

Iwamasa, G. Y. (1997). Asian Americans. In S. Friedman (Ed.), *Cultural issues in the treatment of anxiety* (pp. 99–129). New York: Guilford.

Iwamasa, G. Y., & Pai, S. M. (2003). Anxiety disorders among ethnic minority groups. In G. Bernal, J. E. Trimble, A. K. Burlew, & F. T. L. Leong (Eds.), *Handbook of racial & ethnic minority psychology* (pp. 429–447). Thousand Oaks, CA: Sage.

Jackson, F. L. (1992). Race and ethnicity as biological constructs. *Ethnicity & Disease, 2*, 120–125.

Jackson, G. L., Trail, T. E., Kennedy, D. P., Williamson, H. C., Bradbury, T. N., & Karney, B. R. (2016). The salience and severity of relationship problems among low-income couples. *Journal of Family Psychology, 30*(1), 2–11.

Jackson, J. S., Neighbors, H. W., Torres, M., Martin, L. A., Williams, D. R., & Baser, R. (2007). Use of mental health services and subjective satisfaction with treatment among Black Caribbean immigrants: Results from the National Survey of American Life. *American Journal of Public Health, 97*, 60–67.

Jackson, J. S., Torres, M., Caldwell, C. H., Neighbors, H. W., Nesse, R. M., Taylor, R. J., . . . & Williams, D. R. (2004). The National Survey of American Life: A study of racial, ethnic, and cultural influences on mental disorders and mental health. *International Journal of Methods in Psychiatric Research, 13*, 196–207.

Jemal, A., Thun, M. J., Ries, L. A. G., Howe, H. L., Weir, H. K., Center, M. M., . . . & Weir, H. K. (2008). Annual report to the nation on the status of cancer, 1975–2005, featuring trends in lung cancer, tobacco use, and tobacco control. *Journal of the National Cancer Institute, 100*(23). Retrieved from http://seer.cancer.gov/report_to_nation/

Jemal, A., Ward, E. M., Johnson, C. J., Cronin, K. A., Ma, J., Ryerson, B., . . . & Weir, H. K. (2017). Annual report to the nation on the status of cancer, 1975–2014, featuring survival. *Journal of the National Cancer Institute, 109*(9), djx030. Retrieved from https://www.ncbi.nlm.nih.gov/pmc/articles/PMC5409140/pdf/djx030.pdf

Jernigan, V. B. B., Jacob, T., the Tribal Community Research Team, & Styne, D. (2015). The adaptation and implementation of a community-based participatory research curriculum to build tribal research capacity. *American Journal of Public Health, 105*, S424–S432.

Jewell, S. L., Luecken, L. J., Gress-Smith, J., Crnic, K. A., & Gonzales, N. A. (2015). Economic stress and cortisol among postpartum low-income Mexican American women: Buffering influence of family support. *Behavioral Medicine, 41*, 138–144.

Johnson, A., & Jackson Williams, D. (2015). White racial identity, color-blind racial attitudes, and multicultural counseling competence. *Cultural Diversity and Ethnic Minority Psychology, 21*, 440–449.

Johnson, R. L., Saha, S., Arbelaez, J. J., Beach, M. C., & Cooper, L. A. (2004). Racial and ethnic differences in patient perceptions of bias and cultural competence in health care. *Journal of General Internal Medicine, 19*, 101–110.

Jones, E. (1953). *The life and work of Sigmund Freud* (vol. 1). New York: Basic Books.

Jones, J. M. (1992). Understanding the mental health consequences of race: Contributions of basic social psychological processes. In D. N. Ruble, P. R. Costanze, & M. E. Oliveri (Eds.), *The social psychology of mental health: Basic mechanism and applications* (pp. 199–240). New York: Guilford.

Jones, J. M. (2003). TRIOS: A psychological theory of the African legacy in American culture. *Journal of Social Issues, 59*(1), 217–242.

Jones, M. L., & Galliher, R. V. (2015). Daily racial microaggressions and ethnic identification among Native American young adults. *Cultural Diversity and Ethnic Minority Psychology, 21*, 1–9.

Jones, N. A., & Bullock, J. (2012). *The two or more races population: 2010* (2010 Census Briefs). U.S. Census Bureau. Retrieved from https://www.census.gov/prod/cen2010/briefs/c2010br-13.pdf

Joslin Diabetes Center. (2018). *One in two Asian Americans develop diabetes or pre-diabetes in their lifetime.* Retrieved from https://aadi.joslin.org/en/diabetes-mellitus-in-asian-americans#

Jourdan, A. (2006). The impact of the family environment on the ethnic identity development of multiethnic college students. *Journal of Counseling & Development, 84*, 328–340.

Jung, C. (1967). *Collected works.* Princeton, NJ: Princeton University Press.

Kaltman S., Green, B. L., Mete, M., Shara, N., & Miranda J. (2010). Trauma, depression, and comorbid PTSD/depression in a community sample of Latina immigrants. *Psychological Trauma: Theory, Research, Practice, and Policy, 2*, 31–39.

Kane, E. W. (2000). Racial and ethnic variations in gender-related attitudes. *Annual Review of Sociology, 26*, 419–439.

Kang, S.-M. (2006). Measurement of acculturation, scale formats, and language competence: Their implications for adjustment. *Journal of Cross-Cultural Psychology, 37*, 669–693.

Kang, S. K., DeCelles, K. A., Tilcsik, A., & Jun, S. (2016). Whitened résumés: Race and self-presentation in the labor market. *Administrative Science Quarterly, 61*(3), 469–502.

Karon, J. M., Fleming, P. L., Steketee, R. W., & DeCock, K. M. (2001). HIV in the United States at the turn of the century. *American Journal of Public Health, 91*, 1060–1068.

Kawachi, I., Daniels, N., & Robinson, D. E. (2005). Health disparities by race and class: Why both matter. *Health Affairs, 24*, 343–352.

Kawahara, D. M., & Fu, M. (2007). The psychology and mental health of Asian American women. In F. T. L. Leong, A. G. Inman, A. Ebreo, L. H. Yang, L. Kinoshita,

& M. Fu (Eds.), *Handbook of Asian American psychology* (2nd ed., pp. 181–196). Thousand Oaks, CA: Sage.

Kennedy, H. R., & Dalla, R. L. (2014). Examining identity consolidation processes among ethnic minority gay men and lesbians. *Journal of Gay & Lesbian Social Services: The Quarterly Journal of Community & Clinical Practice, 26*, 465–501.

Kessler, R. C., Birnbaum, H. G., Shahly, V., Bromet, E., Hwang, I., McLaughlin, K. A., . . . & Stein, D. J. (2010). Age differences in the prevalence and co-morbidity of *DSM-IV* major depressive episodes: Results from the WHO World Mental Health Survey Initiative. *Depression and Anxiety, 27*, 351–364.

Kessler, R. C., Chiu, W. T., Demler, O., & Walters, E. E. (2005). Prevalence, severity, and comorbidity of twelve-month *DSM-IV* disorders in the National Comorbidity Survey Replication. *Archives of General Psychiatry, 62*, 617–627.

Kessler, R. C., McGonagle, K. A., Zhao, S., Nelson, C. B., Hughes, M., Eshleman, S., . . . & Kendler, K. S. (1994). Lifetime and 12-month prevalence of *DSM-III-R* psychiatric disorders in the US: Results from the National Comorbidity Survey. *Archives of General Psychiatry, 51*, 8–19.

Kessler, R. C., & Merikangas, K. R. (2004). The National Comorbidity Survey Replication (NCS-R). *International Journal of Methods in Psychiatric Research, 13*, 60–68.

Khan, S. R. (2014). Post 9/11: The impact of stigma for Muslim Americans. *Peace and Conflict: Journal of Peace Psychology, 20*(4), 580–582.

Khawaja, N., Moisuc, O., & Ramirez, E. (2014). Developing an acculturation and resilience scale for use with culturally and linguistically diverse populations. *Australian Psychologist, 49*, 171–180.

Kiang, L., Witkow, M. R., Baldelomar, O. A., & Fuligni, A. J. (2010). Change in ethnic identity across the high school years among adolescents with Latin American, Asian, and European backgrounds. *Journal of Youth and Adolescence, 39*, 683–693.

Kiberstis, P. A., & Marx, J. (2002, July 26). The unstable path to cancer. *Science, 297*, 543–569.

Kibria, N. (1993). *Family tightrope: The changing lives of Vietnamese Americans.* Princeton, NJ: Princeton University Press.

Kim, B. S., Li, L. C., & Ng, G. F. (2005). The Asian American values scale—multidimensional: Development, reliability, and validity. *Cultural Diversity & Ethnic Minority, 11*, 187–201.

Kim, I. J., Lau, A. S., & Chang, D. F. (2007). Family violence among Asian Americans. In F. T. L. Leong, A. G. Inman, A. Ebreo, L. H. Yang, L. Kinoshita, & M. Fu (Eds.), *Handbook of Asian American psychology* (2nd ed., pp. 363–378). Thousand Oaks, CA: Sage.

Kim, I. J., & Zane, N. W. (2004). Ethnic and cultural variations in anger regulation and attachment patterns among Korean American and European American male batterers. *Cultural Diversity & Ethnic Minority Psychology, 10*, 151–168.

Kim, J. Y., & Sung, K. (2000). Conjugal violence in Korean American families: A residue of the cultural tradition. *Journal of Family Violence, 15*, 331–345.

Kim, S. Y., & Ge, X. (2000). Parenting practices and adolescent depressive symptoms in Chinese American families. *Journal of Family Psychology, 14*, 420–435.

Kim, S. Y., Wang, Y., Orozco-Lapray, D., Shen, Y., & Murtuza, M. (2013). Does "tiger parenting" exist? Parenting profiles of Chinese Americans and adolescent developmental outcomes. *Asian American Journal of Psychology, 4*(1), 7–18.

Kim, U. (2001). Culture, science and indigenous psychologies: An integrated analysis. In D. Matsumoto (Ed.), *Handbook of culture and psychology* (pp. 51–76). Oxford: Oxford University Press.

Kim-Ju, G. M., & Liem, R. (2003). Ethnic self-awareness as a function of ethnic group status, group composition, and ethnic identity orientation. *Cultural Diversity & Ethnic Minority Psychology, 9*, 289–302.

King, J. L., & Hunter, K. (2005). *On the down low: A journey into the lives of "straight" Black men who sleep with men.* New York: Random House.

King, K. R. (2005). Why is discrimination stressful? The mediating role of cognitive appraisal. *Cultural Diversity & Ethnic Minority Psychology, 11*, 202–212.

Kinzie, J. D., Boehnlein, J. K., Leung, P. K., Moore, L. J., Riley, C., & Smith, D. (1990). The prevalence of post-traumatic stress disorder and its clinical significance among Southeast Asian refugees. *American Journal of Psychiatry, 147*, 913–917.

Kinzie, J. D., Leung, P. K., Boehnlein, J., Matsunaga, D., Johnston, R., & Manson, S. M. (1992). Psychiatry epidemiology of an Indian village: A 19-year replication study. *Journal of Nervous and Mental Disease, 180*, 33–39.

Kleinman, A. M. (1977). Depression, somatization, and the "new cross-cultural psychiatry." *Social Science & Medicine, 11*, 3–10.

Kleinman, J. C., Fingerhut, L. A., & Prager, K. (1991). Differences in infant mortality by race, nativity status, and other maternal characteristics. *American Journal of Disease in Children, 145*, 194–199.

Klonoff, E. A., & Landrine, H. (1999). Cross-validation of the schedule of racist events. *Journal of Black Psychology, 25*, 231–254.

Kluckhohn, C. (1961). The study of values. In D. N. Barrett (Ed.), *Values in America.* Notre Dame, IN: University of Notre Dame Press.

Kluckhohn, C., & Strodtbeck, F. L. (1961). *Variations in value orientation.* New York: Harper & Row.

Knight, G. P., Roosa, M. W., & Umaña-Taylor, A. J. (2009). *Studying ethnic minority and economically disadvantaged populations: Methodological challenges and best practices.* Washington, DC: American Psychological Association.

Kochanek, K. D., Murphy, S. L., Xu, J., & Tejada-Vera, B. (2016). *Deaths: Final data for 2014*. Atlanta: Centers for Disease Control and Prevention.

Kotchick, B. A., Dorsey, S., Miller, K. S., & Forehand, R. (1999). Adolescent sexual risk-taking behavior in single-parent ethnic minority families. *Journal of Family Psychology, 13*, 93–102.

Kovács, Á. M., & Mehler, J. (2009). Cognitive gains in 7-month-old bilingual infants. *Proceedings of the National Academy of Sciences, 106*(16), 6556–6560.

Krysan, M., Couper, M. P., Farley, R., & Forman, T. (2009). Does race matter in neighborhood preferences? Results from a video experiment. *American Journal of Sociology, 115*, 527–559.

Kulis, S., Marsiglia, F. F., & Hurdle, D. (2003). Gender identity, ethnicity, acculturation, and drug use: Exploring differences among adolescents in the Southwest. *Journal of Community Psychology, 31*, 167–188.

Kunitz, S. J., Gabriel, K. R., Levy, J. E., Henderson, E., Lampert, K., McCloskey, J., . . . & Vince, A. (1999). Alcohol dependence and conduct disorder among Navajo Indians. *Journal of Studies in Alcohol, 60*, 159–167.

Kuo, B. C. H. (2014). Coping, acculturation, and psychological adaptation among migrants: A theoretical and empirical review and synthesis of the literature. *Health Psychology & Behavioural Medicine, 2*, 16–33.

Kurtz-Costes, B., Swinton, A. D., & Skinner, O. D. (2014). Racial and ethnic gaps in the school performance of Latino, African American, and White students. In F. T. L. Leong (Ed.), *APA handbook of multicultural psychology: Vol. 1, Theory and research* (pp. 231–246). Washington, DC: American Psychological Association.

Kwok, J., Atencio, J., Ullah, J., Crupi, R., Chen, D., Roth, A. R., . . . & Brondolo, E. (2011). The Perceived Ethnic Discrimination Questionnaire—Community Version: Validation in a multiethnic Asian sample. *Cultural Diversity and Ethnic Minority Psychology, 17*(3), 271–282.

LaFromboise, T., Coleman, H. L. K., & Gerton, J. (1993). Psychological impact of biculturalism: Evidence and theory. *Psychological Bulletin, 114*, 395–412.

Landrine, H., & Klonoff, E. A. (1994). *African-American acculturation: Deconstructing "race" and reviving culture*. Thousand Oaks, CA; Sage.

Landrine, H., & Klonoff, E. A. (1995). The African American Acculturation Scale II: Cross-validation and short form. *Journal of Black Psychology, 21*, 124–152.

Landrine, H., & Klonoff, E. A. (1996). Cultural diversity and methodology in feminist psychology. *Journal of Black Psychology, 22*, 144–168.

Landrine, H., Klonoff, E. A., Corral, I., Fernandez, S., & Roesch, S. (2006). Conceptualizing and measuring ethnic discrimination in health research. *Journal of Behavioral Medicine, 29*, 79–94.

Lane, S. D., Rubenstein, R. A., Keefe, R. H., Webster, N., Cibula, D. A., Rosenthal, A., & Dowdell, J. (2004). Structural violence and racial disparity in HIV transmission. *Journal of Health Care for the Poor and Underserved, 15*, 319–335.

Langdon, S. E., Golden, S. L., Arnold, E. M., Maynor, R. F., Bryant, A., Freeman, V. K., & Bell, R. A. (2016). Lessons learned from a community-based participatory research mental health promotion program for American Indian youth. *Health Promotion Practice, 17*, 457–463.

LaSala, M. C., & Frierson, D. T. (2012). African American gay youth and their families: Redefining masculinity, coping with racism and homophobia. *Journal of GLBT Family Studies, 8*, 428–445.

Lau, A. S. (2010). Physical discipline in Chinese American immigrant families: An adaptive culture perspective. *Cultural Diversity and Ethnic Minority Psychology, 16*(3), 313–322.

Lau, A. S., & Fung, J. (2013). On better footing to understand parenting and family process in Asian American families. *Asian American Journal of Psychology, 4*(1), 71–75.

Lawson, W. B., Hepler, N., Holladay, J., & Cuffel, B. (1994). Race as a factor in inpatient and outpatient admissions and diagnosis. *Hospital and Community Psychiatry, 45*, 72–74.

Lee, D. L., & Ahn, S. (2013). The relation of racial identity, ethnic identity, and racial socialization to discrimination–distress: A meta-analysis of Black Americans. *Journal of Counseling Psychology, 60*, 1–14.

Lee, E. (Ed.). (1997). *Working with Asian Americans: A guide for clinicians*. New York: Guilford.

Lee, E., & Lu, F. (1989). Assessment and treatment of Asian-American survivors of mass violence. *Journal of Traumatic Stress, 2*, 93–120.

Lee, J., Lei, A., & Sue, S. (2001). The current state of mental health research on Asian Americans. *Journal of Human Behavior in the Social Environment, 3*, 159–178.

Lee, M. J., Bichard, S. L., Irey, M. S., Walt, H. M., & Carlson, A. J. (2009). Television viewing and ethnic stereotypes: Do college students form stereotypical perceptions of ethnic groups as a result of heavy television consumption? *Howard Journal of Communication, 20*, 95–110.

Lee, R. E., & Cubbin, C. (2002). Neighborhood context and youth cardiovascular health behaviors. *American Journal of Public Health, 92*, 428–436.

Lee, R. M. (2003). Do ethnic identity and other-group orientation protect against discrimination for Asian Americans? *Journal of Counseling Psychology, 50*, 133–141.

Lee, S.-K., Sobal, J., & Frongillo, E. A. (2003). Comparison of models of acculturation: The case of Korean Americans. *Journal of Cross-Cultural Psychology, 34*, 282–296.

Lee, Y.-T., & Ottati, V. (1993). Determinants of in-group and out-group perceptions of heterogeneity: An investigation of Sino-American stereotypes. *Journal of Cross-Cultural Psychology, 24*, 298–318.

Lenski, G. E. (1966). *Power and privilege: A theory of social stratification*. New York: McGraw-Hill.

Leong, F. T. L. (1986). Counseling and psychotherapy with Asian Americans: A review of the literature. *Journal of Counseling Psychology, 33*, 192–206.

Leong, F. T. L. & Okazaki, S. (2009). History of Asian American psychology. *Cultural Diversity & Ethnic Minority Psychology*, *15*(4), 352–362.

Leong, F. T. L., Comas-Díaz, L., Hall, G. C. N., McLoyd, V. C., & Trimble, J. E. (Eds.). (2014). *APA handbook of multicultural psychology*. Washington, DC: American Psychological Association.

Leong, F. T. L., Inman, A. G., Ebreo, A., Yang, L. H., Kinoshita, L. M., & Fu, M. (Eds.) (2007). *Handbook of Asian American psychology* (2nd ed.). Thousand Oaks, CA: Sage Publications.

Lerner, M. (1980). *Belief in a just world: A fundamental delusion*. New York: Plenum.

Lévi-Strauss, C. (1966). *Pensée savage* [The savage mind]. Chicago: University of Chicago Press.

Lewis, T. T., Everson-Rose, S. A., Powell, L. H., Matthews, K. A., Brown, C., Karavolos, K., . . . & Wesley, D. (2006). Chronic exposure to everyday discrimination and coronary artery calcification in African American women: The SWAN Heart Study. *Psychosomatic Medicine*, *68*, 362–368.

Lewis-Fernandez, R., Aggarwal, N. K., Baarnhielm, S., Rohlof, H., Kirmayer, L. J., Weiss, . . . & Lu, F. (2014). Culture and psychiatric evaluation: Operationalizing cultural formulation for *DSM-5*. *Psychiatry*, *77*(2), 130–154.

Lie, M. L. S. (2006). Methodological issues in qualitative research with minority ethnic research participants. *Research Policy and Planning*, *24*, 91–103.

Light, M. T., Miller, T., & Kelly, B. C. (2017). Undocumented immigration, drug problems, and driving under the influence in the United States, 1990–2014. *American Journal of Public Health*, *107*, 1448–1454.

Lilienfeld, A. M. (1972). *Cancer in the United States*. Cambridge, MA: Harvard University Press.

Lilienfeld, S. O. (2017). Microaggressions: Strong claims, inadequate evidence. *Perspectives on Psychological Sciences*, *12*, 138–169.

Lim, K. V., Heiby, E., Brislin, R., & Griffin, B. (2002). The development of the Khmer acculturation scale. *International Journal of Intercultural Relations*, *26*, 653–678.

Lindsay, B. (1979). Minority women in America: Black American, Native American, Chicana, and Asian American women. In E. C. Synder (Ed.), *The study of women enlarging perspectives of social reality*. New York: Harper & Row.

Lines, L. M., Sherif, N. A., & Weiner, J. M. (2014). *Racial and ethnic disparities among individuals with Alzheimer's disease in the United States: A literature review*. Research Triangle Park: RTI Press.

Link, B. G., Susser, E. S., Factor-Litvak, P., March, D., Kezios, K. L., Lovasi, G. S., . . . & Cohn, B. A. (2017). Disparities in self-rated health across generations and through the life course. *Social Science & Medicine*, *174*, 17–25.

Liu, T., & Wong, Y. J. (2016). The intersection of race and gender: Asian American men's experience of discrimination. *Psychology of Men & Masculinity* (November 10), n.p.

Liu, W. M. (2002). Exploring the lives of Asian American men: Racial identity, male role norms, gender role conflict, and prejudicial attitudes. *Psychology of Men & Masculinity*, *3*, 107–118.

Longshore, D., & Grills, C. (2000). Motivating illegal drug use recovery: Evidence for a culturally congruent intervention. *Journal of Black Psychology*, *26*, 288–301.

Lopez, G. E. (2004). Interethnic contact, curriculum, and attitudes in the first year of college. *Journal of Social Issues*, *60*(1), 75–94.

López, S. R. (1989). Patient variable biases in clinical judgment: Conceptual overview and methodological considerations. *Psychological Bulletin*, *106*, 184–203.

López, S. R., & Guarnaccia, P. J. J. (2000). Cultural psychopathology: Uncovering the social world of mental illness. *Annual Review of Psychology*, *51*, 571–598.

López, S. R., & Guarnaccia, P. J. (2005). Cultural dimensions of psychopathology: The social world's impact on mental illness. In J. E. Maddux & B. A. Winstead (Eds.), *Psychopathology: Foundations for a contemporary understanding* (pp. 19–38). Mahwah, NJ: Lawrence Erlbaum.

Lopez, V., Corona, R., & Halfond, R. (2013). Effects of gender, media influences, and traditional gender role orientation on disordered eating and appearance concerns among Latino adolescents. *Journal of Adolescence*, *36*(4), 727–736.

Lorentzen, L., Chun, K. M., Gonzalez, J., & Do, H. (Eds.). (2009). *On the corner of bliss and nirvana: The religious lives of new immigrants in San Francisco*. Durham, NC: Duke University Press.

Losen, D. J., & Orfield, G. (2002). *Racial inequality in special education*. Cambridge, MA: Harvard Education Press.

Lowman, R. L. (2013). (Ed.). *Internationalizing multiculturalism: Expanding professional competencies in a globalized world*. Washington, DC: American Psychological Association.

Lu, L., & Nicholson-Crotty, S. (2010). Reassessing the impact of Hispanic stereotypes on White Americans' immigration preferences. *Social Science Quarterly*, *91*, 1312–1328.

Lucal, B. (1996). Oppression and privilege: Towards a relational conceptualization of race. *Teaching Sociology*, *24*, 245–255.

Lugaila, T., & Overturf, J. (2004, March). *Children and the households they live in: 2000; Census 2000 Special Reports* (CENSR-14). U.S. Census Bureau. Retrieved from https://www.census.gov/prod/2004pubs/censr-14.pdf

Lui, P. P. (2015). Intergenerational cultural conflict, mental health, and educational outcomes among Asian and Latino/a Americans: Qualitative and meta analytic review. *Psychological Bulletin*, *141*(2), 404–446.

Lynch, J. W., Kaplan, G. A., & Shema, S. J. (1997). Cumulative impact of sustained economic hardship on physical, cognitive, psychological, and social functioning. *The New England Journal of Medicine*, *337*, 1889–1895.

Lyons, A. L., Carlson, G. A., Thurm, A. E., Grant, K. E., & Gipson, P. Y. (2006). Gender differences in early risk factors for adolescent depression among low-income urban children. *Cultural Diversity & Ethnic Minority Psychology, 12*, 644–657.

Ma, J., & Baum, S. (2016, April). Trends in community colleges: Enrollment, prices, student debt, and completion. *College Board Research, Research Brief.* Retrieved from https://trends.collegeboard.org/sites/default/files/trends-in-community-colleges-research-brief.pdf

Macartney, S., Bishaw, A., & Fontenot, K. (2013, February). *Poverty rates for selected detailed race and Hispanic groups by state and place: 2007–2011; American Community Survey Briefs* (ACSBR/11-17). U.S. Census Bureau. Retrieved from https://www.census.gov/prod/2013pubs/acsbr11-17.pdf

Macklin, R. (2000). Informed consent for research: International perspectives. *Journal of the American Medical Women's Association, 55*, 290–293.

Maddux, J. E., & Winstead, B. A. (Eds.). (2005). *Psychopathology: Foundations for a contemporary understanding.* Mahwah, NJ: Lawrence Erlbaum.

Malott, K. M., Paone, T. R., Schaefle, S., Cates, J., & Haizlip, B. (2015). Expanding White racial identity theory: A qualitative investigation of Whites engaged in antiracist action. *Journal of Counseling & Development, 93*, 333–343.

Mandara, J., & Murray, C. B. (2002). Development of an empirical typology of African American family functioning. *Journal of Family Psychology, 16*, 318–337.

Mantsios, G. (2004). Media magic: Making class invisible. In P. S. Rothenberg (Ed.), *Race, class, and gender in the United States: An integrated study* (6th ed., pp. 560–568). New York: St. Martin's.

Mantwill, S., Monestel-Umaña, S., & Schultz, P. J. (2015). The relationship between health literacy and health disparities: A systematic review. *PLoS One, 10*(12), e0145455. Retrieved from http://journals.plos.org/plosone/article?id=10.1371/journal.pone.0145455

Marger, M. N. (2015). Ethnic stratification: Power and inequality. In M. N. Marger (Ed.), *Race and ethnic relations: American and global perspectives* (10th ed., pp. 27–48). Stamford, CT: Wadsworth/Cengage Learning.

Marian, V., & Neisser, U. (2000). Language-dependent recall of autobiographical memories. *Journal of Experimental Psychology: General, 129*, 361–368.

Marín, B. V., Pérez-Stable, E. J., Marín, G., & Hauck, W. W. (1994). Effects of a community intervention to change smoking behavior among Hispanics. *American Journal of Preventive Medicine, 10*, 340–347.

Marín, G. (1984). Stereotyping Hispanics: The differential effect of research method, label, and degree of contact. *International Journal of Intercultural Relations, 8*, 17–27.

Marín, G. (1992). Issues in the measurement of acculturation among Hispanics. In K. Geisinger (Ed.), *Psychological testing of Hispanics.* Washington, DC: American Psychological Association.

Marín, G. (1993). Defining culturally appropriate community interventions: Hispanics as a case study. *Journal of Community Psychology, 20*, 375–391.

Marín, G., Balls Organista, P., & Chun, K. M. (2003). Acculturation research: Current issues and findings. In G. Bernal, J. E. Trimble, A. K. Burlew, & F. T. L. Leong (Eds.), *Handbook of racial & ethnic minority psychology* (pp. 208–219). Thousand Oaks, CA: Sage.

Marín, G., & Gamba, R. J. (1996). A new measurement of acculturation for Hispanics: The Bidimensional Acculturation Scale for Hispanics. *Hispanic Journal of Behavioral Sciences, 18*, 297–316.

Marín, G., & Marín, B. V. (1991). *Research with Hispanic populations: Vol. 23, Applied social research methods series.* Newbury Park, CA: Sage.

Marín, G., Pérez-Stable, E. J., & Marín, B. V. (1989). Cigarette smoking among San Francisco Hispanics: The role of acculturation and gender. *American Journal of Public Health, 79*, 196–198.

Marín, G., Sabogal, F., Marín, B. V., Otero-Sabogal, R., & Pérez-Stable, E. J. (1987). Development of a short acculturation scale for Hispanics. *Hispanic Journal of Behavioral Sciences, 9*, 183–205.

Markides, K. S., Coreil, J., & Ray, L. A. (1987). Smoking among Mexican Americans: A three-generation study. *American Journal of Public Health, 77*, 708–711.

Marks, A. K., Patton, F., & Coll, C. G. (2011). Being bicultural: A mixed-methods study of adolescents' implicitly and explicitly measured multiethnic identities. *Developmental Psychology, 47*, 270–288.

Marks, G., Garcia, M., & Solis, J. M. (1990). Health risk behaviors of Hispanics in the United States: Findings from HHANES, 1982–84. *American Journal of Public Health, 80*(Suppl.), 20–26.

Marks, J. (1995). *Human biodiversity: Genes, race, and history.* New York: Walter de Gruyter.

Markus, H., & Kitayama, S. (1991). Culture and the self. *Psychological Review, 98*, 224–253.

Marsella, A. J. (1998). Toward a "global-community psychology": Meeting the needs of a changing world. *American Psychologist, 53*, 1282–1291.

Marsiglia, F. F., Kulis, S., Hecht, M. L., & Sills, S. (2004). Ethnicity and ethnic identity as predictors of drug norms and drug use among preadolescents in the US Southwest. *Substance Use & Misuse, 39*, 1061–1094.

Mastro, D., & Tukachinsky, R. (2012). The influence of media exposure and the formation, activation, and application of racial/ethnic stereotypes. *The International Encyclopedia of Media Studies*, 5:2:13.

Matsumoto, D., & Juang, L. (2017). *Culture and psychology* (6th ed.). Belmont, CA: Wadsworth/Cenage Learning.

Matsunaga, M., Hecht, M. L., Elek, E., & Ndiaye, K. (2010). Ethnic identity development and acculturation: A longitudinal analysis of Mexican-heritage youth in the Southwest United States. *Journal of Cross-Cultural Psychology, 41*, 410–427.

Maxwell-McCaw, D., & Zea, M. C. (2011). The Deaf Acculturation Scale (DAS): Development and validation of a 58-item measure. *Journal of Deaf Studies and Deaf Education, 16*, 325–342.

Mayne, S. L., Auchincloss, A. H., Stehr, M. F., Kern, D. M., Navas-Acien, A., Kaufman, J. D., . . . & Diez Roux, A. V. (2017). Longitudinal associations of local cigarette prices and smoking bans with smoking behavior in the multi-ethnic study of atherosclerosis (MESA). *Epidemiology, 28*(6).

McGill, R. K., Hughes, D., Alicea, S., & Way, N. (2012). Academic adjustment across middle school: The role of public regard and parenting. *Developmental Psychology, 48*(4), 1003–1018.

McGlothlin, H., & Killen, M. (2006). Intergroup attitudes of European American children attending ethnically homogeneous schools. *Child Development, 77*, 1375–1386.

McIntosh, P. (2004). White privilege: Unpacking the invisible knapsack. In P. S. Rothenberg (Ed.), *Race, class, and gender in the United States: An integrated study* (6th ed., pp. 188–192). New York: Worth.

McIntyre, A. (2008). *Participatory action research.* Thousand Oaks, CA: Sage.

McKee, M., Schlehofer, D., & Thew, D. (2013). Ethical issues in conducting research with deaf populations. *American Journal of Public Health, 103*, 2174–2178.

McLoyd, V. C. (1990). The impact of economic hardship on Black families and children: Psychological distress, parenting, and socioemotional development. *Child Development, 61*, 311–346.

McLoyd, V. C. (1998). Socioeconomic disadvantage and child development. *American Psychologist, 53*, 185–204.

McLoyd, V. C., Cauce, A. M., Takeuchi, D., & Wilson, L. (2000). Marital processes and parental socialization in families of color: A decade review of research. *Journal of Marriage and the Family, 62*, 1070–1093.

McLoyd, V. C., Harper, C. I., & Copeland, N. L. (2001). Ethnic minority status, interparental conflict, and child adjustment. In J. H. Grych & F. Fincham (Eds.), *Interparental conflict and child development: Theory, research, and applications.* Cambridge: Cambridge University Press.

McMahon, S. D., & Watts, R. J. (2002). Ethnic identity in urban African American youth: Exploring links with self-worth, aggression, and other psychosocial variables. *Journal of Community Psychology, 30*, 411–432.

McNair, L. D., & Prather, C. M. (2004). African American women and AIDS: Factors influencing risk and reduction to HIV disease. *Journal of Black Psychology, 30*, 106–123.

McNeely, M. J., & Boyko, E. J. (2004). Type 2 diabetes prevalence in Asian Americans: Results of a national health survey. *Diabetes Care, 27*, 66–69.

Meeus, W. (2011). The study of adolescent identity formation, 2000–2010: A review of longitudinal research. *Journal of Research on Adolescence, 21*, 75–94.

Mehrotra, M. (1999). The social construction of wife abuse. *Violence Against Women, 5*, 619–640.

Mena, F. J., Padilla, A. M., & Maldonado, M. (1987). Acculturative stress and specific coping strategies among immigrant and later generation college students. *Hispanic Journal of Behavioral Sciences, 9*, 207–225.

Mendes, W. B. (2007). Stereotype-busting people can spur stress, reduce cognitive performance. *Journal of Personality and Social Psychology, 92*, 11–23.

Meredith, L. S., Wenger, N., Liu, H., Harada, N., & Kahn, K. (2000). Development of a brief scale to measure acculturation among Japanese Americans. *Journal of Community Psychology, 28*, 103–113.

Mereish, E. H., & Bradford, J. B. (2014). Intersecting identities and substance use problems: Sexual orientation, gender, race, and lifetime substance use problems. *Journal of Studies on Alcohol and Drugs, 75*, 179–188.

Merianos, A. L., King, K. A., Vidourek, R. A., & Nabors, L. A. (2015). Recent alcohol use and binge drinking based on authoritative parenting among Hispanic youth nationwide. *Journal of Child and Family Studies, 24*(7), 1966–1976.

Miller, M. J., Alvarez, A. N., Li, R., Chen, G. A., & Iwamoto, D. K. (2016). Measurement invariance of the people of Color Racial Identity Attitudes Scale with Asian Americans. *Psychological Assessment, 28*, 116–122.

Miller, S. J. (2011). African-American lesbian identity management and identity development in the context of family and community. *Journal of Homosexuality, 58*, 547–563.

Miller-Cotto, D., & Byrnes, J. P. (2016). Ethnic/racial identity and academic achievement: A meta-analytic review. *Developmental Review, 41*, 51–70.

Mio, J. S., Barker, L. A., & Domenech Rodríguez, M. M. (2016). *Multicultural psychology: Understanding our diverse communities* (4th ed.). New York: Oxford University Press.

Miranda, A. O., & Matheny, K. B. (2000). Socio-psychological predictors of acculturative stress among Latino adults. *Journal of Mental Health Counseling, 22*, 306–317.

Miranda, A. O., & Umhoefer, D. L. (1998). Depression and social interest differences between Latinos in dissimilar acculturation stages. *Journal of Mental Health, 20*, 159–171.

Miranda, J., Bernal, G., Lau, A., Kohn, L., Hwang, W., & LaFromboise, T. (2005). State of the science on psychosocial interventions for ethnic minorities. *Annual Review of Clinical Psychology, 1*, 113–142.

Miranda, J., Duan, N., Sherbourne, C., Schoenbaum, M., Lagomasino, I., Jackson-Triche, M., & Wells, K. B. (2003). Improving care for minorities: Can quality improvement interventions improve care and outcomes for depressed minorities? Results of a randomized, controlled trial. *Health Services Research, 38*(2), 613–630.

Miranda, J., Siddique, J., Belin, T. R., & Kohn-Wood, L. P. (2004). Depression prevalence in disadvantaged young Black women: African and Caribbean immigrants compared to U.S.-born African Americans. *Social Psychiatry and Psychiatric Epidemiology, 40*, 253–258.

Mishel, L., Bernstein, J., & Boushey, H. (2003). *The state of working America 2002–2003*. Ithaca, NY: Cornell University Press.

Mitsch, A.J., Hall, I., & Babu, S. (2016). Trends in HIV infection among persons who inject drugs: United States and Puerto Rico, 2008–2013. *American Journal of Public Health, 106*, 2194–2201.

Miville, M. L., & Ferguson, A. D. (2014). Intersections of race-ethnicity and gender on identity development and social roles. In M. L. Miville & A. D. Ferguson (Eds.), *Handbook of race-ethnicity and gender in psychology* (pp. 3–21). New York: Springer.

Miville, M. L., Mendez, N., & Louie, M. (2016). Latina/o gender roles: A content analysis of empirical research From 1982 to 2013. *Journal of Latina/o Psychology, 5*(3), 173–194.

Mollica, R. (1994). Southeast Asian refugees: Migration history and mental health issues. In A. J. Marsella, T. Bornemann, S. Ekblad, & J. Orley (Eds.), *Amidst peril and pain: The mental health and well-being of the world's refugees* (pp. 83–100). Washington, DC: American Psychological Association.

Molina, Y., Lehavot, K., Beadnell, B., & Simoni, J. (2014). Racial disparities in health behaviors and conditions among lesbian and bisexual women: The role of internalized stigma. *LGBT Health, 1*, 131–139.

Moon, J. R., Capistrant, B. D., Kawachi, I., Avendaño, M., Subramanian, S. V., Bates, L. M., and Glymour M. M. (2012). Stroke incidence in older US Hispanics: Is foreign birth protective? *Stroke, 43*, 1224–1229.

Morales, L., Lara, M., Kington, R. S., Valdez, R. O., & Escarce, J. J. (2002). Socioeconomic, cultural, and behavioral factors affecting Hispanic health outcomes. *Journal of Health Care for the Poor and Underserved, 13*, 477–503.

Morawski, J. G. (2004). White experimenters, white blood, and other white conditions: Locating the psychologist's race. In M. Fine, L. Weis, L. P. Pruitt, & A. Burns (Eds.), *Off white: Readings on power, privilege, and resistance* (pp. 215–231). New York: Routledge.

Morling, B., & Fiske, S. T. (1999). Defining and measuring harmony control. *Journal of Research in Personality, 33*, 379–414.

Mossakowski, K. N. (2003). Coping with perceived discrimination: Does ethnic identity protect mental health? *Journal of Health and Social Behavior, 44*, 318–331.

Mroczkowski, A. L., & Sánchez, B. (2015). The role of racial discrimination in the economic value of education among urban, low-income Latina/o youth: Ethnic identity and gender as moderators. *American Journal of Community Psychology, 56*, 1–11.

Mueller, P. S., Plevak, D. J., & Rummans, T. A. (2001). Religious involvement, spirituality, and medicine: Implications for clinical practice. *Mayo Clinic Proceedings, 76*, 1225–1235.

Muñoz, R. F., & Mendelson, T. (2005). Toward evidence-based interventions for diverse populations: The San Francisco General Hospital Prevention and Treatment manuals. *Journal of Consulting and Clinical Psychology, 73*, 790–799.

Murry, V. M., Brown, P. A., Brody, G. H., Cutrona, C. E., & Simons, R. L. (2001). Racial discrimination as a moderator of the links among stress, maternal psychological functioning, and family relationships. *Journal of Marriage and Family, 63*, 915–926.

Musu-Gillette, L., Robinson, J., McFarland, J., KewalRamani, A., Zhang, A., & Wilkinson-Flicker, S. (2016). *Status and trends in the education of racial and ethnic groups 2016*. Institute of Education Sciences, National Center for Education Statistics (NCES 2016-007). Retrieved from https://nces.ed.gov/pubs2016/2016007.pdf

Myers, H. F. (2009). Ethnicity- and socio-economic status-related stresses in context: An integrative review and conceptual model. *Journal of Behavioral Medicine, 32*, 9–19.

Myers, H. F., & Rodriguez, N. (2003). Acculturation and physical health in racial and ethnic minorities. In K. M. Chun, P. Balls Organista, & G. Marín (Eds.), *Acculturation: Advances in theory, measurement, and applied research* (pp. 163–185). Washington, DC: American Psychological Association.

Nadal, K. L. (Ed.) (2011). *Filipino American psychology: A handbook of theory, research, and clinical practice*. Hoboken, NJ: Wiley.

Nadal, K. L., Davidoff, K. C., Davis, L. S., Wong, Y., Marshall, D., & McKenzie, V. (2015). A qualitative approach to intersectional microaggressions: Understanding influences of race, ethnicity, gender, sexuality, and religion. *Qualitative Psychology, 2*, 147–163.

Nápoles, A. M., Santoyo-Olsson, J., Karliner, L. S., Gregorich, S. E., & Pérez-Stable, E. J. (2015). Inaccurate language interpretation and its clinical significance in the medical encounters of Spanish-speaking Latinos. *Medical Care, 53*(11), 940–947.

National Academies of Sciences, Engineering, and Medicine. (2017). *The value of social, behavioral, and economic sciences to national priorities*. Washington, DC: The National Academies Press.

National Archive. (n.d.). *"I have a dream . . ." (Copyright 1963, Martin Luther King, Jr.): Speech by the Rev. Martin Luther King at the "March on Washington"*. Retrieved from https://www.archives.gov/files/press/exhibits/dream-speech.pdf

National Cancer Institute. (2005). *SEER cancer statistics review*. Retrieved July 3, 2005, from http://seer.cancer.gov/csr/1975_2002/results_merged/topic_race_ethnicity.pdf

National Center for Chronic Disease Prevention and Health Promotion. (2002). *Diabetes: Disabling, deadly, and on the rise*. Washington, DC: U.S. Government Printing Office.

National Center for Chronic Disease Prevention and Health Promotion. (2017). *National diabetes statistical report, 2017*. Washington, DC: U.S. Government Printing Office.

National Center for Cultural Competence, Georgetown University. (n.d.). *Foundations: Conceptual frameworks/*

models, guiding values and principles. Retrieved January 24, 2018, from https://nccc.georgetown.edu/foundations/framework.php

National Center for Health Statistics. (2002). *National Health and Nutrition Examination Survey.* Retrieved from http://www.cdc.gov/nchs/about/major/nhanes/nhanes01-02.htm

National Center for Health Statistics. (2006). *Health, United States, 2005: With chartbook on trends in the health of Americans.* Hyattsville, MD: Author.

National Center for Health Statistics. (2016). *Health, United States, 2015.* Hyattsville, MD: Author.

National Center for Health Statistics. (2017). *Health, United States, 2016: With chartbook on long-term trends in health.* Hyattsville, MD: Author.

National Institute of Allergy and Infectious Diseases. (2004). *Factsheet: How HIV causes AIDS.* Retrieved August 8, 2007, from http://www.niaid.nih.gov/factsheets/howhiv.htm

National Institute on Drug Abuse. (2015). *Overdose death rates.* Rockville, MD: Author.

Navas, M., García, M. C., Sánchez, J., Rojas, A. J., Pumares, P., & Fernández, J. S. (2005). Relative Acculturation Extended Model (RAEM): New contributions with regard to the study of acculturation. *International Journal of Intercultural Relations, 29*, 21–37.

Neal, A. M., & Turner, S. M. (1991). Anxiety disorders research with African Americans: Current status. *Psychological Bulletin, 109*, 400–410.

Neblett, E. W., Jr., & Carter, S. E. (2012). The protective role of racial identity and Africentric worldview in the association between racial discrimination and blood pressure. *Psychosomatic Medicine, 74*, 509–516.

Neff, K. (2003). Understanding how universal goals of independence and interdependence are manifested within particular cultural contexts. *Human Development, 46*, 312–318.

Neff, K. D. (2001). Judgments of personal autonomy and interpersonal responsibility in the context of Indian spousal relationships: An examination of young people's reasoning in Mysore, India. *British Journal of Developmental Psychology, 19*, 233–257.

Neff, K. D., & Harter, S. (2002a). The authenticity of conflict resolutions among adult couples: Does women's other-oriented behavior reflect their true selves? *Sex Roles, 47*, 403–417.

Neff, K. D., & Harter, S. (2002b). The role of power and authenticity in relationship styles emphasizing autonomy, connectedness, or mutuality among adult couples. *Journal of Social and Personal Relationships, 19*, 827–849.

Neff, K. D., & Harter, S. (2003). Relationship styles of self-focused autonomy, other-focused connectedness, and mutuality across multiple relationship contexts. *Journal of Social and Personal Relationships, 20*, 81–99.

Negy, C., Shreve, T. L., Jensen, B. J., & Uddin, N. (2003). Ethnic identity, self-esteem, and ethnocentrism: A study of social identity versus multicultural theory of development. *Cultural Diversity & Ethnic Minority Psychology, 9*, 333–344.

Neighbors, H. W., Caldwell, C., Williams, D. R., Nesse, R., Taylor, R. J., Bullard, K. M., . . . & Jackson, J. S. (2007). Race, ethnicity, and the use of services for mental disorders: Results from the National Survey of American Life. *Archives of General Psychiatry, 64*, 485–494.

Nelson, L. R., Signorella, M. L., & Botti, K. G. (2016). Accent, gender, and perceived competence. *Hispanic Journal of Behavioral Sciences, 38*, 166–185.

Neville, H. A., & Cross, W. E., Jr. (2017). Racial awakening: Epiphanies and encounters in Black racial identity. *Cultural Diversity and Ethnic Minority Psychology, 23*, 102–108.

Neville, H. A., Gallardo, M. E., & Sue, D. W. (Eds.). (2016). *The myth of color blindness: Manifestations, dynamics, and impact.* Washington, DC: American Psychological Association.

Ngo, V. H. (2008). A critical examination of acculturation theories. *Critical Social Work, 9*(1). Retrieved from http://www1.uwindsor.ca/criticalsocialwork/a-critical-examination-of-acculturation-theories

Nguyen, A. B., Chawla, N., Noone, A.-M., & Srinivasan, S. (2014). Disaggregated data and beyond: Future queries in cancer control research. *Cancer Epidemiology, Biomarkers & Prevention, 23*, 2266–2272.

Nguyen, A.-M. T. D., & Benet-Martínez, V. (2007). Biculturalism unpacked: Components, measurement, individual differences, and outcomes. *Social and Personality Psychology Compass, 1*, 101–114.

Nguyen, H. H. (2006). Acculturation in the United States. In D. L. Sam, & J. W. Berry (Eds.), *The Cambridge handbook of acculturation psychology* (pp. 311–330). Cambridge: Cambridge University Press.

Nguyen, H. H., & von Eye, A. (2002). The Acculturation Scale for Vietnamese Adolescents (ASVA): A bidimensional perspective. *International Journal of Behavioral Development, 26*, 202–213.

Nguyen, H. T., & Kellogg, G. (2010). "I had a stereotype that American were fat": Becoming a speaker of culture in a second language. *The Modern Language Journal, 94*, 56–73.

Nicolini, P. (1987). Puerto Rican leaders' views of English-language media. *Journalism Quarterly, 64*, 597–601.

Nisbett, R. E., Peng, K., Choi, I., & Norenzayan, A. (2001). Culture and systems of thought: Holistic versus analytic cognition. *Psychological Review, 108*, 291–310.

North American Spine Society. (2006). Herbal supplements: "Natural" doesn't always mean safe. Retrieved August 22, 2007, from http://www.spine.org/Documents/herbalsupplements_2006.pdf

Nosek, B. A., Greenwald, A. G., & Banaji, M. R. (2005). Understanding and using the Implicit Association Test: II. Method variables and construct validity. *Personality and Social Psychology Bulletin, 31*(2), 166–180.

Nuñez, A., González, P., Talavera, G. A., Sanchez-Johnsen, L., Roesch, S. C., Davis, S. M., . . . & Gallo, L. C. (2016). Machismo, marianismo, and negative cognitive-emotional factors: Findings from the Hispanic Community Health Study/Study of Latinos Sociocultural Ancillary Study. *Journal of Latina/o Psychology*, *4*, 202–217.

Nwadiora, E., & McAdoo, H. (1996). Acculturative stress among Amerasian refugees: Gender and racial differences. *Adolescence*, *31*, 477–487.

Obasi, E. M., & Leong, F. T. L. (2010). Construction and validation of the measurement of acculturation strategies for people of African descent (MASPAD). *Cultural Diversity and Ethnic Minority Psychology*, *16*, 526–539.

Office of Management and Budget. (1997). *Revisions to the standards for the classification of federal data on race and ethnicity*. Retrieved from https://obamawhitehouse.archives.gov/omb/fedreg_1997standards

Office of Minority Health, U.S. Department of Health and Human Services. (n.d.). *The national CLAS standards*. Retrieved January 24, 2018, from https://minorityhealth.hhs.gov/omh/browse.aspx?lvl=2&lvlid=53

Ogbu, J. (1978). *Minority education and caste*. New York: Academic Press.

O'Hara, B., & Caswell, K. (2013, July). *Health status, health insurance, and medical services utilization: 2010; Household Economic Studies* (P70-133RV). U.S. Census Bureau. Retrieved from https://www.census.gov/prod/2012pubs/p70-133.pdf

Okagaki, L., & Sternberg, R. J. (1993). Parental beliefs and children's school performance. *Child Development*, *64*(1), 36–56.

Okazaki, S., & Sue, S. (1995). Methodological issues in assessment research with ethnic minorities. *Psychological Assessment*, *7*, 367–375.

Okazaki, S., & Sue, S. (1998). Methodological issues in assessment research with ethnic minorities. In P. Balls Organista, K. M. Chun, & G. Marín (Eds.), *Readings in ethnic psychology* (pp. 26–40). New York: Routledge.

Orengo-Aguayo, R. E. (2015). Mexican American and other Hispanic couples' relationship dynamics: A review to inform interventions aimed at promoting healthy relationships. *Marriage & Family Review*, *51*(7), 633–667.

Organista, K. C. (2007). *Solving Latino psychosocial and health problems: Theory, practice and populations*. New York: John Wiley.

Ortiz, M. S., Baeza-Rivera, M. J., Salinas-Oñate, N., Flynn, P., & Betancourt, H. (2016). Atribución de malos tratos en servicios de salud a discriminación y sus consecuencias en pacientes diabéticos mapuche [Healthcare mistreatment attributed to discrimination among Mapuche patients and discontinuation of diabetes care]. *Revista Médica de Chile*, *144*(10), 1270–1276. Retrieved from http://www.scielo.cl/scielo.php?script=sci_arttext&pid=S0034-98872016001000006

Osibogun, O., & Pankey, B. (2017). Racial, residential segregation and poor health. *American Journal of Public Health*, *107*, e31.

Oskamp, S. (Ed.). (2000). *Reducing prejudice and discrimination*. Mahwah, NJ: Lawrence Erlbaum.

Oskamp, S., & Jones, J. M. (2000). Promising practices in reducing prejudice: A report from the President's Initiative on Race. In S. Oskamp (Ed.), *Reducing prejudice and discrimination* (pp. 319–334). Mahwah, NJ: Lawrence Erlbaum.

Ozer, E. J., Best, S. R., Lipsey, T. L., & Weiss, D. S. (2003). Prediction of posttraumatic stress disorder and symptoms in adults: A meta-analysis. *Psychological Bulletin*, *129*(1), 52–73.

Ozer, S. (2013). Theories and methodologies in acculturation psychology: The emergence of a scientific revolution? *Psychological Studies*, *58*, 339–348.

Pacheco, C. M., Daley, S. M., Brown, T., Filippi, M., Greiner, K. A., & Daley, C. M. (2013). Moving forward: Breaking the cycle of mistrust between American Indians and researchers. *American Journal of Public Health*, *103*(12), 2152–2159.

Padilla, A. M. (2001). Issues in culturally appropriate assessment. In L. A. Suzuki, J. G. Ponterotto, & P. J. Meller (Eds.), *Handbook of multicultural assessment: Clinical, psychological, and educational applications* (pp. 5–27). San Francisco: Jossey-Bass.

Padilla, A. M., & Olmedo, E. (2009). Synopsis of key persons, events, and associations in the history of Latino psychology. *Cultural Diversity & Ethnic Minority Psychology*, 15, 363–373.

Padilla, A. M., & Perez, W. (2003). Acculturation, social identity, and social cognition: A new perspective. *Hispanic Journal of Behavioral Sciences*, *25*, 35–55.

Palloni, A., & Arias, E. (2004). Paradox lost: Explaining the Hispanic adult mortality advantage. *Demography*, *41*, 385–415.

Parent, M. C., DeBlaere, C., & Moradi, B. (2013). Approaches to research on intersectionality: Perspectives on gender, LGBT, and racial/ethnic identities. *Sex Roles*, *68*, 639–645.

Parham, T. A., White, J. L., & Ajamu, A. (2000). *The psychology of Blacks: An African centered perspective* (3rd ed.). Upper Saddle River, NJ: Prentice Hall.

Park, I. H., & Cho, L. J. (1995). Confucianism and the Korean family. *Journal of Comparative Family Studies*, *26*, 117–134.

Parke, R. D., Coltrane, S., Borthwick-Duffy, S., Powers, J., & Adams, M. (2004). Assessing father involvement in Mexican-American families. In R. D. Day & M. E. Lamb (Eds.), *Conceptualizing and measuring father involvement* (pp. 17–38). Mahwah, NJ: Lawrence Erlbaum.

Parker, G., Fletcher, K., & Hadzi-Pavlovic, D. (2012). Is context everything to the definition of clinical depression? A test of the Horwitz and Wakefield postulate. *Journal of Affective Disorders*, *136*, 1034–1038.

Parks, C. A., Hughes, T. L., & Matthews, A. K. (2004). Race/ethnicity and sexual orientation: Intersecting identities. *Cultural Diversity & Ethnic Minority Psychology*, *10*, 241–254.

Passel, J. S., & Cohn, D. (2008, February 11). *U.S. population projections: 2005–2050*. Pew Research Center, Social

& Demographic Trends. Retrieved from http://assets.pewresearch.org/wp-content/uploads/sites/3/2010/10/85.pdf

Patel, A. I., & Schmidt, L. A. (2017). Water access in the United States: Health disparities abound and solutions are urgently needed. *American Journal of Public Health, 107*, 1354–1355.

Pattnayak, S. R., & Leonard, J. (1991). Racial segregation in Major League Baseball. *Sociology and Social Research, 76*, 3–9.

Pedersen, P. B. (2003). Reducing prejudice and racism through counselor training as a primary prevention strategy. In G. Bernal, J. E. Trimble, A. K. Burlew, & F. T. L. Leong (Eds.), *Handbook of racial and ethnic minority psychology* (pp. 621–632). Thousand Oaks, CA: Sage Publications.

Peguero, A. A., Bondy, J. M., & Shekarkhar, Z. (2017). Punishing Latina/o youth. *Hispanic Journal of Behavioral Sciences, 39*, 98–125.

Peng, K., & Nisbett, R. E. (1999). Culture, dialectics, and reasoning about contradiction. *American Psychologist, 54*, 741–754.

Pennell, B.-E., Bowers, A., Carr, D., Chardoul, S., Cheung, G.-q., Dinkelmann, K., . . . & Torres, M. (2004). The development and implementation of the National Comorbidity Survey Replication, the National Survey of American Life, and the National Latino and Asian American Survey. *International Journal of Methods in Psychiatric Research, 4*, 241–269.

Pérez, D. J., Fortuna, L., & Alegría, M. (2008). Prevalence and correlates of everyday discrimination among U.S. Latinos. *Journal of Community Psychology, 36*, 421–433.

Perez, W., & Padilla, A. M. (2000). Cultural orientation across three generations of Hispanic adolescents. *Hispanic Journal of Behavioral Sciences, 22*, 390–398.

Perilla, J. L., Norris, F. H., & Lavizzo, E. A. (2002). Ethnicity, culture, and disaster response: Identifying and explaining ethnic differences in PTSD six months after Hurricane Andrew. *Journal of Social & Clinical Psychology, 21*, 20–45.

Perkins, E. K. (2014). Challenges to traditional clinical definitions of depression in young Black men. *American Journal of Men's Health, 8*(1), 74–81.

Perlmann, J. (2002). Second-generation transnationalism. In P. Levitt & M. C. Waters (Eds.), *The changing face of home: The transnational lives of the second generation* (pp. 216–220). New York: Russell Sage Foundation.

Pernice, R. (1994). Methodological issues in research with refugees and immigrants. *Professional Psychology: Research and Practice, 25*, 207–213.

Perugini, M. (2005). Predictive models of implicit and explicit attitudes. *British Journal of Social Psychology, 44*, 29–45.

Pescosolido, B. A., Gardner, C. B., & Lubell, K. M. (1998). How people get into mental health services: Stories of choice, coercion and "muddling through." *Social Science & Medicine, 46*, 275–286.

Peterson, S. H., Wingood, G. M., DiClemente, R. J., Harrington, K., & Davies, S. (2007). Images of sexual stereotypes in rap videos and the health of African American female adolescents. *Journal of Woman's Health, 16*, 1157–1164.

Pettigrew, T. F. (1998). Intergroup contact theory. *Annual Review of Psychology, 48*, 65–85.

Pettigrew, T. F. (2004). Justice deferred a half century after. *American Psychologist, 59*, 521–529.

Pew Research Center. (2014). *Remittance flows worldwide in 2012.* Washington, DC: Author.

Pew Research Center. (2015, June 11). *Multiracial in America: Proud, diverse and growing in numbers.* Washington, DC: Pew Research Center. Retrieved from http://www.pewsocialtrends.org/2015/06/11/multiracial-in-america/

Pew Research Center. (2016). *2016 Global Attitudes Survey.* Washington, DC: Author.

Pham, T. B., & Harris, R. J. (2001). Acculturation strategies among Vietnamese-Americans. *International Journal of Intercultural Relations, 25*, 279–300.

Phillips, K. W. (2014). How diversity works. *Scientific American, 311*, 43–47.

Phinney, J. S. (1989). Stages of ethnic identity development in minority group adolescents. *The Journal of Early Adolescence, 9*, 34–49.

Phinney, J. S. (1990). Ethnic identity in adolescents and adults: Review of research. *Psychological Bulletin, 108*, 499–514.

Phinney, J. S. (1992). The Multigroup Ethnic Identity Measure: A new scale for use with diverse groups. *Journal of Adolescent Research, 7*, 156–176.

Phinney, J. S. (1993). Multigroup group identities: Differentiation, conflict, and integration. In J. Kroger (Ed.), *Discussions on ego identity* (pp. 47–73). Hillsdale, NJ: Lawrence Erlbaum.

Phinney, J. S. (1996). When we talk about American ethnic groups, what do we mean? *American Psychologist, 51*(9), 918–927.

Phinney, J. S., Chavira, V., & Tate, J. D. (1993). The effect of ethnic threat on ethnic self-concept and own-group ratings. *Journal of Social Psychology, 133*, 469–478.

Phinney, J. S., Horenczyk, G., Liebkind, K., & Vedder, P. (2001). Ethnic identity, immigration, and well-being: An interactional perspective. *Journal of Social Issues, 57*, 493–510.

Phinney, J. S., Lochner, B. T., & Murphy, R. (1990). Ethnic identity development and psychological adjustment in adolescence. In A. R. Stiffman & L. E. Davis (Eds.), *Ethnic issues in adolescent mental health* (pp. 53–72). Thousand Oaks, CA: Sage.

Phinney, J. S., & Ong, A. D. (2002). Adolescent-parent disagreements and life satisfaction in families from Vietnamese- and European-American backgrounds. *International Journal of Behavioral Development, 26*, 556–561.

Phinney, J. S., & Ong, A. D. (2007). Conceptualization and measurement of ethnic identity: Current status and future directions. *Journal of Counseling Psychology, 54*, 271–281.

Phinney, J. S., Ong, A. D., & Madden, T. (2000). Cultural values and intergenerational value discrepancies in immigrant and non-immigrant families. *Child Development, 71*, 528–539.

Phinney, J. S., & Rosenthal, D. A. (1992). Ethnic identity in adolescence: Process, context, and outcome. In G. R. Adams, T. P. Gullotta, & R. Montmayor (Eds.), *Advances in adolescent development: Vol. 4, Adolescent identity formation* (pp. 145–172). Thousand Oaks, CA: Sage.

Pickren, W. E. (2009). Liberating history: The context of the challenges of psychologists of color for American psychology. *Cultural Diversity & Ethnic Minority Psychology, 15*, 425–433.

Pike, F. B. (1992). *The United States and Latin America: Myths and stereotypes of civilization and nature*. Austin: University of Texas Press.

Piña-Watson, B., Castillo, L. G., Jung, E., Ojeda, L., & Castillo-Reyes, R. (2014). The Marianismo Beliefs Scale: Validation with Mexican American adolescent girls and boys. *Journal of Latina/o Psychology, 2*, 113–130.

Plunkett, S. W., & Bamaca-Gomez, M. Y. (2003). The relationship between parenting, acculturation, and adolescent academics in Mexican-origin immigrant families in Los Angeles. *Hispanic Journal of Behavioral Sciences, 25*, 222–239.

Pole, N., Best, S. R., Metzler, T., & Marmar, C. R. (2005). Why are Hispanics at greater risk for PTSD? *Cultural Diversity & Ethnic Minority Psychology, 11*, 144–161.

Ponterotto, J. G., Casas, J. M., Suzuki, L. A., & Alexander, C. M. (2001). *Handbook of multicultural counseling* (2nd ed.). Thousand Oaks, CA: Sage.

Ponterotto, J. G., Gretchen, D., Utsey, S. O., Stracuzzi, T., & Saya, R., Jr. (2003). The Multigroup Ethnic Identity Measure (MEIM): Psychometric review and further validity testing. *Educational and Psychological Measurement, 63*, 502–515.

Ponterotto, J. G., & Park-Taylor, J. (2007). Racial and ethnic identity theory, measurement, and research in counseling psychology: Present status and future directions. *Journal of Counseling Psychology, 54*, 282–294.

Population Reference Bureau. (2002). Foreign-born make up growing segment of the U.S. Black population. *Population Today*. Retrieved from http://www.prb.org/Publications/Articles/2002/ForeignBornMakeUpGrowingSegmentofUSBlackPopulation.aspx

Portes, A. (1999). Immigration theory for a new century: Some problems and opportunities. In C. Hirschman, P. Kasinitz, & J. DeWind (Eds.), *The handbook of international migration: The American experience* (pp. 21–33). New York: Russell Sage Foundation.

Portes, A., & Rumbaut, R. G. (2001). *Legacies: The story of the immigrant second generation*. Berkeley: University of California Press.

Portes, A., & Rumbaut, R. G. (2014). *Immigrant America: A portrait* (4th ed.). Berkeley: University of California Press.

Posner, S. F., Stewart, A. L., Marín, G., & Pérez-Stable, E. J. (2001). Factor variability of the Center for Epidemiological Studies-Depression Scale (CES-D) among urban Latinos. *Ethnicity & Health, 6*, 137–144.

Poston, W. C. (1990). The Biracial Identity Development Model: A needed addition. *Journal of Counseling & Development, 69*, 152–155.

Powell-Hopson, D., & Hopson, D. S. (1988). Implications of doll color preferences among Black preschool children and White preschool children. *The Journal of Black Psychology, 14*, 57–63.

Purkiss, S. L., Perrewé, P. L., Gillespie, T. L.,, Mayes, B. T., & Ferris, G. R. (2006). Implicit sources of bias in employment interview judgments and decisions. *Organizational Behavior and Human Decision Processes, 101*, 152–167.

Pyke, K. D., & Johnson, D. L. (2003). Asian American women and racialized femininities: "Doing" gender across cultural worlds. *Gender & Society, 17*, 33–53.

Quinn, K., Dickson-Gomez, J., DiFranceisco, W., Kelly, J. A., St. Lawrence, J. S., Amirkhanian, Y. A., & Broaddus, M. (2015). Correlates of internalized homonegativity among Black men who have sex with men. *AIDS Education and Prevention, 27*, 212–226.

Quintana, S. M. (1998). Children's developmental understanding of ethnicity and race. *Applied & Preventive Psychology, 7*, 27–45.

Quintana, S. M. (2007). Racial and ethnic identity: Developmental perspectives and research. *Journal of Counseling Psychology, 54*, 259–270.

Rainwater, L. (1970). *Behind ghetto walls: Black life in a federal slum*. Chicago: Aldine.

Ramirez, M., & Castaneda, A. (1974). *Cultural democracy and bicognitive developmental education*. New York: Academic Press.

Rankin, B. H., & Quane, J. M. (2000). Neighborhood poverty and the social isolation of inner-city African American families. *Social Forces, 79*, 139–164.

Rassool, G. H. (2014). *Cultural competence in caring for Muslim patients*. New York: Palgrave.

Rattansi, A. (2011). *Multiculturalism: A very short introduction*. Oxford: Oxford University Press.

Read, J. G., & Gorman, B. K. (2006). Gender inequalities in US adult health: The interplay of race and ethnicity. *Social Science & Medicine, 62*, 1045–1065.

Redfield, R., Linton, R., & Herskovits, M. J. (1936). Memorandum on the study of acculturation. *American Anthropologist, 38*, 149–152.

Reese-Cassal, K. (2014, September). *2014/2019 Esri Diversity Index*. Redlands, CA: Author. Retrieved from https://www.esri.com/library/whitepapers/pdfs/diversity-index-methodology.pdf

Rehm, J., Üstün, T. B., Saxena, S., Nelson, C. B., Chatterji, S., Ivis, F., & Adlaf, E. D. (1999). On the development and psychometric testing of the WHO screening instrument to assess disablement in the general population. *International Journal of Methods in Psychiatric Research, 8*, 110–123.

Rencher, W. C., & Wolf, L. E. (2013). Redressing past wrongs: Changing the common rule to increase minority voices in research. *American Journal of Public Health, 103*, 2136–2140.

Rentfrow, P. J., McDonald, J. A., & Oldmeadow, J. A. (2009). You are what you listen to: Young people's stereotypes about music fans. *Group Processes & Intergroup Relations, 12*, 329–344.

Rhodes, S. D., Song, E., Nam, S., Choi, S. J., & Choi, S. (2015). Identifying and intervening on barriers to healthcare access among members of a small Korean community in Southern USA. *Patient Education and Counseling, 98*, 484–491.

Richter, B. E. J., Lindahl, K. M., & Malik, N. M. (2017). Examining ethnic differences in parental rejection of LGB youth sexual identity. *Journal of Family Psychology, 31*, 244–249.

Rivas-Drake, D., Seaton, E. K., Markstrom, C., Quintana, S., Syed, M., Lee, R. M., Yip, T. (2014). Ethnic and racial identity in adolescence: Implications for psychosocial, academic, and health outcomes. *Child Development, 85*, 40–57.

Rivas-Drake, D., Syed, M., Umaña-Taylor, A., Markstrom, C., French, S., Schwartz, S. J., & Lee, R. (2014). Feeling good, happy, and proud: A meta-analysis of positive ethnic-racial affect and adjustment. *Child Development, 85*, 77–102.

Roberts, R. E., Phinney, J. S., Masse, L. C., Chen, Y. R., Roberts, C. R., & Romero, A. (1999). The structure of ethnic identity of young adolescents from diverse ethnocultural groups. *The Journal of Early Adolescence, 19*, 301–322.

Roberts, R. E., Vernon, S. W., & Rhoades, H. M. (1989). Effects of language and ethnic status on reliability and validity of the Center for Epidemiologic Studies-Depression Scale with psychiatric patients. *The Journal of Nervous and Mental Disease, 177*, 581–592.

Robins, L., & Regier, D. (Eds.). (1991). *Psychiatric disorders in America: The Epidemiologic Catchment Area study.* New York: Free Press.

Rodriguez, M. A., & Garcia, R. (2013). First, do no harm: The US sexually transmitted disease experiments in Guatemala. *American Journal of Public Health, 103*, 2122–2126.

Rodriguez, N., Myers, H. F., Mira, C. B., Flores, T., & Garcia-Hernandez, L. (2002). Development of the Multidimensional Acculturative Stress Inventory for adults of Mexican origin. *Psychological Assessment, 14*, 451–461.

Rogers, B. K., Sperry, H. A., & Levant, R. F. (2015). Masculinities among African American men: An intersectional perspective. *Psychology of Men & Masculinity, 16*, 416–425.

Rogers, L. O., Scott, M. A., & Way, N. (2015). Racial and gender identity among black adolescent males: An intersectionality perspective. *Child Development, 86*, 407–424.

Rogler, L. H. (1999a). Implementing cultural sensitivity in mental health research: Convergence and new directions. *Psychline, 3*, 5–11.

Rogler, L. H. (1999b). Methodological sources of cultural insensitivity in mental health research. *American Psychologist, 54*, 424–433.

Rogler, L. H., Cortes, D. E., & Malgady, R. G. (1991). Acculturation and mental health status among Hispanics. *American Psychologist, 46*, 585–597.

Rohner, R. P. (1984). Toward a conception of culture for cross-cultural psychology. *Journal of Cross-Cultural Psychology, 15*, 111–138.

Rohner, R., & Pettengill, S. (1985). Perceived parental acceptance-rejection and parental control among Korean adolescents. *Child Development, 56*, 524–528.

Rojas, A. J., Navas, M., Sayans-Jimenez, P., & Cuadrado, I. (2014). Acculturation preference profiles of Spaniards and Romanian immigrants: The role of prejudice and public and private acculturation areas. *The Journal of Social Psychology, 154*, 339–351.

Romero, A. J., Edwards, L. M., Fryberg, S. A., & Orduña, M. (2014). Resilience to discrimination stress across ethnic identity stages of development. *Journal of Applied Social Psychology, 44*, 1–11.

Romero-Gwynn, E., Gwynn, D., Grivetti, L., McDonald, R., Stanford, G., Turner, B., . . . & Williamson, E. (1993). Dietary acculturation among Latinos of Mexican descent. *Nutrition Today, 28*, 5–12.

Root, M. P. P. (1990). Resolving "other" status: Identity development of biracial individuals. *Women & Therapy, 9*, 185–205.

Root, M. P. P. (1992). Back to the drawing board: Methodological issues in research on multiracial people. In M. P. P. Root (Ed.), *Racially mixed people in America* (pp. 181–189). Newbury Park, CA: Sage.

Root, M. P. P. (1998). Multiracial Americans: Changing the face of Asian America. In N. W. S. Zane & E. Lee (Eds.), *Handbook of Asian American psychology* (1st ed., pp. 261–287). Thousand Oaks, CA: Sage.

Root, M. P. P. (2003). Racial identity development and persons of mixed race heritage. In M. P. P. Root & M. Kelley (Eds.), *Multiracial child resource book* (p. 41). Seattle: Mavin Foundation.

Rosario, M., & Schrimshaw, E. W. (2014). Theories and etiologies of sexual orientation. In D. L. Tolman, L. M. Diamond, J. A. Bauermeister, W. H. George, J. G. Pfaus, & L. M. Ward (Eds.), *APA handbook of sexuality and psychology: Vol. 1, Person-based approaches* (pp. 555–596). Washington, DC: American Psychological Association.

Rosario, M., Schrimshaw, E. W., & Hunter, J. (2004). Ethnic/racial differences in the coming-out process of lesbian, gay, and bisexual youths: A comparison of sexual identity development over time. *Cultural Diversity & Ethnic Minority Psychology, 10*, 215–228.

Rosenblum, K. E., & Travis, T.-M. C. (2015). *The meaning of difference: American constructions of race and ethnicity, sex and gender, social class, sexuality, and disability* (7th ed.). New York: McGraw-Hill.

Rosenthal, D., Ranieri, N., & Klimidis, S. (1996). Vietnamese adolescents in Australia: Relationships between perceptions of self and parental values, intergenerational conflict, and gender dissatisfaction. *International Journal of Psychology, 31*, 81–91.

Rossa, M. W., Dumka, L. E., Gonzales, N. A., & Knight, G. P. (2002). Cultural/ethnic issues and the prevention scientist in the 21st century. *Prevention & Treatment, 5*, 21–36.

Rotheram, M. J., & Phinney, J. S. (1987). Ethnic behavior patterns as an aspect of identity. In J. S. Phinney & M. J. Rotheram (Eds.), *Children's ethnic socialization: Pluralism and development* (pp. 210–218). Beverly Hills: Sage.

Rothman, R. A. (2005). Inequality and social stratification. In R. A. Rothman (Ed.), *Inequality and social stratification: Race, class, and gender* (5th ed., pp. 2–25). New York: Routledge.

Rowatt, W. C., Franklin, L. M., & Cotton, M. (2005). Patterns and personality correlates of implicit and explicit attitudes toward Christians and Muslims. *Journal for the Scientific Study of Religion, 44*, 29–43.

Roysircar, G. (2005). Culturally sensitive assessment, diagnosis, and guidelines. In M. G. Constantino & D. W. Sue (Eds.), *Strategies for building multicultural competence in mental health and educational settings* (pp. 19–38). Hoboken, NJ: Wiley.

Roysircar, G. (2014). Multicultural assessment: Individual and contextual dynamic sizing. In F. T. L. Leong, L. Comas-Díaz, G. C. N. Hall, V. C. McLoyd, & J. E. Trimble (Eds.), *APA handbook of multicultural psychology* (vol. 1, pp. 141–160). Washington, DC: American Psychological Association.

Rudd, R. A., Aleshira, A., Zibbell, J. E., & Gladden, R. M. (2016). Increases in drug and opioid overdose deaths—United States, 2000–2014. *American Journal of Transplants, 16*, 1323–1327.

Rudmin, F. W. (2003). "Critical history of the acculturation psychology of assimilation, separation, integration, and marginalization": Correction to Rudmin (2003). *Review of General Psychology, 7*, 250.

Rumbaut, R. G., & Portes, A. (Eds.). (2001). *Ethnicities: Children of immigrants in America*. Berkeley: University of California Press.

Ryan, C. (2013, August). *Language use in the United States: 2011; American Community Survey reports* (ACS-22). U.S. Census Bureau. Retrieved from https://www.census.gov/prod/2013pubs/acs-22.pdf

Ryan, C. L., & Bauman, K. (2016, March). *Educational attainment in the United States: 2015; Population characteristics* (P20-578). U.S. Census Bureau. Retrieved from https://www.census.gov/content/dam/Census/library/publications/2016/demo/p20-578.pdf

Ryan, W. (1972). *Blaming the victim*. New York: Vintage.

Sabogal, F., Marín, G., Otero-Sabogal, R., Marín, B. V., & Pérez-Stable, E. J. (1987). Hispanic familism and acculturation: What changes and what doesn't? *Hispanic Journal of Behavioral Sciences, 9*, 397–412.

Saéz-Santiago, E., & Bernal, G. (2003). Depression in ethnic minorities: Latinos and Latinas, African Americans, Asian Americans, and Native Americans. In G. Bernal, J. E. Trimble, A. K. Burlew, & F. T. L. Leong (Eds.), *Handbook of racial & ethnic minority psychology* (pp. 401–428). Thousand Oaks, CA: Sage.

Safdar, S., & Berno, T. (2016). Sojourners. In D. L. Sam & J. W. Berry (Eds.), *The Cambridge handbook of acculturation psychology* (2nd ed., pp. 173–195). Cambridge: Cambridge University Press.

Safren, S. A., Gonzalez, R. E., Horner, K. J., Leung, A. W., Heimberg, R. G., & Juster, H. R. (2000). Anxiety in ethnic minority youth: Methodological and conceptual issues and review of the literature. *Behavior Modification, 24*, 147–183.

Sakuma, K.-K., Felicitas-Perkins, J. Q., Blanco, L., Fagan, P., Pérez-Stable, E. J., Pulvers, K., . . . & Trinidad, D. R. (2016). Tobacco use disparities by racial/ethnic groups: California compared to the United States. *Preventive Medicine, 91*, 224–232.

Salas-Wright, C. P., Robles, E. H., Vaughn, M. G., Cordova, D., & Perez-Figueroa, R. E. (2015). Toward a typology of acculturative stress: Results among Hispanic immigrants in the United States. *Hispanic Journal of Behavioral Sciences, 37*, 223–242.

Sallis, J. F., & Owen, N. (2015). Ecological models of health behavior. In K. Glanz, B. K. Rimer & K. Viswanath (Eds.), *Health behavior: Theory, research, and practice* (pp. 43–64). San Francisco: Jossey-Bass.

Sam, D. L. (2006). Acculturation and health. In D. L. Sam & J. W. Berry (Eds.), *The Cambridge handbook of acculturation psychology* (pp. 452–468). Cambridge: Cambridge University Press.

Sam, D. L., & Berry, J. W. (Eds.). (2006). *The Cambridge handbook of acculturation psychology*. Cambridge: Cambridge University Press.

Sam, D. L., & Berry, J. W. (Eds.). (2016). *The Cambridge handbook of acculturation psychology* (2nd ed.). Cambridge: Cambridge University Press.

Sam, D. L., Jasinskaja-Lahti, I., Ryder, A. G., & Hassan, G. (2016). Health. In D. L. Sam & J. W. Berry (Eds.), *The Cambridge handbook of acculturation psychology* (2nd ed., pp. 504–524). Cambridge: Cambridge University Press.

Sampson, E. E. (1999). *Dealing with differences: An introduction to the social psychology of prejudice*. Orlando: Harcourt Brace.

Sanchez, J. I., & Fernandez, D. M. (1993). Acculturation stress among Hispanics: A bidimensional model of ethnic identification. *Journal of Applied Social Psychology, 23*, 654–668.

Sanders, R. G. W. (2002). The Black church: Bridge over troubled water. In J. L. Sanders & C. Bradley (Eds.), *Counseling African American families* (pp. 73–84). Alexandria, VA: American Counseling Association.

Sanders Thompson, V. L., Bazile, A., & Akbar, M. (2004). African Americans' perceptions of psychotherapy and psychotherapists. *Professional Psychology: Research and Practice, 35*, 19–26.

Sandil, R., Robinson, M., Brewster, M. E., Wong, S., & Geiger, E. (2015). Negotiating multiple marginalizations:

Experiences of South Asian LGBQ individuals. *Cultural Diversity and Ethnic Minority Psychology, 21*, 76–88.

Santiago, C. D., & Miranda, J. (2014). Progress in improving mental health services for racial-ethnic minority groups: A ten-year perspective. *Psychiatric Services, 65*(2), 180–185.

Santisteban, D. A., Suarez-Morales, L., Robbins, M. S., & Szapocznik, J. (2006). Brief strategic family therapy: Lessons learned in efficacy research and challenges to blending research and practice. *Family Process, 45*, 259–271.

Santos, S. J., Ortiz, A. M., Morales, A., & Rosales, M. (2007). The relationship between campus diversity, students' ethnic identity and college adjustment: A qualitative study. *Cultural Diversity & Ethnic Minority Psychology, 13*, 104–114.

Santrock, J. W. (2004). *Life-span development* (10th ed.). Boston: McGraw-Hill.

Santrock, J. W. (2005). *A topical approach to life-span development* (2nd ed.). New York: McGraw-Hill.

Sarno, E. L., Mohr, J. J., Jackson, S. D., & Fassinger, R. E. (2015). When identities collide: Conflicts in allegiances among LGB people of color. *Cultural Diversity and Ethnic Minority Psychology, 21*, 550–559.

Savage, S. L., & Gauvain, M. (1998). Parental beliefs and children's everyday planning in European-American and Latino families. *Journal of Applied Developmental Psychology, 19*, 319–340.

Schaefer, R. T. (1996). *Racial and ethnic groups* (6th ed.). New York: HarperCollins.

Schaefer, R. T. (Ed.). (2008). *Encyclopedia of race, ethnicity, and society* (vols. 1–3). Thousand Oaks, CA: Sage.

Schillinger, D., Barton, L. R., Karter, A. J., Wang, F., & Adler, N. (2006). Does literacy mediate the relationship between education and health outcomes? A study of a low-income population with diabetes. *Public Health Reports, 121*, 245–254.

Schofield, J. W., & Hausmann, L. R. M. (2004). School desegregation and social science research. *American Psychologist, 59*, 538–546.

Schoon, I., Bynner, J., Joshi, H., Parsons, S., Wiggins, R. D., & Sacker, A. (2002). The influence, timing, and duration of risk experiences for the passage from childhood to midadulthood. *Child Development, 73*, 1486–1504.

Schraufnagel, T. J., Wagner, A. W., Miranda, J., Peter, P., & Roy-Byrne, M. (2006). Treating minority patients with depression and anxiety: What does the evidence tell us? *General Hospital Psychiatry, 28*, 27–36.

Schuman, H., Steeh, C., & Bobo, L. (1985). *Racial attitudes in America*. Cambridge, MA: Harvard University Press.

Schwartz, R. C., & Feisthamel, K. P. (2009). Disproportionate diagnosis of mental disorders among African American versus European American clients: Implications for counseling theory, research, and practice. *Journal of Counseling and Development, 87*(3), 295–301.

Schwartz, S. J., Unger, J. B., Baezconde-Garbanati, L., Benet-Martínez, V., Meca, A., Zamboanga, B. L., . . . & Szapocznik, J. (2015). Longitudinal trajectories of bicultural identity integration in recently immigrated Hispanic adolescents: Links with mental health and family functioning. *International Journal of Psychology, 50*, 440–450.

Schweigman, K., Soto, C., Wright, S., & Unger, J. (2011). The relevance of cultural activities in ethnic identity among California Native American youth. *Journal of Psychoactive Drugs, 43*, 343–348.

Sciacca, K., & Thompson, C. M. (1996). Program development and integrated treatment across systems for dual diagnosis: Mental illness, drug addiction and alcoholism, MIDAA. *Journal of Mental Health Administration, 23*, 288–297.

Sears, D. O., Fu, M., Henry, P. J., & Bui, K. (2003). The origins and persistence of ethnic identity among the "new immigrant" groups. *Social Psychology Quarterly, 66*, 419–437.

Seaton, E. K., & Taylor, R. D. (2003). Exploring familial processes in urban, low-income African-American families. *Journal of Family Issues, 24*, 627–644.

Segall, M. H., Lonner, W. J., & Berry, J. W. (1998). Cross-cultural psychology as a scholarly discipline: On the flowering of culture in behavioral research. *American Psychologist, 53*, 1101–1110.

Serrano, E., & Anderson, J. (2003). Assessment of a refined short acculturation scale for Latino preteens in rural Colorado. *Hispanic Journal of Behavioral Sciences, 25*, 240–253.

Serrano-Villar, M., & Calzada, E. J. (2016). Ethnic identity: Evidence of protective effects for young, Latino children. *Journal of Applied Developmental Psychology, 42*, 21–30.

Settles, I. H., & Buchanan, N. T. (2014). Multiple groups, multiple identities, and intersectionality. In V. Benet-Martínez & Y.-Y. Hong (Eds.), *The Oxford handbook of multicultural identity* (pp. 160–180). New York: Oxford University Press.

Shavers-Hornaday, V. L., Lynch, C. F., Burmeister, L. F., & Torner, J. C. (1997). Why are African Americans underrepresented in medical research studies? Impediments to participation. *Ethnicity & Health, 2*, 31–45.

Shek, Y. L., & McEwen, M. K. (2012). The relationships of racial identity and gender role conflict to self-esteem of Asian American undergraduate men. *Journal of College Student Development, 53*, 703–718.

Shelton, J. N., Richeson, J. A., Salvatore, J., & Trawalter, S. (2005). Ironic effects of racial bias during interracial interactions. *Psychological Science, 16*, 397–402.

Shi, L. (2001). The convergence of vulnerable characteristics and health insurance in the United States. *Social Science Medicine, 53*, 519–529.

Shih, M., Pittinsky, T. L., & Trahan, A. (2006). Domain-specific effects of stereotypes on performance. *Self and Identity, 5*, 1–14.

Shih, M., & Sanchez, D. T. (2005). Perspectives and research on the positive and negative implications of having multiple racial identities. *Psychological Bulletin, 131*, 569–591.

Shin, H. B., & Bruno, R. (2003, October). *Language use and English-speaking ability: 2000; Census 2000 Brief* (C2KBR-29). U.S. Census Bureau. Retrieved from https://www.census.gov/prod/2003pubs/c2kbr-29.pdf

Shive, S. E., Ma, G. X., Tan, Y., Toubbeh, J. I., Parameswaran, L., & Halowich, J. (2007). Asian American subgroup differences in sources of health information and predictors of screening behavior. *California Journal of Health Promotion, 5*, 112–127.

Shore, N., Ford, A., Wat, E., Brayboy, M., Isaacs, M.-L., Park, A., Streinick, H., & Seifer, S. R. (2015). Community-based review of research across diverse community contexts: Key characteristics, critical issues, and future directions. *American Journal of Public Health, 105*, 1294–1301.

Siegel, M. P., & Carter, R. T. (2014). Emotions and white racial identity status attitudes. *Journal of Multicultural Counseling and Development, 42*, 218–231.

Simon, C. E., Crowther, M., & Higgerson, H. K. (2007). The stage-specific role of spirituality among African American Christian women throughout the breast cancer experience. *Cultural Diversity & Ethnic Minority Psychology, 13*, 26–34.

Simonds, V. W., & Christopher, S. (2013). Adapting Western research methods to indigenous ways of knowing. *American Journal of Public Health, 103*, 2185–2192.

Simons, R. L., Murry, V., McLoyd, V., Lin, K. H., Cutrona, C., & Conger, R. D. (2002). Discrimination, crime, ethnic identity, and parenting as correlates of depressive symptoms among African American children: A multilevel analysis. *Development and Psychopathology, 14*, 371–393.

The Singapore statement on research integrity. (2010, July 24). 2nd World Conference on Research Integrity, Singapore. Retrieved from http://www.singaporestatement.org/statement.html

Singelis, M. T. (1994). The measurement of independent and interdependent self-construals. *Personality and Social Psychology Bulletin, 20*, 580–591.

Singh, A. A. (2013). Transgender youth of color and resilience: Negotiating oppression and finding support. *Sex Roles, 68*, 690–702.

Skewes, M. C., & Blume, A. W. (2015). Ethnic identity, drinking motives, and alcohol consequences among Alaska Native and non-native college students. *Journal of Ethnicity in Substance Abuse, 14*, 12–28.

Skinner, O. D., & McHale, S. M. (2017, May 5). The development and correlates of gender role orientations in African-American youth. *Child Development.*

Smedley, B. D. (2008). Moving beyond access: Achieving equity in state health care reform. *Health Affairs, 27*, 447–455.

Smedley, B. D., Stith, A. Y., & Nelson, A. R. (Eds.). (2003). *Unequal treatment: Confronting racial and ethnic disparities in health care.* Washington, DC: National Academy Press.

Smetana, J., & Gaines, C. (1999). Adolescent-parent conflict in middle-class African American families. *Child Development, 70*, 1447–1463.

Smith, T. B., & Silva, L. (2011). Ethnic identity and personal well-being of people of color: A meta-analysis. *Journal of Counseling Psychology, 58*, 42–60.

Smith, T. W. (1990). *Ethnic images* (GSS Topical Report No.19). Chicago: National Opinion Research Center.

Smokowski, P. R., Evans, C. B. R., Cotter, K. L., & Webber, K. C. (2014). Ethnic identity and mental health in American Indian youth: Examining mediation pathways through self-esteem, and future optimism. *Journal of Youth and Adolescence, 43*, 343–355.

Snowden, L. R., & Cheung, F. K. (1990). Use of inpatient mental services by members of ethnic minority groups. *American Psychologist, 45*, 347–355.

Snowden, L. R., & Hines, A. M. (1999). A scale to assess African American acculturation. *Journal of Black Psychology, 25*, 36–47.

Snowden, L. R., Masland, M., & Guerrero, R. (2007). Federal civil rights policy and mental health treatment access for persons with limited English proficiency. *American Psychologist, 62*, 109–117.

Snowden, L. R., & Thomas, K. (2000). Medicaid and African American outpatient mental health treatment. *Mental Health Services Research, 2*, 115–120.

Social Science Research Council. (1954). Acculturation: An exploratory formulation. *American Anthropologist, 56*, 973–1002.

Sodowsky, G. R., Lai, E. W., & Plake, B. S. (1991). Moderating effects of sociocultural variables on acculturation attitudes of Hispanics and Asian Americans. *Journal of Counseling & Development, 70*, 194–204.

Soldier, L. L. (1985). To soar with the eagles: Enculturation and acculturation of Indian children. *Childhood Education, 10*, 185–189.

Solomon, R. C., & Higgins, K. M. (1997). *A passion for wisdom: A very brief history of philosophy.* Oxford: Oxford University Press.

Speer, I. (2016). Race, wealth, and class identification in 21st-century American society. *The Sociological Quarterly, 57*, 356–379.

Spencer, M. S. (2015). Insider-outsider reflections from a Native Hawaiian researcher and the use of community-based participatory approaches. *Australasian Psychiatry, 23*, 45–47.

Sperber, A. D., Devellis, R. F., & Boehlecke, B. (1994). Cross-cultural translation: Methodology and validation. *Journal of Cross-Cultural Psychology, 25*, 501–524.

Stahl, G. K., Makela, K., Zander, L., & Maznevski, M. (2010). Applying a positive organizational scholarship lens to multicultural team research: A look at the bright side of multicultural team diversity. *Scandinavian Journal of Management*, 26, 439–447.

Stahl, G. K., Maznevski, M. L., Voigt, A., & Jonsen, K. (2009). Unraveling the effects of cultural diversity in teams: A meta-analysis of research on multicultural work groups. *Journal of International Business Studies, 1*, 1–20.

Stanfield, J. H., & Dennis, R. M. (Eds.). (1993). *Race and ethnicity in research methods.* Newbury Park, CA: Sage.

Steele, C. M. (1997). A threat in the air: How stereotypes shape intellectual identity and performance. *American Psychologist, 52,* 613–629.

Steele, C. M., & Aronson, J. (1995). Stereotype threat and the intellectual test performance of African Americans. *Journal of Personality and Social Psychology, 69,* 797–811.

Steenbergen-Weijenburg, K., van der Feltz-Cornelis, C., Horn, E., van Marwijk, H., Beekman, A., Rutten, F., & Hakkaart-van Roijen, L. (2010). Cost-effectiveness of collaborative care for the treatment of major depressive disorder in primary care. A systematic review. *BMC Health Services Research, 10*(1), 19.

Stein, G. L., Cupito, A. M., Mendez, J. L., Prandoni, J., Huq, N., & Westerberg, D. (2014). Familism through a developmental lens. *Journal of Latina/o Psychology, 2*(4), 224–250.

Stein, J., Nyamathi, A., & Kington, R. (1997). Change in AIDS risk behaviors among impoverished minority women after a community based cognitive-behavioral outreach program. *Journal of Community Psychology, 25,* 519–533.

Steinberg, L. (2001). We know some things: Parent-adolescent relationships in retrospect and prospect. *Journal of Research on Adolescence, 11,* 1–19.

Steinman, K. J., & Zimmerman, M. A. (2004). Religious activity and risk behavior among African American adolescents: Concurrent and developmental effects. *American Journal of Community Psychology, 33,* 151–161.

Stephenson, M. (2000). Development and validation of the Stephenson Multigroup Acculturation Scale (SMAS). *Psychological Assessment, 12,* 77–88.

Stepney, C. T., Sanchez, D. T., & Handy, P. E. (2015). Perceptions of parents' ethnic identities and the personal ethnic-identity and racial attitudes of biracial adults. *Cultural Diversity and Ethnic Minority Psychology, 21,* 65–75.

Stern, M. P., Knapp, J. A., Hazuda, H. P., Haffner, S. M., Patterson, J. K., & Mitchell, B. D. (1991). Genetic and environmental determinants of type II diabetes in Mexican Americans: Is there a "descending limb" to the modernization/diabetes relationship? *Diabetes Care, 14,* 649–654.

Sternberg, R. J. (1985). *Beyond IQ: A triarchic theory of human intelligence.* New York: Cambridge University Press.

Sternberg, R. J. (2004). Culture and intelligence. *American Psychologist, 59*(5), 325–338.

Stevenson, H. W., Chen, C., & Uttal, D. H. (1990). Beliefs and achievement: A study of Black, White, and Hispanic children. *Child Development, 61,* 508–523.

Stock, M. L., Gibbons, F. X., Gerrard, M., Houlihan, A. E., Weng, C.-Y., Lorenz, F. O., & Simons, R. L. (2013). Racial identification, racial composition, and substance use vulnerability among African American adolescents and young adults. *Health Psychology, 32,* 237–247.

Stock, M. L., Gibbons, F. X., Walsh, L. A., & Gerrard, M. (2011). Racial identification, racial discrimination, and substance use vulnerability among African American young adults. *Personality and Social Psychology Bulletin, 37,* 1349–1361.

Stokols, D. (1992). Establishing and maintaining healthy environments: Toward a social ecology of health promotion. *American Psychologist, 47,* 6–22.

Strasburg, J. (2002, April 8). Abercrombie & glitch: Asian Americans rip retailer for stereotypes on T-shirts. *San Francisco Chronicle,* p. A-1. Retrieved from http://www.sfgate.com/news/article/ABERCROMBIE-GLITCH-Asian-Americans-rip-2850702.php

Stuart, J., & Ward, C. (2011). A question of balance: Exploring the acculturation, integration and adaptation of Muslim immigrant youth. *Psychological Intervention, 20,* 255–267.

Sturgeon, J. (2005, January/February). *The many languages of medicine.* Retrieved April 29, 2005, from Unique Opportunities: The Physician's Resource, at http://www.uoworks.com/articles/language.html

Suarez-Balcazar, Y., Balcazar, F., García-Ramirez, M., & Taylor-Ritzler, T. (2014). Ecological theory and research in multicultural psychology: A community psychology perspective. In F. T. L. Leong, L. Comas-Díaz, G. C. N. Hall, V. C. McLoyd, & J. E. Trimble (Eds.), *APA handbook of multicultural psychology* (vol. 1, pp. 535–552). Washington, DC: American Psychological Association.

Suárez-Orozco, C., & Suárez-Orozco, M. M. (1995). *Transformations: Migration, family life, and achievement motivation among Latino adolescents.* Stanford, CA: Stanford University Press.

Substance Abuse and Mental Health Services Administration. (2006). *Results from the 2005 National Survey on Drug Use and Health: National findings* (NSDUH Series H-30, DHHS Publication No. SMA 06-4194). Rockville, MD: Author.

Substance Abuse and Mental Health Services Administration. (2014). *Improving cultural competence.* Treatment Improvement Protocol (TIP) Series No. 59 (HHS publication No. [SMA] 14-4849). Rockville, MD: Author. Retrieved from https://store.samhsa.gov/shin/content/SMA14-4849/SMA14-4849.pdf

Substance Abuse and Mental Health Services Administration. (2015). *Behavioral Health Barometer: United States, 2015* (HHS Publication No. SMA-16-Baro-2015). Rockville, MD: Author.

Sudano, J. J., & Baker, D. W. (2006). Explaining US racial/ethnic disparities in health declines and mortality in late middle age: The roles of socioeconomic status, health behaviors, and health insurance. *Social Science & Medicine, 62,* 909–922.

Sue, D. W. (2003). *Overcoming our racism: The journey to liberation.* San Francisco: Jossey-Bass.

Sue, D. W. (2004). Whiteness and ethnocentric monoculturalism: Making the "invisible" visible. *American Psychologist, 59,* 761–769.

Sue, D. W., Capodilupo, C. M., Torino, G. C., Bucceri, J. M., Holder, A. M., Nadal, K. L., & Esquilin, M. (2007). Racial microaggressions in everyday life: Implications for clinical practice. *American Psychologist, 62,* 271–286.

Sue, D. W., Ivey, A. E., & Pedersen, P. B. (1996). *A theory of multicultural counseling and psychotherapy.* Pacific Grove, CA: Brooks/Cole.

Sue, D. W., & Sue, D. (1999). *Counseling the culturally different* (3rd ed.). New York: John Wiley.

Sue, D. W., & Sue, D. (2008). *Counseling the culturally diverse: Theory and practice.* Hoboken, NJ: John Wiley.

Sue, S. (1999). Science, ethnicity, and bias. *American Psychologist, 54,* 1070–1077.

Sue, S. (2006). Cultural competency: From philosophy to research and practice. *Journal of Community Psychology, 34,* 237–245.

Sue, S., Fujino, D., Hu, L., Takeuchi, D., & Zane, N. (1991). Community mental health services for ethnic minority groups: A test of the cultural responsiveness hypothesis. *Journal of Consulting and Clinical Psychology, 59,* 533–540.

Sue, S., & Okazaki, S. (1990). Asian-American educational achievements: A phenomenon in search of an explanation. *American Psychologist, 45,* 913–920.

Sue, S., Sue, D. W., Sue, L., & Takeuchi, D. T. (1998). Psychopathology among Asian Americans: A model minority? In P. Balls Organista, K. M. Chun, & G. Marín (Eds.), *Readings in ethnic psychology* (pp. 270–282). New York: Routledge.

Sue, S., Zane, N., Hall, G. C. N., & Berger, L. K. (2009). The case for cultural competence in psychotherapeutic interventions. *Annual Review of Psychology, 60,* 525–548.

Suinn, R. M., Rickard-Figueroa, K., Lew, S., & Vigil, P. (1987). Suinn-Lew Asian Self-Identity Acculturation Scale: An initial report. *Educational and Psychological Measurement, 47,* 401–407.

Suls, J., & Rothman, A. (2004). Evolution of the biopsychosocial model: Prospects and challenges for health psychology. *Health Psychology, 23,* 119–125.

Sumathipala, A., & Murray, J. (2000). New approach to translating instruments for cross-cultural research: A combined qualitative and quantitative approach for translation and consensus generation. *International Journal of Methods in Psychiatric Research, 9,* 87–95.

Sun, S., Hoyt, W. T., Brockberg, D., Lam, J., & Tiwari, D. (2016). Acculturation and enculturation as predictors of psychological help-seeking attitudes (HSAs) among racial and ethnic minorities. *Journal of Counseling Psychology, 63,* 617–632.

Sung, M. R., Szymanski, D. M., & Henrichs-Beck, C. (2015). Challenges, coping, and benefits of being an Asian American lesbian or bisexual woman. *Psychology of Sexual Orientation and Gender Diversity, 2,* 52–64.

Sussman, J., Beaujean, A. A., Worrell, F. C., & Watson, S. (2012). An analysis of Cross Racial Identity Scale scores using classical test theory and Rasch item response models. *Measurement and Evaluation in Counseling and Development, 46,* 136–153.

Swarns, R. L. (2004, August 29). "African-American" becomes a term for debate. *New York Times,* p. 01. Retrieved from http://www.nytimes.com/2004/08/29/us/african-american-becomes-a-term-for-debate.html

Syed, M., & Azmitia, M. (2010). Narrative and ethnic identity exploration: A longitudinal account of emerging adults' ethnicity-related experiences. *Developmental Psychology, 46,* 208–219.

Szapocznik, J., & Kurtines, W. (1980). Acculturation, biculturalism and adjustment among Cuban-Americans. In A. M. Padilla (Ed.), *Acculturation: Theory, models and some new findings* (pp. 139–159). Boulder, CO: Westview.

Szymanski, D. M., & Sung, M. R. (2010). Minority stress and psychological distress among Asian American sexual minority persons. *The Counseling Psychologist, 38,* 848–872.

Szymanski, D. M., & Sung, M. R. (2013). Asian cultural values, internalized heterosexism, and sexual orientation disclosure among Asian American sexual minority persons. *Journal of LGBT Issues in Counseling, 7,* 257–273.

Tadmor, C. T., & Tetlock, P. E. (2006). Biculturalism: A model of the effects of second-culture exposure on acculturation and integrative complexity. *Journal of Cross-Cultural Psychology, 37,* 173–190.

Tajfel, H. (1981). *Human groups and social categories: Studies in social psychology.* Cambridge: Cambridge University Press.

Takaki, R. T. (1979). *Iron cages: Race and culture in nineteenth century America.* Seattle: University of Washington Press.

Talbot, M. (1997, November 30). Getting credit for being White. *The New York Times Magazine, 30,* 116–119. Retrieved from http://www.nytimes.com/1997/11/30/magazine/getting-credit-for-being-white.html

Tam, V. C. W., & Detzner, D. F. (1998). Grandparents as a family resource in Chinese-American families. In H. I. McCubbin, E. A. Thompson, A. I. Thompson, & J. E. Fromer (Eds.), *Resiliency in Native American and immigrant families* (pp. 243–262). Thousand Oaks, CA: Sage.

Tang, C. S. K., Cheung, F. M. C., Chen, R., & Sun, X. (2002). Definition of violence against women: A comparative study in Chinese societies of Hong Kong, Taiwan, and the People's Republic of China. *Journal of Interpersonal Violence, 17,* 671–688.

Taylor, P., Lopez, M. H., Martínez, J., & Velasco, G. (2012, April 4). *When labels don't fit: Hispanics and their views of identity.* Retrieved from http://www.pewhispanic.org/2012/04/04/when-labels-dont-fit-hispanics-and-their-views-of-identity/

Taylor, S. (2015). *Health psychology* (9th ed.). New York: McGraw-Hill.

Telzer, E. H. (2010). Expanding the acculturation gap-distress model: An integrative review of research. *Human Development, 53,* 313–340.

Thoma, B. C., & Huebner, D. M. (2013). Health consequences of racist and antigay discrimination for multiple minority adolescents. *Cultural Diversity and Ethnic Minority Psychology, 19,* 404–413.

Thomas, V., & Azmitia, M. (2014). Does class matter? The centrality and meaning of social class identity in emerging adulthood. *Identity: An International Journal of Theory and Research, 14,* 195–213.

Thomas, W. I., & Znaniecki, F. (1918). *The Polish peasant in Europe and America.* Boston: R. Badger.

Thompson, T. L., Kiang, L., & Witkow, M. R. (2016). "You're Asian; you're supposed to be smart": Adolescents' experiences with the Model Minority Stereotype and longitudinal links with identity. *Asian American Journal of Psychology*, *7*, 108–119.

Thorndike, R. L. (1977). Content and evaluation in ethnic stereotypes. *The Journal of Psychology*, *96*, 131–140.

Titzmann, P. F., & Sonnenberg, K. (2016). Adolescents in conflict: Intercultural contact attitudes of immigrant mothers and adolescents as predictors of family conflicts. *International Journal of Psychology*, *51*(4), 279–287.

Torres, A. (1992). Nativity, gender, and earning discrimination. *Hispanic Journal of Behavioral Sciences*, *14*, 134–143.

Torres, J. B., Solberg, V. S. H., & Carlstrom, A. H. (2002). The myth of sameness among Latino men and their machismo. *American Journal of Orthopsychiatry*, *72*, 163–181.

Townsend, S. S. M., Fryberg, S. A., Wilkins, C. L., & Markus, H. R. (2012). Being mixed: Who claims a biracial identity? *Cultural Diversity and Ethnic Minority Psychology*, *18*, 91–96.

Tran, C., & Des Jardins, K. (2000). Domestic violence in Vietnamese refugee and Korean immigrant communities. In J. L. Chin (Ed.), *Relationships among Asian American women* (pp. 71–96). Washington, DC: American Psychological Association.

Triandis, H. C. (1990). Cross-cultural studies of individualism and collectivism. In J. J. Berman (Ed.), *Cross-cultural perspectives: Nebraska Symposium on Motivation, 1989* (pp. 41–133). Lincoln: University of Nebraska Press.

Triandis, H. C. (1994). *Culture and social behavior*. New York: McGraw-Hill.

Triandis, H. C. (1995). *Individualism and collectivism*. Boulder, CO: Westview.

Triandis, H. C. (2002). Subjective culture. *Online readings in psychology and culture*, *2*(2). Retrieved from https://scholarworks.gvsu.edu/cgi/viewcontent.cgi?article=1021&context=orpc

Triandis, H. C., & Gelfand, M. J. (1998). Converging measurement of horizontal and vertical individualism and collectivism. *Journal of Personality and Social Psychology*, *74*, 118–128.

Triandis, H. C., Marín, G., Lisansky, J., & Betancourt, H. (1984). *Simpatía* as a cultural script of Hispanics. *Journal of Personality and Social Psychology*, *47*, 1363–1375.

Trickett, E. J. (1996). A future for community psychology: The contexts of diversity and the diversity of contexts. *American Journal of Community Psychology*, *24*(2), 209–234.

Trimble, J. E. (2007). Prolegomena for the connotation of construct use in the measurement of ethnic and racial identity. *Journal of Counseling Psychology*, *54*, 247–258.

Trimble, J. E., Scharrón–del Río, M., & Casillas, D. M. (2014). Ethical matters and contentions in the principled conduct of research with ethnocultural communities. In F. T. L. Leong, L. Comas-Díaz, G. C. N. Hall, V. C. McLoyd, & J. E. Trimble (Eds.), *APA handbook of multicultural psychology* (vol. 1, pp. 59–82). Washington, DC: American Psychological Association.

Tropp, L. R., Erkut, S., Coll, C. G., Alarcón, O., & Garcia, H. A. (1999). Psychological acculturation development of a new measure for Puerto Ricans on the U.S. mainland. *Educational and Psychological Measurement*, *59*, 351–367.

Tseng, V., & Fuligni, A. J. (2000). Parent-adolescent language use and relationships among immigrant families with East Asian, Filipino, and Latin American backgrounds. *Journal of Marriage and Family*, *62*, 465–476.

Tseng, W.-S. (2006). From peculiar psychiatric disorders through culture-bound syndromes to culture-related syndromes. *Transcultural Psychiatry*, *43*(4), 554–576.

Tseng, W.-S., & Streltzer, J. (2008). *Cultural competence in health care*. New York: Springer Science.

Tucker, J. A., Phillips, M. M., Murphy, J. G., & Raczynski, J. M. (2004). Behavioral epidemiology and health psychology. In T. J. Boll (Series Ed.) & R. G. Frank, A. Baum, & J. L. Wallander (Vol. Eds.), *Models and perspectives in health psychology: Vol. 3, Handbook of clinical health psychology* (pp. 435–464). Washington, DC: American Psychological Association.

Tung, E. L., Baig, A. A., Huang, E. S., Laiteerapong, N., & Chua, K. P. (2017). Racial and ethnic disparities in diabetes screening between Asian Americans and other adults: BFRSS 2012–2014. *Journal of General and Internal Medicine*, *32*, 423–429.

Turner, S. M., DeMersr, S. T., Fox, H. R., & Reed, G. M. (2001). APA's guidelines for test users' qualifications: An executive summary. *American Psychologist*, *56*, 1099–1113.

Twine, F. W., & Gallagher, C. (2008). The future of Whiteness: A map of the "third wave." *Ethnic and Racial Studies*, *31*, 3–24.

Tynes, B. M., Umaña-Taylor, A. J., Rose, C. A., Lin, J., & Anderson, C. J. (2012). Online racial discrimination and the protective function of ethnic identity and self-esteem for African American adolescents. *Developmental Psychology*, *48*, 343–355.

U.S. Census Bureau. (2014). *People reporting ancestry: 2014, American Community Survey* (B04006). Retrieved from https://factfinder.census.gov/faces/tableservices/jsf/pages/productview.xhtml?src=bkmk

U.S. Census Bureau, Population Division. (2008, August 14). *Table 6: Percent of the projected population by race and Hispanic origin for the United States: 2010 to 2050* (NP2008-T6). Retrieved from https://www.census.gov/data/tables/2008/demo/popproj/2008-summary-tables.html

U.S. Department of Health and Human Services. (n.d.). *National culturally and linguistically appropriate services standards*. Retrieved from https://www.thinkculturalhealth.hhs.gov/clas/standards

U.S. Department of Health and Human Services. (1998b). *Tobacco use among U.S. racial/ethnic minority groups*. Rockville, MD: Author. Retrieved from https://www.

cdc.gov/tobacco/data_statistics/sgr/1998/complete_report/pdfs/complete_report.pdf

U.S. Department of Health and Human Services. (1999). *Mental health: A report of the Surgeon General.* Rockville, MD: Author.

U.S. Department of Health and Human Services. (2000). *Policy guidance on the Title VI prohibition against national origin discrimination as it affects persons with limited English proficiency.* Rockville, MD: Author.

U.S. Department of Health and Human Services. (2001). *Mental health: Culture, race, and ethnicity (A supplement to Mental health: A report of the Surgeon General—Executive summary).* Rockville, MD: Author.

U.S. Department of Health and Human Services. (2006). *Child health USA 2006.* Rockville, MD: Author.

U.S. Department of Health and Human Services. (2010). *Healthy People 2020: Social determinants of health.* Rockville, MD: Author.

U.S. Department of Health and Human Services. (2011). *HHS action plan to reduce racial and ethnic health disparities: A nation free of disparities in health and health care.* Retrieved from https://www.minorityhealth.hhs.gov/assets/pdf/hhs/HHS_Plan_complete.pdf

U.S. Department of Health and Human Services. (2014). *The health consequences of smoking—50 years of progress.* Rockville, MD: Author.

U.S. Department of Health and Human Services. (2015). *HHS Action Plan to reduce racial and ethnic health disparities: Implementation progress report, 2011–2014.* Office of Minority Health. Rockville, MD: Author.

U.S. Department of Health and Human Services. (2016). *Facing addiction in America: The Surgeon General's report on alcohol, drugs, and health.* Rockville, MD: Author.

U.S. Department of Health and Human Services. (2017). *Annual update of the HHS Poverty Guidelines.* Rockville, MD: Author.

Uba, L. (1994). *Asian Americans: Personality patterns, identity, and mental health.* New York: Guilford.

Umaña-Taylor, A. J. (2016). A post-racial society in which ethnic-racial discrimination still exists and has significant consequences for youths' adjustment. *Current Directions in Psychological Science, 25,* 111–118.

Umaña-Taylor, A. J., Diversi, M., & Fine, M. A. (2002). Ethnic identity and self-esteem of Latino adolescents: Distinctions among the Latino populations. *Journal of Adolescent Research, 17,* 303–327.

Umaña-Taylor, A. J., Quintana, S. M., Lee, R. M., Cross, W. E., Rivas-Drake, D., Schwartz, S. J., & Seaton, E. (2014). Ethnic and racial identity during adolescence and into young adulthood: An integrated conceptualization. *Child Development, 85,* 21–39.

Unger, J. B., Gallaher, P., Shakib, S., Ritt-Olson, A., Palmer, P. H., & Johnson, C. A. (2002). The AHIMSA acculturation scale: A new measure of acculturation for adolescents in a multicultural society. *Journal of Early Adolescence, 22,* 225–251.

United Nations General Assembly. (2006, December 16). *International covenant on economic, social and cultural rights.* Resolution 2200A (XXI). Retrieved from http://www.ohchr.org/Documents/ProfessionalInterest/cescr.pdf

University of Rhode Island, Department of Psychology. (2015). *Multicultural Psychology Definition.* Retrieved from https://web.uri.edu/psychology/files/Multicultural-Psychology-Definition-3.19.15.pdf

Van der Zee, K., Benet-Martínez, V., & van Oudenhoven, P. (2016). Personality and acculturation. In D. L. Sam & J. W. Berry (Eds.), *The Cambridge handbook of acculturation psychology* (2nd ed., pp. 50–70). Cambridge: Cambridge University Press.

Vandiver, B. J. (2001). Psychological nigrescence revisited: Introduction and overview. *Journal of Multicultural Counseling and Development, 29,* 165–173.

Vandiver, B. J., Fhagen-Smith, P. E., Cokley, K. O., Cross, W. E., Jr., & Worrell, F. C. (2001). Cross's nigrescence model: From theory to scale to theory. *Journal of Multicultural Counseling and Development, 29,* 174–200.

Vanman, E. J., Saltz, J. L., Nathan, L. R., & Warren, J. A. (2004). Racial discrimination by low-prejudiced Whites: Facial movements as implicit measures of attitudes related to behavior. *Psychological Science, 15,* 711–714.

Van Oudenhoven, J. P., Stuart, J., & Tip, L. K. (2016). Immigrants and ethnocultural groups. In D. L. Sam & J. W. Berry (Eds.), *The Cambridge handbook of acculturation psychology* (2nd ed., pp. 134–152). Cambridge: Cambridge University Press.

Van Oudenhoven, J. P., & Ward, C. (2013). Fading majority cultures: The implications of transnationalism and demographic changes for immigrant acculturation. *Journal of Community & Applied Social Psychology, 23,* 81–97.

Van Zee, A. (2009). The promotion and marketing of OxyContin: Commercial triumph, public health tragedy. *American Journal of Public Health, 99,* 221–227.

Vega, W., Warheit, G., Buhl-Autg, J., & Meinhardt, K. (1984). The prevalence of depressive symptoms among Mexican Americans and Anglos. *American Journal of Epidemiology, 120,* 592–607.

Vega, W. A., Gil, A. G., & Kolody, B. (2002). What do we know about Latino drug use? Methodological evaluation of state databases. *Hispanic Journal of Behavioral Sciences, 24,* 395–408.

Vespa, J., Lewis, J. M., & Kreider, R. M. (2013, August). *America's families and living arrangements: 2012; Population characteristics* (P20-570). U.S. Census Bureau. Retrieved from https://www.census.gov/content/dam/Census/library/publications/2013/demo/p20-570.pdf

Vijver, F. V., & Hambleton, R. K. (1996). Translating tests: Some practical guidelines. *European Psychologist, 1,* 88–99.

Vu, L., Choi, K.-H., & Do, T. (2011). Correlates of sexual, ethnic, and dual identity: A study of young Asian and Pacific Islander men who have sex with men. *AIDS Education and Prevention, 23,* 423–436.

Wade, C., & Tavris, C. (2017). *Psychology* (12th ed.). Upper Saddle River, NJ: Pearson.

Wade, J. C., & Rochlen, A. B. (2013). Introduction: Masculinity, identity, and the health and well-being of African American men. *Psychology of Men & Masculinity, 14*, 1–6.

Walker, J. N. J., Longmire-Avital, B., & Golub, S. (2015). Racial and sexual identities as potential buffers to risky sexual behavior for Black gay and bisexual emerging adult men. *Health Psychology, 34*, 841–846.

Wallen, G. R., Feldman, R. H., & Anliker, J. (2002). Measuring acculturation among Central American women with the use of a brief language scale. *Journal of Immigrant Health, 4*, 95–102.

Wang, P., Lane, M., Olfson, M., Pincus, K., & Kessler, R. C. (2005). Twelve-month use of mental health services in the United States: Results of the National Comorbidity Survey Replication. *Archives of General Psychiatry, 62*, 629–640.

Ward, C., & Geeraert, N. (2016). Advancing acculturation theory and research: The acculturation process in its ecological context. *Current Opinion in Psychology, 8*, 98–104.

Ward, C., & Kus, L. (2012). Back to and beyond Berry's basics: The conceptualization, operationalization and classification of acculturation. *International Journal of Intercultural Relations, 36*, 472–485.

Ward, C., & Mak, A. S. (2016). Acculturation theory and research in New Zealand and Australia. In D. L. Sam & J. W. Berry (Eds.), *The Cambridge handbook of acculturation psychology* (2nd ed., pp. 314–336). Cambridge: Cambridge University Press.

Warren, R., & Warren, J. R. (2013). Unauthorized immigration to the United States: Annual estimates and components of change, by state, 1990 to 2010. *International Migration Review, 47*, 296–329.

Waters, M. C., & Pineau, M. G. (2015). *The integration of immigrants into American society.* Washington, DC: The National Academies Press.

Way, N., Okazaki, S., Zhao, J., Kim, J. J., Chen, X., Yoshikawa, H., . . . & Deng, H. (2013). Social and emotional parenting: Mothering in a changing Chinese society. *Asian American Journal of Psychology, 4*(1), 61–70.

Weaver, C. N. (2005). The changing image of Hispanic Americans. *Hispanic Journal of Behavioral Sciences, 27*, 337–354.

Weaver, C. N. (2007). The effects of contact on the prejudice between Hispanics and non-Hispanic Whites in the United States. *Hispanic Journal of Behavioral Sciences, 29*, 254–274.

Weaver, C. N. (2008). Social distance as a measure of prejudice among ethnic groups in the United States. *Journal of Applied Social Psychology, 38*, 779–795.

Weinstein, R. S., Gregory, A., & Strambler, M. J. (2004). Intractable self-fulfilling prophecies fifty years after *Brown v. Board of Education. American Psychologist, 59*, 511–520.

Weiss, J. W., & Weiss, D. J. (2002). Recruiting Asian-American adolescents for behavioral surveys. *Journal of Child and Family Studies, 11*, 143–149.

Westermeyer, J., Callies, A., & Neider, J. (1990). Welfare status and psychological adjustment among 100 Hmong refugees. *Journal of Nervous and Mental Disease, 178*, 300–306.

Whaley, A. L. (2000). Sociocultural differences in the developmental consequences of the use of physical discipline during childhood for African Americans. *Cultural Diversity & Ethnic Minority Psychology, 6*, 5–12.

Whaley, A. L. (2001). Cultural mistrust: An important psychological construct for diagnosis and treatment of African Americans. *American Psychologist, 32*, 555–562.

Whaley, A. L. (2004). A two-stage method for the study of cultural bias in the diagnosis of schizophrenia in African Americans. *Journal of Black Psychology, 30*, 167–186.

Whaley, A. L., & Davis, K. E. (2007). Cultural competence and evidence-based practice in mental health services: A complementary perspective. *American Psychologist, 62*, 563–574.

Wheeler, D. L. (1997, December 12). 3 medical organizations embroiled in controversy over use of placebos in AIDS studies abroad. *The Chronicle of Higher Education*, A15–A16.

White, R. M. B., Liu, Y., Gonzales, N. A., Knight, G. P., & Tein, J. Y. (2016). Neighborhood qualification of the association between parenting and problem behavior trajectories among Mexican-origin father–adolescent dyads. *Journal of Research on Adolescence, 26*(4), 927–946.

White, R. M. B., Liu, Y., Nair, R. L., & Tein, J.-Y. (2015). Longitudinal and integrative tests of family stress model effects on Mexican origin adolescents. *Developmental Psychology, 51*(5), 649–662.

Whitley, B. E., Jr., & Kite, M. E. (2006). *The psychology of prejudice and discrimination.* Belmont, CA: Thomson Wadsworth.

Whitley, R. (2012). Religious competence as cultural competence. *Transcultural Psychiatry, 49*, 245–260.

Wilbert, J. (1976). *Enculturation in Latin America.* Los Angeles: University of California, Los Angeles, Latin American Center.

Wilkes, R. E., & Valencia, H. (1989). Hispanics and Blacks in television commercials. *Journal of Advertising, 18*, 19–25.

Williams, C. B. (1999). Claiming a biracial identity: Resisting social constructions of race and culture. *Journal of Counseling & Development, 77*, 32–35.

Williams, D. R. (2015). Racial bias in health care and health. *JAMA, 314*, 555–556.

Williams, D. R., & Collins, C. (1995). U.S. socioeconomic and racial differences in health: Patterns and explanations. *Annual Review of Sociology, 21*, 349–386.

Williams, D. R., Haile, R., Gonzalez, H. M., Neighbors, H., Baser, R., & Jackson, J. S. (2007). The mental health of Black Caribbean immigrants: Results from the National Survey of American Life. *American Journal of Public Health, 97*, 52–59.

Wilson, P. A., Meyer, I. H., Antebi-Gruszka, N., Boone, M. R., Cook, S. H., & Cherenack, E. M. (2016). Profiles of resilience and psychosocial outcomes among young Black gay and bisexual men. *American Journal of Community Psychology*, *57*, 144–157.

Wilson, W. J. (1974). The new Black sociology: Reflections on the "insiders" and "outsiders" controversy. In J. E. Blackwell & M. Janowitz (Eds.), *Black sociologists: Historical and contemporary perspectives.* Chicago: University of Chicago Press.

Winterowd, C., Montgomery, D., Stumblingbear, G., Harless, D., & Hicks, K. (2008). Development of the American Indian Enculturation Scale to assist counseling practice. *American Indian and Alaska Native Mental Health Research*, *15*, 1–14.

Woltmann, E., Grogan-Kaylor, A., Perron, B., Georges, H., Kilbourne, A. M., & Bauer, M. S. (2012). Comparative effectiveness of collaborative chronic care models for mental health conditions across primary, specialty, and behavioral health settings: Systematic review and meta-analysis. *American Journal of Psychiatry*, *169*(8), 790–804.

Wong, C. A., Eccles, J. S., & Sameroff, A. (2003). The influence of ethnic discrimination and ethnic identification on African American adolescents' school and socioemotional adjustment. *Journal of Personality*, *71*, 1197–1232.

Wong, Y. J., Owen, J., Tran, K. K., Collins, D. L., & Higgins, C. E. (2012). Asian American male college students' perceptions of people's stereotypes about Asian American men. *Psychology of Men & Masculinity*, *13*, 75–88.

Wong, Y. J., Tsai, P.-C., Liu, T., Zhu, Q., & Wei, M. (2014). Male Asian international students' perceived racial discrimination, masculine identity, and subjective masculinity stress: A moderated mediation model. *Journal of Counseling Psychology*, *61*, 560–569.

Woodzicka, J. A., & Ford, T. E. (2010). A framework for thinking about the (not-so-funny) effects of sexist humor. *Europe's Journal of Psychology*, *6*, 174–195.

World Bank (2016, April 13). *Remittances to developing countries edge up slightly in 2015.* Migration and Development Brief 26. Retrieved from http://www.worldbank.org/en/news/press-release/2016/04/13/remittances-to-developing-countries-edge-up-slightly-in-2015

World Health Organization. (1948). *Constitution of the World Health Organization.* Geneva, Switzerland: World Health Organization Basic Documents.

World Health Organization. (2012). *Social determinants of health.* Geneva, Switzerland: Author.

World Medical Association. (1964/2013). *Declaration of Helsinki: Ethical principles for medical research involving human subjects.* Retrieved from https://www.wma.net/policies-post/wma-declaration-of-helsinki-ethical-principles-for-medical-research-involving-human-subjects/

Worrell, F. C., Mendoza-Denton, R., Telesford, J., Simmons, C., & Martin, J. F. (2011). Cross Racial Identity Scale (CRIS) scores: Stability and relationships with psychological adjustment. *Journal of Personality Assessment*, *93*(6), 637–648.

Wright, R. J., & Fischer, E. B. (2003). Putting asthma into context: Community influences on risk, behavior and intervention. In I. Kawachi, I. F. Berkman (Eds.), *Neighborhoods and health.* New York: Oxford University Press, 233–262.

Wrobel, N. H. (2016). Research measures: Psychometric methods and challenges to valid assessment of constructs. In M. A. Amer & G. H. Awad (Eds.), *Handbook of Arab American psychology* (pp. 361–375). New York: Routledge.

Xu, J. Q., Murphy, S. L., Kochanek, K. D., & Arias, E. (2016). *Mortality in the United States, 2015.* NCHS Data Brief, no. 267. Hyattsville, MD: National Center for Health Statistics. Retrieved from https://www.cdc.gov/nchs/data/databriefs/db267.pdf

Yap, P. M. (1974). *Comparative psychiatry: A theoretical framework.* Toronto: University of Toronto Press.

Yee, A. H., Fairchild, H. H., Weizmann, F., & Wyatt, G. E. (1993). Addressing psychology's problem with race. *American Psychologist*, *48*, 1132–1140.

Yee, B. W. K., Huang, L. N., & Lew, A. (1998). Families: Life-span socialization in a cultural context. In L. C. Lee & N. W. S. Zane (Eds.), *Handbook of Asian American psychology* (1st ed., pp. 83–135). Thousand Oaks, CA: Sage.

Yen, I. H., & Kaplan, G. A. (1999). Neighborhood social environment and risk of death: Multilevel evidence from the Alameda County Study. *American Journal of Epidemiology*, *149*(10), 898–907.

Yick, A. G. (2000). Predictors of physical spousal/intimate violence in Chinese American families. *Journal of Family Violence*, *15*, 249–267.

Ying, Y. (1990). Explanatory models of major depression and implications for help-seeking among immigrant Chinese-American women. *Culture, Medicine, and Psychiatry*, *14*, 393–408.

Ying, Y. (1999). Strengthening intergenerational/intercultural ties in migrant families: A new intervention for parents. *Journal of Community Psychology*, *27*, 89–96.

Yinger, J. (1988). Examining racial discrimination with fair housing audits. *New Directions for Program Evaluations*, *37*, 47–62.

Yip, T. (2014). Ethnic identity in everyday life: The influence of identity development status. *Child Development*, *85*, 205–219.

Yip, T., Douglass, S., & Shelton, J. N. (2013). Daily intragroup contact in diverse settings: Implications for Asian adolescents' ethnic identity. *Child Development*, *84*, 1425–1441.

Yip, T., & Fuligni, A. J. (2002). Daily variation in ethnic identity, ethnic behaviors, and psychosocial well-being among American adolescents of Chinese descent. *Child Development*, *73*, 1557–1572.

Yoo, H. C., Jackson, K. F., Guevarra, R. P., Jr., Miller, M. J., & Harrington, B. (2016). Construction and initial validation of the Multiracial Experiences Measure (MEM). *Journal of Counseling Psychology*, *63*, 198–209.

Youn, G., Knight, B., Jeong, H.-S., & Benton, D. (1999). Differences in familism values and caregiving outcomes among Korean, Korean American, and White American dementia caregivers. *Psychology and Aging*, *14*, 355–364.

Zaff, J. F., Blount, R. L., Phillips, L., & Cohen, L. (2002). The role of ethnic identity and self-construal in coping among African American and Caucasian American seventh graders: An exploratory analysis of within-group variance. *Adolescence*, *37*, 751–773.

Zane, N., Aoki, B., Ho, T., Huang, L., & Jang, M. (1998). Dosage-related changes in a culturally responsive prevention program for Asian American youth. *Drugs and Society*, *12*, 105–125.

Zane, N., Bernal, G., & Leong, F. T. L. (Eds.). (2016). *Evidence-based psychological practice with ethnic minorities: Culturally informed research and clinical strategies.* Washington, DC: American Psychological Association.

Zane, N., & Mak, W. (2003). Major approaches to the measurement of acculturation among ethnic minority populations: A content analysis and an alternative empirical strategy. In K. M. Chun, P. Balls Organista, & G. Marín (Eds.), *Acculturation: Advances in theory, measurement, and applied research* (pp. 39–60). Washington, DC: American Psychological Association.

Zane, N. W. S., Takeuchi, D. T., & Young, K. N. J. (Eds.). (1994). *Confronting issues of Asian and Pacific Islander Americans.* Thousand Oaks, CA: Sage.

Zea, M. C., Quezada, T., & Belgrave, F. Z. (1994). Latino cultural values: Their role in adjustment to disability. *Journal of Social Behavior and Personality*, *9*, 185–200.

Zhang, A. Y., & Snowden, L. R. (1999). Ethnic characteristic of mental disorders in five communities nationwide. *Cultural Diversity & Ethnic Minority Psychology*, *5*, 134–146.

Zhang, Q. (2010). Asian Americans beyond the model minority stereotype: The nerdy and the left out. *Journal of International and Intercultural Communication*, *3*(1), 20–37.

Zhou, M. (1999). Segmental assimilation: Issues, controversies, and recent research on the new second generation. In C. Hirschman, P. Kasinitz, & J. DeWind (Eds.), *The handbook of international migration: The American experience* (pp. 196–211). New York: Russell Sage Foundation.

Zhou, M., & Lee, J. (2017). Hyper-selectivity and the remaking of culture: Understanding the Asian American achievement paradox. *Asian American Journal of Psychology*, *8*(1), 7–15.

Zhou, Y., Dominici, F., & Louis, T. A. (2007, May 7). *Racial disparities in mortality risks in a sample of the U.S. Medicare population.* Johns Hopkins University, Department of Biostatistics Working Papers, no. 145. Retrieved from http://biostats.bepress.com/cgi/viewcontent.cgi?article=1145&context=jhubiostat

Ziegert, J. C., & Hanges, P. J. (2005). Employment discrimination: The role of implicit attitudes, motivation, and a climate for racial bias. *Journal of Applied Psychology*, *90*, 553–562.

Zimmerman, M. A., Ramirez-Valles, J., Washienko, K. M., Walter, B., & Dyer, S. (1996). The development of a measure of enculturation for Native American youth. *American Journal of Community Psychology*, *24*, 295–310.

Zuckerman, M. (1998). Some dubious premises in research and theory on racial differences: Scientific, social, and ethical issues. In P. Balls Organista, K. M. Chun, & G. Marín (Eds.), *Readings in ethnic psychology* (pp. 59–72). New York: Routledge.

Photo Credits

Chapter 1 Istock.com/kzenon 3
Chapter 2 Istock.com/LightFieldStudios 29
Chapter 3 Istock.com/DragonImages 47
Chapter 4 Istock.com/ebstock 81
Chapter 5 Istock.com/monkeybusinessimages 109
Chapter 6 Istock.com/ajr_images 135
Chapter 7 Istock.com/XiXinXing 153
Chapter 8 Istock.com/shakzu 173
Chapter 9 Istock.com/Giselleflissak 199
Chapter 10 Istock.com/bowdenimages 233

Index

Abe-Kim, J., 244
ableism
  definition of, 182*b*
  and microaggressions, 190
academic achievement, family and, 164–66
acceptance
  in biracial identity development, 125
  in biracial identity resolution, 124
acculturation, 20, 66, 81–108
  definitions of, 83–86
  and ethnic identity, 122
  and family, 154–55
  and health disparities, 219–20
  levels of, 105–6
  measurement of, 101–4, 102*b*, 104*b*–5*b*
  and mental health services, 244–46
  models of, 86–94
  mutuality in, 93
acculturation mismatch/gap, 97
  and parent-child relationship, 163–64
Acculturation Rating Scale for Mexican Americans–Revised, 105*b*
acculturative strategies, 89–90, 90*f*
acculturative stress, 90, 98–101
  reasons for migration and, 99–101
achieved ethnic identity, 118*b*, 120
acquaintance potential, 192
acquiescent response, 60
acute diseases, 201
addictive disorders, 239–40
adjustment, psychosocial, 233–55
  biracial identity and, 130–31
  class identity and, 132–33
  ethnic identity and, 128–30
  family and, 158–70
  gender identity and, 146–48
  perspective on, 234
  racial identity and, 126–28
  sexual identity and, 148–50
adult-onset diabetes mellitus, 212
advertising, and stereotypes, 177–78
African American Acculturation Scale, 103–4, 104*b*
African Americans
  and AIDS, 214, 214*b*
  and cancer, 211
  college enrollment, 14, 15, 15*t*
  and coming out, 145–46
  definition of, 8*b*
  educational attainment, 14*t*
  and gender identity, 138–40, 147
  and hypertension, 210
  income, 15
  leading causes of death among, 209*b*
  and mental health services, 245–46
  and parenting, 159–62
  as percentage of U.S. population, 11*t*
  and psychological disorders, 239
  and religion, 170
  surveys of, 236
  term, 2
  types of higher education and, 15*t*
agency
  African American women and, 139
  family, 155
AIDS, disparities in, 213–15
AI-SUPERPFP. *See* American Indian Services Utilization and Psychiatric Epidemiology Risk and Protective Factors Project
Alaska Natives
  college enrollment, 15
  definition of, 8*b*
  leading causes of death among, 209*b*
  as percentage of U.S. population, 11*t*
Alba, R., 86–87
alcohol consumption, 218–19
Alegría, M., 237, 245
Allen, C., 75
Allport, G., 191–92
Amayreh, W. M., 182
ambivalent sexism, definition of, 182*b*
American Community Survey, 247
American Educational Research Association, 49*b*
American Indians
  college enrollment, 15
  definition of, 8*b*
  as percentage of U.S. population, 11*t*
  term, 2
American Indian Services Utilization and Psychiatric Epidemiology Risk and Protective Factors Project (AI-SUPERPFP), 236
American Psychological Association, 49, 49*b*, 59, 178, 182, 183, 223, 241, 243*b*, 249
  and history of multicultural psychology, 22*b*–23*b*, 23, 24*b*
  Presidential Task Force on Preventing Discrimination and Promoting Diversity, 194
Ananeh-Firempong, O., II, 228
ancestry, 9–12
  versus culture, 32
  definition of, 9, 32*b*
  largest groups in U.S., 10*t*
Anderson, L. P., 251
Anderson, Norman B., 23*b*
Angel, R., 33
Anglin, D. M., 248, 249
anthropology, 19
Antonio, A. L., 7
anxiety disorders, 237–39
Asian American Multidimensional Acculturation Scale, 105*b*
Asian Americans
  age and, 12
  college enrollment, 14, 15, 15*t*
  and coming out, 144–45
  definition of, 8*b*
  diversity among, 9, 66*b*
  and education, 9, 166
  educational attainment, 13, 14*t*
  and gender identity, 137–38, 147
  income, 15
  leading causes of death among, 209*b*
  and mental health services, 244–45
  and parenting, 162–63
  as percentage of U.S. population, 11*t*
  and psychological disorders, 238
  surveys of, 236
  term, 2
  types of higher education and, 15*t*
Asian American Values Scale, 104*b*
assessments, culturally sensitive, 250–52, 251*b*
assimilation, 84, 86–88
  as acculturative strategy, 89–90
  in IAM, 92, 93*f*
assumption of intragroup homogeneity, 64
asylees, 71
ataque de nervios, 243*b*, 248
attachment, and ethnic identity, 112–13
attitudes, in-group, and ethnic identity, 113
Australia Department of Families, Community Services and Indigenous Affairs, 50*b*
authoritarian parenting, 158–59, 159*t*
authoritative parenting, 159, 159*t*
aversive racism, definition of, 182*b*
Awad, G. H., 182
awareness, in culturally sensitive assessment, 250, 251*b*

back translation. *See* double translation
balance, and acculturation, 97
Baptiste, D.-L., 252
Barreto, R. M., 244
Bazron, B. J., 228
behavioral lifestyle, and health disparities, 216–19
beliefs
  and ethnic identity, 113
  and families, 157–58
  stereotypes as, 174
benevolent sexism, definition of, 182*b*
Bernal, Martha, 22*b*
Berry, J. W., 6, 19, 42, 89–91, 203
Betancourt, J. R., 228
bias
  health care providers and, 186, 215, 246–47
  types of, 60, 247
biculturalism, 94–95
  and parenting, 163
Bidimensional Acculturation Scale for Hispanics, 102, 102*b*, 105*b*
bigotry
  banalization of, 19
  See also prejudice

bilingualism, 95
and research instruments, 60
binge drinking, 218–19
biomedical model, of health, 200–201
biopsychosocial model, 201–2, 201*f*
biracial identity
and adjustment, 130–31
development of, 122–26
and drug use, 219
resolution strategies, 124–25
Black
term, 2, 34
See also African Americans
body image, gender identity and, 147
Bogardus, E. S., 184
Bourhis, R., 92
Boykin, K., 214
Breslau, J., 249
British Psychological Society, 50*b*
Brown v. Board of Education, 191, 193
Burnett, M. N., 189

caballerismo, 141
Cabassa, L. J., 103
Canada, demographic terminology in, 8
cancer, disparities in, 211–12
caretaking, African American women and, 139
Carney, Hampton, 178
Carrillo, J. E., 228
case studies, 54–55
caste systems, 39
Cauce, A. M., 53
causal factors, 216
CBPR. *See* community-based participatory research
CBRI. *See* Color-Blind Racial Ideology
Center for Epidemiological Studies Depression Scale (CES-D), 60–61
CFI. *See* Cultural Formulation Interview
CHA. *See* complementary health approaches
Chavis, Benjamin, Jr., 224
Chen, J., 245
Chesla, C., 57
Chin, Robert, 22*b*
chronic diseases, 201
Chun, K., 57
cigarette smoking, disparities in, 217–18
Civil Rights Act, Title VI, 247
Clark, K. B., 22*b*, 189
Clark, M. K., 189
Clark, R., 188
CLAS. *See* Culturally and Linguistically Appropriate Services Standards
class identity, 114
and adjustment, 132–33
and intersectionality, 109–34
classism, definition of, 182*b*
class systems, 39–42
and within-group variability, 68
clinician bias, 246–47
Clinton, Bill, 77*b*, 193
close monitoring, of children, 161–62
cognitive debriefing, 62
cohesive-authoritative parenting style, 160*t*, 160–61
Cole, E. R., 140
collaborative care, 252–53
Collaborative Psychiatric Epidemiology Surveys (CPES), 236
collectivistic cultures, 37–38
and families, 157–58
college
enrollment, 14–15
types of institutions, 15*t*
Collins, J. F., 125
colonization, 91
colonizing perspective, 78
Color-Blind Racial Ideology (CBRI), 188
coming out, issues with, 144–46
commitment
CBPR and, 57
and ethnic identity, 112–13
in racial identity formation, 115, 115*b*
communication
culturally appropriate, 50*b*
and health care, 229
community
and ethnic identity, 121
and health disparities, 217, 221–22
community-based participatory research (CBPR), 55–58
translation and, 63
community interventions, culturally appropriate, 50*b*
Community Preventive Services Task Force, 231
comorbid (co-occurring) disorders, 240–41
complementary health approaches (CHA), 229–30, 230*b*
conceptual equivalence, 59
confidentiality, research and, 75–76
conflict
in biracial/multiracial identity development, 122–23
generational, 97, 163–64
conflict-authoritarian parenting style, 160, 160*t*
confusion, in biracial identity development, 125
construct(s), 30
latent, 112
multidimensional, 30
construct bias, 60
construct validity, 59
contact hypothesis, 191
contextualization, of research, 51–52
control group, 53
Whites as, issues with, 72
controlling images, 138
coping, families and, 169–70
core culture, 85
coronary heart disease
disparities in, 208–11
risk factors for, disparities in, 210
cost/benefit balance, 76–77
Council of National Psychological Associations for the Advancement of Ethnic Minority Interests, 49*b*
couple relationships, 166–68
CPES. *See* Collaborative Psychiatric Epidemiology Surveys
Cross, T. L., 228
Cross, W. E., Jr., 114–16
cross-cultural psychology
term, 20
See also multicultural psychology
cultural assimilation, 84
cultural bias, 247
cultural competencies, 50*b*, 227–28
multicultural psychology and, 19–20
cultural dimensions, 37
cultural effects hypothesis, 208
Cultural Formulation Interview (CFI), 241–42
cultural humility, 252
cultural idioms of distress, 234, 241–44, 243*b*, 248
cultural integration, 84
Culturally and Linguistically Appropriate Services Standards (CLAS), 228
culturally appropriate research, 47–80
characteristics of, 51*b*
perspectives on, 50*b*
culturally competent health care, 227–31
culturally competent individual, 19
culturally sensitive mental health practice, guidelines for, 249–54
cultural psychology
term, 20
See also multicultural psychology
cultural socialization, 112
cultural values, and families, 157–58
culture, 30–33
and adjustment, 234
definition of, 5, 31, 32*b*
dimensions of, 31–32
and education, 17–18
and health, 203–5
as multidimensional construct, 30–31
and psychological distress, 234, 241–44, 243*b*
and psychological processes, 32–33
culture-related syndromes, 37, 241–42

Dankwa-Mullan, I., 222
data analysis, culturally appropriate, 71–72
death, causes of, by ethnic group, 209*b*
DeBlaere, C., 110
decolonizing research, 78
defensive-neglectful parenting style, 160*t*, 161
deficit models, 72
Dennis, K. W., 228
dependent variable, 53
depression, 60–61, 236–37
desegregation, of schools, 191, 193
Devos, T., 176
dhat syndrome, 243*b*
diabetes
complications of, 212–13
disparities in, 212–13
Diagnostic and Statistical Manual of Mental Disorders (*DSM*), 241–42
diagnostic procedures, disparities in, 211, 214–15

Dialogue Across Difference, 192
diffusion, and ethnic identity, 118*b*, 119
disaggregation, 65–70
  lack of, and health disparities, 206–7, 211
disciplinary methods, parents and, 162
discrimination, 7, 91, 173–97
  current status of, 185
  definition of, 175*b*
  effects of, 183*b*
  experience of, 184–85
  forms of, 182*b*
  and health disparities, 223
  institutionalized, 40–41
  measurement of, 183–84
  motivations for, 185–88
  nature of, 181–88
  protection against, ethnic identity and, 129–30
  reducing, 190–94, 194*b*
disparagement humor, role of, 187–88
dissonant acculturation, 97
distress, psychological, 234
  cultural idioms of, 234, 241–44, 243*b*, 248
distributive system model, 40–41, 41*f*
diversity, 6
  benefits of, 194–95
  on campus, effects of, 192
  and identity, 110
  support for, multicultural psychology and, 18–19
  in United States, 4–5, 7–9
  within-group, 9, 64–65, 66*b*–67*b*
domestic violence. *See* intimate partner violence
dominant group, 43
Doty, M. M., 221
double jeopardy, 42, 139–40
double minority status, 142
double rejection, in biracial/multiracial identity development, 123
double translation, 62, 62*b*
down-low, men on, 214
downward assimilation, 91
drinking, 218–19
dropout rates, 14
drug use
  disparities in, 219
  undocumented migrants and, 222
drug use risk
  ethnic identity and, 129
  gender identity and, 147–48
  racial identity and, 127
DSM. *See Diagnostic and Statistical Manual of Mental Disorders*
dual diagnosis, 240–41
dual focus approach to translation, 63
dynamic sizing, 250

ECA. *See* Epidemiological Catchment Area study
ecological model(s)
  of biracial identity development, 126
  of physical health, 202–3
ecological perspective, 154
  of family functioning, 154–56, 155*f*
ecological validity, 58
ecologies, 154
education
  and anxiety, 238
  attainment, 13–14, 14*t*
  college enrollment, 14–15, 15*t*
  culture and, 17–18
  desegregation and, 191, 193
  family and, 164–66
  high school persistence rates, 14
  and poverty, 16
  reading achievement gaps, 13
ELLs. *See* English-language learners
emersion, in racial identity formation, 115, 115*b*
emic constructs, 61
encounter, in racial identity formation, 115, 115*b*
enculturation, 95–97
English-language learners (ELLs), 13
Environmental Protection Agency, 225
environmental racism (injustice), 224–25, 224*b*
Epidemiological Catchment Area (ECA) study, 235
epidemiological paradox. *See* immigrant health paradox
epidemiological surveys
  of ethnic minority communities, 235–36
  general, 235
  issues with, 235
epidemiology, 205
Erkut, S., 63
Esri Diversity Index, 12
ethics
  and mental health practice, 249–54
  and research, 74–77
ethnic behaviors, and ethnic identity, 113
ethnic enclaves, 100–101
ethnic identity, 33
  and adjustment, 128–30
  components of, 112–13, 112*b*
  definition of, 112
  development of, 117–22, 118*b*
  and intersectionality, 109–34
  and racial identity, 111
ethnicity, 33–35
  assessment by, problems with, 34–35
  versus culture, 32
  definition of, 32*b*
  and health, 203–5
  in U.S. population, 11–12, 11*t*
ethnic psychology
  research and, 47–80
  term, 20
  See also multicultural psychology
ethnic-racial identity, term, 111
ethnic stereotypes, 174
ethnocentrism, 33–34
ethnogenesis, 87
ethnographies, 55
etic constructs, 61
evaluation, and ethnic identity, 113
evidence-based interventions/treatment, 218, 253–54
exclusion, in IAM, 92, 93*f*
experimental group, 53
experiments, 53–54
exploration
  in biracial identity development, 125
  in culturally sensitive assessment, 250, 251*b*
  and ethnic identity, 113
external validity, 58

facial diversity, 6
Fadiman, Anne, 226*b*
familialism, 67, 158
  and sexual identity, 144
family, 153–72
  ecological perspective of, 154–56, 155*f*
  and ethnic identity, 121
  and health, 133
  and multiracial identity, 131*b*–32*b*
  and sexual identity, 145
  socialization and adjustment, 158–70
  structures, factors affecting, 156–58
family agency, 155
family composition, and poverty, 16
family stress model, 169
fathers, 161–62
Feisthamel, K. P., 247
female-headed households, 157
  and poverty, 16
field experiments, 53–54
filial piety, 158, 168
findings, dissemination of, CBPR and, 56–57
Fine, M., 193
Fishman, J. A., 103
focus groups, 54
Foner, N., 87
forced-choice dilemmas, in biracial/multiracial identity development, 122–23
foreclosure, 113
  and ethnic identity, 118*b*, 119
Foronda, C., 252
forward translation. *See* one-way translation
Fox, M., 220
Freud, S., 31, 52

Gallagher, C., 36
gaman, 168
Gans, H., 85
Gardiner, H. W., 52
gender, 41
  and acculturative stress, 99
  and intersectionality, 110, 118
  and poverty, 16
  and smoking, 218
  and within-group variability, 67–68
gendered racial socialization, 139–40
gendered racism, 180–81
gender identity
  and adjustment, 146–48
  definition of, 136
  formation of, 137–42
  and intersectionality, 135–51
gender roles, 136
  and abuse, 168
  and couple relationships, 166–67

gender typing, 136
  formation of, 137–42
generalizability, 53
generational status
  and acculturation, 91–92, 97
  and enculturation, 95–96
  labels in, 69, 69*b*
  and language use, 103
  separation of, in analysis, 69–70
  and within-group variability, 68–69
generation 1.5, 69*b*
German ancestry, 10, 10*t*
globalization, 82
  and media, 105–6
  and remote acculturation, 96–97
Gordon, M., 84–85
Gray, F., 76
Green, A. R., 228
Guarnaccia, P. J., 234, 241, 242
Guavain, M., 33
Gullet, L., 188
Guthrie, R., 35, 71

Hall, C. C. I., 5
harmonization, 62
Hattam, V. C., 36
health
  physical, 199–232
    acculturative stress and, 100
    class identity and, 132–33
    culture and ethnicity and, 203–5
    experience of, 199–200
    gender identity and, 146–47
    models of, 200–203
    racial identity and, 127–28
    racism and, 189
    social determinants of, 228
  social determinants of, 228
Health Canada, 49*b*
health care, culturally competent, 227–31
health care barriers
  at clinical level, approaches to, 229–31
  at organizational level, 228–29
  at structural level, 229
health care disparities
  in access, 215–16, 221
  in affordability, 221
  in quality, 215–16
health care providers, and bias, 186, 215, 246–47
health disparities, 205–16
  definition of, 206–7
  examples of, 207–15
  factors associated with, 216–19
  reduction of, 227
health equity, 206
health insurance, 246
health literacy, 222
health services
  culturally appropriate, 50*b*
  multicultural psychology and, 19
healthy migrant hypothesis, 208
Herskovits, M. J., 84
heterosexism, definition of, 182*b*
high private regard, 127
high school persistence rates, 14
Hilton, J. L., 174
Hispanic paradox, 100, 220
Hispanics
  term, 2
  See also Latinos
HIV, disparities in, 213–15
Hofstede, G., 37
Holmgren, A. L., 221
homonegativity, 144, 146
horizontal collectivism, 38
horizontal individualism, 38
hostile sexism, definition of, 182*b*
household arrangements, factors affecting, 156–58
Hrdlička, A., 35
humility, in practice, 252
humor, disparaging, role of, 187–88
Hunter, J., 143
hypertension, 210

IAM. *See* Interactive Acculturation Model
identification, and biracial identity resolution, 124–25
identity diffusion, 118*b*, 119
identity foreclosure, 118*b*, 119
identity formation, 143
identity integration, 143
ideology, 42
  and privilege, 44
IDUs. *See* injection drug users
immersion-emersion, in racial identity formation, 115, 115*b*
immigrant health paradox, 100, 220
immigrants
  and acculturation, 81–108
  as percentage of U.S. population, 12
  See also acculturation; migration
implicit attitudes, role of, 186–87
implicit bias, 215
importance, and ethnic identity, 113
incidence, definition of, 205
incorporation, 84
independent construals of self, 37
independent variable, 53
individualism, in IAM, 92, 93*f*
individualistic cultures, 37–38
individuation, 164
inequality, 42
  CBPR and, 56
  and health disparities, 223
infant mortality, disparities in, 208
information, in culturally sensitive assessment, 250, 251*b*
information analysis, culturally appropriate, 71–72
informed consent, 74
infusion, in biracial identity development, 125
in-groups, 33
injection drug users (IDUs), and AIDS, 213, 214*b*
Institute of Medicine, 186, 215, 223
institutional review boards, 74
instruments, psychological
  characteristics of, 58–64
  interpreters for, 63–64
  standardized, 60
  tests, 59
  translation of, 60–63
insulin-dependent diabetes mellitus, 212
integration
  as acculturative strategy, 90
  in IAM, 92, 93*f*
intelligence, culture and, 17–18
Interactive Acculturation Model (IAM), 92–93, 93*f*
interculturalism, 6
interdependent construals of self, 37
intergroup contact
  effective, characteristics of, 191–92
  and reducing prejudice, 190–92
intergroup racism, 188
intermarriage, 69
internalization, in racial identity formation, 115, 115*b*
International Organization for Migration of the United Nations, 85
International Test Commission, 59
interpreters, 63–64
  and mental health services, 247–48
intersecting identities, 110–11
  gender and sexuality, 135–51
  racial, ethnic, class, 109–34
  and stressors, 142–44, 149
  term, 110
intersectional inquiry, 4
intersectionality, 4
  and stereotypes, 180–81
interviews, 54
intimate partner violence (IPV), 167–68
intragroup homogeneity, 64–65
intragroup racism, 188
involuntary immigrants, 70–71
Isaacs, M. R., 228
item bias, 60
Iwamasa, G. Y., 248

Jackson, J. S., 246
Jones, J. M., 31–32
Jung, C., 31
just world hypothesis, 44
juvenile-onset diabetes mellitus, 212

khyâl cap, 243*b*
Kim, U., 31
kufungisisa, 243*b*
Kuo, B. C. H., 98, 99

labels
  of convenience, 65, 111
  and ethnic identity, 112
  issues with, 2, 34–35
  and stereotypes, 181
laboratory experiments, 53
LaFromboise, T., 95

languages
  accented, and stereotyping, 180
  and acculturation measurement, 102, 102*b*, 103
  and family relationships, 164
  and health care, 229
  maintenance of, 13
  and mental health services, 247–48
  and parent-child conflict, 164
  spoken in U.S., 13
  use and proficiency, among ethnic groups, 13
latent constructs, 112
Latinos
  age and, 12
  and coming out, 145
  college enrollment, 14, 15, 15*t*
  definition of, 8*b*
  diversity among, 66*b*–67*b*
  educational attainment, 13, 14*t*
  and gender identity, 140–42, 147
  leading causes of death among, 209*b*
  and mental health services, 245
  as percentage of U.S. population, 11*t*
  and psychological disorders, 239
  surveys of, 236
  term, 2, 11, 34
  types of higher education and, 15*t*
Lévi-Strauss, C., 31
LGBTQ identities, 142–44
  and adjustment, 148–50
  coming out, issues with, 144–46
lifestyle, and health disparities, 216–19
lifetime prevalence, 235, 236
Link, B. G., 207, 248
Linton, R., 84
logos, ethnic minority groups and, 178
López, S. R., 234, 241
loss of face, 167–68, 248

machine-assisted translation, precautions with, 61
machismo, 140–42
major depression, 236–37
major psychological disorders, prevalence and risk of, 235–41
Mak, W., 101, 105
maladi moun, 243*b*
Mandara, J., 159–61
Marger, M. N., 33
marginalization, as acculturative strategy, 90
marianismo, 140–42
Marín, Gerardo, ix, 50*b*
marketing, and stereotypes, 177–78
Marsella, Anthony, 7
Marx, Karl, 39
mascots, 178
McIntosh, P., 43
Measurement of Acculturation Strategies for People of African Descent, 104*b*
media
  and acculturation, 102*b*, 105–6
  and stereotypes, 177–78
mental health, 233–55
  biracial identity and, 130–31
  class identity and, 132–33
  ethnic identity and, 128–29
  experience of, 233–34
  racial identity and, 127
  sexual identity and, 148–50
  stigma and, 248
mental health services
  acceptability barriers, 248–49
  culturally sensitive, guidelines for, 249–54
  factors affecting, 244–49
  utilization of, 244
mentally ill and chemical abuser (MICA), 240–41
meritocracy, 42
method bias, 60
microaggressions, 189–90
  definition of, 189
  examples of, 191*b*
microassaults, 189–90
microinsults, 189–90
microinvalidations, 189–90
migration
  aspects of, and within-group variability, 70–71
  and families, 156
  and mental health services, 244–46
  reasons for, and acculturative stress, 99–101
  and trauma, 238
  See also acculturation; immigrants
mind-body dualism, 200
minority, term, 42
Minority Health and Health Disparities Research and Education Act, 206
minority status, 42–44
  and family, 154
minority stress theory, 149
Miranda, J., 245, 253
mistrust, of mental health services, 246–47
mixed second generation, 69*b*
model minority, 9
Moradi, B., 110
moratorium, and ethnic identity, 118*b*, 119–20
morbidity, 205
mortality, 205
  disparities in, 207–8
motivations
  for discrimination, 185–88
  for stereotyping, 176–77
multiculturalism, 188
  benefits of, 194–95
  definition of, 6
  effects of, 6–7
multicultural psychology, 3–27
  concepts in, 29–46
  definitions of, 5–6, 5*b*
  growth of, 21–24
  history of, 22*b*–23*b*
  and multiculturalism, 6
  publications in, 21, 21*b*
  study of, rationale for, 17–20
  terminology in, 20–21
multidimensional construct, 30
multiethnic background, 12, 67
Multigroup Ethnic Identity Measure–Revised, 118*b*
multiple jeopardy, 42
  and stress, 149
multiracial identity, 12, 67
  development of, 122–26, 131*b*–32*b*
Murray, C. B., 159–61
Muslims
  disparagement humor and, 187
  stereotypes of, 176
mutuality in acculturation, 93
Myers, H. F., 220

National Center for Cultural Competence, Georgetown University, 50*b*
National Comorbidity Survey (NCS), 235
National Comorbidity Survey Replication (NCS-R), 235, 244
National Health and Nutrition Examination Survey (NHANES), 210–11
national identity, and ethnic identity, 113
National Institute of Mental Health, 241
National Institute on Minority Health and Health Disparities, 205, 227
nationality, 32
  definition of, 32*b*
National Latino and Asian American Study (NLAAS), 236, 244–45
National Survey of American Life (NSAL), 236, 245–46
National Survey on Drug Use and Health, 219, 240
Native American Acculturation Scale, 105*b*
Native Americans
  and gender identity, 136
  leading causes of death among, 209*b*
  and mascots, 178
  and psychological disorders, 239
  and research participation, 72–73
  surveys of, 236
  term, 2
  See also American Indians
Native Hawai'ians
  definition of, 8*b*
  as percentage of U.S. population, 11*t*
NCS. *See* National Comorbidity Survey
NCS-R. *See* National Comorbidity Survey Replication
Nee, V., 86–87
Neff, K. D., 38
negative stereotyping, 34
neighborhood
  and health, 133
  and mental health, 127
  See also community
Nguyen, H. H., 100, 103
NHANES. *See* National Health and Nutrition Examination Survey
nigresence, 114–15, 115*b*, 116
NLAAS. *See* National Latino and Asian American Study
non-insulin-dependent diabetes mellitus, 212
nontraditional interventions, 252
NSAL. *See* National Survey of American Life
nuclear family, 156
nutrition, ethnic food and, 199–200, 204*b*

Obama, Barack, 77, 188
Obamacare, 215, 227
obesity, 210–11
objective social status, 132
observation, in culturally sensitive assessment, 250, 251, 251*b*
obsessive-compulsive disorders, 237–39
OCF. *See* outline for cultural formation
Office of Environmental Justice, 225
Office of Management and Budget, 8–9
Office of Minority Health, 50*b*, 227, 228
Ogbu, J., 70, 99–100
Okagaki, L., 17
Okazaki, S., 72, 166
One America Program. *See* President's Initiative on Race
one-way translation, 61–62
Ong, A. D., 112–13, 118, 119–20
opioids, 219
orientation, culturally sensitive, 250
otherness status, 122
Ousman, K., 252
out-group homogeneity effect, 176
out-groups, 33
outline for cultural formation (OCF), 241, 242
outmarriage, 69
Owen, N., 202
OxyContin, 219

Pacific Islanders
  college enrollment, 14–15
  definition of, 8*b*
  leading causes of death among, 209*b*
  as percentage of U.S. population, 11*t*
Padilla, A. M., 22*b*, 59, 71
Pai, S. M., 248
parachute kids, 157
Parent, M. C., 110
parenting
  Asian American mothers, 162–63
  ethnic minority fathers, 161–62
  relationship with child, 163–64
  styles, 158–63, 159*t*
participants, 53
  disaggregating, 65–70
  identification and description of, 64–71
participation
  freedom to discontinue, 74–75
  limited, problems of, 72–74, 73*b*
participatory action research. *See* community-based participatory research
Patient Protection and Affordable Care Act, 215, 227
patrilineal family structure, 158
pediatric AIDS, disparities in, 213
Perceived Ethnic Discrimination Questionnaire (PEDQ), 184
Pérez-Stable, E. J., 222
permanent migrants, 71
permissive parenting, 159, 159*t*
Pettigrew, T. F., 192
Phelan, J. C., 248
Phinney, Jean, 33, 112–13, 117, 118, 119–20, 128, 164
Pickren, W. E., 24
Pittinsky, T. L., 179
place-based interventions, 222
pluralism, 6
policy, and health disparities, 217, 223, 229
Portes, A., 69, 71, 86, 87, 91, 92
Poston, W. C., 123–24
post-traumatic stress disorder (PTSD), 238–39
poverty, 15–16
  correlates of, 16–17
  culture of, 169
  and families, 169
  and health disparities, 221–22
  and mental health services, 246
  and within-group variability, 68
power, 43–44
preassessment, culturally sensitive, 250
preencounter, in racial identity formation, 114–15, 115*b*
prejudice, 34, 173–97
  definition of, 175*b*
  effects of, 183*b*
  experience of, 173–74
  forms of, 182*b*
  measurement of, 183–84
  nature of, 181–88
  reducing, 190–94
President's Initiative on Race, 193
pretherapy intervention, culturally sensitive, 250
prevalence, definition of, 205
preventive care, disparities in, 211, 215–16
privacy, research and, 75–76
privilege, 6, 43–44
process-based universalistic approach, 63
psychiatric epidemiology, 205, 235
PTSD. *See* post-traumatic stress disorder

quasi-experiment, 53
questioning, in biracial identity development, 125

race, 35–36
  as construct, 36
  definition of, 32*b*
  in U.S. population, 11–12, 11*t*
racial identity
  and adjustment, 126–28
  definition of, 111–12
  development of, 114–17, 115*b*
  and ethnic identity, 111
  and intersectionality, 109–34
racial identity schemas, 126–27
racial microaggressions, 189–90
  definition of, 189
racial socialization, 111
  parenting and, 160–61
racial stereotypes, 174
racial tracking, 165
racism
  current status of, 188
  definition of, 175*b*, 188
  effects of, 188–89
  gendered, 180–81
  and health disparities, 223
  nature of, 188–90
  perceptions of, racial identity and, 128
  protection against, ethnic identity and, 129–30
  reducing, 190–94
RAEM. *See* Relative Acculturation Extended Model
reconciliation, 61
Redfield, R., 84
Reese-Cassal, K., 12
refugees, 71
  families of, 157
  trauma and, 238
refusal, in biracial identity development, 125
Reinholdt, M. M., 252
relationships, CBPR and, 57
Relative Acculturation Extended Model (RAEM), 93–94
relative functionalism, 166
reliability, 58
religion
  and families, 155, 158
  and gender identity, 137
  and health, 225–27
  and sexual identity, 146
  and social capital, 169–70
  stereotypes and, 176
remittances, 17
remote acculturation, 96–97
remote enculturation, 96–97
research, 47–80
  ethics and, 74–77
  poor practices in, 48
research methods
  culturally appropriate, 52–53
  selection of, 53–58
resolution, in biracial identity development, 125
responsible, culturally appropriate research, 47–80
  characteristics of, 51*b*
  declarations on, 49*b*–50*b*
  definition of, 50–51
  ethics and, 74–77
  implementing, 51–58
  issues in, 58–72
  nature of, 49–51
risk/benefit balance, 76–77
risk factors, 205
  disparities in, 210
Rodriguez, N., 220
Rogler, L. H., 53, 242
role models, lack of, in biracial/multiracial identity development, 123
Rosario, M., 143
Rosenblum, K. E., 44
Rothman, R. A., 39
Roysircar, G., 59
Rumbaut, R., 69, 71, 87, 91, 92
rural residence, and within-group variability, 68

salience
  and ethnic identity, 113, 117–18
  of phenomenon, 242

Sallis, J. F., 202
salmon bias effect, 208
Sam, D. L., 6, 203
SAMHSA. *See* Substance Abuse and Mental Health Services Administration
Sanchez, D. T., 122–23, 130–31
Sánchez Hidalgo, Efrain, 22*b*
Santiago, C. D., 253
SASH. *See* Short Acculturation Scale for Hispanics
Savage, S., 33
school desegregation, 191, 193
Schwartz, R. C., 247
scientific-mindedness, 250
Scrimshaw, E. W., 143
secondary data analysis, 55
second generation, 69*b*
Segal, S. P., 244
segmented assimilation, 86–88
  definition of, 87
segregation, in IAM, 92, 93*f*
selective migration hypothesis, 100, 220
self, views of, across cultures, 37–39
self-categorization, and ethnic identity, 112
self-esteem
  biracial identity and, 130
  ethnic identity and, 128
  racial identity and, 126–27
separation, as acculturative strategy, 90
SES. *See* socioeconomic status
sexual identity
  and adjustment, 148–50
  definition of, 136–37
  and intersectionality, 135–51
sexual identity formation, 142–44
sexual identity integration, 143
sexual orientation, 41–42
Shih, M., 122–23, 130–31, 179
Short Acculturation Scale for Hispanics (SASH), 105*b*
Simon, C. E., 226
simpatía, 37, 101, 141
Singapore statement on research integrity, 49*b*
single head of household families, 157
  and poverty, 16
Sisson, K., 189
Skinner, B. F., 52
slave systems, 39
Smedley, B. D., 223
smoking, disparities in, 217–18
Snowden, L. R., 239, 246
social capital, 169–70
social class
  and within-group variability, 68
social construction, 111
social context model of acculturation, 91–92
social determinants of health, 228
social distance, 184
socialization, 95
  family and, 153–72
  See also racial socialization
social norms, 31
social orientations, 37
Social Science Research Council, 84
social stratification, 39–42
social stress hypothesis, 100, 220
socioeconomic status (SES), 15–16, 40, 114
  and families, 156–57
  and health disparities, 221–22
sociology, 19
sojourners, 71, 83
soul food, 202, 204*b*
Southeast Asian refugees, trauma and, 157, 238
Spanish Americans
  term, 2
  See also Latinos
spirituality
  and health, 225–27
  See also religion
sports mascots, 178
standardized instruments, 60
status inconsistency, 168
Steele, C., 179
stereotype content, 174, 175–76
stereotypes, 173–97
  definition of, 175*b*
  development of, 176–78
  and education, 165
  effects of, 179–81
  ethnic labels and, 181
  and intersectionality, 180–81
  nature of, 174–81
stereotype threat, 179–80
Sternberg, R. J., 17
strategies
  for acculturation, 89–90, 90*f*
  for acculturative stress, 99
  for biracial identity resolution, 124–25
  for reducing racism, 190–94, 194*b*
stress, stressors
  acculturative, 90, 98–101
  disorders related to, 237–39
  and families, 157, 169–70
  intersecting, 142–44, 149
  racism and, 188–89
structural assimilation, 84–85
subjective social status, 132
subjects, 53
  See also participants
substance, term, 239–40
Substance Abuse and Mental Health Services Administration (SAMHSA), 217, 219
substance-related disorders, 239–40
substance use/abuse, disparities in, 219
Sue, D. W., 43–44
Sue, S., 72, 166, 249–50
Suinn, Richard M., 23*b*
Suinn-Lew Asian Self-Identity Acculturation Scale, 104*b*
Sumner, Francis C., 22*b*
Sun, S., 246
suppression, in biracial identity development, 125
Surgeon General, 218, 219, 253
surveys, 54
susto, 243*b*
symbolic racism, definition of, 182*b*
symbolic violence, 86

television, and stereotypes, 177–78
temporary migrants, 71
temporary protected status (TPS), 71
Thayer, Z., 220
Thomas, K., 246
Thomas, W., 87
Tienda, M., 33
Title VI, 1964 Civil Rights Act, 247
tobacco use, disparities in, 217–18
tolerance, term, 239
toxic environment, disparagement humor and, 187
TPS. *See* temporary protected status
traditional healers, 230
Trahan, A., 179
transferability, 58
transgender individuals, 147
translation
  double, 62, 62*b*
  dual focus approach to, 63
  process of, 61–63
  of research instruments, 60–61
transnationalism, 6
trauma
  disorders related to, 237–39
  and families, 157
Travis, T.-M. C., 44
treatment, 53
Triandis, H. C., 31
triangulation, 53
Trickett, E. J., 17
triple jeopardy, 42
Turner, Alberta B., 22*b*
Tuskegee Syphilis Study, 76, 77*b*
Twine, F. W., 36
two-dimensional model of acculturation, 89–91, 90*f*
two-spirited individuals, 136
type 1 diabetes, 212
type 2 diabetes, 212

unauthorized (undocumented) migrants, 71
  health status of, 222
unemployment, and poverty, 16
unidirectional model of acculturation, 88–89, 88*f*
United Kingdom, demographic terminology in, 9
United Nations General Assembly, 49*b*
United States
  current status of racism in, 188
  demographics of, 9–17
  diversity in, 4–5, 7–9
  population of, 11
urban residence, and within-group variability, 68
U.S. Census Bureau, 2, 8–10, 247
U.S. Department of Health and Human Services, 50*b*, 202, 217, 227, 228
utilization, in culturally sensitive assessment, 250, 251*b*

validity, 58
values
  and ethnic identity, 113
  and families, 157–58
value structures, 37

Vargas-Bustamante, A., 245
variables, 53
Vasquez, Melba, 23*b*, 194
vertical collectivism, 38
vertical individualism, 38
victim-blaming approach, 38–39, 44
voluntary immigrants, 70–71
von Hippel, W., 174
von Luschan, F., 35

Wadhwa, P. D., 220
Weaver, C. N., 183, 184
Weber, Max, 33, 40
well-being, 199–232
West, T. V., 188
Whiteness, 36
White privilege, 43, 117
Whites
  as control group, 72
  definition of, 8*b*
  college enrollment, 14, 15, 15*t*
  educational attainment, 14*t*
  leading causes of death among, 209*b*
  as percentage of U.S. population, 11*t*
  racial identity of, study of, 116–17, 116*b*
  types of higher education and, 15*t*
Williams, C. B., 122
Williams, D. R., 215
Williams, Lindsey, 204*b*
withdrawal, term, 239–40
within-group differences/variability, 9
Woods, Sylvia, 204*b*
working poor, 221
World Health Organization, 228
World Medical Association, 50*b*
Wright, Logan, 23*b*

xenophobia, 7

Yap, P. M., 242
Ying, Y., 248

Zane, N., 101, 105
Zhang, A. Y., 239
Zhou, M., 97, 100
Znaniecki, F., 87
Zucker, A. N., 140